Avery Cardinal Dulles, SJ
A Model Theologian, 1918-2008

Patrick W. Carey

PAULIST PRESS
New York/Mahwah, NJ

All photographs are from Cardinal Dulles' personal archives, courtesy Anne-Marie Kirmse, OP, and Nicholas Lombardi, SJ, with the following exceptions: pages 9 courtesy Marion Seymour; 20 courtesy Joan Buresch Talley; 87, 395 courtesy Abbot Gibbs, OSB; 117, 571 courtesy Ryan J. Stellabotte and Fordham Public Relations; 469 courtesy Bruce Gilbert; and 518 courtesy Monica Des Marais Murphy. The author and publisher express their gratitude.

Author photo, jacket back flap, courtesy of Dan Johnson, Marquette University
Jacket and book design by Lynn Else

Library of Congress Cataloging-in-Publication Data

Carey, Patrick W., 1940–
    Avery Cardinal Dulles, SJ : a model theologian, 1918–2008 / Patrick W. Carey.
    p. cm.
    Includes bibliographical references (p.   ) and index.
    ISBN 978-0-8091-0571-7 (alk. paper)
    1. Dulles, Avery, 1918–2008. I. Title.
    BX4705.D867C37 2010
    230'.2092—dc22

[B]
                                                                                2010014358

Published by Paulist Press
997 Macarthur Boulevard
Mahwah, New Jersey 07430

www.paulistpress.com

Printed and bound in the
United States of America

Dedication
To Gerald P. Fogarty, SJ, mentor and friend,
and to Jesuit friends and colleagues at Fordham and Marquette

CONTENTS

Contents

Contents

Contents

FOREWORD
Joseph A. O'Hare, SJ

ON JULY 30, 1948, I entered the Jesuit novitiate at St. Andrew on Hudson in Poughkeepsie, New York. It is an imposing building with impressive views of the Hudson River and is now occupied by the Culinary Institute of America. Those first few weeks of introduction to Jesuit life were not always comfortable, but a festive note was struck on August 15, the feast of the Assumption, when those novices who had just completed their two years of novitiate took their first vows as Jesuits.

Among those newly minted Jesuits was a tall, angular figure—at twenty-seven years of age, he was slightly older than the others, in a generation when most entering novices were recent high school graduates. Avery Dulles, a graduate of Harvard and a former naval officer, was spared the necessity of the two years of classical studies that awaited the younger men and jumped ahead of his classmates by leaving immediately for studies at Woodstock College in Maryland.

Forty years later, it was my privilege to welcome Avery Dulles back to Fordham University, where he had taught as a Jesuit scholastic, as the first occupant of the newly established McGinley Chair in Religion and Society, a position he held until his death in 2008. At the time of his death, the *Times of London* called him "the most important American Catholic theologian of the 20th century." The author of twenty-five books and more than eight hundred articles, Fr. Dulles was made a cardinal on February 21, 2001, in recognition of his contributions to Catholic theology.

The son of John Foster Dulles, who served as secretary of state in the Eisenhower administration, Avery Dulles, the Catholic theologian, had a most distinguished and interesting family lineage. The story of his life, which Patrick W. Carey tells so well in this rich and well-documented volume, is, as Cardinal Dulles once called it, a "testimonial to grace."

PREFACE

CARDINAL AVERY DULLES, SJ (1918–2008), was perhaps the foremost Catholic theologian in American history. He lived nearly thirty years longer than his fellow Jesuit theologian John Courtney Murray, SJ (1904–1967), the most prominent American Catholic theologian prior to and during the Second Vatican Council (1962–1965); during those last thirty years alone, Dulles wrote more than 530 articles and fourteen books, and at the time of his death he was working on his fifteenth. Dulles was not only the most prolific American Catholic theologian (25 books and about 850 articles) but also the most widely read American theologian in the Catholic world. No other American theologian, Protestant or Catholic, as far as I know, has had as many of his works translated into foreign languages as has Dulles. What he represents, in fact, is the emergence, developing maturity, and impact of an American Catholic theology upon worldwide Catholicism during the period after the Second Vatican Council. Theology became a significant and sometimes contentious part of the American Catholic experience in the post-conciliar period, and Dulles was one of the principal participants in this new development.

For Dulles, faith and theology were his life. He once told a university audience, "Since the age of twenty I have looked upon God as the ultimate source and goal of my life, and have considered my relationship to him far more interesting and important than any other relationship. What could be more intriguing and absorbing than to ponder God's message of salvation?"[1] Theology was not just an academic enterprise for him; it was a personal, faithful, and creative search to understand the revelation of God in Christ, Dulles' own conversion to Christ, and his commitment to the Catholic Church.

It has been a daunting task, but also a learning experience, to write the first biography of this talented scholar and humble person who came into the Catholic Church from a distinguished family of Presbyterian ministers and American diplomats. In 2003, Paulist Press's Dr. Christopher Bellitto invited me to prepare this biography, and, after some hesitation, I agreed to do so. I hesitated because it is difficult to take the measure of any human being whose life is a mystery that cannot be fully told, and because it is particularly formidable to write a biography of a contemporary. Contemporaries do not have the historical distance from their subjects that is necessary to place them and their lasting contributions in the long corridors of time. This first biography suffers from the lack of critical distance. Nonetheless, it attempts to place Dulles in the times in which he lived and to assess his contributions to his generation.

Although difficulties arise in writing a biography of a contemporary, some advantages come from a personal knowledge of the man and from contacts with members of his immediate family, his colleagues, and close associates. I have grown in my appreciation and admiration of the man, as I hope the biography shows, and have shared a number of his views, making me less critical than perhaps other biographers will be. But the biography is not hagiography; it tries to show Dulles' personal weaknesses as well as his strengths and contributions, and it strives to be an academically critical analysis of the man and his thought. I have one major consolation in writing the first biography. I know that others will follow to fill in the gaps, provide alternative interpretations, and have the historical distance that enables judgments about lasting contributions.

Some biographies suffer from a dearth of sources. This one has the opposite problem: a superabundance of published work and unpublished documents and letters from ninety years of life. Dulles and his parents saved almost everything he wrote, including a letter to Santa when he was about five years old. Dulles was an academic since his high school days, and he preserved his unpublished as well as his published adolescent and college papers. He left an extensive record of the development of his mind; trying to discern his intellectual and theological development from his multiple extant sources has been the primary focus of the biography.

In writing this biography, I have struggled to keep a balance between Dulles' personal development over the years, and the thematic issues in his theology (the fundamental issues of revelation and faith, ecclesiology, and ecumenism) where continuity and development are evident. To avoid too much repetition of thematic issues, I have at times selected events where theological issues came to the fore to indicate how Dulles dealt with specific pastoral and ecclesiological and theological issues at different times in his life. In this way I hope to show how his theological journey dealt with change, development, and continuity in the Catholic tradition. In his early theological career, he emphasized development in continuity; later in life, continuity in development. But the two, continuity and development, were always in some kind of dialectical tension and synthesis in his thought. I have had to keep in mind the dialectical nature of his perspectives, and this has not been an easy task. Because of this dialectical mentality, I have countered the simplistic or one-dimensional, conventional labels (for example, liberal or conservative) that have periodically been applied to his theological positions. Dulles himself, though, frequently used these unhelpful labels to characterize others.

This biography focuses, on the one hand, on Dulles' distinctive personal journey of faith and theology, and, on the other, on the representative nature of his experiences and his thinking within the American Catholic community. His family heritage and upbringing had an enduring influence on his life, personality, character, and habits; and he was conscious of the benefits and privileges he had been given because of his family's social and political status in American society. As a young man, prior to becoming a Catholic, he had the advantage of some of the best education Europe and the United States had to offer; on periodic trips abroad, his mother fostered his knowledge and love of the French language and culture and introduced him to European art and architecture. Because of his father's prominence and position, Avery was early on acquainted with the world of politics and international relations. His father, moreover, illustrated and taught him the Protestant work ethic, the habits of a strenuous life, the necessity of periodic withdrawal from work to relax and recreate with family and friends, and the art of acting diplomatically and with tolerance of diverse opinions without sacrificing principle. Avery also learned from his father the responsibilities that came with the personal gifts he had been given and the privileges he had because of the social and economic circumstances in which he lived. Such lessons were deeply ingrained in his character. He was always conscious of having lived in a high-profile American religious and political family and of his family's heritage and status. From his undergraduate days at Harvard, because of his family name and his personal talents and his dramatic conversion to Catholicism, he was the object of front-page news stories. He never, however, used that public prominence for personal gain.

Dulles' life was very public, but it was also a long, private, religious pilgrimage from his college days to his death, and it provides us with one window into the continuities and discontinuities of the broader American Catholic community since 1940, when he was first received into the Catholic Church. He lived his adult life in the periods before and after the Second Vatican Council, the defining event of his life and that of the Catholic Church in the twentieth century. Since he had one foot in the preconciliar Catholic Church and one in the postconciliar, and his head in both, his biography offers an entry point into much that has happened in American and worldwide Catholicism in the sixty years after his reception into the Catholic Church. He absorbed and reflected much of the preconciliar Catholic ethos, the immediate postconciliar theological euphoria, creativity, and speculation, and the later postconciliar reactions to the cultural and ecclesiastical excesses of the 1960s and early 1970s. In the period immediately after the council, Dulles became one of the primary interpreters of the new directions the council envisioned for Catholics in the modern world, without, however, neglecting the doctrinal heritage. By the late 1970s, after the various revolutions of the 1960s, he interpreted the council in light of its continuities with the previous Catholic doctrinal tradition, without losing sight of what was truly innovative. Because of his emphasis on development in continuity, and continuity in development, he became a target of criticism from both the ultra-conservatives within the church in the period immediately after the council and the radical reformers and ecclesial critics during the papacy of John Paul II (1978–2005).

Dulles lived in a postconciliar period of great innovations, developments, conflicts, and polarizations as well as continuities in the American and global church. In this period he became very much a theologian for the times, writing and lecturing for a variety of audiences (ordinary believers as well as theologians), and speaking out from within the Catholic tradition on a host of contemporary issues that were of interest and concern to his age. His theology was an attempt to address these American and worldwide experiences in a way that rose above the fray and tried to heal the wounds of division and discord without compromising doctrine and without invoking the intervention of authoritative ecclesiastical artillery. In this approach he was a theological diplomat, combining in his person a long family tradition of theology and discretion. His theological statesmanship was not an attempt to reach peace in the church and society at any price, but a negotiation that depended on principle and a sound analysis of the Catholic tradition and the signs of the times.

His critics called him a liberal and a relativist in the period immediately after the council and a reactionary conservative in his later career. He did indeed change his theological emphases at different points in his life, depending on how he read the signs of the times and what theological medicine he thought was needed for them. Emphasis on what was new and innovative in the tradition was called for in the period after the council as the church addressed the needs of a rapidly changing world. Emphasis on continuities in the tradition was necessary when a new generation rose up whose moorings were not well grounded in the basics of the faith. In all periods of his life, though, he took the dialectical approach, seeking to bring forth from his vast knowledge of the tradition the old as well as the new.

Dulles was very skeptical about the value of his own biography. To an author who tried unsuccessfully to have a biographical sketch of Dulles published in a major secular journal, Dulles responded in 1997, "My life does not have that much of the dramatic about it, nor would I wish it to. I am pleased to be no more important than my work, rather than a celebrity."[2] When Christopher Bellitto suggested to Dulles that Paulist Press publish his biography, Dulles responded that the results of such an endeavor "may well prove disappointing, since I have never 'done' anything. By deliberate choice I have not been a man of action....I have expressed judgments from time to time, but I have done nothing to see that my judgments are carried through in policies."[3] To another correspondent he wrote, "I don't think my life lends itself to a biography, since I have never done anything significant. But someone may try to write such a volume anyway."[4] I decided to do the biography "anyway," and I hope the results are not "disappointing" to the reader, even though I am myself not satisfied that I have done justice to the man and his times.

Theologians will recognize that the subtitle I have given to the work, *A Model Theologian*, is a fundamental characterization of his theology of models in the post–Vatican II years. Understanding his models methodology—which he applied to faith, revelation, the church, and a host of other theological and ecclesial issues of his day—helps to relate him to his times and to place him on the spectrum of theological options taken by postconciliar theologians. Although the subtitle of the book indicates my interpretation of Dulles' contribution in a contentious age, it is not my own creation. I borrowed it from Dr. John Bolt of Calvin Theological Seminary, who in responding to one of Dulles' addresses in 2002 noted that he would one day like to write an article called "Avery Dulles: Model Catholic Theologian." Dulles' address that day was "clear, articulate, and stimulating," demonstrating once again "that he is not only a model theologian but a master teacher and effective pastor."[5] I hope the biography can show some of these characteristics.

A radical theological pluralism exploded after the Second Vatican Council, and Dulles' theological stance and contributions need to be seen within that context. Some moral theologians challenged official church teachings on ethical issues, and others opposed the challengers. Some fundamental theologians called for a public theology that appealed to verifiable criteria without an explicit appeal to faith in order to make the Christian tradition credible, and others thought that project an impossibility. Some theologians focused on historical research to understand and retrieve or to challenge and declare outmoded specific ecclesial traditions and doctrines. Some systematic theologians questioned long-held Catholic doctrines or the historical formulations of those doctrines and called for an updating or reformulation. Other theologians denied the sole or unique mediatorship of Christ for the salvation of the world and called for a recognition of the salvific role of other world religions. Still other theologians called for a restoration of orthodoxy and criticized the innovators as heterodox. Dulles' theology of models must be seen within this context of theological ferment and contentions. He lived in a period of theological pluralism, conflict, and polarization, and in the cultural and religious wars that erupted in the church and society.

Dulles' models theology was an attempt to acknowledge the various theological systems of thought and to discern within them what was valuable and consistent with the biblical and ecclesial tradition. His models approach aimed to bring healing, unity, and tolerance to a volatile ecclesial and social situation. From his Harvard undergraduate thesis, *Princeps Concordiae* (1941) on Giovanni Pico della Mirandola (1463–1494), to his posthumously published *Evangelization for the Third Millennium* (2009), Dulles was the prince of theological harmony. His major contribution to theology and to the church of his day was his attempt to point theologians and believers to the fullness of the trinitarian mystery of the faith and the church. He did so with the skills of a synthetic mind, a facile pen, and a deep faith that came from a late adolescent conversion experience that endured and deepened over the years. His models methodology, reflective of the postconciliar theological pluralism, revealed his enduring concern to keep differing theological systems in a kind of dialectical tension that allowed the mystery of the Christian faith to break forth in the limited perspectives of the various theological systems of thought. His contribution to the postconciliar period of Catholic life was his fundamental reminder that what was important through all the vicissitudes of history and the conflicts of theological formulations was the mystery and reality of God in Christ, reconciling the world to himself. The dogmas, languages, concepts, theological systems were all limited and inadequate, though necessary, servants of that mystery, which required faithfulness and loyalty. He was ultimately an evangelical, Catholic, ecclesial theologian who called theologians and other believers to transcend their ideological differences and contentions for the sake of the mystery they were called to serve.

ACKNOWLEDGMENTS

IT IS A PLEASURE TO acknowledge the many debts I have incurred in the process of writing this biography. I am deeply grateful to the many institutional and personal archives where I have been allowed to examine papers relating to the biography. First and foremost I want to acknowledge that Cardinal Avery Dulles, SJ, gave me his full cooperation and complete access to unpublished papers in his personal archives at Fordham University in New York. This is not, though, an authorized biography. I thank especially Dr. Anne-Marie Kirmse, OP, research associate to Cardinal Dulles, and her assistant, Mrs. Maureen Noone, who provided pleasant working conditions during the five consecutive summer trips I made to investigate Dulles' unpublished papers. They were particularly gracious hosts, and they responded generously to my repeated requests for photocopies of hundreds of documents.

During those summers, moreover, the Fordham Jesuit community furnished me with housing and hospitality at Spellman Hall, making my trips enjoyable experiences. I am indebted, too, to Joseph Lienhard, SJ, a family friend and colleague, who arranged for my lodging with the Jesuits.

I thank the many archivists and other persons mentioned here who gave me access to Dulles' personal papers or papers relating to this biography. The late John Watson Foster Dulles, Cardinal Dulles' brother, and the archivists at Harry Ransom Humanities Research Center at the University of Texas, Austin, made available many Dulles family papers, especially the correspondence between John Foster Dulles and his son John Watson Foster, letters between Avery and his brother John, and maps and logs of the sailing trips that the Dulleses took during their summer vacations together. Numerous helpful family papers were also provided by

Judith Dulles, the wife of the Cardinal's nephew, John Foster Dulles II. Mrs. Louise Mercier Des Marais allowed me to examine her diary of her relationship with Dulles during their years together at St. Benedict Center (1941–1946), and Robert Johnson Lally, the archivist of the Archdiocese of Boston, sent me the text, which is located in the Boston archives. Dr. James O'Toole of Boston College initially called my attention to this helpful document.

Abbot Gabriel Gibbs, OSB, of St. Benedict Abbey, Still River-Harvard, Massachusetts, enabled me to analyze the Dulles-Catherine Goddard Clarke correspondence of the World War II years and offered typical Benedictine hospitality during my trip to the Abbey. Frederick O'Brien, SJ, archivist of the New York Jesuit Province, summarized for me data from personnel documents I could not have access to in the New York Jesuit Province Archives. Leon Hooper, SJ, director of the Woodstock Center at Georgetown University, gave me access to Dulles' personal papers relating to his experiences at Woodstock College, and Lynn Conway and Scott S. Taylor, archivists at Georgetown, provided comfortable working conditions for my examination of those papers. Drs. Timothy Meagher and William J. Shepherd, archivists at the Catholic University of America, helped locate papers relating to Dulles' involvement in the Catholic Theological Society of America before and after his presidency of that organization and furnished pleasant working conditions in the archives. Dr. James Massa, executive director of the United States Conference of Catholic Bishops' Secretariat for Ecumenical and Interreligious Affairs, allowed me to study the unpublished papers of the Lutheran/Catholic Dialogue during the years (1971–1996) Dulles was involved in the dialogue. Mark J. Williams of Mendham, New Jersey, gave me copies of Dulles' correspondence with his godfather, Msgr. Christopher Huntington.

During the course of writing the biography, I interviewed Cardinal Dulles many times, as well as people who had some significant knowledge of Dulles as a person and theologian, and I am grateful for the time and insights the following persons gave me: John Watson Foster Dulles, Joan Buresch Talley, Patrick Burns, SJ, Philip Rossi, SJ, Joseph Lienhard, SJ, Joseph Fitzmyer, SJ, Gerald Blaszczak, SJ, George Tavard, AA, John Reumann, Kenneth Hagen,

Acknowledgments

Abbot Gabriel Gibbs, OSB, Richard John Neuhaus, Monica and John Murphy, Jeffrey Gros, FSC, and Cardinal Theodore E. McCarrick. None of them, of course, is responsible for judgments made in this text. The same applies to those persons who read the entire manuscript or specific chapters of the text prior to publication, supplied helpful suggestions for improving the text, and saved me from making some factual or literary blunders: Anne-Marie Kirmse, OP, Joseph Lienhard, SJ, Joseph Komonchak, James Massa, Christopher Bellitto, Robert Imbelli, John Laurance, SJ, and Philip Rossi, SJ.

Nicholas Lombardi, SJ, Marion Seymour, Monica Murphy, Anne-Marie Kirmse, Abbot Gabriel Gibbs, and Joan Buresch Talley helped me locate and scan pictures for the book. To them also I am indebted.

I received valuable assistance from the following graduate research assistants during the course of this project: Dr. Nathan Schmiedicke, Mark Chapman, Christopher Ganski, and Dr. Constance Nielsen. I am especially grateful to Constance Nielsen, who from the beginning of the project worked diligently on it, supplied me with numerous valuable insights as she read and summarized the bulk of Dulles' theological opera, typed the oral interviews and the index, hunted down obscure references, proofread various drafts, and offered many suggestions for improving the text.

The John Raynor Library at Marquette University and especially its interlibrary loan office under the direction of Joan Summers uncovered and obtained resources that were difficult for me to locate.

The biography could not have been completed without a reduced teaching load and the generous and indispensable funding that I received from Marquette University's William J. Kelly, SJ, Chair in Catholic Theology, the Way-Klinger Sabbatical Grant for a 2006–2007 sabbatical, and the Lawrence G. Haggerty Award for Research Excellence in 2008.

Paulist Press's Dr. Christopher Bellitto gave good advice and continual encouragement throughout the course of researching and writing the biography. For this also I am grateful.

My wife, Phyllis Knight Carey, has been my companion on this journey of scholarship and has given me her love and the assistance of a sharp, critical, editorial eye that has saved me from some infelicitous literary constructions.

Last, but not least, I want to thank Father Joseph O'Hare, SJ, former president of Fordham University, for agreeing to write the foreword to this text.

I dedicate this text to my good friend and mentor, Gerald P. Fogarty, SJ, who was a guiding light during my years in graduate school and has been an example of solid historical scholarship ever since. I also include in the dedication the Fordham and Marquette Jesuits, who have been my teachers, friends, and colleagues for more than thirty years.

LIST OF ABBREVIATIONS

ACUA   Archives, the Catholic University of America

ADGUSC   Avery Dulles Woodstock Papers, Georgetown
              University Library, Special Collections Division,
              Washington, D.C.

AMUC   The Amalgamated Molders of the Upper Crust
              (Choate School Alumni)

ASBA   Archives of St. Benedict's Abbey, Still River,
              Massachusetts

BCEIA   Bishops' Committee on Ecumenical and Inter-
              religious Affairs

CCC   *Catechism of the Catholic Church* (1994, 1997 revision)

CDF   Congregation for the Doctrine of the Faith

Church and   *Church and Society: The McGinley Lectures 1998–*
Society   *2007* (New York: Fordham University Press, 2008)

Cons   *The Constitutions of the Society of Jesus*, transl. with
              intro. and comm. by George E. Ganss (St. Louis:
              Institute of Jesuit Sources, 1970)

Crowl   Philip A. Crowl's interview with Avery Dulles for
interview   the John Foster Dulles Oral History Project,
              Princeton University: "A Transcript of a Recorded
              Interview with Father Avery Dulles," Woodstock

College, Maryland, July 30, 1966. The transcript
and other Dulles family papers are available at the
Mudd Library at Princeton University.

CTS   College Theology Society

CTSA   Catholic Theological Society of America

DH   *Dignitatis humanae*, Vatican II's Declaration on
           Religious Liberty (1965)

DPFU   Avery Dulles Papers, Fordham University

DV   *Dei verbum*, Vatican II's Dogmatic Constitution on
           Divine Revelation

ELCA   Evangelical Lutheran Church of America

EV   *Evangelium vitae*, Pope John Paul II's encyclical
           The Gospel of Life (1995)

GS   *Gaudium et spes*, Vatican II's Pastoral Constitution
           on the Church in the Modern World

HRHC,TX   Dulles Family Papers, Harry Ranson Humanities
           Center, University of Texas at Austin, Texas

JFDP   John Foster Dulles Papers, Princeton University

LCA   Lutheran Church of America

LG   *Lumen gentium*, Vatican II's Dogmatic Constitution
           on the Church

L/RC   Lutheran/Catholic Dialogue

NA   *Nostra aetate*, Vatican II's Declaration on the
           Relationship of the Church to Non-Christian
           Religions

List of Abbreviations

NCCB	National Conference of Catholic Bishops
NCR	*National Catholic Reporter*
Pastoral Letters	*Pastoral Letters of the United States Catholic Bishops*, 6 vols., vols 1–5, ed. Hugh J. Nolan, vol. 6, ed. Patrick W. Carey (Washington, DC: National Conference of Catholic Bishops/United States Catholic Conference, 1984–1998)
Proceedings, CTSA	Annual *Proceedings* of the Catholic Theological Society of America
Testimonial to Grace	*A Testimonial to Grace*: *Reflections on a Theological Journey* (1946; Kansas City, MO: Sheed & Ward, 1996)
TS	*Theological Studies*
UR	*Unitatis redintegratio*, Vatican II's Decree on Ecumenism
USCC	United States Catholic Conference
USCCB	United States Conference of Catholic Bishops
WCC	World Council of Churches

1
DULLES FAMILY HERITAGE

ON A HOT AND SULTRY DAY, August 24, 1918, in
Auburn, New York, while a world war was raging in Europe during
the reign of Woodrow Wilson, a child was born to Janet Pomeroy
Avery (1891–1969) and John Foster Dulles (1888–1959)—a child
who was destined to become one of the most prolific and internationally recognized Catholic theologians of the twentieth century.
This child was also to become the only English-speaking nonepiscopal theologian since John Henry Newman to be created a cardinal of the Catholic Church. That child was christened in the
Presbyterian Church as Charles Avery Dulles, although he was
called Avery in his family, as his father had been called Foster.[1]

Avery was born and raised in a family that had a long and distinguished tradition in American political and religious life. His
father, who was in Washington, D.C.—where the family lived at
the time of the child's birth—was a lawyer whose interests and
growing expertise in international affairs would eventually make
him a distinguished secretary of state during the presidency of
Dwight David Eisenhower. His mother, who had returned to her
parents' home in Auburn to give birth to the child, came from a
prominent Auburn family. Janet Dulles' mother, Lillias Pomeroy
Avery (1860–1933), was a member of the Auburn community, and
her husband, Charles Irving Avery (1859–1927), after whom the
child was named, was a successful lawyer who drowned in a boat-
ing accident on Lake Owasco before his grandson Avery had much
of a chance to know him. The Dulles family history that the future
cardinal would himself make efforts to preserve and pass on was
rich in documented memories.

The Dulles family came from Ireland to the United States in
the late eighteenth century, although some in the family trace the

1

Dulles name back forty generations to Charlemagne.[2] The Irish origin of the clan stems from William Dulles (whose original surname may have been Douglas), a military man from Scotland who fought in the Battle of the Boyne in 1690. After the battle he settled in Ireland and married a woman from Limerick, where they gave birth to William Dulles II. The second William Dulles (d. ca. 1777), a merchant in Limerick, Ireland, fathered a son, Joseph (1755–1818), who in 1779, at the age of twenty-five, emigrated to Charleston, South Carolina, and established the Dulles clan in the United States. A year after his arrival, during the British siege of Charleston, he fought against the British and was taken prisoner when Charleston fell. When the British were defeated in the South in 1781, Joseph Dulles was released and founded a successful import business in the city. After the war, on February 7, 1785, he married Sophia Heatly (1762–1840), who was from a well-established and prosperous slaveholding South Carolina family. Joseph spoke French fluently, which would have been useful in Charleston's mixed French- and English-speaking population in the early nineteenth century, and was gifted musically. He adapted himself to southern culture, owning slaves whom he willed to his wife after his death, and became relatively prosperous. Sophia gave birth to six children, only two of whom survived into adulthood. One of the surviving children, Joseph Heatly Dulles (1795–1876), brought the Dulles family line to Philadelphia.

Joseph H. Dulles graduated from Yale College in 1814 and moved to Philadelphia, where he married Margaret Welsh (1797–1897) on April 21, 1819. The couple gave birth to eight children, the third of whom, John Welsh Dulles (1823–1887), was Avery Dulles' great grandfather. Joseph H. Dulles became a prominent member of the community as director of the Camden and Amboy Railroad, manager of the American Sunday School Union for forty years, a founder of the Philadelphia Mercantile Library, and a founder of the Calvary Presbyterian Church, which the Dulles family attended. Joseph H. was a successful businessman and an active Presbyterian layman at a time when voluntary religious associations such as the Sunday School Union became significant and effective means of Christian evangelization in the United States.

2

Joseph's son, John Welsh, also a graduate of Yale College (1844), decided after studying medicine at the University of Pennsylvania (1844–1845) to become a Presbyterian minister. In preparation for the ministry, he attended Union Theological Seminary in New York City (1845–1848), which was the third largest seminary in the United States at the time and one that reflected the New School or revivalist side of the Presbyterian tradition.[3] Princeton Theological Seminary would have been closer to his Philadelphia home, but Princeton represented the Old School tradition that had criticized revivalism and had a stricter interpretation of the Westminster Confession. The decision to enter Union, therefore, was probably determined by his prior theological and religious orientation to the New School. On September 20, 1848, after graduating from Union, John Welsh married Harriet Lathrop Winslow (1829–?). Shortly after their marriage the couple joined the foreign mission movement, which had been fostered at Union Theological Seminary. They bore six children, including Allen Macy Dulles (1854–1930), their fifth child and Avery Dulles' grandfather. John Welsh spent the years 1848 to 1853 in Madras, India, as a Presbyterian missionary. Forced to give up his missionary activities because of poor health, he returned to Philadelphia, where he became secretary of the American Sunday School Union (1853–1857), served on the Presbyterian Publications Committee (1857–1870), and became secretary of the Presbyterian Board of Publications (1870–1887). In 1855 he wrote his first book, *Life in India*, a publication of the American Sunday School Union.[4] On February 2, 1865, a few years after his first wife Harriet died, John Welsh married Mary Nataline Baynard (1829–1876) with whom he had two more children.

Allen Macy Dulles followed his father into the Presbyterian ministry. After graduating from Princeton College (1875), where he became competent in foreign languages, he taught for a year at Princeton Preparatory School in New Jersey. From 1876 to 1879, he attended Princeton Theological Seminary, earning an AM degree in 1878. Thereafter, from 1879 to 1881, he continued studying theology at universities in Leipzig, Berlin, and Göttingen. After finishing his studies in Germany, he took a trip to the Holy Land, returning by way of Paris, where in June 1881 he met Edith Foster

(1863–1941), the daughter of John Watson Foster (1836–1917), who was at the time U.S. minister to Russia. Shortly thereafter Allen Macy began courting her, and on January 13, 1886, after five years in the Presbyterian ministry in Detroit, he married her. They had five children, the first of whom was John Foster Dulles, born in 1888 in Washington, D.C., at his maternal grandparents' home. When his first child was born, Allen Macy was in Detroit, where he had been pastor of the Trumbal Avenue Church (1881–1887). He was preparing to move the household to Watertown, New York, where he had recently received a call to serve the First Presbyterian Church.[5]

John Foster Dulles' maternal grandfather, after whom he was named, helped to shape his interests and his career. John Watson Foster had been a brigadier general during the Civil War and, at the time of his grandson's birth, was a Washington lawyer specializing in international law, a prominent member of the Republican Party, and a former American minister to Mexico under Ulysses S. Grant's presidency (1869–1877); to Russia in 1880 under the presidency of Rutherford B. Hayes (1877–1881); and to Spain between 1883 and 1885 under the presidency of Chester A. Arthur (1881–1885). Shortly after his grandson's birth, as a private citizen he became a legal agent for the U.S. government in helping to negotiate treaties with Spain, Brazil, Austria-Hungary, and Germany. During the presidency of Benjamin Harrison (1889–1893), John Watson Foster was appointed secretary of state (1892–1893). After his tenure as secretary of state, he returned to his legal practice, taught at George Washington University, and helped to establish the American Society for International Law (1906) and the Carnegie Endowment for International Peace (1910).[6]

On all his foreign missions for the U.S. government, General Foster was accompanied by his daughters (Edith and Eleanor), whose international experience would have a shaping influence on their own choices and on the families they raised later in life. Edith Foster Dulles' sister, Eleanor Foster Lansing, helped to shape the political context in which the Dulles children matured. In 1890, she married the Washington lawyer Robert Lansing (1864–1928), a Democrat, who had developed an expertise in international law and would become secretary of state (1915–1920) during Woodrow

Wilson's presidency (1913–1921). Robert Lansing, whom the Allen Macy Dulles children called "Uncle Bert," was secretary of state when Avery was born. He was another link to American politics and international affairs for the Dulles family.[7]

The Foster family particularly influenced the lives of Allen Macy and Edith Foster Dulles' children, but especially so John Foster Dulles; his brother, Allen Welsh Dulles, who would become head of the Central Intelligence Agency during the Eisenhower era; and their sister Eleanor Lansing Dulles (named after Eleanor Foster Lansing), an economist with a doctorate from Harvard who would also become involved in various offices in the American government, particularly in the State Department, for nearly twenty years after 1942. As an expert in international economic affairs in the State Department, she participated in post–World War II economic planning in Austria and Germany. Later Eleanor would teach economics at Georgetown University.

The religious context for the family, though, was provided by Allen Macy Dulles. As a pastor in Watertown, he led religious services in his church and formed his children through regular Bible reading and other religious practices and discussions within the home, the domestic church for the Dulles children, where they learned their religious tradition. One practice in which Allen engaged the children, one that his son John Foster would follow for a brief period, entailed asking the children to summarize and discuss the contents of the sermons they had heard on Sundays and Wednesdays. The children absorbed the religious and moral atmosphere of a liberal Protestant home where they frequently discussed religious life and the moral principles derived from the Bible and their Presbyterian practices.

Allen Macy served in Watertown from 1887 to 1904, when he was elected to the newly created chair of Theism and Apologetics at Auburn Theological Seminary. Like Union Theological Seminary in New York City, Auburn Seminary had its origins in the New School revivalist side of the Presbyterian tradition. In 1903, before his appointment, Allen had delivered an annual Auburn Seminary public lecture, which he entitled "Righteous or Hebrew Christianity." In 1904, the year he joined the faculty, he gave an Auburn lecture on "The True Church" that he expanded into a book of the same title in 1907.[8] On September 20, 1905, he delivered a lecture, entitled "The New Apologetic," to inaugurate the new chair.[9] He conceived of apologetics as a necessary seminary discipline—one that prepared students to "understand religion in general and their own religion in particular as a mode of thought, feeling and action, in relation to the thoughts which constitute the world-view of the times (Weltansicht)." The new apologetic, he argued in agreement with certain unnamed German theologians, outlined the "generic idea of religion" and was not focused on the defense of particular doctrines. The real issue in apologetics, as far as he was concerned, was "whether it is rational to be religious at all, whether it is reasonable to be religious in some particular way." The new apologetic focused on the "spiritual valuation" of all phenomena. Allen Macy argued that the spiritual realities under all phenomena resonated with the spiritual identity of the human soul. Examinations of external evidences and doctrines would not lead one to a truly spiritualized religious experience. Allen Macy's professorship would focus on this new and generic approach to apologetics. George William Knox of Union Theological Seminary in New York attended the inaugural and wrote that Allen Macy Dulles' address revealed a man who had "himself felt the storm and stress of our time and who is prepared to wrestle with its real problems. And it is to such men that we must look for the arguments which will make our faith once more possible for living men in this living age."[10] Avery Dulles, too, would later take up apologetics as a focus of his own study.

Allen Macy taught at Auburn Seminary until his death in 1930. Simultaneously, from 1905 to 1916, he served as pastor of the Second Presbyterian Church in Auburn. Although educated at Princeton Theological Seminary, known for its conservative theological positions, he identified himself with the late nineteenth-century liberal Protestant tradition and the progressive wing of the Presbyterian Church. As Allen Macy Dulles' book *The True Church* reveals, he had been exposed in his German theological education to such Protestant liberal thinkers as Albrecht Benjamin Ritschl (1822–1889) and Adolf von Harnack (1851–1930), and he was acquainted with the American social gospel tradition of Josiah Strong (1847–1916) and Walter Rauschenbusch (1861–1918) as well as the historical-theological publications of Arthur Cushman McGiffert (1861–1933).[11] Seventy-five years after his grandfather published *The True Church*, Avery Dulles, as a Catholic theologian, evaluated it within the context of examining the liberal Protestant tradition.[12]

After 1916, Allen Macy focused his efforts exclusively on his teaching in a seminary that tended toward the liberal side of the Presbyterian tradition.[13] He identified himself with the liberals within the Presbyterian Church, as is somewhat evident in his own inaugural address, *The True Church*, and other books and addresses that he published.[14] Earlier in his career, Allen Macy had supported, but with some minor reservations, the modernist biblical scholar Charles Briggs (1841–1913) of Union Theological Seminary when Briggs was attacked by Presbyterian conservatives in the early 1890s. Later on, in the 1920s, he sided with Harry Emerson Fosdick (1878–1969) in opposition to Fundamentalist attacks upon Fosdick's Presbyterian ministry. Allen Macy also signed the so-called Auburn Affirmation (1924, the "chief symbol of the liberal movement within the church"), which opposed Fundamentalist attempts to require restrictive orthodoxy tests for ordination in the Presbyterian Church, and encouraged his lawyer son to defend these causes in Presbyterian Church synods.[15] In 1912, Allen Macy became a cofounder and charter member of the American Theological Society, a society limited to one hundred of the most prestigious Protestant theologians in the United States. He was elected president of the society in 1921–1922. In 1971, fifty years later, in a more ecumenical age, his grandson Avery, a Catholic, was elected a member of the society, and in 1978–1979 he too became its president.

Allen Macy and Edith both had considerable experience in foreign travel, and they wanted their children to be exposed to the international scene. In 1903, after their son John Foster Dulles graduated from Watertown's high school at the age of fifteen, they took the family on a trip to France and left John Foster with a family in Switzerland, where his international education was furthered. Again, in 1908, after John Foster had graduated from Princeton, the Dulles family, with the exception of Eleanor Dulles, returned to Paris for a summer vacation. Such experiences set a pattern that would be followed by John Foster Dulles in raising his own family.

Allen Macy and Edith Dulles also made sure their children had plenty of time and opportunities for relaxation, recreation, and play, especially during the summers. Allen Macy was an athlete, a member of Princeton sports teams when he was there, and he encouraged his children to exercise and enjoy athletic events. Edith's father, John Watson Foster, provided the opportunity for such recreation. By the early twentieth century General Foster had become comfortably wealthy because of his numerous legal contracts with Wall Street magnates. Some time in the late nineteenth or early twentieth century he built a large house, called "Underbluff," and several guest cottages at Henderson Harbor, New York, on Lake Ontario, a short distance from his daughter's home in Watertown. The home at Henderson and the cottages were places where John Watson Foster entertained leading American politicians, banking magnates, statesmen, and foreign dignitaries such as William Howard Taft, John W. Davis, Andrew Carnegie, and Bernard Baruch. The Foster summer home also provided lodging for the Fosters, the Dulleses, and the Lansings, until the Lansings built their own summer home, called "Linden Lodge," close by the Foster home.

With the financial assistance of his father-in-law, Allen Macy Dulles built "Greyledge," a summer home near Underbluff and Linden Lodge. These summer homes remained in the Dulles, Foster, and Lansing families in the twenty-first century and continued to be a gathering place for the extended Dulles clan. During the summers especially, even after General Foster's death, the grandchildren and great grandchildren had a place where they learned how to swim, sail, fish, and relax in other recreational sports. Summer was a time for family fun. Greyledge was where Edith and the Dulles children spent most of their summers. The eldest son, John Foster, vacationed frequently at Henderson Harbor, hobnobbing in his early years with the elites that his grandfather brought to his home and learning the ways of the lake. He would grow to love sailing in particular; it became for him a form of relaxation, where he learned how to put his face against the elements and how to cooperate with nature in order to move a vessel forward. Henderson Harbor would be a place, too, to which he would regularly bring his own children for fun and relaxation in the summers, especially during the month of August, which he reserved for family vacations. As a youngster and throughout his life, Avery returned frequently to Greyledge, the scene of so many enjoyable times with his family. One of Avery's cousins, Joan Dulles Talley, the daughter of Allen Dulles, recalled in 2009 that Greyledge had a long front porch facing Lake Ontario and on Sundays the assembled Dulles family gathered on the porch to sing hymns as they watched the sun set.[16]

Greyledge, Underbluff, and Linden Lodge at Henderson Harbor

John Foster Dulles, unlike his father and paternal grandfather, was not drawn to the ministry but to a life of the law, politics, and statecraft.[17] At the age of sixteen, he entered his father's alma mater, Princeton University, graduating magna cum laude with the second-highest ranking in his class in 1908. He had majored in philosophy, but he had also taken courses from Woodrow Wilson in constitutional government, which sparked his interests in politics and international affairs. During his college years, he accompanied his grandfather John Watson Foster to the Second Hague Peace Conference (1907). There because of his fluency in French John

9

Foster Dulles was appointed secretary to the Chinese delegation. After graduating from college and winning a fellowship for foreign study, John Foster Dulles spent a year (1908–1909) studying philosophy with Henri Bergson and international law at the Sorbonne. At some point during that year, he met a young lady, Janet Pomeroy Avery from Auburn, New York, who was studying at a finishing school there. Returning from the summer vacation, he began studying law at the George Washington Law School while living with his grandparents in Washington, D.C. After finishing law school and passing the bar examination in 1911, he joined, with the help of his grandfather Foster, the prestigious Wall Street law firm of Sullivan and Cromwell.

The year 1912 was a significant year for young Foster, as he was called. He had a position in a law firm, and after courting Janet Avery for more than a year, he married her on June 26, 1912. His sister Eleanor recorded that he had much in common with Janet, especially their international experience and their mutual love of French literature, and that "once having fallen in love with her, he never fell out of love with her."[18] After their marriage in Auburn, Dulles and his new bride returned to New York City, where they rented an apartment and began to raise a family. The couple had two children during those early years in New York: John Watson Foster Dulles (1913–2008), named after his father and his paternal great grandfather, and Lillias (1914–1987), named after her maternal grandmother.[19]

Three Dulles children: John, Avery, Lillias, 1928

Avery with sister Lillias, Henderson Harbor, 1978

In 1912, John Foster Dulles began the legal work in international law for which he had prepared himself. His career in law would be enhanced somewhat by the presidential election that year of Woodrow Wilson, his former professor at Princeton. He worked in the law firm in New York City until the United States entered World War I on April 6, 1917. Thereafter, he, along with his brother Allen and their sister Eleanor, became involved in the war effort.[20] Robert Lansing, their uncle, was then secretary of state, and he saw to it that they worked in the State Department and, in John Foster's case, the Commerce Department of the U.S. government. John Foster served as legal aide on the War Trade Board during the war (when his son Avery was born); immediately after the war he became a member of the U.S. delegation to the Paris Peace Conference as Bernard Baruch's chief legal adviser. After the Versailles Treaty, in the fall of 1919, he returned to Washington, D.C., and in early 1920 moved his young family back to New York City where he rejoined his law firm. His international experience and expertise paid off, and Foster moved up so rapidly in the firm's ranks that, at the age of thirty-eight, he was made a senior partner and in 1926 head of Sullivan and Cromwell.

By the time of his son Avery's birth, the young John Foster had already been recognized for his legal abilities in international affairs, had absorbed some of the moral idealism of the age of Wilson, and had well-placed friends and acquaintances and business associates in government as well as on Wall Street. He was also "very much a family man," who was involved in his children's lives. Avery reported that his father "liked to come home and play games, whether it was Ping-Pong or bridge or tennis or backgammon or conversation, and so forth. We really did do things together a great deal, considering how busy he was." The Dulleses were "a very closely knit family."[21] Avery had fond memories of a home of love and security.[22]

Avery Cardinal Dulles

Playing tennis at Henderson Harbor, July 1982

2
HOME AND EDUCATION, 1920-1940

AVERY'S HOME LIFE, at least during the early years of his childhood, was permeated with a religious atmosphere that came from the liberal Presbyterian heritage of his paternal grandparents. As Avery grew to maturity, however, the Dulles home was affected by the Roaring Twenties and the Depression. Avery's father became an increasingly successful Wall Street lawyer who provided the family with the amenities of the good life and the privileges that come with moderate wealth and position in society. Avery had the advantages of an excellent academic education in some of the best private schools in the United States and Europe. The good life in the Dulles household during the 1920s and an early education in a primarily secular atmosphere seem, however, to have trumped the early stages of Avery's religious formation. During his college years at Harvard, though, Avery, like many in his family, found religion in the midst of serious intellectual pursuits.

During the early 1920s and for much of the remainder of his life, John Foster Dulles was an elder of the Park Avenue Presbyterian Church in New York City, and in the early 1920s he was a regular participant in Sunday services. The children attended services with their parents, and the parents made Sunday a day of worship, with a festive dinner, hymn singing at home in the evenings, and religious conversation. Avery remembers that his father would, as his grandfather had done with his children, question the children about the sermons they heard on Sundays. The Dulles parents created something like an American Puritan Sabbath experience for their children. "No games would be played on Sundays," Avery reported, "and, for reasons I could not understand, the shades were kept lowered."[1] Evidence of Avery's early religious upbringing is found, among other places, in his 1946 account of his conversion to Catholicism, *A Testimonial to Grace*, where he revealed that for the first time in years, during his junior year at Harvard, he prayed on his knees "as my mother had taught me."[2] Although Avery's father and mother were not particularly pious, they followed and passed on to their children religious traditions that they had inherited from their own families.

John Foster also contributed to the liberal side of Presbyterian church life as a lawyer in the 1920s and early 1930s. He defended in ecclesiastical courts liberal Presbyterian churchmen like Henry Van Dusen and Harry Emerson Fosdick, who had been charged with heresy because of their opposition to traditional teachings on the virginal conception of Jesus, the bodily resurrection, or the literal inerrancy of the Bible. Although John Foster never revealed his own views on these subjects, he defended the liberal theologians who questioned them and did so on ecclesiastical procedural grounds. He argued that the New York Presbytery had the right to license preachers within its own presbytery and that the Presbyterian General Assembly had no ecclesiastical authority to interfere in such local procedures, as William Jennings Bryan and other Fundamentalists within the Presbyterian General Assembly were maintaining.[3]

In the midst of the Roaring Twenties, as John Foster Dulles' wealth increased, the Puritan Sunday gave way to the recreational Sunday. In 1928, Dulles rented a house in Cold Spring Harbor (on Long Island) and then in 1929 purchased it. He also purchased Duck Island in Lake Ontario, west of Henderson Bay, in 1941, and later built a cabin there. These homes outside of New York City were places of retreat and relaxation on weekends and during the summers. Once they began going to Cold Spring Harbor on weekends, the Dulleses abandoned their regular Sunday religious practices and replaced them with dinner parties for family and acquaintances, sailing, golf, tennis, bridge, Ping-Pong, and backgammon. The weekends, Sundays, and the summers were times of recreation.[4] The Dulleses were joining in their own more limited ways the days of F. Scott Fitzgerald's *The Great Gatsby* (1925). By the time Avery was ten years old, religion or religious practice was no longer a matter of great moment in his life.

Sailing in Henderson Harbor, August 1985

Before the purchase of the Cold Spring Harbor home, the Dulles children regularly spent their summers at the Avery family summer home on Owasco Lake near Auburn, New York, or at the larger Dulles and Foster and Lansing family homes at Henderson Harbor. As a young child, Avery spent many of his summers at Henderson Harbor, playing with siblings and cousins, getting to know his grandparents, learning to swim, to sail, and to enjoy other recreational water sports. Weekends and summers at Cold Spring Harbor, too, were memorable events, when the family could relax together by playing tennis or learning to sail and race on Long Island Sound.

Early Education

From 1924 to 1930, Avery's formal education took place at St. Bernard's School, a private school in Manhattan at which he was given the benefit of a first-rate elementary education. In 1930, when he was twelve years old, his parents decided that he should have the benefit of education abroad as his father and mother, grandfather and grandmother had had before him. On a trip to Europe that

About the age of twelve

15

summer, therefore, they enrolled Avery at the Institut Le Rosey, a prestigious international boarding school founded in 1880 for French and English college preparatory education, with two campuses at Rolle and Gstaad, Switzerland. Prior to the trip to Switzerland, his grandfather Allen Macy wrote to Avery encouraging him to make the best of his new experience in Switzerland.

> I am sure that it must seem rather dreadful to you to go so far away and be separated from your old association of home & family, the things you are accustomed to. But, the strangeness of the new situation will soon wear off and you will [indecipherable] to enjoy that wonderful, new, world which now seems almost terrifying. You will find Switzerland glorious, grand, beautiful, inspiring.

His grandfather went on to encourage him, probably knowing the anxiety the child felt, to make new friends. "Anticipate great good, and you will get it," he told the youngster.[5] The letter was the last Avery would receive from his grandfather, who died three months later, on November 13, 1930. Avery spent two years at the school, learning French as well as English language and culture and developing a love for French life and culture that he carried with him for the remainder of his life. In his maturer years he considered himself a Francophile. The twelve-year-old Avery also learned how to negotiate foreign travel while at Le Rosey, returning home aboard ship by himself during the summer of 1931.

The experience in Le Rosey was not Avery's first in Europe and would not be his last. In 1926, at the age of eight, he had traveled with his family to France for a summer vacation; in 1930, on his way to Switzerland he had visited Italy with his family; in the spring of 1931, his mother took him and his sister to Versailles for a brief vacation; and in the spring of 1932, he vacationed with his mother and his sister in Italy again. On those trips, as he has revealed, his mother made sure, particularly in Italy and Paris, that the children were introduced to the art museums and to European culture. Avery recalled with fond memories these early experiences with medieval and modern art and architecture and the sensitivity and knowledge his mother brought to this part of his early education. This initial introduction to art and medieval culture would have a long-lasting influence upon his sensitivities to sign and symbol. In 2001, he recalled that the 1932 spring vacation in Italy had impressed him with the "inner coherence between the religious themes and the aesthetic quality of the masterpieces" of the high Middle Ages and the Renaissance.[6] His increasing love of the beautiful he accredited to his mother, asserting that in the aesthetic side of his nature he was more like his mother than his father.[7] His own early education, though, like that of his father's and his mother's, had an international dimension to it that could not be obtained solely from formal schooling.

Choate

In the fall of 1932, after returning from Le Rosey, Avery enrolled in the Choate School in Wallingford, Connecticut, a prestigious preparatory school modeled somewhat after British schools like Eton.[8] Founded by the Episcopalian Judge William G. Choate in 1896 as a boarding school for boys who were intent on a high-level preparation for college, the Choate School had become by the 1930s one of a small number of private schools that primarily served the country's elite and wealthy families. Paul Mellon, son of the Gilded Age robber baron, was a graduate of the school, and the year before Avery enrolled, John Fitzgerald Kennedy began his secondary education there. Avery and the young Kennedy would also go on to Harvard, graduating in the same year (1940). Although they were acquaintances and their paths crossed periodically throughout their lives, they never developed a personal relationship, and though they were cohorts in their allegiance to American political institutions and values, they were in different political camps.

Avery had an excellent preparation for Choate and while there developed his mind and his writing skills. He published some poems and articles in the student paper, the *Choate Literary Magazine*, between 1932 and 1936. These first of many publications reveal a well-informed teenage mind with critical abilities that would rarely be found in American teenagers during the 1930s or in the early twenty-first century. Many of his published poems and essays disclose his interests in medieval, Renaissance, and modern art. During the third form (that is, the freshman year in most American high schools) at Choate, for example, he published "Perugino"—an article on the Italian Renaissance artist Pietro Vannucci's (or Perugino's) altarpiece in a small church in Florence on the "Mysterious Crucifixion." The article demonstrated an unusual knowledge of Renaissance art for a high school student.[9] At the end of the third form, the headmaster, George St. John, reported that Avery "doesn't plan his time as carefully as he might but if the results are this good we can't complain. Heaven knows that we don't want to force Avery into a mould—his own individual shape is far too interesting."[10] During his junior year, he published "Contemporary Van Gogh,"[11] an essay that won First Honorable Mention in the *Atlantic Monthly*'s essay contest for high school students.[12] Dulles argued that although Vincent van Gogh was of the epoch of Chavannes, Hugo, and Liszt, he belonged to the age of contemporary art—the art of Marin, Stein, and Shostakovitch. By the time Avery was a senior at Choate, he was wrestling with the relationship between individuality and tradition in art, as three of his essays from that year indicate.[13] In one of those essays on Paul Cézanne he opined, "We are at last escaping from the idea that tradition implies imitation; we are perceiving that tradition should serve only as a guide to creative expression."[14]

Choate provided Dulles with a solid academic background and introduced him to the stimulating life of the academy in the search for meaning and truth and beauty. In his last year at Choate he had read and written on, among other classics, Aeschylus's *Prometheus Bound*, Goethe's *Faust*, Ibsen's *Enemy of the People*, O'Neill's *Hairy Ape*, Joyce's *Portrait of the Artist as a Young Man*, and Maritain's *Art and Scholasticism*, the last two being, as he admitted in 1993, his introduction to Thomism even before entering college.[15] His focus, though, was on art, not on philosophy or religion.

Choate had a chapel on its campus where all students were required to attend weekly religious services. Although the school and the chapel services were ostensibly nondenominational, they had a distinctly Episcopalian flavor that reflected the founder's and the headmaster's religious tradition. Dulles attended these services regularly but, as he later testified, he believed more in the progress of science and humanity during his teenage years than in religion and had little or no appreciation for a supernatural religion.

> In my prep school days, [Dulles reported in 2005], whatever faith I had was eroded by instructors, assigned readings, and personal study. The evidence available to me seemed to indicate that if God existed at all, there was no real function for such a being. Everything seemed to be explicable in principle by natural causes and human agency. The study of human and cosmic origins, I believed, had done away with any need for the hypothesis of a Divine Creator or of a Provident Governor of the Universe. The materialistic evolutionism that captivated me in those years is still widespread in our day and seriously harmful to faith.[16]

This later recollection may have been something of an exaggeration of the state of his mind during his Choate years, but one of Avery's teenage essays indicated that he saw the medieval church as an impediment to freedom and individuality, a standard and long-ingrained Whig and Presbyterian interpretation of medieval history. The church had suppressed the monks' individuality because they "submitted to a Church which gave them nothing." The "fall of cloistered Christianity" was accompanied by the modern "rise of individuality."[17] He had absorbed much of the school's intellectual atmosphere, and his interpretations of religion were governed by that tradition of education. Like Ralph Waldo Emerson, Dulles believed that art was itself the finest expression of the divine within humanity. "Trained as I was in the habits of skepticism," he later acknowledged, "the act of faith was for me a terrible stumbling block....In a sense it seemed to be the surrender of that which I valued more than anything else: intellectual honesty."[18]

Avery's father, also an intellectual, was more circumspect about the powers of the mind. When Avery graduated from Choate in 1936, his father delivered an address entitled "The Futility of Intelligence," telling the eager young graduates that "people who were intellectually inclined tended to overestimate the power of intelligence."[19] There were other things in life besides intellectual power, and many people were motivated to act more by the power of their intuitions and feelings than by their speculative calculations. It is not clear how Avery reacted at the time to this message from his father, but later in life he, too, would make analogous declarations as a theologian critical of the excessive intellectualism of neo-scholasticism.

During the summers of his high school and college years, Dulles relaxed with his family at Cold Spring Harbor or vacationed in Europe, and usually in August he accompanied his family on weekend and month-long sailing excursions into the Great Lakes.

John Foster Dulles sailing on *Menemsha* in Henderson Harbor

In 1927, John Foster had purchased a forty-foot yawl, the *Menemsha*, which he anchored at Chaumont and Henderson Harbor on Lake Ontario. From 1927 until 1941, the Dulleses, particularly John Foster and his two sons, sailed throughout the Great Lakes, taking excursions to the Georgian Bay in Canada, the western edge of Lake Superior, through the St. Lawrence Seaway to Halifax, Nova Scotia, the Bay of Fundy, and Long Island Sound.[20]

Summer sailings were occasions when father and sons could relax, enjoy each other's company, swim, fish, visit sites along the journeys, and learn the ways of the water as they learned how to sail. The father, too, could teach his sons something about life itself on these cruises. Looking back in 1966, Avery reported that his father "liked wrestling with the adverse contingent circumstances that were beyond people's control. This exercise of battling with elements that he couldn't control was the kind of thing that he enjoyed—the kind of thing he enjoyed his whole life, I think." Sailing was for John Foster Dulles an "allegory of life itself."[21]

John Foster taught his sons about reading charts, plotting courses, and guessing or betting (based on their calculations of the wind and the waves) when they would reach certain destinations. He was "training us, I think," Avery told Philip Crowl, "to estimate various factors and circumstances and to make a prudent calculated guess. And he felt the act of doing this could be acquired by practice and experience." He also taught them not to oppose directly a force of nature (like sea winds) that was greater than they were. One could not, for example, directly pull on a backstay against the wind. One time when Avery was trying to do just that, John Foster told him that it was "impossible to pull directly against the force of the wind because the wind was much stronger than I was." One had to "take one loop around the cleat and then to pull indirectly on an angle."[22]

There was a principle in this lesson that John Foster Dulles applied to circumstances in practical life, according to Avery. "He wouldn't directly oppose a hostile force which was strong, but he would try to find some indirect way of opposing it and making progress against it." This lesson Avery also learned well, as his later theological career revealed. The two sons especially cherished these sailing excursions, not only because of the lessons about life that they learned, but also because the trips offered the young men an opportunity to commune with their father, who was so frequently absent from the home during the year because of his legal practice.

Harvard

Dulles' high school years, the challenge of sailing, and his continuing international travels prepared him for the academic life of higher education. When he finished Choate, he had to decide where to go to college. He considered three options: Princeton, a natural choice since it was the school of his grandfather, father, uncle Allen, and brother; Yale, the choice of many of his classmates; or Harvard. After visiting the schools and examining the faculty and programs, he chose Harvard because he felt that his interests in medieval and Renaissance art and history would be best served by the Harvard faculty. While he was still at Choate, moreover, a Harvard student, James Laughlin, had written Dulles expressing an interest in his "Paul Cézanne" article and inviting him to continue his interests at Harvard by doing art criticism for the *Harvard Advocate*, an undergraduate student literary magazine.[23]

There was no doubt Avery would continue his education beyond high school. But unlike many of his peers, he had no career goals in mind when choosing a college. He had the kind of intellectual curiosity that academics love to see in students. He wanted to pursue his interests in art and medieval history. In this he imitated his father, whose education at Princeton was not governed by careerism; John Foster had majored in philosophy because of his inquisitiveness. Avery went to college at a time in American higher education when only a few high school students went on to college, when it was possible for those who went to college to pursue their academic aspirations, and when college-educated graduates did not have to be concerned about excessive competition for the best jobs in American society. Avery was well prepared for college because of the privilege of a previous superior education, but he also had the intellectual gifts to match the privilege.

In 1936, Harvard, like many other colleges and universities, had not yet experienced the expansion that would take place because of the GI Bill after World War II and the massive government support for research during the Cold War. Harvard had a steady increase in the number of students and faculty throughout the early part of the twentieth century, and by the 1935–1936 school year, the year before Dulles enrolled at the school, Harvard College had 3,726 students, representing most of the states and some foreign countries, and 332 faculty. By the standards of the early twenty-first century, it was a relatively small institution. During the presidency of Abbott Lawrence Lowell (1909–1933), however, Harvard had developed a superior educational climate that encouraged academic excellence among its students.[24]

Long before Avery's arrival at Harvard, religion had been relegated to a disciplinary speciality; it was confined primarily to the Divinity School, where professionals were educated for ministry or academic positions in colleges and universities. By 1936, the Harvard College undergraduate curriculum was largely indifferent to the religious dimension of education. That did not mean, however, that professors neglected the topic of religion in courses in history, philosophy, art, and other disciplines in the humanities, as numerous Catholic Harvard students themselves have testified.[25] Harvard may have been secular in its curriculum, but a good number of the professors were not themselves secularists. Some Boston Catholic clergy and bishops, as well as some clergy and bishops in other parts of the country, though, made periodic reference to the godless education at Harvard, or, as Msgr. Augustine Hickey, pastor of St. Paul's in Cambridge, reported to Cardinal William O'Connell of Boston in April 1930, "Certain teachers do say things occasionally which are detrimental to the Catholic Church. These statements simply reflect their outlook on life. Harvard is utterly indifferent to religion and maintains an attitude by which religious faith and religious principles are utterly ignored."[26] Nevertheless, the Harvard that Avery Dulles entered was not a Sodom and Gomorrah where one would inevitably lose one's soul. Dulles would say much later in life that "Harvard made us Catholics," echoing John Henry Newman's dictum "Oxford made us Catholics," a reference to the conversions of Oxford divines to Catholicism in the 1840s.[27] In Avery's case, though, it took some time before Harvard made him Catholic.

Avery's first year at Harvard was "wild and chaotic." Like many other first-year college students, he felt the newborn freedom of college life, without the supervision of headmasters, tutors, and parents. All-night parties, heavy drinking, and absence from classes characterized much of his freshman year. The liberty that led to licentiousness ended to some extent in April 1937, when he and two of his close friends and classmates went on a drunken spree one night and got in trouble with the law. The three of them stole a taxi, were caught by the police, and were put in jail for the weekend. Avery's uncle Allen (his parents were in Europe at the time) hired a lawyer to get him released. Almost immediately the incident was reported to the Harvard deans who called the young men in to give an account of their criminal activity, rebuked them, and sent them back to their dorms. Eventually the Harvard authorities decided to dismiss Avery's two friends. Avery was reprimanded but not tossed out. He believed that he was not discharged because of his excellent academic performance. (His two friends had been less than adequate students.) The episode had a sobering effect on him and awakened him to the serious consequences of a frivolous student lifestyle.[28]

In his postwar conversion account, as he explained his movement toward Catholicism and the great distance that existed between his previous life and his Catholic life, he recorded that his freshman year "did little to upset the scheme of values which I had formulated and espoused while in preparatory school." He claimed that he had been an eighteen-year-old positivist and atheist and was not interested in things religious. A revealed religion he "relegated to the realm of superstition, and morality exposed in its true guise, as a sort of social contract expressive of the general desires of the community." His intellectual interests outweighed all other values. A true intellectual could not be honest and accept a world view based on faith or unsubstantiated claims.[29]

Much later in life, Dulles gave a more positive interpretation of his freshman year. In 1993, forty-seven years after *A Testimonial to Grace*, he asserted, "My religious development was accelerated by some courses I took as a freshman."[30] In this later biographical account, he was arguing the thesis that "Harvard made us Catholics" and therefore stressed Harvard's unintentional academic role in his conversion. He noted the overall favorable impact his freshman classes had on his religious development, mentioning in particular Professor Roger B. Merriman's survey of European history since the fall of the Roman Empire as a contribution to his understanding of the church's role in history.[31] In that course, he had also read Emile Mâlé's books on religious art in France during the Middle Ages, art he greatly admired. In a freshman course on French literature, Professor Louis Allard introduced him to Pascal's *Pensées* and Chateaubriand's *Mémoires d'outre-tombe*, books to which he took a liking.

These differing accounts of his Harvard freshman year more than likely reflect a tension he felt, a tension between an intellectual agnosticism and a somewhat careless lifestyle and an emerging attraction to the virtuous life. Although he may have experienced in his late teens an intellectual agnosticism, as he records in 1946, he also experienced, as was evident in his earliest writings, a certain tension in his thinking between individuality, which came to the fore in his thinking during these years, and communal tradition, which was emerging in his study of art and history. But the tension itself made him receptive to intellectual influences that would be a part of his Harvard education during his last three years as an undergraduate.

During the summer of 1937, after his freshman year, Dulles went to Paris with his family. That trip would have a transforming effect on his father's life and on Avery's.[32] John Foster went to Paris to preside over one of the biennial meetings of the Institute of Intellectual Cooperation, the International Studies Conference, held under the auspices of the League of Nations. This gathering of intellectuals, politicians, and economists from various nations met to discuss ways of peaceful change in the world. The conference disappointed John Foster because it was unable to transcend the vested national interests that were represented at the meeting.

After the "failed" Paris meeting, John Foster went, as an invited lay delegate, to the 1937 Oxford Protestant conference entitled "Church, Community, and State," a meeting organized by the "Life and Work" segment of the Protestant ecumenical movement. That conference impressed him because the religious leaders discussed transcendental values that provided a solid ground for a just and durable peace. On board ship, on his return to the United States, he began writing on his ever-present legal pad his views on the principles for world peace, a text that he would publish in 1939 as *War, Peace and Change*. On that return voyage, Avery sat with his father on the deck discussing his father's disappointment over the Paris meeting and his newfound respect for the religious principles that had guided the discussions at Oxford.[33] During the next two years, as Avery reported, he proofread and helped revise the text his father was writing. His father sent him various drafts of the text and incorporated some of his suggested revisions in the final draft.[34] This would not be the last time that father consulted son on what he was writing.

While his father was attending conferences and the family was vacationing in Paris and then in London, Avery and his mother visited Chartres and the famous cathedral there. With Felix Barker, a friend and classmate from England who had attended Choate for a year, Avery also toured Normandy and Brittany, bicycling around Vire and Avranches, seeing the sites and being especially impressed with the beauty of Mont Saint Michel. Avery purchased Henry Adams's *Mont-Saint-Michel and Chartres* and a French history of Mont Saint Michel and read them during the vacation. He was particularly struck by the fact that the library of the old monastic settlement, as he told his mother, contained a twelfth-century manuscript of Abelard's *Sic et Non*.[35] This trip too contributed to his sensitivity to the artistic creations of the medieval world and his receptivity to the religious dimension of life.

When Dulles returned to Harvard in the fall of 1937, he began to study Greek and scholastic philosophy in greater earnest. It was his study of philosophy, especially his sophomore-year examinations of Aristotle, Plato, and some of the scholastics, that put him on the road to Catholicism.[36] That year he had courses in philosophy from Raphael Demos, for whom he read extensively in Aristotle and Plato, and in the intellectual history of the Middle Ages from Charles H. Taylor, for whom he read, among other works, Etienne Gilson's *Spirit of Medieval Philosophy* and the *Philosophy of St. Thomas*. Reading Aristotle and Plato helped Dulles escape from the positivism and scientism and skepticism of his immediate past and gave him a new sense of reason's orientation and capacity to grasp reality. From the Greeks and the scholastics, he appropriated a philosophical realism. Aristotle persuaded him that reason "reflected the structure of reality," and Plato convinced him of the objective and universal nature of virtue and the moral law; from Plato he learned that moral laws were universal because they were grounded in a structure of reality that transcended the individual and the collective will.[37]

Like Augustine's encounter with Cicero and the Neoplatonists, Dulles' reading of Aristotle and Plato was a prelude to his conversion story. These two philosophers freed him from the purely empirical and led him to the moral, spiritual, and transcendental dimensions of the human condition. Very much like his contemporary fellow convert to Catholicism, Thomas Merton, he discovered particularly in Gilson's various works on the scholastics a sense of being that awakened him to a realistic metaphysic that he had never before considered.[38]

The discovery of being and God as Being liberated him, he later asserted, from the pragmatism, relativism, and subjectivism of modern philosophy. The ancients had something to teach the moderns, and what he learned in his classes on philosophy and intellectual history moved him intellectually to a philosophical realism that would with some modifications remain with him for the rest of his life. Reality had a structure to it, and it was the responsibility of the human mind to discover that structure and live according to it.

Dulles also came under the influence of Wilhelm Koehler and Charles R. Post, whose courses on Renaissance art appealed to his previous interests in art and gave him a solid foundation in Renaissance history, which would bear fruit in his senior thesis. The person who had perhaps the most significant influence on his college career, however, was Paul Doolin, his tutor at Harvard. Doolin, a recent convert to Catholicism who moved to Georgetown University at the end of Dulles' sophomore year, introduced him to the history of France, but Doolin's impact extended well beyond his expertise as a historian. Dulles spent many an hour in Doolin's room discussing literature, philosophy, politics as well as history. This one-on-one contact with a Harvard tutor who had a deep sense of spiritual values and a vigorous critique of the materialism and subjectivism of modern liberal culture awakened Dulles' inquisitive search for meaning. Here was Dulles' first substantial contact with a committed Catholic intellectual, and he drank deeply from Doolin's well of wisdom. Though Dulles was well aware of Doolin's Irish eccentricities, flamboyant exaggerations, and frequent use of hyperbole in critiquing modern culture, he found in Doolin a tutor who directed him to the spiritual dimensions of reality. Dulles called Doolin a Platonist or Augustinian because of his philosophy of love. But it was not just Doolin's philosophy that appealed to the nineteen-year-old Dulles; it was the fact that Doolin had incorporated that philosophy into his own character, making him a powerful and credible presence.[39] It would be another year, however, before Dulles began to consider the personal consequences of what he was learning from his Harvard education. He had been presented with an intellectual feast, but he was not yet ready to taste the delights; he looked on from afar at the table set before him.

During his college years, Dulles joined a few college clubs that were primarily academic in nature. The society with which he had the longest consistent association had been formed while he was at Choate. During his last year at Choate, he and ten of his classmates organized "The Amalgamated Molders of the Upper Crust" (AMUC). The eleven Choate members, all called "crumbs," met socially on a fairly regular basis from 1936 to 1941 throughout their college years. On June 15, 1936, they wrote a constitution for their group outlining their rules and purposes. The Amalgamated Molders was formed, as the constitution stipulated, "to make fun of all human institutions worthy of being made fun of." At each of its regular gatherings, moreover, each member was to prepare a paper on a topic of choice. By examining each other's ideas, the group hoped "to bring together enough crumby ideas to make the world a butter [sic] place to live in."[40] The playful constitution had an academic purpose, and the papers presented by the members over the first six years of its existence indicate the serious intent of the youthful organization.

In 1936, the members of the "Upper Crust" were on their way to Harvard, Princeton, Yale, St. Lawrence (Kingston, Ontario, Canada), Dartmouth, Brown, and a few other East Coast schools. They met during their college years at Choate, at a restaurant in New York City, or at the home of one of the members. Throughout these years they prepared papers on international and national social or political concerns (for example, the war in Europe, propaganda for American participation in the war, grounds for peaceful change in the world, labor problems in the United States), discussed those papers at their regular meetings, and had them printed in a privately distributed bulletin.[41] From the beginning, the group was preoccupied with issues surrounding war, and most of the members, including Dulles, were ardent opponents of American participation in the war. The papers that Dulles prepared for the group indicate clearly the direction and evolution of his mind while at Harvard, and in many instances they reflect his emerging philosophical and religious as well as his political perspectives.

After he returned from his 1937 summer vacation in France, Dulles prepared his first major production for the "Upper Crust," a paper on "The Necessity for Peaceful Change in the Anarchy of Nations."[42] To some extent the paper reflected ideas he had discussed with his father on his return from his Paris vacation. Dulles chose the subject of peaceful change for discussion because "no topic should more interest us as socially conscious members of the world than the elimination of war, which is at present the world's greatest bane. As individuals it should concern us, too, because war

28

in the near future seems inevitable; and it will, when it comes, affect all our lives deeply and directly." The question was how to bring about peaceful change in the world. In this regard the League of Nations had been inept and a failure because it had no way of reducing tensions between sovereign nations and no way of diminishing the social and economic boundaries that the nations had constructed between themselves.

The real problem was national sovereignties and the unwillingness of the nations to give up voluntarily any of their control. Dulles suggested that one way of overcoming the problem was to develop a new world order in which individual sovereignties came under a federal system. The U.S. Constitution had wisely provided for a system that limited the powers of local sovereignties and provided ways of peaceful coexistence. The ultimate aim of Dulles' paper was to find ways of abolishing war and of increasing cooperation among the nations as means of peaceful change in the world. Like his father, Dulles was not an American isolationist but an internationalist who wanted to transcend powerful and self-centered national sovereignties.[43] But there was a systemic international problem here that called for more than moral platitudes.

In 1938 and 1939, Dulles and the other "crumbs" wrote papers on the American government's propaganda efforts in favor of the United States' entrance into the European war.[44] In response to these efforts, Dulles prepared "Some Personal Reflections on the Present Crisis," arguing, with the aid of Sidney Rogerson's *Propaganda in the Next War* (1938), that the government would more than likely bill the entrance into the war as a "fight between Democracy and Dictatorship"—a view that distorted the present crisis. Americans in particular, Rogerson maintained, were "more susceptible than most peoples to mass suggestion." Dulles intimated that the propaganda would be played out in the United States, and Americans needed to be warned against such a simplistic portrayal of the war.

> All of us, as I see it, are more or less victims of a zeal for moral action which predisposes us to regard every conflict as a clash between good and evil, the idea of a conflict between two equal evils being dramatically unsatisfying.

29

The art of propaganda is primarily the art of taking advantage of this human tendency by means of disguising selfishness as principle.[45]

In 1939, as it was becoming clearer that Americans might be drawn into the war, Dulles wrote "Liberalism in Retrospect" for the "crumbs" to discuss.[46] This essay is well worth some extensive analysis because it reveals Dulles' developing religious philosophy, his maturing sense of the spiritual and transcendental foundation of society and community, and his opposition to liberalism narrowly defined. The rise of totalitarian governments was, he opined, "an extreme and disastrous reaction against liberalism." It was necessary, however, to examine the tenets of liberalism in order to assess the reaction against it. Liberalism arose in the eighteenth and nineteenth centuries and was difficult to define, but Dulles found beneficial Pope Leo XIII's definition of liberalism as the doctrine that "each man is a law unto himself."[47] Dulles' essay was studded with quotations from Plato, Aristotle, Mill, Kant, and Catholic sources besides Leo XIII, including Dante, Gilson, Jacques Maritain, and Karl Adam—revealing what he was reading during his last year at Harvard College.

Quoting Maritain approvingly, Dulles noted that eighteenth- and nineteenth-century liberalism had an effect upon society and culture in that it made "each abstract individual and his opinions the source of all right and truth." Dulles' neo-Thomism began to emerge in a major way in this essay as he identified liberalism with individualism and subjectivism, two philosophical orientations that undermined order and its instrumental means—authority—in society and culture. "Experience was equated with knowledge," Dulles asserted with respect to the classical liberals, "and therefore it was thought that knowledge must be, like experience, incommunicable. Neither God nor man was respected as an authority, since no knowledge was recognized which was not the fruit of individual trial and error." Like his father during this period of his life, Dulles was searching for the transcendental values that bound societies and cultures together, but unlike his father, he was discovering those values in scholastic sources with which his father had little acquaintance. And his critique was centered more on the philosophical tenets that he thought gave rise to modern liberal culture than on the nations' vested and pragmatic political decisions that his father had criticized in *War, Peace and Change* (1939).

In the previous century, Dulles argued, "individualism and relativism corroded the very foundations of communal life." He quoted favorably Karl Adam's view that "the autonomous man, cut off from God, and the solitary man cut off from the society of his fellow-men, isolated from the community, is now severed also from his own empirical self. He becomes a merely provisional creature, and therefore sterile and unfruitful, corroded by the spirit of 'criticism,' estranged from reality, a man of mere negation."[48] The liberals of the nineteenth century made absolutes out of doubt, diversity, and change and, in fact, deified change itself. This attitude was all consuming, manifesting itself in the relentless egoism of capitalism, a metaphysical rejection of dogmatism, a retreat from realities to conceptions of reality, an emphasis on self-realization and development in education, a utilitarianism and subjectivism in ethics, and a universal and abstract regard for the sacred right of individuals (without regard for how the right was used) in politics. History and progress, moreover, were conceived within this broad definition of liberalism as "a monstrous dialectic of conflicting errors, in which each clash of interests was predestined, by the requirements of its very nature, to be resolved in synthesis on a higher plane." All of this led ultimately to a classless society.

In order to avoid the extreme totalitarian reactions against liberalism, Dulles maintained, nations had to purge themselves of these weaknesses and limits of liberalism. "Man neither is nor desires to be an end in himself." Dulles called for a new appreciation of the dignity of the individual person as a rational and social being.

> The individual must be made aware of belonging to a community and to a cosmos, and he must understand that title to this membership involves duties as well as rights....Man feels a certain exultation in the practice of such virtues as trust, courage, obedience, loyalty. In the liberal society, however, virtues of this order have no place: doubt is substituted for faith, pleasure for hope,

31

and egotism for charity. Not only occupation, but state and family as well, are degraded into precarious contractual partnerships contingent on mutual benefit. Labor possesses no dignity because it is regarded simply as a means of self-advancement. Love, fidelity, and the instinct to serve are said to be the marks of feeble and dependent natures.

This interpretation of modern society fits in with an early twentieth-century Catholic critique of modern culture that was evident in, among other sources, Jacques Maritain's *Trois Reformateurs* (1925). The scholastic critique reflected the Catholic search for an order in society that was based upon transcendental realities and values. In this youthful essay, Dulles asserted, very much like the Catholic Workers in the United States, that the task at hand was to build families, churches, industries, cities, states, and nations into true societies—personalist, not individualist; communal, not collectivist. In order to achieve such a sense of community, Dulles concluded, "The student must receive moral and religious as well as intellectual training." By 1940 he had come to the conclusion that reshaping the world order could not take place without a spiritual revival. This was not mere pietism, though. He was considering a spiritual revival that undergirded an intellectual transformation. It was not a spiritual retreat, but a spiritual penetration of the intellectual that worked itself out in building a just and durable peace in the world. Dulles' battle with liberalism, as he defined it in this essay, would not end in his early twenties but would recur periodically throughout his career as a Catholic theologian. Like Orestes Brownson and John Henry Newman before him, he saw an alternative to a liberal culture that he thought led to chaos.

In May 1940, just prior to final examinations at Harvard, the "crumbs" met in Wallingford, Connecticut, for a social evening and a discussion of another of Dulles' papers, "Observations on Sovereignty and the War System."[49] The group had kept together during their four years of college, and many of them were graduating with honors—Dulles with a summa cum laude. Honors, however, were not on their minds when they met. War was. Dulles repeated a thesis that he had articulated at an earlier meeting: that national sovereignties were inevitably productive of war, not peace. The *Federalist Papers* taught, he argued, "that the presence in one neighborhood of a multitude of disconnected sovereignties is inevitably productive of recurrent hostilities." The presence in the world of sixty legally autarchical sovereignties without responsibility for one another, as was the current case throughout the world, was "the exact equivalent of anarchy within the state. It is unworkable for exactly the same reason that anarchy is unworkable— because the natural egoism of men leads them to oppress others for the sake of their particular advantage." Sounding very much like the Protestant theologian and ethicist Reinhold Niebuhr (1892–1971), he believed that anarchy among states was far more disastrous than among individuals because "nations are far more selfish than individuals."

One of the major evil consequences of the sovereign state system, Dulles continued to argue, was the tendency of one state to deify itself while it demonized its enemy—a tendency that was all too apparent in the current world crisis. And the idea of some kind of equality among sovereign states was a hoax, because the powerful states could always oppress the weaker ones. International law, moreover, was unable to control selfishness among the nations. War was the natural concomitant of the inherently evil sovereign system. Force was the only method by which the oppressed could achieve freedom and the poor could improve their lot. The present war, he believed, manifested the struggle for economic security, a struggle against the unjust settlements after World War I, and a revolt "of energetic peoples who have felt that they were denied equal opportunity under the domination of England, France, and the United States."[50] Germany, Italy, and Japan felt the burdens of economic injustice or lack of opportunity that made peaceful reform seem impossible. Dulles was not justifying the rise of the totalitarian regimes and the preemptive strikes against neighboring states; he was trying to explain what he considered the systemic causes of the expanding European war. He suggested that the way to avoid this recurring problem was to break up the European system of sovereignty.

One year later, on May 16, 1941, the AMUC college graduates met for one of their last social gatherings prior to the United

States' entry into World War II. That meeting acknowledged the group's individual achievements over the past six years, mentioning in particular Dulles' publication of his senior thesis, the Harvard Phi Beta Kappa Prize essay, *Princeps Concordiae: Pico della Mirandola and the Scholastic Tradition*.[51] The "crumbs" had matured during their college years, were actively and intellectually engaged with world problems, and had come to realize that life was earnest and they had a responsibility in society to bring about a "butter world." Before long many of them, including Dulles, would enlist in the armed services to aid their country during World War II. They may not have given up on the kind of internationalism they were trying to foster during their college years, but Pearl Harbor created a situation that moved them to support America's entrance into the war.

While he was discussing issues of peace and war with his fellow students, Dulles was simultaneously studying medieval, Renaissance, and Reformation history and literature. During his junior year he took courses in Michelangelo, the intellectual history of the Middle Ages, and "Transitions from Medieval to Modern Culture." These courses, as he told his mother, were "right up my alley, since the principal authors taken up are Dante, Chaucer, Villon, and Montaigne, all of whom I already know fairly well."[52] He continued during his junior and senior years to read in philosophy and history and focused his study on the history and philosophy of the Italian Renaissance and to some extent on the English Protestant Reformation. He took courses in history, particularly from professor Charles Howard McIlwain (1871–1968), whose course on the constitutional history of England was, in Samuel Eliot Morrison's judgment, one of Harvard's "most famous courses in the social sciences."[53]

In one of those history courses Dulles prepared two extended research papers: "The Place of Wolsey in English History" and "Does the Ecclesiastical Establishment of Edward VI or That of Mary Show the Wider Divergence from the Precedents Set by Henry VIII?" The papers revealed little about his own religious leanings at the time; they show a certain academic distance from any particular religious interpretation of the changes he examined. Cardinal Wolsey he interpreted as a self-interested time server, a churchman whose motivations were more political than religious. In Dulles' interpretation, Wolsey, and even more so Henry VIII, capitulated to the growing patriotism and secularism of the Renaissance. In his study of the political and religious policies of Henry VIII, Edward VI, and Mary, he concluded that the sixteenth-century English struggle of the two faiths, Catholic and Protestant, had ultimately produced "the abeyance of religion and the unquestioned triumph of the lay state."[54]

Princeps Concordiae

Dulles' undergraduate interests in history and philosophy came together during his senior year as he prepared a thesis on Giovanni Pico della Mirandola (1463–1494), the young Italian Renaissance scholar. Dulles read Pico's major works, the significant modern studies of them, contemporary English, French, German, and Italian histories of the Italian Renaissance, and scholastic philosophy and theology, and, prior to writing the thesis, consulted with experts in the field (for example, professors John Goheen of Queens College, an authority on scholastic philosophy; Paul Oskar Kristeller, professor of medieval and Renaissance philosophy at Columbia University; and his tutor at Harvard, Dana B. Durand).

During the Christmas vacation of his senior year, as he was testing out his thesis, he sent Kristeller a draft of his project and asked for an interview to discuss it. In a letter to Dulles prior to their meeting, Kristeller suggested that though he believed Dulles' emphasis on the Paduan scholastic influence on Pico's thought was correct, he warned the young man not to discount the Platonic influence—an influence that Pico had derived from his reading of the Florentinian Marsilio Ficino's *Theologia Platonica*. Nonetheless Kristeller encouraged the young scholar to examine the Aristotelian and scholastic philosophical background of Pico's thought, as Dulles intended to do, because much more work needed to be done in that direction.[55]

Dulles acknowledged in his thesis on Pico that there were three dominant interpretations of Pico's work. One set of interpreters asserted that Pico was a Platonist, coming predominantly under the influence of the Renaissance Florentine Platonic school of thought.

Another emphasized his fascination with Cabbalist thought, "searching after hidden meanings in ancient Oriental manuscripts." A third school of interpretation represented him as an idealist who embodied ideas that anticipated Hegelianism. Dulles took issue primarily with the third school, arguing that Pico was not an idealist in the modern sense but a medieval realist. He went on to argue throughout the thesis that Pico's philosophy "was primarily a scholastic synthesis."[56] He devoted successive chapters to demonstrating how Pico's ontology, cosmology, anthropology, psychology, and theology were consistent with traditional medieval doctrines.

The senior theses at Harvard had developed into a superior academic exercise during the presidency of Abbott Lawrence Lowell. In 1936, Samuel Eliot Morrison wrote that "we often have honors dissertations for the AB nowadays that would have been thought worthy of a PhD thirty years ago."[57] Arthur M. Schlesinger Jr.'s 1938 Harvard senior thesis on Orestes A. Brownson was so well done that it was published a year later and became for years a standard biography, particularly important because of Schlesinger's analysis of Brownson's political and social thought during the age of Andrew Jackson.[58] Dulles' senior thesis was likewise so well researched and convincingly argued that it won the Harvard Phi Beta Kappa Prize for 1940, a prize that had been awarded only six previous times, and, in 1941, after the thesis was revised,[59] Harvard University Press published it.

The book was a major first step in Dulles' career as a publishing scholar, and it received some favorable reviews with the requisite academic notations of its limitations.[60] The research and writing for the text, too, reflected his intellectual development at Harvard College and influenced the future direction of his intellectual interests. Many years after his research on Mirandola, Dulles acknowledged that "I found myself bitten by the theological bug. My supreme interest would never again be anything but theology."[61] In 2008, at a conference on Dulles' theology during his ninetieth year, the British Catholic theologian Aidan Nichols, OP, analyzed *Princeps Concordiae* as a seed bed for many of the themes in Dulles' later theology.

Nichols argued that Dulles, like the subject of his book, was a Prince of Concord. Throughout his career, Dulles, like Pico, had attempted to bring peace to the philosophical and scholarly community, by bringing apparently conflicting intellectual traditions (in Pico's case the Aristotelian and the Platonic, the Thomist and the Scotist) into harmony. This project was not a facile syncretism that tolerated "blatant contradictions" or erroneous opinions, but a synthetic, dialectical, and irenic project that acknowledged the benefits as well as the limits of different systems of thought and tried to combine the perspectives and insights of different approaches and schools of thought. Such a synthetic approach was a humble acknowledgment that reality could not be captured in any single system of reflection. *Princeps Concordiae* also demonstrated Dulles' fundamental and long-lasting interest in the mind's and the heart's reception of revelation, the nature of theology as a distinctive discipline distinguished from philosophy, the role of culture in the shaping and development of intellectual traditions, and the catholicity of Catholicism evident in Pico's search for sources of divine wisdom in pagan sages as well as in scripture and the church's tradition.[62]

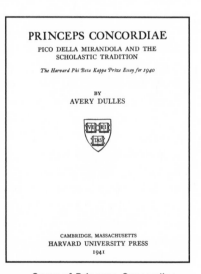

PRINCEPS CONCORDIAE

PICO DELLA MIRANDOLA AND THE
SCHOLASTIC TRADITION

The Harvard Phi Beta Kappa Prize Essay for 1940

BY
AVERY DULLES

CAMBRIDGE, MASSACHUSETTS
HARVARD UNIVERSITY PRESS
1941

Harvard graduation portrait   Cover of *Princeps Concordiae*

During his senior year, while he was preparing his thesis, Dulles was vice president of Harvard's Foreign Relations Club, a student organization. The students (one of whom was the future Protestant

37

theologian Langdon Gilkey) who belonged to this club were, like many students throughout the country in 1939–1940, opposed to American intervention in the European war. During the early months of 1940, the club, with the support of faculty advisers, one of whom was the former chancellor of Germany, Heinrich Bruening, organized a national conference of college students to discuss ways of maintaining peace throughout the world. The club invited more than twenty colleges to the conference. Each college was to send delegates who would represent the issues of specific countries. Harvard chose to represent the interests of Germany; Dartmouth elected Great Britain; and Cornell chose the United States. Other schools impersonated other countries at this supposed international conference.[63] During the conference, the student delegates were to propose ways of avoiding war and determine principles that should govern any settlement of conflicts between nations; the whole concept of a settlement based on victory or defeat in war, the Harvard students wrote to their fellow students, had to be abandoned.

The invitations sent to the different colleges indicated that an international organization based on federalism rather than independent national sovereignties was the real solution to the grievances among the nations. The League of Nations failed, the students wrote (reflecting an earlier paper that Dulles had prepared), because it did not compel governments to surrender any of their sovereign powers. A new international organization based on federalism was needed that would overcome the weaknesses of the sovereign system. The federal system that the students envisioned was one that did not require unanimous consent of the participating nations; such an unrealistic method of decision making would not check the sovereign system. The Harvard students were convinced that a federalism of some type would provide the peaceful means necessary to solve world problems, but they asked all the student delegates to consider what type of international federation would be practical. The student delegates were also to prepare position papers for the conference that would address international disputes that usually centered on the most neuralgic problems: economics, colonization, immigration, and national boundaries.[64]

The conference, "Peace through a New International Order," was held at Harvard from April 12 to 14, 1940. After listening to four keynote addresses by prominent professors, including Bruening,[65] the students began to discuss their position papers. Dulles led the Harvard delegation of students. Prior to the conference he had prepared a position paper, "German Economic Cooperation," that argued that "Germany can solve its economic problems by peaceful means."[66] The problem, however, was that the Versailles Treaty ruined any opportunity for that to happen, because the treaty exacted inordinate reparations from Germany after the war, and the victorious countries, including France, Great Britain, and the United States, put excessive tariff barriers in Germany's way. The Great Depression of 1929, too, led to competitive currency devaluations. Dulles' paper suggested that the way to peaceful change for Germany was "economic cooperation between countries, and an exchange of goods based on economic principles, rather than the desire for self-sufficiency." If the nations involved could gradually lower tariffs and come to some monetary agreements, Germany could eventually solve its economic problems and would not have to resort to war. Germany was endowed with abundant natural resources and a genius for industrial organization, but it needed raw materials from other countries for its industries to operate effectively, and other countries needed what Germany could produce. Some kind of economic agreement was necessary to ensure Germany's success as well as that of other countries. The Harvard student delegation discussed and later revised and adopted much of Dulles' position paper for its own contribution to the conference, "Advance Report of the German Delegation."

Despite the fact that the Yale delegation, representing France, walked out of the conference on the second day,[67] the conference organizers judged the conference an "unqualified success." The eighty or ninety delegates from the twenty colleges had reflected on peaceful ways of determining a just peace. They were "convinced of the imperative necessity of a conclusive change in the conduct of world affairs." They seemed to have agreed, too, that a new international order "based on realities" was needed, although they did not have enough time to discuss the kind of order that was necessary. The conference, widely reported in local and national papers as well as in the *Harvard Crimson*, focused primarily upon economic matters since they "are at the root of most international disputes."[68]

The years at Harvard College, Dulles confessed in 2005, "were formative in a way that no other could be for me."[69] His home life, his summer vacations, and his privileged educational opportunities encouraged him to face and struggle with major philosophical and political issues. Even as a young man, he came to know the strenuous intellectual life and developed the stamina to pursue it with vigor. The world that he experienced during the late 1930s and early 1940s was in turmoil. His own intellectual discoveries and his personal pursuit of perfection and the good life, as Plato understood the good life, led him to raise some serious questions about what was ultimately good, true, and beautiful. As a result of his studies, he told a commencement audience in 2005, "I became a Christian believer and a Catholic, the best decision I have ever made. My entire adult life has been molded by what I learned in my college days, and I hope that you who are graduating today will be able to say the same sixty-five years from now."[70] For it was during his college years that his own religious life became a matter of ultimate concern for him.

3
BECOMING A CATHOLIC, 1937-1941

WHILE PURSUING HIS academic work at Harvard and engaging fellow students in discussions of world affairs, Dulles was also searching for a meaningful religious life, one that reflected the realism he was encountering in his study of medieval and scholastic thought. He had formed his views of world affairs in communion with his father, his Choate classmates, and his own studies at Harvard. But during his last two years at Harvard, other interests had dominated his intellectual horizon and indeed had an effect on his views of international and national problems. His last two years as an undergraduate and his first years as a student at Harvard Law School brought about deeply personal religious and intellectual changes.

Personal Awakening and Discovery

One turning point came in his junior year, 1938–1939, when the Greek and scholastic philosophy he had been studying during his sophomore year started to sink in and he began thinking about the goal of human life and his own life. What was it that drove people to live beyond the pleasure principle? What was it that caused them to transcend their own personal needs? Neither he nor his closest friends were particularly self-centered or focused on the pleasure principle. They saw themselves as dedicated to goals that transcended self-gratification, but they found personal satisfaction in serving the progress of humanity, "the liberation of the toiling masses from the chains of capitalist greed," or world peace or some other cause that served the human condition. They were not hedonists.[1] But could these humanitarian ideals draw forth from the human heart a love and loyalty that lasted? Or could they evoke a dedication that was commensurate with one's final end? What was the ultimate purpose of life? Those were the big questions Dulles faced in his junior year.

Dulles was awakened to the personal importance of those questions one day in February 1938 while he was reading a chapter of Augustine's *City of God* for one of his courses in medieval history. As he records in *A Testimonial to Grace*, he stopped reading the chapter and went on a long walk along the Charles River, where he had what could be called a religious experience, a new revelation about divine "purposiveness."

> As I wandered aimlessly, something impelled me to look contemplatively at a young tree. On its frail, supple branches were young buds attending eagerly the spring which was at hand. While my eye rested on them the thought came to me suddenly, with all the strength and novelty of a revelation, that these little buds in their innocence and meekness followed a rule, a law of which I as yet knew nothing. How could it be, I asked, that this delicate tree sprang up and developed and that all the enormous complexity of its cellular operations combined together to make it grow erectly and bring forth leaves and blossoms? The answer, the trite answer of the schools, was new to me: that its actions were ordered to an end by the only power capable of adapting means to ends—intelligence—and that the very fact that this intelligence worked toward an end implied purposiveness—in other words, a will.[2]

This "revelation" of the presence of a divine will in the world awakened him to the presence of God in his own life, and it elicited from him an act of faith. He returned to his room, fell down upon his knees, as his mother had taught him to do when he was a little boy, and prayed "for the first time in years."[3] He prayed the Our Father with a new conviction of the divine presence and with a fresh sense of its meaning for him personally. This was the beginning of a religious search for meaning that would continue throughout the remainder of his life. His study of history and philosophy had led him to this point and made him receptive to the new revelation, but it was not the source of the experience. His act of faith was the result of a revelation of the presence of God.

After his Charles River religious experience, Dulles decided that he would prayerfully read and meditate upon at least one chapter from the New Testament each day. He also decided that he would begin to attend church services regularly. As his religious experience and search deepened, he "felt the need for some living institution which would bring Christ closer as a Person and apply His lofty principles to the circumstances of this remote age."[4] Throughout the second semester of his junior year and his entire senior year, therefore, he did much church-hopping. He was searching for a religious home, one that corresponded with his experience and his studies of history and philosophy.

On Sundays during the school year, Dulles attended services in several Cambridge and Boston Protestant churches (including Episcopalian, Presbyterian, Baptist, Methodist, Unitarian, and even some nonsectarian), listened to the sermons, and made judgments about the theologies and styles of worship he observed. He found none of them entirely satisfactory. In his 1946 account of his conversion to Catholicism, he indicted them all in a fashion that corresponded to typical Catholic critiques. His disillusionment with Protestant forms of worship reflected his emerging philosophical realism. For the most part, the Protestant forms of worship and the preachers had "failed to emphasize that radical inversion of human values which had been wrought by the Cross on which Christ died. Instead, they appealed primarily to human wisdom and to humanitarian sentiment." To Dulles many of the sermons he heard were little more than "homely disquisitions on self-improvement."[5]

Disappointed with his experiences in the Protestant churches, Dulles decided to attend Mass in a Catholic church. For a Protestant with a substantial Presbyterian heritage and pedigree, this was no minor decision. He knew very little about Catholic forms of worship. He had had few contacts with Catholics during his young life. Some of his Choate and Harvard classmates, like

John Fitzgerald Kennedy, were Catholics, but he had had little substantial communication with any of them. His tutor during his
sophomore year, Paul Doolin, was a convert to Catholicism, and
Dulles respected him greatly. But, going to a Catholic church in
search of "some living institution" was a different matter.

One Sunday during his junior year, he went to Mass, but he
was disappointed with the experience. His Protestant formation
came to the fore, and he was actually repulsed by the sacrificial
symbolism of the Mass and found the sermon "dry in content and
dryly delivered." He realized after attending that Catholic service
that he preferred the "cold chastity of Protestant worship." He also
found disdainful the "sugary sentimentality" that characterized the
popular Catholic religious art and religious emotionalism that was
so much a part of the church's devotionalism in the late 1930s and
early 1940s.[6] In the original manuscript of *A Testimonial to Grace*, in
the parts he deleted for the publication, he was even more forceful.
He noted, for example:

> Nothing was more repugnant to me at this stage than the
> pompous display of embroidered vestments and gilded
> chalices. How far a cry, I thought, from the simplicity of
> the Master!...In the painted statues of saccharine
> Madonnas and of insipidly smiling priests and nuns I
> experienced a positive obstacle to the raising of one's
> mind to God.[7]

But he was attracted to Catholic theology and philosophy as he
found it in his study of medieval and Renaissance thought.

In 2001, Dulles reported that he had learned at Harvard
College that Catholic Christianity, "when deeply held in the hearts
of a people, was capable to [sic] generating an intellectual and artistic culture of the highest caliber."[8] American Catholicism had not in
1940 reached that high caliber of artistic and intellectual expression,
but Dulles had certainly experienced some of it in his various trips to
Europe as a young man. He also discovered during his last two years
of college that the faith and philosophy he so admired in the patristic and medieval authors he was reading for his Harvard courses "was
not simply a thing of the past."[9] Dulles found on Church Street in

Harvard Square a Catholic bookstore, St. Thomas More, that sold and lent books by authors of the Catholic intellectual renaissance of the 1920s and 1930s, and was drawn to the contemporary Catholic neo-scholastic revival. He began reading the works of Etienne Gilson, Jacques Maritain, Karl Adam, Otto Karrer, E. I. Watkin, C. C. Martindale, Cuthbert Butler, Martin D'Arcy, Ross Hoffman, and Paul Hanley Furfey, among others. Quickly he became a regular client at the store, feeding his voracious reading habit.

Dulles made the acquaintance of the store manager, Catherine Goddard Clarke, and her assistant, Louise Mercier, the daughter of Harvard professors Zoé and Louis J. A. Mercier of the French Department. Both women were well read and became his guides in the selection of contemporary as well as medieval Catholic authors. Clarke played an especially important role in his conversion to Catholicism and became his godmother when he was received into the Catholic Church. Louise Mercier recalled years later that Dulles asked her and Clarke for recommendations on what to read, and he "frequently left with dozens of borrowed books."[10] As Louise's youthful diary from this period of her life shows, she had a late teenager's crush on Dulles.[11] Dulles had an affection for her, as he did for a few other women in his Catholic circle, but it was not the same kind of affection that Louise in her early adult years had for him. Nevertheless, she remained one of Dulles' lifelong friends. And years later after she married, she and her husband, Philip Des Marais, frequently invited Dulles to their home.[12]

The St. Thomas More bookstore and lending library was the scene of much of Dulles' contact with Catholics and Catholic authors during his college days. The store had been established in January 1936, by Evangeline Mercier, Mary Stanton, and Martha B. Doherty, all graduates of Emmanuel College.[13] The store was named after St. Thomas More (1478–1535), who was martyred under the reign of King Henry VIII, and in 1935 was canonized as the patron saint of lawyers. The bookstore was a vital center of Catholic activity during the Catholic literary, artistic,[14] and scholastic renaissance of the 1930s and 1940s. It was primarily Catholic intellectual life—its insistence on doctrine, its medieval philosophical and theological realism, and its contemporary neo-scholastic continuity with this medieval tradition—that gradually moved

Dulles toward Catholicism. He discovered increasingly that he was more comfortable with and attached to Catholic patterns of thought than he was with Protestant thought as he had experienced it in Protestant religious services. Dulles' appreciation of Catholic intellectual life preceded his appreciation of American Catholic liturgies, devotional practices, and popular religious art.

By his senior year, Dulles was going to High Mass regularly on Sundays. Clarke helped him select a missal, the *St. Andrew's Missal*, that guided him through the celebration of Mass and answered his questions about Catholic ritual and practices. What impressed him in these liturgical experiences was the large number of those who filled the Cambridge Catholic churches on Sundays and holy days. The multitudes saw something in Catholic ritual and symbolism that he did not at first see. He realized that his initial abhorrence of Catholic symbolism and popular devotional practices and art was caused in part by "a personal unwillingness to succumb to any religious emotion before I had answered intellectually the religious problem. I was determined not to let sentiment draw reason in its wake." Gradually, however, he overcame his initial aversion to popular devotional practices and art, but only after he had professed his faith in the Catholic Church. Then he acknowledged that "in religious art,...devotional value properly takes precedence over purely esthetic considerations."[15]

The power of the ancient faith over ordinary, working-class Catholics in Cambridge served as a witness to Dulles of the potent attractiveness of Catholic worship, and it was something he repeatedly mentioned not only in his *Testimonial* but in his theological writings throughout his life. The "Catholic faith," he told a Polish audience in 2001, "had an extraordinary hold on the minds and hearts of the common people....They were remarkably faithful in their religious observance. Their piety was governed by the same revelation that had inspired the great artists and poets of earlier centuries."[16] The witness of popular Catholicism was another contributing factor in his process of conversion, and he repeatedly reflected upon this sense of the faith that he found in the churches in his later theological writings.[17]

As he was in the process of examining and experiencing Catholic life and thought, Dulles was simultaneously involved in

Republican politics. During the summers of 1939 and 1940, he worked for Thomas E. Dewey (1902–1971), the New York district attorney and Dulles' father's good friend and fellow Republican, who was anticipating a run as the Republican candidate for the presidency. In the summer of 1939, Dewey had hired Dulles to work for what was called the Transcontinental Research Incorporation, a cover for Dewey's presidential aspirations. Dulles spent the summers of 1939 and 1940 doing research on presidential campaigns since 1912. Dewey was interested in the techniques used for capturing the enthusiasm of the electorate. Dulles examined historical studies of the campaigns and newspapers in the New York Public Library, trying to determine "why the person who had won had won" and then prepared reports that summarized the results of his research.[18]

The reports revealed an incisive and synthetic mind analyzing the major campaign issues, the styles of campaigning, and the probable reasons for the results. In addition, Dulles indicated his own personal assessments of the campaigns and the lessons they taught. In analyzing, for example, the circumstances surrounding Wilson's nomination as the presidential candidate, Dulles concluded "that political organization, where it was vigorously carried on, was as effective as the speaking tours were ineffective."[19] In his assessment of the 1920 campaign, Dulles passed rapidly over Ohio's Governor James M. Cox's campaign against Warren G. Harding, asserting that it was instructive "only as an example of everything which a candidate for President ought not to do. In the first place, the Cox campaign was based on a complete misunderstanding of the mood of the nation."[20] Cox was aggressive, moreover, used immoderate language against his opponents, denounced minorities in a most intolerant manner, complained of being persecuted by the newspapers and big business, and held on to a Wilsonian idealism that was dead in the country.

In a paper on neutrality legislation from 1933 to 1939, Dulles warned Dewey against any isolationist positions relative to the current war in Europe, but he also thought that President Roosevelt's signing of the Neutrality Act of 1936 left him vulnerable to charges of inconsistency. "One may," Dulles wrote, "profitably contrast these words [of Roosevelt's on neutrality when signing the

Neutrality Act of 1936] with those used by the President today."[21] In the end, Dulles argued for maintaining "our neutrality legislation" with some changes to remedy the defects; but he did not advocate a "complete neutrality" because such a stance would be impossible without sweeping embargoes that would damage trade unnecessarily.[22] Dulles' reports were object lessons for Dewey to consider as he anticipated a nomination as the Republican candidate for president in the June 1940 Republican Convention, which Avery attended with his father.

At the end of July 1940, after the Republican Convention, Dewey thanked Dulles for his research assistance.[23] The research had been helpful even though the Republican Party had selected Wendell Willkie (1892–1944) over Dewey as its presidential candidate; Willkie was more of an interventionist with respect to the war in Europe than were Dewey and John Foster Dulles. In 1944 and 1948, however, Dewey, with the help of John Foster Dulles, won the Republican nomination for president and ran a vigorous campaign. Avery attended the 1944 Republican Convention, too, but in 1948 he was in the Jesuit novitiate and far removed from politics.

After working behind the scenes on Dewey's 1940 presidential aspirations, Dulles joined his father for their August outing on the *Menemsha*. They started their trip to the northern shores of Lake Superior from the Detroit Yacht Club, where the boat had been taken by Robert Hart. During the excursion, Dulles reread Augustine's *Confessions* and continued to contemplate the direction of his own religious life, but no one in the family had a clue that he was considering a change in his life. After returning from their summer sailing journey, Avery was off to Harvard Law School.

Becoming a lawyer seemed natural. He was following in his father's footsteps. When he returned to Harvard in the fall, he dutifully began to study the law, but deep down he was more interested in philosophy, literature, and religion than in the law. Indeed he spent more time reading in religion and theology than he did in law. He continued, too, to be involved in discussing world affairs. Like Thomas Dewey and his father, he opposed what he considered the increasing interventionist propaganda by those who supported American entrance into the war. In 1939 he had joined the Harvard chapter of the American Independence League, and in

September 1940 he prepared a position paper that he sent out to other students encouraging them to join the league in opposition to the American interventionists.

The purpose of the league, he declared, was primarily academic: that is, to inform students of the issues involved and to create a sense of collaboration among "students all over the country, ready to demonstrate and exercise every possible pressure to *keep this country out of war*." The league opposed two attitudes that were emerging: what Dulles called "international romanticism" and "mass fatalism." "We found out in the last war," Dulles argued in opposition to the international romanticists, "that when we fight to save democracy abroad we only risk losing it in all countries." It was useless, moreover, to "impose a settlement by force unless we are prepared to maintain it by force—unless we make ourselves a totalitarian state organized for war." The other attitude, "mass fatalism," was equally opposed to peace. The fatalists declared that it was "inevitable that we will get drawn into the war." Dulles rejected this attitude, writing that "it is impossible for that to happen so long as there is a *strong, organized, vocal opinion against war*." Students were needed to resist the movement toward war, and Dulles encouraged them to join the league and pay the ten-cent token membership fee.[24]

In the midst of these and other activities as a law school student during the fall of 1940, Dulles was personally moving more and more toward a decision to become a visible member of the Catholic Church. The intellectual and esthetic clues and evidences for such a decision had been mounting and converging since he was a sophomore in college. He had been drawn to the philosophical and theological realistic metaphysics of the Greek philosophers, the medievalists, and the neo-scholastics and found in the contemporary Catholic intellectual revival a powerful alternative to the liberalism that had been so much a part of his earlier life. Like Orestes Brownson and John Henry Newman in the nineteenth century, he developed a crucial critique of liberalism, especially in his autobiographical account of his conversion. *Liberalism* became for him, as it had for Brownson and Newman, a code word for everything that was wrong with contemporary intellectual culture. His earlier Harvard College essays, as we have already seen, defined his opposition to liberalism. He found in the contemporary Catholic Church, as he indicated in his autobiography, not only a metaphysical realism as an alternative to liberalism but also a vigorous and explicit critique of the liberal mentality.[25]

Catholic social philosophy, too, had become an attractive intellectual option for him. He found in that philosophy an understanding of the human person, the family, and the state that offered a potent alternative to some modern notions. The human person, in this view, was dependent on fellow human beings for personal survival and development. Such a philosophy of the human person as a connected entity countered the contemporary "gross overemphasis on the autonomy of the human person." In such a philosophy, furthermore, the family and the state were not perceived as pure creatures of the human will but as part of a divinely ordered reality.[26]

Dulles also discovered in the course of his life the beauty and aesthetic qualities of Catholic art and architecture. His trips to Europe in particular made him aware that the Catholic way of life gave rise not only to an attractive and compelling philosophy of life but also to a religious artistic achievement that was unparalleled. His initial negative reaction to liturgical symbolism and to American Catholic devotional practices was gradually overcome by his examination of that symbolism and his frequent attendance and limited participation in Catholic liturgical services. His church hopping as an undergraduate had acquainted him only with alternative forms of worship that had a limited, not a compelling, attraction. He became especially drawn to the powerful drama of the Triduum services of the death and resurrection of Christ during Holy Week in 1940.[27]

His regular meditative and prayerful reading of the Bible since his junior year in college also contributed to his religious awakening. In scripture, he discovered Christ as the source and mediator of salvation for his soul, and his reading deepened the longing of his mind and heart for the salvation that comes from identification with Christ. Salvation became available to the world through the incarnate Christ, and the "logic" of the incarnation required a visible, organic, community of faith to put subsequent generations of believers in communion with Christ. Reading the Bible and Catholic sources eventually convinced him of the intimate and inherent connection between Christ and the Catholic Church. The salvation of Christ came to the individual, he began to believe, through the church's sacraments, ministry, and authority. Dulles records in his autobiography that he heard in his mind the divine reply to his search and longing for Christ and salvation: "In My Church, came the gracious reply, you will find Me indeed."[28] The divine reply was an invitation to examine the church's claims as the logical extension of the incarnation, as the fullest realization of the four marks of the church, as an infallible and indefectible institution established by the will of Christ. "None of the Protestant denominations," he asserted, even claimed, as did the Catholic Church, to "safeguard the integrity of the faith, to spread the Gospel to all nations, to enunciate the moral law, and to administer the Sacraments."[29] Dulles investigated these claims and became convinced that they were justified.

Dulles found some confirmation of his understanding of the Catholic intellectual, moral, aesthetic, and religious tradition in the multitudes of simple Catholics who attended Mass on Sundays and holy days in the Cambridge churches. He also found some confirmation of this in the Catholics that he met in and around the St. Thomas More bookstore and in discussions with Catholic college students in and around Cambridge. Many years after he left Cambridge, Dulles recorded that at Harvard Law he met graduates from Catholic colleges whose confidence in their faith was a "counterpoise to the relativism that pervaded the air."[30]

Doubts and Decision

No one of these clues or pieces of evidence, nor the convergence and combination of all of them, however, were enough to make Dulles decide to join the Catholic Church. At the most, they removed obstacles in the way of a decision, or they made joining the Catholic Church a truly viable option for him. But roadblocks to a decision were also present. His intellectual search had not compelled him toward a determination; he had unresolved doubts about apparently contradictory teachings in the Bible and lingering hesitancies about unanswered questions on the Catholic tradition. He continued to be uncomfortable with certain popular devotional practices within Catholicism. In addition, as a twenty-two-year-old, he had some "last-minute" doubts about the finality involved in joining the Catholic Church. Was he ready to submit himself to Catholic authority and commit himself for life to the Catholic Church? The church demanded no less, and even though that was an attractive feature, it also "appalled" him. He worried, further-more, about how his family and his friends would take his decision if he became a Catholic. He had a natural reluctance to "take any action which would estrange me from my family and friends."[31]

Nonetheless, by mid-September 1940, Dulles decided that he needed to make some serious inquiries about joining the Catholic Church. Once he made up his mind, he went to the St. Thomas More bookstore and asked Catherine Clarke how he might become a Catholic. She told him he would have to take instructions and directed him to Fr. Edwin A. Quain, a Jesuit priest who was getting a doctorate in Greek and Latin at Harvard. Dulles met Quain in mid-September and for about six weeks Quain prepared Dulles for reception into the Catholic Church.

The decision, as Dulles himself indicated, was a leap of faith that transcended both his reasons for and his reasons against it. In the midst of the mounting evidence and converging clues as well as lingering doubts, he put his trust in God and attributed his deter-mination to a grace-given act of faith. "That I did eventually make this act of faith is attributed solely to the grace of God. I could never have done so by my own power."[32] But faith was not an act of blind trust or an irrational act; it was done in the midst of clues and evidences and reasons that he had been investigating. Much later in life, Dulles acknowledged that he "could hardly imagine any adult coming to Christian or Catholic faith without having deliberated for some time and having found good reasons for adopting the faith. (Certainly I myself found reasons)."[33] Nonetheless, he just could not get over the hump of the negative reasons without a trusting confidence in a power that transcended his own abilities and natural resistances. Ultimately, his trust in God transcended, but did not annihilate, the evidences of reason.[34]

During his instructions with Quain, Dulles decided rather firmly that he wanted to become a Catholic. Quain believed that he was well prepared and could be received into the church.

Throughout his college years and into the fall of 1940, Dulles had kept his leanings toward Catholicism to himself. He, of course, had been close to Catherine Clarke and the Mercier sisters, and he made known the direction of his life to them, but he had not explicitly shared his inclinations to join the Catholic Church with his parents. He thought that they must have known the direction of his mind.[35] But parents do not always know what their children, especially their adult children, are thinking, and Dulles' parents were completely unaware that he was leaning toward Catholicism. Originally, according to Louise Mercier's diary, Dulles was planning on being baptized on November 1, 1940, but the baptism was postponed "because of complications in the family."[36]

Apparently Dulles had informed his parents during late October of his intention to join the Catholic Church, and they were surprised and disturbed by the news. He realized then that he needed to explain to them his reasons for becoming a Catholic, so he deferred his baptism. On November 3 his mother sent him a telegram, now lost, inviting him home and apparently asking him to discuss his decision with his parents. In response to the telegram, he wrote to his mother saying that he could not come home at the moment because he had to prepare his first legal brief for one of his law school classes. He also tried to soften the blow of his decision by intimating that although his decision was almost inevitable, he was willing to wait before acting on it. He had in fact, if Louise Mercier's diary can be trusted, made up his mind before writing the letter. Nonetheless, in an attempt to break the news to his parents as gently as he could, he told his mother:

> I am not doing anything about entering the Catholic Church for the moment. It is largely a question of how much I can dare to disbelieve, having strong reasons for believing so much. Christianity is not a thing that can be done by halves. If one admits it at all he must consent to be entirely reborn. The comfortable middle position, which is so inviting, is utterly untenable. I do not know whether conscience can long allow me to remain without commitment, but for the moment I am resolved to wait.[37]

By the middle of November, however, he determined to wait no longer and told his parents that he was going to join the Catholic Church.

As soon as they received the news, Dulles' mother called him and asked him to come home to discuss his resolution with his father. She was upset, and so was his father, as his brother John Watson Foster Dulles remembers. Avery went to New York on November 24 to explain to his father the reasons for his resolve. According to Avery's brother, his father tried to talk Avery out of his decision.[38] This assessment was not how Avery himself remembered it. He has said that his father was definitely "surprised" by his decision, but after a long conversation, his father accepted it because he believed it was based on Avery's strong conscientious convictions. Dulles' parents were not anti-Catholic, but, Avery reported in 1997, "they didn't think the Catholic Church was quite respectable. They were brought up in a Protestant culture in which Catholics, on the whole, were people at the lower social and intellectual level."[39] In 1966, he recalled the conversation with his father, noting in particular that his father

> didn't have a very favorable view of Catholicism at that time. I think that his own closest contact with Catholicism was when he was a boy in Spain, which was a country where there was a great deal of official Catholicism, but he felt that the moral standards were very low. You know, coming as a Presbyterian from up-state New York—he was struck by the contrast. This was in 1909, the year when he studied in Paris. He learned Spanish and lived with a Spanish family, I think. Anyway, this was pretty much his picture of Catholicism, and it was not a very favorable one. So, he felt that the main argument against Catholicism was not anything of a theoretical or theological or of a philosophical nature, but simply that it didn't work out in practice, because you could get situations like this where social and moral standards were deplorably low.
>
> But again, he respected my reasons as my own and didn't try to exercise any kind of pressure on me not to become a Catholic.[40]

Nonetheless, his parents were deeply upset and somewhat hurt by Avery's choice. He was turning his back on a long Presbyterian family heritage and entering a religious tradition they considered authoritarian and spiritually superficial. They tried to convince him to delay his entrance into the church until his grandmother Dulles, who was in bad health and close to death, had passed away. Dulles, however, felt he could not delay what he called the "grace of conversion" and preferred to explain his decision to his grandmother than postpone it any longer.[41]

When he returned to Harvard, the day before he was received into the Catholic Church, he wrote to his parents thanking them for the opportunity to discuss his decision with them and explaining again the reasons for his resolution. The letter is worthy of some considerable attention because it outlines something of his mind at the time of his conversion. He had become convinced of the divinity of Christ, he told them, and "it would be hardly possible for me to admit the Divinity of Christ and to deny the authenticity of the Church." The gospel, he believed, called him to that church that Christ had established. He perceived, moreover, a continuity between what Christ taught and what the Catholic Church taught, a continuity he did not find in the Protestant churches, he told his parents.

> Finally, the Catholic Church is the only Church today which teaches what Christ seems to have taught. Christ believed in the power of devils, most of the Protestant Churches do not. Christ believed in eternal punishment for those who deliberately sin against God, and do not repent. Christ believed that prayer was an effective means of obtaining both spiritual and material rewards. Christ believed that this world was primarily a preparation for the next, and repudiated the humanitarianism which has come to dominate the Protestant churches. He taught that Christian doctrine must be the basis of our social relations. He believed that the most important thing in the world was the salvation of souls. He said that those who disbelieve, contrary to their better judgment, would be condemned. He insisted on absolute ortho-

doxy, while most the the [sic] Protestant churches today think that faith is of no importance except insofar as it affects what we do (utilitarianism).[42]

Christ emphasized the necessity and radical nature of faith, and Dulles found that same radical demand in the Catholic Church. He wanted his parents to know that he was joining the Catholic Church because he felt called by Christ to a radical decision and "that there are good rational bases for my belief." Dulles' later interests in apologetics stems to some extent from his personal experience in explaining to his parents the reasons for the faith that was in him.

His parents prudently had cautioned him to wait to make sure his decision was based on permanent and not fleeting convictions. Dulles assured them:

You may well think that I ought to wait a while to make sure that I will always believe as I now believe. But I am quite sure that any further development of my personality will not alter my views. Catholicism is not made for people of only one temperament, as anyone who knows many Catholics could tell you, and as you undoubtedly know from your experience. I am not going into the Church merely for my own pleasure. I feel it is a duty.

Dulles also wanted to persuade his parents that his admiration for Catholicism was not just a result of his medieval studies. In fact, he told them it was his love of Plato that first gave him a sense of the personal direction of his life. Plato convinced him "that moral and intellectual values are absolutely transcendent, and not relative to the individual." Those convictions he also found in Catholicism. His current thinking, moreover, was not governed by the influence of Catholic friends or teachers. "I would assure you that the road to Catholicism is one which I have taken alone." Most of his close Harvard friends were "complete unbelievers." He had almost no close friends who were Catholic. Since his sophomore year, furthermore, he had not studied under any Catholic teachers at Harvard. When he returned to Harvard in the fall of 1940, he began to make a few Catholic friends who shared with him an understanding of Catholicism he could not find in books.

He concluded this long letter by assuring his parents that his allegiance to Catholicism would in no way decrease his love and respect for and his allegiance to them. "The Catholic Church is almost alone today in insisting on the sanctity of the family. It emphasizes the duty of every Christian to honor his father and his mother." Dulles knew, moreover, that his parents accepted his decision even though they themselves had many doubts. He believed that their doubts were "more for my sake than for your own. But I feel quite confident that I am taking the right step—indeed what is for me the only step."

On November 26, 1940, the day after this letter to his parents, in a small private ceremony at St. Paul's Church in Cambridge, Fr. Quain baptized Dulles conditionally, as was then the common practice when the Catholic Church received Protestants into the fold. He chose November 26 because it was the feast day of St. John of Berchmans (1599–1621), a young Jesuit scholastic known for his exceptional piety and devotion to the Jesuit rule of life. His godparents were Catherine Clarke and Christopher Huntington, an assistant dean of freshmen at Harvard and a recent convert to Catholicism from a renowned Episcopalian family.[43] After the ceremony, Dulles hosted a dinner for a few friends at the Commander Hotel in Cambridge.

After his reception into the church, he wrote to his grandmother Dulles to explain the reasons for his decision. His father, however, had already informed her of that decision so she would not be unprepared for Avery's announcement. After receiving Avery's letter, Grandmother Dulles wrote to him, telling him that he had been in her thoughts ever since his father had told her that he had decided to enter the Catholic Church.

In 1934, a few years before she had become ill, Avery's seventy-one-year-old grandmother had written an autobiography that she had privately printed for all her grandchildren. *The Story of My Life* recorded contacts with the Catholic Church while she and her sister accompanied her father, John Watson Foster, on his diplomatic missions to Catholic countries. She noted in great detail the Holy Thursday ceremonies she attended with her family, other foreign dignitaries, and the royal family in Madrid. She was particularly impressed by the washing of the feet at the Spanish royal palace where the Holy Thursday Mass took place. Archbishop Mariano Rampolla del Tindaro (1843–1913), the Apostolic Nuncio to Spain, presided at the Mass, at which were, among others, thirteen poor men and twelve poor women. During the Mass, King Alfonso XII (1824–1885) washed the feet of the men, and Queen Maria Christina (1858–1912), with the assistance of Archbishop Rampolla and members of the Spanish nobility, washed the feet of the women.[45] After the Mass, the king and Spanish nobility served a fifteen-course meal to the poor who were the guests of honor.[46] Prior to the Mass, moreover, the king and queen had provided the poor men and women with new sets of clothing. These impressive events remained in Edith Foster Dulles' memory. She understood the power and symbolism of the Spanish Last Supper ceremonies.

In 1940, while confined to bed by her illness, she assured Avery that he as well as all her grandchildren were constantly in her thoughts and prayers. On his decision to enter the Catholic Church, she told him, "I feel that I can understand perhaps better than any of the others your attitude." She had herself spent all of her childhood years in Mexico, where she was regularly and directly in contact with the Catholic Church; then in France, "where the beauty of Notre Dame and many others made their impression on me"; and then the two years in Spain, where

> as we came in contact with the royal family we also came in contact with their many religious ceremonies. Then of course, I have read the lives of so many of the beautiful saints and enjoyed the churches at Assisi and Perugia. While all these things did not convert me, from the faith in which I had been so seriously brought up, yet it helps me to understand your position.[44]

She told her grandson that she was proud that he had taken such a serious interest in religion, particularly at a time when, as the news reports seemed to indicate, so many young people had abandoned religion. "I only wish," she continued, "that the Protestant church in which I firmly believe could draw its members so closely to itself and what it represents as the Catholic church seems to do."[47]

When she had first learned of Avery's decision, she told him, she had been saddened and feared that it would create a division in the family, but the longer she thought about it the more she began to realize that

> after all, the one essential of religion is to feel and be conscious of the Presence of God and as we come into His presence to more and more follow the teachings of Jesus. Therefore that sadness has passed and I feel that perhaps we are closer than ever as we have discussed these vital matters of religion. So I hope that all joy and happiness may come to you in your new experiences of religion.

The letter was a great comfort to Avery, and after receiving it he visited his grandmother in Auburn, New York, and thereafter frequently corresponded with her until her death on June 8, 1941.

Avery's grandmother kept up her nurturing role until she died. Her correspondence with Avery during her last months reveals the kinds of insights into her grandson's soul that some grandmothers are privileged to have. Avery and his grandmother corresponded about literature, devotional reading, prayer, and family matters. At one point in discussing literature, she revealed that she may have understood Avery better than he did himself at that point in his career. "The study of Law," she wrote, "must be a great contrast to the other literature which means so much to you." She also periodically requested that Avery send her some good devotional literature that she could have read to her in the mornings and in the evenings. She had *A Diary of Private Prayer* (1936) by the Scottish Presbyterian John Baillie (1886–1960), but she could not find in his work "any thoughts which will help me through the day."[48] Avery responded to her requests, periodically finding Catholic devotional literature in the St. Thomas More bookstore that he thought his grandmother might find fruitful during her last days. He sent her devotional works, among which were Pierre Charles's *Prayer for All Times* (1925 and many subsequent editions), Joseph McSorley's

Think and Pray (1936), and other meditation books. At one point, his grandmother wrote that the devotional literature he sent was being read to her every morning and she was finding great comfort in it. "I always think of you and thank you when we have read our chapter."[49]

She was proud, too, that her daughter Margaret was giving talks on the Bible in New York, that Avery's father was doing so much good work for the churches in New York, and that Avery himself was contributing to the benefit of the world through his religious activities. At one point Avery told her of the good work that the Baroness Catherine de Hueck (1896–1985), founder of Friendship Houses in Toronto (1930) and in Harlem in New York City (1938), was doing for the "needy colored children" in New York City and how his young Catholic friends from Boston were going to New York to aid de Hueck's work among the poor. After hearing about de Hueck's work, his grandmother wrote to Avery agreeing with him that "it is wonderful as you say to find the old Mystical spirit appearing again." As she moved toward her final days, she was encouraged that the religious upbringing that she and her husband had tried to communicate to the family was evidenced in the works of her children and grandchildren. She told Avery, "It gives me great joy to know that so many members of the family are giving help where it tis [sic] so much needed today"[50]—a continual refrain in many of her letters to Avery.

She was also proud of her family's literary efforts, especially so of Avery's newly published book, *Princeps Concordiae*, on Pico della Mirandola, which Avery sent her in February 1941. She could not read Avery's book, as she could not read her daughter Eleanor's book on economics,[51] because they were beyond her capacity. But she was delighted "that we have children and grandchildren who can surpass us in both economica and Italian art [sic]."[52] She also purchased copies of Avery's book to give to her friends. "I find that several people are interested in your book and I have given several away myself."[53]

Avery's mother, too, was gratified by his accomplishments as a scholar and writer, purchasing numerous copies of his book and sending it to relatives and friends. John W. Davis, one of the family's longtime friends, a retired lawyer from a prestigious Manhattan law firm (Davis, Polk, and Wardwell) and a Democratic presidential candidate in 1924, read Avery's book with much interest. He reported back to the proud mother that he had read the book with great pleasure and was not surprised that it had won the Harvard Phi Beta Kappa Prize. The book, Davis continued, "gives evidence not only of great research but of an unusual power of analysis. Congratulate him for me." The seventy-year-old former law partner predicted that Avery would have great success if he continued on in the law, but, he insisted, the "best thing I can wish for him—and I am quite serious about this—is that as he approaches seventy these [philosophical] topics may seem as interesting and important to him as they do today."[54]

In the spring of 1941, Avery received the sacrament of confirmation from Bishop Richard J. Cushing. When Catholics received this sacrament they were asked to choose a confirmation name, usually a name of one of the saints, indicating their own personal commitment to follow a life of holiness. Dulles chose the name Robert after one of his favorite saints, the Jesuit theologian Robert Bellarmine. Dulles had first learned of Bellarmine in a Harvard undergraduate class on the history of political thought in the West. Charles H. McIlwain's "respectful presentation" of Bellarmine's work in that class piqued Dulles' interest, and during his first semester at Harvard Law, he read James Brodrick's *The Life and Work of Blessed Robert Francis Cardinal Bellarmine* (1928). Dulles continued his interest in Bellarmine's work off and on throughout his later career as a theologian and historian of apologetics, considering him, as a 1994 essay argued, "A Moderate in a Disputatious Age."[55]

St. Benedict Center

Shortly before and after his acceptance into the Catholic Church, Avery had become increasingly more active in promoting religious and intellectual life among Catholic students in the Boston area. Before and while he was taking instructions from Fr. Quain, he joined the St. Andrew's Club, a gathering of Catholic students from Harvard, Radcliffe, MIT, Cambridge Junior College, Emmanuel, and other colleges in the area. Students from these schools met regularly in the living room of a wealthy Catholic convert, Mrs. Francis Gray, to discuss issues of faith and philosophy. By the early months of 1941, the club had outgrown her living room. The students needed more space and a more permanent structure for Catholic student discussions and lectures on religious, philosophical, and literary topics. In response to this need, Dulles, Catherine Clarke, Margaret Knapp, and Christopher Huntington found an empty building across from St. Paul's Catholic Church in Cambridge, negotiated a low rent, and moved the student group into the new building in the spring of 1941, calling the place St. Benedict Center.

The center became controversial in the Catholic community in the late 1940s when Fr. Leonard Feeney, SJ, the leader at the center after 1942, began teaching that no salvation existed outside of the visible Catholic Church, a doctrine that got him in trouble with church authorities. Eventually, because of disobedience, he was excommunicated.[56] These controversies, however, arose in the late 1940s, long after Dulles had separated himself from the center.

The center offered enough space for a lending library for students and faculty in the area who were interested in books on a variety of Catholic topics. During the summer of 1941, Dulles spent much time and contributed some of his financial resources to furnishing the new center. Although the center periodically supplied student volunteers to assist Catherine de Hueck's Friendship House in Harlem and Dorothy Day's Catholic Worker Movement, it was primarily, according to Dulles, a cultural and intellectual center rather than a social action club. At the beginning the center had no overarching philosophy; it was simply a place where lay students and faculty could meet and discuss their faith. Even though the group received periodic visits from clergy, it had no permanent priest or theologian. It was primarily a lay group and movement. Nor was the center a part of the Harvard Catholic Club, a low-key group that was reluctantly but officially acknowledged by the Boston Archdiocese.[57]

During Dulles' time in Boston, furthermore, the center had no "integral Catholic culture" that was suspicious of all values outside its own circle, as would become the case under the influence of Fr. Feeney a couple of years after the end of World War II. In the early years, the center was, in fact, open to the secular education at Harvard and other places. Dulles, in particular, found no signs at Harvard of any fierce anti-Catholicism. "Certainly the people I studied under, while most of them were not Catholics, were highly respectful of the Catholic tradition."[58]

While they were establishing the center in the late spring of 1941, Dulles, together with Catherine Clarke and Madeleine Mercier, went to visit Sr. Evangeline of Jesus at the Carmelite Convent in Roxbury. Sr. Evangeline had been aware of Dulles' journey to Catholicism and had been in frequent communication with her family about his developments. The visit had an impact upon Dulles, as he revealed in a letter to Zoé Mercier. The letter intimated that he had a yearning for the religious life. He reported that "after two hours of conversation with Sister Evangeline of Jesus I felt that in leaving I was going away from the one place where things really happen, away from the dynamo of grace & truth, and into the 'world' which is so full of motion but so empty of the pure, the divine, activit[y] of perfect rest."[59] Nothing less than total commitment would satisfy him.

After the center was up and running under the management of Catherine Clarke and after his first year as a law student, Dulles returned to his home in New York City during the summer of 1941 to work again for Thomas Dewey in the district attorney's office, but this time as a law assistant assigned to work primarily in the Racket Bureau, a task that Dewey noted "called for qualities of penetration and discretion."[60] Avery's father had that summer purchased Duck Island in Lake Ontario as a vacation retreat and invited his son John to join him there to "do some miscellaneous sailing" on the lake. He hoped, too, that Avery could join them, "if we can get him away from the District Attorney's office where he is now very busily engaged breaking up rackets and dealing with thugs and gunmen."[61] The three of them met at Duck Island and boarded the *Menemsha* for what would be their last sailing excursion together on Lake Ontario. The trip gave the three of them a relaxing opportunity to discuss world affairs and philosophy as well as family matters.

During this trip, as his brother John remembers it, his father made sure that on Fridays they served fish for the dinner meal in respect for Avery's Catholicism.[62] In September John Foster sold the *Menemsha*, "much to my grief," as he told his son John.[63] The three Dulles men had fond memories of these sailing trips, breathing in the fresh air off the lakes, fishing, swimming (even in the ice cold water), seeing new sights every year, and, most of all, being together as a family. In the midst of World War II, John Foster Dulles kidded with his son John that he hoped a recent fishing expedition that John had had "showed more results than you and Avery generally produced."[64] John Foster Dulles thoroughly delighted in his time with his sons. As he told his son John during the war, he yearned for the day "when you and Avery and I can again do something like that together."[65] Avery in his eighties and John in his nineties shared their father's sentiments about these trips during their youth, as my interviews with them confirmed.

Dulles became a Catholic during a period of great world turmoil and insecurity, and he, like other English-speaking intellectuals since the 1920s, found in the Catholic Church an emphasis upon Christ and transcendental realities that were not evident to him in the other religious traditions he investigated. By joining the Catholic Church, Dulles was identifying himself with a religious community that had always been something of a minority tradition in the United States. He was well aware of that at the time. Forty years later, when speaking of the relationship between discovery and revelation, he acknowledged that "those who have had an intense experience of personal conversion are in a position to stand within a cognitive minority. They do not cherish the illusion that the majority is always right."[66]

After Dulles united himself with the Catholic Church, he continued his opposition to American entrance into the war until the summer of 1941, prior to Pearl Harbor, when he applied for a commission in the U.S. Naval Reserve. By then, he, like many other students, was convinced that the United States could not avoid the war. He was aware of the imminence of war, and he did not want to be drafted into the Army. He believed he was more fit for the Naval Reserve, a branch of the service where he had some skills that would be useful. He was not a pacifist, but an internationalist, and although he opposed war as a means of settling international disputes, he was enough of an American pragmatist to see that the country needed to be prepared for the eventuality of a war. Like many others of his age, he supported his country in a time of trouble and joined the Naval Reserve to demonstrate his obligation; in doing so, he became a part of Tom Brokaw's "Greatest Generation."[67]

4

THE NAVY YEARS, 1941–1946

WHEN HE RETURNED TO his New York City home from the August 1941 sailing trip, Dulles enlisted for the U.S. Naval Reserve and applied for a commission as ensign. John Fitzgerald Kennedy, his fellow Harvard classmate, was doing the same in Boston, as were numerous other college and high school graduates across the country. It was becoming evident, even for someone like Dulles who had opposed America's entrance into the war, that the United States needed to be prepared for that terrible eventuality. Dulles, however, would not be called into the Naval Reserve until after Pearl Harbor. After enlisting, he returned to Cambridge to begin his second year in Harvard Law School.

His return to Harvard Law was short-lived. The bombing of Pearl Harbor, the "day of infamy" (December 7, 1941), would change his life and that of many other young men. The day of the bombing, Dulles was at Mass at the German Church in Boston, listening to the Von Trapp Family singing hymns. On December 19, 1941, Dulles announced to friends at St. Benedict Center the "shocking news," as the young and lovestruck Louise Mercier put it,[1] that he was to leave and join the Navy, and for the next five years he would be involved in the war effort.[2] Pearl Harbor had energized the nation and brought out the old war spirit that former isolationists had dreaded and that internationalists, like Dulles, had previously criticized. But the world situation had changed, and America was under siege. Dulles and most of his Harvard and St. Benedict Center friends supported the call for war in defense of the country and in opposition to worldwide totalitarianism. The situation in the United States had changed since Dulles' more optimistic days, when he believed that the United States could stay out of war and lead the world to peace through some kind of world organization that would bring countries together both to discuss their grievances and to find peaceful ways to secure justice and equity in the world. He had not given up on the need for peaceful means of reconciling international hostilities, but, in view of Pearl Harbor, he supported the country's need for self-defense and his own duty to contribute to that defense.

Modern War and Christian Conscience

After Pearl Harbor, Dulles reexamined his opposition to American entrance into the war. Ever the academic, he sat down in April 1942 and wrote out for himself "Modern War and the Christian Conscience," a paper that considered the injustices of most modern wars, the possibility and conditions of a just war, the just powers of the state in a time of war, and the obligations of a citizen in a time of war. Using the traditional just war theory, Dulles put forth the legitimate reasons for a government's use of force and its right in some instances to inflict death. The ruler, he wrote, quoting St. Paul, "beareth not the sword in vain: for he is a minister of God, an avenger to execute wrath upon him that doth evil" (Rom 13:4). The Christian conscience had no inherent difficulty with a declaration of war in certain prescribed instances. "To declare war against a foreign power that seeks to oppress one's own subjects is not only a right but a duty."[3] There were strict limits, however, for declaring a war just, and from Dulles' perspective, most modern wars did not meet the legitimate criteria.

Most modern wars were waged for purposes of economic or political domination. Governments indoctrinated their peoples to some kind of "fanatic hatred" for the enemy and proclaimed a "most inordinate self-righteousness." Preemptive wars of belligerent governments were generally, Dulles declared, promoted by governments who "judge their enemies by standards which they would shrink from applying to themselves" and "trick their enemies by the fabrication of lies and the suppression of truth. Domestic liberties are heedlessly trampled under foot." These unjust modern wars slaughter "innocent non-combatants," spread famine and disease and the "wanton destruction of the bounty of nature and the choicest treasures of art."[4]

Nonetheless, there were times in the modern world when a state had to exercise its legitimate powers to resist belligerent governments that had prosecuted unjust wars. In such cases, citizens of a state under siege were duty-bound to support the state in its declaration of war. The citizen had the duty when a just war was declared to serve as "an instrument of the State in the execution of justice." The citizen who became a soldier, moreover, was obliged to follow orders. "Unless, then, the war is manifestly unjust, the soldier who is called by the State to fight is no more responsible to see to the justice of that act than is the executioner who is ordered to put to death a duly tried, though possibly innocent, convict. There must be a strong presumption that the authority, antecedently delegated to the State, has been legitimately exercised." In all of this, of course, the Christian must remember that "God is to be obeyed rather than men." Dulles had come to terms intellectually with the necessity of the American declaration of war and became a willing participant in it, considering it a privilege to be an "instrument of the state."[5]

He was still in New York City at the time he wrote "Modern War and the Christian Conscience" and read it to his father, who "objected to the whole notion of social justice. He said that nobody knew what was just in social relations, but only what was expedient for the community as a whole. Of course he was willing to recognize the concept of charity, but he said that Christ didn't say anything about justice, so far as he knew." In other words, Dulles told his godfather Christopher Huntington, "the article, written for myself and for you, will not have much meaning for non-Catholics."[6]

Christopher Huntington wrote to Dulles after receiving his article and wondered why he had not applied his principles to the present war. Dulles admitted that principles need to be applied if they were to mean anything, "but under modern conditions I don't see how the citizen of any state can attempt to pronounce on such matters."[7] Application demanded a knowledge of facts, and most citizens just did not have the facts at their command. One could presume that the authorities had the facts upon which they based their decisions, and Dulles was willing to presume that they made the right decision. He was exercising here what he would later call a "hermeneutics of trust" with respect to decisions made by ecclesiastical as well as civil authorities. But such a presumption and such a hermeneutic left much room for ambiguity and was not a call for blind faith.

Avery sent his position paper on war to Margaret Knapp, a member of St. Benedict Center and young woman who would soon join a convent. She wrote back to Avery while he was in Chicago at the Naval Reserve Training Center and, among other things, commented on the paper, interpreting it within the context of her knowledge of Avery's former positions. She believed that the paper was speculative and that Avery himself had not yet taken a decisive position on the war. He could not accept, she surmised, the total pacifism of the Catholic Worker type,

> though I do think that privately everyone must follow his conscience in matters not pronounced upon by the Holy See. But for those who believe that the wisest thing is to go along with the Government, realizing that although they deplore war personally and morally, the Government is purely temporal and must do its best in temporal matters, and that an individual cannot see the whole thing accurately.[8]

Knapp believed that Avery's paper certainly supported such a point of view. He was personally and morally opposed to war, but he saw it as a necessary evil under specified conditions. He had not become a war hawk.

Naval Intelligence and Excursions

In late December 1941, Dulles was assigned to the U.S. Naval Intelligence operation in New York City, serving as a civilian investigator, and in the early months of 1942, he was sent to the School of Naval Intelligence in Washington, D.C., thereafter returning to duty to the New York City office of Naval Intelligence. In March 1942 Dulles was commissioned as an ensign, and in May he was sent to Chicago's Northwestern University Naval Reserve Station for officer training. He reported that we live here, six in a room, many hundreds of us together, living a highly regimented life & taking a sort of cram course in navigation, gunnery, seamanship & allied subjects....For all the marching, mustering, and mathematics, and all the restrictions on liberty of movement, I don't mind the life here, at least not after getting "broken in."[9]

John F. Kennedy was also sent to Northwestern for the same purposes. During the remainder of the summer (August 5 to October 1), Dulles served on the USS *Ranger*, an aircraft carrier based in Norfolk, Virginia, and operating along the North American Atlantic coast. In October 1942, he was sent to the Subchaser Training Center at Miami, where he received further training for antisubmarine warfare. During World War II, the submarine chaser was a 110-foot warship with a crew of about thirty men, a part of the splinter fleet of the Navy, manned primarily by members of the

Navy lieutenant, 1943

Naval Reserve. These small ships periodically led landing craft into assault beaches, protected them from enemy fire, fought off air attacks, swept for mines, laid down smokescreens, and patrolled the seas for enemy submarines.[10]

In December 1942, after completing his training in Miami, Dulles was commissioned as a lieutenant, junior grade, and was sent to Houston, Texas, where he was assigned as a gunnery and communications officer to the subchaser USS *PC* (Patrol Craft) *1251*. While in Houston, awaiting sea duty, Dulles wrote a paper on "Religious Tolerance" in response to a controversy between the American Catholic hierarchy and the Federal Council of Churches in 1942, a controversy in which his father was involved. He sent his private notes to Christopher Huntington and his father. The controversy arose when the United States Catholic Bishops' 1942 "Statement on Victory and Peace" decried Protestant proselytizing of Catholics in Mexico, Central America, and South America because such efforts were, among other things, a "disturbing factor in our international relations." The Federal Council of Churches, a Protestant ecumenical organization that had its origins in 1908, protested against the religious intolerance of the bishops' statement. During the discussion prior to the press release of the Protestant reaction, John Foster Dulles, a leading member of the Federal Council, advised against issuing such a statement because "we are starting a fight with the Roman Catholic Church" and the Protestant statement might be "disastrous to the efforts to provide a united Christian front." Avery Dulles did not understand his father's reasons for protesting against the Federal Council's statement and sought to provide in "Notes on Religious Tolerance" his own reasons behind the bishops' concerns. He did not expect his father to agree with his Catholic reasons, but he hoped that his father might at least understand them. His career as an ecumenist started with his family; he told his father, "Mutual understanding, I am confident, will somewhat dispel that atmosphere of mutual distrust which so impedes collaboration—not to speak of reconciliation—between the two great branches of the tree of Christendom."[11]

Dulles' "Notes on Religious Tolerance" reflected a personal Catholic view that he shared with Huntington and his father. He argued that faith was a free act and could not be forced by any power. All human beings had or should have the freedom of faith and worship. But, society, while having the responsibility to preserve freedom of conscience, had a duty "to protect the minds of the faithful from false doctrine." Heresy had no right to exist because it was detrimental to society and to the ultimate end of humanity. The state, furthermore, "should jealously promote the things of God," and therefore it was "proper for the state to seek to restrain heresy." Such a view, he admitted, applied fully only where the Catholic religion was constitutionally established; that was not the case in the United States, where such laws against heresy could not be achieved without endangering the peace of society. In a letter to Christopher Huntington, Dulles acknowledged that in the paper on tolerance he did not take up the issue of "the coercive power of the Church" because of his ignorance of the subject. He believed, however, that Catholics should be up front in explaining Catholic doctrine to Protestants on the church-state issue. "I hate that policy which truckles to public opinion and seeks to pretend that the doctrine of separation of Church and State has not been solemnly condemned by the Holy See, not once but repeatedly." Dulles' opinion on this topic would change dramatically after his encounter with John Courtney Murray and the Second Vatican Council. At this point in his career, though, it reflected a view that was shared by those who considered themselves uncompromising Catholics.[12]

When he had time on his hands, as at Houston, he frequently put pen to paper to clarify his thoughts. But his days of waiting for sea duty in Houston were coming to an end. From February until December 19, 1943, he went to sea, patrolling the Caribbean on *PC 1251*. While he was aboard the subchaser, General Mark Clark and the Fifth American Army occupied Sicily and several Mediterranean islands and then in September invaded the Italian mainland, more than a month after the Italians themselves had ousted Benito Mussolini (1883–1945) and his Fascist regime.

After this long sea duty in the Caribbean, he was given a leave (December 22, 1943, to January 10, 1944) to visit his parents in New York City. He also used the occasion to visit friends at St. Benedict Center in Boston, where he talked to Fr. Leonard Feeney, SJ, whom he had first met in the fall of 1942.[13] Throughout the war, Dulles was in periodic corre-

Visiting family in Cold Spring Harbor while in the Navy, 1943

spondence with Feeney, whose charm and charisms Dulles admired, as did most of his associates at St. Benedict Center. Feeney's rigorous interpretation of the dictum "No salvation outside the church" had not developed during the war years, the years when Dulles had most of his contact with Feeney.[14]

After his brief leave, Dulles was assigned as liaison officer on the F.N.S. *Le Cimeterre*, a French Navy subchaser, which he served from January 26, 1944, to April 22, 1944. Dulles was at first sent to Nashville, Tennessee, where the Nashville Bridge Company, through the United States' lend-lease program, was building *Le Cimeterre* (*PC 1250*) for the Free French Navy. He spent a month or so in Nashville observing the building of the new ship, making sure the equipment functioned properly, acquainting himself with the French naval officers and the skeleton crew who were to man *Le Cimeterre*, and preparing himself as a liaison officer to the French Navy. While in Nashville, he took up Louis J. A. Mercier's *College French* (1935) to brush up on his French. He also read French works that his mother sent him or he purchased, a reading practice that he continued in his spare time throughout the war.[15] To sharpen his linguistic skills, moreover, he began writing to his mother in French.

Dulles boarded *Le Cimeterre* once it was seaworthy, and sailed from Nashville to Memphis, New Orleans, Key West, Miami, and Norfolk. He spent May and part of June 1944 at the U.S. Naval Training Center in Miami. During the first week of June, American forces liberated Rome from Nazi control and stormed Normandy for the D-Day battle (June 6).

After finishing further education at the training center, Dulles had a short leave (between June 24 and July 10, 1944) to visit his parents who were in Chicago at the time. He flew to Chicago and then with his parents to New York City and spent a weekend with friends in Boston. While in Boston in July, he and Fr. Feeney visited John F. Kennedy, who was in the New England Baptist Hospital recovering from an unsuccessful surgery on his back, almost a year after his PT-109 had been rammed and split in half by a Japanese destroyer in the South Pacific. Dulles also enjoyed July 4 with his friends, swimming, cooking out, and talking philosophy.[16]

On July 15, after his leave, he was sent to Casablanca, Morocco, as a coding officer and remained in Casablanca for less than a month engaged in "communications duties." Whenever he had the time, he went to a nearby French church for Mass, rosary, and/or benediction, as he reported to his godmother, Catherine

Clarke. "The French seem to recite their public prayers and sing their Latin hymns more beautifully than do our own congregations. It has been very pleasant living here, and in many ways I should like to be staying on here a few months."[17] Dulles may not have known it at the time of his letter to Clarke, and if he did he could not let on that he was about to be engaged in the invasion of southern France. But that was to be his next assignment.

On August 4 he took up his new duties as liaison officer aboard *Le Fantasque*, a large destroyer of the French Navy. He worked on board the destroyer helping to coordinate American and French naval enterprises in the successful Allied invasion of southern France, an effort that lasted until September 4 when he was relieved of his duties aboard *Le Fantasque*. The French government appreciated his work during this invasion and awarded him the Croix de Guerre with a silver star after the war.

In September 1944 Dulles was transferred to the USS *Philadelphia* (CL-41), a light cruiser, and served as flag secretary and liaison officer with the French Navy. During September and October, moreover, he served as personnel officer for Commander U.S. Naval Forces, Northwest African Waters, aboard the USS *Catoctin*, a combined operations and communications headquarters ship. He was also assigned to the USS *Brooklyn*, another light cruiser, during November. Even though he had been assigned to different ships at different times, he remained stationed at Naples, Italy, spending most of his time ashore from December 1944 to October 1945. As the war was coming to an end, Dulles served in the American naval headquarters at Naples as a personnel officer, far removed from the imminent danger of the battles that were taking place elsewhere in Europe and Asia. During Dulles' stay at Naples, President Franklin Delano Roosevelt died (April 12, 1945), Germany fell on May 7, 1945, and Japan surrendered shortly after the United States dropped the atomic bombs on Hiroshima and Nagasaki on August 6 and 9, 1945.

Navy Life, Letters, Literature, and Travel

During the years of the war, from 1942 to 1945 (except for August 1944 when he was aboard *Le Fantasque* during the invasion of southern France), Dulles led a rather routine life as a commissioned officer on board ship or ashore. Throughout the war years he was in continual contact with his family, especially through his sister Lillias and his mother, who wrote him almost every week, and his many friends in the Boston area, especially Catherine Clarke and the three Mercier sisters (Louise, Madeleine, and Evangeline). The women back home in Boston and New York were particularly solicitous about his material welfare and provided a spiritual support system for him throughout the war, as their many letters disclose.

Dulles' almost weekly letters to his mother were intended primarily to ease her anxiety about his safety. He wrote frequently to assure her, as he did on July 18, 1944, for example, that he was "in excellent health, and *perfectly* safe" on board *Le Fantasque*; again on August 28, 1944, he told her that "at present I am in the best of health and as safe as you could wish." Many letters to her or any of his other correspondents did not contain much concrete news, because of naval orders prohibiting detailed descriptions of naval operations or specific locations,[18] but he regularly sent his mother brief notes just to "let you know that I am alive, well, and entirely safe," as he wrote on September 6, 1944. On November 13, 1944, he sent his mother a short, handwritten V-Mail (Victory Mail),[19] saying that he was "sorry not to be able to furnish more personal details, but I am afraid that my correspondence from now on will contain even less than usual. At least I will try to write frequently enough to stop you from worrying. I assure you that I couldn't be safer at home."[20] He was trying to assuage her legitimate parental worries and fears about his safety.

His mother's letters to him were continual reminders of how concerned she was, but they also informed him about family affairs and especially about his father's work and writings. Prior to and during the war, John Foster Dulles made significant contributions to the Federal Council of Churches. The Federal Council was organized to express fellowship and catholic unity among Protestant denominations and to secure united efforts to improve the moral and social conditions of all peoples by applying Christian principles to all relations of human living. During World War II, John Foster Dulles presided over the Federal Council's Commission on a Just and Durable Peace (established in 1941), preparing numerous position papers for the council and the commission on the postwar establishment of international peace and generating public support for a United Nations organization. Avery's mother and his Boston friends sent him many of these papers and reports on them from the New York City and Boston papers. Avery read them and commented on them periodically in his letters to his mother and friends. He was particularly supportive of his father's efforts on behalf of a United Nations organization, and he agreed with his father's attempts to relate Christian principles to international problems of peace, even though he and his father did not always agree on specifics or have the same notions of political expediency and pragmatism. On February 25, 1945, for example, he wrote to his father on his birthday agreeing with the Federal Council's "Message to the Churches" (January 1945), a consensus position paper that was published after a meeting of the Federal Council of Churches in Cleveland.[21]

Although Dulles agreed in general with his father and the Protestant ecumenical statement on religious involvement in international issues of justice and peace, he believed that statement was compromised by what he had recently read in a *Time* magazine article. The piece pointed out that some prominent Protestants who belonged to but did not represent the Federal Council (including the Princeton theologian John Alexander MacKay, 1889–1983) had protested against the Vatican's involvement in politics. As reported in *Time*, their protest asserted that "establishments of religion, however widely representative, however exalted, have no place at the council tables of the state." Avery told his father that "such extreme views about the separation of the Church from political affairs" seemed to contradict statements on the relations of politics and religion that were coming forth from the Federal Council of Churches, especially the Cleveland "Message to the Churches." The neuralgic reaction of some Protestants to Vatican attempts to address political issues disturbed Avery.[22]

Avery was also well informed about his father's activities on behalf of the Republican Party and especially his work on the presidential election campaign of 1944. His former boss, Thomas Dewey, was running for the presidency that year, and his father was one of Dewey's primary advocates. Avery followed the campaign as best he could from the Mediterranean, but he was not surprised by Dewey's eventual loss. "I didn't expect that Dewey would get elected," he told his mother, "and from a personal point of view, as I have said before, I did not desire it, but I find myself a little more disappointed than I thought I would be....I wonder if things will go better for the Republicans in 1948."[23] They did not. Earlier, on Election Day, he told his sister Lillias that the polls seemed to indicate a very close race, "but, because of my self-protective pessimism perhaps, I am incredulous. Tomorrow, I suppose, will tell. It is strange, isn't it, how one can keep hoping for a thing that one does not want personally? Viz., D's election."[24] Dulles did not want to see Dewey elected because he believed that Dewey would then make his father secretary of state, and at this point in his life he did not fancy being the son of a secretary of state. He also believed that office would place a great burden on his father.[25]

Avery was also kept informed somewhat about his uncle Allen Dulles' spy activities in Switzerland during the war. Avery received clippings from the Boston *Herald* and the New York *Herald* on his uncle and was informed that the *Saturday Evening Post* had published an article on him. In one of his letters to Louise Mercier, Avery indicated that from hearsay he had also been informed that his uncle "had been of importance in the surrender of the German armies in North Italy," which was indeed the case.[26]

During the war, Avery's Boston Catholic friends kept him aware of events at St. Benedict Center, repeatedly indicating that they were praying for him, and encouraged him to keep them in his prayers. Many members considered him the spiritual father of the center. He frequently wrote to them encouraging them to keep the center focused on what was of real worth: the sanctification and salvation of souls. In a November 1943 letter to members of the center, a letter that was eventually published by the center, Dulles outlined his own understanding of the group's fundamental goals. "Nothing," he wrote, "is more thrilling than to be able to work with you in the great work of establishing the kingdom of Christ in our own souls and thus bringing fire on the earth." First and foremost the center was a place of study, to gain increasing knowledge of Christ, and of prayer, to express the love of Christ. The center also provided for "a life in common, the life of those who are trying to live Catholic lives in a world that is largely hostile or indifferent....By means of the Centre we have found out that there is a specifically Catholic way of having a tea, a breakfast or a dance, and, in general for doing everything that it is human to do."[27]

Members of the center were engaged in social and apostolic work, but that mission was not primary. The apostolic mission of the center was secondary in the nature of things, since "we cannot give what we do not already have....We are called to be apostles, but only because we have already been called to be saints."[28] The center was a spiritual communion—a community of prayer, a mutual support for faith and Christian discipline, a refuge from a world of materialism and conflict. It was like a family, an *ecclesiola*, a little church. Although it was a cell of Christian perfection in Dulles' mind, it was not isolated or alienated from the world and from engagement with the world. Dulles knew, too, that places like St. Benedict's could not live by the spirit alone, and he sent monthly checks to the center to help sustain it.

Dulles' extensive correspondence during these war years reveal that his interior life was anything but routine. Letters to his friends at St. Benedict's were filled with his deepening sense of the spiritual life, reflecting much of what he was reading and contemplating. He was particularly conscious of Ignatian spirituality. He told Catherine Clarke at one point that he disagreed with Thomas à Kempis on the use of material things and that he preferred the way Ignatius of Loyola approached the subject. Like Ignatius, he believed that "the very capacity of nature to be used for sensible pleasures should be availed of as a means of giving glory to God." Glory to God in all things. Our Lord, he continued, must have enjoyed the taste of wine. But whether we eat or whether we abstain, he quoted St. Paul, we should give glory to God—"that is the standard we should adopt."[29]

During Lent 1944, Dulles wrote a prayer expressing grief and anguish at the terrible effects of war: the desecration of holy places, the destruction of homes and convents, the slaughter of human persons. The causes of such evils were multiple, but he singled out the human unbridled lust for pleasure, covetousness, anger at offenses received, envy, and "avarice in refusing to share advantages possessed." He desired during Lent to make reparation for the sins of the world and join his sacrifices to those of Christ. "Grant especially, O Heavenly Father," he ended his prayer, "that my penances may extinguish in my own soul the greed, vengefulness, cruelty, intolerance, and coldness of heart by which I have made myself a guilty partner in the outrages being committed in the world. Through Jesus Christ Our Lord, Amen."[30] The war years were times of reflection, introspection, contemplation, and prayer. He was preparing himself for a different life.

Periodically Avery received letters from young women who, like him, were considering a religious vocation or who were going into the convent and would continue to pray for his safe return to Boston to lead the center again.[31] He also received, through the letters and packages of the Carmelite Sr. Evangeline of Jesus, devotional books, scapulars, and prayers from the convent in Roxbury, Massachusetts. Her total commitment to the life of prayer and sanctification was particularly appealing to the young Navy man. There was so much activity in the world, he told her, and so much value placed on it that the world at times forgot the true goals of human existence. He found in previous conversations with her that the real meaning of human existence could be found in the work of the religious orders, in the cultivation of perfection, in the contemplation of the source of beauty, truth, and virtue, and in the "prayer which moves mountains."[32] He found all these ideals realized in her life, and he was attracted to it. That life, he frequently asserted, was real—meaning a life contemplating Being itself. The Navy man, in Sr. Evangeline's opinion, as she reported it to her sister, was "a very special person and God must love him with a 'special' love."[33] In a letter to Avery she reminded him that Our Lady would protect him, and she sent him "the brown Carmelite scapular[34] which thousands of boys are wearing....Remember that Carmel is *always* praying for you."[35]

Even those like Fr. Leonard Feeney, who had only a brief acquaintance with Avery, perceived that he was called to a religious vocation. "It is a great dream that some day you will come back here as a priest," he told Avery in 1943, "and take over this work yourself, for it truly belongs to you."[36] The seeds of a religious vocation had already been planted at the time of his conversion to

Catholicism in 1940. Years later, he told a correspondent that, prior to joining the Jesuits, he had the idea that he "would like to become a priest and a Jesuit, since I felt that in that way I could best devote myself to the work of the Church, given my own particular gifts and limitations."[37] He had the war years to discern the ultimate direction of his desires.

Periodically throughout the war, Avery complained to family and friends that he did not have enough to do with respect to his naval duties. He had much time on his hands both on board ship and ashore, but he was not bored because he filled up his spare time with reading, writing, and visiting the sites around the places where he was stationed. In addition to reading his father's many position papers during the war years, Avery had access to the U.S. military newspaper, the *Stars and Stripes*, and periodically friends sent him issues of *Thought* and the *Catholic Mind*. Family and friends also sent him books, and wherever he was he purchased volumes to keep his mind occupied. As his correspondence indicates, he read widely: devotional books and studies on spirituality,[38] examinations of contemporary religious problems,[39] philosophy,[40] novels and other literary works,[41] and some history and biography.[42]

Life in the Navy was not all monotonous, routine work. When Avery was on leaves or on shore he had occasions to visit museums, listen to operas and symphonies, and periodically go to movies. While in Miami at the naval base, for example, he saw the popular *Going My Way*, which, he told his mother, was "an excellent moving picture."[43] Bing Crosby's and Barry Fitzgerald's acting in that movie swept the 1944 Academy Awards and was the most successful movie since *Gone with the Wind* (1939). Navy life and spiritual contemplation did not separate him from popular American culture.

Dulles spent his Navy years—much as he had spent his time after his freshman year in college—thinking about the good, the true, and the beautiful, and thinking about those ideals in the light of their foundation in God as being. His thinking reflected his study of and identification with the Greek philosophers (Plato and Aristotle), the scholastics, and the modern neo-Thomists. Writing also occupied much of his time. He kept up an extensive correspondence, much of which he did late in the evenings or on

Sundays or when he was on duty with not much else to do. As is already clear, he wrote frequently to family and friends. But he also wrote periodically to members of the military on official business. On one occasion, for example, he wrote to the Catholic military ordinary, Francis Cardinal Spellman (1889–1967), to protest the Navy's requirement that men in the Navy carry contraceptives with them when they went ashore. Dulles wanted to know what were his own responsibilities as an officer when he was under orders to distribute such devices to the enlisted men. In response to his inquiry, Auxiliary Bishop John F. O'Hara, CSC (1888–1960), military vicar, wrote, "A contraceptive is essentially evil; therefore, no Catholic can ever recommend its use. He may, under orders, act as a passive agent in handing them out if he is forced to do this by military authorities. He should in this case make known his own opposition to the practice." O'Hara, however, knew of no written Navy orders in this regard and requested Dulles to send him a copy of any written orders to this effect, and O'Hara would then bring it to the attention of the secretary of the Navy.[44]

In one of his other letters during the war, Dulles referred to what he called the "G.I. Joe standard of values," which he found understandable but appalling.[45] Years later, when he was in the Jesuit philosophate at Woodstock, Dulles wrote an open letter to prospective Catholic inductees into the armed services and warned them about the temptations to the faith that they would encounter in the services. Many young Catholic inductees would find that military service would either make or break them as Catholics. Group dynamics, military culture, and even military leadership at times supported and encouraged immorality: cursing and uncouth language, pin-up art, pornographic magazines, drunkenness, and brothel visits. Moral corruption, which abounded "in every barracks," was the major threat to religion. One needed a strong faith, supported by frequent practice, to overcome the dynamics of military life on some bases. But, Dulles acknowledged, it was possible to find a support system for one's faith and moral life in the military. One had to seek out those who shared one's faith in order to build a community of faith and moral living within the military.[46]

Dulles also wrote a few essays on philosophical and religious topics, two of which we have already analyzed, during his stay in the Navy. While in Houston, he sent his father an essay he had written on religious pragmatism, an article that dealt with issues his father had touched upon in some of his writings and owed something to "our talks. You will note that I do not criticise the pragmatic method, but only the pragmatic philosophy."[47] "Religious Pragmatism" was later published in the *Journal of Religious Instruction*, a Catholic journal on religious education.[48] Dulles defined pragmatism as utilitarianism, and for the utilitarians, morality was what was useful or that which was satisfying to one's internal desires or some external benefit. Utilitarianism became humanitarianism when the supreme good was perceived as the temporal advantage not necessarily of the self but of the human race as a whole. The utilitarians were not in general opposed to religion, but they valued it for its utility for the self, society, or the human race as a whole. Whether in its utilitarian or humanitarian form, pragmatism tended to divorce the good from the true in order to wed it to the useful and the temporal.

Christianity was indeed useful for the self, society, and the human race, but, according to Dulles, its value lay not in its utility. Its value lay primarily in its revelation of humanity's origin in God and its destiny in God through the mediation of the Christ. This revelation and mediation motivated and made possible a love for neighbor and God that was beneficial to the individual and society. The kind of morality that emerged from Christianity, moreover, was not based on an indifference to truth. Christianity did not define truth as that which worked. Christians insisted that moral virtue was doing the will of God as that will was made known through revelation and natural law. Christians understood virtue as a knowledge and love of God.

In the Christian conception of morality, according to Dulles, the mind was to be put in conformity with the truth and the heart with the good, both of which were identified with Being. There was, in other words, an objective foundation for all morality. It was based on the natural law, was universal, and was binding on conscience. "Rights and duties have some force and meaning when they emanate from the objective order of being and from the eternal purposes of the Creator."[49] Dulles' neo-scholastic mentality came through in his approach to morality.

While Dulles was in the Navy, he started thinking more seriously about the steps that led to his conversion to Catholicism, as many of his letters reveal. He wanted, moreover, to give his parents and his family a fuller account of why he became a Catholic. During the times when he was not preoccupied with Navy business, therefore, he began in the fall of 1944 to write out an account of his conversion, an account that he eventually published in 1946 as *A Testimonial to Grace*, echoing a theme in the Christian tradition that goes back to Paul's conversion story and Augustine's *Confessions*. Originally he had not planned to publish his account, intending it for the private use of his family and friends. After he typed up the manuscript, he showed it to Fr. Harold V. Stockman, SJ, a chaplain aboard *Le Cimeterre*, who recommended that it be published and "perhaps Sheed and Ward would be interested."[50] Dulles thereafter sent the manuscript to Catherine Clarke, who gave it to Fr. Feeney for his perusal. After the war, Feeney sent it to Sheed & Ward to be published.

Reading, writing, and travel occupied much of his time while Dulles was in the Navy. But of the three, travel was the one activity that began to wear on him. Occasionally, particularly toward the end of the war, Avery told friends and family that he was tired of the incessant travel and the recurring changes in naval assignments. His life during the years of the war was in continual flux, and he yearned for some rest and personal peace. In June 1944, he reported to Louise Mercier that he was sick of the constant movement. "When this war comes to an end, I don't think I will ever travel again!"[51] Almost a year later, he told her partly in jest, as he had others, "In my old age [he was not yet thirty] I am becoming increasingly attached to stable and predictable things! Above all, I hate travel."[52]

Nonetheless he had enjoyed the travel during the early years and the visits to different port cities and the great diversity of peoples and new sights that he observed. He had years earlier fallen in love with French culture and enjoyed the French naval officers that he came to know during the war. In Casablanca, he came in contact with Arab culture and was delighted with what he discovered there, observing the mosques and other forms of Islamic architecture and the Moslem daily call to prayer. In Naples, he had come to know the Italians in ways that defied the stereotypes (for example, that Italians were superstitious, nonpracticing Catholics) that were sometimes operative in the United States. From his base in Naples, moreover, he went to the beaches of Capri and swam in the Mediterranean and took day trips to Vesuvius, Pompeii, and Herculaneum, a site he thought surpassed Pompeii in beauty and interest. Periodically, too, he took short trips to small churches in and around Naples, reporting on the religious customs of the area to his American family and friends. In one letter he described in great detail the feast of the Nativity of Our Lady in Naples, "characterized by much street-dancing and hilarity, of a sort that is not characteristic of religious solemnities at home." The feast in Naples had not "been laicized" as had some feasts like Christmas and St. Patrick's Day in the United States. He delighted in describing the Italian custom, demonstrating his appreciation for the catholicity of cultural expressions of the Catholic faith.[53]

Three times during the war he went to Rome, and for the first time in his life as a Catholic, he visited the tourist sites. Twice during these trips he was part of a general audience with Pope Pius XII.[54] Once (December 1944) while in Rome he had a special audience with the pope. While touring the Vatican with two other naval officers, he asked a Swiss guard

> if it would be possible to see the pope. He said wait a few minutes and I'll see. He came back in five or ten minutes and said, "I just talked to the papal chamberlain who told me that the pope is holding an audience for Italian doctors." I told him that we had two doctors from the American Navy and could they get into the audience to see the pope. And the papal chamberlain said "yes."

The three of them got into the special audience, but Dulles "was so nervous that the pope might ask me something about where I had gone to medical school and something about practicing medicine in the American Navy" that he worried through the entire affair.[55] Years later he told a group of students in jest, "I was worried that if I lied to the Pope I would spend a thousand years in Purgatory."[56]

In September 1945 Dulles contemplated a trip to visit his parents in London. Dulles' father was in London attending a meeting of the Council of Foreign Ministers, representatives of the UN Security Council, who were meeting to conclude the essential features of five peace treaties with Italy, Hungary, Rumania, Bulgaria, and Finland. The American secretary of state, the Democrat James F. Byrnes, influenced by Republican senators, had appointed John Foster Dulles to the American delegation to offer legal advice on these international arrangements and to make the meeting bipartisan. Earlier in April, and for some of the same reasons, John Foster had been made a legal adviser to the American delegation in San Francisco during the establishment of the UN charter. In order to avoid any suspicion of an entanglement of church and state, John Foster had resigned from the Federal Council of Churches and his presidency of the Commission on a Just and Durable Peace so that he could take part in the UN meetings. His participation in the London meeting, therefore, was another step in his increasing participation in the establishment of American foreign policy after the war.

At the end of September, Avery flew to London and stayed with his parents during the last days of the Foreign Ministers' meetings, meetings that failed to achieve their objectives.[57] Previously Avery had written a letter to his mother saying that he would like to visit them in London, but later he reported that he did not think he could get away. Then he received an unexpected cable from COMNAVEU (Commander of Naval Forces, Europe) in London ordering him to report there "at once for temporary duty." "That was all it said," Avery later reported. "I was worried that I was about to be reprimanded because I'd done something wrong in my work as personnel officer, and I could not figure out what papers I should take with me." As it turned out, his parents had also wanted to see him, and therefore his father "had gotten word to the naval people that he'd like to see me, and they brought me to London for several days. I stayed at Claridges with my parents."[58]

During his London visit, Avery spent some quiet time with his mother, attended with his father some of the Foreign Ministers' open meetings, joined his parents at receptions held for the foreign ministers, and met notables like the American ambassador to the Soviet Union, Averill Harriman; Secretary of State James Byrnes;

James Clement Dunn, a member of the State Department; Jefferson Caffrey, ambassador to France; and Lady Nancy Witcher Astor, a member of the British Parliament.[59]

On October 3, after the London conference concluded, Avery's parents departed for the United States and Avery tried to get a plane back to Naples, but he had to take a circuitous route, flying first to Paris, where he had a brief layover giving him time to visit some of the sites, then on to Rome, and eventually to Naples, arriving on October 8. During his last day in London, he felt feverish, and by the time he got to Paris he was beginning to feel some weakness in his left leg and right arm. The condition worsened by the time he got to Rome, and when he arrived at Naples, he went to bed immediately hoping that the condition would pass. But it did not. The next morning he went to the dispensary where he was confined for five days, diagnosed with grippe (influenza). When discharged from the dispensary, however, he discovered that he was unable even to stand. Immediately, he was sent to the Army hospital in Caserta, where he was "confined on charges of infantile paralysis [polio]." The paralysis, he reported to his mother, "evidently is not very serious."[60]

While in the hospital, Dulles entertained himself with reading his father's speech before the Council of Foreign Ministers and religious texts sent to him by friends. His room, he playfully informed his mother, was private, one usually reserved for generals. "In the morning I am often greeted with 'how are you today General (or Admiral)?' or some such phrase."[61] His contraction of polio was more serious than he originally had thought and hospitalized him for the next four months. The effects of polio would return when he was in his eighties, weakening the muscles in his left leg and restricting his movement, and in his ninetieth year making him unable to talk or swallow.

Return to St. Benedict Center

At the end of October 1945, Dulles was transferred from Naples to the Naval Hospital at Bethesda, Maryland, where he began treatments for polio and had an opportunity to continue his reading and writing. On February 17, 1946, after a four-month stay at Bethesda, he was sent to the Naval Hospital in Chelsea, Massachusetts, for further treatments, but this time as an outpatient. He took up residence in Cambridge, and in July, after the strength in his arm and leg had been sufficiently restored, he resigned from the Navy. During his years in the Navy, he began to see the world in new ways that would have a significant impact on the rest of his life. He had plenty of time on board ship and on shore to think about the world and his role in it and particularly about his vocation in the years to come after the war concluded.

While residing in Cambridge, from February 17 until he left for the Jesuits on August 14, he visited his old friends at St. Benedict Center and became involved again in their activities. By 1946, Fr. Leonard Feeney was clearly in charge of the center, and he was the focus of attention, giving the Thursday night lectures to college students and faculty who came for discussion and fellowship. The Thursday night lecture was the "most popular event of the week,"[62] but it was not the only one. Almost every night of the week some activity (a discussion, a prayer group, a lecture) drew together several students and faculty.

A significant number of college-aged women and men who belonged to the center eventually became Carmelites, Benedictines, Dominicans, Jesuits, or diocesan priests. Religious vocations emerged out of the life of the center before as well as after Fr. Feeney's involvement. He certainly fostered vocations to the religious life, but at its beginnings and even in 1946, as Dulles characterized it, the center had a "thriving lay spirituality." It was the "age of the laity," as Feeney liked to say in the 1940s. Feeney focused much of his attention on developing Christian laity with a solid piety and encour-

With Leonard Feeney, SJ, and Catherine Goddard Clarke

aged students to look upon marriage as a religious vocation. Many who were involved with the center went to daily Mass, had their own daily hour of private meditation and prayer, and took part in periodic retreats. In the spring of 1946, for example, Dulles, like some other lay Catholics, took part in a three-day silent retreat given by Leonard Feeney's brother, Thomas Butler Feeney, SJ. The center provided a place and occasions for students with similar interests in their faith to meet each other. Out of these encounters came vocations to the married life.

Even in 1946, though, Dulles later reported, the group at the center, under Feeney's direction, was beginning to close in upon itself, a development Dulles considered "unhealthy." In the last months of 1946, Feeney was beginning to direct the center as if he were a novice master within a religious order. The group was beginning to isolate itself from "other influences, even Catholic influences....Any disagreement became almost a form of disloyalty." After Dulles left the center, it developed as a "sort of quasi-religious community" that increased its polemical confrontations with those outside the group.

In its original spirit and even under Feeney's direction, the center nurtured a vibrant intellectual life with a strong sense of "devotion to the Catholic tradition, especially to the Catholic theological tradition." Feeney had an ardent affection for the Virgin Mary and the communion of the saints, and he encouraged students to study the writings of the saints and particularly the doctors of the church, whom he considered the "great guardians of orthodoxy."[63] Dulles, like Feeney, was attracted to the church's doctors, and in the spring of 1946 he began writing a book on them. The book was never finished because of Dulles' decision to enter the Jesuits, but four chapters (three unpublished and one published) are extant and reveal something of Dulles' approach to the Catholic theological tradition as a young lay scholar.

The four chapters that he wrote during April and May were on the lives and teachings of Saints Athanasius, Ephrem, Hilary, and Cyril of Jerusalem.[64] Each essay of a little more than ten typed pages introduced the authors, provided a brief character sketch, and analyzed one or two of their major writings. Dulles argued throughout these four chapters that the doctors were all champions of orthodoxy. They all had to meet heresy in their day, and sometimes they did it at significant personal costs; three of them were exiled repeatedly from their episcopal sees because of the machinations of their heretical clerical and episcopal enemies and the power of an Arian-infected empire. Of Athanasius, for example, Dulles wrote:

> Through these dark years Athanasius was one of the few powerful leaders in the Greek world who could be relied upon both to proclaim the truth as long as life was in him and to confirm his brethren in professing the faith which they had received from Christ "though an angel of heaven should teach them otherwise." *Athanasius contra mundum*, the saying goes. For his championship of the divinity of the Incarnate Word he amply deserves the title which the Church has conferred upon him, "the Father of Orthodoxy."[65]

The doctors Dulles examined were all defenders of the faith, of the received tradition, and shapers of a theological tradition. Although as human beings and as theologians, they had their personal, idiosyncratic, and intellectual limitations (some of which, like their severe polemical stances, were detrimental to the good of the church), they contributed to what Dulles called the "development of Christian doctrine." St. Hilary illustrated in a striking way

> a fact noted frequently by theologians from St. Augustine to Cardinal Newman—that the definition of Catholic doctrine has often been assisted by the rise of heresies. St. Hilary himself explicitly recognized this to be the case. "Great is the force of truth," he declared, "for, although it can be known by itself, still it shines more brightly in the midst of contradictions. Remaining immovable in its own nature, it becomes daily more firmly established when challenged." It is a property of the Church, he notes, that "it is victorious when assailed, it is best known when most contested, and most powerful when most abandoned." The heretics can prevail

against each other, but are powerless against the truth. Indeed their errors are mutually destructive of each other. "Lis eorum est fides nostra" [Their contention is our faith].[66]

Dulles learned something of the doctrine of development from studying these church fathers, but he also learned of the need for moderation in theology, particularly moderation in dealing with heresy. Hilary again offered an example. Some of his contemporaries and even subsequent scholars had criticized him for being either too conciliatory or too harsh with heretics. In Dulles' view, "the truth of the matter is that, while uncompromising in matters of doctrine, he was exceedingly patient in dealing with those whom he considered to be in good faith." Some of Hilary's "more fanatical" orthodox contemporaries charged that his approach was too indulgent. But Hilary's policy was not only "consistent with the demands of Christian charity, but it proved eminently successful in bringing about the restoration of orthodoxy."[67]

These essays on the doctors of the church were clearly consistent with the emphasis Feeney placed upon orthodoxy and the Catholic tradition at St. Benedict's, but they also demonstrated an awareness of the historically conditioned and developmental nature of Christian doctrine, the limits of theological formulations and speculations, and the need to be open to those who were in good faith but not exactly accurate in their understandings and formulations of doctrine. Already, as a young man, Dulles was beginning to mark out for himself a theological position that would come to characterize his role as a theologian later in life. His own theological moderation separated him from the isolationist and integralist tendencies that would later characterize Feeney's direction of St. Benedict's, his rigorous and unorthodox interpretation of "no salvation outside the church," and his obstinate resistance to ecclesiastical correction that put him outside the church.

In 1946, though, those separatist tendencies at the center were only emerging; they were not yet fully developed. Most members of the center were more interested in studying and learning about their Catholic faith than in defining the meaning of *extra ecclesiam nulla salus*. The study of the writings of the church's doctors was not only the focus of Dulles' proposed book; it was also a central focus of discussions at the center. In addition to preparing brief essays for his book, Dulles wrote papers on theological texts that members of the center were discussing. He delivered these papers before the group to initiate discussions on the texts they were reading. In April and May 1946, for example, the members were reading and discussing St. Bernard of Clairvaux's (1090–1153) *On the Love of God* and his *Sermons on the Canticle of Canticles* as well as Thomas Aquinas's treatise on the angels in the *Summa theologiae*. In preparation for the discussion, Dulles prepared two papers, one on each of St. Bernard's texts.[68]

Dulles' paper on the *Love of God* distinguished between Aristotle's view of the moral virtues and the Catholic view of the theological virtues. Aristotle described virtue as the "means between opposite extremes, which represent respectively the excess and the defect of the quality in question." Thus fortitude was the mean between timidity and rashness. The theological virtues, on the other hand, bear on God as the ultimate end of human existence and were not characterized as means between extremes. "Their object being infinite, faith, hope and charity cannot be carried to excess." The love of God, for example, could never be extreme because the object of the soul's desire was unlimited and inexhaustible.[69]

Like Dulles, those who belonged to the center were interested in writing out their ideas and their religious discoveries for their fellow members. Out of this desire came the idea that the center ought to publish a journal in which the members could express their thoughts on the Catholic tradition and communicate them to a larger audience. With this idea in mind, Dulles, Fr. Feeney, Catherine Clarke, Bill Macomber, and Fakhri Maluf went to Archbishop Richard James Cushing of Boston to obtain ecclesiastical permission for a new magazine to be called *From the Housetops* (a title taken from Matthew 10:27: "What I say to you in the dark, say in the light; and what you hear whispered, proclaim from the housetops"). When Cushing was asked about censorship of the magazine, he told Feeney "censor it yourselves," a decision he may have regretted later on.[70] From the beginning, the new journal was conceived as a quarterly. Dulles edited the first issue and published an article in it.

The first issue contained an opening article by Leonard Feeney that took a particularly scholastic or Thomistic approach to the relationship between reason and faith.[71] Other articles focused on issues that were central to discussions at the center. Daniel Sargent wrote on Gerard Manley Hopkins, William F. Macomber on existentialism, Margaret T. O'Brien on secularism in American colleges, Fakhri Maluf on Plato and liberal education, and Thomas B.

FROM THE HOUSETOPS

Vol. I, No. 1   September, 1946

CONTENTS

Front page, *From the Housetops*

Feeney and Lyra Riberio prepared poems. Dulles concluded with "On Keeping the Faith."[72]

Dulles' article highlighted the progressive growth of faith by the habitual and frequent contemplation of the mystery of God. But the contemporary American culture, with its nominal Christianity and its practical atheism, affected many, even Catholics,

> with a spirit of doubt and compromise. The precious principles for which we stand, although not presently under the stress of physical assault, are being constantly subjected to the incursions of an alien culture. For every culture which is not Catholic is in some degree anti-Catholic. Where Christ is concerned, there can be no neutral position.[73]

Dulles had not entirely escaped from that attitude that he later criticized as the fortress mentality of Fr. Feeney and of St. Benedict Center. But his article was not exclusively nor even primarily on the cultural atmosphere in which Catholics must live; it was on the need to develop one's spiritual life.

Dulles asserted later on in the essay that Catholics like those at the center should not concentrate on apologetics or even on criticizing the culture in which they lived but on "saving our own souls" by making frequent and fervent acts of faith.[74] Faith, like any virtue, needed to be exercised in order to grow and develop; faith atrophied without habitual expression. He suggested to the readers, moreover, practical ways in which the desire for God and the expression of faith might be put into regular practice: through mental prayer, reading and "hard thinking" on Catholic books, conversations with others, and imploring "Our Lady, under her title of Mediatrix of all Graces" for the gift of perseverance. Praying, reading, writing, and discussing were the practical ways toward the increase in faith. This prescription characterized in fact what was taking place at the center. He concluded this article with a prayer: "May we, on departing this life, be able to echo on our lips and in our hearts the glorious boast of the Apostle of the Gentiles, 'Cursum consummavi, fidem servavi' [I have finished the race, I have kept the faith, 2 Tim 4:7]."[75]

After Dulles finished editing the first issue, he departed from Boston to join the Jesuits, with whom he already had an affinity. He had studied the history of Jesuits in his courses on late medieval and Reformation history at Harvard, had been instructed in the faith by a Jesuit, and was drawn to the Jesuits' intellectual and spiritual tradition and mission.

5

BECOMING A JESUIT, 1946-1958

EVER SINCE BECOMING a Catholic, Dulles was attracted to the religious life, as is clearly evident in his letters before and during the war. A relatively large number (more than a hundred by some estimates) of persons associated with St. Benedict Center prior to its separation from the Catholic Church had decided to become priests or religious. Fr. Leonard Feeney had encouraged those vocations, but they were generated even before he became connected to the center. Dulles' inclination to become a priest and a Jesuit was strengthened during the war. When he returned to the center in 1946, he told Feeney, who had earlier encouraged him to become a priest and return to the center to direct it, that he wanted to become a priest and a religious. Feeney's first reaction, according to Dulles, was to say, "This is the age of the laity."[1] Dulles reported this conversation when he was trying to emphasize that Feeney was not dragging St. Benedict's members into religious life; he wanted to develop a vibrant lay spirituality as much as he wanted to encourage vocations to the priesthood and the religious life. Nonetheless, Dulles told his godfather, Christopher Huntington, on the eve of his joining the Jesuits that "without the guidance which I received from Father Feeney I do not see how I would have been able to arrive at any secure decision" about becoming a Jesuit priest.[2]

In June 1946, once he had made up his mind to become a Jesuit, he informed his father by telephone that he was applying for admission to the Jesuits. In a subsequent letter to his mother he wrote that he was not telling people about his decision until he was accepted and "everything is set." In a week, he continued, he was to be interviewed by four or five Jesuits as part of his application process. He was concerned, though, about his parents' reaction to his decision. He told his mother:

> I am sorry that you will inevitably regret this step, and I know that all I can ask of you for the present is your patient acceptance of my action, since you know that I would not do it unless I were convinced that it is best for my own sanctification and for the service of God. It will mean some degree of separation from you and from my friends in the world. It will mean leaving our Center here, which has surpassed all my expectations as a place where God is genuinely loved and where we love one another very dearly in Christ. But the step will be essentially a joyous one, for the priesthood is a tremendous privilege—the greatest that man can enjoy in this life. And I trust that God will find a way of overcoming my personal defects which would otherwise render me totally unworthy.[3]

After receiving this letter, his mother wrote to him to let him know that his parents had accepted his decision. Her letter brought him "great consolation." His decision, he wrote back to her, was reached after "much prayer and deliberation. It is frankly based on the premises of the faith which I hold, and not on natural considerations. But, as St. Paul says, the foolishness of God is wiser than the wisdom of men; or, as St. Aloysius put it, it is better to be the servant of God than to be ruler of the whole world."[4] Dulles also sent his mother Evelyn Waugh's *Edmund Campion* (1946) to introduce her to Jesuit life in the sixteenth century.

Dulles' decision became a front-page news item once it was more widely known. "Son of Protestant Leader to Study for Priesthood" ran a story in the *Boston Globe*. Instead of becoming a lawyer like his father, an expert on international relations, and a major advisor to Protestant church bodies, the article reported, Dulles would begin studies leading to the priesthood.[5] The *Boston Pilot*, the archdiocesan Catholic newspaper, followed suit, acknowledging Dulles as the author of a major study of Pico della Mirandola, the son of a Presbyterian layman, and a recent convert to Catholicism whose *A Testimonial to Grace* was about to be published.[6]

Front page, *Boston Evening Globe*, August 14, 1946

Before he entered the novitiate, Avery visited his parents, who gave him a going-away party at their Cold Spring Harbor home. Only the immediate family were present. His brother, John, and his wife, Eleanor Ritter Dulles, had come to New York from their home in Monterrey, Mexico, and his sister, Lillias, and her husband, Robert Hinshaw, were there. In the midst of the family gathering, as Eleanor was playing the piano, Avery came over to her and said, "You know I am going to become a Jesuit. Can you teach me how to sing?" He was already contemplating his first Mass, but his sister-in-law found the question very amusing because although she knew he had great literary talents, it would be difficult to teach the man to sing.[7]

Becoming a Jesuit priest was normally a long and arduous thirteen-year experience prior to ordination, with an additional year of theological education and another year in tertianship after ordination. A young man spent two years in a Jesuit novitiate (at the end of which the novices took simple vows of poverty, chastity, and obedience), two years studying the humanities, three years in the study of philosophy, three years in what the Jesuits called "regency" (usually teaching some subject in one of the Jesuit schools), four years studying theology (he was ordained to the priesthood after the third year of theology), and after finishing theology, the Jesuit priest spent one year, called the "tertianship"; that is, a "third year" of novitiate—to renew and reinvigorate his spiritual life. He then took final vows, either immediately or a year or more after tertianship. Jesuits preparing to be priests were called "scholastics" as soon as they entered the novitiate and until they made final vows; thereafter they were considered fully incorporated into the Society. The entire experience from the novitiate until tertianship was an attempt to develop the Jesuit's heart and mind, integrating his piety and learning in preparation for serving his neighbor. The purpose of the Society of Jesus, as Ignatius of Loyola articulated it in the Jesuit *Constitutions* (written in the 1550s), was "to devote itself with God's grace not only to the salvation and perfection of the members' own souls, but also with that same grace to labor strenuously in giving aid toward the salvation and perfection of the souls of their fellowmen."[8]

Novitiate

On August 14, 1946, after receiving a letter of acceptance from the New York Jesuit Provincial,[9] Dulles began his life as a Jesuit in the novitiate at St. Andrew-on-Hudson, which was located about 80 miles north of New York City in Poughkeepsie. Like many of the Jesuit novitiates in the United States, it was situated in a bucolic setting, far removed from city life. The rural atmosphere, the rolling hills and fertile fields, the beauty of the Hudson River Valley, the quiet, and the slow pace of life that mirrored the rhythms of nature provided an ideal atmosphere for an introduction to a religious way of life that had its own regular cycle of prayer, study, manual labor, exercise, recreation, and rest. Here at St. Andrew, Dulles spent two years of his life learning the Jesuit methods of spiritual discernment, discovering the desires of his own soul, reading, as had St. Ignatius of Loyola during his own retreat, the lives of the saints and other spiritual treatises (like Thomas à Kempis's *Imitation of Christ*, ca. 1418, and Alphonsus Rodriguez's *The Practice of Christian Perfection*, Eng. trans. 1697–1699). It was a time of retreat and withdrawal from the world in order to come into communion with God, to be transformed by the experience, and to be prepared in this atmosphere to direct others in the one thing that counted, the salvation of their souls. Before one could serve one's neighbor in this regard, however, one had to experience personally the saving power of Christ in one's own life. This is what the novitiate was about. It was an extensive introduction to a new way of life, one that Dulles had desired for some time, and one that he had contemplated throughout the protracted years of the war. The novitiate was the place where beginners in the Jesuit way came to terms with their vocation to lead lives of poverty, chastity, and obedience in the service of God and their neighbors. This was Ignatius's vision, clearly articulated in the Jesuit *Constitutions* that he formulated prior to his death.

Dulles entered the novitiate in August 1946 with thirty-eight other young men who anticipated becoming Jesuit priests. The large number of novices was not unusual for Jesuit novitiates in the immediate pre- and postwar years; in fact, the large numbers reflected the general expansion of American Catholicism during these years. Vocations to religious and clerical life increased dramatically from 1920 to 1945: a phenomenal 82 percent increase in the number of clergy (from 21,019 to 38,451), a 140 percent increase in seminarians, and an 83 percent increase in women religious. The growth continued in the immediate postwar years (between 1945 and 1965), although not as dramatically: a 52 percent increase in clergy, a 127 percent increase in seminarians, and a 30 percent increase in women religious.[10] The American Jesuits, too, experienced an astonishing increment: from 200 in 1872 to 5,141 in 1936.[11] Dulles' vocation to the Jesuits was part of a larger movement in American Catholicism during these years.

Of the thirty-eight young men who entered the Jesuit novitiate at St. Andrew in 1946, twelve left before the end of the novitiate, and four others left the Jesuits before ordination.[12] Twenty-six of the thirty-eight who entered were in their teens and were primarily graduates of high schools; they had little experience beyond their own parochial surroundings. Ten of the novices were in their twenties, some of whom were college men or had already graduated from college. Four of these ten were in their mid-twenties (twenty-five to twenty-seven years of age) and, like Dulles, were veterans of World War II.[13] In 1951, Dulles counted twenty-four veterans who were studying for the priesthood with him at Woodstock College.[14]

In Jesuit novitiate, Poughkeepsie, New York, 1946

Dulles, however, stood out among the new Jesuit recruits. He had turned twenty-eight years old, had come from a prominent New York Presbyterian family, had graduated from a prestigious university, had already published two books, had been to law school, had legal experience in the New York City district attorney's office, had extensive international travel, and had been to war. Having converted from Protestantism, moreover, he, unlike many of the eighteen-year-olds who entered with him, had a much clearer idea of what Catholicism meant for him, and he had an historical appreciation of the Jesuit order that many of them would take some years to learn. Nonetheless, he, like his fellow novices, entered St. Andrew with the same intentions of learning the Jesuit way, and he shared the same experiences of prayer, spiritual exercises, and menial manual labor that was expected of all novices.

The two years Dulles spent in the novitiate were years of withdrawal from the world and entrance into the spiritual life of Christian perfection. The first week or ten days in the novitiate, called the "first probation" or "candidacy," was a testing period, a time to examine one's vocation in the light of probing questions (*Examen*) that Ignatius had required all applicants to consider prior to their admittance into the order. This period of self-examination was followed by the second probation, a prolonged period of almost two years in which candidates continued their self-reflection in the light of the *Examen* and the *Spiritual Exercises*, to which the novices were first introduced in October, in a thirty-day retreat of prayer and silence. The remainder of the novitiate was spent putting the principles of the Jesuit spiritual tradition into practice in preparation for a life of spiritual discernment and development. The retreat, which would be repeated during tertianship, was followed in the novitiate by two eight-day retreats in the months of August, five three-day retreats throughout the year, and periodic days of recollection. The daily spiritual life of a Jesuit, too, had a certain rhythm to it—a rhythm that Jesuits were to follow throughout their lives by spending an hour at spiritual reading, one or two meditations a day, and twice a day, once at noon and once in the evening, an examination of conscience. For the remainder of his life, moreover, Dulles, like other Jesuits, would every year have an eight-day retreat. Throughout these two years in the novitiate,

Dulles and the other novices were under the guidance of a novice master, a Jesuit known for his spiritual insight, who introduced the recruits to the *Spiritual Exercises* and the Jesuit *Constitutions*, so they would understand clearly to what they were committing their lives.

As his later life revealed, Avery took seriously the *Spiritual Exercises*. What stands out in his later life is his fundamental commitment to the lordship of Christ, the Ignatian rules for thinking with the church, the rules for the discernment of spirits, the task of "working against" (*agere contra*) the temptations of the soul, and the presupposition "that every good Christian ought to be more eager to put a good interpretation on a neighbor's statement than to condemn it." He would later apply these Ignatian guidelines for Christian living not only to his own interior life but to the life of the church. Ignatius, for example, advised his followers to work against desolation and temptations that impeded communion with God. Dulles expanded the *agere contra* principle to include a working against not only the interior desolation of the spirit but the temptations of the culture that weakened the church's commitment to Christ as Lord.[15] At times the cultural temptations were not just external but matched the interior tendencies of the mind and heart, and Dulles tried repeatedly to discern how best to work against them in his own soul as well as in the church and the culture.

The novitiate was a regimented life that could be considered quotidian if one forgot the intent of the life: a probing self-examination and an ever-increasing purification of one's life that led to ever-greater communion with Christ and with the mission of the Society of Jesus. The order of daily life could be monotonously routine if it were not for the internal spiritual journey, which was anything but ordinary. Daily life followed a pattern that gave discipline to the novice's life: rising every morning around 5:00 a.m., spending an hour in prayer or meditation, then attending Mass with a period of spiritual thanksgiving thereafter. Breakfast followed the early waking spiritual exercises, and thereafter the novices were employed in the early morning hours with what Jesuits called *manualia*—that is, work chores like washing dishes, cleaning the floors and bathrooms, working outside the house on the lawns, or other jobs that were necessary for the physical maintenance of the buildings and grounds. After completing these regular tasks, the novices would attend a class given by the novice master, who introduced them to the Jesuit rules and constitutions or gave spiritual conferences that focused on the personal appropriation of the theological and moral virtues or outlined points of good order and manners that novices needed to become Christian gentlemen. After the morning class, lunch was served, during which, as at all meals, monastic silence was observed so that the novices could listen to the reading of a biography of one of the saints or some other spiritual treatise. On special feast days and on other occasions, however, the novice master would declare a *Deo gratias* (Thanks be to God), meaning that the monastic silence was vacated and the novices were free to engage in conversation during the meal.

After lunch the novices could do some physical exercise, or together with two others, take a stroll around the grounds. All Jesuit novitiates, in keeping with the *Constitutions*, emphasized the need for exercise to keep mind and body sound. Periodically during the week, moreover, the novices engaged in organized team sports or were free on Sundays and feast days to take long walks or exercise. The period of exercise was followed by a class in Latin and/or Greek on a regular basis to prepare students for their future study in philosophy and theology. Latin, too, became the language of the novitiate as the novices became more and more familiar with the language and were required to communicate with one another in Latin. The novices, too, were trained on certain days in the art of reading out loud (called *schola anglica* or *toni*) for public audiences, in preparation for their later careers as preachers and teachers. The afternoon's activities were followed by a half-hour's meditation (called *flexoria*) prior to dinner, recreation after dinner, self-examination and prayer at the end of the day, and lights out for bed around 9:00 p.m. Since the Jesuit founders considered idleness the devil's workshop, they left little room in the novice's daily horarium for leisure.

In the *Constitutions*, Ignatius provided that the novices would have some time during the novitiate years to do some apostolic work. He suggested, for example, that novices spend a month or longer during the novitiate serving in hospitals, and/or that they be engaged in some form of catechesis, explaining Christian doctrine to boys and other simple persons, and/or spend a month in some kind of pilgrimage.[16] These prescriptions were adjusted to American life, but many novices did indeed spend some time working in hospitals. During the second year of his novitiate, Avery spent a couple of weeks teaching catechism in a Poughkeepsie boys' high school. During the 1940s, though, there was not much emphasis on apostolic work in the Jesuit novitiates. The primary stress was on spiritual formation.

Jesuit novices were not totally removed from the world they left. Dulles, for example, kept in touch with his family and members of St. Benedict Center through written correspondence. Periodically, he received visits from family and friends like Catherine Clarke and Fr. Leonard Feeney, and learned from them what was going on in the world he left behind. Fr. Feeney, for example, came to the novitiate in April 1948, gave a talk to the novices, and visited with Dulles about the events taking place at St. Benedict's and the lives of his spiritual "sisters" there.[17] It is not clear how much the novice Dulles knew about the emerging unorthodox view of "No salvation outside the Church" that members of the center were beginning to propagate in 1948, but he had been receiving numerous letters from Catherine Clarke since 1943 detailing an increasing hostility between the center and Harvard (as well as other secular colleges in the Boston area), and Feeney's and other members' severe criticisms of liberal or "*Commonweal* Catholicism" (including criticisms of Catholic colleges for being less than orthodox).[18]

As a novice, Dulles received visits from his mother, sister, and some of his New York cousins. In April 1948, after one such visit from his mother and his cousin Robert Edwards (a distant relative of the famous Puritan Jonathan Edwards) and Robert's wife, he wrote to Catherine Clarke that the visit was pleasant, and he hoped

> that some or all of them may have received some hidden grace which Our Lord will bring to fruition as he knows how. Without getting into any religious discussion (timidity or tact on my part?) I did get some pretty definite ideas about what's being taught at Union Theological [Seminary in New York where his sister was matriculating], and discovered that I am not yet beyond

being shocked. A complete denial of every Christian dogma—the Virgin Birth dismissed as a fairy tale—denial of the possibility of any denomination getting a full and comprehensive grasp of Christian doctrine—denial of the importance of truth—study of psychiatry to get new and modern lights on the nature of sin. Against all this what can one do or hope for?[19]

Dulles was expressing here attitudes that he had earlier identified with liberalism, and in this reaction he was very much in conformity with the American Catholic spiritual tradition of the early postwar years. A Catholic could have heard Fulton Sheen, whom Dulles had admired, articulating the antiliberal line on the *New York Catholic Hour* radio program in the late 1940s. Dulles would soften some of his criticisms of the liberal mentality in the 1960s, but he never completely departed from the kinds of criticisms he made here on what he tagged religious liberalism.

Although Dulles shared some of the anti-liberalism of his St. Benedict's associates, his form of it was never as radical as theirs. Immediately after Dulles completed his novitiate years, Feeney and the young intellectuals at St. Benedict's had become so unorthodox that the Jesuit superiors in August 1948 tried to remove Feeney from the center, but he refused to go. Thereafter Dulles had no more communication with Feeney, other members of St. Benedict's, or even his godmother Catherine Clarke, who had been so instrumental in his movement toward Catholicism. In fact, Dulles never reconnected with his godmother before her death and did not communicate with other members of the center until 1980, after Feeney (in 1972) and some prominent members of the center (in 1974) were reconciled to the church. Dulles never accepted their radical interpretation of *extra ecclesiam*, nor did he accept their extreme sectarianism, which had developed after he left the center.

At the end of the novitiate years, in August 1948, Dulles took simple and perpetual vows of poverty, chastity, and obedience. Simple vows were given before the novice master and committed the novice to the Society, but they did not bind the Society to the Jesuit candidate. The candidate still had to prove himself capable of the academic work that was required to become a priest in the

Society. Normally after the novitiate, a candidate would enter what the Jesuits called the "juniorate," that is, the first two years of college in which they would study the humanities. Since Dulles already had his college degree, he was sent immediately to Woodstock College in Maryland, where he began in September 1948 his three-year study of philosophy.

Woodstock College Philosophy

Woodstock College was the flagship school for the philosophical and theological education of Jesuit priests. Established in 1869 in the Patapsco River Valley 25 miles west of Baltimore, Woodstock was the sole national center for educating Jesuit priests throughout most of the nineteenth century. In the immediate post–Civil War period it was, like its distant neighbor Princeton Theological Seminary, a center of conservative theological thought. Its first dean and chief theologian, Camillo Mazzella, SJ (1833–1900; dean 1869–1878), like Professor Charles Hodge at Princeton, claimed that he taught nothing new (*nova non docere*, as he wrote in the preface of his *Praelectiones de Virtutibus* in 1871). Aemillio de Augustinis (1829–1898), another of Woodstock's Italian scholastic theologians, "laid no claim to the dangerous gift of originality in theology, for originality bordered too closely on the precipice of heresy to suit his mind" as one of his students reported.[20] Like Princeton, too, Woodstock had established its own press, which published multiple theological texts written by its own professors. In 1872, moreover, it launched the *Woodstock Letters*, which provided an opportunity for students as well as faculty to publish their works.

In 1948, the philosophy faculty at Woodstock taught primarily out of the neo-scholastic manuals that were prominent in many Catholic seminaries and colleges. The Woodstock faculty consisted of Gustave Weigel[21] (on cosmology for one year before being assigned to teach theology), Charles Denecke on epistemology, Edward Hanrihan on general metaphysics, Joseph Clarke on cosmology, Ralph Dates on natural theology, John McLaughlin on ethics, and James Conway on the history of philosophy. These were not the names of prominent philosophers. By the time Dulles got to Woodstock, the Suarezian neo-scholasticism[22] that dominated so much of the nineteenth- and early part of the twentieth-century philosophical education at Woodstock and other places was dying out and being replaced by what Dulles called a "genuine Thomism." "At Woodstock we were much more influenced by Maréchal and others of the Transcendental Thomists."[23]

Dulles called what he received in his courses at Woodstock a "purer version of Thomism" than the Suarezianism of the past. He meant that students read Aquinas's two great *summas* and not merely the commentators upon those texts. Dulles, always ready to read more than was required in class, studied some of Aquinas's other texts, the *De veritate* and the commentary on Peter Lombard's *Sentences*. He was particularly drawn to the "magnificent phenomenology of love" that he found in Aquinas's commentary on the *Sentences*. This reading outside the normal class requirements and his continued reading in Etienne Gilson and Jacques Maritain convinced him, he wrote in 1996, that Aquinas was not, as some charged, removed from experience nor a "dry and abstract" thinker. Dulles' formal study of philosophy at Woodstock expanded his "vision by presenting a view of the whole of reality, both created and uncreated." For him "philosophy was an aid to the spiritual life." It enhanced his "sense of dependence on God, and of gratitude to him for all that was beautiful and good."[24]

At the time he was taking philosophy classes at Woodstock, Dulles himself saw philosophy not merely as a discipline that gave the Jesuit an introduction to highly technical concepts expressed in precise Latin and that conveyed rational arguments for the existence of God, the spirituality of the soul, and human freedom—a discipline, in other words, that was a handmaid to and a preparation for theology. No, for him philosophy was not utilitarian or instrumental; it was a discipline with its own integrity; it held a key to reality itself.

> For philosophy has as its first and immediate effect to make a man at home in the universe in a way in which no other branch of learning can do....It shows us what it means to exist, to live, to know, to love, to do.... Philosophy brings a deeper appreciation of the world in which you dwell....For every chain of philosophic rea-

soning leads eventually, by an inescapable inner logic, from relative beings to Absolute Being, to the Supreme Font of all beauty, truth, and goodness.[25]

Philosophy, from this perspective, was for everyone who desired to become an "intellectual Christian" or "cultured man."[26] In fact, philosophy for Dulles was an introduction to the reflective life, a life in search of wisdom. In this view, he reflected the classical Greek and scholastic sapiential notions of philosophy. In the 1990s, Dulles would return to the philosophical roots of the Hellenistic and scholastic traditions that he had been introduced to as a young man, arguing that for the sake of progress the church needed a "relatively stable philosophical tradition." At that point in his life, after a post–Vatican II period of excessive criticism of the Greek and scholastic traditions of philosophy, he called for a retrieval of what Catholics used to call the "perennial philosophy."[27]

In 1949, while he was studying philosophy, Dulles received an invitation from Fr. John A. O'Brien (1893–1980)—a lecturer on Catholicism for twenty years at the University of Illinois, a professor at the University of Notre Dame in the 1940s and 1950s, and author of more than forty books—to write an account of his conversion for a text O'Brien was editing for publication. The proposed book, *Where I Found Christ,*[28] was to feature the conversion stories of "a group of noted scholars and writers." Among the notables to be invited were Jacques Maritain, Hugh Scott Taylor, Graham Greene, Arnold Lunn, Christopher Hollis, and Thomas Merton. O'Brien wanted Dulles to write a short account of his conversion for a popular audience in the hope that his and other accounts of conversion would be "both a light for the footsteps of many pilgrims and a channel of divine grace for many searchers for the truth."[29]

Dulles prepared a short essay, "Coming Home," that eventually appeared in the published text and was condensed for the *Catholic Digest.*[30] The first draft, however, was not entirely acceptable to the editor. He suggested that Dulles remove some of the technical philosophical and theological terms that were of "questionable value in speaking to the ordinary layman." He also thought that Dulles had exaggerated the lack of religion in his early life when he wrote that "the first twenty-two years of my life [were] in almost unbroken ignorance of the whole purpose of my existence." Such a characterization, moreover, contradicted what he had actually said about the early religious training he had received at home. "After all," O'Brien told him,

> your childhood was a good deal more "religious" than that of many Catholic children; the influence of your sister, for example. And if you were validly baptized, the Triune God dwelt within you, you were endowed with those operative habits of good, the infused virtues of faith, hope and charity. You are thinking chiefly of your lack of cooperation with God moving familiarly within you, yet the whole period of twenty-two years is with difficulty presented as of uniform indifference to His inspirations.[31]

Dulles took out the exaggerated sentence and modified the draft according to O'Brien's editorial suggestions, making the essay more readable for a general audience. "Coming Home" was the story of the Prodigal Son going home to his father after a frivolous and materialistic life. As in *A Testimonial to Grace*, Dulles gave credit to Plato and Aristotle for preparing him for his eventual conversion; in fact, they brought about a "Copernican revolution in my outlook" during his sophomore year at Harvard. Dulles wrote that he believed "there is a vacuum in the hearts of our generation due to the atmosphere of doubt and debunking in which we have grown up." The Catholic Church had a great opportunity to counter those tendencies by emphasizing the faith that saved. Once he himself had realized that he had been called by God to a higher life, he did not hesitate to join the Catholic Church as the means of salvation. "If I should reject the present grace," he wrote, "how could I expect like graces in the future?"[32] His conversion was a story of grace, being drawn home to a gracious God.

Before writing the article, Dulles sent O'Brien's invitation to his father and asked his father what he thought he might do in response to the invitation. He also told his father that in addition to the account of his conversion, he was to prepare a brief biographical sketch that would precede the essay in O'Brien's book. John Foster Dulles, a U.S. senator from New York in August 1949, responded by telling his son that he did not want to "express any opinion of my own in regard to so personal a matter" as his conversion story, but that he would "prefer that my name should not be brought into the biographical sketch."[33] His father offered no reason for his preference, and it would be pure speculation to suggest any. Avery decided to write the account and sent a copy to his father, whose name was not included in the biographical sketch. His father liked the little piece. He thought it was better than *A Testimonial to Grace*. Although as literature it was not as good as the book, the article was "more solid—more appeal to reason & less to sentiment—with still emphases on faith 'the evidence of things not seen.'"[34]

Avery protested throughout his life that his relationships with his parents were warm and affectionate, before as well as after his conversion to Catholicism. His own correspondence with his parents certainly verify his contention. Some letters, however, as we have seen, reveal a few ideological tensions between father and son. Avery, too, was saddened that he could not share his deeply felt religious sentiments with his parents, as letters to some of his Catholic friends indicate. Father and son continued to communicate on matters of importance, even though there was an intermittent strain in the affectionate bond that united them.

Avery had written his father letters while in the philosophate, usually discussing ideas that he knew his father entertained. On one such occasion he suggested to his father that communism was inherently linked to violent methods and that it could not coexist with Christianity in the world. His father responded that under Stalin that was clearly the case. Coercion to impose conformity was at the heart of Stalin's approach to communism, but, he told his son, communists were not the only ones to use coercion to induce conformity. "Various Christian groups have at one time or another thought and acted that way, and so also have the Moslems. Such beliefs and practices have, however, largely passed away and it is conceivable that they may pass away as an aspect of communism." Eventually communists would learn that it was inexpedient and counterproductive to use violence to accomplish their ends—because of the opposition that generally builds up in response to such terrorism. John Foster ended his long letter to his son by saying:

I know you have a contempt for "expediency," but that is
what in fact determines most people's conduct, and when
you ask whether as a practical matter communism can be
expected to give up violent methods without first becoming converted to a Christian view of the nature of man,
my answer is that all history proves that such a development is quite possible.[35]

Nonetheless, Foster wrote in another letter to his son that those
who possess a righteous faith will for a long time be "a minority.
The majority are largely guided by custom, habit and expediency
and such fact is a reality which is, I think, to be taken into account
in estimating the future."[36]

Although the idealist son and the pragmatic father disagreed
over the issue of expediency, they were united in their opposition
to communism, as were many Americans, and especially Catholic
Americans, in the postwar period. That preoccupation with communism was only to increase in the next few years with the rise of
Joseph McCarthy—a politician whose violent opposition to alleged
communists within the American government both father and son
considered wrongheaded. According to Avery, McCarthy's tactics
"violated Christian principles."[37]

During 1949, John Foster Dulles was in the midst of his political campaign in New York to retain his seat in the U.S. Senate, and
that may be one of the reasons he did not want his name associated
with his son's conversion story. During the campaign, however,
John Foster would find his son to be a political benefit. In July the
Republican governor of New York, Thomas Dewey, appointed
John Foster to the United States Senate seat that Robert Wagner
had resigned for health reasons. Dulles was appointed to fill out
Wagner's remaining four-month term, and in the process he
decided to campaign for the Senate seat. He ran against the
Democratic candidate, Herbert H. Lehman. The campaign got
nasty, and both sides began slinging mud at each other. The
Republican side implied that Lehman and the Democrats were soft
on communism, and the Democrats, trying to preserve the
Catholic vote, hinted periodically that Dulles was against popery
and had disinherited his son because of his conversion to

Lunch with John Foster Dulles, 1950

Catholicism. One of Dulles' campaign leaders, the Catholic lawyer Roderick L. O'Connor, suggested that the slurs had to be addressed directly. O'Connor called upon Fr. Robert Gannon, SJ, former president of Fordham University, who was an avid Republican, to see if Gannon could manage to get Avery, who was in the philosophate at Woodstock, to visit his parents in New York to negate the rumors. Gannon got Avery to New York, where the press had opportunities to take pictures of father and son enjoying lunch together at the family home on Ninety-First Street.[38]

Avery knew why he was being brought to New York and willingly cooperated with the Republican intentions because, as he later reported, "I knew it was for political purposes. But I was willing to serve because the kind of things that were being said had to be stopped."[39] The attempt to sway the Catholic vote did not work, and Dulles lost the race by 200,000 votes. After the election, John Foster wrote his son saying that though he lost New York City by a big margin, he had drawn to his side some Catholic voters who would normally have voted Democratic. "It was grand to have seen you," he wrote to his son, "and I think your appearance here did considerable to counteract the evil rumors that had been set on foot."[40]

Regency at Fordham University

Avery returned to Woodstock after his New York trip and finished his licentiate in philosophy in the spring of 1951; shortly thereafter he was assigned to Fordham University to teach philosophy during his two-year regency. As envisioned by Ignatius of Loyola, the period normally called the "regency" was a time in a Jesuit's formation when he would take a break from his studies to teach or serve in some other capacity in one of the Jesuits' schools or missions. The change from one Jesuit institution to another, according to the Jesuit constitutions, was intended to be useful for the scholastics' "better progress in spirit or in learning; or because it is useful for the universal good of the Society." As in all other phases of Jesuit formation, the regency ultimately aimed at the "greater service of God our Lord."[41] In the 1950s in the United States, Jesuits normally spent a three-year regency teaching Latin and Greek or some other subject in one of the Jesuit high schools. Dulles, like a few other Jesuits, was assigned to teach philosophy at the college level.

Fordham was not totally unfamiliar to Dulles. He had taken Catholic instructions when he was at Harvard from Fr. Edwin Quain, SJ, who was subsequently in the early 1950s academic vice president at Fordham. The president of Fordham at the time was Fr. Laurence J. McGinley, SJ (1949–1963), who had previously taught biblical studies at Woodstock College (1942–1949) while Dulles was in the philosophate. McGinley articulated values that many in the American Catholic community, including Dulles, shared at the time. In an October 1952 Mass of the Holy Spirit, a Mass that usually marked the beginning of a school year in Catholic colleges and universities, McGinley indicated what he believed were the fundamental threats of the age that a Catholic college education should counter: communism, fascism, and militarism. But he also took aim at the "colorless banner of those pale men who have no values, the Liberals in education, in the U.N., in the journals, and in the diplomatic service—the Liberals for whom no good thing exists in heaven or upon earth that can transcend themselves...the pale men without values, the unhappy Liberals, desperately unhappy—and desperately dangerous."[42]

111

Catholic education offered an alternative to an education in the "liberal" tradition. Dulles was joining a Catholic university that was a significant part of the Catholic culture of the early 1950s, a culture that still reflected the values of its immigrant Catholic roots and one that was emerging into a postwar expansiveness that had at the time unforeseen consequences as Catholics in greater numbers moved to the suburbs, into the growing middle class, and into the mainstream of American culture. The Catholic colleges and universities were in part agents of this period of expansion and transition. Dulles was a part of this new generation of postwar Catholics, and he joined a faculty who were emerging into the new era together: antiliberal (as they defined that term) but open to some values outside their own tradition.

Dulles came to Fordham during a period of high enrollment. Fordham, like all American colleges and universities, was experiencing great expansion because of the Serviceman's Readjustment Act (popularly known as the GI Bill). Prior to the war, enrollment at Fordham stood at about 8,000; it declined to 3,086 (2,000 of whom were women) by 1944, and by 1949 it had risen to 13,200—a phenomenal growth. In the early 1950s the enrollment remained at about the 1949 level.[43]

Fordham's Catholic students were shaped by the Cold War anticommunism of the emerging McCarthy era,[44] the threat of a nuclear holocaust, the resurgent Republicanism of Dwight David Eisenhower, and a burgeoning Catholic expansionism that built and filled Catholic parishes, schools, convents, and seminaries. Many of the Catholic students at Fordham came from parochial schools and Catholic high schools, and a number came from prestigious Jesuit Catholic high schools from across the country. Fordham continued to provide a moral and religious as well as a secular education to these students, serving them *in loco parentis* (that is, taking a parental role in shaping student lives away from home).

Dulles was a part of this formative and educational culture that characterized most Catholic colleges and universities in the early 1950s, and contrary to his later testimony, he believed in the early 1950s that a secular education for Catholics was a danger to their faith. In secular colleges, he wrote in 1951, a Catholic student,

112

one generally not prepared for rational attacks on the faith, would soon find himself "in possession of much better arguments against his religion than in its favor"—even though that was not part of his own experience at Harvard.[45] That attitude of the early 1950s toward secular higher education, though, reflected sentiments that were widely shared in the Catholic educational community.

In 1952, in the middle of his regency at Fordham, Dulles became particularly interested in the Republican campaign for the presidency. His father was heavily engaged in the campaign in favor of the Republican candidate, Dwight David Eisenhower. In that year, too, Fordham University granted Dulles' father an honorary doctorate for his work in international affairs. Avery was himself a Republican and favored Eisenhower over Adlai Stevenson, as did most of the students at Fordham (by a 2-to-1 margin),[46] and, according to some polls, at least 45 percent of American Catholics, who by large majorities in the previous presidential elections had voted Democratic.[47] During the campaign, John Foster wrote the foreign policy statement for the Republican Party platform and published an account of it, "A Policy of Boldness," in *Life* magazine.[48] It was clear from his work for the Republican Party that John Foster Dulles would be a strong candidate for the next secretary of state if Eisenhower won, which he did by a landslide. Dulles became the secretary of state during the Eisenhower era, and in the

John Foster Dulles receiving honorary degree at Fordham, 1952

midst of a very busy life, he continued to discuss some major issues with his son and to correspond with him and his brother, John. With his father as secretary of state, the scholastic Dulles was something of a celebrity on campus.

Although Avery Dulles observed the presidential campaign from his office at Fordham with eager anticipation of a Republican win, he was primarily preoccupied with teaching philosophy. The "official doctrine" of Fordham's department of philosophy was Thomism,[49] and Dulles was aligned with that tradition. Fordham's philosophy department, however, was becoming increasingly diverse in its philosophical orientations, breaking the hegemony that neo-scholasticism and neo-Thomism had had on the department in the past. The department to which Dulles belonged housed distinguished philosophers, but not all of them were Thomists or neo-Thomists. The French neo-Thomist, anti-fascist, and anti-Franco advocate Jacques Maritain, in 1942 had encouraged Fordham's president, Robert I. Gannon, SJ, to hire Dietrich von Hildebrand (1889–1977), an exile from Nazi Germany and an avid anti-Nazi. Fordham hired Hildebrand, who introduced students and other Americans to German phenomenology, Augustinian philosophy, and the philosophy of love through his teaching and writings (more than a hundred articles and thirty books).

Fordham had also hired in 1944 the Belgian Jesuit Joseph Donceel (1901–1994), a Transcendental Thomist, who quickly became a favorite among the undergraduate student population. The department also housed Robert C. Pollock, who introduced students to the philosophy of Ralph Waldo Emerson and William James, and Robert J. Roth, SJ, who arrived the year Dulles left Fordham and who was to teach courses in the classical American philosophical traditions of Charles Peirce, William James, Josiah Royce, and John Dewey. William F. Lynch, SJ, who would later become famous for his *Christ and Apollo: The Dimensions of the Literary Imagination* (1960), focused on the relationship between religious belief and aesthetic appreciation. In the early 1950s, though, the undergraduates were primarily introduced to the philosophical tradition of St. Thomas Aquinas, and it is this tradition that Dulles taught to the undergraduates during his two years at the university.

In 1955, two years after he left Fordham, Dulles published, together with James Demske and Robert O'Connell, *Introductory Metaphysics*, a philosophical textbook intended to introduce undergraduate students to the Thomistic understanding of being. The book was written during the summers of 1951 and 1952, while Dulles was teaching at Fordham, and is worth some attention because it reflects Dulles' approach to philosophical education at Fordham and indicates what he thought of his future as a Jesuit educator. The authors tried to come to terms with problems they had encountered in teaching scholastic philosophy to undergraduates. Introductory courses in scholastic philosophy (whether in logic, psychology, cosmology, general metaphysics, or natural theology), they argued in the preface, presupposed material taught in other courses. *Introductory Metaphysics* fused the essentials of general metaphysics, cosmology, and natural theology into a "single continuous treatise" that could serve as a general introduction to the synthesis of the philosophical enterprise.[50]

The principal goal of a philosophical education, in their estimation, was to make students wise, and that did not mean that students were to inherit passively a particular system of philosophy but that they were to engage the wisdom of past philosophical writings "as guides, not as substitutes, for our personal reflection."[51] Philosophy's aim was to instill in students a love of wisdom, a love of learning and reflection that encountered the reality of things. Throughout the text, the authors identify themselves as "moderate realists."[52] Like Thomas Aquinas, they were moderate rationalists in that they simultaneously acknowledged the capacities of reason to perceive reality (being) while they gave due consideration to the weakness of the human intellect. Like Aquinas, moreover, they realized that experience did not explain itself and could only be explained by realities that lay beyond itself.[53]

They wanted, furthermore, to preserve the truths of the rationalism of someone like Baruch Spinoza (1632–1677) and likewise the truths inherent in the "metaphysical agnosticism" of Immanuel Kant (1724–1804). The scholasticism they wanted to convey to their students, therefore, was in dialogue with modern philosophy, not simply an inheritance to be accepted without philosophical reflection and engagement. More than one-half of the text was devoted to a discussion of natural theology. It was in philosophy classes in the 1950s that most students in Catholic colleges were exposed to a systematic study of the rational grounds of theology and religion. Dulles had put much time and energy into preparing himself in philosophy because he believed, as did some in Fordham's philosophy department, that he was on the Jesuit track to teach philosophy in the future.

Like many other Jesuits in colleges and universities, Dulles not only taught while he was at Fordham, but he also became a moderator of Fordham's Catholic Evidence Guild and an assistant moderator of the Sodality of the Blessed Virgin Mary, nationally organized extracurricular Jesuit societies for students interested in learning more about their faith, developing their spiritual lives, and putting into practice the social justice dimensions of their Catholicism. The Sodality had been in Jesuit colleges and universities since the sixteenth century, but it had received significant national focus and leadership under the direction of the St. Louis Jesuit Daniel Lord. Dulles' work with the local Fordham Society was primarily as a spiritual and intellectual director of the group of students who met together on a regular basis to discuss issues of faith and justice and to plan retreats and times for prayer and meditation. His own experience at St. Benedict Center at Harvard had prepared him well for leading such a group at Fordham.

Theodore McCarrick, later the cardinal archbishop of Washington, D.C., was elected president of the sophomore Sodality and had much contact with Dulles during his sophomore year. Years later, when he was a cardinal, he testified about Dulles' work with the Sodality.

> We knew him from his father. We knew the history; we knew he'd been a convert; we knew that this was going to be one of the great brilliant men. We weren't sure in what area that brilliance was going to manifest itself, but we knew he was going to be one of the brilliant men of the Society in our time. He was fun. He was very good. He would never impose. He'd be with us, and he would listen, and he may make a suggestion here and there,

Fordham Sodality Council, 1952, with Avery Dulles seated left
and Theodore McCarrick, second student from right;
Cardinals Avery Dulles and Theodore McCarrick, 2001

which was always good and well taken by us, because we
were looking for direction.[54]

In 2001, when both he and Dulles were elevated to the cardinalate, McCarrick recalled some of his student days with Dulles:
"We all expected him to be an intellectual who would not have a lot
of warmth, who would be a cold, dry scholar. And he wasn't. He
was a scholar, no doubt about that, but he had a wonderful sense of
humor, and he had that wonderful laugh, which he still has—that
deep, hoarse laugh."[55] Another former student, Anthony L.
Adolino, wrote to Dulles in 1972 to thank him for his "inspired
teaching when I was your philosophy student....I have never forgotten what I learned from you."[56] Periodically Dulles received letters from grateful students, and this was especially the case after he
received the red hat in 2001. Abbott R. Morgan, for example, a former student, recalled his happy days with Dulles in the Ramskeller,
a Fordham student hangout, and remembered Dulles' quip after
congratulating Avery when his father was appointed secretary of
state. Dulles responded, "Thank you. I deserve it."[57]

Dulles also established on campus a Catholic Evidence Guild,
and with the guidance of Frank Sheed, of the publishing firm of

Sheed & Ward, he set up a local chapter at Fordham.[58] Frank Sheed and his wife, Maisie Ward Sheed, had been involved since the early twentieth century in street preaching in London and in establishing Catholic Evidence Guilds in England and later in the United States. The Evidence Guilds were evangelical attempts to spread the faith and make known the grounds of Catholic beliefs and practices. On Catholic college campuses, they served the function that St. Benedict Center served for Catholic students in the Boston area.

Woodstock College Theology

Dulles had spent a busy two years of regency at Fordham teaching, giving spiritual direction, and evangelizing students. At the conclusion of his second year, in the early summer of 1953, he returned to Woodstock, where he began his four-year course in theology. In 1953, Woodstock was one of five Jesuit theologates in the United States, but it was the most influential and prestigious. All of the professors at Woodstock had been educated in the neo-scholastic or Thomistic theology of the era, but some were beginning to branch out of the scholastic womb to apply their theology to new areas of consideration, and some were beginning to employ new methods in theology and biblical studies. During and after the war, Woodstock was in a period of transition.

The theologate was well served by an able and distinguished publishing theological faculty, two of whom, John Courtney Murray[59] and Gustave Weigel, would eventually become *periti* at the Second Vatican Council. Murray and Weigel had both received their doctorates from the Gregorian University in Rome and had been significantly influenced by Thomistic theology, the reigning theology of the Roman schools in the late 1930s. Murray's Roman education was in fundamental theology, while Weigel's was in dogmatic theology. Under the direction of the historical theologian Edgar Hocedez, SJ, Weigel completed his dissertation on the semi-Pelagianism of Faustus (ca. 408–490), the bishop of Riez in southern France. Weigel had also taken classes at the Gregorian from Sebastian Tromp, SJ, the silent author of Pope Pius XII's encyclical *Mystici Corporis* (1943).

Woodstock housed *Theological Studies*, the most important Catholic theological journal in the English-speaking world at the time, a periodical established in 1940 and since 1941 edited by John Courtney Murray, who had been a Woodstock faculty member since 1938 and was fast becoming the leading American Catholic theological theorist on religious liberty and church-state relations. Weigel came to Woodstock in 1948, focusing his teaching and research since 1949 on ecclesiology, revelation and the act of faith, and ecumenism. Murray had asked him to become the local expert in American Protestant theology and ecumenism and to write on these topics for *Theological Studies*. After 1950, Weigel became one of the first American Catholic theologians to take Protestant life and thought seriously and to examine it from its own sources, earning a reputation in the ecumenical movement. Murray and Weigel in particular would make some significant contributions to ecclesiology, ecumenism, and the doctrine of religious liberty during their careers as editors and teachers and would help to influence theological and ecumenical directions at the Second Vatican Council.

Other members of the Jesuit faculty would also contribute significantly to the renewal of systematic theology, historical theology, and biblical studies prior to and after the council: for example, Walter J. Burghardt[60] in patristics and historical theology, Robert McNally in medieval theology, George Glanzman in Old Testament, Vincent O'Keefe and Francis McCool in New Testament. There were others whom Dulles considered excellent teachers, but they were largely unknown outside of Woodstock because they published very little of their work: Thomas Brophy and Joseph Sweeney in dogma, Harold V. Duhamel in moral theology, John Reed and Joseph Gallen in canon law, and Paul Palmer and Patrick Sullivan in sacramental theology.

The renewal of theology was not accomplished without conflict among theologians in the United States, and Woodstock was, both prior to and during Dulles' theological education, at the center of some major disputes in theology. In 1942 and 1943, in the midst of the continuing Cold War between American Protestants and Catholics, John Courtney Murray, with the help of some other Jesuits, began writing articles in *Theological Studies* on a theological basis for intercredal cooperation in American society. Those articles were attacked by some theologians at the Catholic University of America—Paul Hanley Furfey, Joseph Clifford Fenton, and

Francis J. Connell, CSSR—who considered Murray's approach a manifestation of religious indifferentism. This theological debate was followed in 1944 and subsequent years by disagreements over the kind of theology that should be taught to lay college students.

After the war, from about 1947 to the mid-1950s, Murray entered into a long and contentious dispute with Fenton and others on a Catholic understanding of religious liberty and separation of church and state, a theological controversy that ended in 1955 when Murray was silenced by his Roman Jesuit religious superiors. Later, at the Second Vatican Council, Murray's position would be vindicated. Weigel, too, entered into new areas of theology in the early 1950s when he began studying and writing on Protestant theology, an area that some American Catholic theologians believed would also lead to religious indifference. Going to Woodstock's theologate put Dulles on the path of theological renewal and controversy that was taking place in a few other isolated institutions in the American church at the time. In 1953, however, the new directions of theology were only beginning to emerge.

Among the professors at Woodstock, Weigel had the greatest impact on Dulles' theological development and his later career as a theologian. Murray, the more creative and insightful theologian, had less of an influence on Dulles because Murray had been relieved from teaching at Woodstock so that he could spend more time on his research, editing, and publishing; his teaching was, by Dulles' account, not very effective or inspiring.[61] Weigel, on the other hand, was an engaging teacher when he was prepared (and that was not always the case), and he took a personal as well as professional interest in the students he perceived to be talented. Dulles was in that group of students whose careers Weigel helped to shape. Dulles' first close contact with Weigel came in courses on the church and the act of faith in the 1953–1954 school year. When Weigel died in 1964, Dulles testified that he was "a dynamic teacher with a flair for the dramatic, he delighted in making challenging statements that would arouse passionate disagreement." Weigel had a lasting impact on Dulles' interest in modern Protestant theology. But when Dulles told Weigel that he was interested in reading Protestant theology and told him that he thought he ought to know something about Protestant thought

At Woodstock, Maryland, 1953

since he was a convert from Protestantism, Weigel shot back: "If that's your best reason, you might as well drop the project."[62] Dulles thought of better motives.

Both inside and outside the classroom, Weigel provided students with guidance and modeled for them a way of life that included relaxation as well as hard work, humor as well as seriousness. He poked fun at others and enjoyed being the object of others' pranks. Jesuit scholastics periodically produced skits that made fun of the faculty members. During one of these skits, Dulles played the role of Cardinal Ottaviani, who in the name of the Holy Office anathematized one of Weigel's books and cast it into a roaring fire. Weigel enjoyed the skit, according to Dulles.[63]

Weigel had the most important, but not the only, influence on Dulles' theological development. Through Weigel, Dulles was introduced to the systematic study of ecclesiology, fundamental theology, Protestant theology, and ecumenism—abiding interests throughout his later career as a theologian. At Woodstock, Dulles was also introduced to the renaissance of Catholic biblical scholarship, a renewal that had been given some impetus in 1938 by the organization of the American Catholic Biblical Association and in 1943 by Pope Pius XII's encyclical *Divino Afflante Spiritu*. That papal document stressed the need to follow the literal meaning of scripture but also opened the way for a legitimate study of literary forms and biblical criticism. By 1953, George Glanzman and Francis McCool were teaching courses in biblical studies at Woodstock that introduced students to the new critical issues of contemporary scholarship. Dulles found these courses stimulating and discovered systematic issues on the nature of revelation that the newer biblical studies posed for apologetics and fundamental theology.[64]

At Woodstock, as at many seminaries in the United States in the 1950s, professors used the Latin theological manuals (Pesch, Dieckmann, Pohle, Garrigou-Lagrange)[65] that had been written in the nineteenth and early twentieth centuries to guide seminarians through the various doctrinal tracts of theology (from the doctrine of God to the doctrine of eschatology). The manuals provided an introduction and an understanding of the major issues and interpretations in theology, the competing theses, and the sources (from scripture and tradition) for the substantive Christian doctrines. In 2005, Dulles acknowledged that the manual style of theology had gone out of fashion, but it gave him "a thorough exposure to the classical theological questions and debates."[66]

Dulles' theological education, like almost all his previous education, was not confined to the classroom nor to the arid theological manuals assigned in class. Weigel introduced Dulles to the works of Maurice de la Taille and Odo Casel, and he read some of their major works outside of classroom requirements. During his Harvard days, he had read Karl Adam, especially *The Spirit of Catholicism*,[67] and he continued to read many of Adam's other texts. Dulles was particularly drawn to the theologians of the *nouvelle théologie*.[68] Francophile as he was, he read some works of Yves Marie-Joseph Congar, Henri de Lubac, Jean Daniélou, and Marie-Dominique Chenu. He also read some of Karl Rahner's works, "devouring," he later noted, Rahner's articles in *Zeitschrift für Katholische Theologie* and the first volume of his *Schriften zur Theologie* (1960) before he finished his theological education. Many of these authors, except perhaps Karl Adam, were not well known in American Catholic theological seminaries in the 1950s, but they would be major contributors to the renewal of Catholic life and thought at the Second Vatican Council. Dulles used the biblical works of Roland de Vaux, Pierre Benoit, David Stanley, and John L. McKenzie, among others, moreover, as complements and corrections to the scholastic manuals. He also read the works of Protestant theologians, including Oscar Cullmann, Rudolf Bultmann, Karl Barth, and Paul Tillich, as well as works produced by the World Council of Churches. Weigel in particular had encouraged him in this ecumenical direction of his theological education.[69]

During the theologate, Dulles not only read widely; he also published reviews and a few articles that demonstrated what he was learning. His most extensive essays during this period reflected three interlocking theological subjects that were at the heart of his theological education and would continue to interest him throughout the remainder of his life. Like his theological mentor, Weigel, Dulles' writings centered on ecclesiology, and particularly on the unity of the church. He also wrote on the Bible, reflecting the new critical approaches to the Bible. In these writings, he demonstrated a fundamental theological interest in the nature of revelation, its relation to the Bible, and the Bible's relationship to the church. And finally, he wrote on the relationship of Catholic theology to contemporary Protestant thought and on the Catholic Church's relations to the Orthodox churches. Such an early interest in ecumenism would continue to shape his career as a theologian in the post–Vatican II era. He also wrote short reviews of philosophical works and an essay or two on the Legion of Decency and positivism. But his fundamental focus was on theology.

Dulles' first major theological article as a Jesuit scholastic was on Cyprian's *De ecclesiae unitate*, a third-century treatise on the church, the fourth chapter of which on the primacy has two versions, a longer and a shorter one. Dulles published his article in the *Theologian*, a periodical for Woodstock's own students that Dulles edited during his last year of theology. Well aware of the critical problems associated with the two versions[70] of Cyprian's text, Dulles argued that "the notion of an acephalous episcopate cannot without violence be thrust upon Cyprian," that Cyprian's ecclesiology demanded union between the local church and a "principal church" that was the means of preserving that unity, and that his theory was reinforced by his own experiences in the episcopate. Rome, in Cyprian's view, was the only local church that was called "mother church," as the source or womb of the unity of all the churches.[71] He emphasized in particular Cyprian's focus on Roman primacy as a means of preserving unity of doctrine within the church universal and Cyprian's appeal to the biblical warrant for Petrine primacy as an essential part of his ecclesiology. This emphasis on Roman primacy was a core part of the church's liturgical tradition and was clearly evident in a convert's profession of faith upon entering the church: "I recognize the Holy, Roman, Catholic and Apostolic Church as the mother and teacher of all the Churches."[72]

Dulles' theological commitment to the church's unity and to the Roman primacy as a means of preserving a unity of doctrine and ecclesial life reflected his own conversion experience. Although he did not share the rigorous interpretation of the doctrine "no salvation outside the church" as did some of his old friends in Boston's St. Benedict Center, he did share with them a strong sense of the church's unity of doctrine and life and a commitment to the primacy of the Roman See. That fundamental commitment, although nuanced in later years, remained a part of his core ecclesial experience.

For most Catholics, the unity of the church was not the result of any examination of patristic sources like Cyprian's *De ecclesiae unitate*; it was part of their liturgical experience. In 1955, Dulles addressed this Catholic sense of unity when he wrote on the Eucharist as the sacramental means and realization of the church's unity. It was at the Eucharist where Catholics came into mystical union with Christ and with other members of the church, and it was in the Eucharist where Catholics had a concrete experience of that unity. Writing in *Worship*, the premier journal of the pre–Vatican II American Catholic liturgical revival, Dulles outlined his own views of the mystical body of Christ as a core part of his understanding of sacramental unity.[73] Dulles' ecclesiology was being shaped by his studies of patristics and sacramental theology in the 1950s, as is evident in his early writings as a scholastic.

Although reared in a Protestant home, Dulles had read very little Protestant theology before his conversion to Catholicism. His most recent experience of the Protestant world was very much like that of most other Catholics who looked upon Protestantism from the outside. Protestantism seemed to represent a sea of diversity with no essential core of common doctrine or life. In the theologate, however, he began, under the direction of Weigel, to study some contemporary Protestant theology in a more systematic way than he had ever done in his past, and that examination also influenced Dulles' ecclesiology.

Since 1950, Weigel had been publishing articles and books on the American Protestant churches and American Protestant theology, and he was leading his students into the same area of research. It is not too clear, given the present state of scholarship, how widespread was the reading of Protestant theologies in Catholic seminaries, but in the 1950s, Protestant theology was being read in places like Woodstock and St. John's University Seminary (Collegeville, Minnesota), and Catholic theologians like Weigel and George Tavard (1922–2007)[74] were awakening the Catholic reading public to the importance of studying Protestant theology from Protestant sources. This ecumenical dimension of American Catholic life in the 1950s has been overshadowed in historical literature by the focus on Protestant fears of Catholic power, as was evident in the organization of Protestants and Others United for the Separation of Church and State (1948) and in the popularity of Paul Blanshard's *American Freedom and Catholic Power* (1949). The early Catholic participation in ecumenism would be overlooked by post–Vatican II Catholic involvements in church unity movements. In the 1950s, though, there was what could be called a slight thawing in the ice-cold war between Protestants and Catholics. Dulles became a part of this new dimension of Catholic interest in the search for ecclesial unity in the postwar period, when the emphasis on consensus was not only evident in American biblical, historical, and sociological studies but also in Murray's intercredal and religious liberty projects.

In 1955, to acquaint the clergy with the ecumenical movement, Dulles published an article on "The Protestant Concept of the Church" in the *American Ecclesiastical Review*, a periodical whose primary audience was American Catholic parish priests. The article reflected a traditional Catholic reading of Luther's, Calvin's, and Barth's understandings of the dichotomy between the invisible and visible church and a Catholic understanding of the sacramental unity of the church's mystical and hierarchical dimensions. Nonetheless, the essay called attention to the dissatisfaction in the contemporary Protestant community with the ecclesiastical divisions that did exist and the Protestant movement toward more organic unity, as was evidenced by the organization of the World Council of Churches (WCC, 1948). Dulles also pointed out that he believed the new emphasis on the "relationship between the Church and the churches is perhaps the major issue in contemporary Protestant theology."[75] Wilhelm A. Visser't Hooft, secretary general of the WCC, Dulles informed his readers, decried the broken unity of the churches, a disunity that was manifested clearly by the inability of the churches to meet together at the Eucharist. The WCC was organized to correct this situation.

Within the contemporary Protestant community, according to Dulles, two opposing understandings of church unity existed: the "conservative ecumenists" emphasized the necessity of a unity of doctrine and worship; the more "radical" approach saw the futility or impossibility of agreeing on doctrinal issues and interpretations of Christ's message and stressed the unity in the life of Christ without demanding conformity to one rule of faith and order. The Catholic approach to church unity, which was "repugnant to all Protestants," asserted that "all Christians should achieve dogmatic unity through submission to a single authorized magisterium." Though a positive movement toward church unity existed within contemporary Protestantism, Dulles declared that "we cannot do better than to insist that the Church is a society of love as well as a society of law, and that our obedience to the Vicar of Christ is a means to achieving closer and more vital union with God....For the authority of the Church is the power of her Spirit, and her Spirit is the Spirit of God."[76] Dulles' ecumenism reflected that of Weigel, his mentor, but it also revealed an early interest that would mature over the years. In the United States of the 1950s, that Catholic interest was innovative, though from the perspective of the post–Vatican II era it seems antiquated.

During his last year in the theologate, after his ordination to the priesthood in 1956, Dulles published an article on "The Orthodox Churches and the Ecumenical Movement" for the *Downside Review*,[77] a British Benedictine periodical, which reflected some of his previous resistance to official Catholic participation in the ecumenical movement, but the tone was slightly different from his earlier article, and the subtext was much more open to Catholic involvement in the ecumenical movement than he was prepared to acknowledge in a published article. While he justified the Catholic refusal to take part in the Protestant ecumenical movement or in the WCC, he acknowledged that the Orthodox churches had been involved in the Faith and Order side of the ecumenical movements since 1925 and that many of those churches had joined the WCC. Like the Catholic Church, moreover, the Orthodox churches had insisted on doctrinal unity as a basis for intercommunion, the visibility of the church, the church's relationship to the scriptures, the role of the human will in the process of salvation, mariology, the irreformability of dogma, the sacredness of tradition, apostolic succession, the veneration of the saints, and the seven sacraments— and yet their participation in the WCC had "not sucked [them] into Protestantism."[78]

On the positive side of things, Dulles noted, "Both Orthodox and Protestants have profited by the ecumenical contacts of the past half century. There is no evidence that Orthodox theology has been undermined by Protestant concepts, or that the Orthodox and Protestants are joining in a 'united front' against the Catholic Church."[79] The unarticulated message here was that the Catholic Church had nothing to fear by entering the ecumenical movement and perhaps much to gain by the very dialogue that took place in those meetings. But that message was clearly not acceptable in many Catholic circles, or, that is at least what Dulles thought at the time, some months prior to his tertianship in Europe, where he learned of a much more positive Catholic approach to the ecumenical movement.

Dulles' interest in Protestant theology was also evident in his study of Paul Tillich. For some years Weigel had been introducing students to Tillich's theology, and in 1956 Weigel published an article that introduced Tillich to a wider Catholic audience.[80] That same year, Dulles, following his mentor's example, published a sympathetic but critical analysis of "Paul Tillich and the Bible" in *Theological Studies.*[81] Dulles presented Tillich's understanding of the relationship between revelation and the Bible, an issue that would become central to Dulles' work as a theologian, with an emphasis on Tillich's distinctive symbolic understanding of biblical language. He also demonstrated how Tillich's critical "Protestant principle" operated in his approach to the Bible and in theology in general. Dulles found much in Tillich that Catholic theologians could admire, particularly his criticism of biblical literalism, his notion of the insufficiency of the Bible as the sole criterion of theology, his appreciation of the function of tradition in theology, his view of the legitimate development of dogma, and his critiques of an excessive supernaturalism in reaction to an exaggerated naturalism. Tillich, moreover, avoided the kind of biblicism that Dulles believed characterized the thought of the liberal Protestantism of Albrecht Benjamin Ritschl and Adolf von Harnack.

Dulles also valued Tillich's use of philosophy in his theology and his bold ontology, but he found things in Tillich's thought that troubled his Catholic sensibilities: for example, Tillich's almost total rejection of the supernatural (that is, that God can act on creatures from without), his transpersonal understanding of God, and philosophical presuppositions that were indebted to Friedrich Schelling's idealism, Friedrich Schleiermacher's subjectivism, Rudolf Otto's phenomenalism, and Martin Heidegger's existentialism. Dulles did not oppose these particular philosophies or the use of philosophy in the examination of revelation, but he believed that Tillich's philosophy trumped the revealed message; he did not allow revelation to "correct, enlarge, and inwardly transform" the philosophy that he used as a method to explicate his systematic theology.[82] Nonetheless, in Dulles' view, Tillich's system "holds exceptional interest for the Catholic theologian."[83]

Dulles' writings during the theologate years also indicate that he was something of a participant in the biblical revival that was taking place in American Catholicism at the time. Prior to his theological studies, Dulles had what could be called a precritical, almost literal, approach to the Bible, very much like the approach taken by his friends at St. Benedict Center and indeed by Dorothy Day and many in the Catholic Worker Movement in the 1930s and 1940s. By the time he reached the theologate at Woodstock, the younger biblical scholars, those trained in the ancient biblical languages and modern criticism, were beginning to expose students to various critical studies of the Bible. By the mid-1950s, the American Catholic Biblical Association had, in Gerald P. Fogarty's characterization, "come of age."[84]

Students like Dulles were becoming aware of the importance, for example, of historical criticism for "any sound hermeneutic," as is evident in an article he published on "Pentateuchal Criticism."[85] That article was an attempt to present the latest trends in biblical scholarship on the Pentateuch and to demonstrate why he believed Catholic scholars (like Roland de Vaux) sided more with the "traditio-historical" school of the Scandinavian Uppsala Lutherans than with the "literary-critical" school of Julius Wellhausen and his followers in Germany, England, and the United States. In Dulles' opinion, the bulk of contemporary evidence seemed to justify the conclusion on the Mosaic origins of the first five books of the Bible (against the Wellhausen school), but they were Mosaic only in the sense that they bore "the impress of Moses' personality."[86] Like many in the Uppsala school, Dulles discerned multiple sources of the Pentateuchal tradition. "Most Catholic scholars today," he also noted, "readily acknowledge that the Mosaic books are compilations from various sources, and were cast into their present form long after the time of Moses."[87]

In this balancing act, Dulles maintained some continuity with the earlier Catholic teaching of Mosaic authorship and simultaneously affirmed the conclusions of recent biblical scholarship. This was a method that would come to characterize much of his approach to theology in the future: an acknowledgment of the substance of previous teachings while recognizing what John Courtney Murray called the "growing edge of the tradition." Although Dulles acknowledged the benefits of historical criticism of the Bible, he was aware that biblical criticism itself posed some serious systematic questions on the nature of revelation, inspiration, and inerrancy—theological issues that Dulles did not take up in his article on the Pentateuch but issues that he would address later in his theological career.

At the end of his third year of theology, as was customary with Jesuits, Dulles was ordained a priest. His ordination, unlike that of most Jesuits, became a highly publicized event because his father was the secretary of state, and the ordaining prelate was Francis

Family portrait, 1957

Cardinal Spellman of New York. His ordination together with that of thirty-six other Jesuits, took place at Fordham University Church in the Bronx on June 16, 1956. John Foster and Janet Dulles, their daughter, Lillias, and other immediate members of the Dulles family attended the ordination ceremony at Fordham. The event became a photo opportunity for journalists and was the subject of front-page articles in the *New York Times*. John Foster Dulles, the *Times* reported, was an elder of the Brick Presbyterian Church on Park Avenue. He told reporters, "I feel very happy that my son has found a faith and the satisfaction of his faith. I have three children, all of whom are devout and religious. They have each in their own way found a communion with God, and for that I am very happy."[88]

The reporter went on to record that Fr. Dulles gave his first blessing, considered a special privilege in the Catholic tradition, to Fr. John LaFarge, SJ, the founder of the Catholic Interracial Council, but that he did not bless members of his immediate family publicly. The family gathered privately at Fordham after the ceremony to celebrate. The event also gave his father an opportunity for an extended private conversation with Cardinal Spellman, the nature of which was never revealed in the press. The day following his ordination, Dulles celebrated his first Mass at Fordham.

Since he was generally inept at ceremonies and did not know how to organize this event, he telephoned. Theodore McCarrick, his former student at Fordham and at the time a seminarian at Dunwoodie Seminary, saying, "I've no idea how you prepare for something like that. We'll probably have to have a reception afterwards, and we'll probably have to get servers." And, he asked, "Can you do that?" McCarrick told him he would take care of everything and that Dulles need not worry about the affair. The first Mass was celebrated with what McCarrick, who served at the Mass, later called "evident faith and holiness."[89]

A week after his first Mass, Dulles celebrated, in the presence of family and friends and Jesuit colleagues, a solemn High Mass at the Dahlgren Chapel at Georgetown University. His godfather, Christopher Huntington, who had been ordained a priest in 1952 for the Diocese of Brooklyn, New York, delivered the homily, which focused on the power of Christ through the instrumentality of the priest at the Eucharist. The priest had the privilege of proclaiming Christ as the salvation of the world, but that task of "restoring all things in Christ is not restricted to the priesthood. Since God took upon Himself a Human Nature, He has chosen all humanity as His instrument." Huntington asserted nonetheless that Dulles had the qualities necessary for proclaiming the kingdom of Christ, "and he comes from a family in which, for generations, a concern that the Will of Christ be done, and that the Peace of Christ prevail, has motivated untiring labor of the most extensive kind."

What a wealth of strengthening tradition will ever be in Fr. Dulles' mind, Huntington continued, as he reads the words of St. Paul [1 Cor 4:7]: 'What hast thou that thou hast not received?'" And what he received he received from Christ and from family. Like Christ, the priest was to be a mediator of salvation, transmitting to others "the stream of life which flows from the sacraments." The priest was "the custodian of the life of souls." God could have saved the world in any number of ways, but in fact he did so through the sacrifice of Christ, and he could have "saved us without ordaining Fr. Dulles. The fact is: He did ordain Father Dulles. Let us thank Him for this. For it is by this that we are enabled to *continue* to *live*."[90] Huntington wanted to emphasize the fact that the priesthood was the most powerful instrument in the world, and it was not because of a human choice of a vocation but because of Christ's choice of the instrument through which he mediated salvation to the world. The sermon reflected the very high view of the priesthood in the 1950s. In the 1990s, Dulles would call for a re-emphasis on this cultic dimension of the priesthood.

After the ordination and first Mass festivities, the thirty-seven-year-old Fr. Dulles returned to Woodstock for his final year of theology. His theological interests were uppermost in his mind, but during the theologate years, he also addressed other issues in print. Shortly before he was ordained, for example, *America* published an article he wrote on the "Legion of Decency," a Catholic institution organized by the American bishops to guide Catholics in their assessment of the moral value of movies. In that essay, Dulles argued that the Legion had a social role to play in American culture. It was a force against the weakening of the "moral fabric of society." The annual pledge Catholics gave at Mass to avoid immoral films, moreover, accentuated the social dimension of the Legion's purpose. "It is not enough," he argued, "for Catholics to be on their guard against personal mortal sin. They must be alert to the social aspects of motion-picture morality."[91] Dulles' interest in the role religion played in American culture would continue in later years.

Dulles had become something of a celebrity in the Catholic community in the late 1950s, and the St. Thomas More Catholic Lawyer Association invited him to give a keynote address at their annual meeting in New Orleans on September 11, 1956. His address, "The Contemporary Flight from Ideas," warned lawyers about the temper of the modern mind that was "thoroughly positivistic." The "triumph of positivism" was not a total flight from the significance of ideas or the use of reason, but positivism had placed technical over intuitive reason. The effect of all this was a collapse of consensus in society, the increase of fragmentation, and an inability to sustain a common universe of discourse. The denial of an objective order of things and the inability to discern an order of truth that transcended mere facts would ultimately lead society down the path to disintegration. The scholastic view of reason had something valuable to offer society in this time of relativism. The moderate rationalism of the Christian tradition needed to come to the fore in all areas of human living to preserve order and meaning in society. By a "moderate rationalism," Dulles meant a reason that was open to and completed, not destroyed, by revelation—a reason that functioned under the inspiration of Christian belief. This moderate rationalism was needed in all fields of human endeavor to provide coherence, order, stability, and justice in society. Dulles called for the restoration of what Walter Lippmann called the *Public Philosophy*, a text he repeatedly quoted.[92]

When Dulles entered the theologate, he believed that he was to finish his theology course and then obtain a doctorate in preparation for teaching philosophy in one of the Jesuit schools. Weigel, however, saw in him a theologian, and by the end of Dulles' years of studying theology, Weigel encouraged the Jesuit superiors to send Dulles to Rome for a doctorate in theology, preparing him to teach at Woodstock. Dulles' own inclinations and interests had been, since his last days at Harvard, more theological than philosophical, and the decision to send him to Gregorian University met with his own desires. Before he began studies in Rome, however, he took a ten-month period of tertianship; that is, as said earlier, a "third year" of novitiate.

Tertianship in Münster, Germany

For Jesuits in the 1950s, the year of tertianship normally took place immediately after the last year of theology. St. Ignatius envisioned the year of tertianship as an opportunity to continue one's spiritual regeneration after long, hard years of academic pursuits. Ignatius was clear about the purpose of this period of Jesuit formation:

> After those who were sent to studies have achieved the diligent and careful formation of the intellect by learning, they will find it helpful during the period of the last probation to apply themselves in the school of the heart, by exercising themselves in spiritual and corporal pursuits which can engender in them greater humility, abnegation of all sensual love and will and judgment of their

own, and also greater knowledge and love of God our
Lord; that when they themselves have made progress
they can better help others to progress for glory to God
our Lord.[93]

Tertianship was a time in which the Jesuit completed his spiritual formation in the Society, a kind of retreat from worldly and
academic endeavors in order to rekindle his spiritual life prior to
his apostolic assignment in the Society. It was analogous to the
novitiate in purpose. During tertianship, Dulles experienced again
the thirty-day retreat. After nearly fifty previous retreats of various
kinds during his prior Jesuit formation, there was really nothing
new in terms of content in the tertianship retreat. It was a period of
prayer and self-examination about familiar and basic biblical
themes and Christian truths. The emphasis during the tertianship
was on deepening his love of Christ and neighbor so that his service might stem from a sense of love and not merely from a sense
of duty. For this reason, the tertianship period has been called a
"school of love."

Dulles was sent to Münster, Germany, for his tertianship year.
Prior to leaving, his father sent him a letter telling him that he was
sure Avery would find it interesting in Germany and that he was

Tertianship in Münster, 1957–1958 (second step, far left)

letting "some of our German friends" know of his stay in Germany.[94] They could help him get around. His father also wrote him periodically while he was in Münster, and his mother visited him there, as she had done before when he was a student in Switzerland. While in Münster, Dulles was periodically invited to the home of Pusso and Anne-Marie Peus for gatherings of local Münster elite and foreign students and dignitaries. Pusso Peus was at the time mayor of Münster, and he and his wife had enjoyed especially meeting many foreign Jesuits who were in the town for their tertianship year or who were studying at the university. Dulles became lifelong friends with the Peus family and visited them repeatedly on trips to Europe.

The time in Germany allowed Dulles the opportunity not only to complete his formation as a Jesuit but also to visit many of the European centers of ecumenical activity. By 1957, his interests in the ecumenical movement had been growing, and he took advantage of his European sojourn, prior to his doctoral studies in Rome to visit centers of ecumenical activity: Paris, Amsterdam, Berlin, Paderborn, Heidelberg, Mainz, and Niederaltaich. During the summer of 1958, he visited and worked at two ecumenical institutes at the universities of Münster and Heidelberg, attending seminars conducted by two leading Lutheran ecumenists, Ernst Kinder and Edmund Schlink. He also visited Paderborn's Catholic Johann Adam Möhler Ecumenical Institute, where the periodical *Catholica* was published, and the Benedictine Abbey of Niederaltaich in lower Bavaria, where *Una Sancta* was published and where he attended a Lutheran-Catholic conference on "The Lord's Supper and the Eucharist," listening to papers by Alois Grillmeier, Henry Fischer, and Paul Althaus.

Dulles was greatly impressed by the ecumenical activities that he observed in Europe and reported in *America* that American Catholics needed to understand the questions that Protestants were raising in order to better understand Catholic theology itself. He also indicated that Germany was far ahead of the United States in real ecumenical activity between Protestants and Catholics. In the United States, Catholics could no longer accept the fact of religious divisions with fatalism. American Protestants and Catholics needed to take each other's thinking more seriously than in the past, read and understand each other's works, and thereby explore problems of common concern. Dulles implied that it was time for American Catholics to become more seriously involved in the ecumenical movement.[95]

Dulles' tertianship year was fruitful as a continuation of his spiritual development and as an introduction to the European ecumenical movement. At the end of his tertianship, he was now ready to enter his life's work as a theologian and professor of theology. To prepare himself for that mission within the Society, he left Germany for Rome.

6

FROM THE GREGORIAN TO WOODSTOCK, 1958–1965

THE NEWLY PROFESSED Jesuit priest began his two-year study of theology ("biennium") leading toward the doctorate during a momentous month in the history of Roman Catholicism. Dulles arrived in Rome at the Gregorian University on October 10, 1958, the day after the death of Pope Pius XII. By the time he returned to Woodstock College in 1960 to begin his teaching career as a professor of theology, an ecumenical council, the full import of which he could not have realized during his two years of intense doctoral studies, had been convoked, and the United States was in the midst of a presidential campaign involving his Harvard classmate John Fitzgerald Kennedy. In addition, the five years following his return to the United States erupted with some revolutionary political and social transformations as well as expectations and intimations of reforms in theology and church life.

Gregorian University and Pope John XXIII

The world's press corps during October busied itself with news from the Eternal City and the Vatican, where Pope Pius XII had died on October 9, bringing to a conclusion an aloof magisterial style of leadership that had characterized the papacy in the twentieth century. The press, however, could not have and did not predict that the death of Pius XII was the end of a particular expression of Catholicism. The *New York Times*, for example, simply recorded the death of the old pope and the impending election of a new one without much reflection on the end of an era.[1] The *Times* also quoted remarks of several American notables, including John

Foster Dulles, on the death of Pius XII. The secretary of state noted that the "passing of this great spiritual leader, who has ever been in the forefront of the defense of Christian civilization, is a profound loss for all peoples of the world. His dedicated devotion in the cause of peace and justice has been a truly great inspiration providing hope to all mankind in difficult and troubled times."[2] Present at the ceremonies were dignitaries from across the world, including John Foster Dulles and his wife Janet, among others representing the United States. Avery met his father and mother at the airport and spent a few days with them at events surrounding the death of the pope.

Reunion in Rome At the North American College i Rome U.S. Secretary of State Joh Foster Dulles and Mrs. Dulles had a family reunion with thei son, Father Avery Dulles, S.J., a convert who is studying ther Mr. Dulles had attended the funeral Mass of Pius XII as on of President Eisenhower's representatives.

With parents in Rome, 1958

When one pope dies, as the Romans say, they make a new one. The press speculated, as they are wont to do, about the election of a new pope, but few of the newspaper accounts predicted the election of the elderly Angelo Giuseppe Cardinal Roncalli, the archbishop of Venice. On October 28, the newly elected pope chose the name John XXIII.[3] He did some surprising things during his first months in office. The press followed the warm and engaging new pope as he visited prisons, hospitals, and parishes in the city of Rome and candidly spoke with the press. Ninety days after his election, moreover, he announced that he was going to convoke an ecumenical council, an announcement that astonished almost everyone, including the cardinals of the Catholic Church, the Vatican curia, Catholic theologians, and Catholic people around the world, as well as the press. He also convoked a diocesan synod for the Roman diocese, over which he presided as the bishop of Rome. The last Roman Synod was held in 1461, so this announcement, too, sparked a great deal of interest in Rome and throughout the world.

On November 9, 1958, within a month of his arrival in Rome, Dulles received some national attention in the United States when he preached a regular Sunday sermon at San Silvestro.[4] Present at the Mass was an American reporter who published an article on the sermon in the *New York Times*.[5] Dulles was "surprised by all the publicity it was given," as he told his mother when he sent her a copy of the sermon. The sermon was on Matthew 16:18 ("You are Peter, and on this rock I will build my church"), an appropriate text for the day's feast of the Cathedral of St. John Lateran, the pope's cathedral. Dulles acknowledged at the beginning of his sermon that "it is a great privilege, which we foreigners cannot help but appreciate, to be here in the city of Rome, in so many ways the heart of the Catholic Church." It was particularly "thrilling" to be in Rome in the past month, when great numbers had witnessed the impressive funeral of one pope and the election and coronation of another. These events "have made us all feel proud to call ourselves spiritual subjects of our Holy Father, the Pope."[6]

After setting the historical background for the biblical passage and giving a homiletical exegesis of the passage, Dulles launched into a commentary on the needs of the times. One of the primary needs of the day, and one that the new pope himself had addressed, was the broken unity of the church, "which should be a source of sadness to each one of us." Quoting Pope John XXIII's first address on Christian unity ("We open our heart and extend our arms to all those who are separated"), Dulles acknowledged the hopeful signs that pointed toward more "cordial relations." He ended the sermon with a call for all Catholics to imitate the attitudes of the church itself toward non-Catholic Christianity. That attitude is

> not one of boasting or pride or complacency, nor, on the other hand, one of doubt, boredom or discouragement, but an attitude of zeal, courage, patience, charity, hope, and prayer. Above all, I should say, of prayer. For if we pray in union with Christ the Good Shepherd that all his sheep may become one flock, we may be sure that God will greatly bless our prayers.[7]

The restoration of Christian unity would be a subject of Dulles' studies for years to come.

These were exciting days to be in Rome, especially for young Jesuits who were studying at the Gregorian University, a Jesuit institution established in 1551 that had been at the center of Vatican affairs for generations and whose theological professors had made significant contributions to the various Vatican congregations and papal encyclicals and statements. In the 1990s, Dulles himself characterized the theology taught at the Gregorian in the following terms: "The Gregorian University, in close alliance with the papacy, promoted [by the middle of the nineteenth century] a new vintage of scholasticism, which survived down to Vatican II. This theology, heavily apologetic in tone, became the basis of seminary textbooks and apologetic literature throughout the Catholic world."[8]

Some Jesuit theological professors (for example, Sebastian Tromp and Charles Boyer) at the Gregorian were advisors to many Vatican congregations and had some influence upon preparations for the Vatican Council. Dulles worked with these professors and met some of the best and brightest of the young Jesuit scholars from around the world who had been sent to Rome to develop their theological skills. Since the middle of the sixteenth century (when it was called the Roman College), the Gregorian has been considered the premier Jesuit institution of higher education.

Like his Woodstock professors Murray and Weigel, Dulles was sent to the Gregorian in preparation for a teaching career in theology at the Woodstock seminary. Like his theological mentor, Weigel, moreover, Dulles had developed a keen interest in fundamental theology (the issues of revelation and ecclesiology, key issues in Catholic theology since at least the First Vatican Council) and the modern ecumenical movement. He would refine his ecumenical theology at the Gregorian by eventually writing a dissertation on the subject of the *vestigia ecclesiae* (explained later in this chapter).

The biennium course of studies at the Gregorian concluded with a written dissertation, a chapter of which had to be published prior to the granting of the STD (the doctorate in Sacred Theology). Dulles chose courses that corresponded to his interests and that prepared the way for writing a dissertation. During the first year of the biennium, he took four courses: from Antonio Orbe, a "great expert on Valentinian Gnosticism and Irenaeus,"[9] on Irenaeus's response to Gnosticism and other heresies of the second century; from Zolton Alszeghy—dean of the theological faculty and professor of dogmatic theology and of the history of theology—on medieval theology; from Stanislaus Lyonnet, professor of New Testament, on the exegesis of the letters to the Colossians and Ephesians; and from Jan Witte, professor of Protestant theology, on the function of the Holy Spirit in the work of redemption according to Lutherans and Calvinists. The Dutch-born Witte eventually became Dulles' dissertation director because his area of expertise was Protestant theology, the subject of Dulles' dissertation, "The Protestant Churches and the Prophetic Office."[10]

In the midst of Dulles' first year at the Gregorian, his father became extremely ill and had to be hospitalized at Walter Reed Hospital in Washington, D.C. John Foster Dulles had had an operation in 1956 when the physicians discovered and removed some intestinal cancer. The cancer, however, had returned in late 1958, although he thought his intestinal pain, which was severe, was diverticulitis. By February 1959 the pain had become unbearable, and he went to the hospital to have an operation on a hernia, but the surgeons discovered that the cancer had returned and it was terminal. He was told that he had probably less than six months to live. Avery and the rest of the family were informed of his condition,[11] although his brother John had already had some intimations

John Foster Dulles' Christmas card to his son, 1958

that something was radically wrong. In December 1958, when John Foster was in Mexico City for the inauguration of the new president, Adolfo López Mateos, Avery's brother John had been shocked to learn that his father's health had already deteriorated badly.

On April 16, 1959, when John Foster realized that his situation was hopeless, he resigned his office as secretary of state. Shortly thereafter, Avery returned home to be with his father and family during the final days. He visited with his father in the hospital every day for the month before he died. When pneumonia set in, and John Foster realized that the end was near, he asked Avery for his priestly blessing. They talked, too, about essential things, discussing, as Avery later revealed, the doctrine of the Trinity, the deepest convictions father and son shared.[12] John Foster died on Trinity Sunday, May 24, 1959, after a public life of struggle for a just and durable peace.

The funeral for John Foster Dulles was a state affair, so ordered by President Dwight Eisenhower. The funeral ceremonies took place in the Washington Cathedral, attended by heads of state and foreign dignitaries and longtime diplomatic friends from various parts of the world. Politicians, especially prominent statesmen like John Foster Dulles, receive the public accolades and criticisms of their admiring and opposing peers throughout their lifetimes. At the time of their deaths, the politicians' careers are rehearsed in the newspapers, and they are judged according to their political accomplishments.[13] Churchmen from the United States and other countries sent their condolences and their assessments of Dulles' career. Pope John XXIII sent letters of condolence to President Eisenhower and to Fr. Dulles,[14] and the newly appointed apostolic delegate to the United States, Archbishop Egidio Vagnozzi, called Dulles "a staunch bulwark against tyranny and the man who preserved in the hearts of so many people hope and confidence in the future of mankind."[15]

Statesmen like Dulles, however, are not only politicians; they are husbands, parents, and brothers. The parental bond is not available to the press, nor are family members ever able to articulate adequately the meaning of that bond. John Foster Dulles' funeral was not just a state affair. During the days preceding the funeral, during the state celebration of his life and death, and for a long time after the funeral, Avery's mind and feelings were caught up in a flood of memories of good times together on the summer sailing trips, the continual support he had received from his Presbyterian father even when he had become a Catholic and a Jesuit priest, the conversations and ideas they shared and exchanged about a lasting peace among the nations, and most of all the love that nurtured him into his mature years. These memories never leave even in one whose belief in the resurrection and eternal life transcend the death of one's parent.

After the funeral and the days of mourning with family and friends, Avery left his mother, siblings, and relatives to return to Rome to finish his doctorate. On his way to Rome in the fall of 1959, he stopped off at Paderborn, Germany, to attend a meeting of the Catholic Conference for Ecumenical Questions, hosted by the city's archbishop, Lorenzo Jaeger. The conference, originally formed in August 1952, had met annually in various European cities since its founding; it aimed to create a true collaboration between bishops and theologians in exploring a *rapprochement* between the Catholic Church and other Christian communities.[16] The 1959 meeting was attended by Jan Willebrands, a Dutch theologian and the conference's prime mover and charter member, Yves Congar, C. J. Dumont, Bernard Leeming, and Hans Küng, among others.

The Paderborn event was particularly stimulating because of the new opportunity many participants saw for influencing the Second Vatican Council, which had been announced at the beginning of the year. The theologians and bishops at the conference discussed ways that they might influence the council on ecumenical concerns and in fact had formed a steering committee that had prepared a paper on issues that needed to be considered at the council. They sent it to Roman Cardinals Alfredo Ottaviani, Domenico Tardini, and Eugene Tisserant as well as to a few bishops around the globe. The steering committee listed, among suggestions to be considered at the council, the need to avoid language of "return" to Rome as the immediate or only goal of ecumenism; the need to balance the emphasis on the church's holiness with an expression of the phenomenal reality of the church as a community of sinners; and the need to consider a legitimate diversity in the church's liturgy, canon law, and theology as a manifestation of the church's true catholicity (that is, catholicity should not be identified with uniformity). Some of these proposals eventually ended up in *Unitatis redintegratio*, the Second Vatican Council's decree on ecumenism. Dulles' connections with his Dutch professor, Jan Witte (who, like Willebrands and some other Dutch bishops and theologians, had developed a strong interest in the ecumenical movement during the immediate postwar years), and his observance of the Paderborn event deepened his knowledge of the European Catholic ecumenical movement. But, it is fair to say, his initial interest in the ecumenical movement had been sparked earlier at Woodstock by Gustave Weigel.

After the conference, Dulles moved on to Rome to complete his second year and write his dissertation. During the 1959–1960 school year he took four more courses: from Witte on the theology of Karl Barth; from Juan Alfaro, a systematic theologian, on the gratuity and immanence of the supernatural order (a course that emphasized nature's openness to grace but saw no need for Karl Rahner's supernatural existential, a view that Alfaro criticized); from Edward Dhanis, professor of fundamental theology, on the historical Jesus (on the Son of Man theme in the Gospels, on historicity, and on Rudolf Bultmann's theories); and from Sebastian Tromp, professor of fundamental theology and the well-known ghost writer of Pope Pius XII's *Mystici corporis* (1943), on the Holy Spirit as the soul of the mystical body (the title of one of Tromp's books),[17] a course that reflected the theology of *Mystici corporis*.

Dissertation

When Dulles first came to the Gregorian, his theological interests were divided between medieval scholasticism and contemporary ecumenism.[18] And in fact he had initially proposed to Bernard Lonergan a dissertation topic on illumination in the thought of Thomas Aquinas, but Lonergan delayed his response. In the meantime Dulles decided to work with Jan Witte on the subject of *vestigia ecclesiae*, that is, the traces of the true church. John Calvin and some of his theological successors had used the term *vestigia ecclesiae* to describe the marks or traces of the true church that had been preserved in the Roman (papal) church. Catholic theologians in the twentieth century, most notably Yves Congar, used the term to designate, as Dulles indicated in his dissertation, "the positive realities subsisting in the dissident Confessions."[19] Dulles' choice of a topic in ecumenical theology reflected the new Catholic preoccupations with Protestant theology generated by the calling of an ecumenical council. Dulles noted at the beginning of his dissertation that the old polemic between Protestants and Catholics was slowly dying, and a new irenic atmosphere was emerging to end the war between the various churches. Many Catholic theologians were coming to the conclusion that Catholics had much to learn from the achievements of Protestants "both in the speculative and in the practical order." Dulles' dissertation was a Catholic attempt to examine one topic that could "open up new paths of doctrinal development."[20]

In the summer of 1959, Dulles decided to limit the dissertation to "Protestant churches and the prophetic office in those churches, as a manifestation of *vestigia ecclesiae.* But Witte was not too happy with the limitation." Witte wanted Dulles to tackle the larger issues related to the *vestigia.* Dulles, however, "was afraid it would take five years to do a dissertation on such a topic because the field was so vast."[21] Ultimately Dulles prevailed, and the topic was narrowed to the ground and role of the prophetic mission in the classic Lutheran and Calvinist traditions. Dulles' dissertation was not concerned with the individual status of Protestants within the church but with the ecclesial status of the Protestant churches.

Although Dulles was well aware of the need to address the priestly and the kingly offices within these two Protestant magisterial traditions, his own dissertation, "Protestant Churches and the Prophetic Office," was limited to the prophetic (that is, preaching and teaching) office. The dissertation was primarily an exercise in speculative, not positive or historical, theology, meaning that he was raising a theological problem that he believed Catholic theologians needed to address: Was there a truly prophetic office or mission within these Protestant traditions?

Dulles addressed specifically the ministry of the word within the Protestant churches. Was the prophetic function within the Protestant churches a legitimate *vestigium* of the true church? Or,

145

more directly, "To what extent [could] a Protestant Church, while remaining faithful to its Protestant principles,...contribute positively to the faith of its members?"[22] Protestants were convinced that they proposed the word of God with salutary power. What, Dulles asked, "must the Catholic theologian say about this claim?" That was the problem of his dissertation, and it was particularly problematic within the context of Pope Pius XII's encyclical *Mystici corporis* (1943). Because Pius had identified the mystical body of Christ with the Catholic Church's unicity and visibility, it was difficult to see, from the perspective of Catholic theology, how one could attribute a salvific function to Protestant churches as churches.

On the basis of Catholic theological principles and Catholic sources, Dulles argued that Protestant churches did not possess the prophetic office (because they did not belong to the unity and visibility of the Catholic Church), but they exercised a certain prophetic function, and their members who adhered to that preaching of the Christian revelation could make acts of theological faith. Protestant churches had the assistance of the Holy Spirit in carrying out their prophetic function, but that function was actually and ultimately dependent on the prophetic office in the true church.

Dulles' argument was carried out in seven chapters. He identified in chapter 1 the Catholic Church and the prophetic office, outlining four essential attributes of prophetic utterance: accuracy, credibility, authority, and spiritual power. The second chapter addressed the possibility of Christian faith and salvation among Protestants. The next four chapters demonstrated how the prophetic function operated within the Protestant churches, reflecting the essential attributes of prophetic utterance: accuracy (chapter 3), credibility (chapter 4), authority (chapter 5), and spiritual power (chapter 6). In their prophetic function, in Dulles' argument, the Protestant churches fell short of the fullness of the prophetic office that was evident in the Catholic Church, but they did participate in that office (chapter 7) when they preached Christ and the Christian message with accuracy, credibility, authority, and power.

Dulles published the sixth chapter of his dissertation in 1960, thereby fulfilling the Gregorian requirement for the reception of

With John Courtney Murray, SJ, 1966

his doctoral degree. He sent the chapter to John Courtney Murray, editor of *Theological Studies*, who read it and suggested that he revise it slightly (by reducing footnotes and the dissertation apparatus) and return it to him for publication.[23] Chapter 6, "The Protestant Preacher and the Prophetic Mission," was published in *Theological Studies* and later as an independent pamphlet.[24] He reiterated the thesis of the dissertation and argued against the "ecclesiological rigorism" of theologians like Charles Journet, who overemphasized the juridical and canonical mission to preach and depreciated "the power of the prophetic elements" in "dissident churches."[25] Dulles maintained that without an official mandate, Protestant preaching could have the *gratia sermonis* and thereby participate in the prophetic function in the church.

To support his argument, he invoked the authority of Aquinas, who maintained in an analogous situation that women who did not have an official mandate to preach in the church had the *gratia sermonis* to engage in private teaching and speaking informally.[26] Dulles also supported his case by reasoning, in conjunction with Congar, that even the laity need not wait for a commission to give witness to the faith; in their baptismal grace, they possessed a certain apostolic mission. Because of baptism, Protestants also possessed the infused virtues of faith and charity, a fact that was clearly evident in their constancy in witnessing to the faith and in their martyrdoms in concentration camps. Because of their baptisms, Protestant ministers possessed the priestly and prophetic powers of Christ and therefore participated in the prophetic function, which invoked genuine faith.

Preaching in the Protestant churches, though, was not merely a reflection of a baptismal mandate. Protestant churches had the *vestigium* of ordination, and although Protestant ministers did not exist within the apostolic line (that is, they did not possess the power of orders and jurisdiction), they did exist within the prophetic line. More than that, Dulles argued, Protestant ordination indicated that Protestants had the desire (*votum*) for the sacrament of ordination. If Catholics argued, as the Holy Office did in its 1949 decision *Suprema haec sacra* against the Boston Feeneyites, for the desire of baptism, why could Catholic theologians not argue for an "ordination in desire," applying the doctrine of the *votum* to sacraments like holy orders? Dulles asked why a person may not "actually desire properly sacerdotal graces." The Protestant ordination rite, if it expressed such a *votum sacramenti*, would deserve to be called a "quasi sacrament." Even though defective and not part of the "objectively valid apostolic mission," the institutional structure of the Protestant churches tended to foster the ministerial vocation and indeed contributed to the prophetic mission of the church.[27] That was the least that could be said about Protestant preaching, which was an effective agent in evoking faith. Here Dulles was trying to provide theological reasoning for a Catholic acceptance of one significant *vestigium ecclesiae* in the Lutheran and Calvinist churches.

Dulles never published the entire dissertation because, as he later admitted, it was already outdated by the time he had returned to the United States and what he had argued in the dissertation was "common doctrine" after the Second Vatican Council.[28] Reading the dissertation from the perspective of the post–Vatican II era, one would have to agree with Dulles that it was outdated by 1965. In fact, the argument to acknowledge the ecclesial status of Protestant churches seems from the perspective of the early twenty-first century to be extremely tortured and minimally ecumenical. Reading the dissertation makes one aware of how rapidly the ecumenical atmosphere changed in the United States in the early 1960s. Nonetheless, when measured against the ecumenical situation in the American Catholic Church in 1960, the dissertation made an advance in ecumenical theology and demonstrated Dulles' grasp of the signs of the times.

The general Catholic approach to Protestants in the United States on the eve of the Second Vatican Council had been significantly shaped by Pius XII's *Mystici corporis*, which appealed to Protestants to return to the true visible church even though it acknowledged that in desire and intention individual Protestants were oriented to the mystical body and through their desire and intention they could be saved.[29] Fr. Edward F. Hanahoe, SA—a member of the Franciscan Friars of the Atonement, promoter of the Chair of Unity Octave, and a *peritus* at the Second Vatican Council assigned to the Secretariat for Promoting Christian Unity—represented this approach to what he called *Catholic Ecumenism*.[30] In 1959, Hanahoe had explicitly denied that any *vestigia ecclesiae* resided in non-Catholic communities, although *vestigia* could be found in Protestant individuals as individuals.[31]

American Catholic theologians and apologists, for the most part, treated Protestants as individual Christian seekers with no ecclesial reality of their own. How widespread Hanahoe's views were is not clear; what is clear is the innovative character of Dulles' dissertation in this American context. He was attempting to deal with the ecclesial realities that existed within the Protestant (Reformed and Lutheran) churches, and it appears that very few American Catholic theologians were thinking along these lines in 1960. His view went well beyond the generally accepted Roman curial views at the time.

Dulles' dissertation was more in line with the thought of other American Catholic theologians (for example, Gustave Weigel, George Tavard, James Cunningham, and Gregory Baum—all of whom were appointed *periti* at the Vatican Council and were members of the Secretariat for Promoting Christian Unity) who were making more positive assessments of Protestant life and thought. Gustave Weigel, Dulles' professor at Woodstock, had throughout the 1950s made serious attempts to overcome the divide between Protestants and Catholics by studying Protestant theological and doctrinal sources and by engaging Protestants in open and warm personal relations. But his type of ecumenism did not raise the kinds of issues that Dulles was concerned with in his dissertation. Dulles was raising issues that transcended an era of good feeling, questions that Catholics needed to consider in light of the four hundred years of Protestant expressions of Christianity, an historical experience that could not be reduced to manifestations of individual experiences of Christianity. Protestants, in other words, related to the church by something more than an implicit or explicit intention or desire because, in Catholic theology, all graces, as the intentions and desires were, had a visible and sacramental character. Catholics, Dulles argued, needed to come to terms with the visible, sacramental, and ecclesial character of grace that existed outside the Catholic Church. In this he was raising issues that were new in the American Catholic theological tradition.

Dulles was more favorable to the approach to ecumenism taken by Gregory Baum, who argued that papal documents "are not the place where the ecumenism of the church is normally exercised; this is properly speaking the work of theologians." Nonetheless, Baum interpreted many papal documents as having a trajectory toward the modern ecumenical movement and held that they could be interpreted as acknowledging, at least implicitly, that Protestant communities of faith could be seen as media of salvation (because they mediated baptism, the word of God, faith, and holiness). He believed that Protestants were to be dealt with more as communities of faith than as individuals with no mediated access to the sources of Christian life.[32]

George Tavard, too, educated under Henri de Lubac, had also made some significant contributions to an emerging American Catholic ecumenical movement. Tavard had maintained against Hanahoe's "unionist integralism" that the theologian had the responsibility to consider ecumenical issues and questions not yet treated by the popes. Hanahoe had shown too little respect for non-Catholic Christians and had an inaccurate understanding of them. He simply could not dismiss, for example, the idea of *vestigia ecclesiae* because he could not find that notion in papal documents.[33] Dulles' dissertation was part of this emerging American Catholic ecumenism, and his dissertation helped to prepare him for his official appointment to the American Lutheran/Catholic Dialogue in 1972, joining Tavard, a charter member of that group.

After defending his dissertation, for which he received the highest commendation at the Gregorian, and before returning to the United States, Dulles took a trip to Germany, Austria, Switzerland, and France. The "high point" of his sojourn was a visit to Taizé, a Protestant ecumenical and international religious community founded in 1940 by the Swiss-born Br. Roger Schutz.[34] Located in the south of Burgundy, France, near Cluny and between Chalon-sur-Saône and Macon, the Taizé community had developed a monastic-like life of prayer, celibacy, material and spiritual sharing, and great simplicity of life. There Dulles met Br. Schutz, one of whose books on the principles of ecumenism he would later review favorably.[35] While there he also had a long conversation on the ecumenical movement with Max Thurian, whom he later called the "leading theologian" at Taizé,[36] who later converted to Catholicism and was in 1992 appointed (with Dulles) to the Vatican's International Theological Commission. This trip reinforced Dulles' desire to encourage the ecumenical movement in the United States.

Dulles had seen firsthand during this and previous trips to ecumenical institutes the effects of the ecumenical movement on the European churches, Catholic as well as Protestant. In Germany in particular, he later wrote, there was a "greater openness, greater mutual understanding, greater concern for the visible unity of Christians in the one Church of Christ." As a result of interaction and discussion between Catholics and Lutherans, "Catholicism in Germany tends to be more evangelical than in other lands; and Protestantism in Germany is perhaps more ecclesiastically-oriented than elsewhere." Americans could learn from the German experiment, even though the religious situation in the United States differed from Germany. "As I see it," Dulles wrote in 1961, "we [Americans] are still in a pre-dialogue phase. Before we discuss detailed points of agreement and disagreement, we should try to get to know each other better."[37] Part of his mission as an American theologian and as a professor at Woodstock would be to promote the ecumenical movement in the United States and to acquaint his students with current Protestant theology.

Woodstock College in Changing Times

After his summer European working vacation, he returned to the United States and Woodstock to begin preparation for his classes. For nearly three years Dulles had been educated in the European Catholic ecumenical environment. His experiences in Rome for two years were exciting and eventful, not only because of the theological education he was receiving at the Gregorian but because of the atmosphere in Rome during the first years of Pope John XXIII's reign. Rome, too, was the center of Catholic information and activities, buzzing with ecclesiastical scuttlebutt and new rumors every day. Returning to the rolling hills and pastoral setting of Woodstock College would have been a dramatic change for almost any other year than that of 1960, when the country, and Woodstock College in particular, was alive with discussions of the presidential election and talk about the new pope and the upcoming ecumenical council.

John Fitzgerald Kennedy was nominated during the July Democratic convention. The Republicans chose Richard Nixon, who had been Eisenhower's vice president and a close associate of Dulles' father. Avery also knew Nixon; when Nixon published his autobiography in 1988, Dulles wrote him a congratulatory note.[38] With the beginning of the school year, the campaign began to heat up. On September 2, 1960, Kennedy started campaigning in Maine, and the news media followed him. The religious issue came to the fore when Norman Vincent Peale, the nationally renowned pastor of the Marble Collegiate Church in New York City, and other prominent Protestants, attacked Kennedy as the Catholic candidate, asserting the old bromide that a Catholic who had allegiance to the pope could not fully serve his country. A Catholic had to be first of all obedient to the pope, and in such a situation, religious liberty in the United States was in great danger.[39]

During the primaries, the topic of Kennedy's Catholicism came to the fore again when the Episcopalian bishop of California, James A. Pike, published a book asking the American voter "to weigh the degree of his own trust in not only the [Catholic] candidate but in the candidate's Church."[40] The attacks upon Catholicism were what some in the American Catholic community, including some of the professors at Woodstock College, had feared would happen if a Catholic ran for president.[41] The ghost of Al Smith, a Catholic and a presidential candidate in 1928, was not yet dead in the Catholic community in 1960.

Kennedy decided to meet the attack head on and read a position paper on the issue of religious liberty at a September 12, 1960, meeting of the Greater Houston Ministerial Association, where he asserted:

> I believe in an America where the separation of church and state is absolute—where no Catholic prelate would tell the President (should he be a Catholic) how to act and no Protestant minister would tell his parishioners for whom to vote—where no church or church school is granted any public funds or political preference—and where no man is denied public office merely because his religion differs from the President who might appoint him or the people who might elect him.[42]

Before giving that Houston speech, Theodore Sorensen, Kennedy's press secretary and campaign organizer, read it to John Courtney Murray, who made a few corrections but later insisted that one could not respond over the phone to a quick call on such an issue. Kennedy's position, Murray later acknowledged, was much more separationist than his own more nuanced view.[43] Earlier, in 1958, while Kennedy was in the U.S. Senate, his office had consulted Murray on the Catholic understanding of the First Amendment. Prior to the campaign, moreover, and in the midst of the 1960 spring primaries, Sheed & Ward published Murray's *We Hold These Truths: Catholic Reflections on the American Proposition*. Frank Sheed, the publisher, had anticipated that the issue would come up in the presidential campaign and had asked Murray to write the text, giving a Catholic assessment of pluralism in the United States and a Catholic reflection on the issue of church and state.

The religious issue in the campaign was a hot topic at Woodstock. Woodstock's two leading theologians, Murray and Weigel, periodically weighed in on the question. They responded to the Peale bomb shortly after it was dropped in the *New York*

Times. Murray was livid, asserting, "The brutal fact becomes increasingly clear. The 'oldest American prejudice,' as anti-Catholicism has rightly been called, is as poisonously alive today as it was in 1928, or in the Eighteen Nineties or even in the Eighteen Forties. Its source is the same, political and religious ignorance. Its result is the same, a disastrous confusion of politics and religion."[44] Although Weigel did not support Kennedy and did not vote for him,[45] he presented a theological argument for the separation of religious and secular issues that seemed to favor Kennedy's candidacy. In response to the Peale statement, he spoke on the religious-political issue at the Church of the Blessed Sacrament in Washington, D.C., on September 27, 1960. It was absurd to think, he argued, that the Catholic Church would exercise political control over a Catholic president, or to believe that a Catholic president would destroy religious liberty in the United States, or to hold that a Catholic president would be bound by Catholic morality in deciding public issues. Catholics in the United States had a long tradition of supporting the First Amendment, and that was not going to change. Weigel maintained, and his views were quoted in the *New York Times* as "authoritative," that the function of civil law was not to teach theology or even the moral views of legislators.[46]

Weigel also made a radical distinction between morality and civil law, asserting in the Blessed Sacrament lecture that the "toleration of immorality, if such toleration is demanded by the common good, is good law, and in accord with the morality of political action."[47] Weigel's separationist position, as articulated in this speech, drew the fire of Protestant as well as Catholic commentators who believed that Weigel had excessively secularized the state. Avery Dulles, who, like Weigel, did not favor Kennedy as a presidential candidate, joined the critics, maintaining in an interview in the 1990s that Weigel's distinction between the moral and civil orders was "overly simplistic."[48]

The Woodstock to which Dulles returned in 1960 was also alive with discussions of the new pope and the upcoming council. Weigel and Murray participated directly as theologians at the council. Faculty and students at Woodstock followed closely the conciliar debates—informed by Murray and Weigel about the proceedings, but also, as Dulles himself has indicated, by reading the accounts of the conciliar conflicts that were published by Xavier Rynne[49] in the *New Yorker* magazine and later in widely read books on the council. Those articles and books by a priest-scholar turned journalist provided Americans with historical and theological insights into the council that were not available in other journalist accounts. Dulles as well as others at Woodstock found them clearly informative and enlightening.[50] They helped to shape Dulles' early interpretation of the council.

The *New Yorker* articles, "Letters from Vatican City,"[51] presented an insider's view of the day-to-day operations and discussions within the council and the machinations that took place outside the council floor to influence the results of the conciliar debates. The "Letters" were closely followed by the theological faculty and students at Woodstock and other seminary faculty and students across the country. Many of the bishops at the council, moreover, eagerly awaited the installments. Rynne's writings were theologically well informed, full of ecclesiastical gossip and church politics, candid, honestly forthright about the personalities and foibles of the conciliar participants, and bold in siding with and favorably interpreting the positions of the progressive wing at the council.

Readers of Rynne's "Letters" learned firsthand about the diversity that characterized worldwide Catholicism, East and West, North and South. He focused on the conciliar battles between the so-called liberals and conservatives, categorizations that were repeatedly used to interpret conciliar proceedings, and showed very precisely how they split on a host of issues. He frequently asserted that the majority at the council were on the progressive side on almost all the issues that came before the council—even though, as he presented it, a very strong conservative minority, mostly associated with the Roman Curia and in control of most of the initial schemata presented to the council, had an enormous influence beyond their numbers in trying to protect the *status quo ante* in the church. The future belonged to the progressives in Rynne's telling of the story, and all the major turning points in the council were interpreted in terms of the victory of the progressives over the intransigents. Such an interpretation had an enormous impact on Dulles and on many others who followed the council.

One of the early key turning points during the first session was the debate over the "sources of revelation." The progressives, in Rynne's interpretation, saw the original document as simply a manifestation of scholastic intransigence and a failure to take into account twentieth-century Protestant and Catholic scholarship on the issue. The original document, moreover, was unnecessarily insensitive to Protestant and Orthodox views. The progressives wanted to scotch the document completely and start over. A vote was called, but the progressives failed to muster the necessary two-thirds majority (only 1,368 out of 2,209 voted to nullify the document; only 822 voted to continue the debate on the original document) that would have halted the discussion on the original schema. Pope John XXIII, though, intervened to save the day for the progressives. He had heard the voice of the majority at the council and decided to return the original document to the Theological Commission, headed by conservatives like Alfredo Cardinal Ottaviani of the Holy Office. He also ordered the Secretariat for Promoting Christian Unity, headed by the more liberal Augustine Cardinal Bea, to join the Theological Commission in revising and, in fact, creating a new schema on revelation that the majority at the council could accept. For Rynne, that was a major turning point in the council, giving a decided victory to the progressive forces. In the 1960s and early 1970s, Dulles, like many other Americans interested in the council, accepted this interpretation and periodically used Rynne's dichotomous terminology—of liberals versus conservatives, progressives versus intransigents, conciliar battles, and victories for one side over another—to describe the council and its outcomes.

Like many other theologians outside the council, Dulles followed the debates on "The Sources of Revelation." They were particularly pertinent to the courses he was teaching at Woodstock. The progressives at the council, whom Dulles favored, were ecumenically sensitive to the views of contemporary Protestants and aware of the shortcomings and historically conditioned nature of the Post-Tridentine view of the "two sources [scripture and tradition] of revelation." Dulles, of course, was not privy to the actual original draft of the document on revelation, nor to the discussions on the council floor, except as they were revealed in the press, and particularly in Xavier Rynne's accounts in the *New Yorker*.

In Rynne's view, the progressives were in line with the mind of Pope John XXIII, and the conservatives were the prophets of doom and gloom. They associated nearly all changes, whether in doctrinal formulations or in disciplinary and pastoral policy, with the late nineteenth- and early twentieth-century heresies of modernism. This characterization of the debates at the council would have a long-lasting popular impact on how the council was understood in American Catholicism—and would influence present and future theologians as well as large numbers of people in the pews.

Dulles generally sided with the progressives. But the progressives were not always well received in some circles in the early 1960s. In 1963, shortly after John Courtney Murray was appointed (at the invitation of Francis Cardinal Spellman) a *peritus* for the Second Vatican Council, the president of the Catholic University of America refused to allow four theologians (Murray, Weigel, Godfrey Diekmann, and Küng) to speak there. Such censorship reflected a control over education and information that infuriated some within the American Catholic community and ironically provided publicity that enabled Küng to carry on a very successful national speaking tour to many Catholic and non-Catholic colleges and universities across the country, speaking on reforms that might be anticipated at the council. Dulles had met Küng in the late 1950s and was well acquainted and favorably impressed with his work on Karl Barth, the ecumenical movement in Germany, and on his calls for reform in the church. The Küng whirlwind speaking engagement across the nation stirred up again interests in the council after the first session had concluded and helped to give support to the voices for renewal within the church.[52] Dulles was sympathetic with these movements at the time.

Prior to the council and in anticipation of it, Küng had published *The Council: Reform and Reunion.*[53] In response to Pope John XXIII's call for a council that had as one of its primary aims the restoration of Christian unity, Küng outlined what he saw as the necessary conditions for reunion. This council would not aim at reunion in the way some previous councils had, but it would, he suggested, focus, as the pope intended, on the internal and external renewal of the church itself as a first step or preliminary condition for Christian unity. Reform, he advised his readers, was not the preserve of Protestantism but was consistent with the long Catholic tradition. Catholics could and should own the fact that the church was always in need of reform, although Küng, like most Catholics, preferred to speak of renewal rather than reform in order to preserve continuity with tradition. Like the pope, moreover, Küng invoked *aggiornamento* (the modernization of pastoral work and ecclesiastical discipline) as one of the necessary conditions for the renewal of the church. He also called for some healthy self-criticism within the church, because it was not only a divine creation but a church of sinful human beings. And, he believed, the church was in a strong position to be able to bear a sound critical assessment of its own internal weaknesses.

Küng ended the short treatise by boldly suggesting things that needed to be renewed in the church, starting with the necessity to renew doctrinal formulations that no longer met the aspirations of the modern world. He was not so much calling for a reform of doctrine but a development of dogmatic statements that were, in fact, historically conditioned articulations of the faith. New formulations were required to meet the sensitivities and reflect the perspectives of the present age. He also made suggestions for the reform of the episcopal office to restore the full value of that office in the church—underlining what would be called "collegiality" and "subsidiarity" within the church, moving away from an excessive Roman centralization that had developed in the most recent centuries. He saw this suggestion as a key objective for the upcoming council—"a restoration of the office of the bishop, and of the local church which he embodies, both at the level of dogmatic theory and at that of practical organization; and through this, a radical, interior renewal of the life of the church: all as a necessary preparation for ultimate reunion."[54]

Dulles reviewed the 1961 French translation of Küng's book as well as the 1962 English translation,[55] emphasizing the fact that Küng saw the Holy Spirit as the source of renewal, and Christ and the gospel as the norm of renewal. Some, Dulles opined, might consider the book "radical and dangerous" because of some of its bold recommendations for reform, but Dulles thought that it could stimulate some "healthy debate" within the church. Dulles, however, thought that Küng's proposals for decentralization created "delicate problems," like the possibility of the tyranny of a local ordinary or the development of unchecked power at the local ecclesiastical level, that Küng had not fully investigated. Küng's book, though, was worthy of a great deal of consideration because it focused attention on issues that needed to be discussed at the upcoming council. "Nearly everyone these days," Dulles reported in 1963, "is anxious to read something by Hans Küng." While generally favorable to Küng's perspective in the 1960s, Dulles noted that Küng had a tendency "to over paint the dark side of the picture," particularly with respect to his statistics on practicing Catholics.[56]

Despite the occasional criticism of Küng, Dulles shared with Küng many of the same anticipations and expectations about the council. By January 1965, before the last session of the council, Dulles could speak of the council in terms of "Luther's Unfinished Reformation." By that he meant that Vatican II had gone beyond Trent in its approach to Luther and the Protestant movement because it admitted that Luther had some valid concerns and that he had not originally wanted to create a separate church. Luther had emphasized the Bible as more important than Aristotle, the need for a vernacular liturgy, the restoration of the role of the laity, a ministerial clergy, and better preaching—values that had sustained Protestantism throughout the centuries and values that Vatican II was now reasserting. Luther, moreover, brought a new sense of self-criticism into the church, and Vatican II was now following his lead. Catholics at the council were not only becoming self-critical, but they were more open to criticisms and critiques that came from contemporary Protestant theologians. Citing Dietrich Bonhoeffer, Dulles asserted that Luther wanted a reformed, not a new church, and if all this was true, one could conclude that "Luther's Reformation is still an ongoing thing."[57] The council was for Dulles a supreme moment of self-reflection, self-criticism, and self-reform.

The year 1963, in the middle of the council, was particularly eventful for Dulles personally and for the country. Between the first and second sessions of the council, on August 15, 1963, Dulles took his solemn vows, completing the period of formation as a

Jesuit. The Jesuit pronounced perpetual solemn vows of poverty, chastity, obedience, and a fourth vow, unique to Jesuits, of special obedience to the pope in matters regarding mission, promising to undertake any mission the pope might choose.

Dulles took these vows during a year in which Francis Cardinal Spellman invited John Courtney Murray to be a *peritus* at the council; the Catholic University refused to allow four theologians to speak there; Hans Küng went on his national tour speaking of anticipated reforms; Martin Luther King Jr. marched on Washington, D.C.; the second session of the council opened; Dr. John Rock published *The Time Has Come: A Catholic Doctor's Proposals to End the Battle over Birth Control*, a book that was widely distributed and raised considerable interest among Catholics in the contraceptive pill he had developed; and President John Fitzgerald Kennedy was assassinated. These were momentous times that might have made the taking of solemn vows as a Jesuit insignificant in comparison. But Dulles was a Jesuit, and he continued, in the midst of these events and the regular routine of teaching and lecturing, to develop his life as a committed religious for whom the internal discernment of one's spiritual progress was the chief concern of one's life. Taking solemn vows was another step in marking his own religious development and commitment.

Like Karl Rahner, who was one of his favorite contemporary theologians, Dulles never separated theology and spirituality or his work as a theologian and his personal religious experience as a Catholic Christian and a Jesuit. In the early 1960s, when so much interest in religious experience reemerged, Dulles used Rahner's theology to explain his commitment to an Ignatian spirituality that focused on finding God in all things.[58] Dulles, like Rahner, emphasized the simultaneity of the personal, the sacramental, and the ecclesial in all religious experience, modifying to a considerable extent the almost exclusive emphasis in the 1960s on the individualistic or purely subjective spiritual search for meaning.

Dulles agreed with Rahner's insistence, for example, on the ecclesial dimension of the communion of souls with God. "The Word became flesh, Rahner reminds us, in order to unite to himself a holy people. But this cannot be merely interior communion of souls invisibly linked together in grace. Granted the spatio-temporal quality of human life, the communion of saints must realize itself as a corporate, socially organized body." One's own personal search for communion with God always involved a dialectical and dynamic union of "the uncreated and the created, the Christic and the Marian, the sacramental and the personal, the ecclesial and the individual, the sacred and the secular, the institutional and the charismatic." This Ignatian mysticism, as Rahner and Dulles analyzed it and practiced it, was "compounded of an absorbing preoccupation with God's utter transcendence and an astonishing ability to find him in the actual situations of life, in the here and now."[59] Finding God in all things required daily prayer and reflection, sacramental grace, the constant exercise of the theological and moral virtues, a high degree of humility, and, especially for the Jesuit, a willing response to the evangelical vows of poverty, chastity, and obedience. Finding God's will was the goal of the Christian life and the continual aim of a Jesuit theologian's work.

On January 3, 1964, in the midst of Dulles' fourth year (1963–1964) of teaching at Woodstock, Gustave Weigel died suddenly after a brief illness. Weigel had been Dulles' mentor and colleague, a major figure at Woodstock, and a much beloved colleague among many American Protestant theologians and journalists at the council. Weigel's death was a great loss for Woodstock and had consequences for Dulles. Prior to Weigel's death, Dulles had taught courses on revelation and apologetics, fundamental and foundational issues for theologians. Weigel had been primarily responsible for the courses on ecclesiology and ecumenism. After Weigel's death, those courses were assigned to Dulles. Revelation, ecclesiology, and ecumenism were core issues at the council, and they were the issues closest to Dulles' own interests. He took up the new courses and continued to publish his own research in the areas of revelation, apologetics, and ecumenism—but in ways that reflected the transformations that were taking place in those fields through the work of the council.

Woodstock, like many American Catholic seminaries and colleges, experienced the excitement of the council and the impact of multiple social and cultural transformations in the United States. The presidential campaign and the prospects of the council evoked much discussion among faculty and students at Woodstock in the fall of 1960, but the main business at Woodstock was theological education. Although profound ecclesiastical, theological, and social changes were in the air in Rome and in the United States during the years of the council, they had little effect on the structures at Woodstock. Woodstock College remained relatively traditional. One student who was at Woodstock during those years has indicated that the council had "very little impact [on the college]. It was pretty much pre–Vatican II traditional text-book theology. Better than average maybe...we had some good people there, but it was very traditional."[60] The student body, the academic structures, the curriculum, the teaching style, and the rural location were relatively stable during these years, though there were some signs that things were changing.

The students at Woodstock in the early 1960s, because of the Jesuit system of education, were older than those in the free-standing diocesan seminaries, where students would generally have been in their early twenties. The Jesuit scholastics were in their late twenties and some in their early thirties; they were born during the Depression and came to maturity in the post–World War II era of prosperity; they and their families were a part of the gradual but confident emergence of Catholics into American cultural, social, economic, and political life. Many of them, moreover, had previous educations that had prepared them in other disciplines; some had already received doctorates in disciplines other than theology. They were a part of the new generation of Catholics, too, who identified with John Fitzgerald Kennedy's emergence, whether or not they supported him politically. Since the mid-1950s, professors in Catholic seminaries across the United States had noticed the emergence of a new type of seminarian. The new recruits were much more Americanized than had been true of earlier generations, had been more exposed to the cultural and political and social values of the post–World War II economic prosperity, and had imbibed the dynamics of American freedom.

The number of students in classes at Woodstock during the years of the council (1962–1965) remained relatively large and relatively stable. About 315 students had matriculated there in 1958, declining to about 300 by 1965. The decrease of scholastics at Woodstock, about 4 percent from 1958 to 1965, matched that in the entire U.S. Jesuit Assistancy.[61] By 1965, few at Woodstock or any other American Catholic seminary could have anticipated the precipitous drop in the number of scholastics and seminarians that would take place in the postconciliar period.

The academic structure at Woodstock during these years followed the older patterns of education that had served Jesuits for generations. The ultimate end of theological education was ordination, not a degree in theology. Classes in theology were structured to provide the scholastics with enough theological understanding that they could pass the oral examinations at the end of their education, allowing them to be ordained to the priesthood. The Jesuit form of education, like that in many other seminaries, focused on moving students from one year of theological formation to another; education was measured in terms of the gradual advancement in theological understanding, not in terms of the number of credit hours one had taken in theology. More than 50 percent of the curriculum was devoted to dogmatic theology, and the rest of the curriculum was divided up between courses in moral theology, scripture, some church history, and courses in practical pastoral theology.

For all scholastics, class attendance was obligatory. In class, theology was communicated primarily by lectures, and students listened, took notes, and asked questions when appropriate. It was a practice at Woodstock, and many other places, that in class and in preparation for oral examinations students used theology lecture notes that had been prepared by previous generations of students. In 1960, Dulles, like many of the theology professors, taught in the old style, a style that some scholastics considered uninspiring or simply boring; he taught the way he had himself been taught—by lectures, and he prepared his lectures on the basis of certain Latin theses he wanted to demonstrate in class, very much in the way the old theological manuals presented materials. The content of Dulles' courses in theology, though, reflected not only the manual tradition, but the new theology of Rahner, Küng, Congar, de Lubac, Danielou, and other German, French, Dutch, and Belgian Catholic theologians, the theologies of prominent Protestant theologians, and, gradually, the influences from the Second Vatican Council. He translated numerous excerpts from various theologians' writings and handed them out in his classes—to modify the manual approach to theology and to keep students abreast of what was going on in the newer approaches to theology. But, all in all, there was little structural change in theological education before the end of the council.

During the council years, the governance of Woodstock College and the living arrangements within the college reflected patterns that had served the Jesuits well for decades, if not centuries. The college was governed in hierarchical fashion, with the Jesuit superior and the rector having the final say about decisions affecting college life. Professors within the college, too, had total control over the curriculum and established the grounds and criteria for monitoring student progress in theological education and for passing examinations. Scholastics had little or no participation in the governance of the college. It was a hierarchical institution. The separation between the scholastics and the professed fathers who taught was also evident in the living arrangements. The professors had their own recreation and dining rooms, and the students had theirs.

Woodstock professors, and especially the spiritual director, kept a close scrutiny over the students' spiritual development as they prepared for the priesthood. Progress in spiritual development was almost as important as progress in theological formation—although in the Jesuit *Constitutions*, Ignatius of Loyola had stipulated that during the scholasticate, spiritual exercises and pious practices within the colleges should not trump intellectual development. Ignatius wanted a balanced formation program that paid due attention to the students' intellectual, spiritual, social, and physical health. But spiritual formation was an integral part of the seminary education, and all professors were supposed to be sensitive to this aspect of Woodstock's educational aims.

English had been used in theological instruction in American seminaries and scholasticates for some years, even though some textbooks were in Latin. Rome decided in 1962 to change that practice and to require the use of Latin in theological education, a decision that seemed at the time to be contrary to other directions coming from Rome. Before the council opened in October 1962, Pope John XXIII issued *Veterum sapientia* (February 22, 1962), promoting the retention and use of Latin in the church and in seminary education. Dulles, like other professors in seminaries, lectured in Latin after the papal declaration, for at least the first fifteen minutes of class, but he discovered after a few weeks that the Latin lectures were just ineffective. Ironically, *Veterum sapientia*, in Dulles' estimation, "pretty much brought about the demise of Latin in the classroom."[62]

Dulles settled into Woodstock and developed a rhythm of life that he followed throughout his career as a theologian. He studiously prepared lectures for his teaching and for the many public lectures that he was invited to give to audiences of priests and laity interested in the new developments in theology and church life. Teaching and public lecturing led to publishing, where he developed his theology by putting it in communion and at times in tension with the received theological tradition. Like some theologians in the *nouvelle théologie* tradition, he perceived the necessity of creative adaptation to modern thought as well as historical retrieval. His teaching, public lecturing, and publications in the early 1960s reflected a balance of tradition and innovation in his theology.

Fundamental Theology at Woodstock

In his teaching, public lecturing, and publishing during the years of the council, Dulles tackled some key issues in fundamental theology. He focused in particular on the meaning of revelation in its relation to history and faith, researched the history of the theology of revelation, and, increasingly influenced by historical consciousness, investigated the relationship between historical fact and faith. He addressed the traditional Catholic understanding of the relationship of scripture and tradition, trying to reshape the issue in the light of twentieth-century studies in scripture and history. He developed, too, a new approach to Christian apologetics, one that took into consideration the emergence of historical criticism in biblical and doctrinal studies and examined the relationship between the historical Jesus and the Christ of faith. The American ecumenical movement also became a subject of his reflections and publications. In all of these areas he demonstrated an emerging awareness of the historical consciousness that was characteristic of the *nouvelle théologie* and developments taking place at the council.

During his first years at Woodstock, Dulles' energies were almost totally given to preparing his classes on revelation (which included a systematic examination of biblical inspiration and apologetics) and an introduction to scripture. The introduction to the New Testament and the Gospels was a course in fundamental theology, focusing on the issues modern biblical scholarship was raising for theology. In these years, Dulles was developing a theology of revelation—a project that would occupy him for the remainder of his life—in his classes and publications. The class, *De Revelatione Christiana*, covered Catholic and non-Catholic notions of revelation.

His lecture notes on revelation presented ten theses defining revelation, its possibility, necessity, facticity, signs of its credibility, and the fundamental mystery of the person of Jesus.[63] In the midst of ten lectures, he outlined in a forty-page handout some prominent non-Catholic notions of Christian revelation. Like his own mentor, Weigel, he introduced students to Protestant biblical and theological scholarship within the framework of a traditional thesis approach to fundamental theology. His method was historical as well as systematic. He presented the issue of revelation, for example, historically, focusing on the question as it had arisen in writers since the Protestant Reformation (Deists as well as Protestant; liberal as well as conservative post-Reformation Christians). He appealed to Pius XII's encyclical *Humani generis* (1950) on the need to study non-Catholic sources not only to understand their errors but also to examine the truth that was in them. He focused significantly on the subjective dispositions for the reception of revelation and took up recent questions in biblical theology (for example, on methods of interpreting the New Testament, on the question of the historical Jesus and the Christ of faith, on the Messianic Secret in Mark, on whether or not the apostles knew prior to Jesus' death of his divinity, and on Jesus' resurrection as a historical fact).

During each section of the course, Dulles introduced students to current literature on revelation. When he left the Gregorian, he borrowed René Latourelle's class notes on revelation to use in his classes at Woodstock. He translated, too, an article by Latourelle on what he called the "Catholic Notion of Christian Revelation."[64] Catholic magisterial notions or definitions of revelation, since they were born in very particular historical circumstances and tended to resonate with those circumstances, had to be interpreted with a great deal of care. Latourelle advised students to consider not this or that single historical document to be exhaustive of a doctrine on revelation but to consider the totality of the church's utterances. From that totality one could get a grasp of the meaning of the doctrine. What Latourelle suggested for the doctrine of revelation could also be applied to other areas of church teaching. Revelation itself had a historicity to it, and that must be taken into account in accessing and interpreting the revealed record.

In 1964, Dulles wrote a substantive article, "The Theology of Revelation," that was primarily a review of Latourelle's *Théologie de la révélation* (1963), published shortly after the first major debates on revelation at the council. Dulles' article put the twentieth-century preoccupation with the theology of revelation within its larger historical context, noting that prior to the Reformation, theologians used revelation primarily to defend particular Christian doctrines against heretical assertions; after the Reformation, attention shifted to the scripture and tradition issue, and the methods of discovering what was contained in revelation; in the post-Enlightenment period, because of rationalism and modernism, attention again turned to defending supernatural revelation itself; and in the twentieth century theologians focused on developing a theology of revelation, which had an immediate ecumenical urgency. Protestants had worked in this area of revelation since the Protestant Reformation and the Enlightenment. Catholics were behind the times in this regard. In the immediate past, Catholics had focused so much attention on the sacraments as the means of grace that they tended to neglect the "salvific power of the word of God."[65]

Latourelle's new book, the fruit of a decade of work, was a welcome Catholic contribution to the issue. Although Latourelle's method was quite traditional, his focus, like that of other recent theologians (Marie-Dominique Chenu, de Lubac, Congar), centered on the christocentric, historical, interpersonal, and biblical dimensions of revelation and criticized the excessively apologetical, abstract, and propositional approaches of the twentieth-century neo-scholastic manual tradition. In Dulles' view, however, Latourelle left some questions unanswered and issues underdeveloped or undeveloped: among other things, the universality of revelation and its ongoing reality beyond apostolic times, the extradoctrinal dimensions of revelation, the ultimately mysterious and unfathomable and symbolic nature of revelation.[66]

Latourelle had made a major contribution to the Catholic theology of revelation, but he had also left much room for improvement in that theology, a task Dulles would continue to pursue throughout his life. After publishing the article on revelation, Dulles received a letter from Latourelle thanking him for pointing out the weaknesses in his own position and congratulating him on the publication of a perceptive article on the needs in contemporary Catholic approaches to revelation.[67]

Dulles used the German theologian Gottlieb Söhngen, one of Pope Benedict XVI's teachers, to argue for a "historical component in Christian revelation."[68] According to Söhngen, the "Christ mystery is no kingdom of 'pure' values like the kingdom of 'eternal truths.'" In Christianity, truth itself was incarnate in history, and the "validity of its affirmation is inseparable from its historical origin or revelation." This emphasis on historicity is evident in Dulles' early class notes. He agreed, too, with Söhngen that theology could not be legitimately separated into historical and speculative branches. The fundamental and doctrinal theologian needed to be reminded that

> no dogma ever reaches a believer except by being revealed by God and proclaimed by the Church. The theological understanding of the dogma, moreover, can never with a good conscience prescind from the history of its revelation and proclamation. Christian theology must be an inner unity of historical and speculative theology. One should not regard speculative theology as genuine theology and historical theology as a mere propaedeutic to it. The Enlightenment would consider that truths of fact have their value as preparation for truths of reason; the positive factor in religion would be propaedeutic to rational religion. But a Christian theologian cannot with good conscience speak of the propaedeutic character of historical theology. Historical theology is just as genuinely theology as speculative the-

ology, or rather genuine theology is a living totality of historical and speculative theology.[69]

After giving his class a fairly comprehensive introduction to the history of Catholic notions of revelation, he urged his students to consider carefully the "nuggets of solid gold" that one could find in non-Catholic theories of revelation and to learn from the way in which non-Catholics themselves criticized "one another with remarkable acumen" to point out the weaknesses and shortcomings of their respective positions. Students could learn much from the various Protestant theories on revelation of the past four centuries, but they also needed to learn how to bring various theories into some kind of synthesis after an analysis of disparate notions and different sides of the question of revelation. After an analytical approach to the various elements of revelation, the student needed

> to show how the Christian revelation can be God's pure word and yet received into finite human minds; how it can be perfective of man and yet transcend all human possibility; symbolic and yet doctrinal, mysterious and yet intelligible, real and yet verbal, social and yet personal, beyond verification and yet discernible—to be able to synthesize all these apparently incompatible attributes without arbitrarily sacrificing some to others—such is the task which non-Catholic theology has left unsolved.[70]

Historical retrieval, systematic analysis, and dialectical synthesis would characterize Dulles' theological method and work for much of his life.

Dulles' own published works during the years of the council indicated that he was moving gradually away from the more cautious systematic theological approach he had taken in his Gregorian dissertation. He was becoming more and more affected by what *periti* at the council called "historical consciousness" with respect to revelation, ecclesiology, ecumenism, and a host of other theological issues. *Historical consciousness* was the buzzword that seemed to characterize all progressive theology at the council. Historical criticism had of course influenced biblical studies for some time, but the appeal to historical consciousness came more and more into prominence in the American Catholic theological community during and after the council.

Dulles was particularly impressed with Michael Novak's characterization of what had been taking place in theology because of the council. In *The Open Church* (1964), Novak described what many foresaw as the clear separation of the new, historically conscious approach to theology from what he called the "non-historical, or anti-historical orthodoxy" of the theology of the immediate past.[71] And, for him, the struggle at the council was between these two kinds of theology; the victory in this battle belonged to the historically conscious theologians.

In a chapter entitled "The School of Fear," Novak characterized the nonhistorical theologians as the "prophets of doom." Their "entrenched" theology, which had predominated in the church for the past four hundred years, was presented as immobile, abstract, and triumphalistic. It was a theology that favored a kind of speculation that ignored historical fact, past or present. It defended "a system of propositions as orthodox while refusing to commit itself to the world of investigating that system's historical justification, or making it relevant to the historical realities of the present." It defended an "orthodoxy suspended, as it were, outside of history, in mid air." This nonhistorical orthodoxy was impervious to criticism and change and, moreover, it was absolutely self-righteous, arrogant, proclaiming its own view as self-evident truth. Quoting Lord Acton, Novak presented this kind of theology as "intellectually lazy; as isolated from contact with unbelievers; as jealous of its own authority; as unscrupulous in its treatment of other schools; as fearful of sources of evidence outside its own system."[72] For the nonhistoricals, one could say, original research was original sin. What is amazing about this characterization of the theology of the previous four hundred years was that it was done without a single reference to a concrete historical text or representative theologian. Such caricatures of the past were not entirely uncommon in the 1960s in the popular press and in some theologians. And, Dulles was not entirely freed from such exaggerations in the mid- to late 1960s.

What was important for the progressive school of theology at the council, Novak argued in agreement with Pope John XXIII's opening address, were two things: the principle of historical development and the principle of concrete reality.

> Both of these principles insist upon attention to concrete history: to the men, movements, and events of history. Both principles insist that the man who uses them must enter the stream of history and work from within it, conscious that his words and his concepts are conditioned by it (the principle of development), and that his theories must meet the test of concrete facts, movements, and events (principle of concrete reality). The first principle is aimed against the idea that words have meaning outside of their historical context, or are unconditioned by their origins. The second is directed against the idea that ideology is "pure" and should be judged only in the light of logic; it insists on judgment of institutions, men, and events as they appear in fact as well as in theory. Both principles deny the man who uses them the right to claim that he or his ideas are uninfluenced by history, or that he need not undertake the work of bringing his ideas and methods to the bar of concrete reality.[73]

According to Novak, it was the historically conscious theologians who were emerging during the council, and that kind of theology was to be the wave of the future.

Although Dulles did not accept entirely Novak's characterization of past or present theology, he did move in the direction of what could be described as a historically conscious theology. This kind of theology was evident in his publications on ecumenism, revelation, and apologetics prior to and during the years of the council. As a fundamental theologian, he periodically pointed to the limits of the older manual theology,[74] emphasized the benefits of a more historically conscious Catholic theology (John Henry Newman, Marie-Dominique Chenu, Henri de Lubac, Yves Congar, Romano Guardini, Karl Rahner, and so on), and interacted with modern Protestant biblical and systematic scholars in his classes and in his publications. His interests were primarily in understanding the dynamic and synthetic interrelationship of reve-

171

lation, the Bible, tradition, church, faith, history, and dogma—the constitutive elements of fundamental theology. His own approach to theology was changing in the process of trying to reexamine the relationship of these various elements within the Catholic theological tradition.

Dulles had moved away from the older apologetical approach to history and to the Gospels as historical narratives, and at the same time, he appropriated elements of scientific or academic history and especially of the so-called historical-critical method in biblical studies and theology. But, he continued, too, to criticize what he saw as some of the inherent limits of scientific history and the historical-critical methodology when used exclusively in theology and interpreting the Bible.

Throughout the years of the council and immediately thereafter, Dulles regularly gave summer lectures and periodically participated in summer schools that were organized for priests and laity who were interested in modern theological developments. His first major published book, *Apologetics and the Biblical Christ* (1963), was a collection of five lectures given to priests of the Archdiocese of Chicago in the summer of 1961 on the impact of modern biblical studies on Christian apologetics.[75] The five lectures dealt with (1) the relationship between apologetics and historicism; (2) the Gospels and scientific history; (3) the Gospels as confessional documents, integrating fact and interpretation, fact and faith, history and faith; (4) the resurrection as history and confession; and (5) the divinity of Christ as history and confession.

The lectures made three major points. First, Dulles argued that the older manual-style apologetical approach to the Bible was inadequate and needed to be replaced. His criticisms of the older manual theology would be a recurring theme throughout his career, but they were especially emphasized in the 1960s and early 1970s. The older manual approach to apologetics was unsatisfying because it looked upon the Bible and the Gospels in particular as historical narratives that presented miracles and prophecies as historical evidence of the divinity of the Christian tradition. The Bible could not legitimately be treated as a historical narrative; it was written by believers for believers and intended to arouse faith, not establish historical fact. The manual approach, moreover, misunderstood the fundamental motives that evoked faith. Although the apologist had to rely on "purely human evidence," he or she could not treat the Bible as an academic historian might treat it.[76]

Second, Dulles emphasized the value of modern biblical scholarship as an aid to apologetics. But he criticized certain aspects of the historical-critical school as he had criticized the older Catholic apologetic. In essays in the early 1960s, Dulles argued that scientific history, as that was understood in the German historical-critical, value-free school of thought, could not account for the divine authority of miracles.[77] He was particularly averse to the tendency in some historical-critical biblical scholarship and in some theologies to separate or to distinguish too sharply biblical theology (as narrative or descriptive) and systematic theology (as normative), what a text meant and what a text means, fact and faith. In 1963, he took issue with H. E. W. Turner's *Historicity and the Gospels* precisely because Dulles believed that the "criteria of academic history are hardly sufficient" in judging the credibility of gospel narratives that are "wholly concerned with the extraordinary words and deeds of an utterly unique person."[78] The objective, noncommittal, value-free approach was all well and good, but it was not theology. The distinction between what the Bible meant and what it means was invalid in theology, especially from a Catholic perspective, because what it meant is "still normative," and for Dulles the Bible was "permanently authoritative." The theologian's task, in the end, was "to set forth the contents and implications of God's revelation, as he himself understands it within the tradition of the church to which he belongs."[79] Although theology could be served by the historical method, theology was not a historical science. Theology was inherently confessional in the sense that it required faith and that faith came to theologians as it came to all Christians in and through the church.

Third, Dulles wanted to preserve a role for apologetics in theology, but he considered apologetics part of a fundamental theology that presupposed faith. *Apologetics and the Biblical Christ* argued against an historicist (whether from the evidentiary school or from the value-free school of historians) apologetic in favor of what Dulles preferred to call a "confessional apologetic." The Bible could be a part of such an apologetics if one had a wider view of the

Bible, reason, and evidence than was evident in either the manual tradition or an exclusively historical-critical method. The Bible was not purely a historical narrative, solely accessible to the historian's workshop. Nonetheless, the scriptures could still be used in apologetics, but in an apologetics that was addressed not to the scientific historian but to the religious inquirer. Dulles argued that it was possible "to show that the narratives of the New Testament make a powerful, and in some ways decisive, contribution to the credibility of the Christian revelation."[80] And, for him, that task was consistent with the traditional notion of the apologist's role "to show the reasonableness of the assent of faith."[81] Dulles was calling for a confessional apologetic, not one based solely on reason or historical evidence as that evidence was conceived of in the manualist's and the historian's workshops.

Dulles concluded that it was necessary in apologetics to

treat the New Testament writings as religious testimony—a testimony embracing both factual memories and spiritual insights. The attributes of the testimony are such that the prudent man in search of religious truth can find it satisfying. The intrinsic sublimity of the message, its coherence, and its adaptation to man's religious needs make it eminently worthy of consideration as a revelation from God.[82]

The New Testament, in other words, had its own inherent compelling motive for acceptance as revelation. The religious inquirer could find in the Bible religious testimony that resonated with the inherent desires and inclinations of the human mind and heart.

The scriptures offered not scientific or evidentiary proofs but authoritative testimony that had the potential to arouse faith. Such testimony brought with it a "distinct font of knowledge."[83] Testimony, and especially the testimony of the church, played a significant role in communicating and evoking faith and in developing a solid epistemological foundation for the credibility of Christianity. The older Catholic approaches to apologetics and the Bible were excessively rationalistic and extrinsic; they relied too heavily on external signs and proofs to move reason to accept the credibility of

Christianity. What Dulles was proposing in the early 1960s was an approach to the Bible and apologetics that acknowledged the totality of the human epistemological response to Christian testimony. The old manual tradition had put too much confidence in reason and reason's ability to discern the divine within the historical records of the past. Dulles was proposing to the Chicago priests a new way of looking upon apologetics, modern biblical scholarship, and the Bible. The small book was printed more than eight times in English and was translated into French, Korean, Polish, and Chinese. Most of the fourteen or more book reviews were overwhelmingly positive, indicating that his approach had an appeal or resonated with his readers' notions.[84]

Within his classes as well as in his publications, Dulles dealt at some length with the primarily Protestant distinction between the so-called historical Jesus and the Christ of faith. What concerned him most in the nineteenth-century liberal Protestant quest for the historical Jesus was the tendency to "put aside the supernatural and produce an enlightened, moral teacher whom the moralistic, scientifically minded European of the late nineteenth century could accept and admire." But the twentieth-century reactions to this movement were also unsatisfactory because Protestants like Martin Kähler, Otto Dibelius, Rudolf Bultmann, and to some extent, Paul Tillich tended to emphasize faith over history or faith without history, and this "cleavage between faith and fact" was "unacceptable from the Catholic point of view."[85]

Also unsatisfactory were those contemporary Protestant theologians (for example, Joachim Jeremias, Nathaniel Taylor, Gregory Dix, Ernst Käsemann, John A. Robinson) who stressed the significance of the historical Jesus for Christian faith but failed to relate adequately faith and fact. Using the academic discipline of history, one could not, in Dulles' view, identify the historical Jesus with the Christ of faith. But if history were understood as "the full reality of the past, with all its significance for weal and woe, including its decisive impact on the shape of things to come, then we must give a very different answer" to the question, "Is the historical Jesus the same as the Christ of faith?" In this understanding of history, "the Christ of faith, and he alone, is the Jesus of history." Only the faith of the church, in the light of the Easter and Pentecost mysteries, was capable of "grasping the secret of this man," and that faith reflected the fuller notion of historical reality.[86]

Dulles was trying to shape his fundamental theology to avoid the extremes of the kind of dogmatism he found in the manual tradition and the tendencies to historicism that he discovered in some forms of liberal Protestantism and Catholic modernism. He took up issues, as we have seen, that arose from historical criticism, historical consciousness, and the new methods of biblical scholarship. Prior to the council he also hoped that it would focus on scripture and tradition. Trent had established the necessity of tradition but had not clarified adequately the relation between scripture and tradition. A question remained. Were there things revealed in tradition that were not in scripture? Dulles thought that the Second Vatican Council would not define this relationship too narrowly, leaving room for theologians to work out the finer technicalities of the relationship.[87]

During the council, Dulles continued to investigate the meaning of tradition and the connection between scripture and tradition. Like some *nouvelle théologie* and Transcendental Thomist theologians, he adopted the French philosopher Maurice Blondel's (1861–1949) "dynamic notion of tradition" because it steered a path between the pitfalls of dogmatism and historicism and anticipated "some of the best thinking of Vatican II."[88] Although Blondel was not always easy to understand, any contemporary Catholic engaged in fundamental theology had to have a firm grasp of Blondel's thought. For Dulles there was a dynamic relationship between faith and fact; faith did not control or absorb fact, nor did fact determine or judge faith. The two retained their independence while remaining in a symbiotic relationship, the one with the other. By the end of the council (1965), Dulles had not yet articulated a comprehensive, systematic view of the relationship between faith and history, but he had clearly identified the extreme boundaries that he found unacceptable for theology.

The relation between scripture and tradition received much attention during the council, and Dulles weighed in on the issue, publishing three reviews of Catholic authors who addressed the subject. In 1963, James Patrick Mackey published *The Modern Theology of Tradition*, a book Dulles considered "the most serviceable Catholic monograph" available in English on a topic that had gained high interest since the beginning of the council. Unlike some of the manual theologians, Mackey did not accept the idea that tradition was summed up by the teaching of the magisterium. Like an "increasing number" of theologians, however, he held that the "witness of the Fathers and theologians, and the *sensus fidelium*, have their own proper value as sources." Although Dulles praised Mackey for his enlarged views of tradition, he faulted him for being preoccupied with doctrinal issues, underrating liturgy, neglecting the role of the Holy Spirit, and, in an ecumenical age, failing to consider tradition "outside the borders of Roman Catholicism."[89]

Dulles also commented briefly on Gabriel Moran's *Scripture and Tradition* (1963), noting that it was useful because it outlined the contending Catholic views, surveyed some of the best French, German, and English authors on the subject, and concluded with a "judicious" final chapter listing four points on which partisans of the contending sides could agree: (1) that Trent did not definitively define the existence of a constitutive tradition; (2) that scripture and tradition were not "sources," "except in the sense of being 'channels' or 'manifestations' of revelation"; (3) that tradition was not a stream of truths, completely separated from scripture, flowing down from the apostles to the present; and (4) that not all dogmas were contained in scripture in "its obvious sense."[90]

Moran was involved in catechesis and religious education and saw the contemporary theologies of revelation as a necessary propaedeutic for doing religious education. After writing his book on *Scripture and Tradition*, he began a doctoral dissertation on the theology of revelation and wrote to get advice from Dulles, who was, in Moran's view, one of the few theologians in the American Catholic community who were interested in the topic. He asked Dulles four questions on the subject of revelation, seeking to discover whether Dulles thought his views were "too far out or on dangerous territory or whether I am hitting at the right spots." First, he wanted to know, "Does not the inner union of revelation and grace, worship and sanctification take place in Christ, the process reaching a high point in the paschal event?" Moran had just read Latourelle's *Théologie de la révélation* (1963) and found it inadequate. Moran wanted to avoid the difficulties of identifying revelation with "truths, judgments, or propositions," and he found Latourelle's views unable to avoid the problem of such identification because he had neglected to perceive that, according to Moran, "revelation reaches its fullness in the knowledge which Christ has." Latourelle, and almost all Catholic theologians on the subject, seemed to reject such a notion. How did Dulles understand this issue?[91]

Second, Moran wanted to make a "clear distinction between revelation and the *depositum fidei*," but he could not square that view with magisterial pronouncements in the twentieth century. Third, he believed that Latourelle's attempts to balance the objective and the subjective elements in revelation were insufficient. "Isn't," Moran asked, "the Christian gospel not the revelation but a norm for interpreting revelatory experience? Isn't everything in human experience capable of bearing supernatural revelation with the gospel held to be the unsurpassable Christian testimony of faith to the human experience of God?" Fourth, Moran asked whether Latourelle's understanding of an inherent relationship between revelation and sacrament was simply wrong. Latourelle seemed to treat sacrament as the culmination of revelation. For Moran, "nothing completes revelation; sacramental actions complement the preaching of the gospel but both are within the process of revelation and faith."[92]

Moran's letter called for an extensive response from Dulles— a response that Dulles gave with apologies for its brevity (a characteristic apology that Dulles gave theologians who either sought his advice or argued with his positions). Moran's four questions deserved a serious response because they centered on issues crucial to a theology of revelation. First, Dulles liked Moran's view that "revelation reaches its fullness in the knowledge which Christ has." But he felt that the issue of Christ as a recipient of revelation was a "thorny question," which called for more serious reflection than he could provide in a letter. Although Dulles acknowledged, in conformity with church teaching, the completeness of revelation in Christ, he asserted that the completeness of revelation in apostolic times "cannot be naively defended" because our understanding or conceptualization of the faith is "not the same as that of the apostolic Church." Dulles, however, believed that a deposit of faith existed upon which all later developments depended and could not subscribe to Moran's view that "'apostolic knowledge (however implicit [that] knowledge may be)' is not at 'the base of the development.'"[93]

Second, with respect to Moran's understanding of the closing of revelation, Dulles responded that

> revelation as a process (*revelatio activa sumpta*) by no means ends with the apostles. But post-apostolic revelation has an Incarnate structure. It comes to the modern Christian through the avenues of scripture-tradition and brings us into a community of faith with the church of apostolic times, so that we profess no other faith than that which was delivered to the saints.

The *depositum fidei*, therefore, does not change, but, of course, doctrine does grow, "at least in explicitness." Third, Dulles was not as inclined as was Moran to emphasize revelation as experience, particularly an experience that was anything other than the revelation "in Christ to the Church." Dulles also emphasized more than Moran the content of revelation. Fourth, Dulles agreed with Moran on the integral relationship among revelation, word, and sacrament; both theologians asserted that the ministry of sacraments had a revelatory dimension.[94]

In 1965, as seminaries across the country were reexamining their curriculum in light of the council and changing times, Dulles was asked to critique the seminary course on revelation and suggest ways of making it more apostolic. Dulles prepared a paper on the subject, criticizing the manual approaches to revelation and then proposed the elements that should be included in a new course. He suggested that the course should include the following elements: a focus on what reason can and cannot accomplish without revelation; revelation as a response to the limits of the human condition; the Old Testament notions of revelation (connecting word and work); the person of Jesus as the *verbum visibile* (the complete integration of word and work); the New Testament as the inspired record of Christ's self-revelation; the church as the community in which revelation takes places and in which it is passed on from generation to generation; the personal appropriation of revelation; and the universal and eschatological nature of revelation, reminding students that "revelation appears in its true character as a drama in which all men are involved."[95] During the years of the council, Dulles was laying a foundation and sorting out issues that he would take up in some of his major publications on revelation and faith in the latter part of the twentieth century.

Ecumenism

The doctrine of revelation was one of Dulles' key theological research interests. Another, closely related to revelation, was ecumenism. In fact, for Dulles a renewed and revitalized Catholic understanding of revelation would, he believed, contribute to Christian unity. His first publications after the dissertation were focused on the rising Catholic appreciation of the ecumenical movement, a new movement in Catholicism that was gradually replacing the older controversial theology and the almost exclusively polemical approach to the Protestant churches and Protestant theology. During the council years, his own approach to ecumenism changed from a very cautious assessment of what could be accomplished in the ecumenical movement at the very beginning of the 1960s to a much more positive acceptance of the possibilities for Christian unity by 1965.

After his dissertation, Dulles periodically indicated what he thought the council might do for Catholic ecumenism. Prior to the opening of the council, Dulles and others were asked by *America* to respond to the question, "What Hopes and What Misgivings Do You Entertain Regarding the Currently Emerging Religious Dialogue in America?" Dulles, anticipating objections from some Catholic readers, held that ecumenism, especially as it was understood and practiced in Europe for the past decade, did not mean "doctrinal indifferentism" or a loss of Catholic identity or a degeneration into a polemical or sterile debate with those outside the Catholic tradition. The highest goal of a Catholic ecumenism was "getting closer to Christ" and a "mutual enrichment" of those Christians who engaged in dialogue, a view he maintained throughout his life. Dulles had "high hopes" that these goals of spiritual renewal and mutual understanding of Protestant, Catholic, and Orthodox traditions could be achieved.[96]

For their part Catholics needed to overcome the narrowness of the past, old habits of thought and ingrained prejudices, and join together with non-Catholics in defending the "fundamental principles of Christianity and natural law."[97] Dulles, nonetheless, reminded an audience at the National Catholic Education Association annual meeting in 1962 that "the Catholic Church can never take her place at any council table as one church among equals, nor can she even consider the possibility of retracting an iota of her faith."[98] This kind of language was considerably diminished toward the end of the council.

Dulles knew that some Catholics feared that ecumenism could lead to religious relativism, indifferentism, compromises, or strident polemics and refutations. Nonetheless he believed that such approaches of the past were being overcome by the ecumenical good will generated by Pope John XXIII and continued by Pope Paul VI.[99] Other Catholics and some Protestants, during the first stages of the council, suffered from what Dulles called a "holy impatience" with the council's halting movements and with its mixed messages on ecumenism.[100] After the council had promulgated The Constitution on the Church and the Decree on Ecumenism, Dulles spoke, unlike earlier, in terms of a "reciprocal or dialogical" relationship between Catholics and other Christians and of the mutuality, equality, and cooperation in the ecumenical movement. The Catholic Church needed to receive as well as give in the ecumenical dialogue. By 1965 Dulles used the language of working together with dialogue partners to learn from the divine word; he no longer used the language of unequal partners, even though he continued a Catholic confessional approach to dialogue.

The change in language reflected to some extent the influences of discussions at Vatican II and Dulles' own participation in ecumenical activities in the United States. In 1963, he was invited to lecture at Concordia Lutheran Seminary in St. Louis. He also participated in the first major Protestant-Catholic-Orthodox dialogue in the United States, held at Harvard University from March 27 to March 30, 1963. Organized by members of the Harvard Divinity School (primarily by Samuel H. Miller and G. Ernest

Wright) in response to the new atmosphere created by the council, the meeting involved 160 scholars who heard papers and participated in seminar discussions on various topics of ecumenical interest (for example, relationship of scripture and tradition and authority, public worship and liturgy, meaning of reform, common ethical questions in a pluralistic and relativist society). Most of the participants were Americans, but Augustin Cardinal Bea and Msgr. Jan G. M. Willebrands of the Vatican's Secretariat for Promoting Christian Unity were also present. In the organizers' view, the ecumenical conference added to the "mounting indication of a radical change in the religious climate of the world....Ten years ago the Colloquium would have been an impossibility."[101] Dulles, too, found the colloquium a "landmark" in Protestant-Catholic relations in the United States, and even though it did not cover all the issues that divided the churches, it was a "thrilling and gratifying" experience for "those who were privileged to attend."[102]

In July 1964, too, Dulles participated in a conference in New York City on the renewal of Catholic seminary education. That conference, in addition to discussing the revision of various theological courses, focused on the need, in the light of Vatican II, to give greater attention to "the teachings and practices of our separated brethren" and for seminaries to engage in dialogue with

Harvard reunion, 1965

Orthodox, Protestant, and Jewish theologians and seminaries.[103] By the time the Decree on Ecumenism was promulgated (November 21, 1964), American Catholic ecumenical language and attitudes and practices were significantly changed, and Catholics could be said to be significantly involved in the ecumenical movement. Dulles' own change of language during the council years reflected a more general openness in the American religious culture.

Robert McAfee Brown, Protestant theologian at Stanford University, had been an ecumenical partner with Gustave Weigel in the early 1960s. After Weigel's death, Brown, who had been somewhat pessimistic about the pending results of Vatican II's approach to ecumenism,[104] had by the end of 1965 changed his tune, as he indicated in a letter to Dulles:

> We are living in exciting times, and as a new year begins I am thankful that there are people like you dedicated to the furthering of the ecumenical spirit, into which, in a few short years, we have been led so much further, and so much more rapidly, than anyone could ever have anticipated.[105]

In five short years the ecumenical climate had changed so much that the old Catholic language and concepts were no longer useful for describing the changed reality. Ecumenism was a new adventure, but it was just beginning, as subsequent years were to show.

Rockhurst Reform of Theological Education

Other changes were taking place, too, that would directly affect seminaries like Woodstock. Throughout the United States during the council years, seminaries and colleges here and there were experimenting with curricular changes, academic governance, and lifestyle issues. By 1965, the transformations in student attitudes, the renewals called for by the Second Vatican Council, and the changing social circumstances caused the Jesuits in particular to reassess what they were doing in their educational institutions, particularly in the theologates. During Easter week of 1965, therefore, the deans of all the Jesuit theologates met at Fordham University to discuss what needed to be done in the seminaries to meet the needs of the day. At the Fordham meeting, the deans established what they called an "Inter-Faculty Program Inquiry" (composed of selected faculty members from the Jesuit theologates), appointed Dulles to chair the committee, and gave the faculty a mandate to revise the courses of theology, assign the number of hours for each course, determine the sequence of courses, and to work out, "in as minute detail as possible, a complete syllabus for each course." The deans anticipated that Vatican II and the Thirty-First General Congregation of Jesuits (May 1965)[106] "will grant rather wide powers to various regions for the devising of seminary programs best suited to local conditions." They wanted the faculty to exercise their creativity and originality in reorganizing seminary education and hoped that the faculty "will not feel bound by past Church and Society [of Jesus] legislation regarding the particulars of seminary training." Dulles chaired a steering committee (composed of Frederick W. Crowe, Dennis J. McCarthy, and Richard McCormick) that was to preside over a meeting on the curriculum to be held at Rockhurst College (Rockhurst, Kansas) from November 7 to 13, 1965.[107]

Prior to the Rockhurst meeting, the various Jesuit theologates in the United States and Canada discussed in their own institutions how they might revise the curriculum to meet the needs and complaints of students about the old curriculum. At Woodstock Dulles sent to the faculty questionnaires on revisions, convoked meetings with the faculty in September and October 1965, and then devised a report on the curriculum that summarized the discussion. The report was then made available to Jesuits at the Rockhurst meeting.[108] The same or similar processes took place at other theologates.

Twenty professors of theology from the Jesuit theologates in the United States and Canada met at Rockhurst and produced what was called the "Inter-Faculty Program Inquiry Report" ("Rockhurst Report"), which would have a significant impact on subsequent Jesuit education in theology and would transform the academic structure that had been characteristic of Jesuit education for four hundred years.[109] Dulles presided over the meeting, and much later in life he noted with a grin, "We changed the curriculum in the course of a weekend."[110] That characterization was not far from the truth. Joseph M. Becker has described the report that came out of the conference as a "watershed marking the academic transformation of the theologate."[111] A Jesuit scholastic at the time, Justin S. Kelly, called it "a radical change in theology—a transformation of the basic conception of theologate formation."[112] The professors involved came to nearly unanimous decisions on all the recommendations they made to the deans of the Jesuit theologates and to the provincials. They suggested that their recommendations be implemented at once, during the 1966–1967 school year, and that the recommendations they were making for the graduate and professional levels of theology include a consideration of moving the theologates to major universities, because an adequate implementation of the graduate phase of theology demanded "close contact with a full university complex to insure a proper range of offerings."[113]

The Rockhurst Report divided theological education into four major categories (biblical, historical, systematic, and theologico-pastoral) and made recommendations for all levels of theological formation, from the novitiate to the doctorate. The Jesuit theologians recommended, for example, that equal weight be given in the curriculum to all four areas of theology, replacing the previously very heavy emphasis on dogmatic theology. One of the more innovative suggestions in this division of theology was what the report called "historical theology." Prior to Rockhurst, very few, if any, Catholic theological programs in the United States had a discipline called "historical theology." And Catholics generally did not use the term "systematic" theology to describe any course in theology. In fact, what Rockhurst did was create two new fields of theology (historical and systematic) out of what was formerly called dogmatic theology. Historical theology was to include not only Church History, "but also patristics, and the history of theology, heresies, and dogma; the intention is that these subjects should be treated from a more historical perspective and with the measure of autonomy proper to history."[114]

Justin Kelly, a Jesuit scholastic, saw the division of dogmatic theology into historical and systematics as perhaps the "key to the success or failure of the Rockhurst program." In Kelly's understanding, historical theology treated "certain past ideas *as historical,* that is, as past, no longer current. It presupposes the possibility of achieving historical perspective—some degree of distance, of separation, from the theological views of the past." Historical theology did not deal with "our questions" or issues in the contemporary world but with what those in the past believed to be true. Systematic theology dealt with "a *contemporary* theological problematic: that is, a contemporary framework of questions and methods which is distinct from the framework of the sixteenth century, or the thirteenth, or the fourth." For Kelly, historical theology "discusses the theological questions and answers of the past; systematic theology explores *our* questions." Systematic theology was primarily thematic, theoretical, or speculative in that its aim was not to discover what was said in the past about a particular issue "but to discover what an intelligent Christian believer might say today." This definition of the difference between historical and systematic theology underlined one of the central motifs of the Rockhurst conference—what Kelly described as a "movement towards a new and more relevant theology."[115] Making theology relevant to the modern world was a response to the cries of the irrelevance of dogmatic theology that had emerged or were beginning to emerge among many scholastics and also among some of the younger professor-theologians. By separating as radically as it did historical and systematic theology, the Rockhurst Report unwittingly and ironically laid the foundation for an ahistorical approach to the Catholic faith that would soon emerge in some circles in American Catholicism.[116]

The Rockhurst Report made other suggestions that would change the way theology was taught and appropriated in the theologates. It suggested, among other things, that the Jesuit Provincials ought to increase the number of competently trained professors in all areas of theology; that all teaching of courses in cycle be eliminated and replaced by a high degree of electives; that the four years of theology be replaced by the credit hour system, thereby making possible the reduction of the number of years a scholastic would need to complete a course in theology; that the requirement of class attendance be dropped, allowing students the option of attending classes when they needed to do so to pass the examinations; that possibilities for specialization be increased, especially at the graduate level; that courses focus on how theology related to contemporary conditions in society; and that liturgy be a part of all four areas of theology. In addition to these recommendations, the Rockhurst Report provided a sample syllabus for each of the major areas of theology, with a corresponding bibliography for each.

Behind the suggestions were three educational and theological principles, which Kelly designated as relevance, diversification, and comprehension. The principle of relevance has already been discussed. The principle of diversification acknowledged the individual scholastics' needs and allowed them to take courses that corresponded to those needs. Thus, in Kelly's judgment, theological education in the future would focus more on personal appropriation than coverage of content. The principle of comprehension focused on the students' grasp of theology rather than on the number of hours logged in the classroom. The examinations, therefore, would be geared toward testing such a comprehension.[117]

At the end of the Rockhurst meeting, Frederick Crowe, SJ, of Regis College, Ontario, Canada, asked that he be allowed to register a gentle complaint about what the faculty had just done in revising theology into the four disciplinary approaches to theology. He believed the entire newly constructed program of theological education lacked "theoretical considerations that would enable us to grasp the whole range of theological disciplines in a unitary view and to relate them to one another organically." In his view, the new program reflected the "weaknesses of the modern university— many disparate fields in almost complete isolation from each other." He agreed with his colleagues that they had legitimately identified four distinct areas of theological inquiry, but he thought that the new program gave "no account of their relations to one another or of principles governing transition from one to another."[118] Crowe had identified a problem that would continue in Jesuit theologates and in various other schools of Catholic theology in the period after 1965, because most American Catholic programs in theology would follow the example of Rockhurst or something analogous to it.

Looking back on the Rockhurst Plan in 2005, Dulles acknowledged that "on paper it looked all right, but we did not have people prepared to teach what we had in mind." There were other problems with the plan too. The separation of dogmatic theology into historical and systematic did not work very well.

> Our idea was that historical theology was to introduce the decisions of the councils; and we separated patrology and church history [from dogmatic theology] and so forth....Historical theology was to show the context in which councils operated, the development of various theological schools of thought, and the abiding and binding decisions, how the theological questions had changed over time. So, it could have worked.[119]

In 2005 Dulles was less enthusiastic about the Rockhurst Plan than he had been in 1965. By 2005, he realized that the recommendations were made without much consideration of the consequences and without the personnel needed to carry out the various provisions of the plan.

Nonetheless, in 1965 the Rockhurst Plan reflected optimism about change, diversity, relevance, adaptation, and reform that was in the air because of the council, the Jesuits' Thirty-First General Congregation, and the student movements in American society. And the Rockhurst Plan, which would be implemented in the 1966–1967 school year, would have some major consequences for Jesuit education and lifestyle in the years to come. It was an attempt to accommodate theological studies to a new generation of students, to reflect conciliar directions in theology, and to reverse an emerging decline of interest in theology among the scholastics. The intentions were noble, but the plan, hastily devised, manifested a desire for change that would soon erupt in directions that were not foreseen at the time.

After Rockhurst, Dulles returned to Woodstock, where he and others awaited the euphoric celebration of the conclusion of the Vatican Council and anticipated the spiritual and ecclesiastical reforms that would be implemented in the postconciliar period. Things were already changing in the church, as was evident in Pope Paul VI's trip to the United Nations (October 4, 1965), when he called for "no more war"; Paul VI's and Athenagoras I's removal of the mutual excommunications of 1054 between the Roman and the Orthodox churches (December 7, 1965); the closing of the council (December 8, 1965); and the promulgations of the Vatican decrees on revelation, religious liberty, and the church in the modern world. These were heady days of expectations of a new era in the life of the church. These were also the days of emerging conflict in the church. Fr. Gomar de Pauw, a professor of theology and academic dean at Mount Saint Mary's Major Seminary in Emmitsburg, Maryland, launched the Catholic Traditionalist Movement in 1965, resisting the changes promulgated by the Second Vatican Council.[120] Catholic faculty at St. John's University in Jamaica, New York, battled with the university's administration over faculty rights and academic freedom. A new age of enthusiasm, experimentation, reform, and conflict was emerging in the Catholic Church in 1965 and would continue in subsequent years.

7

FROM VATICAN II TO THE CLOSING OF WOODSTOCK, 1966–1974

THE IMMEDIATE POSTCONCILIAR years were fraught with momentous changes in society and the church: the escalation of the Vietnam War and the subsequent and at times radical and organized protests, the highly publicized trials of peace protesters in various cities, the murders of significant public figures (Senator Robert F. Kennedy and Martin Luther King Jr.), the race riots and massive destructions in many of the inner cities across the country, the violence associated with the Democratic Political Convention in Chicago in 1968, the Supreme Court's *Roe v. Wade* (1973) decision in favor of abortion and the beginning of a protracted national debate on abortion, the political coverup of the Watergate burglars (1972) and the resignation of President Richard Nixon (1974) because of it. Nixon's resignation became the supreme symbol of a corrupt establishment during the era.

Within the American Catholic Church, too, revolutionary changes and protests erupted throughout the period. In response to the Second Vatican Council and the changing times, theologians and public opinion makers called for numerous and varied ecclesiastical reforms—in the liturgy, church structures, ecclesiastical practices, and attitudes toward the modern world and American society. Academic freedom became an issue not only at St. John's University (1965) but also at the University of Dayton (1966) and especially at the Catholic University of America (1967), where Fr. Charles Curran was denied tenure. Because of organized protests, the Catholic University administration reversed its decision and granted him tenure. The Catholic charismatic movement arose in the mid-1960s and continued to influence the church and theology throughout the next decade and beyond. The Catholic peace movement emerged in the early 1960s and gained strength and visibility in the late 1960s and early 1970s, culminating in the 1968 trial of Fr. Daniel Berrigan, SJ, and eight other Catholic peace activists and protesters at Catonsville, Maryland. In 1968, too, Pope Paul VI published *Humanae vitae*, condemning artificial means of birth control, an action that gave rise to a series of public protests against the encyclical by some theologians, clergy, and numbers of laity around the United States. In the midst of these and other rapid and radical transformations, Catholic institutional statistics began to reflect a serious decline—in the departures of numbers of clergy and women religious, a precipitous decrease in the number of seminarians, the closing of many primary and secondary Catholic schools, and a radical fall in the number of Catholics celebrating the sacraments.

Implementing Rockhurst

Dulles' life was affected by the changes going on around him in the postconciliar church and society. In 1964, even before he became involved in planning and preparing and implementing the Rockhurst Plan, Dulles became a major force in proposing what was called at Woodstock an "American Institute of Spirituality." Jesuit faculty and students at Woodstock proposed the establishment of an institute on spirituality to bring about a revival of ascetical or spiritual theology that would correspond with the earlier successful biblical and liturgical revivals. The proposed institute was to be an interdisciplinary research and teaching center located at one of the Catholic universities. The proposal focused on the need to develop an American-based spirituality that would synthesize the biblical, liturgical, and theological renewal and put those developments in dialogue with moral, psychological, and sociological studies. The goal was to develop a specifically American spirituality for Jesuits and for American Catholics in particular and for other Americans who might find such a spirituality appealing. The goal, the proposal stated, was to "seek the renewal of Christian living in America, the renewal of religious life in all religious and clerical communities, both men and women, and therefore, automatically, the renewal of the Society of Jesus."[1] Dulles eventually took a leading role in advancing the proposal. He chaired a number of meetings at Woodstock to get Jesuits from around the country acquainted with the proposal and interested in the project. Twenty-four Jesuits from various theologates met at Woodstock in September 1964 to discuss the project. The meeting proved successful in winning the support of Jesuits outside of Woodstock. Dulles, as chair of the project, sent the Jesuit Provincials of Maryland, New York, and Buffalo the proposal, seeking their approval, their financial support, their assignment of young Jesuits to study in areas essential to the future of the institute, and their appointment of an administrator to establish and administer the institute.[2] The provincials approved it, named Christopher Mooney, SJ, as its director, and located it at Fordham University, where it was eventually called the Bea (named after Augustin Cardinal Bea, SJ) Institute of Spirituality.[3] In 1965 and thereafter, Mooney organized theological conferences to discuss the relationships between spirituality and American culture—conferences that invited experts from various disciplines, not just theology, to participate. In the mid-1960s Dulles took part in many of these conferences, taking copious notes, as was his custom when he was not directing the discussions.

In the midst of these activities, the Woodstock faculty began to implement the Rockhurst reform plan that affected the seminary's curriculum, lifestyle, governance, and location. Jesuit theologates like Woodstock changed the curriculum, incorporating the spirit of Vatican II, contemporary revisions in theology, and the demands of the students themselves for more choice in the direction of their own education. Already in January 1966, Woodstock faculty and students received a memorandum on implementing Rockhurst. The curriculum "experiment" at the bachelor level was slated to begin in September 1966, and the new graduate program was to begin in the 1967–1968 academic year.[4] In February, the Woodstock students themselves put together a forty-two-page set of recommendations for changing the curriculum. Their recommendations reflected to a considerable extent Justin Kelly's understanding of the relationship between historical and systematic theology. Historical theology dealt with the past "as past, no longer current," and systematic theology dealt with the questions "contemporary men are asking." Systematic theology "should be the department where the theologizing is done, not where the previous formulations of dogma are merely handed on." The students' recommendations were followed by a student-faculty meeting in March in which their proposals were discussed. At that meeting, Walter Burghardt asked the students, "Should contemporaneity or revelation itself be the norm of what was to be treated in systematics?"[5] The issues were not resolved at this meeting, and some students continued to look upon systematic theology almost exclusively in terms of its contemporary relevance.

Rockhurst had not in fact divided theological education into four independent departments—biblical, historical, systematic, and theologico-pastoral—but the relations between the different approaches to theology had not been clarified. The connection between historical and systematic continued to call for reflection. The relationship between biblical and the other disciplines within theology became another problem in the post-Rockhurst era, and Dulles periodically called attention to this issue. In response to one Woodstock attempt to articulate the role of biblical studies in theological education, Dulles remarked that the "'scientific understanding of the Biblical books' is quite alright, but the main point in a theologate is theological understanding of these books. Is 'scientific' here taken to include theological or to mean theologically neutral?...I do not think that the biblical area has satisfactorily defined itself with relation to other areas." Dulles in fact wanted more integration in theological education and a better way of articulating the close connections and overlappings of the various methodological approaches to theological education.[6] Understanding the relations of biblical studies to systematic theology would be an ongoing issue for him throughout his career as a theologian.

By 1966, Jesuit scholastics had come to have a significant role in making changes in the curriculum, governance, and lifestyle at Woodstock, although the faculty continued to make the final decisions. Change, innovation, and planning were recurring themes in the postconciliar period at Woodstock, as at other Catholic institutions. Everything seemed to be subject to change and in flux.

Students, faculty, and administrators seemed to be oblivious to the long-term consequences of such dynamics.

By 1969, Dulles was becoming a bit weary with continual change in the curriculum. He wanted some stability and the maintenance of high standards in theological education, as some of his memos to the dean of studies at Woodstock reveal. In one memo, for example, he found it necessary to argue for the continuation of comprehensive examinations in theology prior to ordination. Apparently some were arguing that these examinations were no longer needed. Rockhurst and the Jesuits' universal norms for theological education, the *Normae Generales*, he maintained, had required such comprehensives. "When a decision has been made, the next stage is to carry it into execution with firmness of purpose, rather than constantly to be going back over the question whether some other decision ought to have been made—a procedure which in effect amounts to preventing any decisions from really being decisions." Comprehensives held students accountable for what they were learning, made faculty aware of weaknesses in the program, and were pedagogically useful in guiding students in their study and reading. The Rockhurst Plan could not be put into full effect without comprehensives. "No educational institution," he told the dean,

> can frequently overturn its program, since plans have to be made in terms of certain fixed assumptions. The curriculum which has been adopted for Woodstock, but thus far not fully been put into effect, is based on the assumptions that comprehensives are given, that they are a serious and demanding test, and that it is certain to every student when he enters Woodstock that he will have to face such examinations before getting his BD degree from Woodstock. Only if these assumptions are made clear can the full possibilities of the present program be achieved.[7]

In Dulles' mind, the Rockhurst reform in the curriculum was intended to help students make greater achievements in theology, not to loosen up standards of theological education.

The Woodstock implementation of Rockhurst gradually developed a new curriculum that provided for many more electives than in the past and allowed students the choice of attending classes, whether electives or required courses. Many of the faculty, moreover, reduced the number of classes assigned for their subjects and tried to educate by means of discussion rather than exclusively by lectures.[8] The theologates were loosening up and entering a new era of freedom and choice—one that in fact focused on the needs of students and less on the demands of the discipline of theology. Many professors, including Dulles to a certain degree, accommodated themselves to the new situation. Some were good at a new style of teaching, and others, like Dulles, were not especially adapted to the style, and some students found his classes (whether by discussion or lecture) less than stimulating. Jesuit scholastics, in fact, periodically quipped, "dull, duller, and Dulles" to characterize his teaching and lecturing style—even when they found his courses well organized and substantive in content.

Postconciliar students at Woodstock have been variously characterized. Some of them had "genuine intellectual interests,"[9] while others saw theological education as simply a means to ordination (for them theology was fundamentally pastoral). Like numbers of seminarians across the country, these students were becoming known, at least by 1964, as the "new breed."[10] The emerging "new breed" were not very many in 1964, but they were important and their numbers increased in subsequent years. As Andrew Greeley characterized them, they were not the complacent and apathetic students of the mid-1950s; they were preoccupied with the values of honesty, integrity, and authenticity, and they were a questioning bunch. Greeley quoted a Jesuit college administrator who noted, "For four hundred years we have been in the apostolate of Christian education, and now we suddenly find that our seminarians are demanding that we justify this apostolate." Another Jesuit administrator corroborated, saying, "Jesuit seminarians are the most radical people in the American church—bar none." The new breed were not disobedient or disrespectful of authority, but they raised critical questions. They were also characterized as worrying about fulfillment, anxious about loving and being loved, more interested in people than ideas, and concerned about human suffering and willing to get involved in alleviating it. Having experienced many changes in their own lives, they continued to expect more changes in the future; they also wanted freedom and wanted it immediately. They were not gradualists with regard to change. Greeley summarized the general characteristics of the new breed in this way:

> They are a paradoxical bunch, supremely self-confident, yet anxious and restless; they are organizationally efficient and yet often diplomatically tactless; they are eager to engage in dialogue and yet frequently inarticulate in what they want to say; they are without ideology and yet insistent on freedom; they are generous with the poor and suffering and terribly harsh in their judgments of their elders and superiors; they are ecumenical to the core and yet astonishingly parochial in their tastes and fashions; they want desperately to love but are not sure that they know how to love. They want to scale the heights yet are mired in the foothills.[11]

Between 1966 and 1974, Woodstock College tried to meet the aspirations of the "new breed." Reform, adaptation, change, excitement, and confusion were evident almost everywhere where seminary leaders tried to accommodate the seminaries to the changing climate. The "new breed" seminarians were coming into their own during these years, but for the first time in history there was a notable decline in the number of seminarians. After 1965 the decline became alarming at most seminaries, including Woodstock, where the number of scholastics decreased from about 300 in 1965 to 150 in 1971, a 50 percent decline in six years. The entry-level classes were smaller than in the early 1960s, and more than 65 Woodstock scholastics left the Jesuits between 1965 and 1973.[12] Some Woodstock faculty priests, too, were beginning to leave the priesthood, adding to the sense of contraction. Something had to be done to stop the leakage, and several experiments were tried to make seminary life more attractive and relevant to the new generation of seminarians and faculty.

Seminaries and theologates across the country experimented with a host of changes in lifestyle and governance as well as curriculum in order to respond to the reforms of the council and the new students. At Woodstock in Maryland, the Jesuit superiors tried to establish a new collegial atmosphere by creating common dining and recreation areas for faculty and students, eliminating the previous separate dining and recreation areas in an attempt to break down barriers between faculty and students. The rigorous discipline of the past, moreover, was gradually loosened up in an attempt to create an atmosphere of greater individual responsibility among the students for the direction of their own education and lives. Student-faculty committees were created for consultation on a host of curricular, lifestyle, and ad hoc social activist issues. In 1968, for example, faculty and students created the Committee on the Washington Statement (COWS) in response to Cardinal Joseph O'Boyle's suspension of a few priests, including some Jesuits, who had protested publicly against Pope Paul VI's encyclical *Humanae vitae*. The committee's purpose was to support the suspended clerics.[13]

Students at Woodstock in Maryland were involved in various forms of social activism, as was illustrated by COWS. And, for some students, theology that was not socially relevant was unworthy of study. In Dulles' view, some students "came in with such assurance that there was nothing worthwhile teaching them unless it related to the secular and affected society."[14] A few Woodstock students were involved in activist programs in Washington, D.C., and/or in Baltimore during their last years in Maryland. Some scholastics were working with real estate groups in these cities on behalf of fair housing, others were working with the poor in the inner cities, and still others were peace activists supporting the antiwar movements of the time. At one point in 1968, the scholastics decided that they would all participate in an organized protest in Washington, D.C., against the Vietnam War. The day before the protest, Dulles is reported to have said to his class, "I gather that there is not much point in my attempting to conduct class tomorrow."[15] So class was cancelled. Social activism could and did at times trump theological education at Maryland's Woodstock in the late 1960s, and the more activist-inclined student leaders could apply pressure on fellow students to join their social protests.

The trial of the Jesuit Daniel Berrigan and the Catonsville Nine, which took place in 1968, drew scholastics periodically to

Baltimore to observe the proceedings instead of going to class. One or two of the more activist scholastics were involved in destroying draft records in Washington, D.C., as part of their protests against the Vietnam War.[16] The students' involvement in the peace protests and some of the illegal activities involved in those protests drew the FBI to Woodstock to investigate some of the student activism, but nothing seems to have resulted from the investigation.[17] Although Dulles never publicly protested against the various forms of social activism, he was not happy with these developments at an institution dedicated to theological education and formation. These were "difficult years" in the classroom as far as Dulles was concerned.[18]

Dulles also faced some personal difficulties in trying to comfort his mother in the decade after his father's death. "Having spent much time with my own mother," he told a correspondent whose father had died in 1994, "I know how such a loss can be felt, especially by a devoted wife."[19] Dulles' mother lived in Washington, D.C., when he was at Woodstock in Maryland, and he made frequent visits to her. When his brother, John, came to Washington, the two of them would meet at their mother's home, play tennis together, and then enjoy a meal with her. As indicated earlier, he was very close to his mother and had her sensitivity to art and French culture. After her husband's death, though, she never really ventured much beyond her home or outside of Washington. In the late 1960s, her health began to deteriorate, and in 1969 she was hospitalized. Avery visited with her in the hospital, realizing that her end was near. On May 14, 1969, she died; a funeral service was held for her at the Georgetown Presbyterian Church, after which she was buried at Arlington.[20] Avery attended the wake and the funeral, feeling the pain of such a loss and receiving the condolences of family, friends, and those diplomats who had known her and her husband. One former ambassador sent Avery his condolences, recalling that he and his wife "will always be grateful to your mother for the many acts of kindness that she extended to us during our stay in Washington. We were among those who enjoyed the hospitality of her home innumerable times and we had the pleasure of entertaining her and your late father in our embassy and when they came to Manila in our home."[21] Traveling back and forth between Washington and Woodstock during this last year of his mother's life was trying, especially at a time when Woodstock was planning a move to New York City.

The Rockhurst implication (in Resolution no. 8) that theologates consider moving their institutions from rural areas to urban and university centers was taken seriously by all the Jesuits involved in clerical formation in the United States. In 1967, after numerous discussions in the Jesuit community, Woodstock decided that it should move to an urban and university center. The Woodstock buildings were old and in need of much repair; they had been built for large numbers of scholastics who no longer were coming into the Jesuit community, the scholastics themselves were restless in the rural countryside and, in Dulles' interpretation, "We had a fleet of forty cars with students running into the cities day and night. It just wasn't working very well."[22] Staying at rural Woodstock seemed to Dulles to sound the death knell of the institution. The institution had lost its attractiveness for many of the students and faculty. In addition, as Rockhurst envisioned, moving the theologates to urban and university centers had the great advantage of enabling faculty and students to put theological education and theology itself into dialogue with what was emerging in the thinking of Protestant, Jewish, and secular thinkers. Dulles, like the majority at Woodstock, was in favor of the move and supported the reasons for doing so. The question for him and others was, Where should Woodstock move?

Moving Woodstock to New York City

Dulles was appointed to a committee that was given a mandate to select some locations for a move and present the options to the Woodstock community for a decision. The committee looked into various possibilities, including a move to Harvard, Georgetown in Washington, D.C., Morningside Heights in New York City, and Yale. Woodstock hired an accounting firm to do a feasibility study on relocation, assessing in particular the comparative prospects for space and the initial and continuing costs of relocating at either New Haven or New York.[23] While the committee investigated the possibilities, the mayor of New Haven sent a delegation to Woodstock to represent Yale's case. Trying to attract young Jesuits who were interested in social action, the delegation, a Jesuit reported jocosely, said something like, "You don't have to go to New York [which was being seriously considered] to run into drugs or gangs or all that, come to New Haven! We got it all."[24]

For a variety of reasons, not the least of which was Yale's academic reputation, the Woodstock faculty unanimously decided in 1967 that Yale presented the best prospects for the relocation. Yale offered Woodstock a good proposal, and the committee presented it as the best option. Faculty and students at Woodstock enthusiastically received the proposal, and the decision in favor of the move to Yale was sent to the Jesuit General. "Fordham all of a sudden," according to Dulles, "took alarm, and the chairman of the theology department suggested that Woodstock come to New York and be attached to Fordham." Fordham's Christopher Mooney, SJ, chair of the Theology Department, prepared a lengthy paper in which he argued that Woodstock's faculty should not be allowed by themselves to decide a future that would affect "every Jesuit in the East" and that there were considerations for choosing New York of which the Woodstock faculty were unaware. Fordham sent the document to Rome and then "sent a delegation to Rome to present its case. And that caused the General to tell Woodstock to look further into the possibilities of New York."[25]

The committee thereafter investigated the New York option and prepared a proposal for moving there, but to the Morningside Heights area, not to the Fordham campus. The Morningside Heights area was chosen because of its proximity to educational facilities there—Columbia University, Union Theological Seminary, Jewish Theological Seminary, and the Interchurch Center. Although some of the faculty, John Courtney Murray in particular, favored the Yale option over New York City, the decision eventually was made to move to New York. But the move was delayed for some time because of the riots in 1968 and the difficulties of making arrangements for housing and classroom facilities.

By the beginning of the 1969 school year, Woodstock had purchased or rented housing and classroom space in the Morningside Heights area and moved the college in two shifts. About one-half of the college (about seventy-five scholastics and ten faculty) moved to New York in the summer of 1969; the second half, including Dulles, moved in the summer of 1970. The new circumstances differed considerably from the rural Maryland setting and had a great effect on education and community life.

After the move was completed, the Maryland and New York Jesuit Provincials sent a letter to the Woodstock faculty and students asking them to begin during the 1970–1971 academic year to plan for the future of Woodstock in New York City. Whatever Woodstock's apostolate "remains or becomes," they wrote, should be the result of a careful and prayerful choice. Accompanying their letter was a lengthy and detailed "Program for Evaluating the Future of Woodstock College in New York." The new circumstances demanded a reexamination of what they were doing, but even more important was the need to reconsider what the primary objective of Woodstock was to be. Would Woodstock's mission continue to be what it was for the past hundred years, namely "the theological education of Jesuit candidates for priesthood"? Or did Woodstock wish to "select another primary objective that would involve an enlarged theological apostolate in America"?[26]

In response to the provincials' request, an assessment and planning committee—composed of Woodstock faculty, including Dulles, students, laypeople (Louise and Philip Des Marais) from New York, and a representative priest from the New York Diocese—was formed at Woodstock. One member of the planning committee, a scholastic at the time, recalled years later that the committee had a

> wide ranging discussion of the plans for the future of Woodstock College. There was again a lot of confusion. The monsignor [on the committee] went back to the Chancery and said "they don't know what they're doing." His idea was you got a seminary to train priests, you teach courses, teach them how to be priests, why all this talk? He almost quit. He had to be begged back on.

The dynamic of reassessment and constant planning was for this former scholastic "a symbol of the directionless-ness of Woodstock."[27]

The Woodstock planning committee and various segments within the community produced four major proposals for Woodstock's future. Dulles favored retaining the goal of training candidates for the priesthood, but he also wanted Woodstock to take on new responsibilities as a major center for theological research in the United States. New York offered "unique possibilities for an apostolate involving theological reflection," he told one of his colleagues.[28] By the end of a two-year period of discussion and construction of proposals, the planning committees had accomplished very little. By 1972, the Jesuit Provincials were considering closing some of the theologates, and Woodstock would be one of the victims.

To some extent the relocation to New York reflected the dynamics of the times in the aftermath of the Second Vatican Council. As the *New York Times* reported at the time, the Woodstock move illustrated a growing trend among seminaries "to seek sites that provide contact with urban problems and with such secular disciplines as sociology, psychology and literature."[29] The seminary movement also indicated a more general trend in postconciliar Catholicism: a rejection of the preconciliar "withdrawal from the world" approach for educating seminarians and a postconciliar affirmation of involvement in the modern world. Like withdrawal, the engagement syndrome had its own set of advantages and difficulties, both of which would be experienced in the New York setting.

Some scholastics were reported to have been excited about the move to New York and the opportunity to learn firsthand about urban problems, to work in programs for the city's poor, to enjoy the benefits of a university education, and to study Protestant Christianity under Protestants themselves.[30] Once in New York, the spirituality of withdrawal was difficult to maintain, and there emerged a spirituality of engagement that would characterize much of Jesuit life in the city. The Jesuit spirituality of contemplation in action, too, took on a significantly activist emphasis in the midst of city life. Jesuits in the new urban environment had to have more responsibility for the affairs of personal and community life than was needed in the isolation of rural Maryland where personal and communal needs were generally taken care of by the religious superiors and workings of the substructure of seminary life. In the city, scholastics and faculty were now responsible for shopping for food, preparing meals, taking care of their own laundry, and making decisions in their daily routine—decisions that had previously been for the most part an unreflective part of the seminary regimentation in Maryland. The story is told, and it may well be apocryphal, that when Dulles moved into an apartment in New York, he was so unfamiliar with regular household equipment that he once put his laundry into the dishwasher. Dulles, of course, was not as absent-minded as this story reveals. He knew his way around in the kitchen. As a young man he had learned household chores on his father's yawl and in his own apartment during his days as a law student at Harvard. But his style of life in New York was not the more sedate form of life he had experienced in Maryland.

By the late summer of 1970, Woodstock College had leased classrooms at Union Theological Seminary, offices in the Interchurch Center for administrative purposes, and apartments in four major complexes. Fifty of the 158 scholastics lived in thirty-one apartments on Ninety-Eighth Street, where one of the Jesuit scholastics had volunteered to furnish and decorate the new living space. The 158 scholastics and their faculty could no longer live together in one community, as they had in Maryland. They now lived in four smaller communities and had much more participation in the decisions made about their own lifestyles than they had had in the isolation of Maryland. The Woodstockers, moreover, lived in the midst of New Yorkers, and the scholastics had the opportunity to interact with other college, university, and seminary students, women as well as men. And some scholastics more than others took advantage of the opportunity. The isolation, uniformity, order, and structure of the Maryland experience was gradually giving way to a more loosely knit seminary structure in which the role of the superior was at times uncertain and tentative. Freedom and experimentation were the dominant motifs of Jesuit life in the city. The past way of Jesuit formation was perceived by some as rigid and regimented. Other Jesuits saw the new freedoms as fraught with an abandonment of genuine Jesuit values as the new mentality seemed to overlook or deny the values inherent in the old order of a disciplined life.

It would be difficult to characterize the 158 scholastics and the twenty faculty members who eventually moved to New York. Some of the scholastics were clearly enthusiastic about the move; others were more circumspect and cautious; a few thought the move a mistake and left the community or transferred to other theologates. Some of the scholastics, particularly the native New Yorkers, were comfortable in the city, but others, as one of the scholastics at the time recalled, "arrived in Penn station, took a cab to their residence and were terrified for three years, terrified of New York."[31]

In New York City, a few scholastics continued the social activism they had started in Maryland. During the first two years in New York, the activist scholastics became significantly involved in the protest movements against the war in Vietnam and supported other highly visible and controversial causes. These scholastics frowned upon academic life or at least measured all academic life by its so-called relevance to "real" issues in society. Other scholastics were more academically inclined and prepared themselves for future careers in education or some one of the other Jesuit ministries.

Teaching in the midst of these changing expectations became something of a challenge for Dulles, but, of course, the New York scene was not itself the cause of the changing expectations. The variety of student expectations had been evident already in Maryland during the mid- to late 1960s. But in New York there were greater opportunities for distraction from academic work, the primary work of a theologate, and indeed more competition for the scholastics' attention in the social arena. Theology and theological education were not the central focus of all the scholastics' attention, and that made teaching a difficult task.

The new Jesuit experiment in New York, and particularly the social activism and new lifestyle of some of the Jesuit scholastics and faculty, drew some considerable public attention two years after the Jesuits relocated—the kind of attention that contributed eventually to the closing of Woodstock. In August 1971, Garry Wills, a former Jesuit scholastic of the Missouri Province, after a series of interviews with members of the Woodstock community, published an article with revealing, unrepresentative, and semi-sensational pictures on the Woodstock community that was unflattering to say the least and damaging to Woodstock's reputation, especially among Jesuit superiors in the United States and in Rome.[32]

The article focused on the discontinuities with previous Jesuit seminary training, on the innovations in the new urban setting, and on the scandalous or semi-scandalous activities of a few Jesuit scholastics. Wills grabbed the reader's attention by opening with a description of the Jesuit ordinations in May 1971. Prior to the ordination service at Fordham University, a group of peace activists, encouraged by at least two of the Jesuit ordinands, distributed outside the church two flyers: one with a photocopy of Cardinal Terrence Cooke, the ordaining bishop, in an airplane cockpit, ridiculing the cardinal as military vicar, and a second (signed by two of the Jesuit ordinands) accusing the cardinal of war crimes as military vicar. During the ordination service, two of the Woodstock Jesuit ordinands, to the great embarrassment of the Jesuit superiors, refused to give the cardinal archbishop of New York the kiss of peace and went to the microphone to proclaim to all those in attendance, "I am sorry but I cannot give you the kiss of peace until you resign as vicar of the military forces of war." Cardinal Cooke responded by saying to the audience, "Brothers, we look at things in a different way," and then went on to explain that his role as chief of chaplains was not "meant to be political, but only to give spiritual solace to men dying or in danger of their death."[33] This opening incident in the article was intended to illustrate the out-of-control nature of seminary education and the Woodstock experiment.

The article went on to detail other instances that exemplified the shocking trends in seminary education. Wills emphasized the secular tendencies and social activism that affected some of the scholastics, pointing out that after ordination, one Jesuit priest spent a year driving a taxi cab in New York City. Some scholastics were found working at the United Nations, performing in New York drama, playing as a jazz impresario, participating in community relations with local police and firemen, or helping in drug clinics. This kind of secular activism, of course, detracted from serious academic work, and in fact, Wills was quick to point out that "most of the students are bored with theology at this point—indeed, with all formal study (a reaction to the long earlier training imposed on them, so much of which looks useless in light of all the changes since Vatican II)."[34] By Wills's own estimate, Jesuit scholastics spent less than two hours a day, on average, in the study of theology.

Although Wills acknowledged that there were some serious students among the Woodstock scholastics, he emphasized that many of the students doubted the value of their studies, were suspicious of authority, and were uncertain of the purpose of their lives. Wills also stressed, at least implicitly, that the New York City Jesuit lifestyle was incongruent with the vows of poverty. He depicted the apartments where Jesuits were living in the expensive upper west side of New York City, focusing in particular on one house where Jesuit scholastics appeared to live in some luxury and leisure. He quoted one non-Jesuit resident saying "Some rich outfit must be moving in" when the Jesuits moved into his building. One of the Jesuit residences, moreover, was characterized as a "priestly hippie pad" where peaceniks, male and female, gathered to organize various protests. To indicate more graphically the semidissolution of the former Jesuit lifestyle, Wills published a photograph of a Jesuit scholastic gazing at two scantily clad young women sunbathing on the roof of one of the residences where the Jesuits lived.

The Wills article intended to paint a picture of scholastic life at Woodstock as an utter failure. Aimlessness, uncertainty, lack of discipline, and the absence of directive and decisive leadership characterized the new experiment in New York City. In fact, Woodstock's leaders had gone about the task of adapting to New York City with "suicidal efficiency";[35] they were portrayed as enthusiastic and naively optimistic about the experiment in urban seminary education. Woodstock, Wills admitted, was probably not much different from other Jesuit theologates and the general post–Vatican II seminary education. In the end, though, Wills asserted that Woodstock was "not only battered from outside by history, but crumbling by the very throb of its own energies."[36] It was a failure, in his estimation, and he predicted its demise.

A December 1971 article in the *New York Times* also indicated that "the transplanting has produced a radically new style of Catholic theological education." The Woodstock community, like many other seminary communities, was engaging in some bold experiments and new forms of community living that produced a good deal of uncertainty about future Jesuit identity. "Today's Jesuit seminarians are also more sophisticated than their predecessors about the church as a social institution, and they are suspicious about any arrangements that would sacrifice their individual gifts to the needs of the institution—including Jesuit ones." Jesuits, one scholastic was quoted as saying, "operated on the fringes of the church and didn't follow the party line."[37] The anti-institutionalism of the era influenced those inside as well as outside the seminary walls.

Dulles and other Jesuits at Woodstock saw the Wills article and other newspaper reports as caricatures of the real Woodstock, even though they acknowledged that some of the characterizations were true. Dulles, in fact, had written his Jesuit superior, in response to the superior's request for recommendations on community life, to suggest that the superior summon members of one of the New York Woodstock Jesuit houses "to make a manifestation to you sometime in the next month or two. Some, I feel, are drifting and need to be faced with challenges. Are they just passing the time in a reasonably pleasant way, or are they really working at being Jesuits, seminarians, future priests, theology students...?"[38] Dulles himself was well aware that a few scholastics were preoccupied with things other than academic theology, but he had faced that reality already in Maryland. The move to New York City was not the cause of that preoccupation; it was more a product of the times than the result of education in the city. Dulles saw the damaging and scandalous effects of the article, but at the time thought that it was such an exaggeration that Jesuit superiors would not take it seriously. The article, however, got around the world quite quickly and contributed to the Jesuit superiors' decisions on which theologates to close.

Jesuit theology, not just lifestyle issues, came under attack periodically. Dulles was upset, for example, by an article Dan Lyons wrote in *Twin Circle* in August 1972. Lyons cited an Anglican theologian who had been on the faculty of Union Theological Seminary and who had originally thought that when the Jesuit students and faculty came to Union they would have a positive influence on Union and "overcome the secular humanism by emphasizing the supernatural." That was not the case. In fact, the "Jesuit theologians have been corrupted by the humanistic influence that prevails." And, the "Jesuit community has been going out of its way to prove that they are as good Protestants as we are."[39] Dulles suspected that the "orthodox Anglican" whom Lyons cited was the biblical scholar Reginald H. Fuller of the Protestant Episcopal Theological Seminary in Virginia. Fuller had become one of Dulles' friends and colleagues at Union, and Dulles immediately shot off a letter to Fuller to ask whether he was indeed the source of the damaging quotation, and if he was, to whom was he referring? They had been colleagues at theological conferences and knew each other's positions fairly well, so to Dulles it seemed "scarcely possible that you would be criticizing my theology from that angle." The sweeping charge seemed to him to be "incredible" and he asked Fuller for an explanation.[40]

Fuller admitted that he had been the source of the accusations, but that they were offhand, private comments and not part of any public address. He was sorry that such private communications were made public. He had made them in the context of discussing the future of Union Theological Seminary. "My remarks had reference to the general ethos of the Woodstock community as exhibited in the lack of positive effect it has had on the spiritual and liturgical life of Union. It had no reference to the faculty, either individually or collectively, or to the theological teaching at Woodstock." Fuller in fact had confidence in the theology of some of his theological colleagues at both Union and Woodstock, including Dulles, "but this does not alter the fact that the predominant ethos at Union is what I apparently referred to as basically humanist."[41] Dulles was sensitive to charges against the Jesuits and particularly against the New York Woodstock community because he knew that Jesuit Provincials were discussing which theologates to close.

Closing Woodstock

Jesuit Provincials in the early 1970s were facing some serious difficulties in the theologates. The number of Jesuit scholastics throughout the world had been steadily declining since 1966. By 1975, the number of scholastics (3,770) had decreased by more than 65 percent from its peak year of 1958 (11,118).[42] The American Jesuits, who also experienced severe declines, could no longer support five theologates for the formation and education of Jesuit priests. Something had to give, and the ten American Jesuit

Provincials met periodically after 1971 to investigate and to decide which of the five theologates should remain open and which should be closed. Woodstock had the longest history and the most prestigious faculty of all the theologates, but it had also received a considerable amount of bad press over lifestyle issues. In June 1972, the provincials recommended to the Jesuit general, Pedro Arrupe, that three theologates remain open, including Woodstock. The general did not take this recommendation as a final one and asked the provincials to consider some questions, one of which included an examination of Jesuit formation for the priesthood and community life and governance at Woodstock. The provincials met again, and after more investigations and discussion about the theologates, in October sent the general a second recommendation that suggested that Woodstock be closed. In the general's mind, "it was on formation that Woodstock was not chosen as a theologate and formation will be an essential factor in continuing the approval for the three theologates chosen."[43]

The provincials' decision to close Woodstock was based on various concerns, as Robert Mitchell, SJ, a former New York provincial and president of the Jesuit Conference, has indicated. According to him, the provincials considered "the quality of the faculty, ecumenical opportunities, geographical dispersion, housing available for Jesuit students, financial cost of each operation, the location of the undergraduate and philosophical programs for Jesuit students, etc. The ten provincials tried to balance all these considerations in coming to their final decision, which was approved by Fr. Arrupe."[44] Formation of Jesuits and lifestyle issues, too, loomed large, as reports from the provincials and letters from the general reveal.[45] The general accepted the October recommendation and made his decision known in late December 1972.

The general's decision was announced to the Woodstock community and to the press in the early days of January 1973. Secular and Catholic newspapers and journals reported the determination and the disappointments of those at Woodstock. In deciding which theologates to close, the *New York Times* relayed, the issue of the "religious formation" of future Jesuits weighed heavily upon the provincials and the general. In other theologates, moreover, the Jesuit community was not so spread out as was the case in

New York. *Time* reported "A Death in the Family," indicating that Woodstock never really got off the ground with a good start. From the beginning, it was broadcast as a failure by Garry Wills's "acerbic 1971 piece." The closing was another sign "that the Society of Jesus has lost its great vision, its instinct for leadership, its openness to the world."[46]

Prior to the announcement of the decision, the president of Woodstock, Christopher Mooney, and other members of the faculty made their representations to the general, seeking a reversal of the decision, but to no avail. Dulles was in Rome in March 1973, after the decision was announced, preparing to teach a course at the Gregorian University during the second semester. The Woodstock faculty asked Dulles and Walter Burghardt to make one last attempt to present the case against closing Woodstock. In March they met with the Jesuit general and his curia. According to Dulles, the general and curia in Rome "listened courteously and with interest. The American Provincials had…raised many questions and were especially concerned about an article on lifestyle issues that had been published in the *New York Magazine*."[47] Dulles was convinced that the lifestyle issues and community governance were primary reasons for closing Woodstock and that conviction was confirmed in Dulles' and Burghardt's discussions with the general and his curia. The two Woodstockers repeatedly answered questions about Wills's charges against Woodstock. The meeting with the general ended with some understanding of the decision-making process.[48] Although the decision was painful for Dulles, as for others at Woodstock, he accepted the decision and was ready to continue the Jesuit mission wherever that might lead him. During his years at Woodstock, his primary focus was on theological education and theology, not on the Society's administrative decisions. In these years he published some of his most widely read theological essays and books, which the next chapter examines.

8
MODELS THEOLOGY FOR TURBULENT TIMES, 1966–1974

IN THE IMMEDIATE postconciliar years, between 1966 and 1974, in the midst of some radical changes in his own Woodstock community and in the larger American Catholic community, Dulles was in constant demand as a theological adviser, public speaker, university lecturer, author of books, articles, and reviews—earning a reputation as one of the foremost interpreters of Vatican II and as one of the moderately progressive theological reformers of the period. Like many other Catholic theologians, he was caught up in the spirit of reform and renewal in the church. Although he separated himself from some of the more radical proposals for reform and criticized some theologians who, in his view, had been overly zealous in rejecting elements of the preconciliar church, he emphasized, as did many reformers, the historically conditioned nature of doctrinal formulations, the relativity of many church practices and structures, the pluralism within Christianity, the adaptability of the church, and the necessity of accommodating the church to the needs of modernity and "modern man." These themes had budded during the council years, but they came to full flower in the decade following the council.

Vatican II and Dulles

Dulles became increasingly involved as a theological consultor to the nation's bishops, as a conversation partner in national and international theological conferences and symposia, and as a participant in ecumenical endeavors. These were productive years theologically, years in which he published more than 120 articles,

211

chapters for books, essays, and book reviews in addition to seven major books, two of which, *The Survival of Dogma* (1971) and *Models of the Church* (1974), received considerable attention. *Models*, a post–Vatican II classic period piece, was his most widely distributed and popular theological treatise and is still widely used at the beginning of the twenty-first century.

During these years, Dulles became one of the most creative interpreters, supporters, and promoters of the council and an advocate for reforms in theology and church structures. He emerged during these years, too, as a provocative analyst of the signs of the times for a generation of Catholics who were trying to come to terms with changes in the church and in society. He had his critics, from the extreme theological right and the radical left, and he positioned himself in between these two extremes by critiquing positions he considered inconsistent with the documents of Vatican II—criticizing those who either opposed the council's reforms or supported reforms that unjustifiably exceeded its intent. Although he was by temperament conservative, he placed himself within what he repeatedly called the "progressive" or "liberal" wing of postconciliar Catholic theology. That meant various things.

The progressive theologians, after as before the council, were those who attempted to retrieve and reinterpret the Catholic tradition in ways that were meaningful to contemporary Christians and the modern world. Progressive theology meant several things to Dulles in the period immediately after the council, when the enthusiasm for reform and change in the Catholic tradition was at its highest for him, as it was for many in the Catholic community. Like many of the progressive theologians of the era, he tried to interpret the signs of the times and to indicate what was meant by a modernity and a modern world that the Catholic tradition needed to address. Certain ideas and values and attitudes seemed to characterize the modern world: secularity, freedom, autonomy, and a scientific mentality that put a premium on the skeptical and the positive. In the mid-to late 1960s, Dulles saw the emergence of the so-called Death-of-God and secular theologies as major signs of the times and as "symptomatic of many assumptions and attitudes which pervade the air we breathe."[1]

These new theologies, which Dulles did not entirely approve

but which he saw as a challenge to traditional forms of Christianity, revealed to him "the modern antipathy to abstract metaphysical thinking, the prevailing distrust of traditional doctrines, the contemporary concern for relevance and pragmatic results, and the new accent on human freedom."[2] The new theologies were attempting to respond to real problems in contemporary European and American cultures. It was evident to Dulles in 1966 that "the social pressures in favor of religion are rapidly diminishing. In some circles the situation has almost reversed itself: the convinced believer rather than the agnostic is the non-conformist, the independent thinker."[3] In this situation, Catholic theology needed to be rethought, reinvestigated, and perhaps reformulated to meet the demands of the modern intellectual and social movements. On this score, the Second Vatican Council was a good start in Catholic communal attempts to reinterpret and make meaningful the Christian tradition for believers who were living in modern intellectual and social circumstances.

The Vatican Council marked the end of an era for Dulles and the beginning of a new dispensation in Catholic history. During these immediate postconciliar years, he contrasted sharply the pre- and postconciliar eras of Catholic history. The period prior to the council was characterized by the church's repeated assaults upon the modern world; Catholicism during the era was alien to all forms of modernity; it was defensive, counter-reformational, reactionary, authoritarian, and filled with its own smug certitudes. The characterization of the old, "ghetto" church was periodically presented in bold assertions. In 1969, for example, Dulles illustrated his views of the past by saying that "the Catholic doctrine of the magisterium as it developed in the century or two before 1950 represents a progressive alienation from the modern world. In proportion as the thinking of secular society became self-critical, relativist, concrete, and future-oriented, the magisterium became more authoritarian, absolutist, abstractionist, and backward looking."[4]

Dulles used Henri Bergson's terminology to characterize the pre–Vatican II Catholic Church as a closed rather than an open society: "This defensive, closed, static Church of the Counter-Reformation is the one in which most of us were raised and trained."[5] Catholics, particularly those in the United States, lived in a cultural ghetto, from which they were only slowly emerging in the post–World War II period. As Dulles explained to French and Italian readers in 1962 and 1963, American Catholics were conscious of being a minority, and that social consciousness made many of them disinterested in the common good. Prior to the council, many Catholics received from their families little or no cultivation of service to the nation. Even in 1962 and 1963, Dulles was hoping that the council, in response to the needs of the times, would produce a new style of bishop who could lead American Catholics beyond their ghettoes into a genuine concern for the common good and bring about a new style of relating to non-Catholics.[6]

Catholic theology in the post-Reformation era was dominated by the nonhistorical orthodoxy of a neo-scholasticism that was particularly uncreative in its almost complete reliance on Denzinger, a manual of doctrinal and dogmatic statements, for the source of its positions. Because of sociological, not intellectual causes, moreover, Catholics in the United States lacked any creative intellectual tradition, and Catholic theology in the United States, with some notable exceptions, was much poorer than theology in Europe.[7] This characterization (or rather caricature) of the preconciliar church and its theology lasted until the mid-1970s, when Dulles began to present a more nuanced picture of the past.[8]

Dulles' presentation of the past, however, served to justify the advances of the Second Vatican Council and the call to reforms that he truly considered necessary in the modern world. Pope John XXIII had done something new and had changed the course of history for the Catholic church, making possible a new, open church. John XXIII called for *aggiornamento*, a reforming mentality that would bring the church up to date to meet the needs of the modern world. The Vatican Council, which was "dominated by the progressive theologians of Transalpine Europe,"[9] brought about a new mentality in the Catholic Church—one that was historically conscious, developmentalist, accommodationist, open to the contributions of the modern world, respectful of internal diversity and external pluralism and religious liberty, dialogical, ecumenical, humble, self-critical, and reform minded.

Like many other progressive theologians in the immediate postconciliar period, Dulles interpreted the council by emphasizing its innovations and seeing them as more central than its reaffirmations of previous official positions. By following a quasi-hermeneutic of discontinuity, he stressed those elements in the council that were novel.[10] Pope John XXIII "opened the windows" and changed the course of history, leading theologians and others to reconsider the role the church ought to play in the contemporary world. The post–Vatican II church, too, as Dulles interpreted it, differed from its decadent and static past. It would be an open church and relevant to a modern world and a modern mentality that was emerging socially and intellectually even among American Catholics, who were coming out of their self-enclosed ghettoes. The accent during these years was clearly on what was forward looking, on what was wrong with the past, and on what needed to be criticized from the past—reformed and reconsidered and reformulated. For nearly a decade, Dulles, like many of the progressive theologians of the era who were formed in the preconciliar church, took for granted the Catholic tradition and continuity with the past. The progressive middle was not abandoning the preconciliar tradition; they were simply presupposing that it had a grip on the church that needed to be loosened, not given up.

As Dulles read the signs of the times in the late 1960s and early 1970s, though, all was not well in the postconciliar church. The changes in the church and in society made some people feel that there was indeed nothing firm or stable to hang on to, producing in the culture a certain crisis of faith. The various movements of reform in the Catholic Church, moreover, were tearing the church apart, as some were "reluctant to part with what seems tried and true" and others wished "to sweep away with an angry gesture everything that seems to savor of the past. Practically everyone," moreover, "feels at liberty to criticize the institutional Church from his own point of view." The younger generation, who felt the difficulties of the times most acutely, furthermore,

> do not wish to be tied to the ideas and values of a bygone era....[They] do not want to become the tools of a gargantuan bureaucracy; they resent being railroaded into a mass of doctrinal positions the importance of which is by no means evident to them....An increasing number of

younger Catholics feel only casually related to the Church as something rather marginal in their lives.[11]

The times were changing, and Dulles, like other progressive theologians, felt called upon to address the changing mentality that came out of the council and the radical social and religious changes that were being experienced in the American Catholic community. In his openness to change and development and accommodation, he saw himself in conformity with the direction and mind of the church as that mind was revealed in the council documents. As a fundamental theologian, whose task it was to investigate, understand, reinterpret, and communicate the Catholic tradition, Dulles continued to address the issues that were within his competence and of special concern in the postconciliar church: the meaning of revelation, faith, dogma, apologetics, the church, and ecumenism.

Revelation and Dogma

In Dulles' interpretation of the council, one generally shared by a host of interpreters, the debates over the doctrine of revelation, in preparation for the Constitution on Divine Revelation, *Dei verbum*, represented a historical turning point, giving the progressives a major victory that would influence almost all the other conciliar documents.[12] Dulles focused much of his theological attention on the meaning and importance of a renewed understanding of the doctrine of revelation because it was so central to all of theology—fundamental theology, doctrinal or systematic theology, and apologetics. He wrote more than thirty-two articles and four books on the subject,[13] and most of what he published on ecclesiology and ecumenism was dependent on his understanding of revelation, faith, dogma, and apologetics. He focused his attention on reformulating a coherent and intelligible understanding of the relationship among revelation, faith, and dogma, culminating in this period in *The Survival of Dogma* (1971), a collection of twelve previously published and unpublished essays from the late 1960s and early 1970 that represented the most liberal or progressive theological statement of his career.

Protestant and Catholic critical and scholarly approaches to biblical studies, historical consciousness within the church, a more critical assessment of the limits of language and an awareness of the symbolic language of the Bible, a renewed appreciation of negative or apophatic theology, and the secular or agnostic criticisms of revelation since the Enlightenment—all these developments demanded a renewed understanding of the doctrine of revelation, one that was true to the biblical witness and the long tradition of Catholicism. The task of postconciliar theology was to bring about a more comprehensive understanding of revelation than that of the immediate past—one that would in the end provide a solid foundation for fundamental and doctrinal theology and aid the movement toward Christian unity. It was a key issue. Vatican II had opened the doors toward a new understanding, but the council served only "as the starting point of a new and more vigorous line of development." *Dei verbum* had crystalized and incorporated the theological development of the decades before the council; it was the task of the postconciliar theologians to extend that development into a new era.[14]

The title of Dulles' first major book on the subject during this era, *Revelation and the Quest for Unity* (1968), an anthology of previously published and unpublished lectures, indicated a fundamental thrust of his attempts to rethink the nature and meaning of revelation in light of Vatican II's ecumenical sensitivities. The Protestant theologian Robert McAfee Brown asserted that Dulles' book revealed an ecumenical "'style' of theology for the future."[15] His emerging theology took seriously the thought of major Protestant theologians—Oscar Cullmann, Karl Barth, Gunther Bornkamm, Paul Tillich—to learn from them and not just to score points against them.

While coming to terms with a renewed understanding of revelation, Dulles contrasted, as he did in his attempted renewal of apologetics, the preconciliar neo-scholastic-manualist tradition and the conciliar and postconciliar historically conscious approaches. For the neo-scholastic tradition, particularly since Vatican I (1869–1870), revelation was the authoritative word of God, which came to human beings in two sources: the Bible and tradition. This two-source theory conceived of revelation itself in propositional terms, emphasized the objective and extrinsic nature of revelation, tended to equate revelation with the church's dogmatic statements, and focused on biblical miracles, the fulfillment of biblical prophecies, and the church itself as signs or motives of the credibility of revelation. This extrinsic, propositional view of revelation came to be challenged by twentieth-century historical studies of the Council of Trent and of the patristic and medieval periods and by Protestant and Catholic biblical studies.

The new theology of the twentieth century emphasized the primacy of the historical, interpersonal, subjective (personalist), symbolic, intrinsic, and ongoing dimensions of revelation. Dulles had a dynamic and dialogical view of revelation, emphasizing in particular the symbiotic and synthetic relationship among the Bible, tradition, and the church. Revelation itself, moreover, was not just a set of propositions or conceptual truths communicated to human beings but the self-disclosure of God who communicated with human persons through words and deeds; it was a salvific encounter with God. Unlike some of the neo-scholastics, Dulles did not identify dogma with revelation, emphasizing instead the primacy of the mysterious encounter with God over the verbal, and thus secondary, formulations of dogma. This new emphasis on revelation was evident in the council's decree *Dei verbum*, a decree that did not reject the older scholastic approach but certainly modified it by including it within a personalist understanding. The task of theology in the postconciliar period, Dulles frequently wrote, following the lead of Pope John XXIII's opening message to the Second Vatican Council, was to restate the Christian message in the "literary forms of modern thought."[16]

Although he emphasized the newer dimensions of revelation, Dulles, like Karl Rahner, saw his own approach as a mediating one—one between what he sometimes called the "modernist-immanentist" view and the "anti-modernist-extrinsic" view.[17] Dulles appreciated those philosophers and theologians who tried to avoid the Scylla of traditional orthodoxy's view of revelation as mere factual knowledge or information from a higher realm and the Charybdis of modern theological existentialism "which regards revelation as meaning divorced from historical fact." A "dehumanizing objectivism" was as faulty as was the "cult of subjectivism."[18] Likewise, he was well aware of the symbolic nature of biblical language, but one could not lay it down as a principle that "symbolism in a narrative is evidence against its historical realism." It could be said, in fact, that the central Christian mysteries derived their symbolic value from their historical realism.[19]

Although Dulles criticized the older manualist tradition, he thought some theologians like Gabriel Moran had an "excessive tendency" to reject earlier works that emphasized the objective. Dulles wanted postconciliar theology to accent, in the light of Vatican II, revelation as the "salvific encounter which takes place in the here and now" between the believer and God,[20] but not at the expense of historical events or revelation's "determinist structure or communicable content."[21] This concern for theological balance, though, was not always evident in the late 1960s as he emphasized one side of revelation rather than the other. Dulles argued for *The Survival of Dogma*, but in doing so he emphasized over and again that the linguistic, theological formulations of revelation and faith demanded a development and reinterpretation of the Christian tradition, and he tended to relativize (or put relative value on) Scripture, tradition, dogma, and the authority of magisterial statements. What was primary was revelation (the divine self-disclosure) as a salvific encounter.[22]

Dulles' emerging emphasis on the subjective or interpersonal dimension of revelation, especially in *Survival*, called for a new understanding of the role that faith played in this encounter. Revelation could be received only in faith, but how then could one understand the relationship between revelation and faith? Was revelation merely a projection of a faith experience? Was the objective dimension of revelation minimized by emphasizing the necessary role of faith in revelation? Dulles' own formulation of responses to these and other questions was greatly influenced from the mid-1960s on by his reading of Michael Polanyi, the chemist and philosopher of science, whose *Personal Knowledge* had a great impact on Dulles' post-1965 theology.[23]

Dulles came across Polanyi's work quite by accident. One day in the mid-1960s he saw Polanyi's *Personal Knowledge* listed on John Courtney Murray's syllabus for one of his courses. He checked the book out of the library and began reading it. He found it "terrific." "I would say," he told me,

> that I began reading it in about 1965. I started using it in methods courses. I found it very applicable to my own

method in theology, and it was articulating things that I was actually doing and it transformed my consciousness....He was very good at pointing out that there was always something more there than one was able to articulate. He was very much aware that there was always something much more than could be contained in propositions.[24]

For Dulles there was indeed the objective side of revelation, God revealing, but there was also the subjective side, the reception in faith. And that reception in faith was not just a rational assent, nor did it contain mere factual knowledge. It was a personal encounter in which one entered into a kind of knowing (producing what Polanyi called "tacit knowledge") that went well beyond what could be communicated in human language, especially in the language of propositions. It was difficult, except conceptually, to separate faith and revelation, the objective and the subjective, without destroying something of the reality of revelation itself. In Dulles' view revelation was the interaction of the subjective and the objective, and when he considered faith as the subjective dimension of revelation he did not separate faith itself from the objective dimension because of the inherent connection between the two. Faith was a matter of "personal knowledge," and like Polanyi he believed that faith had an objectivity and a reality to it. Personal knowledge was not purely intellectual; it involved the whole person, mind, will, emotions, love and hope. It carried insight into life itself.

Faith was what helped scientists to transcend the confines of a scientific paradigm, and it enabled the religious person to come into contact with God and to penetrate without fully apprehending the mysteries of revelation in nature, in the Bible, in history, in worship, in prayer, and in the creativity of human culture. In his postconciliar approach to the meaning of faith, Dulles was trying to transcend the manualist and neo-scholastic intellectualist reduction of faith to a rational assent that transcended but did not contradict reason. That notion of faith was based upon the authority of God revealing, a God who was reasonable and always acted with human beings in ways that condescended to their nature. That notion of faith was not wrong, but it was reductionist.

In 1967 and 1968, Dulles wrote a series of articles on faith for *America* magazine.[25] These articles were intended for a large audience of reading Catholics, not just for the professional theologian. In these articles and in several others, he emphasized the personalist, existentialist, and historically conditioned nature of all faith experiences and tried to address the so-called crisis of faith that was a center of attention in the popular religious press in the late 1960s and early 1970s. The articles were pertinent, moreover, because they came in response to Pope Paul VI's declaration of 1967 as the "Year of Faith." Historically speaking, Dulles noted, American Catholics had evolved from a childish, naive faith, protected by the Catholic ethnic ghettoes, to the self-assured, assertive adolescent faith of the post-1930s, to the present state of crisis in which the old world of the past was quickly fading, producing an uncertain world of relativity, pluralism, and change. The present situation, with its emerging dynamic, evolutionary view of reality upset the faith of those Catholics who were comfortable in their own parochial world. Vatican II complicated the whole picture for American Catholics by calling for a dialogue with the modern world and reforms and changes in a church most Catholics had associated with the unchanging bastion of unity and stability. Dulles summarized the crisis in this way:

> The more we acknowledge the normative value of modern patterns of thought, including critical scientific method, the more exposed and vulnerable our faith seems to become. The Church, including its solemn doctrinal pronouncements, is viewed as historically conditioned. Many Catholics, who previously felt secure under the aegis of an unassailable authority, today feel that there is nothing firm or stable to hang on to. Many would prefer to return to the womb of a protective Church and to reverse, if they could, the effects of the Johannine revolution.[26]

Other Catholics wanted everything to change and were upset with the pace of change in the old church. In this situation, faith itself came into crisis. What was needed in the new era, for the development of a mature faith, was a renewed understanding of faith that could be true to the tradition while incorporating the insights of modern philosophy and science and the emerging dynamic, evolutionary worldview.

In the new situation, Catholics had to learn to separate or distinguish the experience of faith as an "adherence to God as he discloses himself in Christ" from all the historically and culturally conditioned ecclesiastical expressions of the faith, and even acknowledge and allow for a certain legitimate dogmatic pluralism (historically and currently).[27] Theologians who raised questions about the formulations of the faith did not necessarily undermine the faith itself. Most of the time, theologians were looking for ways to make the faith itself more intelligible to their age. "When man's assumptions and forms of thinking change, the faith must be restated in new ways to prevent misunderstanding."[28]

Some received interpretations, in the light of some forms of modern thought, become incredulous and need to be reinterpreted for the sake of faith itself. Some Catholics and other Christians, for example, used to think Eve was made from a rib of Adam or that Jonah was in the belly of a whale for three days or that at one time a flood covered the whole Earth. These expressions of the biblical tradition needed to be reinterpreted in the light of more sophisticated biblical criticism and in conjunction with modern thought. Faith was not to be placed in the literary forms but in the God revealed in the literary forms. Dulles was here trying to prepare American Catholics for a biblical revival that had been going on for some time in Protestant and Catholic circles and at the same time open them to the possibilities of questioning and criticism within the church without damaging or diminishing faith itself. A mature faith allowed one to live with criticism, uncertainty, and even doubt. Faith was not childish credulity, nor adolescent zeal, but adult humility. "A mature faith is humble enough to criticize its own presuppositions and learn from the science of the day."[29]

The mature faith was not an empty faith, as Dulles knew from his own conversion experience. Faith itself was the result of conversion, some change of mind and heart, that had an ongoing effect on the whole of life. Those who were called men and women of faith "are persons who have experienced, at some privileged moment, an overpowering sense that the divine has manifested itself to them." Such a faith for the Christian was centered on the saving mystery of the cross and resurrection. It demanded of the one who lived in that mystery not only obedience and sacrifice but also love, hope, and grace, which made it all possible. Such a person of faith lived with the confidence that his or her life had a meaning that transcended all the transitoriness and uncertainty of the world: "The man of faith does not know the answer to all speculative questions, but he has a few firm convictions that have burned themselves deep into his soul. The aura of light may be small, but it must be intense."[30] Throughout these articles Dulles focused on faith as a personal experience that carried meaning and insight, but this subjective experience was not without objective warrant or specific content.

Dulles was leery of emphasizing too much the existentialist, subjective dimension of faith, and he wanted to make it clear that his own evolving notion of faith was not entirely subjective. The scholastics did have a point. There was an intelligible content in the faith. To be personal, as faith was, did not mean to be purely relative, arbitrary, or subjective. Although faith, as "a living communion with the God of love," was more than dogma and more than the formulations of doctrine, it was "not an empty sack that can equally well be filled by anything God chooses to say." The Christian faith had a trinitarian and christological structure to it. It flowed from the central Christ-events of the incarnation, cross, and resurrection and there was an "intimate connection between the act of faith and its doctrinal content."[31] And, it was not simply an individual possession, but personal in the sense of being interrelated with a community of faith because faith was never an isolated, individual phenomenon but a communal experience, manifested periodically in the liturgical celebrations when Catholics prayed together the Nicene-Constantinople Creed during Mass. There was a definite and specific intelligible content in the faith.

Dulles sensed the emergence of Catholics out of their cultural ghettoes, as he called them, and he was aware that Catholics who were increasingly college educated needed an approach to their tradition that was much more sophisticated than the approaches they had received in the catechisms of their early formation in the faith.

He was attempting to meet the challenges of historical conscious-ness, the contemporary experiences of change and pluralism, and a general American, dynamic, developmental, or evolutionary view of reality. Under such circumstances, theologians had the task of rein-terpreting faith in its multiple dimensions and weaning Catholics away from what he considered an immature and almost exclusively intellectualist view of faith and a propositional view of revelation. His personalist approach during these years—influenced by Polanyi, John Henry Newman, Martin Buber, Karl Rahner, Maurice Blondel, Louis Monden, and a host of other philosophers and theologians— stressed the absolute priority of faith over dogma.

Dogma and dogmatic statements also came in for some seri-ous reconsideration in the years after the council. Some theolo-gians either reinterpreted or questioned various traditional dogmas (original sin, transubstantiation, the virginal conception, papal infallibility) or raised doubts about their continuing validity. Church teaching in general was repeatedly called into question, particularly after the 1968 publication of Pope Paul VI's encyclical *Humanae vitae* on birth control. Within this context, it was impor-tant to provide an understanding of the meaning of dogma and its functions within the church and in the life of faith. In these years, Dulles sought to articulate an understanding of dogma that would meet the needs of a rapidly changing, increasingly secular, and ecu-menically sensitive religious world. To do this, he criticized the older, manual understanding of dogma and contrasted it with a view he considered more in conjunction with the theology of the council and the insights of those theologians who were more his-torically conscious than the manualists and neo-scholastics. In this regard, he quoted from Pope John XXIII's opening address at the council. The pope encouraged the council fathers to penetrate the church's doctrinal heritage and to form a consciousness that would be in conformity with authentic doctrine, "which, however, should be studied and expounded through the methods of research and through the literary forms of modern thought. The substance of the ancient doctrine of the deposit of faith is one thing, and the way in which it is presented is another."[32]

In several articles and in *The Survival of Dogma*, Dulles rein-terpreted the meaning of dogma, revitalizing and revising the classical concepts in order to preserve the idea of dogma in the Catholic Church.[33] The Counter Reformation Catholic theologians—influenced by Greek intellectualism, Roman legalism, the nonhistorical thinking of the Enlightenment, and the reactionary clericalism of the nineteenth century—had produced a concept of dogma that was nonhistorical, juridical, absolutist, authoritarian, and intellectualist. That notion of dogma emphasized "its identity with revelation, its conceptual objectivity, its immutability, and its universality." Such a static concept of dogma had produced among some contemporary theologians and the laity either a servile conformism or a defiant rebellion.[34] In most of his articles on the subject at the time, Dulles attacked more vigorously the intransigents, those in the contemporary church who were battling change, than the innovators who wanted to overthrow the older conceptions, although he had criticisms for both extremes.

In his interpretation of the postconciliar theological scene, he placed himself on the side of those theologians who emphasized (1) the historically conditioned nature of all dogmatic statements, in contrast to those who emphasized the absolute, immutable, and irreformable nature of dogma; (2) a transcendental in contrast to a propositional view of truth; and (3) the provisional nature of past pronouncements, seen as points of departure, in contrast to past proclamations as deposits of faith or inherited patrimony that needed to be preserved in all their cultural and linguistic details.[35] Those who held to the Counter Reformation or manualist idea of dogma, a relatively recent development in the history of theology, could not deal with the current changes in the church and could not help Catholics to understand what indeed was happening in their church. The serious crisis in the church would not be overcome by simply repeating what had been said in the past. Most Catholics, like most other Christians in the United States, moreover, were greatly disadvantaged in coming to terms with contemporary transformations because they lacked a sufficient sense of history.[36]

The Survival of Dogma, the most radical and relativist of his writings, was a key to this period of Dulles' theological development. Like many of his articles, it focused on the derivative nature of dogmatic statements. They were historically, sociologically, and culturally conditioned conceptualizations and formulations of what was primary—namely revelation (the word of God), a personal and communal encounter with the divine mystery, the fullness of revelation in Christ. The church's dogmatic statements carried the limitations of their times and reflected the evolutionary development of the church's consciousness of the meaning of revelation. Dogmas developed in the church and therefore reflected also the diversity of the times in which they were formulated. The dogmatic language in which the church formulated its understanding of revelation, moreover, was symbolic; it was not scientific or descriptive language.

Since the mid-1950s, Dulles had been interested in the symbolic nature of language as he found it described in the works of Paul Tillich, Karl Rahner, and Michael Polanyi, among others. The mystery of the divine self-communication came to human beings through symbols. Over the years, Dulles would develop his understanding of symbol, and it would increasingly become central to his theology, but in the mid-1960s and early 1970s he defined it as

> a word, gesture, picture, statue, or some other reality which can be made present to the senses or the imagination, and which points to a reality beyond itself. But this other reality is one which cannot be precisely described or defined; it is not knowable, at least with the same richness and power, except in and through the symbol. The symbol has power to evoke more than it can clearly represent because it addresses itself not simply to the senses and the abstractive intelligence, but to the entire human psyche.[37]

Dogmatic language was a means for a personal encounter with God. It was not, however, mere "subjective fantasy" because it had "truth value."

Because the church's dogmatic language was historically conditioned and therefore limited, developmental, and symbolic, it needed to be reformulated, reinterpreted, and adapted to meet the needs of each era. And, it was possible to have not only a diversity of dogmatic expressions in history but also a legitimate pluralism of dogmatic formulations in the present. Some might think in reading some of Dulles' articles of the mid-1960s and early 1970s that he was an historical relativist or subjectivist with respect to church dogmas, and indeed some read him in that way. But emphasizing the historically relative, sociologically contextual, culturally conceptual, and symbolic nature of dogma did not make him a relativist or subjectivist. Even though he was taking issue with the older objectivist and rationalist scholastic approaches to dogma, he did periodically during these years speak of the normative nature of dogmatic statements.

The last chapter of his *Survival*, for example, focused on what he called the "'Irreformability' of Dogma."[38] Terms like *irreformability* and *infallibility* were time-conditioned terms, and in 1970 Dulles believed their usefulness or communicability was questionable.[39] His project, however, was not to relativize dogma but to make it meaningful for his contemporaries. There was something in dogmatic statements that provided a stable and permanent reflection of divine revelation, which demanded fidelity. All Dulles' previous talk of modernization, innovation, and reformulation had to be understood within his understanding of Christian self-identity over time. What was irreformable in dogmatic statements was their truth and meaning, while the conceptual terminology in which they were cast historically was subject to change and reformulation. But even the concepts, propositions, and the symbols of the faith, Dulles argued in conjunction with Rahner and others, contained something more than the subjective attitudes or consciousness of a particular era. He argued throughout the immediate postconciliar period for a reconceptualization of dogma that preserved the reality and truth of dogmatic statements. For this reason, he advised church authorities to be slow to condemn theological speculation and attempts to reformulate dogma. Flexibility in the church was not antithetical to structure. Just as skyscrapers and ocean liners bend in order to preserve their structure, so also should the church as it meets the challenges of the new times that come upon it. He argued, in the end, that there is a normative quality to Christian belief, that the church has the authority to express it, but that historical existence requires reformability of expression,[40] and "because dogma has an inbuilt elasticity it can and will survive."[41] After all, one reconceptualizes in order to preserve the content of the faith. Dulles argued for the survival of dogma but for dogma reconceptualized as a symbolic mode of communication.

In the immediate postconciliar period, Dulles argued primarily against the older conceptions of dogma, but he also criticized those like Gabriel Moran and Leslie Dewart who had excessively challenged or rejected the previous notions of revelation, dogmatic concepts, and propositions. Dulles had a more affirmative approach to dogmatic propositions, for example, than Dewart, who denied the infallibility of magisterial declarations on the grounds that the notion of infallibility did not leave enough room for progressive reinterpretations. Dulles was not opposed to progress and reformulation, but he thought that Dewart's "evolutionary theory of knowledge" and his "conceptual agnosticism" completely relativized dogma and minimized the significance of religious language. Some concepts, Dulles asserted, had an "authentic cognitive role. They enable one to achieve noetic insight into the realities to which they refer; they mediate a contemplative union between the knower and the known."[42] Dulles' own relativizing had its limits. "When Christians proclaim that Jesus is the Incarnate Word or that he rose from the dead, they surely intend to do more than report on their own states of consciousness."[43]

Dulles' conservative critics in the late 1960s and early 1970s interpreted his emphasis on historical conditioning and reformulation as a manifestation of modernism or liberalism or relativism and a capitulation to the contemporary zeitgeist. They caught something of the spirit of Dulles' theology even though they missed many of the qualifications he made in speaking of revelation and dogma. Fellow Jesuit Dan Lyons, for example, writing for the conservative Catholic newspaper *Twin Circle*, asserted that many of Dulles' theological views caused considerable "bewilderment." Lyons listed criticisms of Dulles' positions and singled out his views on dogma. Lyons thought Dulles had undermined the church's authority and its understanding of dogma when Dulles asserted that a "plurality of authentic Christian sources protects the believer from being crushed by the weight of any single authority." Dulles' view that the concept of the immutability of dogma was of "relatively recent vintage" was hard for Lyons to swallow. Such views could be considered an attack on the church's infallibility. Dulles' opposition to the universality of dogma and support for dogmatic pluralism could lead to "dogmatic relativism and seriously undermine, if not eliminate, the authority of the magisterium."[44]

Lyons charged that Dulles' characterization of the preconciliar period as one of "religious adolescence" and immaturity, and his lavish praise of "our present era of turmoil and confusion" was itself immature and detrimental to Catholic faith. His book on *Survival*, furthermore, was more interested in the atmosphere in which questions were raised than in the substantive answers to particular questions.[45] Lyons was concerned that the constant questioning and speculation in postconciliar theology was undermining the faith of the contemporary Catholic, leaving the impression that anything goes in theology. Lyons demonstrated in this article the criticisms that were periodically leveled against Dulles' theology from conservative or ultra-conservative Catholics.[46] Dulles had, in fact, focused much of his own criticism on the theologies of the immediate past and sided with the theological reformers, who, people like Lyons believed, had capitulated to modernism and liberalism.

Progressive theologians (for example, Gregory Baum, Raymond Brown, Bernard Cooke, Michael Fahey) reviewing *Survival* generally agreed, in Fahey's characterization, that Dulles balanced "continuity with innovation" in his attempts to reformulate revelation, faith, and dogma. According to Berard Marthaler, Dulles' theological epistemology was evolving in *Survival*, and the book reflected "important new directions within Catholic theology as a whole." Some progressive reviewers, although generally positive, thought Dulles was too conservative, too cautious, and overly optimistic in his assessment of the magisterial authority of the pope and bishops.[47]

Apologetics

Dulles had come increasingly to accept the historicity of the human condition, and in the post–Vatican II era, he, like many of his theological colleagues, emphasized the relativity of much in the Christian tradition; but since his days as a student at Harvard, he also had an abiding concern for the truth claims of Christianity in general and of Catholicism in particular. And this concern manifested itself, among other things, in his attempts to keep alive within Catholic theology the task of apologetics—or the responsibility of the theologian to come to terms with "objections to religious faith and weigh the legitimacy and rationality of his own commitment."[48] Apologetics was a Christian's attempt to "make your defense...for the hope that is in you" (1 Pet 3:15). Christian faith had its own rationality, and it was the task of Christian apologetics to make that rationality evident by using resources available in contemporary philosophy, science, and other disciplines of the modern university.

Apologetics had been a part of Dulles' course on fundamental theology at Woodstock,[49] and during the council he had written on the subject with respect to new, twentieth-century approaches to biblical studies.[50] He continued after the council to show an interest in the subject, but interest in apologetics had waned considerably in the Catholic theological community since the council.[51] The older neo-scholastic apologetic was considered excessively rationalistic, obscuring the dimensions of mystery and experience that were so much a part of Vatican II and postconciliar theology. Catholic seminary courses in apologetics all but disappeared after the council. The same was true in Catholic undergraduate theology and religious studies programs.[52] In twentieth-century Protestant theology as well, especially under the influence of Karl Barth between 1920 and 1950, apologetics had died out. Within this postconciliar context, Dulles saw the need to refocus Catholic attention on the role of apologetics in the Christian tradition.

Dulles has said, "After Vatican II it became unfashionable to talk about apologetics, and almost everybody called it fundamental theology. It was a rational approach to theology. But in the Italian system [in which Dulles had been educated] fundamental theology was really a part of dogmatics. It was a concentration upon theological method and the sources of theology."[53] For Dulles, apologetics was a part of fundamental theology and clearly a part of dogmatics.[54] It was a part of faith seeking an understanding and an intelligibility that was available to an audience wider than the community of faith. Nonetheless, after the council, Dulles believed that the waning interest in apologetics needed to be addressed. An opportunity to address the issue came to him in 1969 when he was invited to write two volumes on apologetics, one a history of apologetics and the second a systematic examination.

The publishers of the *New Catholic Encyclopedia* in the mid-1960s had made enough money on that project that they decided to form what they called "Corpus Instrumentorum," a corporation intended to produce theological texts in the postconciliar era. They invited Dulles to write two texts on apologetics. He obtained a sabbatical in 1970 to do research on the history of apologetics, publishing it in 1971.[55] A second volume on the theory of apologetics, however, was never published, because by the end of 1971, Corpus had run out of funds to support the project.

Catholics and Protestants in Europe and Protestants in English-speaking countries had previously produced multivolume and single-volume histories of apologetics, but Dulles' *History of Apologetics* was the first comprehensive book on the topic to be published in English by a Catholic. The book aimed to give the reader a descriptive historical account of the major currents and transformations of apologetics in different periods and cultures. Focusing on the shifting goals and methods of apologetics through the centuries, Dulles limited himself to those major thinkers who were committed to Christianity as a revelation, including Protestants as well as Catholics since the sixteenth century. He supported, however, no theory about what apologetics should be. Although Dulles' history was primarily descriptive, he made it clear where his sympathies lay. Among the ancients, he identified more with the Alexandrians (Clement and Origen) than with Tertullian, among the medievals more with Aquinas than others, and among the moderns more with Blondel and Newman than with the traditionalists or neo-scholastics and manualists. He sided with what he categorized as the liberal tradition and indicated that much of official Catholic apologetics in the nineteenth century held an "unduly conservative attitude" to scientific biblical criticism.[56] Dulles was convinced throughout his career that apologetics could not be separated from revelation and theology in general; it was a theological discipline, an emphasis in his thought that would come to the fore in debates with theologian David Tracy after 1974.

Ecclesiological Issues and *Models of the Church*

Ecclesiology

Dulles' primary theological focus was in fundamental theology (that is, in the areas of the theology of revelation and faith, the sources and methods of theology, and apologetics). But, in fact, he is most widely known as an ecclesiologist, and it was in the immediate postconciliar era that he produced what became his most commercially successful book, *Models of the Church* (1974), the book upon which his reputation grew to national and international prominence.[57] He turned to ecclesiology primarily because he was invited by John Courtney Murray, editor of *Theological Studies*, to explain Vatican II to Catholics in the United States, and at the heart of the council was a reformulation of the doctrine of the church. Since 1964, Dulles taught courses on ecclesiology at Woodstock, and after the council he wrote a brief introductory commentary on *Lumen gentium* (LG: the Dogmatic Constitution on the Church) for Walter M. Abbott's edition of the *Documents of Vatican II* (1966), an English translation that was widely distributed and became the *magna carta* for the renewal of Catholicism in the years immediately after the council.

Dulles himself was surprised by the request to write the introduction to *Lumen gentium* because, as he has said, "Ecclesiology was not my main theological focus." Abbott, a fellow Jesuit, however, convinced him to do it.

> Abbott came down to Woodstock and pleaded with me to write it. I said that I could write the introduction to the document on revelation, that I was more qualified to do that document. I told Abbott I was not really qualified to do the commentary on the church. He said that he had already gotten someone to do the introduction to *Dei verbum*. So I decided to do it.[58]

Dulles, of course, had previously given lectures on the church for his classes at Woodstock, but he had written very little explicitly on ecclesiology prior to this request. (His doctoral dissertation, how-

232

ever, and his published articles on ecumenism significantly addressed major issues in ecclesiology.)

Between 1966 and 1974, Dulles wrote more and more directly and indirectly on the doctrine of the church, culminating in *Models*. He developed his own ecclesiology, following the innovations of Vatican II. Abbott's *Documents of Vatican II* was the first major introduction that most reading Americans had to the council's accomplishments. The document on the church (*Lumen gentium*), which Dulles called, in agreement with most theologians, the "most imposing achievement of Vatican II," was the lead document in Abbott's edition. Dulles introduced *Lumen gentium* by placing it in its immediate historical context, noting that in general the twentieth century was the century most focused on ecclesiology. For Catholics, Vatican II's Constitution on the Church had to be perceived as completing and transcending the unfinished business of Vatican I. The excessive and one-sided emphasis of Vatican I on the papacy was brought into balance when Vatican II presented the church within the mystery of trinitarian salvation and placed the papacy and episcopal collegiality in the wider context of the church's mystery. Vatican I's emphases were evident in twentieth-century theological manuals, which stressed the church's hierarchical and juridical elements, and those elements, though modified to some extent by Pope Pius XII's pioneering encyclical *Mystici corporis* (1943), seemed to dominate the first draft of Vatican II's document on the church. That first draft, however, went through a "drastic revision" at the council, producing a "radically different vision of the Church"—one that emphasized the pastoral, christocentric, biblical, historical, and eschatological dimensions of the church.[59]

The final draft of the document, therefore, was an "entirely new document" that was overwhelmingly approved by the council fathers (2,151 in favor; 5 opposed)—emphasizing the mystery of the paradoxical union of the human and the divine, a recurring theme in all the documents of Vatican II. *Lumen gentium* was "strongly ecumenical" in tone, presented authority as service, and had something of a "democratic note" to it. Although the document was an advance over previous twentieth-century approaches to the church, it was not the last word. It was open to development and therefore could be considered a stepping stone to the future.[60]

Dulles' introduction set the tone for the reception of the document in American Catholicism. The document also became a foundation for Dulles' own attempts to present an ecclesiology more in tune with Vatican II, contemporary developments in theology, philosophy, and science, and the needs of an American Catholic community that was rapidly becoming more and more contentious and diverse in religious opinions.

In 1967 Dulles collected and revised various previous lectures on the church and published them in *The Dimensions of the Church*, his first extensive attempt to interpret the achievements of Vatican II and demonstrate their consequences. The major theme of the book was Vatican II's vision of the church's relationship to the total human family. *Dimensions* was structured in terms of the church's triple dialogue with other Christian churches, with other world religions, and with the secular world. Vatican II broke down the walls that had previously separated the Catholic Church from its multiple relationships with the human family and identified itself "with the great concerns of mankind." The book concluded with a chapter on Dietrich Bonhoeffer's "Worldly Christianity" because, in Dulles' estimation, Bonhoeffer was as important for theology in the 1960s as was Rudolph Bultmann after World War II and Karl Barth between World War I and World War II. The modern Catholic Church had, in Dulles' estimation, privatized religion and disengaged it from the world and worldly progress. Bonhoeffer and Vatican II called for a new engagement between the church and the aspirations of the world.[61] By mentioning Bonhoeffer and the other Protestant theologians, Dulles indicated that he was writing for Protestant as well as Catholic audiences. He wanted to demonstrate the Catholic Church's new openness to developments in other Christian theological traditions.

Dulles was emphasizing in *Dimensions* what he considered the direction the council had given in its understanding of the church. Vatican II broke new ground by emphasizing the concrete and historical dimensions of the church rather than the abstract and metaphysical. The older essentialist approach of ecclesiastical documents like *Mystici corporis* could not deal effectively with the church as a concrete, historical, and sinful people of God. Vatican II overcame that limitation and emphasized the human side of the church, its need for constant reformation, and its eschatological reality.

Dimensions was written at "a time of widespread suspicion and restlessness," and it was Dulles' attempt not only to explain the complexities of the full Christian reality to an American audience but to counsel his readers to avoid seeing oppositions and conflicts where there were only tensions and contrasts. Dulles reiterated throughout the book a theme that was increasingly evident in his writings: a contrast and distance between the pre–Vatican II church as a closed society and the postconciliar church as an open society. In the end, Dulles counseled Catholics that "a more positive attitude toward the whole human family is required by fidelity to Christ and the church."[62]

Most reviewers of the book interpreted Dulles' approach to ecclesiology as a sound representation of Vatican II theology. Again and again reviewers noted that Dulles balanced continuity and innovation in his theology of the church. In the contemporary theological world, he represented the middle road between the archconservatives who resisted change and the radicals who were impatient with the halting reforms of Vatican II and wanted to go well beyond the council in their ecclesiologies. He was characterized as sound and safe, not very adventurous, and still preoccupied with some institutional issues. According to one reviewer, he represented "a 'new orthodoxy' which is being surpassed by a radical wing that cannot tarry at this resting point but must press on."[63] Another reviewer thought the book "smacks of universalism."[64] The reviews of Dulles' books in the late 1960s and for some years to come demonstrated the divided opinion in the theological community, placing Dulles in the middle where he could be shot at from both extremes. If one takes the middle or moderate ground, one is bound to be squeezed.

Dulles wrote articles on the missionary and eschatological nature of the church in the years after he published *Dimensions*. Those articles focused on aspects of his ecclesiology that eventually ended up in his *Models of the Church*. He had previously addressed the missionary nature of the entire church, but in the mid-1960s he began to emphasize much more than in the past the need to change the way in which the church exercised its missionary mandate. In the past, the church focused excessively on evangelism and the conversion of non-Christians. In the present, the church needed to retrieve the fundamental idea of witnessing to and dialoguing with non-Christians (who had, as many modern theologians believed, some share in the divine revelation) and with reevangelizing Christians who had increasingly become inured in their secular cultures.

In the non-Christian world, moreover, the church could preach and teach more effectively by serving the needs of that world. The church ought to

> present Christianity in terms which make sense to modern man and are adapted to the current world situation....Amid the present anxiety concerning world hunger, war, and dissension, men look spontaneously to Christianity, with its message of love and reconciliation to make a contribution. We can do this by courageously sharing the joys and hopes, griefs and anxieties of men of our age.[65]

By serving those needs and applying the medicine of the gospel, the church carried out its missionary mandate to make this world a more humane community.

In the past, the church's missionary work, conceived of mostly in terms of conversion, was periodically accompanied by a European or American cultural imperialism that denied or abused human freedom and the cultural and religious values in the countries where missionaries worked. The new missionary task was to listen as well as to preach, to learn as well as to teach. The church has always been missionary, but the way it carried out its missionary charge changed over the course of time. The task in the present was to overcome some of the mistakes of the past and take on a new respect for freedom and cultural pluralism.[66]

This new emphasis in Dulles' approach to missions, however, would be modified here and there in his articles, especially as he reacted to those theologians and churchmen who had failed to acknowledge sufficiently the value of evangelization and conversion or who denied or minimized the ecclesial dimension of missionary work.[67] By 1974, although he continued to acknowledge, as had Vatican II, the social dimension of the gospel as part of the church's missionary work, he could be critical of those who seemed to be excessively preoccupied with that dimension. Missionary work was indeed evangelical. Dulles quoted *Gaudium et spes* to reinforce that idea: "Christ, to be sure, gave his church no proper mission in the political, economic, or social order. The purpose He set before her is a religious one."[68] The religious included the social, but emphasis on the religious was the proper one.

Like many other post–Vatican II theologians, Dulles also stressed the pilgrim or eschatological nature of the church. The church was not the perfect society, as it had been portrayed in post-Tridentine theology. The Catholic Church, too, could not be completely identified with the church of Christ, as had been done in Pope Pius XII's *Mystici corporis* (1943). Vatican II had been more modest in its claims by asserting that the Church of Christ "subsisted" (*subsistit in*, LG 8) in the Catholic Church, a favorite passage that Dulles quoted repeatedly. The church, one interlocking divine-human reality, subject to sin and the vicissitudes of history, was a pilgrim on its way to perfection and to the end for which it had been created. This emphasis upon the pilgrim and eschatological dimension of the church modified, Dulles thought, the previous Catholic arrogance and self-righteousness. Although Dulles acknowledged the distinction between the kingdom of God and the church, he did not place a dichotomy between them, as did, he thought, Hans Küng and some other theologians.[69] But in the mid-1960s Dulles emphasized the "not-yet" side of the church's eschatological nature. Increasingly after 1970 he acknowledged that the promise of divine presence was to some extent already realized in the church's visible manifestations, especially in its public worship. But a tension existed between the already and the not-yet of the divine promise.

Throughout this period, Dulles also pointed out some of the practical implications of Vatican II's emphasis upon the eschatological dimension of the church and summarized them in 1974: that dimension put the sinfulness and weaknesses of the church in perspective, accented the church's historical relativity, combated religious individualism, aided the ecumenical movement, and helped to bridge the gap between the church and the world—all themes that were emphasized in multiple ways in Dulles' ecclesiology during these years.[70]

Humanae vitae

By 1967, tensions within American Catholicism were mounting as differing factions in the church battled over the implementation of the reforms of Vatican II and over the extent to which the church ought to accommodate itself to American culture. Those tensions erupted into open conflict in 1968 after the publication of Pope Paul VI's *Humanae vitae* (July 1968), the papal encyclical on birth control. Moral theologians at the Catholic University of America, joined by those at Woodstock and other seminaries and colleges, along with a host of priests and laypeople, protested openly against the pope's prohibition of unnatural means of contraception. Moral theologians in particular organized mass meetings and signed letters dissenting from official papal teachings, a first in the history of American Catholicism.

Dulles was not a moral theologian and did not pronounce or write explicitly about the substance of the papal teaching, nor did he sign any of the numerous letters of protests that were sent around to the various theologates, seminaries, and colleges. Dulles was in Rome at the time the encyclical was published, and in a private conversation on the encyclical with a fellow Jesuit he is reported to have said, "Here I have been teaching for years…that the Church exists in dialogue with its own members, with other Christian communions, and really with men of good will everywhere. What are we to make, then, of a document that simply sets aside the discussion of the past ten years and retreats into the position of 1931 [*Casti Connubii*, 1930]?"[71] When reminded of this conversation in 1994, Dulles replied that he may indeed have said such things, but "I was trying to sort things out at the very beginning."[72] In 2005, years after the heat of the controversy, Dulles indicated that he "did not take a position, and couldn't stand up and say the pope was wrong. I had been taught before that it was traditional Catholic doctrine."[73]

In 1968, the theologians' public dissent produced open conflict in the church. Dulles did not join the public protests because his "concern was a pastoral one; I was trying to get people to live together in the same church."[74] The primary issue for Dulles, as for Karl Rahner, was ecclesiological. In *Stimmen der Zeit* (September 1968), Rahner, without pronouncing for or against the substantive doctrine of *Humanae vitae*, offered some general ecclesiological reflections on the encyclical that he hoped would transcend the tensions in the church between those who wanted to employ repressive measures to enforce consensus and those whose intemperate language of dissent could undermine respect for the church's official teaching office. In September 1968, in the midst of the conflicts, Dulles approved of Rahner's reactions to the encyclical and its reception and addressed the magisterium's role in the church. In *America* he published an article intended for a general reading public that outlined Rahner's and his own pastorally motivated position on the encyclical.

Like Rahner, Dulles was not convinced by the encyclical's intrinsic arguments and reiterated that the teaching was not irreformable but advised caution in reacting to it. Nature itself was not the sole criterion of morality; human conscience, a part of human nature, had to be considered. When considering the issue of contraception, Dulles advised, theologians should present arguments on both sides; married people could follow their conscientiously formed opinions without feeling guilt; and American bishops should avoid exacting "wooden conformity to the letter of *Humanae vitae* on the part of every Catholic regardless of his conscientious convictions." Dulles protested against what he considered on the one side "undisciplined protest" and on the other "bureaucratic over kill." Like Rahner, moreover, he was convinced that even though the ecclesiastical magisterium was indispensable in the formulation of doctrine, many other factors had to be considered "to achieve a clarity of doctrine." Among the factors to be assessed were such things as the "'sense' of the faithful, new acquisitions of knowledge by individual Christians and theologians, and the 'signs of the times,' which present ever new and varying questions."[75] *Humanae vitae* had raised an important ecclesiological issue for Dulles, that of the role and authority of the magisterium and of the theologians in the church, and he took up that issue in the years immediately following the encyclical.

Authority in government, business, and education as well as in the church came under continual fire during the 1960s. Opinion polls seemed to indicate after the publication of *Humanae vitae* that the authority and teaching function of the papal and episcopal magisterium were severely undermined within the church. In the midst of radical dissent in various segments of society and church, Dulles sought to preserve a role for authority and an official magisterium in the church by reinterpreting or reformulating how ecclesiastical authority and the teaching office in the church ought to function in a new democratic and antiestablishmentarian age. By 1969, he began writing on the issue, developing in the process what could be interpreted as a more democratic, charismatic, and egalitarian approach to the existence and function of ecclesiastical authority and the magisterium than was envisioned in the immediate past. He saw his own perspective as a continuation of the spirit of Vatican II.

Dulles made two arguments, one historical and one systematic, for a comprehensive view of the role of authority and the teaching office in the church. Consistent with his general approach to theology during these years, he made a sharp contrast between the authoritarian and absolutist approach of the magisterium in the post-Tridentine church and the dialogical approach in the Vatican II church. Vatican II, in contrast, opened the doors to the modern world and reinterpreted its own biblical foundations and its long history. Rather than emphasizing its judgmental and juridical function, as in the immediate past, the contemporary magisterium in conformity with Vatican II could become a directive force inspiring, encouraging, stimulating, and sensitizing Catholics to the implications of the gospel message. The systematic task of the late 1960s, in view of the dissent to *Humanae vitae*, was not to dissolve the magisterial role but to reformulate a view of the church and authority that made room for a larger participation in the church's authority and teaching role.

The Prophetic and Charismatic in the Church

All in the church possessed the Holy Spirit and therefore all had a role to play in the church, even in teaching and in the formulation of doctrine. The Pauline epistles and the council acknowledged an ordered diversity of functions in the church, and the contemporary church needed to recover something of this democratic élan within the church's own tradition, retrieving elements that were superseded or lost in the most recent past. The laity had a sense of the faith, and their contributions had to be considered in the church's attempt not only to preserve the apostolic tradition but also to propel the church into the future. In this regard, too, the church should make room for the role of prophets and teachers. They had insights into the faith that came from their charisms and/or from their competence as scholars. The bishops, though, had a necessary role in the church. Their role need not be exclusively that of defining the faith but rather that of listening to the voices in the church and bringing into focus the wisdom of the entire church, present as well as past. There was not just a teaching church (the hierarchy) and a learning church (the laity), as envisioned in the immediate past. "The faithful as a whole, and especially those who have scholarly competence or charismatic insight, participate in the magisterium." Dulles implied that such a reinterpretation of ecclesiastical authority and the magisterium would help to recover the democratic elements of the church's own early tradition and bring the church into a modern, secular society that was "self-critical, relativist, concrete, and future-oriented."[76]

In the late 1960s and early 1970s, in the midst of the rise of the Catholic charismatic movement in the United States,[77] Dulles emphasized the prophetic and charismatic dimension of the church to balance what he considered the excessive previous stress upon the priestly, hierarchical, and juridical dimensions. Restoring these elements would not only be more authentic to the longer tradition but would also have ecumenical potential. But this emphasis on the prophetic was not something entirely new in Dulles' theology. His doctoral dissertation had focused on the prophetic. In the dissertation, though, Dulles identified the prophetic with the proclamation of the word and with the office of the magisterium, although he allowed for authentic and efficacious preaching outside the Catholic Church (in Protestant churches) and therefore a prophetic role outside of the magisterium. By the late 1960s, he focused more and more on the contrast and tension between the prophetic and the sacerdotal roles in the church, identifying the prophetic largely

241

with a critique of the status quo and with a special gift to discern the signs of the times.

Prophets were those with inspired insight who urged a course of action to be taken in the present concrete situation. The church always had a need for prophets and for the prophetic role to keep the church in tune with the will of God, but it also needed the sacerdotal and hierarchical roles to moderate the zeal of the prophetic. The main focus in the late 1960s, however, was on the restoration of a legitimate role for the prophetic and the need for criticism from within and from outside the church.[78] The Holy Spirit, moreover, provided not only a charism of office in the church, but also other gifts that constituted the "nonofficial charisms in the church," which, Dulles noted, should be reemphasized.[79] Vatican II had to a considerable extent accentuated this emphasis upon the prophetic and the charismatic in the whole church, and when speaking of authority in the church in this period of his career, Dulles wanted to give proper weight to these elements.

Küng and the Church

Dulles' willingness to support the prophetic and charismatic, and the demands for ecclesiastical reform, however, was limited, as was somewhat evident in his approach to Hans Küng's theology in this period. Before and during the council, Dulles had been almost universally positive on Küng's prophetic approach to theology and reform. After the council, Dulles joined Küng on the editorial board of *Concilium*, the journal of postconciliar progressive theologians. In the mid-1960s, too, Dulles was generally favorable to Küng's views of dogma and the church. But, when he reviewed Küng's *The Church* in the Jesuit journal, *America*, in 1968, a mostly favorable review, he articulated some reservations about the direction of Küng's postconciliar thought. Dulles was astonished, for example, at some of Küng's conclusions, particularly his assertion that the distinction between the presbyterate and the episcopacy was "merely disciplinary," not dogmatic, and his appeal to *Lumen gentium* to support that view. Küng raised some important questions about theological positions thought previously unassailable, but he had a way of raising issues that called into question his own methodology. He cited "obscure texts as though they were decisive testimonies" and asked "genuinely difficult questions as if they could admit of only one answer."[80] Nonetheless, Dulles thought Küng's book would appeal to Protestants because of its strong biblical base and would be valuable for Catholics in rethinking some ecclesial issues.

Dulles' review and Küng's book were attacked by some clerical readers in a subsequent issue of *America*. How could Dulles recommend a book that he found objectionable in so many particulars? Dulles responded by saying that because Küng raised significant issues that traditional theological textbooks had not considered might mean either that he was wrong or that he was simply making "a creative theological advance." Dulles did not want Küng prematurely condemned by conservatives—as were Newman, Albert Möhler, and Karl Adam—simply because he did not follow the party line in theology.[81]

Dulles' critique did not alienate Küng. In fact, Küng wrote Dulles thanking him for supporting him in Dulles' reply to the *America* critics and apparently invited Dulles to teach for a semester at Tübingen. Almost a year later, Dulles responded to this letter, saying, "It was a pleasure to come to your defense against the zealots in the correspondence columns of *America*."[82] Dulles then invited Küng to consider teaching for a semester at Woodstock once it was fully settled in New York. The theological criticism did not destroy the friendship between the two.

The two, though, were not exactly on the same page theologically, as became manifestly evident when Küng published his *Infallible?* in 1971, after the publication of *Humanae vitae*. *America* again invited Dulles and others to review the book, which had become something of a *cause célèbre* in the theological community, creating the so-called Infallibility debate,[83] because of Küng's opposition to infallibility. In *Church*, Küng had raised issues about the limits of the doctrine of infallibility and the juridical interpretations of its meaning, a position with which Dulles had no difficulties because Küng did not question infallibility itself. *Infallible?*, however, went well beyond the *Church* in this regard.

In preparation for his review of *Infallible?*, Dulles read Rahner's assessment of the book in *Stimmen der Zeit* and Küng's two articles in reply. He also wrote to Leo O'Donovan, SJ, who was then studying in Germany, and asked him to send him Rahner's final response to Küng, the German bishops' response, and any other pertinent German literature on the book.[84] It was clear Dulles saw this book as an important statement that had to be dealt with seriously, particularly given the current reactions to ecclesiastical authority and *Humanae vitae* in the American Catholic Church.

Dulles' review, as most of his reviews, indicated where he agreed with the author and where he parted company. He agreed with Küng's view of the historically conditioned nature of dogma and believed that Küng raised significant questions that would make it difficult to defend traditional rationalistic and juridical notions of infallibility. On the other hand, Dulles did not accept Küng's rejection of the doctrine of infallibility, nor did he think Küng was "fully successful in establishing his own theories" on the church's indefectibility, its "perpetuity in truth." Küng's notion of truth was, for Dulles, too extrinsic, placing truth exclusively in God's saving will "rather than as anything really present in the pilgrim church." Dulles himself believed that a reformulated concept of infallibility, one that acknowledged limitations, was necessary. Unlike Küng, however, he asserted that the church had the ability (charism) to give "authoritative expression to what the gospel means in a particular situation." There was a substantive reality in the church's infallible teachings, one that was irreformable—not, however, in its conceptual framework nor in its terminology. Küng had gone too far. In effect, by identifying *Humanae vitae* with past notions of infallibility, he had defined infallibility much like the conservatives he opposed. In the end, "in repudiating what he understands to be the universal, definitive teaching of the church, Küng exhibits how little content he gives to his affirmation that the church is indefectible in the truth."[85] Dulles' review indicated that his support for progressive theologians had its limits, particularly when he considered their reinterpretations of the Catholic tradition moving radically beyond the boundaries of defined doctrine.

On November 14, 1971, Küng lectured at Columbia University on "Jesus Christ—Challenge to the Church," and Dulles responded to the lecture, giving a more general assessment of Küng's theology. Dulles referred to him as a Catholic Karl Barth.

Like Barth, Küng's theology was largely kerygmatic, biblical, and christocentric. But overemphasis on these genuine elements of theology could lead to errors. It was proper to emphasize, for example, the church as the community that proclaims the word, but it was more important to note the church as a mystery of the divine indwelling. It was appropriate to emphasize the biblical foundations, but not to the extent of subjecting tradition to the Bible. Christocentrism, moreover, was justifiably stressed as a good ground of ecumenical relations, but when other elements in the Christian tradition were neglected, that approach could lead to the loss of specific Catholic identity. By 1971, in Dulles' estimation, Küng's theology had these strengths and parallel weaknesses. Dulles intimated that Küng sometimes gave the impression that he remained in the church simply to fight against the evil present therein, leaving no positive reasons for belonging. In Küng's presence, Dulles did not hide his own view of Küng's arrogance, a term Dulles did not use. Küng "seems to assume he knows the way the Church should move, and that bishops and popes are to be judged by how far they agree with him"—forceful words even for a theological symposium.[86]

Although Dulles could on occasion take on the so-called progressive theologians, like Küng, when he believed they had gone too far, he could also on occasion take on current Vatican declarations that he believed were inadequate to the church's biblical foundations and long theological tradition or were out of tune with what he considered the best theology of the day. On July 5, 1973, the Congregation of the Doctrine of the Faith issued *Mysterium ecclesiae*, a "Declaration in Defense of the Catholic Doctrine on the Church against Certain Errors of the Present Day." Dulles believed that the declaration was part of a postconciliar authoritarian backlash that he periodically criticized. Although the declaration made some valuable observations, it was generally negative in its assessment of certain current theological approaches to the church.

With respect to the infallibility of the magisterium, the declaration presented some significant nuances, but it also made some historical assertions (for example, that "the Church has from the beginning always believed that the magisterium possesses infallibility") that raised serious questions "if only because the term of infallibility was not applied to the magisterium until late in the Middle Ages." Section IV of the declaration, obviously directed against Küng, rejected his thesis on indefectibility but, in Dulles' opinion, it made "no effort" to "meet the exegetical, historical, and systematic arguments Küng has presented." The declaration's purely juridical understanding of infallibility, which Küng had somewhat convincingly, in Dulles' view, demolished in *Infallible?*, was "not theologically viable." Dulles then went on to give his own understanding of what infallibility meant in the church:

> I would hold that the entire Church has a kind of permanence in the truth of Christ that may appropriately be called "infallibility." Going beyond Fr. Küng (as I understand him), I would add that the Church's infallibility may at times come to determinate verbal expression through the pronouncements of Popes, bishops or councils, when it is given to them to see clearly how a controversy should be resolved.[87]

Although Dulles had difficulty with other aspects of *Mysterium ecclesiae*, the issue of infallibility was one of his key concerns because the congregation, he believed, had overreacted against Küng and had not met Küng's arguments.

Reform of Church Structures

The issue of authority was closely tied to the issue of structural reform in the church during these years. Dulles was indeed sympathetic with the various calls for reform, but the progressive advocacy of reform had its limits, as theologian Richard McBrien discovered when he read Dulles' review of his *The Remaking of the Church* (1973), a major proposal for massive structural reforms. The review episode, minor though it was, demonstrates something of the tensions and polarization that existed in the period and reflects the ecclesial experiences that helped to condition Dulles' ecclesiology. Dulles had originally provided a very positive comment on McBrien's book when Harper & Row asked for a dust jacket blurb; the more extended review of the book in *America* was generally favorable, but it also had a critique that disturbed McBrien.

Dulles was in general "sympathetic with the directions" of the book; what McBrien advocated would help to revitalize the church "by feeding into the ecclesiastical sphere the climate of freedom and participation characteristic of the American secular heritage." Most of the thirteen structural reforms (for example, the elections of bishops and popes, married clergy, women's eligibility for priesthood and episcopacy, deliberative vote of laity in diocesan and parish councils) that McBrien supported had been urged here and there throughout the postconciliar period, and Dulles did not say whether or not he agreed with them. He agreed only with the attempts to advance greater freedom and participation in the church.[88]

The review, however, also pointed to an underlying "bothersome implication" in the book "that the most recent is presumably the best. I should prefer to say that some preconciliar theology was good, and some postconciliar theology is a disaster." McBrien blamed the bishops for the current polarization in the church, an interpretation Dulles thought unjustified because there was enough blame to go around to include priests and theologians, and avantgarde Catholics who "go beyond" the council. Some of the so-called progressives in the church, "after proposing irresponsible innovations, added to the confusion by abandoning the priesthood, the religious life or even the Church itself."[89] Dulles was not happy with McBrien's single-minded explanation of complex and complicated current events. Nor was Dulles pleased with McBrien's almost exclusive emphasis on "remaking" the church, giving little attention to the church as mystery and as a place of prayer, worship, and religious experience.

Dulles ended his review with his litmus test for all reform proposals: Would they make the church more Christian and more prophetic, and would they render the members of the church more loyal to Christ and more open to the Spirit than under present conditions? Questions like this periodically occurred in Dulles' reviews and in his essays and books when he did not want to attack a position directly or when he wanted to critique the dogmatic partialism of an approach, whether of the right or the left.

McBrien was unhappy with the review, particularly because none of Dulles' enthusiasm in the original dust jacket blurb (which did not reach the publisher in time for publication) made it into the review. McBrien complained to Dulles that his review would "give many of the bishops just the excuse they need to ignore both the book and its message." Dulles "fortunately" had maintained "some credibility with many of the moderately conservative bishops," making his review even more significant among that group.[90] McBrien correctly sensed how Dulles' review would be used by some conservative Catholics—as part of a more general assault on McBrien's theology.

The two theologians were friends and had a mutual respect for one another. McBrien did not expect that Dulles would whitewash his book if he found flaws in it, and he did not expect that the rather negative review would ultimately harm their relationship. Dulles responded to McBrien's concerns by outlining his distaste for the genre of dust jacket blurbs that did not allow for qualifying comments about a book. Dulles, moreover, was quite frank about his second and more cautious reading of the book.

> I may be wrong, and you have every right to think that I am wrong, but I have to say what I think I see. I think the book, while it makes a good and important contribution, does not help us as much as it might to get beyond the present polarization in the Church....If there is to be any dialogue with the traditionalists (as they may be called) one must speak to their real, and partly justified, anxieties. The task that your present book leaves undone, in my opinion, is to show that the kind of reforms you ask for are consonant with the Church at the deepest level of its being.

Dulles was not concerned, furthermore, with how his review might play among conservatives like the "*Wanderer* crowd. I frankly do not think much about them." Theologians, Dulles believed, needed to critique their colleagues' work, and he was "glad" that McBrien felt his "friendship is strong enough to bear the weight of a few theological differences. I would hate to think that my friends would not want me to say frankly what I think of their work, or would not feel free to challenge my views, even publicly."[91] Shortly after Dulles' review was published, he was informed that it had been quoted in *Our Sunday Visitor* for the purpose of attacking McBrien. The "extreme-right-wing" priest Albert J. Nevins had used Dulles' review to continue his journalistic assaults on McBrien.[92] Nevins quoted Dulles directly, as McBrien had anticipated, to justify Nevins' previous criticisms of McBrien. Nevins used Dulles' review to deny McBrien's claim that Nevins was biased. Even Dulles, one of McBrien's colleagues, Nevins retorted, was troubled by McBrien's understanding of the church.[93] Dulles responded to this review by writing the editor of *Our Sunday Visitor*, asking that to be fair the editor include two paragraphs from Dulles' review that indicated his favorable assessment of McBrien's book, but Dulles anticipated, correctly as it turned out, that his letter would not be published in the paper.[94]

Dulles' ecclesiology emerged from a contentious theological age and was conditioned somewhat by his personal participation in some major ecclesiastical consultative bodies. Many American bishops saw him as a major supporter of Vatican II and a voice of moderation within the church, and they appointed him to ecclesial, ecumenical, and advisory committees in the late 1960s and early 1970s. He became a theological advisor to a number of bishops and episcopal projects and in 1975 was sought out, for example, to provide theological advice on the *National Catechetical Directory*, critiquing drafts and providing detailed suggestions for improvements.[95]

In 1969, the United States Catholic Conference (USCC), the public policy arm of the National Conference of Catholic Bishops (NCCB), appointed Dulles to its newly constituted Advisory Council. The Advisory Council—consisting of five bishops, five diocesan priests, five religious priests, five women religious, and about forty laypeople—was a very diverse body representing different elements of the American Catholic community. Dulles considered the council "quite a miniature of the entire Catholic Church in the United States....I was fascinated with the different perspectives, finding out how different people were thinking." The purpose of the Advisory Council, as Dulles conceived of it, was to "give advice to the bishops on agendas for their semi-annual meetings, and we went over the agendas and made recommendations—whether we approved, disapproved, or wanted changes on the documents that they were preparing."[96]

The Advisory Council met about twice a year and periodically made suggestions and provided advice to the administrative arm of the USCC. The council suggested in 1974, for example, that the bishops establish a Catholic-Moslem dialogue. It advised the bishops, among other things, on shared responsibility in the church, bad conscience marriages, the mission of the USCC, and the advisability of holding a national pastoral council. Dulles was periodically asked, too, to prepare talks that bishops were to give to the full assembly of bishops, as he once did for Joseph Cardinal Bernardin.[97]

As the bicentennial of the United States approached, the bishops considered whether or not they should convoke a national pastoral council to celebrate the centennial. They asked the Advisory Council to determine whether or not such a council would be beneficial and asked the members to provide them with the pros and cons of holding one. At a meeting on May 2, 1970, Dulles suggested that the council hold an interdisciplinary symposium to examine the feasibility of convoking a national pastoral council.[98] In August 1970, in Chicago, therefore, the council organized an interdisciplinary consultation. Dulles gave the plenary address, "The Idea of a National Pastoral Council," at the meeting, outlining the canonical definitions of councils, the theological warrants in Vatican II, the postconciliar developments especially in the Dutch Church, and the issues (purposes, agenda, structure, membership, procedures, authority, relationship to other ecclesial bodies, and objections) that needed to be considered. The consultation published for the bishops various benefits as well as serious objections that could be envisioned in holding a council.[99] In October, Dulles prepared a paper on "The Authority of a National Pastoral Council," outlining various issues that needed to be considered.[100] In September 1971, after considering the issues involved, the members of the Advisory Council recommended that the bishops convene such a council.[101]

The recommendation had little effect one way or another because, as Dulles has said, "There were signals from Rome that they were unhappy with the idea of a national pastoral council. The Dutch Pastoral Council was in the background here." Between 1965 and 1970, the Dutch Catholic Church held six sessions of the Dutch Pastoral Council, a representative group of liberal Dutch Catholics, to implement Vatican II. The Dutch council proposed some rather radical changes in liturgy, use of mass media, catechesis, diocesan administration, and social justice.[102] Because of Rome's fear of such councils, the American bishops decided not to call a national pastoral council, but they still wanted to celebrate in some major way the nation's bicentennial, so they put the question to the Advisory Council: What was a legitimate alternative? Dulles was "in favor of something more doctrinal. But others wanted something else. Sister Marie Augusta Neal from Emmanuel College in Boston was very strongly influenced by liberation theologians, and she proposed something more along the lines of social action."[103] By 1974, therefore, the bishops had decided on what was denominated "Call to Action," a national meeting of representatives of the American Catholic Church to be held in Detroit in 1976. Dulles' involvement in the Advisory Council deepened his sense of the state of American Catholicism at the national level and conditioned his ecclesiological reflections.

During the 1960s and early 1970s, Dulles also took part in ecumenical endeavors that contributed to the development and shape of his ecclesiology. He periodically attended meetings of the International Jesuit Ecumenists in 1969 and 1971 and of the Faith and Order Commission of the World Council of Churches (WCC) in 1971 and chaired a Catholic Theological Society of America (CTSA) committee that examined various statements of numerous bilateral ecumenical conversations in 1971. That same year the bishops appointed him to the Lutheran/Catholic Dialogue in the United States.

Models of the Church

Dulles' experiences with the ecumenical movement, increasing diversity of opinion in the Catholic Church, varied conflicts with ecclesiastical authority, dissent and authoritarian backlashes, varying rates of reform in the church and resistance to innovation, and opposing interpretations of the intent of Vatican II—all these experiences within the post–Vatican II church helped to provide the immediate context in which Dulles wrote his *Models of the Church*. His theology engaged not only the biblical and historical foundations of the church but the needs of contemporary Christians, and as such, it was conditioned by the events of the 1960s and early

1970s. Yet, because it was rooted in traditional sources, it transcended to some extent the times in which it was written.

After 1964, Dulles was becoming more widely known throughout the Catholic Church and beyond as a reliable interpreter of Vatican II and a moderate voice on the side of post–Vatican II reforms and theological creativity. It was within this context that John J. Delaney, an editor at Doubleday Publishing and creator of Doubleday's Image book imprint on Catholicism, solicited Dulles in 1971 to write a book on the theology of the church that would address some of the major ecclesiological issues of the day.

Even before Delaney's invitation to write a text on ecclesiology, Dulles had been toying with the idea of constructing a theology of the church based on a synthesis of various biblical images and historical theological models or paradigms. For some time, he had been using a models approach in theology to acknowledge the varieties of theological perspectives on revelation, faith, and apologetics. By the early 1970s he also applied that approach to ecclesiology, and one of his first major attempts to do so was in a paper he presented to the international meeting of Jesuit Ecumenists in August 1971. That paper, later published in *Theological Studies*,[104] outlined what he considered to be the five major types of ecclesial unity (substantialist, dualist, actualist, eschatologist, and secularist) that had been devised by theologians and church officials in the past hundred years. Later, on November 10, 1972, at a lecture at Gordon-Conwell Seminary, as he examined the relationship between the church and salvation, he used an approach that clearly reflected the institutional, communitarian, sacramental, kerygmatic, and servant categories that he would later use in *Models of the Church*.[105] These five models of the church were based on different biblical images and schools of theology, and all of them could be found in the various documents of the council. By 1971, moreover, he was handing out notes in his class on ecclesiology that incorporated his models methodology.[106] He described various models (that is, ideal types) of the church and put them into dialectical relationship with one another to underline the benefits and limits of such conceptual formulations and to accentuate the fundamental mystery of the church of Christ. One of his students recalled that Dulles "was not the most exciting teacher, though he was very very good both in terms of what he provided from class notes and in his own lecture presentation—very good in bringing together what were and what are the various kinds of positions and ways of thinking through different issues."[107]

By the early 1970s, Dulles was using a models approach as a pedagogical device for introducing students and his readers to the development and paradigmatic shifts in perspective that occurred in the history of theology. But the models approach was not only a pedagogical device for understanding major shifts in historical conceptualization; it was helpful for categorizing the pluralism that existed in contemporary theology. Dulles used models ultimately, however, to forge a theological consensus or synthesis in the community of theologians and in the church—a synthesis that provided for the unity of faith and allowed for a diversity of theological expression.

Dulles wrote the first draft of *Models of the Church* very rapidly in the fall of 1972,[108] polished it during a sabbatical semester teaching at the Gregorian University in the spring of 1973, and published it in 1974. *Models* was not a systematic theology of the church, as Dulles has admitted, but rather "an introduction that might be called a 'dialectics.'"[109] To some extent the book aimed to put different positions in a dialectical relationship, and in this respect it developed "from my scholastic background—the desire to group the *'opiniones'* by schools and to make sure that one had taken advantage of what was valid in them and answered the difficulties they would raise against one's own position."[110] *Models* was primarily an exercise in ecclesiological method.[111]

The book was in reality a period piece in that it aimed explicitly to foster a kind of theological pluralism "that heals and unifies."[112] He wanted to put various models or images or theologies of the church (Protestant as well as Catholic, contemporary as well as historical) into dialogue with one another with the hope that such an approach could get beyond the limitations of particular or isolated or single-minded views of the church. Putting various images of the church together, as had the council, contributed to the ecumenical intent of Dulles' project and underscored the basic fact that the church was itself a mystery that transcended the limitations of singular human images and particular theological constructions or formulations.

In an age of great pluralism, diversity, polarization, and conflict, a models approach to ecclesiology could prove fruitful, Dulles believed, for healing and unifying the church and for enabling people to practice tolerance and live with the current situation. A single model of the church could no longer achieve these aims. In the past, a single model of the church became what Thomas Kuhn, in the realm of science, called a "paradigm." A particular image of the church became a paradigm when it successfully incorporated much of the biblical and historical tradition and solved many ideological and practical problems. Such single models were able to solve issues that previous paradigms were unable to resolve, but in unraveling one set of problems, the new paradigm created others not entirely foreseen in the construction and reception of the new one. Dulles perceived this general principle to be operative in the church's history, particularly since the Protestant Reformation. In that period the church's self-understanding shifted from one major paradigm to another: from the perfect society of the post-Reformation period, to the mystical body of the 1940s and 1950s, to the people of God of Vatican II's *Lumen gentium*, to the servant or healer of Vatican II's *Gaudium et spes*. Dulles presented five different, though complementary, models of the church, no one of which was dispensable and each of which interpenetrated and qualified the other. It was his attempt to respond to the growing discord and pluralism within the church. It was also his contribution to the greater unity between the church and other Christian and religious communities.[113]

Dulles' five major models (the church as institution, as mystical communion, as sacrament, as herald, and as servant) were outlined in terms of their strengths and weaknesses, applied to certain theological issues (eschatology, the marks of the true church, ecumenical relations, ministry, and revelation), and evaluated in light of one another. The first three models were on the church's being, the last two on its mission. The first three models, moreover, reflected a quasi-Hegelian relationship of thesis, antithesis, and synthesis. "Thus the sacramental model retrieves and sublimates the valid elements in the institutional model as well as those of the communion model. The sacramental model therefore cannot be strictly speaking opposed to either of the first two, but in its two-level structure it avoids the distortions to which the first two, taken in isolation, are subject."[114]

Dulles wanted to harmonize what was best in each of the models without overlooking the inconsistencies and indeed the conflicts and contradictions between the different models. All things in the models could not be reconciled. While evaluating the different models, he also predicted that certain trends (modernization of structures, increased ecumenical unity, more internal pluralism, ecclesiastical decisions that were more provisional than immutable, ecclesiastical governance more by persuasion than by force) already evident in the church's most recent history would continue to influence the church in the future. These predictions represented the optimism of church reformers in the decade immediately after the council, but Dulles acknowledged the "staying power of the conservatives, and their determination to adhere to ancient forms." The call "to confront the world of today" would no doubt be blunted by the weight of the church's large historical heritage and by the conservative reactionaries. Dulles' predictions about the future, therefore, were modified by his sense of historical realism—the presence of a considerable conservative force in the church, a trend that was evident in the postconciliar era.[115] *Models*, though, was clearly on the side of the church reformers who called upon the church "to confront the world of today."[116]

It seems fair to say that although Dulles found many strengths in the institutional paradigm, he was in 1974 decidedly negative in his assessment of this "exclusive" model of the church, reflecting to a large extent the anti-institutionalism of the 1960s and early 1970s in the United States. He wanted to bring the five ideal types into a comprehensive synthesis, clearly favoring the sacramental model because he believed it had the greatest power of incorporating the strengths of the others.

Models was well received in the United States and the English-speaking world. In many Catholic seminary, college, and university courses it became a standard resource for courses on ecclesiology. The text went through several reprintings, editions, and translations, and thirty years after it was first published, it continued to be a useful resource for introducing Catholics and others to the various ways in which the church had been and continued to be conceived in the various schools of theology.

The book reviews reflected the diversity of theological opinion in the academy, although most were generally positive. Many reviewers focused on Dulles' creative and innovative use of a models methodology in ecclesiology to deal with the diversity and polarization in church and society. Some reviews noted favorably Dulles' view that the institutional model could no longer be treated as primary; others thought that he had not been critical enough of the dangers inherent in that model, and still others believed that he had caricatured that model.[117] Although one reviewer asserted that Dulles was too liberal and his descriptive use of models only added to the diversity and confusion in the church,[118] another thought him so careful and low-keyed that he had to be tagged a "conservative," the kind of person Pope Paul VI might appoint to the International Theological Commission (an appointment that would indeed happen, but twenty years after this review).[119]

Ecumenism

Since his days as a student in the theologate, Dulles had been involved in ecumenical concerns, and after his dissertation, he continued his theoretical interests in ecumenism and became a participant in the movement in the United States. Ecumenism was an aspect of ecclesiology, but it was a primary focus of his own research and writing prior to his more explicit attention to ecclesiology. In 1968, he admitted that "for a decade now I have felt with increasing urgency that Catholic theology cannot be fully catholic unless it is constantly nourished by fruitful interchange with the theology of all the churches of the East and West. According to Vatican Council II, these churches are not external to the one Church of Christ."[120] Throughout his life as a professor of theology, Dulles saw the practical and the theoretical aspects of ecumenism as intertwined.

Almost as soon as he got to Woodstock as a professor of theology in 1960, Dulles became involved in the ecumenical movement. On January 5, 1962, prior to the council but in response to

Pope John XXIII's call to Christian unity, the new archbishop of Baltimore, Lawrence Joseph Shehan, established a Commission on Ecumenism (later called the Archdiocesan Commission on Christian Unity), and appointed Dulles, among others (for example, Raymond Brown, Walter Burghardt, Gustave Weigel, Harry Kirwin, David Maguire), to it. Baltimore was the first Catholic diocese in the country to organize such a commission, and it became something of a model for other diocesan commissions established during and after the council.[121] Dulles continued to be active on the commission from 1962 to 1970, after which he became much more involved in ecumenical activities at the national level. The commission engaged local Protestant ministers and churches, developed bibliographies, and organized, together with the Maryland Council of Churches, Christian Unity weeks, and in 1964 sponsored a national workshop on ecumenism for other dioceses and interested persons.

After the council, Dulles was appointed consultor to the Papal Secretariat for Dialogue with Non-Believers (now called the Pontifical Council for Dialogue with Non-Believers), an appointment he held from 1966 to 1973. Pope Paul VI had created the secretariat on April 9, 1965, before the end of the council, and appointed Cardinal Franz König as president and other cardinals, bishops, and theological consultors as members. The secretariat had the task of studying atheism and unbelief, encouraging ways of dialoguing with unbelievers, and thereby leading believers themselves to a fuller recognition of human values and a better understanding of matters that concerned religion.[122] Dulles met periodically with American members of the secretariat, including John Courtney Murray and Bishop John Wright of Pittsburgh, and periodically commented on papers prepared by the secretariat, but he never went to any meetings in Rome. "Frankly," he reported, "I didn't think it was worth the time or the money [to go to Rome], because my contribution would have been so slight." Bishop Wright was in charge of the American branch of the secretariat, but he did not organize meetings with any nonbelievers, and the thing "died on the vine" in the United States.[123]

Dulles also participated in the third and fourth meetings of the international congresses of Jesuit Ecumenists. He attended the third meeting (October 5–8, 1969), at North Aurora, Illinois, outside of Chicago, offering a few oral observations on intercommunion, the topic for that meeting, that were later published in *Diakonia*.[124] At the meeting of these professional Jesuit ecumenists, Dulles raised a few questions about the possibility of intercommunion. His intention here was purely speculative, seeking responses to questions that he believed needed to be addressed by professionals in the field. He asked, for example, whether a valid ordination was absolutely necessary for a valid Eucharist. He also suggested that decisions on the possibility of intercommunion ought not to be a matter of legislation but a matter "of discernment in the existential situation."[125] Invoking discernment, of course, Ignatian as it was, could lead to all kinds of flexibility, but he was well aware that the discernment process ultimately belonged to the bishops, and one or two of them in Europe (particularly Léon-Arthur Elchinger, the bishop of Strasbourg) had been most open to allowing intercommunion in specific cases.[126]

In the late 1960s and early 1970s, Dulles had great confidence in and optimism about the emerging unity between the Catholic and Lutheran churches. In 1969, in an era of experimentation and ecumenical openness, Dulles, together with two Lutheran minister-theologians, Carl E. Braaten and Wolfhart Pannenberg, met together for ten days at John Carroll University to give the "Tuohy Lectures." While there, they concelebrated a Eucharist and gave communion to Catholics and other Christians attending the service. Like some other Catholics of the day, Dulles believed that eucharistic sharing in this fashion was acceptable as a reflection of the developing unity of the churches and indeed as a means of furthering that unity. The concelebration, a violation of canon law, reflected his willingness to move the church in new directions, consistent with what he perceived to be the reforming direction of the council. In 2007, however, when he relayed this event to me, he was obviously embarrassed by what he had done in contravention of the church's canonical tradition. He characterized this experience as one of the "crazy things" that was going on in the 1960s. In this period of "confusion" after the council, he, like some other progressive theologians, was open to a variety of new things, and he anticipated what he and others thought was the direction the church would eventually take.[127]

That Cleveland concelebration event was not only uncanonical but also especially uncustomary for the normally cautious and ecclesially conscious Dulles. In none of his published or unpublished writings did he ever address or try to justify concelebration with ministers from other Christian traditions. The possibilities of intercommunion, however, came up again and again in his writings after the John Carroll concelebration, and in these subsequent writings, he became much more cautious than he had been there. In 1973, for example, while summarizing ecumenical statements on intercommunion and the mutual recognition of valid ministries of the different churches, Dulles indicated that certain conditions (not fulfilled at the John Carroll event) would have to be met before intercommunion would be possible. First of all, each church would have to be prepared "to authorize the ministers of the other to preach and celebrate the Eucharist on a regular basis for the faithful of its own community. This would presuppose a fundamental consensus between the churches not only regarding ministry but also regarding all those doctrines, structures, and principles considered essential to Christian faith and life." The present discipline in the Catholic Church, however, forbidding Catholics from ever receiving the Eucharist in a Protestant ceremony, tended to give the "false impression" that the Catholic Church "denies any spiritual efficacy to the Lord's Supper as celebrated by Protestants." He agreed, as he had already done to some extent in his dissertation, with those Catholic theologians who thought it was no longer justifiable theologically for Christians to look upon each other's communion "as devoid of saving value."[128]

At the present time, though, when the churches were in a state of significant doctrinal disagreement, intercommunion would be a "false sign." Allowing intercommunion "would obscure the essential relationship between Church and Eucharist." But Dulles did leave room for some limited intercommunion: "As long as the churches themselves are divided, no more than limited Eucharistic sharing would seem to be appropriate."[129] The Eucharist as a sign of unity generally argued against intercommunion, but the Eucharist as a means of unity argued in its favor, as the Decree on

Ecumenism seemed to indicate. Dulles, however, had problems with this supposed or implied separation of sign and means. The Eucharist, in his theology, as in that of Karl Rahner's, communicated grace by signifying.[130]

The Fourth International Congress of Jesuit Ecumenists (Dublin, August 16–20, 1971), focused on "Diversity in the Doctrine of the Church," and Dulles prepared a formal paper on five different models of Christian unity, reflecting different models of the church and various schools of theology.[131] Four of the five models of church unity originated outside of the Catholic Church, but all five were evident here and there in the conciliar documents. Vatican II, Dulles argued, opened itself to a variety of expressions of unity, not always reconciling one with the other. Unity is conceived in terms of different views of the nature of the true church: Catholics have traditionally and even at Vatican II argued that the Catholic Church is substantially identified with the church of Christ—interpreting that unity either in an exclusivist or an inclusivist fashion. Other notions of church unity focused on the perfect inner, spiritual, and invisible unity as opposed to the imperfect, visible unity; or the fullest manifestation of unity realized in the faith and worship of the gathered community; or unity perceived of as ever unrealizable until the eschaton; or unity achieved in common service to the needs of the world. These five different types of unity, not mutually exclusive, manifested the conceptual pluralism within the Christian community and underlined again the mystery of that unity that belonged to the divine-human communion that constituted the church. Dulles reiterated in this article a recurring theme in his quasi-apophatic theology of the 1960s and early 1970s: his emphasis on the divine mystery at the heart of Christianity and the manifold possibilities for human articulations of that mystery.

Prior to the Dublin meeting, between August 2 and 13, Dulles had attended the World Council of Churches' Faith and Order meeting at Louvain. Earlier, Dulles had written Jan Cardinal Willebrands, president of the Secretariat for Christian Unity, whom he had known personally since 1958, requesting from him an invitation to be one of the Catholic observers at the Faith and Order meeting. He believed that his participation as an observer at that meeting would be of assistance to him in his ecumenical activities in the United States.[132] He received the invitation he solicited, attended the meeting, and prepared a lengthy summary of the proceedings for Catholic theologians in the United States.[133]

The theme of the meeting was "The Unity of the Church and the Unity of Mankind." The theme developed out of a concern with three different questions: What is the function of the Church in relation to the unifying purpose of God for the world? What is the unity of the Church? What is the unity of mankind? The majority at the meeting (excluding the Orthodox members), in Dulles' opinion, seemed to favor less concentration on the traditional doctrinal and ecclesiological concerns of the Faith and Order movement and more focus on the theology of life and action, or they preferred rather to consider the traditional doctrinal and ecclesiological issues in the context of the total needs of "mankind for liberation, healing, and development"—a focus Dulles did not entirely support.[134] He was also mildly critical of the great variety of theological issues that did come in for consideration during the meeting. He would have opted for a narrower focus in order to move gradually toward greater consensus. He also intimated that many of the issues were being discussed by churchmen who had no particular theological competence in the areas they were discussing. But such was the nature of these meetings. All in all, though, he believed that the meeting raised important questions that were being seriously pursued in a collegial atmosphere by fellow Christians from various denominations. It was significant ecumenical work.

The Louvain meeting was the first time that Catholics attended as members of the Faith and Order Commission—an anomaly of sorts, Dulles believed, because Catholics were not members of the parent body, the WCC. Only 8 of the 140 official members of the Faith and Order Commission, however, were Catholics, and of those eight only one, Raymond E. Brown, was from the United States. Dulles himself was invited as an observer. Catholic appointments to Faith and Order, in Dulles' opinion, needed to be rethought; too many Catholic members were from countries that did not have a numerous Protestant population. Catholic active participation in the discussions, moreover, was minimal, as was particularly appropriate, in Dulles' view, for their first official attendance at a Faith and Order meeting.

The meeting afforded Dulles the opportunity to make new acquaintances and renew old friendships. At the meeting, he met European theologians, like Fr. Joseph Ratzinger of Regensburg, whom he had not met before, and reestablished communication with others, like Max Thurian of Taizé, whom he had previously met. The meeting also deepened his interest and knowledge of the international ecumenical movement. In 1982, he would again return to a Faith and Order meeting in Lima, Peru, where a significant ecumenical statement on baptism, Eucharist, and ministry was developed.[135]

One of the reasons Dulles sought an invitation to the Faith and Order meeting at Louvain was his increasing participation at the national level in the ecumenical movement. In June 1971, Carl J. Peter, president of the Catholic Theological Society of America, appointed Dulles to chair a research committee[136] to report on the eight postconciliar bilateral conversations between Catholics and other denominations.[137] The research committee was given a mandate to investigate issues and make recommendations for the future of these dialogues—recommendations that could be passed on to the Bishops' Committee for Ecumenical Affairs. This was one way in which a professional theological organization could provide assistance to the bishops in their assessment of their ecumenical endeavors in the United States. In a letter to Dulles, Peter outlined the kinds of questions to be considered:

> Is there consistency or not between the various positions taken by Roman Catholic theologians in different consultations? Are there serious issues of division that have not been faced either by mutual agreement or perhaps even by oversight? Are there convincing grounds theologically for the conclusions reached? If not, are there at least sufficient grounds for taking the conclusions reached with the utmost seriousness and for testing them further? Finally, what future steps are called for in the view of the Committee?"[138]

The committee examined the various bilateral statements, met twice for all-day meetings in January and May 1972, and thereafter Dulles prepared a draft report of their conclusions, a draft that was revised by committee members and then submitted to the CTSA Board of Directors, who, as was becoming customary with their commissioned study reports, "accepted" the report "without expressing agreement or disagreement with the contents."[139]

The theologians had a difficult time trying to summarize the bilaterals because there was no overall organization, no uniform method, no consistent developmental or progressive approach to doctrinal or pastoral issues, and no issues that were universally discussed in the various bilaterals. Each of the dialogues went its own separate way, focusing on issues that were of apparent concern to the individual groups. One could not accuse the bilaterals of being controlled from above or of having some kind of monolithic structure. They appeared to be free-wheeling discussions without much direction from the national episcopal body or from the various denominational judicatories. The committee's report reflected the diversity that existed in the various dialogues in their understanding of their own goals and their approaches to various issues: doctrines of ordained ministry, status of women, doctrines of the Eucharist, intercommunion, interreligious marriages, and methods of doctrinal agreement. These issues, of course, were not discussed in each of the dialogues. Only three bilaterals, for example, even raised the issue of the goals of their consultation. The committee, though, described and summarized the various documents that had been published, outlined the points of convergence and divergence, evaluated the statements, and then made recommendations for future consideration.

Among the recommendations, the committee suggested that the bilaterals pay much more explicit attention in the future to explicating their own goals and methods, "pursue a systematic plan rather than to jump discontinuously from one topic to another," and that the national Catholic bishops implement in some concrete ways the principles accepted by the bilateral groups; otherwise the dialogues would remain pastorally fruitless for the general Christian population. The committee, too, expressed agreement with the Presbyterian-Catholic dialogue that there were "no clear obstacles to this [the ordination of women] in revelation or Christian dogma" and commended that bilateral for its "courageous" effort in taking up the issue, the only bilateral to do so. But the committee also recommended that the women's ordination issue needed further study. In its general conclusion the committee acknowledged what it saw as the real achievements in the bilaterals.

They have helped to overcome prejudices, to establish friendship and trust, to suggest realistic ecumenical goals, and to prompt a healthy reexamination of the doctrinal positions that have become habitual in the various confessional traditions. The consensus statements studied in this report attest to important convergences in traditionally disputed areas, notably the doctrine of the ministry and the Eucharist.[140]

The experience on the committee proved very fruitful for Dulles as he prepared himself for his episcopal appointment to the Lutheran/Catholic Dialogue.

The bilateral study committee judged that the Lutheran/Catholic Dialogue was "in many ways the most exemplary of the consultations." The publications from that dialogue included not only the consensus statements but also the working papers, and both reflected the high theological caliber of the participants. The statements, moreover, were careful to mention not only the agreements but the serious and lingering disagreements, and above all, the dialogue progressed systematically "from baptism, through Eucharist, to ministry, and in its present phase to teaching authority and papacy."[141]

By the end of 1974, Dulles was in the thick of the ecumenical movement. He was cautiously optimistic about its eventual historical, and certainly its eschatological, outcome, but he was also well aware of the difficulties that had to be faced honestly in ecumenical dialogues with respect to doctrine and practice. The movement toward unity demanded careful theological research, fidelity to the past, creative discernment in the present, and openness to the pluralism of Christian formulations that pointed to and symbolized the Christian mystery. During these early years of his involvement in the ecumenical movement, Dulles became widely known as an ecumenical theologian because of his numerous publications in popular journals of Catholic opinion, like *America* and *Commonweal*, as well as in professional periodicals. He was also on the ecumenical circuit during these early years of ecumenical enthusiasm, giving lectures and keynoting workshops on Christian unity.[142]

In the course of these early years, Dulles insisted repeatedly that agreement on doctrine was crucial for any viable Christian unity, but he also relativized the significance of this issue by emphasizing the existence and validity of doctrinal and systematic pluralism, the historically conditioned nature of dogmatic and confessional statements, and the need for sociocultural adaptations of these historically conditioned statements of the past. Because the Christian reality so far transcended human abilities to conceptualize, it was not necessary to insist, in moving toward doctrinal agreement, on a common system of conceptualization or terminology. It was possible to allow a "certain diversity in the theological formulation of the one faith."[143] Vatican II, moreover, had acknowledged a "hierarchy of truths," meaning that certain dogmatic declarations (like the Marian dogmas) of the past were not as central to the faith as some others. For this reason, Dulles suggested in 1974 that anathemas be lifted on the two most recent Catholic dogmatic statements on Mary's immaculate conception and assumption.[144] That proposal, he believed, would ease the path toward Christian unity. Dulles' position was not one of historicism, or doctrinal relativism, or theological indifferentism, but it sounded so to some Catholic conservatives who held on to earlier Catholic notions of doctrinal fixity.

That Dulles was not a theological historicist is somewhat evident in his critique of the Congregation for the Doctrine of the Faith's (CDF) *Mysterium ecclesiae* (1973) as an ecumenically oblivious document. Although the document acknowledged the historicity of the human subject and the conditioned nature of dogmatic statements, it was clearly intended to warn certain theologians who had minimized or relativized the singular importance of the Roman Catholic Church. To counter this tendency, the declaration focused on the institutional perfection, or relative perfection, of the Catholic Church, and identified the church of Christ with the Roman Catholic Church. Although Dulles appreciated its acknowledgment of the historicity of human subjects and dogmatic statements, he was highly critical of its "reactionary" tenor, insensitivity to Vatican II's ecumenical thrusts, and its lagging "behind the best theology of the day." Dulles implied that it would set back the ecumenical movement if its provisions were fully accepted. While concluding his commentary on *Mysterium ecclesiae*, Dulles was unusually critical: "The philosophy behind this declaration is still predominantly juridical, clerical, authoritarian and objectivistic—somewhat outdated."[145] *Mysterium ecclesiae* was another sign of an authoritarian backlash in the postconciliar period, but it could not ultimately arrest the movement toward reform and Christian unity. These temporary setbacks, in Dulles' opinion, were mere bumps along the road to more openness and creative theological reformulation.

Dulles' interpretation of the CDF document and his critical appraisal did not go unchallenged. Two priests who were obvious admirers of Dulles' theology took issue with his understanding of the relationship of the church of Christ to the Catholic Church. Dulles asserted that the declaration had subtly departed from Vatican II by claiming "a very close, or even absolute, identity between the Church of Christ and the Roman Catholic Church." The council had distinguished between the church of Christ and the Catholic Church, stating that the church of Christ "subsisted in" but was not exclusively identified with the Catholic Church, an interpretation Dulles reiterated frequently in the late 1960s and early 1970s.[146]

One clerical opponent, Daniel S. Hamilton, insisted that whereas the council taught that "elements of the Church of Christ exist outside the Catholic Church, the Church of Christ subsists only in the Catholic Church." He believed that Dulles had overemphasized the distinction between the church of Christ and the Catholic Church. Another priest, Paul F. Palmer, SJ, charged that Dulles had relativized priestly powers in favor of priestly service. Dulles responded to his colleagues' measured criticism by maintaining that he had been deliberately provocative when he asserted that Vatican II, unlike Vatican I, had not claimed that Christ had instituted the Catholic Church. Dulles had not denied, however, any sacramental powers within the priesthood but preferred more than his colleagues to emphasize the service dimension of the priestly office.[147] In his later years, Dulles would revisit these issues and modify his emphases.

Christian unity could also be hastened, Dulles believed, if the various churches involved in the church's missionary efforts could work together rather than compete in that enterprise. The church of Christ was missionary by nature, and ecumenical cooperation in evangelical efforts would enhance the sign value of the unity that was already present in the church of Christ and would serve as a means for increasing and deepening that unity.[148] Cooperation in missionary evangelism included, in his opinion, common proclamation, mutual service to material needs, and dialogue with peoples outside the Christian tradition.

Christian unity could be achieved by what Dulles periodically called "secular ecumenism"—that is, Christian active cooperation in serving the material needs of human beings and collaboration in bringing peace and justice to the contemporary world. This type of ecumenism—one that was less concerned about historical controversies between the churches and more focused on the realities and needs of modern life—was particularly appropriate in the United States, where Christians had a decidedly practical bent and an energy to go along with it, and it was also a feature of Vatican II's Church in the Modern World (*Gaudium et spes*; GS 1).[149]

Dulles and His Critics

Dulles' views on revelation, ecclesiology, and ecumenism did not go uncontested during these immediate post–Vatican II years. The ultra-conservative journals (*Triumph*, *Twin Circle*, and the *Wanderer*) periodically criticized him as a liberal reformer who was hypercritical of the past heritage of the church and excessively optimistic and uncritical in his acceptance of modern developments in thought. Some others, who found his theology generally acceptable, criticized his interpretations of the intentions of Vatican II and his ready willingness to minimize the conservative contributions at the council and the continuing relevance of some traditional positions that were included in the council documents.

Dulles also on occasion received private criticisms of his theological positions. One of his longtime friends from his days at St. Benedict Center in Boston, Bill Macomber, a fellow Jesuit, for example, wrote him after his talk on intercommunion before the

Jesuit Ecumenists in Illinois in 1969: "Our friendship is such as to authorize us to speak our minds to one another without fear of offending." Macomber went on to criticize the way Dulles interpreted the Decree on Ecumenism. Dulles had questioned whether, by acknowledging Protestant groups as ecclesial communities, the council implied that it also recognized their ministry. In Macomber's view, this was not the council's implication. He believed that the council did not recognize "their ordained ministers as true priests with the power to celebrate Mass validly." This implication may not have been Dulles' intention, but "your words lie open to an equivocal interpretation that goes far beyond your premises and the intentions of the council." As Macomber read the signs of "the present confused theological situation," he advised Dulles to avoid by all means "such possible equivocations."[150]

Dulles had raised the question about whether or not a validly ordained ministry was required for a valid Eucharist. Macomber found that question particularly unfortunate since the "teaching of the Church on this question [has] been clear and constant for at least the last sixteen centuries"—a valid ordination was necessary for a valid Mass. Dulles' habit of raising these kinds of questions, according to Macomber, was not merely a speculative enterprise but entertained possibilities that were unjustified and would increase not decrease the confusion in the contemporary theological world. "There are today in the United States altogether too many unbalanced Catholics that are quite ready to turn your theological possibility into an unquestionable certitude that can be used as a basis for practical realizations, even in defiance of the Church's authority." Macomber ended his private letter to Dulles by recommending that he inculcate in the young men he taught that "we can only receive revealed truth by humble docility to the Magisterium of the Church."[151] Dulles' positions did not go unchallenged by friend or foe. He had moved a great distance theologically since the days of his conversion to Catholicism in 1940, and his positions changed considerably after the council.

In a letter to J. Madison King, a Baptist theologian at Furman University, Dulles outlined the changes that he had undergone since he published his *Testimonial to Grace* (1946), a book that "is no longer the proper path for anyone to follow in the early seventies."

In that book and during the period of his conversion, Dulles wrote to King, "I was looking for a kind of authoritative guidance and stability and security which I now believe is not available to man in this world." He admitted that since the Vatican Council, "I have drastically revised my ideas about what the Catholic Church is and what it should be; and I now find myself completely at home in what I myself consider the Catholic Church to be." At the present time, he told King, he considered his own theological positions in line with theologians like Rahner, Edward Schillebeeckx, "and their disciples in all countries." Dulles knew that he was living in dangerous but exciting times, and he knew there would be many mistakes made within the Catholic Church, but he had hope. "I enjoy being a part of the new effort to bring Catholicism into the modern world—a perilous effort and one that will result in the loss of many beautiful things inherited from the middle ages. I hope we do manage to keep alive the robust faith which produced all that beauty and that culture."[152]

To a theological correspondent who had argued for the infallibility of *Humanae vitae* and had taken issue with Dulles' notion of infallibility, Dulles responded with his usual critical distinctions about what constituted an infallible statement. He did not like heresy hunting in the church, and he periodically called for a legitimate pluralism of opinion on certain matters: "It seems to me," he wrote, "that at this point it is impossible to read out of the Church the vast numbers of Catholics who do not accept *Humanae vitae*. Cannot we live with different views on some matters among those who are united in accepting what is clearly divine revelation?" And, then, not to be apodictic, he added, "While I seem to be prepared to tolerate more diversity than seems admissible to you, I respect your right to defend and urge your own views."[153] Throughout most of his life, Dulles could communicate with people on all sides of the theological spectrum, and he periodically called, as he did here, for toleration of legitimate opinions for the sake of ecclesial unity. The tensions in theological positions contributed to the development of doctrine, and tolerance of legitimate differences was necessary for a theologian's humility about his or her own opinions.

In the immediate postconciliar period, in the midst of rapid and radical changes in society and church, Dulles hammered out his theology to meet the times as he conceived them. From the tragic murder of one president to the humiliating downfall of another, American society experienced something of a cultural revolution. From the end of Vatican II until the mid-1970s, the American Catholic Church had its own religious revolution. Rapid and unprecedented changes in society and the Catholic Church gave rise to pluralism and tremendous diversity of opinion, creating polarization and confusion in the body politic and within the church.

Within this context, Dulles considered it his role as a theologian to explain change and provide room for a diversity of opinion within the church in a way that helped to overcome the polarization and confusion that many in the Catholic Church experienced during these years. His own theology made room for change itself and for a legitimate internal pluralism.

Dulles thought of his own theology in very much the same way he thought of the theology of Karl Rahner. Dulles was trying to "escape from the painful dilemma between a Modernistic immanentism and an anti-Modernist extrinsicism."[154] As a son of St. Ignatius, moreover, he wanted to put the best construction upon the theologians whose works he reviewed, trying to discover what was valuable in their perspectives while criticizing their limitations. Throughout the 1960s and early 1970s, for example, he reviewed much of the death-of-God literature and what was called "secular theology," finding in such immanent approaches to theology something of value for the times, but he also critiqued those approaches as devoid of much of the tradition's emphasis on divine transcendence. Some of those theologians seemed to think that "anything goes" as long as it was relevant to current needs. But, for the most part, he was on the side of those world-affirming theologies (for example, those of Bonhoeffer, Harvey Cox, Teilhard de Chardin, and the Church in the Modern World) that emphasized divine immanence without denying transcendence. Although he appreciated the realism of neo-scholasticism, his criticisms during these years fell heavily upon the antimodernist, neo-scholastic manual theology of the immediate past. That theology was nonhistorical, excessively objectivist, essentialist, propositional, and devoid of a sense of human subjectivity.

In the midst of tremendous change and polarization, Dulles conceived of himself as a moderate theologian who was trying to hold together a middle ground in the theological community between those he periodically designated "rigid conservatives" and those he tagged "radical reformers." The contemporary theologian's task, he believed, was ultimately one of spiritual discernment—meaning that the theologian had the responsibility in faith to discern the meaning of the biblical and historical tradition and apply it to the needs of the day in order to keep alive the heritage of faith and build up the church in the present.

Woodstock Theological Center

The decision in 1973 to close Woodstock was a hard one for Dulles, but he accepted it. It was not clear at the time, however, what the closing meant. Could there still be a Woodstock research center in New York after the seminary was shut down? Could the Woodstock library be preserved in connection with a research center? These and other questions remained unanswered for much of 1973 and the early months of 1974.

After the spring 1973 semester at the Gregorian, Dulles returned to the United States to teach a summer course at the University of San Francisco, where he had regularly taught in the summers in the years after the council. In the fall of 1973, he had a sabbatical and then returned to teach at Woodstock for the 1974 spring semester, the last semester he would teach at Woodstock.

From the beginning of the discussion of Woodstock's closing, there was intense interest in preserving something of Woodstock's presence in New York and especially its theological library, one of the best Catholic theological libraries in the country at the time. Various Jesuits, including Dulles, made proposals for keeping Woodstock in the Morningside Heights area and continuing it as a theological research center associated with Columbia University and other educational institutions in the area. The Jesuit general, too, supported some kind of continued theological apostolate in New York City, as was evident in the Dulles-Burghardt 1973 meeting with him.[155] In October 1973, Dulles prepared memos on Woodstock's continued presence in the city, proposing at one point a Woodstock Theological Center, composed of about ten theologians who would interact with various Protestant and Jewish scholars and with various disciplines outside of theology in their research on questions of particular interest to church and society. He also suggested, more specifically, that Woodstock could be a center for ecumenical theology like some ecumenical centers in Europe.[156]

Union Theological Seminary, Fordham University, and Yale all sought the placement of Woodstock's library in their institutions. In the early months of 1973, Dulles initially favored keeping the library in New York. Decisions were moving very quickly, though, because Woodstock was to be closed after the 1974–1975 school year. The various proposals to keep Woodstock in New York as a theological research center did not win favor with the New York and Maryland provincials, and they eventually decided to preserve the library, move it to Georgetown University, and establish there a center for theological research.

As soon as the decision to close Woodstock was publicly announced, Dulles began receiving invitations from colleges and universities to join their theology faculties. He was going to have to move to another school, and he had to decide which one of the invitations he should accept. In the past, he had received many invitations to teach at other institutions. In October 1972, for example, he was invited to apply for the position of dean at the newly established School of Religious Studies at the Catholic University of America. In response to this request, he indicated that he had no intention of leaving Woodstock, but "it may be that there will soon be decisions which could affect the future of Woodstock in one way or another, and therefore I would not want to rule out completely at this point a post such as your committee is proposing."[157]

In the early part of 1974, when it became clear that Dulles would move on to another institution, he sat down with the provincial to discuss the various invitations he had received and to decide which one would be most acceptable. A combination of factors helped him decide to accept the invitation to the Catholic University of America. As he later told one correspondent, he thought that Catholic University had "the best graduate faculty in Catholic theology" in the United States and he had some good friends on that faculty.[158] In the process of decision making, he asked his provincial, "Which one [of the invitations] do you want me to accept? He said he wanted me to go to Washington, to go to The Catholic University and at the same time to work with Walter Burghardt in setting up the Woodstock Theological Center."[159] In the summer of 1974, then, Dulles packed up and headed off to Washington, D.C., for his new appointment.

On Pentecost Sunday, May 1975, Dulles returned to New York City to give the homily for the liturgy that officially closed Woodstock. The homily, based on Acts 2:17 ("Your young men shall see visions, and your old men shall dream dreams"), put the closing into the larger framework of salvation history. The closing was in fact a new Pentecost for young and old Jesuits alike, who were to live in the Holy Spirit and bring "forth fruits worthy of Woodstock's rich tradition." The decision to close Woodstock was not one anyone at Woodstock desired, but the "history of salvation has taught us to rely not on our own strength but on the power that comes from above, not on our own devisings but on the 'vision that faith bestows.'" Not one to be mired in pessimism about the decision to close Woodstock, Dulles talked of continuing the Woodstock tradition of "solid scholarship" and theological formation in the new institutions and ministries to which the Jesuit students and professors would be going.[160]

Preaching at Woodstock College's closing Mass,
Columbia University, May 18, 1975

273

9

A CHASTENED PROGRESSIVISM, 1974–1988

DULLES BEGAN HIS work at the Woodstock Theological Center at Georgetown University and his teaching at the Catholic University of America in the fall of 1974 and remained there until his retirement at the age of seventy in 1988. During these years, he continued as a progressive theologian in the tradition of the Second Vatican Council, but his progressivism was modified or chastened as he responded to events and theological developments. The closing of Woodstock College, "the American Jesuits' most influential seminary" in Michael Fahey's judgment,[1] was a shock and a wake-up call to some Jesuits, including Dulles, even though they were well aware of the possibility in the early 1970s. The nine years after the Second Vatican Council were filled with tumultuous changes within Woodstock, in the Jesuit community in the United States, and in American Catholicism in general. The contrast with the stability and security of theological and seminary education in the 1950s could not have been more dramatic.

Other events in American Catholic history—including a continuing steady decline in the statistics of religious participation of Catholics, the decreasing numbers of seminarians, increasing withdrawals from the priesthood and religious life, and an excessive accommodationist stance in some elements of the Catholic Church—all combined to modify Dulles' earlier enthusiasm and optimism about reform and experimentation in American Catholicism. Dulles had had adult experiences in both eras, and after the closing of Woodstock, he would begin to reexamine the meaning of the experiences of stability and those of change, experimentation, adaptation, and development. Gradually, his progressivism and optimism were subdued by developments he considered violations of the council's documents and directives. The postconciliar reformist mentality, he believed, needed to be assessed in the light of the council's statements, and he contended toward the end of his tenure at Catholic University that "Vatican II embodies greater corporate wisdom and theological maturity than the work of most private theologians since the council."[2] The extremes of some postconciliar reformists and the brokenness of the Catholic tradition in the United States became all too evident to him, and what he wrote in 1982 about American Catholicism in general could well be applied to his own life as a Catholic theologian: "Chastened by the experience of their own fragility, Catholics are groping for a new identity."[3]

Woodstock Theological Center

From 1974 to 1983, Dulles was on the board of the Woodstock Theological Center, serving as a research associate. In such capacity he suggested theological themes the center ought to examine, took part in theological discussions that the center organized, prepared papers for them, and contributed to publications that eventually emerged from the conversations. In 1974, he and Walter Burghardt proposed that the center invite competent theologians to do research on and to discuss, among other things, a theology of power, a theology of freedom, and church-state relations. When other Jesuits suggested that the center focus on issues of justice and peace in the world, Dulles demurred. He was not opposed to such suggestions, but he did not believe "that the Church is a particularly effective agent of social reform, or that social reform ought to be pursued by the Church as such." He preferred that the center "focus on problems more evidently connected with Christian revelation and with the mission of the Church to preach and interpret the revelation and to become a worshiping community." But again he realized that his own preferences would probably not be met with universal approval among his Jesuit colleagues who were involved in setting the agenda for the center.[4]

In 1975, the center organized two symposia to commemorate the publication of Vatican II's Declaration on Religious Liberty (*Dignitatis humanae*; DH) and its Constitution on the Church in the Modern World (*Gaudium et spes*; GS). Dulles had suggested twice that the center focus on a philosophy and theology of freedom because it was theoretically problematic in the Catholic tradition (for example, the *de auxilius* controversy), practically a problem within the church (because of the grave "disorder" to which the cult of freedom had led, and because of the scandalous suppression of freedom within the church), and socially because the Enlightenment quest for unlimited freedom had had a shaping influence particularly on the "American myth."[5] The center did not take up Dulles' rather broad suggestion but instead focused on the council's document on religious liberty and sponsored, together with the Bishops' Committee on Ecumenical and Interreligious Affairs, a symposium on that declaration.

The symposium, held in Washington, D.C., on November 16, 1975, was in commemoration of the tenth anniversary of the Declaration on Religious Freedom and in honor of John Courtney Murray. Dulles presided and introduced the symposium by noting that the subject of religious liberty needed examination to further "the application of the Declaration in the work of the American church today." The issue, too, was not exclusively an inner Catholic issue but an ecumenical and interreligious question. From the beginning of the discussion of religious liberty at the council, the ecumenical and interreligious dimensions of the subject had come to the fore and continued to be of central concern. Dulles introduced also the keynote speaker, Msgr. Pietro Pavan, the Italian theologian who had a long list of accomplishments, one of which was his collaboration with John Courtney Murray at the council in drafting the document on religious liberty. The symposium was a gathering of Catholic theologians, cardinals, bishops, priests, and laity. The Protestant George A. Lindbeck and the Jewish scholar Manfred Vogel were also active participants in the discussion. Papers delivered at the conference were eventually published.[6]

On a handwritten note in his papers, Dulles became unusually personal in reflecting on the meaning of freedom in his own life. "I do not think of freedom as an existential problem for myself. There are many things I lack and desire. I'd like more knowledge, insight, eloquence and power of many kinds. I'd like to be more able to win friends and influence people. In some way all of these desires can be called desires for freedom, but they are not formally or primarily directed toward freedom." He went on to record that he felt no one ever impeded him "from reaching my best potentialities." To some extent, he felt impeded by destiny and by the "general character of the world into which I was born." The world around him, too, he asserted, had lost interest in the questions "I consider most important. This means that I do not find in the secular world and even in great sections of the Church, the kind of intellectual and moral support I desire." Indirectly all of this limited his freedom. "I feel estranged from a world that does not put meaning and value on the things I consider most important." He was trying to define here how he understood the problem of freedom. "I have all the freedom I want or need. What I lack to some extent are the firm structures that reinforce, motivate, and direct the basic thrust of my existence."[7]

The second major 1965 Woodstock-sponsored symposium, held at Manresa-on-Severn near Annapolis, was on the Church in the Modern World. For that consultation, Dulles prepared a paper on "The Situation of the Church: 1965 and 1975," hoping to stimulate discussion on continuity and change in the identity of the church over the previous decade and into the future. His paper was not on *Guadium et spes* but on the historical transformations in American Catholicism from the eve of the council to 1975, focusing in particular on the liberal-conservative polarization in the church since the council. He suggested in this paper, as he had done in other essays and articles, that Vatican II was essentially a "compromise. It combined the vision of the church as a hierarchical and divine society, oriented toward eternal life, with the newer vision of the church as a free society called to serve the larger human community. This compromise seemed at the time, and may well seem today, to be the wisest, if not the only practicable, course."[8] After the council, American Catholics seemed to be going in two different directions, one toward the older model of the church and the other toward the newer one. The polarization that emerged was, in Dulles' opinion, "more deleterious to the Church than any external opposition....A polarized society simply cannot attract new members or new leaders of high quality." Dulles argued that the current and future church could not profitably return to the ghetto Catholicism of the preconciliar period, nor continue to polarize and decline as in the immediate postconciliar period.

What he prescribed for the future was a new kind of sectarianism—one that focused on developing the church as a "little flock," a disciplined community of committed believers, who no longer had the support of a homogeneous cultural environment but who "distanced themselves from the dominant culture" in order to retain any firm beliefs and moral norms. Dulles was not calling for a withdrawal from the world, but he was suggesting that "the Catholics of tomorrow will have a sharpened sense of the ambiguities in all human cultures, and will not find it difficult to appreciate the attitudes of Conservative Evangelicals, including Pentecostals. They will find inspiration in the cosmopolitan, mobile, and pluralistic Catholicism of the ancient Church."[9]

Dulles took part in a few other consultations and symposia at the Woodstock Center in the mid-1970s, preparing papers and contributing to the high-level discussions. He prepared a paper for a 1976 symposium on the faith that does justice,[10] participated in symposia on personal values in public policy and on retrieving and renewing the Catholic human rights tradition,[11] and wrote his last center paper for a symposium on the lordship of Christ.[12] This last paper on the lordship of Christ over the church focused on how that lordship manifested itself through the ecclesial institution and through the charismatic impulses among the priests, prophets, and pentecostals within the church—themes that he had been discussing since his dissertation. This and other Woodstock papers were exploratory pieces. He was being speculative, suggesting possibilities, and trying to determine if new directions in the church could indeed produce the fruits of the spirit (Gal 5:22–25). Woodstock Center offered the opportunity for this kind of theological speculation as Dulles continued his journey as a theologian.

After July 1981, Dulles stopped going to the Woodstock Symposia because of time constraints and probably because the center had shifted to more ethical issues related to church and society. His theological interests were primarily in fundamental theology, ecclesiology, and ecumenism. At the beginning of 1983, therefore, he resigned as research associate at the center, saying that since he had done nothing for the center in the past eighteen months, he did not think it right to continue his association.[13]

Dulles continued at the Catholic University of America his

"solid scholarship" and his previous historical, developmentalist, symbolic, personalist, and world-affirming approaches to theology, reaffirmed the need for reinterpretation of doctrine to meet the needs of contemporary culture, and reasserted the call for change and reform in the church's structures and methods of administration. But by the end of 1974, a new, slightly modified tone began to appear in many of his writings and a discernible shift occurred in his theological emphases, as was already evident in a conference he attended at the University of Calgary celebrating the septicentennial anniversary of the death of Thomas Aquinas. He came away from that meeting with a new appreciation of Aquinas's relevance for some contemporary issues.[14] Dulles had been a student of Aquinas's theology since the 1940s, but Aquinas seems to have drifted into the background or shadows of his theology in the years immediately after the council, when historical awareness, immanentism, and personalism characterized so much of his theology. The metaphysical realism of the Thomistic vision, which Dulles had never denied, gradually returned to his theological considerations, without forfeiting the benefits of historical consciousness.

In the immediate past, of course, he had criticized those theologians—like Gabriel Moran, Hans Küng, Richard McBrien—whom he thought had moved theologically in some respect too far beyond the intentions and directions of Vatican II. He had, though, supported those theologians and others like them who were attempting to address their theology to the needs of the modern world, following in this respect Vatican II's document on the Church in the Modern World. By the end of 1974, however, he began to critique those whom he believed had been excessively preoccupied with the church's social mission to address the material needs of modern human beings. At a 1974 Jesuit conference, Cardinal Stephen Kim gave a paper on the church's evangelical responsibility to social action, emphasizing "the inadequacy of any program of evangelization that would neglect the social and civic aspects of redemption." Dulles responded to the paper by offering something of a caution to this kind of emphasis. "Many of us today have no difficulty in accepting the prophetic task of the church with regard to the social and political order. But we perhaps need to be reminded of the mystical and eschatological dimensions of redemption."[15]

Dulles was becoming more and more critical, in Ignatian *agere contra* fashion, of those who unduly stressed the social dimension of the church's message and mission, an emphasis that overshadowed or overlooked communion with God as the primary aim of the church's message and mission—an aim that ultimately provided the ground for the church's social activism. As he now read the signs of the times, he began to criticize, more than in the immediate past, the overemphasis in the previous decade on what was new in Vatican II, on reform and dissent in the church, on experimentation, on excessive self-scrutiny and self-questioning, and on radical reinterpretations of the gospel and tradition that were suffused with an immanentism and secularism that relied more on critical methods of scientific inquiry and less on the faith experience of the church. Although some major theological and ecclesial advances were made during the 1960s, the excesses of the period had tended to undermine a fundamental sense of divine transcendence and the human need for a radically distinctive religious experience that elevated human beings above the human condition. In this understanding of the times in which he lived, he joined others in calling for a critique of the all-too-secular theological tendencies of the day and for a restoration of a sense of transcendence in popular religious culture as well as in theology. These elements, of course, were evident in his earlier thought, but they came to the fore in the period after 1975 without undermining his former progressive tendencies.

Dulles' participation in four events in the mid-to late 1970s reflects a shift and a periodic oscillation in his thinking. The four events—his participation in the so-called Hartford Appeal for Theological Affirmation (1975); his forthright criticisms of some major theologians in the progressive tradition (1975–1978); his involvement in and reactions to the Catholic Theological Society of America's (CTSA) commissioned study and publication of *Human Sexuality* (1972–1977); and his engagement in the American bishops' bicentennial "Call to Action" convention in Detroit (1976)—demonstrate some discontinuities and continuities with his theological journey during the decade immediately after the council.

Hartford Appeal

The "Hartford Appeal" was a statement of eighteen theologians, most of whom would have been considered progressive centrists, from different denominations and theological orientations. Their appeal called for a recovery of a sense of transcendence in the churches and in theology. In January 1975, the theologians met at Hartford, Connecticut, to discuss a draft statement of theological concerns that had been prepared by Richard John Neuhaus, Lutheran pastor of St. John the Evangelist, Brooklyn, New York, and associate editor of *Worldview*. He and Peter Berger, another Lutheran and a Rutgers University sociologist, had envisioned, organized, and invited various theologians to the conference to consider, debate, and revise the initial statement and to discuss the state of the churches and theology after the revolutionary decade of the 1960s.

In March 1974, Berger and Neuhaus had invited to the conference about fifty theologians whom they thought would "be interested in" and "in all probability be enthusiastic about its aims."[16] Dulles received, as did other theologians invited to the meeting, an initial "General Statement" that outlined twelve theological "anathemas" to be discussed. Dulles hesitated to reply to the invitation because he noted in a memo, "As at present formulated, some of the anathemas seem to me to be too sweeping. At least by suggestion, they seem to condemn good initiatives and good ideas. I would not wish to be associated with a movement that was committed to extinguishing good things." Nonetheless, he was interested in the kinds of problems that the General Statement had identified and was willing to take part in a discussion of issues. He also suggested that they invite Carl Peter of the Catholic University of America because he was a "good systematic thinker."[17] In preparation for the conference, Dulles and Peter eventually formulated a series of twelve positive affirmations that they thought ought to be discussed along with the "anathemas."[18]

For some time Berger and Neuhaus had been commenting on the state of religion in contemporary society and had been discussing among themselves the need to bring theologians together to enter into their conversation. Of course, by 1975 their conversation was part of a much larger new mood, after the downfall of the Nixon presidency, the collapse of the Vietnam War, and the rise and vigor of conservative Evangelical Protestantism.

Religion was by no means dead in American society, but some sociologists were demonstrating that a shift in religious sensibilities was taking place in reaction to the experimentation and changes of the 1960s. Prior to the Hartford convention, a few scholars pointed to a new religious phenomenon, illustrating in particular an increasing divide between the intellectual elites (ecclesiastical bureaucrats and liberal theologians) and the more conservative laity in the churches. Peter Berger's *A Rumor of Angels: Modern Society and the Rediscovery of the Supernatural* (1970), Dean Kelley's *Why Conservative Churches Are Growing* (1972), Jeffrey Hadden's *The Gathering Storm in the Churches* (1969), and James Hitchcock's *The Decline and Fall of Radical Catholicism* (1971) and *The Recovery of the Sacred* (1974), among other texts, indicated a certain reaction to the immanentism of the 1960s and what some would call a religious capitulation to modernity.

Whether or not the invited theologians agreed with the theses of these sociologists and historians of religion, they were conscious that something was amiss in religion and that churches and theologians, including themselves, needed to be recalled to the sacred within Christianity. Some participants cited one or two of the books mentioned, but they were also aware of a pervasive secularism, especially among the intellectuals in American society. They pointed, for example, to the "Humanist Manifesto II" (1973) as one indication of a larger phenomenon of secularism in the society of intellectuals. That document contended that

> as in 1933 [when the first Humanist Manifesto was published], humanists still believe that traditional theism, especially faith in the prayer-hearing God, assumed to love and care for persons, to hear and understand their prayers, and to be able to do something about them, is an unproved and outmoded faith....We find insufficient evidence for the belief in the existence of a supernatural; it is either meaningless or irrelevant to the question of the survival of the human race.[19]

Some, like Dulles, were also concerned with the excessive social activism in some agencies of the World Council of Churches in the 1960s. Dulles quoted, for example, a 1967 report of the Department of Studies in Evangelism that concluded that "it is the world that must be allowed to provide the agenda for the churches."[20]

Although the Hartford participants acknowledged the social responsibilities of the churches that flowed from the gospel, they were unwilling to allow the secular movements and intellectuals to set the agenda for the churches. Some participants were concerned about the experimental liturgies that copied fads in secular society, or the so-called underground churches, many of which imitated the lifestyles of hippie communes, or the denigration of theology and solid theological scholarship as of no practical use in a society beset by so many social problems. Most of the participants, in other words, were conscious that the cry of the 1960s for relevance that had so influenced the churches, their own theological students, and theologians like themselves had its benefits but also its excesses, excesses that they were concerned about.

By 1975, Dulles was one of the most respected and well-known theologians in the country, in both the Protestant and Catholic communities. He was particularly esteemed in the Catholic theological community. He had received the Cardinal Spellman award for distinguished achievement in theology in 1970, was elected to the CTSA's board of directors from 1970 to 1972, was elected vice president of the CTSA in June 1974, and became president in June 1975.

Dulles and seventeen other distinguished theologians met at Hartford to discuss the Neuhaus draft.[21] Because of his national reputation, Dulles' presence at the Hartford convention was significant, and his contributions to Hartford and his subsequent defense of the published appeal revealed something of a change in theological emphasis.

The three-day meeting at Hartford examined Neuhaus's draft and, according to Neuhaus, revised it substantially but preserved the overall structure of the original document.[22] The revised document was sent to all the participants and to others who could not attend the meeting. The participants and a few other theologians unable to attend the meeting signed the document, but some theologians who were invited to sign refused to do so. The signed document was then published and commented on in papers and journals around the country.

The Hartford document, "An Appeal for Theological Affirmation,"[23] consisted of thirteen very concise and general thematic statements that were intended, in Dulles' view, "as a reaffirmation of transcendence against the idolatries of our time." The thirteen propositions listed some of the "pervasive" errors that were "superficially attractive" but in fact "false and debilitating to the church's life and work." The appeal cited no sources and named no adversaries. It was a general shot across the bow of the American ecclesiastical ship and was intended to be a critique of both a radical secularism and an individualistic, privatized religious conservatism inside the churches. It was intentionally provocative in naming the errors of the day and deliberately vague and noncommittal in attributing blame to specific individuals or groups. It was Dulles' opinion in May 1975 that the principal target of the appeal was not theologians "who are generally taken seriously by their colleagues, but rather second-rate popularizers and theological journalists, who have frequently given the impression that they were accurately reproducing the views of theologians."[24] In subsequent weeks and years, though, Dulles and a few others named specific theologians as targets of the Hartford Appeal, creating or illustrating something of a divide in the theological community.

The appeal received extensive coverage in the secular and religious press, and a host of judicious as well as angry reactions from theologians. Kenneth A. Briggs of the *New York Times*, for example, gave a relatively accurate account of the document as an urgent call to Christians "to abandon secular influences that are 'false and debilitating' to the church's work." He summarized then what he considered the major signs of the church's excessively heavy borrowing from the secular. Secularism was manifested in "the concept that religious thought must pass the test of scientific rationality, that all religions are the same, that religion is a manmade creation and that Jesus can be described in purely human terms." But the document was not simply a reactionary theological critique, as Briggs understood it. It was trying to find a middle ground, as George Forell had characterized the document, between the "with-it theology and the madness of fundamentalist fads," giving Christians an alternative to the extremes in the churches. But, the document could be called "liberal," Briggs noted, in its understanding of the church's relations to social-political issues.[25] *Time* magazine summarized the appeal and characterized it as "The Hartford Heresies," wondering, as did Briggs, about the specific targets of the brief statement. But *Time* suggested, unlike Briggs, that the targets probably included Harvey Cox, Joseph Fletcher, Bishop John Robinson, and the popularizers of Teilhard de Chardin and liberation theology.[26]

Numerous theologians, too, reacted to the appeal, demonstrating not only that it had hit a sensitive nerve but also that its generalities were too broad to stick to anyone. Neuhaus's *Worldview* gave critics an opportunity to express themselves. Harvey Cox gave an angry retort, calling the document "a good old raucous theological Scopes trial" that "has already fizzled into a nonevent." The thirteen propositions or themes condemned, in his view, "no sane theologian would want to defend." The document was simplistic, toppling straw men, and caricaturing the contemporary theological scene. Worst of all, it had no christological center.[27] Other theologians, Catholic as well as Protestant, criticized the generalities and the one-sided shotgun approach to broad currents in the churches and in theology. Few denied the fundamental need to assert the reality of the transcendent in Christianity, but a number thought that the appeal was governed by a Lutheran "two kingdoms" split between the church and the world, between divine transcendence and divine immanence.

The theologians who criticized the statement regretted, as did John C. Bennett, professor at the Graduate Theological Union at Berkeley, that it seemed to call "for a retreat from much of the best that the churches have recently been doing to identify themselves with people around the world who are in greatest need of radical social change."[28] Some Catholic commentators like Gabriel Moran, a professor of religious education at New York University, were disturbed by the reactionary tone and by its failure to be critical of the church itself as an oppressive institution. He agreed with the many who were "suspicious of institutions that *denounce*."[29] Like some others, Gregory Baum, professor of theology at St. Michael's College of the University of Toronto, could not imagine which theologians were indicted. He thought that the statement was untimely, particularly in an American culture that was pietistic and individualistic, and unresponsive to the churches' various pronouncements on a "social understanding of the Christian message." It would have been better to have insisted "that divine grace humanizes and socializes human life." Baum thought the whole statement reflected the "neoorthodox religious imagination" of the organizers, presupposed "a radical separation between God and the world," and was "suspicious of the humanistic interpretation of the Gospel."[30]

Other religious papers published theologians' and historians' supportive as well as critical responses to Hartford.[31] The appeal became an event that stirred up the religious and theological communities. In a sardonic column addressed to Berger and Neuhaus, historian Martin Marty of the University of Chicago put the statement in the context of what he thought future historians would consider relevant in the 1970s: "You see, nothing is more 'with it' and 'relevant' in 1975 than attacking the idea of being 'with it' and 'relevant.'" The theological appeal for transcendence, moreover, was supposedly unneeded because "all but .000002 per cent of today's active American Christians would agree with you."[32] The Hartford Appeal reflected a larger cultural shift in reaction to the relevant 1960s; it was part of the zeitgeist of the 1970s.

Relevance was a theme of the Catholic Theological Society of America's annual meeting in June 1975, when the CTSA convention focused on Catholic theology's relationship and rapport with the social and political sciences. The Hartford Appeal was discussed in the hallways and bull sessions at the meeting, but none of the papers delivered at the convention mentioned the document, except for the presidential address. The president of the society, Br. Luke Salm, who was about to hand over the presidential reins to Dulles, spoke on "Past Perspectives and Future Prospects for the CTSA." His theme was that, in the past as in the present, the CTSA had a clear emphasis on its Catholic identity; that was its strong point. It had also experienced some openness to the diversity in American society and in American scholarship, but was "perhaps overly cautious." The future called for the CTSA to enter

more wholeheartedly into a positive dialogue with social movements.[33] In the midst of his talk, Salm called attention to Hartford:

> One of the dangers for the CTSA in the publicity
> attending the recent Hartford statement on the loss of
> transcendence is that we may think that it applies to
> us....But the statement has all the disadvantages of the
> typical Roman condemnations. It is always dangerous
> and difficult to determine those to whom it applies, a
> game that too many in the Catholic community love to
> play.

He then turned the appeal upside down, calling for more
openness. The CTSA should use the thirteen points of the appeal
to "examine whether it has been open enough to modern thought,
to human experience, to other religions, to human potential, to
self-realization in human community, to the oppressive character of
some of our institutions and traditions, to social concern and
action, and to the struggle for a better humanity."[34] The emphases
were not those of Hartford.

At the CTSA's celebration of Mass, Dulles, the society's vice
president (1974–1975), gave a homily on Matthew 5:14 ("You are
the light of the world"). The sermon reflected something of the
liturgy's penitential rite and something of the Hartford Appeal. It
began with a liturgical call for repentance. He asked the theologians to examine how "we as individuals and as a theological community have gone astray." Then he listed the seven capital sins of
theology (pride, presumption, aloofness, indolence, jealousy, ambition, and "fear, by which we shrink from speaking out frankly when
the situation so demands") and provided something of an examination of conscience for theologians before reflecting on how theology should be a source of light in the world. He wanted the
theological community to consider three things: how theology
"works by a borrowed light" (that light being Christ), how it must
be "attached to the community of faith," and how it should be
"pursued communally."[35] Theology, in other words, was a discipline
that was christocentric, ecclesial, and collegial, and, therefore,
theologians ought to be open to admonition and correction. The

primary theme here was that theology had its own light—a light that transcended individual or even communal consciousness but also a light that needed to be received personally and communally.

Dulles and other participants in the Hartford meeting were well aware by the end of the summer that their appeal had received a large but very mixed response from theologians and church people. The participants believed they needed to clarify their intentions and correct some of the unnuanced charges that had been leveled against the appeal. In September, therefore, the group gathered again to collect their thoughts and publish them, which they did in *Against the World for the World*, the title itself indicating their opposition to both capitulation and withdrawal. Several of the participants prepared statements that were a part of the publication. Dulles, responding to charges made against Hartford, argued that from his perspective the appeal was a significant ecumenical statement that did indeed seek to identify what he labeled as "latent heresies" or "secret infidelities," although by those terms he did not mean what the journalists meant when they misled readers by focusing on the "Hartford Heresies." By latent heresy he did not mean a direct or explicit attack on Christian revelation, but a mental universe formed "by a tissue of assumptions that make up the public mind of the day. We are immersed in, dependent on, and influenced by a mental world that lies largely beyond our control. Many of the unspoken assumptions of our culture are out of harmony with Christian faith." In Dulles' view, this was Hartford's real target. There is a certain "tacit knowledge" that comes from living in the secular tradition, and that knowledge and the assumptions that go along with it "can scarcely be verified by objective measurements."[36] Hartford, in other words, was after what was implicit, not explicit, heresy. The danger, too, was more invidious because it was not part of reflective consciousness. Hartford was trying to bring the implicit to conscious examination.

Revisionist Theologians Critiqued

After the Hartford episode in theological affirmation and controversy, Dulles and a few other Hartford participants began to identify theologians who had excessively accommodated themselves to the contemporary zeitgeist. In some book reviews and in his *Resilient Church* (1977), Dulles focused on the limits of reinterpretation and adaptation, modifying, but not denying, his 1960s insistence on the necessity of such. But he did not deal simply in theological abstractions; he identified concrete manifestations of excessive accommodationism by naming theologians he considered to have fallen into that trap.

In June 1976, Dulles published an extensive review of David Tracy's *Blessed Rage for Order: The New Pluralism in Theology* (1975).[37] At the time, Dulles and Tracy were colleagues who were involved in the CTSA as president and vice president respectively; both, too, were considered preeminent in their field. Although respected colleagues and participants in the post–Vatican II progressive theological movement, however, they were not on the same page theologically, as the review clearly demonstrated. That review, too, indicated a certain rift that was taking place in the progressive wing of post–Vatican II theology and reflected something of the spirit of Hartford.

Tracy's *Blessed Rage for Order* presented a view of fundamental theology and a theological method and epistemology that clearly differed from Dulles' approach. Operating within the pluralistic environment of the Divinity School of the University of Chicago, Tracy was less concerned than Dulles with Catholic ecclesiastical reforms and the exposition of the Second Vatican Council and more committed to making theology, systematic as well as fundamental, an appropriate "public discourse." Like Dulles, though, Tracy accepted the "present pluralism of theologies" because he believed that this situation "allows each theologian to learn incomparably more about reality by disclosing really different ways of viewing both our common humanity and Christianity." In his view, this acceptance was not a capitulation to a consumerist mentality, that is, pick and choose whatever theology best fits your current needs. Such a mentality would ultimately result in theological chaos. The theologian must "articulate and defend an explicit method of inquiry, and use that method to interpret the symbols and texts of our common life and of Christianity." Tracy argued for the use of a "revisionist" model of theology. The revisionist finds himself caught in a dilemma. He is committed to the modern world and to the God of Jesus Christ, and "neither traditional Christian self-understanding nor recent modern self-understanding nor any combination thereof will suffice to resolve that dual dilemma." Tracy's theology, therefore, was directed to a "basic revision of traditional Christianity and traditional modernity." By revising both traditions, Tracy intended to demonstrate "that the Christian faith is at heart none other than the most adequate articulation of the basic faith of secularity itself." Thus, a revisionist theology "is best understood as philosophical reflection upon the meanings present in common human experience and the meanings present in the Christian tradition."[38]

Such philosophical reflection, according to Tracy, provided an avenue to appropriate public discourse. Much of Tracy's theological work was directed to the secular academic community and to the task of underlining the religious grounds Christian believers shared with all humankind. He tried to show how "Christian claims to truth are not private but public." For Tracy, theology is "public" when "it provides disclosive and transformative truth available, in principle, to all intelligent, rational and responsible persons." This task of apologetics could be adequately achieved when the theologian critically analyzed the Christian truth claims "without any appeal to personal belief-warrants," developed "public criteria for meaning, meaningfulness and truth," and then applied these criteria to "the questions of religion, God and Christology."[39] If theology was to be a science, Tracy contended, "it must use only publicly verifiable criteria."[40] Thus, Tracy attempted to achieve a critical Christian accommodation with the modern mind.

Dulles had a great deal of respect for Tracy's erudition and insight and shared with him an acceptance of pluralism in church and theology and a sympathetic regard for secularity and modernity. But there were limits to this acceptance as far as Dulles was concerned, and he made those limits evident in his critique of Tracy's method of doing theology. Dulles' view of fundamental theology differed dramatically from Tracy's, and this was not the result of some conservative backlash of the 1970s but an enduring feature of Dulles' fundamental theology. He did not believe that the Catholic theologian could explain Christianity to the modern pluralistic and secular world without an explicit religious commitment to Christianity. It is at this point, in particular, that he disagreed with those like Tracy who believed that on one level, the level of fundamental theology, a firm religious commitment was "unnecessary, even dangerous." Dulles affirmed in 1975, as he had for years, that fundamental as well as dogmatic theology demanded persons committed to Christianity if it was to be "adequately practical." He maintained that the "fundamental theologian may legitimately draw upon the testimony of tradition," because fundamental theology was "inseparable from dogmatics."[41] Thus, in the contemporary world, an adequate apologetic for Christianity presupposed commitment and denied the possibility of a completely scientific objectivity or rationality in fundamental as in systematic theology. In other essays and books in the period after 1975, Dulles battled with the Tracy-like revisionist model for doing theology, seeing it in part as an appropriation of the empirical model of the positive sciences.[42]

At the time he reviewed Tracy's book, Dulles did not link Tracy with the targets of the Hartford Appeal, but in *The Resilient Church* (1977) he did so. That book was Dulles' attempt "to appraise and carry forward the theological work of Catholic ecclesiology in the decade since the Council." In the following terms he situated himself on the theological spectrum in Catholicism:

> Unlike many ecclesiastical conservatives, I hold that adaptation need not be a form of capitulation to the world, but that an adapting church should be able to herald the Christian message with greater power and impact. Unlike certain liberals, I am deeply concerned that the church, in its efforts at adaptation, should avoid imitating the fashions of the non-believing world and should have the courage to be different. Difference is not to be cultivated for its own sake but is to be fearlessly accepted when Christ and the Gospel so require.[43]

In a chapter entitled "Critique of Modernity and the Hartford Appeal," Dulles argued for an "authentic modernization without a new Modernism and without destructive polarization." Theologians like Langdon Gilkey and Tracy, among others, Dulles went on to say, were attempting to work out "some kind of accommodation with the modern mind while avoiding secularity in extreme and virulent form." The extreme form he called secularization, "a philosophy of life that is naturalistic and implicitly atheistic."[44] Nonetheless, both Gilkey and Tracy, in their attempts to reinterpret the gospel message without abandoning secularity, had accepted too much of the secular spirit, did not sufficiently challenge or correct its aberrations, and in fact had conformed much of the Christian tradition to a secular norm. In this chapter on Hartford, it was clear that Dulles believed that both Gilkey[45] and Tracy had succumbed to the seduction of the secular spirit and thereby diluted the power of Christianity to make a distinctive contribution to the world. Dulles implied that theologians like Gilkey and Tracy had accepted "the secular outlook as normative" in their attempts to reconcile Christian values with those of the secular world.[46] Dulles went on to criticize Tracy's understanding of the "Christian story" as a

> "supreme fiction" that had meaning to the extent that it represents authentic human possibilities....To all appearances Tracy is content to say that the early Christians were inspired to invent a good story about Jesus.... Tracy's Christology if I have correctly understood it would seem to fit the widespread tendency to ignore the reality of God's redemptive action in the flesh-and-blood Jesus, and to substitute for this an interest in the power of the Christian story to provide appropriate symbols for expressing a basic human experience.

In another place, Dulles asserted that Tracy's belief in the hope for everlasting life, like that of some others, was "marginal, if not illusory."[47]

Such weakening of the central Christian mysteries was, for Dulles, a disaster. He was not charging the theologians with heterodoxy or heresy, but he saw in their theologies and methodologies tendencies of what he had previously called the "latent heresy" that was at work in the popular and academic culture—a rampant immanentism, secularism, psychologism, and sociologism that left little or no room for transcendence. One could not accommodate or reconcile Christian values with these kinds of assumptions in the culture. Dulles went on to defend the Hartford Appeal, arguing that it was not simply setting up straw men and phantom heresies, as some had charged. There were concrete manifestations of the loss of transcendence in some contemporary theologians. Even some of the signers of the appeal acknowledged their own tendencies, perhaps in the past, to be overly preoccupied with reconciling Christian values with contemporary secular values. The excessive self-criticism within the Catholic Church during the previous decade was only one manifestation of this tendency, and many who opposed Hartford wished to continue "the ecclesiastical masochism and disarray of the previous decade."[48] The inclusion of Gilkey and Tracy with a few Christian secular theologians in this chapter on Hartford brought forth a vigorous response.

Like Dulles, other Hartford signers had also identified targets. The identification was, of course, a response to those opponents who charged that the Hartford heresies were simply creations of a reactionary imagination. Peter Berger, for example, made it clear to the Catholic theological community that he thought the rejection of the supernatural was not a figment of Hartford's imagination but was clearly evident in the theologies of Schubert Ogden, Gilkey, and Tracy.[49]

The religious newspapers, liking a good fight, invited Tracy and Gilkey to respond to the charges Dulles had leveled against them.[50] Both respected Dulles as a theologian, but both considered his charges against them as erroneous and damaging, damaging more so because a generally respected theologian was the source of the charges. They perceived Dulles' accusations and those of Hartford as witch hunts. They also denied that their theologies supported the kinds of charges Dulles and others had made against them, and they rejected in particular the journalistic labels that had been applied to their theologies—that is, that they had exploited the tradition to support the secularist, immanentist, and reductionist mentality of modernity. Both were obviously upset and angry that Dulles had misrepresented the subtlety of their positions and arguments. They felt Dulles had been hasty, irresponsible, and inaccurate in reporting their positions and in associating the two of them with radical positions that they did not hold. They were declared guilty, they charged, by unreasonable association. Both acknowledged their fundamental belief in the Christian tradition's faith in the divinity of Jesus and in life after death, and Tracy asserted that "I will gladly and publicly disown my position as unacceptable even for fundamental theology, much less for dogmatics" if Dulles could ever demonstrate that the charges he made were actually in Tracy's text. They accepted the basic Christian creedal assertions.

Dulles responded to both of these forceful reactions by acknowledging that he continued to consider Tracy and Gilkey his friends and respected theological colleagues; his disagreements with their positions were theological, not personal.[51] Dulles and Gilkey had been classmates at Harvard in the late 1930s, had joined together at Harvard in protesting American entrance into World War II prior to Pearl Harbor, and had a certain respect for each other for more than forty years.[52] No theologian, Dulles argued, ought to be immune from criticism. He had focused his attacks on their unfortunate use of language in a few places and on their theological methodology. He did not charge them personally with heresy, but he reasserted that he believed their language and their methods gave inadequate "theological rationale" for faith and prayer and their own professed beliefs. He continued to believe, moreover, that their approaches to theology reflected, especially in Gilkey's case, the latent heresy Dulles had identified in his defense of Hartford. But the latent heresy that he pointed out in their works was "a pervasive feature of the mental climate of the age, and may be found even in the work of those whose explicit beliefs are entirely orthodox."[53] It was more a matter of proportion and emphasis than false propositions. It was also clear from Dulles' response that he disagreed fundamentally with Tracy's separation of or radical distinction between fundamental and dogmatic theology. Dulles continued to maintain that fundamental theology was a part of dogmatic theology and that one could not separate one's faith and formation in the tradition from one's task as a theologian, whether fundamental or dogmatic.

The theological controversy, indicative of a growing split in the progressive wing of theology in America, ended up with expressions of mutual friendship but did not resolve the differences and left a bad taste that persisted into the future. The fuzzy notion of a latent heresy was difficult to nail down with chapter and verse and open to vast generalizations that could have brought the entire progressive wing of theologians—including Dulles' earlier 1960s enthusiasm for reform, adaptation, and reinterpretation—under condemnation. Nevertheless, the controversy was not about a "diphthong," a reference to Edward Gibbon's charge that the whole world after Nicaea was torn apart by a silly theological battle between the homoiousians and the homoousians with respect to the nature of Christ. This Dulles-Tracy-Gilkey battle was more than a tempest in a teapot; it reflected long-standing conflicts on the way Christians should use and critique the secular tools in communicating the faith, and precisely on what grounds and by what criteria they should accommodate the secular mentality.

Dulles believed by the mid-1970s that some theologians had bent over backward to accommodate the Christian message and were in danger of losing a sense of its distinctive identity and of forfeiting a discriminating stance in which the Christian message could challenge and critique the society in which it lived. If it was a matter of proportion and emphasis, it was nonetheless a matter of serious concern. To some extent this stance was a retreat from Dulles' own emphases in the late 1960s and early 1970s. He had not abandoned the progressive program of Vatican II, but he now saw the need to challenge an excessive accommodationist stance, and this new emphasis[54] came more and more to the fore in subsequent years.

Human Sexuality

The battle within Catholic theology was also evident in the controversial CTSA–commissioned study on *Human Sexuality*, which was "received" by CTSA's board of directors in June 1976 when Dulles was president of the society. In 1972, the society's board had appointed a committee of five theologians[55] to do a study on human sexuality to provide "some helpful and illuminating guidelines in the present confusion" and to prepare a report to the CTSA board on their findings.[56] The five theologians spent two years examining the issue in light of the Bible, Christian traditions, and modern empirical studies, and on the basis of this study recommended certain pastoral guidelines for implementing their theology. The chairman of the research committee, Anthony Kosnik, gave the CTSA a summary report of the committee's findings in June 1975.[57]

During Dulles' presidency of the CTSA (June 1975–June 1976), the news media gave the unfinished study sensational headlines: "A New Catholic View of Sex" and "Church Study Debunks Vatican Views of Sex." Dulles was well aware of the newspaper reports, and the chair of the study committee, Anthony Kosnik, protested against the premature and what he characterized as inaccurate reports in the press, which indicated that the report departed from Catholic moral doctrine.[58] The *Detroit News* quoted Kosnik as saying, for example, "Christ found Himself comfortable with women. He reached out to them, even those rejected by the society of the day. You could call Him a feminist out to change the structures of a society that dehumanized and misused women. He didn't have the hang-ups St. Paul had."[59] In this context of widespread and unwanted and arresting publicity, the CTSA board met several times to discuss the controversial study and advised the committee to seek outside evaluations from competent moral theologians. Dulles and some board members had serious reservations about the study,[60] and in January 1976 he advised Kosnik and the committee to take into consideration the Vatican's recent declaration on sexual ethics.[61]

The board members met again in June 1976 to discuss the study and, in spite of their reticence, decided that they would "receive the Report on Human Sexuality" but made no decision on publishing it at the time. Prior to this decision, as one press report indicated, several members of the board and especially Dulles "argued vigorously for additional 'scholarly review' before acceptance."[62] The board wanted to consult with other theologians and prepare an assessment of the study for the committee, leaving the committee with the final discretion on what advice they would accept or reject.[63] In August 1976, Dulles sent Kosnik a letter detailing some of his own personal objections to the report and providing four pages of editorial revisions, but he indicated that the study was a "real contribution and well deserves publication under the auspices of the CTSA."[64]

Other theologians in the CTSA were not so accepting of the study. Some moral theologians like William E. May of the Catholic University tried to organize theologians against the study,[65] and at the 1977 annual convention, he protested vigorously, but without success, against calling the publication a study "commissioned" by the CTSA.[66] The board, however, had also received letters from theologians supporting the study; some, too, thought it "basically conservative...but a step forward."[67]

The board decided at its June 1977 meeting to have the study published. It agreed to commission the publication, but "these actions," it noted in a foreword to the 1977 published text, "imply neither the approval nor disapproval by the Society or its Board of Directors of the contents of the report."[68] The disclaimer was consistent with the CTSA's past policies on receiving research reports, but it carried with it more than the usual hesitation about accepting the conclusions of theological research, much of which had not been reviewed by the society's membership prior to publication and some of which was seriously challenged within the society.[69] After the publication, Dulles is reported to have said, "I doubt they [the commission members] have taken any positions that haven't been taken by moral theologians writing in the field in the last decade. They're not aiming to break new ground but to synthesize material." He also offered the opinion that "quite a number of confessors have been operating" on the principles articulated in the book.[70] Dulles was being descriptive here, but the statement reflected his confidence in the scholarship and judgment of the theological community at the time. And his view that the book represented standard current thinking in the theological community was apparently accepted by a majority who attended the CTSA annual meetings in 1976 and 1977. Only a small minority protested against the statement.

Human Sexuality's liberal or tolerant acceptance not only of birth control but also of masturbation, homosexual activity, extramarital and premarital sex as long as these actions promoted a creative-integrative human development, made it a prime target for criticisms within the Catholic Church. Some theologians like May had serious difficulties with *Human Sexuality*'s moral consequentialism, historical relativism, poor scholarship, and inadequate

297

methodology. The document, too, indicated how far some theologians were willing to go to adapt or accommodate Catholic teachings to empirical studies and the current cultural mores in American society. These criticisms rendered the book "an inadequate and misleading guide to sexual morality."[71]

Human Sexuality was also not acceptable to the American Catholic bishops.[72] In November 1977, the National Conference of Catholic Bishops' (NCCB) Committee on Doctrine, whose chairman was a bishop and whose members were theologians as well as bishops, reviewed the published text and concluded that it could not be considered a helpful pastoral guideline for beleaguered pastors, priests, counselors, and teachers, nor a guide for Catholics in forming their consciences because it contradicted "theological tradition and the Church's clear magisterial teaching refined over the centuries and recently reaffirmed in the Vatican Declaration on Sexual Ethics and the American Bishops' Pastoral Letter [*To Live in Christ Jesus* (November 1976)]."[73] Two years after the American bishops rejected the document, the Congregation for the Doctrine of the Faith (CDF) commended them for their stand on the study, and in a letter to Archbishop John R. Quinn, the archbishop of San Francisco and the presiding bishop of the NCCB, found it difficult to understand how "a distinguished society of Catholic theologians would have arranged for the publication of this report in such a way as to give broad distribution to the erroneous principles and conclusions of this book and in this way provide a source of confusion among the people of God."[74]

The publication of the document ultimately had some serious consequences in addition to the magisterial condemnations. Some theologians left the CTSA after the publication, Kosnik was removed from his seminary teaching position in 1982,[75] American bishops became increasingly skeptical about the leadership of CTSA theologians, and the gap widened between conservative and progressive theologians.

Dulles had some reservations about the text, which he expressed privately to the authors and to other correspondents and at the CTSA board meetings prior to its publication, but he eventually supported the publication "under the auspices of the CTSA." In the immediate past and in the present, Dulles had supported and even advocated a certain theological pluralism in the theological community, and he supported freedom for theological inquiry and speculation. He could protest that although sponsored, *Human Sexuality* was not approved by the CTSA. His willingness to sponsor the report was consistent with his progressive theological perspectives in the mid-1970s and his nondirective leadership style. But in 1977 he sympathized with Michael Novak's view that "there is a tendency among contemporary theologians to yield far too much to the *Zeitgeist*," a tendency Novak found in *Human Sexuality*. Some theologians in the CTSA, Novak feared, "are too eager to appear enlightened and up-to-date. People on the left, I believe, should be as critical of tendencies on the left as they are of tendencies on the right. Theologians are developing a vested interest in the new. This is becoming an occupational disease." Dulles told Novak in 1977 that the sexuality report would be "pastorally helpful, but I'm not satisfied that the report really supplies what was most needed—namely, a *theology* of sexuality. For my taste there is too little effort to see 'creative growth and integration' in terms of the mystery of Christ and the Church. But then I'm not a moral or sacramental or pastoral theologian."[76]

Dulles pleaded professional incompetence in 1977 on this and other moral issues, a plea he would not make later in his career. By the 1990s he considered the *Human Sexuality* episode and the theological battles with the pastoral magisterium over sexual issues a manifestation of theological accommodation or capitulation to contemporary cultural mores.[77] In his 1996 enlargement of his autobiography, moreover, he indicated that he was "dissatisfied" with the sexuality report and that authors had received some "excellent critiques" from fellow theologians "but they did not make significant changes before they published the report on their own authority."[78] In this way Dulles relieved himself and others in the CTSA from any responsibility for publishing the report.[79] It was solely the work of the authors involved in the study, and, to some extent, this was the tradition of receiving study reports in the CTSA up to the mid-1970s. Nonetheless, the publication was sponsored by the CTSA, and the society reaped some benefits from the royalties received from the sales of the text in order to recuperate the costs associated with sponsoring the study.

Bicentennial Call to Action

Dulles also became involved in a fourth event, the American Catholic celebration of the bicentennial, a part of which illustrated some of the tensions and conflicts of the day and moved him more and more toward a critique of the direction some Catholic activists wanted to take the church. Catholics celebrated the American bicentennial in two phases: through the forty-first International Eucharistic Congress, held in Philadelphia during August 1976; and through the bishops' Call to Action conference, held in Detroit during October 1976. Dulles participated in both events.

The Philadelphia Eucharistic Congress drew ecclesiastical dignitaries from around the world, including Pope Paul VI's personal representative, Cardinal Karol Wojtyla, the future pope, and Mother Teresa of Calcutta. President Gerald Ford was in attendance at the closing ceremony, delivering a brief concluding bicentennial statement. These international congresses were intended to deepen the spiritual life of the Catholic faithful, draw attention to the significance of the Eucharist, and focus on the unity of the church. The Philadelphia event did all of that, reflecting little of the controversies within the Catholic Church, but it was also an academic and ecumenical event. During the meeting, theologians from various religious traditions, but especially the Lutheran, delivered papers on the Eucharist. Dulles gave a paper on intercommunion between Catholics and Lutherans and responded to another paper delivered by George Lindbeck.

Dulles' paper on intercommunion with Lutherans was a summary of positions he had been developing for nearly a decade. He rejected the argument that because the Eucharist was a sign of unity achieved, intercommunion could not be allowed until full ecclesiastical unity or doctrinal unanimity had been restored. He also disapproved the argument that because the Eucharist was a sign of unity imperfectly achieved and indeed a means to fuller unity, intercommunion should be allowed on the basis of minimal doctrinal agreement. His own position, like that of Lindbeck, was somewhere between these two opposing positions.

He summed up his own position by saying that although "one should normally receive communion in a service of one's own confession, occasional acts of intercommunion may be seen as an appropriate sign of the partial but growing unity among separated churches and as an appropriate remedy for their present separations." The episcopal allowance of occasional intercommunion with Lutherans was a possibility, Dulles argued, because of three major preconditions that had already been achieved during the past decade in the Lutheran/Catholic Dialogue: "(1) a basic unity in faith, expressed by common creeds understood in a similar way; (2) a sense of somehow belonging, notwithstanding all the divisions, to the one church of Christ; (3) the will to a more perfect union."[80]

Two other preconditions for intercommunion, however, remained problematic and therefore argued against any regular intercommunion between Lutherans and Catholics. Sacramental sharing would not be appropriate until Lutherans and Catholics had reached a substantial agreement about eucharistic doctrine and had come to recognize each other's services as true Eucharists (and for Catholics this meant a recognition of a valid ministry within the Lutheran churches). These were thorny problems that had yet to be worked out in the bilateral conversations. Nonetheless, Dulles suggested, in union with some European bishops, that under certain specified conditions that were acceptable to the disciplines of both churches, intercommunion might be allowed on limited occasions. In this proposal, he was in basic agreement with Lindbeck, who also sought to enlarge the area of intercommunion beyond the current disciplines in the respective churches.[81]

The second half of the Catholic celebration of the bicentennial, the Detroit Call to Action convention, had a longer history and produced more controversial results than the Philadelphia event and awakened Dulles to some of the limits of ecclesiastical adaptation that he later identified in *The Resilient Church* and other writings. The idea for Call to Action emerged from the bishops' Advisory Council. In 1973 the bishops created a Bicentennial Committee—composed of representative clergy, laypeople, and bishops—to prepare for the Detroit convention. The committee suggested that the convention take seriously Pope Paul VI's *Call to Action* and the International Synod of Bishops' *Justice in the World*, two 1971 statements on the social dimensions of the gospel and apply them to American society and the American church. The

Detroit convention, therefore, would focus on issues of "liberty and justice for all."[82] In preparation for the convention, the committee solicited opinions and advice from more than 830,000 individuals from across the country, encouraged meetings in parishes and dioceses to discuss issues of justice and peace, held seven public hearings in different cities on various issues (humankind, nationhood, the land, the family, work, ethnicity and race, global justice), and appointed writing committees to prepare working papers and proposals for the Detroit meeting.

Dulles participated in the Call to Action process not only through his involvement in the bishops' Advisory Council but also by his testimony before the first public hearing and his appointment to a preconvention committee on ecclesiology that prepared a paper on the church for the delegates' consideration at Detroit. In 1975, the first public hearing in Washington, D.C., focused on "Humankind," one of the themes to be considered at Detroit. Cardinal John Dearden, chairman of the hearing and of the Call to Action conference, invited all those present to assess how "the American Catholic community can contribute to the quest of all people for liberty and justice."[83] Dulles opened up these hearings with an invited paper on the ecclesiological implications of Pope Paul VI's *Development of Peoples* (1967) and the International Synod of Bishops' *Justice in the World* (1971). The keynote of these two documents, Dulles argued, revealed "a much more intimate involvement of the Church and of the concerns of the Gospel with the present situation of world development than one perhaps finds in the earlier social encyclicals which accent, rather, the eternal principles of social justice on a rather abstract level attributed more to the natural law than to a social analysis of the present situation in the world."[84]

Dulles focused the remainder of his comments on the real dilemma he perceived in the church's relations to social problems in the world, a recurring theme in his most recent work. If the church simply articulated general and abstract principles of social justice, teaching from on high, it could justly be accused of irrelevance in the modern world. If, however, it identified the church's teaching with concrete social proposals or programs already in the body politic, it could correctly be accused of exceeding its particular competence (that is, its specific mandate of fostering communion with God). In the face of this problem, Dulles called upon the bishops and the Bicentennial Committee to live creatively in the tension of this dilemma by articulating the general principles that flowed from the gospel and by applying them to concrete social problems, but with certain provisos: the church should in everything that it does emphasize its primary mission of fostering communion with God. But living in communion with God was not separated from living in a world of multiple social problems. The church, though, should speak provisionally in areas where the subject matter itself was tentative. In making prudent applications to social problems, moreover, the church should get the advice of technical experts in the field, demonstrate evidence for the concrete positions it takes, use the language of persuasion (not command), make it clear where disagreement and dissent are possible, and put into practice in the church's institutions the principles of justice articulated in its own documents. Applying the gospel to concrete social situations required technical skill, exposure to and knowledge of the concrete situation, and a consciousness of the mind of Christ that conditioned the other two.[85]

Dulles' opening address was cautionary about the deeply problematic nature of relating the sacred and the secular and the complex problem of living in both simultaneously. When asked how one might reconcile the difficulty of simply stating generalities and articulating highly concrete proposals, Dulles responded by offering no practical blueprint for such a reconciliation. He appealed instead to what he called "concrete discernment," which was a combination of spiritual insight governed by the gospel, technical skill, and concrete knowledge of specific problems.[86]

Six other hearings were held across the United States during 1975 in preparation for the bicentennial event in Detroit. After the hearings were completed, Dulles was appointed to a writing committee that met periodically to prepare a working paper and proposals on ecclesiology for the Detroit convention.[87] Thereafter Dulles and 1,340 Catholic lay and clerical delegates, most of whom were chosen by the bishops themselves, went to Detroit for the Call to Action three-day meeting in October 1976. More than a thousand nonvoting observers, many from the secular as well as religious press, also attended the meeting. The attendance of the press assured that the convention would receive widespread coverage. The meeting, deemed a huge success by its avid proponents and a dismal failure by its opponents, created 182 proposals, some of which were contrary to contemporary church discipline or doctrine.[88] Those proposals were submitted to the National Conference of Catholic Bishops for consideration and for implementation over the next five-year period.

The *New York Times*, among other newspapers, gave daily coverage of the Detroit event, emphasizing the radical experiment in the Catholic democratic consultative procedures and the sensational proposals that "could alter traditional church attitudes on such major issues as birth control, divorce and the role of women in the church."[89] The *Times* and other journals focused on the conventions' recommendations for new policies on the treatment of divorced Catholics and homosexuals, for the ordination of women and married men, and for other hot-button issues that caught the journalists' attention.[90] Many of the bishops who were consulted by the press indicated that they thought it highly unlikely that some of the reform-minded proposals would be approved by the National Conference of Catholic Bishops. The bishops eventually responded to the resolutions but refused to consider or implement the controversial doctrinal and disciplinary suggestions.[91]

Dulles, as the immediate past president of the CTSA and one of the most prominent theologians attending the convention, was periodically sought out by the press to give his impressions of the issues being discussed and the votes that were taken. On the issue of women's ordination, for example, he pointed out to a reporter that "if the rationale for the traditional position is merely cultural...then we have the freedom to move ahead. If the maleness of Christ is involved as a sacramental symbol of the priesthood, then there are serious obstacles." He concluded his comment on the issue by saying that he "would like to see more careful theological studies done."[92]

Dulles did not publish any personal assessment of the Detroit Call to Action convention immediately after the event, an omission that was untypical of his participation in major ecclesiastical meetings. But he was not entirely favorable to the outcome. Although he approved in principle a consultative process in the Catholic Church, he was less than enthusiastic about the practical results of

Detroit. Some very serious theological and disciplinary issues were being discussed and debated and voted on by large numbers of people who had little theological competence.[93] A decade after Detroit, Dulles suggested that during the late 1960s and early 1970s what neoconservatives called the "new knowledge class" had had some considerable influence upon the American Catholic bishops—an influence that "crested" in the mid-1970s. Increasingly after the Call to Action deliberations, however, the bishops aligned themselves more and more with mainline Catholics and not the professional and technical experts. Their pastorals on peace (1983) and the economy (1986), however, Dulles argued, could not be perceived, as they were by Peter Berger and other neoconservatives, as reflecting the undue influence of a new intelligentsia.[94]

Detroit, Dulles implied, had been a wake-up call for the American bishops and others who were unwilling to follow the radical direction set by Detroit. One could argue, too, that Dulles himself saw Detroit as another manifestation that things had gotten somewhat out of control within the American Catholic Church and shifts in priorities were in order. That interpretation is reinforced by what Dulles said much later in his career about Detroit. In the 1996 enlargement of his autobiography, he asserted that

> in three short days, the carefully nuanced working papers were gutted by a series of radical amendments....The Call to Action assembly provided an object lesson in how a small group of militant activists could manipulate a large majority of open-minded liberal delegates, thus aligning the assembly with an agenda that had little in common with the Catholic tradition, the social teaching of the Church, and the concerns of the great majority of worshipers.[95]

Increasingly Dulles interpreted Detroit as the loss of a middle ground he was trying to preserve between the reactionary conservatives and the radical reformers in the post–Vatican II church. Holding the moderate middle in theology became his most concerted effort during these years.

10
THE MODERATE MIDDLE IN THEOLOGY, 1974-1988

THE DETROIT CONVENTION, together with his Hartford experience, his dispute with David Tracy and Langdon Gilkey, and his involvement in the *Human Sexuality* controversy, happening almost simultaneously in the mid-1970s, brought a shift in Dulles' theological emphases in the years after Detroit, as was clearly evident in *The Resilient Church*. The modified emphases, moreover, were also apparent in his approaches to faith, revelation, ecclesiology, and ecumenism—the focal points of his own theological research.

Faith and Revelation

By the mid-1970s, Dulles was reconsidering his own theology of faith and its relationship to various issues in church and society. In 1975, he reflected autobiographically on the two major stages of his own personal journey in understanding faith. He characterized his early years, from about 1940 to 1960, as a quasi-revolt against the emptiness and meaninglessness of a materialistic and self-absorbed modernity and an "obedient hearing of a living and authoritative voice that speaks in the name of Christ....Allegiance to Jesus therefore took me to an authoritative and dogmatic Church."[1] That early mentality stayed with him for his first twenty years as a Catholic and a Jesuit. Around 1960 and for the next fifteen years or so, Dulles' attitudes and interests gradually changed, although it must be said that he never abandoned his initial faith experience. After 1960, however, he became much more conscious of the poverty of human language and concepts to convey the transcendent God, and he became increasingly more aware of the historical and cultural limitations of all human and ecclesial formulations of the faith. Vatican II, moreover, underlined more than in the past the mystery of God and the historicity of the human condition. All of these developments gave him a more nuanced understanding of authority and a more tentative approach to all previous conceptualizations of the faith. By 1975, therefore, he could say that faith itself "seems to me less a set of hard-and-fast answers than a constantly unfolding process."[2] His basic conviction of faith remained, but it led him to deeper levels of understanding and wisdom and made him much more cautious or at least tentative about the absolute authority of previous expressions of the faith.

On different occasions, Dulles spoke of at least three models or ideal conceptualizations of faith: the intellectualist, the fiducial, and the performative. The exclusive formulations of faith as knowledge, as trust, or as action had certain benefits but also weaknesses that Dulles hoped might be overcome by bringing the traditional Catholic, traditional Protestant, and current liberationist or activist formulations into dialogue with one another. Each of the formulations emphasized a significant element of faith. Liberation theology's emphasis on faith as action in favor of justice and universal liberation had certain advantages over the traditional Catholic and Protestant approaches to faith because it was consistent with the biblical notions of freedom and because it overcame the Platonic idealist tendencies of the intellectualist approach and the laissez-faire tendencies of the fiduciary attitude to social activism. Dulles favored the newer liberation emphasis on action in behalf of justice, but he criticized the tendency among some liberationists who identified the gospel itself with a particular social or economic system or who equated social justice with the whole of salvation.[3]

During his years at Catholic University, when Dulles was invited to lecture at various Catholic colleges and universities, Catholic higher education was in the midst of a discussion of its identity in the modern world, and Dulles periodically addressed that issue in terms of the relationship among faith, justice, and the academic disciplines. On May 13, 1978, the Jesuit University of Detroit gave Dulles an honorary degree, one of more than forty he received in the course of his theological career. During the com-

Lecturing in Frankfurt, August 26, 1977

mencement ceremony, he told the audience that a Catholic university was not a catechetical institute, nor was it simply a pragmatic institution for the promotion of knowledge and skills without regard for questions of value, nor did it need to be religiously uncommitted in order to be a bona fide university. A Catholic university had a mission to provide students with a critical and creative understanding of faith in God and an understanding of how that faith had implications for issues of justice in the world—a faith, in other words, that led to just social action. The Second Vatican Council, the postconciliar international episcopal synods, and the Jesuits' General Congregations had all spoken of the inherent relationship between faith and justice, and it was the responsibility of the Catholic university to promote that link.

Theology or religious studies within a Catholic university, critically and creatively examining issues of faith and justice, needed to be in dialogue with the other disciplines, especially in those areas where the findings or hypotheses of the other disciplines have religious or moral implications. In dialogue with one another, the university disciplines should analyze public policies and pronounce, where appropriate, on the arguments behind particular programs, initiatives, issues, and positions in the light of faith's vision of justice. Within this job description, the university "must insist on full academic freedom" to dissent not only from governmental policy and current practices but also from the "rigidities of ecclesiastical dogmatism."[4] Theology's critical, creative, and dialogical roles within the university were not in Dulles' mind separated from the traditional understanding of theology as faith seeking understanding.

Dulles also continued his research into the theology of revelation, and during this period of his career he produced *Models of Revelation* (1983), the book he himself characterized in 1992 as "the most serious and substantial I have written"; for some time thereafter he considered it his most significant theological argument.[5] Because revelation was a more technical topic, the book was not as popular nor as widely distributed as *Models of the Church*. *Models of Revelation*, though, revealed what was at the center of his theology, and the study was the culmination of his research and writing on revelation since the early 1960s. Previous to 1983, he had outlined the history of the theology of revelation and had written several articles and encyclopedia entries on issues related to the nature and function of revelation. Many of these articles were historical and descriptive, and they relied particularly on Vatican II's *Dei verbum* and other conciliar statements, as well as upon past and current Protestant and Catholic theological studies of the issue. He had surveyed broadly what had been written on the issue, and in 1977 he spent a semester at the Woodrow Wilson International Center for Scholars, researching and examining much of the twentieth-century representative Catholic and Protestant approaches to revelation, focusing in particular on what the theologians understood revelation to be (its nature) and the means of its communication to human beings. He also focused much of his Wilson Center study on symbol theory in contemporary philosophical and literary critical studies as well as in contemporary theology.

In December of that year, then, he presented a paper to the Fellows of the Center on the results of his research, arguing that revelation had a symbolic structure and was a symbolic form of communication. In 1980, after revising that paper several times, he published the results in *Theological Studies* under the title "The Symbolic Structure of Revelation,"[6] a seminal article for his *Models*.

"Symbolic Structure" focused on some of the controversial issues in contemporary theology: how revelation was initially communicated, how it made its entrance into the human mind, and what kind of truth it could claim. These were the central issues in contemporary fundamental theology as far as Dulles was concerned, and no consensus existed on them. The twentieth-century theological responses to these issues, he argued, could be divided into five major models or ideal types or paradigms, which he designated as the propositional, historical, mystical, dialectical, and symbolic. He examined each of these ideal types, into which no single theologian fit exactly, in terms of how revelation was communicated and what kind of truth it contained. As in *Models of the Church*, Dulles was here creating mental constructs that helped to demonstrate the legitimate pluralism in theology and the fundamental mystery at the heart of the reality the theologians were attempting to approximate in their own theological systems. Of course, tensions and irreconcilable differences existed among the models of revelation, but Dulles wanted to preserve the benefits of each model while transcending its limitations.

For Dulles, the symbolic model transcended the other models and incorporated the advantages of each of the others. Revelation as a symbolic form of communication gave rise to a participatory knowledge of divine things—a kind of knowledge that simultaneously transformed the participant and surpassed discursive thought. The personal encounter with revelation brought about a new awareness, changed commitments, and modified behavior, all of which initiated the participant into a saving relationship with God. In this symbolic model,

> revelation never occurs in a purely internal experience or as an unmediated encounter with God. It is always mediated through an experience in the world. More specifically, it is mediated through symbol—that is to say, through an externally perceived sign that works mysteriously on the human consciousness so as to suggest more than it can clearly describe or define. Revelatory symbols are those which express and mediate God's self-communication.[7]

When Dulles spoke of revelation as symbolic communication, he had a very definite understanding of what he meant by *symbol*. A symbol, unlike an indicative sign, which merely pointed to a reality outside of itself, contained the reality to which it pointed and invited the person to participate in that reality to such an extent that the experience and knowledge obtained from the participation transcended the person's ability to articulate fully what was known through the experience. Nature, the cosmos, historical events, words, stories, myths, rituals, artistic creations, and persons could all become symbols of divine communication. Symbols, moreover, speak to the whole person: mind, heart, and will, and not just to the intellect.

Periodically Dulles identified himself as a "symbolic realist" rather than a transcendentalist or a conceptualist. "As a realist," he told John McDermott, a fellow Jesuit theologian, "I hold to the inviolability of certain propositions of faith, but as a symbolist I deny that faith is primarily an assent to propositions. I maintain that the realities of revelation are initially mediated by symbols (especially symbolic realities) that carry a spiritual power able to convert and save." In this he separated himself somewhat from Karl Rahner. He did not, as he thought Rahner seemed to suggest at times, think that "faith can be deduced a priori from some generically human experience of faith....I insist more than Rahner does on the historical mediation of grace—a point on which I find Rahner ambiguous rather than wrong."[8]

Dulles concluded his "Symbolic Structure" by maintaining that his approach to revelation was consistent with Vatican II's *Dei verbum* (DV): "This plan of revelation is realized by deeds and words having an inner unity: the deeds wrought by God in the history of salvation manifest and confirm the teaching and realities signified by the words, while the words proclaim the deeds and clarify the mystery contained in them" (DV 2). The first four models of revelation outlined in this article were brought together and reconciled in the fifth, the symbolic approach. "Because revelation occurs as symbolic, it can be both propositional and historical, both mystical and dialectical, without detriment to the proper attributes implied by each of these designations."[9]

Dulles had clearly outlined the main features of his symbolic model of revelation, but the article was not his definitive statement of what he meant by a symbolic approach. In 1980, he was invited to Marquette University's symposium in honor of Karl Rahner, who was that year being given the university's "Père Marquette Discovery Award" for his achievements in theology. Dulles decided to give a talk at the conference on the relationship between revelation and discovery, hoping to transcend the impasses created by exclusive subjectivist or objectivist approaches to revelation. To articulate his own views, he used Michael Polanyi's understanding of discovery as a process of personal knowledge. Discovery, in a Polanyian sense, was not entirely under the control of the observer's explicit efforts. Neo-orthodox theologians in particular thought of revelation and discovery as entirely different realities. They asserted that some modern theologians had put discovery or religious consciousness in the place of revelation. If religious knowledge were discovery, they held, it could not be revelation, and if revelation, it could not be discovery. Dulles' talk was an attempt to overturn this view of things. Revelation and discovery were not polar opposites or merely juxtaposed to one another. He proposed, instead, that "revelation can be brought within the category of discovery, and that it may even be defined as a gifted religious discovery."[10]

These two articles of 1980, "The Symbolic Structure of Revelation" and "Revelation and Discovery," indicated something of the direction of Dulles' thought. He refined his notion of revelation as symbolic mediation during the 1981–1982 school year when he held the Gasson Chair at Boston College. The result of this year of study and reflection was his 1983 magnum opus, *Models of Revelation*, the culmination of more than twenty years of work on the issue.

Models was a tour de force in fundamental theology, surveying some major philosophical objections to the reality of revelation, critically examining five twentieth-century theological models of revelation (propositional, historical, mystical, dialectical, and new awareness), arguing that all five models involved symbolic communication, proposing "symbolic mediation" as a way of integrating the solid values of the five differing systems, and applying his symbolic view of revelation to six issues (Christ, world religions, the Bible, the church, eschatology, and faith) that were directly affected by any theology of revelation. The book differed from his 1980 article on "Symbolic Structure" by designating the fifth model as "new awareness." In this newly constructed "Revelation as New Awareness" model—represented by theologians like Gregory Baum, Gabriel Moran, Leslie Dewart, Ray L. Hunt, and William M. Thompson—revelation was perceived as "a transcendent fulfillment of the inner drive of the human spirit toward fuller consciousness."[11] The new fifth model, no longer called the symbolic model, demonstrated a shift in his thinking about all the models of revelation he had previously identified. He now argued that symbolic communication was inherent in each of the five models.

Unlike *Models of the Church*, Dulles' typological construction in 1983 was not so much concerned with affirming a legitimate pluralism as it was with transcending the polarities that existed in competing approaches. He had characterized that postconciliar context in various ways since 1965, and by 1983 he interpreted his times not only in terms of a legitimate diversity but also in terms of various polarizations and conflicting claims. That understanding of the contemporary situation made reconciling the "warring parties" a primary objective of this book.[12] The cultural and religious situation had changed, or his perception of the situation had changed. By the 1980s, moreover, he charged that "subjectivism" had "invaded many sectors of Catholicism," reducing faith to "private feeling," and as a result "concern for universally valid truth has greatly receded."[13] Dulles acknowledged that his own typological approach to revelation was a time-conditioned theological response to the ideological and cultural pluralism of his own times, but a response that was consistent with the longer biblical, doctrinal, theological, and ecclesiastical traditions. It spoke to the times, but it also transcended the limits of a culturally bound position.

The book was a personal testimony to his self-identity as a theologian in the 1980s. Ever since he was an undergraduate at Harvard, he had been preoccupied with understanding the relationship between faith and reason, revelation and faith. He had developed his own thinking on these issues from a relatively pre-critical sense of the faith, to an acceptance of a critical-historical approach to the faith, to, finally, an acknowledgment of the reductive limits of the critical enterprise and the value of a postcritical restoration of what Dulles, following Polanyi and others, referred to as a "due allowance for tacit awareness and symbolic communication."[14] The book was also a masterful assessment of a vast amount of twentieth-century literature on revelation, introducing his readers to the full spectrum of Christian responses to the issue, from those of conservative Protestant Evangelicals and Catholic neo-scholastics to the neo-orthodox and liberal or progressive Protestant and Catholic positions on revelation. In this respect *Models* was a major guide for students of the subject.

Dulles' identification of symbolic communication in all the models of revelation served to preserve the truths inherent in each of the models, raise them into a new kind of synthesis, transcend the differences among the models, correct some of their deficiencies, and ultimately establish a coherent theology not identified with any one of them. For Dulles, as for some of his Protestant and Catholic theological colleagues, revelatory symbols communicated a kind of knowledge that transcended the purely noetic or discursive. Revelatory symbols allowed the recipient to dwell in the symbol and to participate in the reality that the symbol signified.[15] *Models of Revelation* was a much more systematic work than *Models of the Church* because it moved beyond the descriptive and the analytical to the synthetic.

Dulles' symbolic or postcritical approach to revelation sought to escape both subjectivism and objectivism, and he applied it to a series of dogmatic problems that rounded out his fundamental theology of revelation. He demonstrated in the second half of his text how the symbolic approach viewed Christ as *the* revelatory symbol or the summit of revelation, the presence of revelation in the various religions of the world, the Bible as the document of revelation, the church as a bearer of revelation, the developmental and eschatological nature of revelation, and the meaning of the acceptance of revelation in faith.

Models of Revelation was widely reviewed in various Protestant and Catholic journals of theological opinion and rapidly became a significant textbook in theological education in the English-speaking and -reading world, going into its ninth printing in 2003, twenty years after its initial publication. Although Dulles himself saw the work as a project in fundamental theology and not a comprehensive theology of revelation, one of his reviewers tagged it "the most comprehensive treatment on revelation in the English-speaking world."[16] Other theological reviewers, recognizing the magisterial contribution of Dulles' work, took issue here and there with elements of his perspective. Even while they criticized lacunae in it, almost all the reviewers acknowledged the "worthwhileness" and indeed the necessity of dialoguing with his understanding of revelation in any future work on the subject.[17]

Models of Revelation was Dulles' most significant work in fundamental theology during his years at Catholic University. After it was published, he continued to reflect on faith and revelation and at one point wrote explicitly on Michael Polanyi's insight on these theological issues. Following Polanyi, Dulles argued that there was a fiduciary component in all human knowledge; the fiduciary element in theology, therefore, was not "an anomaly among the cognitive disciplines."[18] Polanyi had pointed to the function of tacit knowing in the scientific enterprise, and Dulles applied that notion to theology. Tacit knowing was the result of focusing attention on the joint meaning of all the clues that were available rather than focusing separately on particular clues. Tacit knowing provided human beings with a knowledge that transcended particulars and that provided a surplus of meaning. Tacit knowing functioned in theology as in many other disciplines, and the fiduciary element in all knowing was the beginning of the discovery process because human beings had to trust their powers to perceive problems, to envision solutions, and to discriminate between correct and counterfeit solutions.[19] The process of discovery and the labor of searching, however, were not always the means of arriving at a solution. At times a solution arrived unexpectedly, and at times when the searcher was not consciously looking for it. It sometimes came as an illumination, as a sheer gift.

Polanyi's analysis of this process of faith, discovery, and illumination exhibited to Dulles the very process of religious discovery and conversion. Many times in religion and theology, as in the scientific enterprise, the discoverer felt no need for confirmation of the discovery. The solution arrived with its own validation because of its inherent intellectual beauty, its acceptability to persons of respect and insight, its own cognitive and practical fruitfulness, and its correspondence with what had been known before the solution arrived. The solution corresponded in fact to the antecedent expectations, the longing inherent in the search, or, in Polanyi's terms, it was "accredited in advance by the heuristic craving which evoked it."[20]

Dulles was well aware that his comparison of the scientific discovery process to the process of religious discovery and personal conversion did not apply to all scientists nor to all believers. Many scientific and religious practitioners did not have those illuminating discoveries or those sudden conversions that a few in their respective communities experienced. Nonetheless the common practitioners in science or in religion took their faith and their understanding from the communities and traditions in which they dwelt. And the novices in these communities were induced as apprentices into their respective communities of faith and meaning by means of teaching and practice. In science, the authoritative leadership of experts provided the links of continuity, stability, and order within the scientific community and passed on their expertise to scholars who came after them. In religion or Christianity, an analogous situation occurred when authoritative leaders exercised a supervision over the standards of admission, the training and education of clerical leadership, and a control over the catechesis to which new members were introduced.[21] Whether in science or in religion, the new member appropriated the wisdom and knowledge of the community by dwelling in it and exercising its practices.

Dulles was a fundamental theologian primarily interested in the theoretical issues that faced the church in the modern world. He tried to dialogue with those academics like Polanyi whose work had a direct bearing on epistemological issues in the Christian tradition. But Dulles was also concerned with the very practical pastoral problems that the Catholic Church faced in the present, and his theoretical positions had a direct bearing on some current ecclesial issues.

Dulles applied Polanyi's insights not only to his understanding of Christian faith and tradition, but also to the very practical issues of communicating the faith in concrete programs of religious education. In April 1985 he gave a keynote address to the annual meeting of the National Catholic Education Association and chose as his topic "The Communication of Faith and Its Content."[22] He proposed to Catholic educators his own symbolic realist approach to Christian epistemology (distinguishing that approach from the dogmatic rationalism, historical positivism, and mystical empiricism that in the past and in the present had influenced Christian education and formation).

A symbolic realist perceived Christian faith itself as a "personal commitment to the joint meaning of the Christian symbols...an imaginative integration of divinely given clues or symbols." Such a view of faith meant that the joint meaning could never be adequately formulated in language but was "tacitly perceived through reliance on the symbols themselves."[23] In light of this view of Christian faith, the task of the religious educator was threefold: to exhibit the credibility of the Christian religion because faith had a cognitive content, to communicate the contents of belief, and to socialize the individual into the community of faith. Religious educators functioned analogously to experts in the field of science; they had the responsibility to induct apprentices into the community of faith, and they could most helpfully do that by immersing the neophytes into the religious and moral practices of Christianity. The experiences within the Christian symbol system and in Christian activities would, they hoped, lead to that surplus of meaning that existed within the Christian tradition.

The socialization process and the maintenance of a close communion of believers with one another was particularly important, Dulles argued, when a gulf existed between "the faith commitment and the prevailing assumptions of the general culture."[24] Dulles was calling upon Christian educators to take a more holistic approach to Christian education than had been envisioned in religious education programs that emphasized exclusively doctrinal content, salvific historical events, or interior religious experience. A triadic approach to Christian knowledge, encompassing all three elements in their multiple symbolic manifestations, was the holistic approach he suggested.

Revelation required a sense of the faith in order to be adequately interpreted, and Dulles was very conscious of the need to clarify the Catholic meaning of the so-called sense of the faithful, particularly in a democratic society that was sensitive to the role of majority opinion. That phrase had been used repeatedly, especially in the postconciliar period, to underline the role of the entire Christian community in the reception and formulation of the faith.

And in a period of polarization and opinion polls on nearly all conceivable issues, Dulles found it necessary to speak out on the meaning of a supernatural sense of the faith, which the Second Vatican Council affirmed. A universal agreement on matters of faith and morals was an infallible index of truth (*Lumen gentium*; LG 12). But, what did that mean? In 1986 Dulles reasserted the infallibility of the *sensus fidelium* and claimed it as a "distinct theological font."[25] Later in his career, Dulles continued to acknowledge the role of the sense of the faithful in church teaching; it had "no juridical standing; it cannot overrule the teaching of the hierarchy, but it can stimulate the hierarchy to formulate new doctrines or reformulate older doctrines."[26]

The supernatural sense of the faith was not a sociological concept; it was not a mere head count; it required responsible communal discernment in the light of scripture, tradition, and religious experience. Sometimes in the history of Christianity, it was true, the faith of the church was maintained by a majority; at other times, however, it was preserved by a faithful remnant against the majority. There was ambiguity here in appealing to the sense of the faithful, and that reinforced the need for discernment. Contemporary theologians, moreover, conscious of the historical, cultural, and social conditioning of all forms of knowing, pointed to the limitations of a universal sense of the faithful as a source of Christian truth. Those who appealed to the sense of the faithful had to be sensitive to its limitations, especially aware of the subtle as well as obvious influences and pressures that public opinion in secular societies had upon the Christian faithful. One also could not discount the effects of fallen human nature on the opinions and judgments of the faithful. Given these limitations, it was nonetheless true, according to Dulles, that the *sensus fidelium* was a nonautonomous but distinct theological source. It was an acknowledgment that the faithful, from the bishops to the laity, were those who, under the guidance of the Holy Spirit, were able to recognize and discern the meaning of the word of God. In the end, the sense of the faithful was a spiritual discernment in conformity with revelation, not public opinion polls.

For Dulles, spiritual discernment was required for an adequate reading and interpretation of scripture, but that was not the only approach to the word of God in scripture. Scripture had been read and interpreted on multiple levels in the past and in the present. Dulles had clearly addressed this issue in *Models of Revelation* and in other writings during his years at Catholic University. He designated his own approach and that of many other Catholic and Protestant theologians as "centrist." The centrist approach was distinguished from the

> "orthodoxy" of recent centuries and from contemporary conservative theology by insisting that the biblical texts must be read in their full historical and literary context and pondered in the light of Christian tradition and present experience. But, unlike radical theology, the centrist positions accept the Bible as a primary embodiment of the word of God and as an indispensable normative source for the church and for theology.[27]

Dulles increasingly insisted that the Bible, as the word of God in the church, was open to multiple readings. It was not, as H. Richard Niebuhr once remarked, solely the book of the historian's workshop. It was the book of the church and could be read and fruitfully interpreted by the faithful, by scholars and professional biblical exegetes, and by the magisterium of the church. It was used by the faithful for prayer (private and liturgical) and spiritual nourishment. It was studied by scholars for the sake of a clear understanding of the various texts and their varied meanings. It was a foundation source for the church's official magisterium, as it helped to clarify and define the meaning of the Christian faith. Tensions and contradictions at times existed between a spiritual, a critical-historical, and a magisterial reading of the Bible. Nonetheless, the theologian had to acknowledge the necessity of preserving the validity of each reading of the Bible in order to capture the mystery of the message contained in it.

These various readings, however, were not mutually exclusive; they could be preserved, Dulles believed, in dialectical tension and synthesis. Talking to a group of charismatic Catholics in the late 1970s, Dulles argued for a reciprocal dependence and coinherence of seemingly diverse approaches to the Bible. He wanted a more dialectical approach to the Bible—one that acknowledged that

> the Church creates the Bible while the Bible creates the Church. The Bible authenticates tradition, but tradition authenticates the Bible. The *magisterium* learns from biblical scholars and at the same time instructs them what they are to believe about scripture. The Bible is the Church's book, but the Church is under the Bible as the word of God. The Bible is not the Church, but the Church can never be without the Bible, nor can the Bible be truly Bible without the Church. Between Bible and Church there is both a profound unity and an ineradicable distinction.[28]

Dulles repeatedly asserted that since the Second Vatican Council, Catholics had paid more attention to the Bible as the word of God, and Protestant scholars had given more credence to the role of tradition. Although major differences continued to exist between Protestant and Catholic approaches to the Bible, there was an emerging consensus that Dulles found fruitful. Although he continued to call for a dialectical approach to the Bible that acknowledged the role of scholarly interpretations as well as a certain spiritual reading of the scriptures, he would also become increasingly more critical of a scholarly historical-critical approach that seemed to undercut his view of the Bible as symbolic communication—a criticism that would become much more pronounced after he retired from Catholic University.

Since his junior year at Harvard, Dulles had become a consistent and avid reader of the Bible for his own spiritual nourishment and as a fundamental source for his understanding of the Christian tradition. More than many other American Catholic fundamental or systematic theologians, he used biblical texts extensively in his own theological writings, revealing a familiarity with the texts that came from many years of reading, contemplating, and studying the Bible. At times his theological arguments were grounded with strings of biblical citations, appealing always to the biblical foundations for positions he was taking. He was doing in his theology what the Second Vatican Council, which called the Bible the "soul of theology," had recommended for theology. He was also an avid reader of biblical commentaries and the most recent critical biblical scholarship. His use of biblical citations, therefore, was many times informed by critical scholarship and was not simply a matter of supplying proof-texts for his theological arguments. His extensive use of the Bible in his theology had an appeal to Protestants, especially Evangelical Protestants, even when they might not agree with his interpretations.

Dulles continued during his years at the Catholic University to argue for the survival of dogma, not dogma as the term was understood in the nineteenth- and early twentieth-century neo-scholastic manuals, but dogma as a form of symbolic communication that mediated the mystery of faith. Dogmas were not fixed in concrete, as the scholastic manuals understood them; they developed historically and were valuable forms for preserving continuity in the faith over time. Although historically conditioned and never fully expressive of the mystery, dogmas, Dulles argued in various essays, have a significant role to play in formulating a community's faith and providing a test for right thinking in the church. In these years, more than in the late 1960s and 1970s, Dulles emphasized the power of dogmas as symbols of faith for promoting orthodoxy and leading to acts of faith, hope, charity, and devotion. He argued against some contemporaries who identified orthodoxy with heresy hunting or magisterial imposition, and insisted that an emphasis on dogma and orthodoxy, rightly understood, was consistent with the New Testament's authentic concern for sound doctrine.[29]

Apologetics

Although as a fundamental theologian Dulles focused most of his attention upon revelation, faith, dogma, and the tasks of theology during his years at the Catholic University, he also on occasion wrote of the need for a more adequate apologetics in a post–Vatican II Catholic Church that had dismissed or neglected the discipline. Although he never prepared a systematic apologetics, he suggested in periodic essays elements that needed to be considered in any contemporary approach to the subject.

A new apologetic was needed that took account of two realities: the fundamental orientation of the human spirit toward the divine and the testimony of the lived experience of faith within the church. The new approach needed to acknowledge that the hungers of the human spirit, made evident in a conglomeration of clues, could not be satisfied apart from faith and that the individual decision of faith rested upon a multitude of unverifiable assumptions. The justification of faith was "necessarily a personal matter," meaning that faith was, in Polanyi's language, personal knowledge. Faith was indeed personal and beyond empirical verification, but it was not blind commitment; it was an intelligible act based on a series of clues, not all of which were the subject of reason's attention. The new fundamental theology and the new apologetic, unlike the older approach, did not seek to prove that Christian commitment was the only proper one; it aimed to make intelligible the process of one's faith decision.[30]

An integral part of that decision of faith included the witness of the church as the symbol of a transformed encounter with God. The church, in this apologetic, was considered the ground or sacrament of God's presence in the world, manifested most clearly in the lived Christianity of its members.[31] Reflection on the interaction of the individual search and the communal demonstration of a lived Christianity needed to be incorporated into a new apologetic for contemporaries, who were conscious of the subjectivity and freedom of the human person and the influence of social circumstances on personal development.[32]

Ecclesiological Issues

Dulles continued his work in ecclesiology while at the Catholic University, although he did not teach courses on ecclesiology, except when Patrick Granfield, OSB, an ecclesiologist, was absent or on leave from the university. Dulles acknowledged in *The Resilient Church* that he aimed to "appraise and carry forward the theological work of Catholic ecclesiology in the decade since the Council."[33] The very title of that book indicates something of what Dulles would emphasize in the late 1970s and thereafter: the church's power "to accommodate itself to the pressures placed upon it" but also its capacity "to respond creatively and to exert counterpressures upon its environment."[34]

Church as Community of Disciples

A major new development in his ecclesiology emerged in the 1980s when Dulles began to speak of the church as a "community of disciples," a model of the church that he believed to be more appropriate to the times than those he had identified in *Models of the Church*, even though he continued to believe that those paradigms had enduring value. This new concentration upon discipleship was part of a larger movement in theological and biblical studies. Dulles had been impressed in the 1960s with Dietrich Bonhoeffer's *Cost of Discipleship* (1937; Eng., 1959) and had read some of the 1960s biblical studies on discipleship in the New Testament.[35] Biblical scholars increasingly examined discipleship in the 1980s, as was evident, for example, in Marquette University's 1982 symposium on "Call and Discipleship: New Testament Perspectives." Dulles had followed, read, and quoted from the proceedings of that conference.[36]

No doubt these studies had an influence on Dulles' interest in discipleship, but Pope John Paul II's first encyclical, *Redemptor Hominis*, The Redeemer of Man (1979), published five months after his election as pope, was the most significant factor in turning Dulles' attention to the topic.[37] The pope wanted to put Christ and his message of universal liberation "back into the center of world history," as two of his biographers have noted.[38] The encyclical was a call for a spiritual renewal in church and society, for freedom for all religious believers, and for a moral regeneration that would lead to justice in society, an equitable distribution of the goods of the earth, and a focus on eternal salvation. What particularly resonated with Dulles' understanding of the times was a paragraph that focused on discipleship, a paragraph he quoted periodically:

> Membership in that body [of Christ] has for its source a particular call, united with the saving action of grace. Therefore, if we wish to keep in mind this community of the People of God, which is so vast and so extremely dif-

ferentiated, we must see first and foremost Christ saying in a way to each member of the community: "Follow me." It is the community of disciples, each of whom in a different way—at times very consciously and consistently, at other times not very consciously and very inconsistently—is following Christ. This shows also the deeply "personal" aspect and dimension of this society.[39]

In his early 1980s essays, Dulles focused on the particular relevance and the meaning of discipleship for contemporary Christians, perceiving Christianity and faith itself as discipleship.[40] This emphasis, of course, was not new. It was a significant element in the New Testament, had been reiterated and practiced in the early church, in the monastic tradition, and Ignatius of Loyola had made it a special feature in the training of his companions. The call to discipleship meant for the New Testament, as for contemporaries, a total commitment to Jesus as master. Discipleship involved "a radical break from the world and its values" and a "total renunciation of family, property, income, worldly ambition, and even personal safety." An emphasis on the church as a community of disciples was especially relevant at a time when convinced Christians were what Peter Berger called a "cognitive minority" or what Dulles repeatedly called a "contrast society" in almost every country in the world. Being a Christian in a secularized society was a difficult task that required conversion and intense formation as disciples.[41]

A solid induction into the community and a thorough socialization were required for the creation of a genuine community of disciples. The formation process called for mature Christians to serve as examples and models for the young and immature or marginal novices in the tradition so that by dwelling within the community they could be attracted to a way of life and learn and practice what it meant to follow Christ. Dulles suggested that such a formation process might best be accomplished in small groups where spiritual leaders could pass on the beliefs and practices of Christian living.[42]

At times Dulles appeared to be advocating a novitiate program, similar to that in religious orders, for all new Christians. Indeed, "vigorous primary communities of faith" were particularly needed in dechristianized cultures.[43] Some might think, moreover, that he was supporting a sect mentality in the midst of what he frequently called a "neo-pagan" world. There is no doubt that he saw the need for a profound and wholehearted conversion that could withstand the pressures of an increasingly secularized world that had all the powerful social and cultural mechanisms to induce the secular mentality. Yet, he was not promoting a withdrawal from the world and its concerns. He wanted the church to take seriously its dedication to Christ and its mission of mediating salvation. Withdrawal and renunciation were necessary for personal and social transformation in Christ. For Dulles, only a faithful, believing church could be a credible church, and only a credible church could be the matrix of faith.[44] For sure, there was a new tone in his ecclesiology of the 1980s, one that emphasized the free, personal, and human component of the disciples' response to Christ.

Dulles saw this new emphasis on the church as the community of Jesus' disciples—stressing free decision in response to a call and the voluntary nature of associating with others who equally felt called to follow Christ—as corresponding well with voluntary elements in American culture. Ironically, such an emphasis enabled the community of disciples to be a "contrast society," to "stand up against the views of many of our compatriots, including perhaps our own family."[45]

Dulles was not proposing that a community of disciples would be the super-model to integrate all the other models of the church. He saw the discipleship model as a "further refinement of ideas" in *Models of the Church*. In 1987, he enlarged his *Models* and incorporated into that text an essay published in 1986 on the "Community of Disciples as a Model of Church." The added chapter brought the book "into alignment with my current thinking."[46] He saw the disciples model as broadly including and incorporating the best elements of the other models but in no way eliminating them. The new stress on discipleship had implications for pastoral ministry, the understanding of community, the sacramental experience, preaching and proclamation, and service within the world.

The sacramental model of the church, a model Dulles formerly thought best able to incorporate the advantages of all the other models, had the distinct advantage, together with some of the other models, of emphasizing the grace dimension of the church and its permanent structural features. But the sacramental model had the disadvantage of being abstract and impersonal, leaving most American Catholics with an image that rarely corresponded to their experience. The discipleship model, on the other hand, although unable to articulate as clearly as the sacramental model the grace dimension, had the distinct advantage of being able to emphasize the free response to a divine call, the voluntary side of identity with the Christian community, and the continual need for spiritual renewal and learning as a disciple. For Dulles, discipleship provided a profound image for the spiritual regeneration of the church and its ministries.

To some extent Dulles' call for a community of disciples reflected his own experience of Catholic formation at St. Benedict Center in Cambridge, Massachusetts, and in the Jesuit novitiate in the 1940s, where he experienced a comprehensive Christian environment in the midst of a world he saw as devoid of spiritual meaning. But it was not a romantic or conservative quest for restoration. He was interpreting the signs of the times and saw among contemporary Christians, and particularly among the young, the loss of a disciplined Christian life and the inability to experience and understand the significance of Christian symbols.[47] Something more than his earlier *Models of the Church* was needed to provide theological insight for a practical renewal of the church. Emphasizing discipleship was one of the ways to bring about more free commitment to Christ and to the mystery of the church's salvific mission. He was not building a new systematic theology of the church, but he saw discipleship as one of the foundation stones for building a more comprehensive ecclesiology.

The Papacy

Discipleship was Dulles' overriding concern in ecclesiology during these years, but he also addressed a host of other ecclesiological issues: for example, the roles and interrelationships of popes, bishops (especially national episcopal conferences), prophets, and teachers (especially theologians) in the community; the meaning of authority, collegiality, freedom, and dissent. He wrote on these and a host of other problems facing the church and was well aware that he was speaking in a democratic, pluralistic, and increasingly secular age that did not share his understanding of religious authorities, obedience, freedom, and dissent. On most of the ecclesiological issues he faced, he took what could be called a "moderately liberal centrist" position, a designation he once used to characterize the theology of fellow Jesuit theologian Francis Sullivan.[48]

Within the postconciliar era, the theological understanding of the papacy and the papal role in the church and society came under closer scrutiny and examination than in perhaps any other period in Catholic history since Vatican I. Patrick Granfield aptly described the period as a *Papacy in Transition*.[49] The popes of the period had broken out of the self-imposed Vatican imprisonment, traveling throughout the world on various missions in support of the global church and addressing a host of social and moral as well as ecclesial issues in the process. In the immediate post–Vatican II period, a few papal initiatives and reforms manifested a new concern for collegiality with the bishops and theologians of the world. Some unpopular papal declarations and Vatican censures of a few theologians, however, seemed to undermine the spirit of Vatican II.

Between 1971 (when Hans Küng published his *Infallible?*) and the early 1980s, theologians (Dulles included), canonists, and journalists responded to these events and produced a flurry of books and essays on the papacy. They reinterpreted its role and meaning for a postconciliar, secular, and ecumenical age,[50] focusing on the biblical foundations, historical developments, and the social and cultural conditions that shaped the Petrine function in the church over time. Several of these studies also proposed various reforms for the papal office and especially for its exercise in the modern world.[51] Dulles spoke to all of these issues during his fourteen years at Catholic University.

In 1985, Dulles opined that Popes Paul VI and John Paul II strove to implement Vatican II, but since Vatican II reflected both traditional elements in Catholic theology as well as progressive ones, neither of which was well integrated in the documents of the council, these two popes tried to preserve both conciliar tendencies—a task that was not easy and certainly one that ultimately reflected the conflicts that were inherent in the council itself. Paul VI "strove loyally to implement it [the Vatican II Council] in an even-handed way. John Paul II, since 1978, has shown himself primarily concerned with reestablishing discipline and overcoming what he describes as the 'disarray and division' left in the wake of the council."[52]

Dulles' former emphasis on the new at Vatican II was fading into the background, but it was not totally eclipsed. He sympathized with the difficult tasks that both popes had, and after 1978 he shared some of Pope John Paul II's interpretation of the signs of the times. Nonetheless, he saw serious tensions in both papacies between the exercise of primacy and the promotion of collegiality, the papal emphasis on universal unity and the diversity inherent in the regional churches, the Vatican attempts at doctrinal control and the reality of theological dissent. The conflicting realities were evident, for example, in Pope Paul VI's 1965 establishment of the International Synod of Bishops as a manifestation of collegiality. Synods met in 1967, 1971, 1974, 1977, 1980, and 1983 and produced documents for the universal church, but the synods were purely advisory; the representative bishops had no deliberative vote, and the popes controlled the agenda and the final documents.

In 1969, moreover, Paul VI established the International Theological Commission to advise the Congregation for the Doctrine of the Faith (CDF), and in 1971 he promulgated new procedures for the examination of doctrinal cases. Thereafter the CDF issued a series of declarations against doctrinally suspect theologians. These CDF preoccupations with doctrinal orthodoxy, particularly under Cardinal Joseph Ratzinger since 1981, are "not unlike the Holy Office under Ottaviani,[53] except it no longer functions as predictably as the neo-scholastic juridicism of earlier generations enabled it to do." Dulles' interpretation of these postconciliar papal activities reflected simultaneously his unhappiness with some papal and Vatican exercises of authority and his acknowledgment that the papacy had a responsibility to protect the integrity of the faith.

Was John XXIII deluded in imagining that errors tend to destroy themselves in the course of time? Was Vatican II mistaken in holding that truth wins over the mind of its own gentle power? Was Paul VI naive in imagining that faith can best be defended by the positive proposal of true doctrine? Taking advantage of the liberty gained by the council, some Catholics undoubtedly carried innovation and dissent to excess. The confusion of the postconciliar period reminds us that severity as well as mercy may be in place and that strong structures of authority, such as the Catholic church has always possessed, may be needed to protect the integrity of revealed truth.[54]

Dulles supported Vatican II's advocacy of the principles of subsidiarity, legitimate diversity, and collegiality, and he saw the need for the exercise of papal authority to preserve the faith, but he worried that some postconciliar exercises of primacy and ecclesiastical authority were as excessive as were the expressions of liberty and dissent.

Dulles was clearly aware of the historically and culturally conditioned nature of the papacy as an institution in the church. Much of what had been historically associated with the papacy—such as the development of the Roman curia, the process of papal elections, and even residency in Rome—were historical developments that were not necessarily a permanent or divinely given part of the Petrine function in the church. Since the mid-1970s Dulles, like other theologians, had called for "a renewed papacy."[55] What that meant for him was a reinterpretation of the doctrine of Vatican I and particularly a renewed attention to the meaning of the divine institution of the papacy. Dulles was conversant with the biblical studies on the Petrine function in the Bible and in the early church and on the limitations of asserting that Christ had personally founded the papacy as an institution. The historical evolution and development of the papacy was consistent and in continuity with the Petrine function in the Bible. The papacy was part of the divine plan but not directly instituted by Christ, as Vatican I and earlier Catholic theology had asserted.

In the mid-1970s and early 1980s, Dulles, like other theologians, suggested reforms for a renewed papacy in the postconciliar era. At one point he proposed the possibility that the Petrine function in the church could be exercised either by a single individual or by "some kind of committee, board, synod, or parliament." He also periodically recommended a more constitutional approach to papal government in the church, with some attention to a balance of powers and gifts within the church, maybe even a separation of powers (into judicial, legislative, administrative), providing a "constitutional evolution somewhat similar to that of England."[56] Papal infallibility, as defined at Vatican I, needed to be reinterpreted in light of the more collegial approach to the church taken at Vatican II, and at one point Dulles would say that the definition at Vatican I, when one considered the various restrictions on it, "really commits one to very little."[57] Dulles also postulated that the exercise of the papacy might be reformed so that the papacy would take on a more "inspirational" and less juridical role in the church. An "affective" mode of papal behavior might enhance the symbolic role of the papacy as an agent of the church's universal unity. These and other kinds of speculative proposals and suggestions for reform indicated something of what Patrick Granfield meant by the *Papacy in Transition*.

Episcopacy and Collegiality

By the early 1980s, Dulles' attention shifted to the episcopal role in the church and especially to the theological significance and teaching authority of national or regional episcopal conferences and the International Synod of Bishops. These issues were, of course, not unrelated to the concerns for reform of the papal office and for postconciliar Vatican reluctance to share responsibility and authority within the church. As a member of the American bishops' Advisory Council between 1969 and 1976, Dulles had close contact with the National Conference of Catholic Bishops and an experiential knowledge of the conference's role in the American church and its relationship with the Vatican. He had been an advocate of collegiality between the bishops and the papacy and a supporter of shared responsibility in the national church between the bishops and their clergy and laity. The Advisory Council was one institutional attempt to implement shared responsibility in the American church, and Dulles had supported those efforts as we have already seen. By the 1980s, however, he focused more and more attention on the teaching authority of the national episcopal conferences and on the role of the International Synod of Bishops.

The question of the status and meaning and authority of national episcopal conferences came to the fore in the early 1980s in the United States because of the American bishops' publication of its pastoral letter on peace, *The Challenge of Peace* (1983), and the prior extensive consultation process that went into the creation of that pastoral. That letter was challenged by scholars and church leaders around the world and stirred up debate in church and society. In Rome, Cardinal Ratzinger of the CDF was having second thoughts about the teaching authority of national episcopal conferences. The experience of the Dutch church in the 1960s and the rapid decline of Catholic allegiance in that church had worried Vatican officials about the theological status and authority of national conferences, and some were hesitant about the new consultative processes in the American church. In 1965, Ratzinger had published an article in *Concilium* arguing that episcopal conferences were a legitimate institutionalization of the collegial nature of the church. By the early 1980s, as prefect of the CDF, however, he suggested that those conferences did not have the *mandatum docendi*, the mandate of teaching—that mandate belonged only to individual bishops in their dioceses or to the college of bishops united with the pope. The Second Vatican Council had not in fact pronounced on the precise authority of the episcopal conferences. It was, therefore, an open theological question, and Dulles offered his own views on the subject in response to questions raised about the authority of the American pastoral on peace.

When the authority of episcopal conferences came into question in the early 1980s, Dulles framed the issue in sacramental, not juridical terms. The bishops had a sacramental mission to teach, and, in fact, the American bishops' conference had issued pastoral letters on a variety of topics that reaffirmed doctrinal issues. Their authority to teach flowed from their sacramental consecration. And, Dulles argued, several Roman congregations, including the CDF, had approved some episcopal conferences' doctrinal statements on sexual morality. The American episcopal conference had a Committee on Doctrine, and that committee had periodically examined the doctrinal soundness of various theological works, including the controversial report on *Human Sexuality* (1977). If the episcopal conferences had no doctrinal authority, such activities would be considered superfluous, but in fact they were not. The conferences, in Dulles' opinion, had some teaching authority.[58] But it was not clear precisely the extent of that authority, and that was an issue that needed further clarification.

Rome had a legitimate concern, Dulles wrote in 1983, about the authority of national episcopal conferences, especially when different national episcopal conferences taught conflicting or potentially conflicting principles on international concerns on justice and peace, as was clearly the case in the different approaches of the German and American episcopal statements on nuclear arms. But, Dulles thought, different statements, appealing to different theological principles, could be of value in creating theological and doctrinal dialogue across national borders, and that could be healthy for theology and for the church. One had to examine episcopal statements, however, with a degree of discernment.

The Challenge of Peace, for example, made it clear that not everything in the pastoral had the same doctrinal weight. One had to distinguish carefully between the moral principles invoked and the application of those principles to very complex problems of justice and peace. The American bishops wisely acknowledged that persons of good will could legitimately disagree with the episcopal applications in certain complex areas of international peace and justice. "In actual practice," Dulles wrote in 1983, "the influence of such statements and the assent that they elicit depend chiefly on the intrinsic qualities of the documents and on the reception accorded to them by discerning critics and by the general public." The authority of the applications the bishops made in the pastoral on peace would ultimately depend on the way in which it was received. But, in fact, Dulles surmised that the way the American bishops went about producing their statement on peace—by study, consultation, and revision—would in the end have an "influence far greater than the juridical status" of the document.[59] Dulles favored the consultation process as a manifestation of collegiality and shared responsibility in the church.

Dulles continued throughout the 1980s to support the doctrinal authority of episcopal conference statements, but he was particularly conscious that specific policy recommendations in some American episcopal statements were "unduly influenced by left-of-center politics," as J. Brian Benestad had argued. Conference statements, though they reflected the collegial nature of the episcopacy, did not necessarily undermine the authority of individual bishops. Dulles reminded his readers in 1985 that an individual bishop can reflect a prophetic voice, when the individual "sees what is not yet evident to the group as a whole."[60] Dulles wanted to provide, even within the national episcopacy, room for the lonely prophetic voice as a part of the church's teaching magisterium.

By 1985, the precise authority of episcopal conferences was not yet clearly defined. The extraordinary International Synod of Bishops, convoked by Pope John Paul II that year, called for a study of the theological status of those conferences because of recurring criticisms of them. Dulles continued over the years since the extraordinary synod to speak on the levels of doctrinal authority in conference statements, and in 1988 he proposed that conferences had what he called a "pastoral magisterium." Such a magisterium was not strictly doctrinal in that a national conference could not impose new doctrines upon the entire church, but the teachings of episcopal conferences, doctrinal and moral, were pastoral and were many times more effective teaching instruments than the voices of individual diocesan bishops teaching in isolation from one another. In Dulles' view, the conferences' "pastoral magisterium" was "indirectly doctrinal" and therefore participated in the authority of the universal magisterium of the church when its teachings were given to the local churches.[61]

Dulles had favored the development of the International Synod of Bishops, even though, as already indicated, he had reservations on how it functioned. Prior to the extraordinary synod in 1985, convoked to reassess postconciliar developments in the church and various interpretations of Vatican II twenty years after the council, Dulles called for the synod to reassert the spirit, principles, and concrete reforms of Vatican II against what he called the "new prophets of gloom who are spreading pessimism and discouragement."[62]

The interpretation of Vatican II itself had become a source of contention during the previous twenty years. In Dulles' opinion, those on the extreme right condemned it for its modernist or Protestant tendencies, and those on the far left dismissed it for its failure "to do away with the church's absolutist claims and antiquated hierarchical structures." Conservative Catholics located the true meaning of the council in those elements that were in continuity with the past, and progressives located it in the innovations. Many of the statements of Vatican II were indeed compromise statements reflecting the traditional as well as more progressive elements. But Dulles believed that it was time for the synod to affirm that the council did set forth "a solid core of unequivocal teaching."[63]

After the synod, Dulles gave a relatively positive report on the results, saying, in effect, that it had indeed reaffirmed the council's solid core of teaching. In the brief period of time that it met, it could not, and did not, address all the major issues that arose in the postconciliar period, and it left some of those controversial issues (for example, women in the church, contraception, status of divorced and remarried, clerical celibacy, powers of episcopal synods, Roman centralization, reorganization of the Roman curia, theological dissent) completely untouched, primarily because the issues themselves were complex and needed more time for mature reflection and examination.

The synod, though, did bring to the fore six new emphases or priorities: the call to personal holiness; modification of the concept of the people of God, by stressing the mystery of grace and communion; a prominence given to missionary witness and evangelization; a less optimistic view of the signs of the times than was evident at Vatican II; a reassertion of the theology of the cross; and a new focus on the meaning of inculturation.[64] The synod represented something of a shift in priorities that Dulles seemed to approve. He believed it could help overcome the extreme polarization without diminishing legitimate diversity, dialogue, debate, and theological inquiry.

Prophetic and Charismatic Offices

Off and on since his dissertation, Dulles had spoken not only of the pope's and bishops' roles within the church but also of the prophetic and charismatic functions. The church was not the church of Christ without what Karl Rahner had called the "dynamic element." Inspired prophets and charismatics had a role to play in the church, and Dulles periodically advised those in the papal and episcopal office to listen carefully to what these figures in the past and present church were saying about the gospel and Christian life in the modern world. The charismatic renewal in the church, especially since the mid-1960s, was a clear indication that the charismatic gifts were not, as some supposed, gifts given only at the church's beginnings. The prophetic and the charismatic were recurring events in the total life of the church, even though they were discontinuous and unpredictable aspects of the dynamic element in the church.

In his dissertation Dulles had tied the prophetic element in the church to the preaching office, and in the mid-1960s he emphasized the prophetic role of reading the signs of the times in attempts to address the word of God to what was new and evolving. By the early 1980s, he was calling for the recognition of all prophetic ministries of the word and for a balance of the institutional and charismatic elements in the church. The inspired prophetic dimension could be found in popes (John XXIII), in the lonely prophetic bishop within a conference of bishops, the priest witness (Max Metzger), the monk (Thomas Merton), or the social activist (Dorothy Day). All of these could be considered modern types of prophetic witness to the word of God.[65] The institutional (that is, the prescribed, typical, stable, clearly defined) elements in the church were distinct from the charismatic (the spontaneous, personal, temporary, fluid), but both elements were at once autonomous and interdependent, and both contributed to the church's upbuilding.

In the midst of ecclesiastical polarization and the secular cultural wars of the 1980s, Dulles called for a synthesis of the two elements in the church, aware that historically the two elements had at times clashed and one had to be open to such conflicts in the present and future church. In such a historical situation of tension, Dulles counseled submission to the lordship of Jesus Christ, who ruled not only through the institutional structures but also through the varied ministries and activities of the charisms in the church. There was no magic solution to historical tensions within the church. He admonished all elements within the church to "recognize their limitations and treat the others with patience, respect, and charity." Time was needed to sift the wheat from the chaff

(Matt 13:24–30). Only through a spiritual discernment, a discernment process that took time, could the church in any period of historical controversy arrive at a genuine consensus that deepened faith, hope, and love in the church. The institutional needed the charismatic, and the charismatic needed the institutional in order to keep the church itself faithful to its one Lord.[66]

Theologians and the Magisterium

The succession of apostles in the church was necessary for oversight; the succession of prophets was necessary for inspired imagination to interpret the signs of the times; and the succession of teachers (especially theologians) was necessary to provide synthetic and critical reflection that satisfied the human need to understand. Each of these three ministries of the word provided insight and knowledge and wisdom for the disciples of Christ. Dulles continued to emphasize the theologian's prophetic role in the church. Theology, as a systematic study of the faith from the perspective of faith, had a crucial role to play in the church's life.

From the late 1960s until the end of his career, Dulles took up the special issue of the relationship between the magisterium of the pope and bishops and the magisterium of the theologians, an issue that had become a bone of contention in the church since the theologians' public protests against the teaching of *Humanae vitae*. In the summer of 1969, Dulles prepared a paper for the annual meeting of the College Theology Society, an association of lay and clerical theologians who taught in colleges and universities, on what has become known as Dulles' theory of the dual magisterium.[67] The college teachers published Dulles' paper in their proceedings, entitled, appropriately in the "Age of Aquarius," *Theology in Revolution*, emphasizing discontinuity with the past. Dulles' paper sought to put things in perspective with respect to teaching in the church, and he made three principal points: (1) there exists in the church an unofficial or nonhierarchical teaching; (2) the existence of an official or hierarchical teaching office flows from the nature of faith itself; and (3) the two different types of teaching need to be related more effectively than they had been in the immediate past.[68] Teaching as a function had existed in many forms in the church's history and flowed from the nature of the church itself as an organic community united in Christ and in the Holy Spirit. One could say, therefore, Dulles argued in agreement with other theologians, that "sound doctrine does not in every case flow down to theologians and the laity from the top officials in the church." There was a bottom-up teaching in the church that had to be acknowledged, as, in fact, Vatican II had done. Nevertheless, the church was not simply a society for the advancement of religious knowledge but a creedal and witnessing community that by its nature demanded a determinative teaching office lest it be overrun by the winds of changing public opinion. Dulles did not question the existence of an official magisterium, but he believed that theologians had to re-think the nature of that official magisterium in light of the presence of the nonhierarchical teaching of the laity and theologians. To exercise their doctrinal responsibility, the bishops' "juridically supreme teaching power" needed to be properly related to "the equally undeniable right of the faithful in general, and competent experts in particular."[69]

Dulles outlined the relationship between the theologians ("the competent experts") and the hierarchy. He argued for a qualitative difference between the "authentic magisterium of the hierarchy and the doctrinal magisterium of the scholar." They had different functions to play in the church. The hierarchical magisterium's task was to give public expression to teaching and provide juridical definitions. The theologians' magisterium was to investigate the wisdom of the past, analyze the present situation, and open new channels for what John Courtney Murray had called the "growing edge of the tradition." Within this dual function of teaching in the church, tensions have and will inevitably arise, and, therefore, Dulles suggested that "it might be desirable to institutionalize to some degree the participation of theologians in the church's decision-making processes."[70] Such a suggestion was not a radical innovation because in the past theologians had had a deliberative vote in some of the church's ecumenical councils. When one considered the magisterium as a function and not just as a deliberative office, therefore, it was clear that the bishops were not the sole teachers in the church.

By the mid-1970s, Dulles was at the peak of his institutional involvement with the community of theologians in the United States. He was president of the Catholic Theological Society of America (CTSA; June 1975–June 1976) and president of the American Theological Society (1978–1979), a primarily Protestant organization. His voice on the theologian's role in the church, therefore, was given some extraordinary attention in the theological community. Dulles had a very high regard for critical theology, but also an awareness of the temptations and "sins" of the theologians that could make them a source of darkness rather than light in the church.

In June 1976, as president of the CTSA, Dulles delivered a seminal address, "The Theologian and the Magisterium," developing his theory of the dual magisterium in the church. The address must be interpreted as an attempt to counter a nineteenth- and early twentieth-century neo-scholastic manual view of theology's task—a juridical task "which had impaired the proper relationship between official teaching and scholarly integrity." The manuals had restricted the term *magisterium* to the episcopal and papal offices within the church. Teaching, thus conceived, was a juridical task, commanding the will to obedience. In this view, theologians had "only a subordinate and instrumental role" in teaching. Their task was simply to present and defend the teaching of the hierarchical magisterium. Dulles countered this view and developed an alternative statement of the relationship between theology and the church's magisterium. At a time of much theological dissent from official church teachings and a growing alienation between theologians and the hierarchy (a reversal to some extent of the cooperation between them that was evident at the Second Vatican Council and during the immediate post–Vatican II years), Dulles' talk was timely. He acknowledged that in spite of signs of cooperation between some theologians and some bishops, "the mutual relationship between theology and the hierarchical magisterium is still fraught with misunderstanding, tension, distrust, and occasional bitterness."[71] He intended to address the situation by shedding light on the relationship between the two teaching functions.

At the beginning of his talk, Dulles confessed that theology had been the all-consuming devotion of his life since his early days at Harvard. And it was the wisdom of Catholic theology that attracted him to Christian faith, the Catholic Church, the religious life, and the priesthood.

> For me faith has always been first of all a wisdom—an all-encompassing view of reality as perceived through a total personal response.…The wisdom of Christian theology, as I initially found it in authors of the Catholic tradition, has continued to guide my days, and it is from this perspective that I have found my association with the Catholic Theological Society so gratifying.[72]

This personal testimonial set the stage for his reflections on the relationship between theologians and the hierarchy.

Dulles' presidential address aimed to present a speculative proposal on that bond. He focused on teaching in general as an enlightenment of the mind, not an imposition on the will, although enlightenment usually led to a freely chosen commitment. Teaching aimed at understanding, freedom, and maturity in the life of faith. Dulles argued that one could speak of two magisteria in the church: "that of the pastors and that of the theologians." The biblical tradition and the longer history of Catholic thought demonstrated that there was a variety of charisms in the church, and when one considered teaching in the church, one had to take the longer view of things, acknowledging that the bishops, as supreme pastors, had "legitimate doctrinal concerns, but they are not the dominant voices on all doctrinal questions. The *magistri*, teachers by training and by profession, have a scientific magisterium, but they are subject to the pastors in what pertains to the good order of the church as a community of faith and witness."[73] Neither one of these teaching offices in the church was self-sufficient. They complemented and mutually corrected one another in the history of the church. The relationship was not one of subservience, because theologians had the freedom of inquiry to carry out their task, and the bishops had the authority of office to protect fidelity to the Christian revelation.

The two teaching tasks in the church were not equal. They had different aims and different authority, but they both served the upbuilding of the Christian community, the ultimate biblical criterion for the genuineness of different charisms in the church. The

bishops or the hierarchical magisterium had the authority to protect the integrity of the faith for the entire Christian community,
and the theologian had a personal authority that flowed from his or
her competence to investigate and speculate on the intelligibility
and meaning of that faith.

In this essay, Dulles did not specify who were the theologians
he had in mind nor did he outline in detail what his theory of the
two magisteria might mean in the present practice of the church,
but he did suggest that representative theologians, chosen by the
body of theologians themselves, should have more involvement in
writing church documents and a more deliberative voice in deciding doctrinal issues, as had been the practice in some of the
medieval councils. He also suggested that the current hierarchical
magisterium needed to be more open to the results "of critical
scrutiny and constructive [theological] speculation." In the immediate past, the hierarchy had been too hasty in prematurely condemning theological innovations and speculations, speculations
that were later accepted by the magisterium. He also advised theologians themselves to be more cooperative and to "avoid unnecessary confrontation with the hierarchy." He wanted the CTSA,
moreover, to continue, as in the past, to resist taking corporate
positions as a society, "for in so doing we would inevitably embar-
rass those of our members who did not concur with the majority."[74]
He also opposed theologians developing party loyalties in opposition to the hierarchy and creating in effect a theological caste in the
church. The CTSA should preserve its primary objective as a study
and research society in the pursuit of theological wisdom. Dulles'
address was one more attempt to overcome the polarization that
was developing in the postconciliar church.

Because of his call for the participation of theologians in the
church's decision-making processes and his allowance of dissent,
especially the dissent of the theologically competent, some traditionalists in the church considered Dulles a flaming liberal. Shortly after
the talk, Dulles told George Higgins that he hoped it "won't land me
and the CTSA in trouble." He complained, moreover, that a first
draft of a national Catholic news story was "very deceptive" and that
he got them to kill it and to substitute a second that was "slightly less
misleading."[75] Higgins had congratulated Dulles after the talk and

later wrote to tell him that Bishop Edward W. O'Rourke of Peoria, who was "rather rigid in his theological views," was "very disturbed" by the address.[76] Some liberals in the church agreed that Dulles belonged in the liberal camp because they interpreted his analysis of a double magisterium as attributing equal authority to the hierarchy and theologians (a position he did not hold).

In the midst of radical dissent and authoritarian backlash, Dulles considered himself a moderate in a contentious age, very much like the "moderate" theologian Robert Bellarmine, whom Dulles had admired earlier in his career.[77] In 1970, he wrote, "Neither the extreme traditionalist nor the extreme modernist position can come through with a positive program that holds out any prospects of success in the long run. A restoration of consensus demands an enlargement of the moderate center, which insists upon discipline and restraint but rejects blindness and rigidity."[78]

Dulles' CTSA talk, unfinished as a speculative argument, failed to indicate who he had in mind when he spoke of theologians. Were all theologians with degrees, all those teaching in colleges and seminaries, as well as those who were acknowledged experts in the field considered to be the potential representative theologians he had in mind to advise the hierarchy about church documents? If representative theologians were drawn into the church's official teaching and were to be chosen by theological societies and not, as was currently the practice, by the hierarchical magisterium, how were they to be selected by the theologians themselves? These and other questions were left unaddressed in the talk. In later essays, though, Dulles would develop his thinking more fully on these issues.

In the years after his presidential address, Dulles continued to do research and write on the magisterium and theology: on the history of the changing conceptions of the relationship between professional theology and the hierarchical magisterium, and the need to examine the role of theological dissent in the church;[79] on the acceptance of authority in theology as consistent with theology's critical enterprise;[80] on avoiding historicism and excessive existentialism in a historically conscious theology attuned to the needs of the day;[81] on the validity of a pluralism of theological methods against those who asserted a primacy of the historical-critical method;[82]

and on the necessity of dialectical and critical methods within a context of faith.[83]

Dulles' own reflections on the two magisteria fit into a much larger discussion. Involved in the discussion were other theologians, canonists, and bishops, who had been trying since the mid-1960s to work out a viable understanding of the relationship between theologians and the hierarchical magisterium.[84] In 1980, in fact, the CTSA established a joint committee with the Canon Law Society to examine the relationship and to create guiding principles for cooperation between theologians and bishops and for resolving disputes. The joint committee produced a report on *Cooperation between Theologians and the Ecclesiastical Magisterium* (1982)[85] and a document on the topic that was endorsed by the CTSA and sent to the bishops in 1983.[86] That document, revised and emended over the years, became the basis of the American bishops' 1989 statement on *Doctrinal Responsibilities*.[87]

While the joint committee was preparing its report, Dulles again addressed the issue of "The Two Magisteria: An Interim Reflection," continuing to articulate his earlier dual magisterium thesis and attempting to provide more theological justification for various teaching functions in the church.[88] The two magisteria, the hierarchical and the theological, participated in the church's magisterium and functioned, as indicated previously, in different ways in shaping the church's teaching. In this essay, unlike his earlier ones, Dulles stipulated what he called the qualifications for membership in each magisterium. By ordination, of course, bishops shared in the teaching office (*munus docendi*). Membership in the theological magisterium was determined by theological competence—it was a matter of learning and of specific skills. "Theologian" applied "more properly to creative and influential thinkers than to the pedestrian, run-of-the-mill college or seminary professors."[89]

Dulles went on to argue that it was not necessary to receive a "canonical mission" in order to be considered a Catholic theologian; that juridical approach ought not to define what constituted a Catholic theologian as was being considered at the time by the International Theological Commission and other elements in the church. Just as the lay apostolate and Catholic Action were not necessarily a participation in the hierarchy's mission, so also the

Catholic theologian's role in the church was not determined by a canonical commission from the hierarchy. Theologians had their own functions as part of a scholarly or theological magisterium. Dulles wanted to preserve what he considered an interdependence and relative autonomy of the two teaching functions in the church. The theological and the hierarchical magisteria provided a system of healthy checks and balances within the church.

Theological Dissent

Periodically during his years at Catholic University, Dulles spoke on the authority, freedom, obedience, and legitimate dissent of theologians. This was not just an exercise in theological speculation but an attempt to provide guidance in a time of clashing opinions within the church, and particularly within Catholic University. His dual magisterium theory was one attempt to provide theological wisdom in trying times.

The immediate context for Dulles' discussion of these issues was the so-called Charles Curran controversy at Catholic University. Since 1967, Curran had been a source of contention because some of his opinions on sexual ethics were at variance with official Catholic teaching. His leadership in the public theological protest against the papal encyclical *Humanae vitae* dramatized theological dissent within the American Catholic Church. The issue of dissent was not just a matter of one individual's theological opinion. More than seven hundred theologians signed petitions against the encyclical, demonstrating that theological dissent was fairly widespread in the mid-1960s. Dissent carried on into the 1970s and beyond, on a variety of doctrinal as well as moral-sexual issues. The very fact that Curran was elected vice president of the CTSA in 1968, the year of the protest, became president in 1969, and received the CTSA's John Courtney Murray prize for distinguished theological achievement in 1972 indicated that he had support for his dissenting opinions in the major Catholic theological society in the country. Although largely unknown to the public, the Vatican's CDF began examining Curran's positions in 1979, concluding in 1986 that Curran was no longer "suitable nor eligible to teach

Catholic theology."[90] He was eventually removed from teaching theology at Catholic University.

In 1984, prior to the CDF's decision against Curran, the Theology Department at Catholic University voted (13 to 4, with 3 abstentions) to support him in his controversy with the CDF and signed a petition to Cardinal Ratzinger in Curran's favor. Five past presidents of the CTSA (but not Dulles), four past presidents of the College Theology Society, and 750 other Catholic theologians likewise supported Curran. Dulles signed none of the group letters nor statements of support for Curran, but he did write personally to Cardinal Ratzinger, indicating that Curran's views were comparable to those of many of his peers in moral theology not only in the United States but also in Europe and other continents. Curran was respectful of Catholic tradition and willing to explore new questions. Dulles had read very little of Curran's work, he wrote, and had no special competence in moral theology, but he knew that Curran was esteemed by his colleagues and was held in high regard at Catholic University. He concluded by saying that "it would be very detrimental to our university if disciplinary action were taken against Fr. Curran. I sincerely hope that the present case can be resolved to the satisfaction of all concerned."[91]

Dulles was extremely cautious in public with respect to the Curran case. Although he acknowledged at times that organized public dissent might be to the church's benefit, he was personally uncomfortable with organized public expressions of dissent, seeing them more as power plays in the ecclesiastical body than as teaching moments for the church. Nevertheless, in 1988, two years after the Vatican condemnation of Curran, Dulles acknowledged that the case "was exceedingly complex," and he was troubled by the oversimplifications in the press and the "common tendency to make harsh and simplistic judgments against either side." Dulles thought a 1988 book on the Curran case was a "teaching moment" because it dealt with serious issues in moral theology from the perspectives of Curran's theological supporters as well as his opponents. After reviewing the book, Dulles judged that "the decision of the trustees of Catholic University to withdraw Fr. Curran's canonical mission without debarring him from teaching at the University in the field of his competence is an indication that the complexity of the question is appreciated." By 1988 Dulles had become more and more supportive of magisterial authority because he believed that "in our age it is imperative for the Church to maintain firm authority structures in order to preserve its united witness in a largely dechristianized society."[92]

Since the mid-1960s, Dulles had personally spoken out in favor of legitimate theological dissent from some noninfallible church teachings, as long as the dissent was expressed respectfully, with fidelity to tradition, probative arguments, and openness to correction from peers and the hierarchy. An individual Catholic theologian also had to have a basic presumption in favor of the church's hierarchical magisterium, a presumption, however, that could at times be overcome by critical evidence and argumentation.

Dissent had been a part of the church's historical experience and was justified theologically by an understanding of faith, the church's pilgrim status, the developmental nature of doctrine and tradition, and the hierarchy of truths. Living or dwelling within a doctrinal or religious tradition, Dulles argued in conjunction with Michael Polanyi, did not impede but rather enhanced one's ability to "break out" of the tradition in order to develop, revitalize, and enrich it.[93] Dissent did not overturn the tradition but provided growth at its edges. For the most part, Dulles argued, the post-Tridentine church allowed very little or no theological dissent, and in fact came down hard on theological innovation or dissent, particularly in the nineteenth and early twentieth centuries. Vatican II changed the situation. In the mid-1970s, Dulles argued that although the council reaffirmed the obligation to "assent to the ordinary, noninfallible magisterium of the Roman pontiff," it had in fact approved the theological vision of some theologians who had previously been condemned or at least silenced by the Vatican. Vatican II, he insisted, had worked "indirectly…to legitimate dissent in the Church. This it did in part by insisting on the necessary freedom of the act of faith and by attributing a primary role to personal conscience in the moral life." Even though the council failed to pronounce explicitly on the legitimacy of dissent, the bishops at the council had in practice dissented from some of the official Vatican-prepared documents, had approved some theological innovations that had been previously considered unorthodox or heterodox, and "quietly reversed earlier positions of the Roman magisterium on a number of important issues."[94]

In the 1960s, some national episcopal conferences, the German and American, for example, had laid down certain conditions for legitimate dissent from noninfallible official teachings, and Dulles had approved those conditions (for example, the reasons must be serious and well founded, the expression of dissent must not impugn the church's teaching authority, and the dissent should not give scandal). But there were also in his mind levels of dissent that needed to be distinguished. Dissent could be internal, private, public, and/or organized. Each level of dissent, moreover, had its own justifying conditions, and one had to reflect seriously about the reasons for the exercise of dissent within a community of faith. Dissent, like faith itself, required discernment, and at any given period in history it was not easy "to discern exactly which doctrines are mistaken."[95]

Dulles rarely made any public judgments about specific cases of theological or cultural dissent within the church and infrequently pronounced on conflicts between specific theologians and the Vatican. Basically, he wanted to heal the polarization in the church and usually therefore had admonitions for both sides of a conflict—generally warning against premature dissent and hasty condemnations. Time could sometimes heal differences or make for development or prove the fruitfulness of either hierarchical authority or dissenting opinions. At any rate, Dulles counseled patience to let the Holy Spirit work through the process of history to bring the church into all truth. But in all this, he was opposed in principle neither to expressions of theological dissent nor to the exercise of magisterial judgment for the sake of truth and unity in the church.

Some might interpret Dulles' reactions to dissent by the 1980s as ambivalent. He was anything but ambivalent, however. He tried to keep in balance the mutual and beneficial need for authority and freedom within the Christian community because they were both inherent in faith itself. Faith had its origins in the authority of God revealing. In the Johannine sense, Christian discipleship and commitment to the word of God brought knowledge of the truth, and truth made for freedom. In the Pauline sense, obedience was always an element of faith.[96] Theologians and Christian scholars—

as committed, obedient, and free—had the right, as the Second Vatican Council had declared, "to express their minds humbly and sincerely about those matters in which they enjoy competence."[97] There were, in other words, theological reasons for the expression of dissent; it was a serious scholarly enterprise, not simply a culturally conditioned reaction to Roman and Vatican statements. The church was neither a debating society nor an army, but a community of faith in which freedom and authority resided together, sometimes in a tense synthesis.

By the 1980s, a "culture of dissent," as some called it, had arisen in the American Catholic Church. Although Dulles accepted in principle legitimate grounds for theological dissent in the church, he was becoming increasingly disturbed by the 1980s with the widespread cultural dissent within the church and by some serious questioning of fundamental Catholic doctrines. The postconciliar dissent and protests were "too frequent, too sweeping, and too strident," manifesting many times a rebelliousness that was harmful to a Christian community that was bound together by an established set of beliefs. He believed that things had gotten out of hand, and even defined dogmas of the church were not exempted from questioning. In fact, some in the Catholic community were glorifying dissent and unorthodoxy as signs of freedom and personal insight and accusing those who upheld officially stated doctrines as timid or insincere. On the other hand, the hyper-orthodox did not distinguish between doctrines that were essentials of the faith and those that were official but reformable teachings.[98] By the late 1980s, Dulles was criticizing the widespread culture of dissent and the selective appropriation of Catholic doctrines more than he had earlier in his career, when he supported pluralism and a responsible theological dissent.

Toward the end of 1987, shortly after his retirement party at Catholic University, Dulles experienced another death in his immediate family. His sister Lillias Dulles Hinshaw, after a long struggle with cancer, died on December 1, 1987. Although her death was not unexpected, it was a blow to Avery. She was an assistant to the ministers of the Madison Avenue Presbyterian Church, had been educated in theology at Union Theological Seminary in New York City, and had periodically engaged Avery in theological discussions. They had common theological interests and, as Avery told a relative who had sent him condolences, they had a mutual fondness for one another, and she was "closest to him" in the family in age and in sympathies.[99] In many ways he carried on with her an irenic ecumenical conversation that had been going on periodically in the immediate family since Avery was in his early twenties.

Dulles' official involvement in the ecumenical movement was most pointedly illustrated in his twenty-five-year participation in the Lutheran/Catholic Dialogue. His engagement in that ecumenical adventure is the subject of the next chapter.

11
THE ECUMENIST, 1971–1996

DULLES BECAME ONE of the foremost American Catholic ecumenists in the latter half of the twentieth century. Almost as soon as he returned from Rome in 1960, he became involved in ecumenical activities as a theologian seeking ways to articulate the faith for an age seeking more amicable relations and a fuller understanding of the various Christian traditions. He was a theological ecumenist who worked primarily with theologians to forge firmer bonds of doctrinal communion between the ecclesiastical traditions. In the early 1970s, Dulles was very optimistic and enthusiastic about the future possibilities of an emerging unity, even though he acknowledged that church union was going to be a long-term process.[1] His most extensive work in ecumenism took place primarily in the twenty-five years (1971–1996)[2] he served on the Lutheran/Catholic (L/RC) Dialogue. A significant portion of his life was spent in this ecumenical work, and it had an effect on his theology and his sense of responsibility as a theologian for accurately representing the Catholic Church's teachings. To one correspondent in 1980, Dulles expressed his desire, expectations, and realism about Christian unity: "I share your desire that all Christians have full fellowship with one another. But the implementation of that desire requires that they come to have the same beliefs, adopt the same sacramental usages, and the same behavioral standards."[3]

Of all the ecumenical activities, the most important for him and for the American Catholic Church was the L/RC Dialogue. That consultation had been organized in 1964, prior to the end of the Second Vatican Council,[4] and by 1971 it had produced four major statements,[5] which many people consider the most substantial ecumenical statements on doctrine. That dialogue discussed in organic fashion decisive and divisive doctrinal issues, had the most effective methodology and procedures, involved many reputable theologians in the country,[6] and made the most significant agreements of all the bilaterals in the United States, articulating in the process the areas of continuing disagreements and the needs for further research and examination. The L/RC bilateral, although officially sanctioned by the United States Catholic Bishops and the U.S. branch of the Lutheran World Federation, did not have any authority to speak for the churches they represented, as the Lutheran and Catholic theologians themselves admitted in their document on *Teaching Authority and Infallibility in the Church* (1980): the "agreements of theologians are not yet the consensus of the churches." Nevertheless, as the prefaces of almost every published statement of the bilateral indicated, "As competent and responsible theologians their views merit serious attention and carry considerable weight."[7]

Structure of Lutheran/Catholic Dialogue

Understanding Dulles' participation in the L/RC Dialogue depends to a considerable extent on understanding its structure and some of its procedures. The National Conference of Catholic Bishops appointed a bishop to chair the dialogue from the Catholic side, and the USA National Committee of the Lutheran World Federation (now called Lutheran World Ministries) appointed a Lutheran (eventually a church president or bishop) to share chairing duties. Both the Catholic and the Lutheran national bodies also appointed the theologians who were primarily responsible for setting the agenda, preparing position papers in the areas of their competence (biblical, historical, or systematic), discussing the papers and the issues, and writing the common statements that the dialogue ultimately produced. Between 1971 and 1996, the dialogue met twice each year in various cities throughout the United States, conducting about fifty meetings during those years. Each meeting lasted about three days, with three separate sessions each day. The theologians decided, after considerable discussion, what were the basic agreements, what were not church-dividing issues, and what were the continuing differences between the two churches. All of these were demanding and time-consuming tasks.

Some theologians realized after their experience on the dialogue that it demanded too much time, and they decided they could no longer participate.

The meetings were not only well organized, they were well chronicled in detailed minutes. At first the discussions were tape-recorded and then transcribed verbatim, providing a thorough report of the proceedings. Later, individual participants served as secretaries of the conversations, and those minutes, too, were extensive, but not as exacting as the earlier ones. The minutes were helpful not only for the long-term participants but also for the new members who came to the dialogue, providing them with a history of the discussions.[8] Those minutes reveal an earnest desire for unity between Catholics and Lutherans, a faithfulness to their respective traditions, an openness to one another's doctrinal and theological positions, a willingness to get beyond the polemics and some of the historically, culturally, linguistically, and socially conditioned doctrinal and theological expressions of the past, and a forthrightness in holding firmly to those positions they each considered non-negotiable. As the context of past L/RC relations was contentious and polemical, so the present context was affable and ecumenical. As the past context, moreover, conditioned the previous positions taken, so the present ecumenical context conditioned the results of the consultation. These ecumenists were not willing to compromise, as some in both churches charged, but they were open to new ways of looking at the past and future, new methods that aimed at mutual understanding and ultimately at a more viable visible unity that reflected the divine will. And in this, they were more hard-headed realists than easy optimists and certainly could not be charged with undue compromising. It was clear from the minutes that the theologians discovered in responding to questions raised by their theological partners that their traditions needed much more theological research and reflection on certain doctrinal and theological issues. The dialogue itself, in other words, helped to set a theological agenda for future research; this was certainly the case for Dulles, who was stimulated by the questions raised by his Lutheran dialogue partners and by some of his Catholic colleagues.

The topics selected for discussion at the meetings usually flowed organically from previous discussions. The discussion on papal primacy (the first discussion Dulles attended), for example, followed from the previous years of discussion on the Eucharist and Ministry, and the years of discussion on Teaching Authority and [Papal] Infallibility in the church followed that of papal primacy.

Each meeting was preceded by the preparation of position papers written by individual theologians in their areas of competence. At times, too, the dialogue commissioned outside theological experts to present papers on areas where the dialogue partners had no particular competence or needed additional help from other *periti*. In the process of discussing these various papers and commissioned studies, the dialogue partners discovered where their respective traditions agreed, where they continued to disagree, and where they could agree that some of their differences (linguistic and cultural and theological) were not as church dividing as some had considered in the past. In the course of the discussions, surprising convergences emerged.

The end point of the discussions was the development of a common statement in which Lutherans and Catholics could indicate precisely where their agreements, disagreements, and non-church-dividing differences lay. Selected members of the dialogue were designated to prepare a draft statement of their common concerns, and that statement was then subjected to another round of discussions, editing suggestions, and emendations until a document could be produced that reflected the consensus of the group. Once revised and agreed upon, the common statement was published, along with selected position papers prepared by individual theologians to give the readers a sense of what research and reflection lay behind the common statement.

After a common document was produced, it was at times sent to the Catholic episcopal chair of the Bishops' Committee on Ecumenical and Interreligious Affairs (BCEIA), who periodically sent it on to the prefect of the Vatican's Secretariat for the Promotion of Christian Unity. When the common statement on papal primacy was sent to Archbishop William Baum, Fr. John Hotchkin, director of the BCEIA, wrote the archbishop that the dialogue was submitting its conclusions "to wider review and broader judgment to test how they can be either confirmed or bettered."[9] That was all part of the ecumenical process, and in this, the Lutherans followed suit, submitting the common statement to national ecumenical offices in the respective Lutheran churches (Lutheran Church of America [LCA], Lutheran Church–Missouri Synod, and later to the Evangelical Lutheran Church of America [ELCA]).

It has been said that these ecumenical common statements received little or no response from higher church authorities, were not received by the larger communities, and therefore remained ineffective or stagnant ecumenical exercises. There may be some truth in these charges, especially with reference to the larger reception of these documents within the respective churches. It has been Vatican policy, however, not to respond to national but only to international bilateral consultations. In the case of the document on papal primacy, however, the Vatican secretary of state, Cardinal Jean-Marie Villot, responded to Archbishop Baum by sending two Roman evaluations of the common statement, indicating the positive advances as well as some defects that at least two members of Vatican congregations (the individuals were not identified) found in the documents. The Roman evaluations considered the common statement a good "study document."[10] From this view, there were still too many problems worldwide with L/RC relations to consider the statement anything more than a generally good move in the right direction, with advances beyond other ecumenical statements of the past.

What is not clear from the archival evidence, however, is precisely why the Vatican secretary of state responded to this document; that was not usual Vatican policy, and no other Vatican responses were in the files of Bishops' Ecumenical Affairs offices. In the 1960s, 1970s, and 1980s, the common L/RC ecumenical statements seemed to have received little or no institutional response from the larger religious communities. That would change a bit in the 1990s. But the failure of official reception was a problem that would trouble some of those who were engaged in the dialogical process.

The topics considered during Dulles' tenure on the L/RC Dialogue flowed from one discussion to another. Dulles entered the dialogue when it was in the midst of discussing "Papal Primacy and the Universal Church" (seven sessions, lasting from 1970 to 1973), followed by nine sessions on "Teaching Authority and Infallibility in the Church" (from 1974 to 1978), ten on "Justification" (from 1978 to 1983), thirteen on the "One Mediator, the Saints and Mary" (from 1983 to 1990), and four on "Scripture and Tradition" (from 1990 to 1992). After these sessions were finished, Dulles was appointed to a coordinating committee (1993 to 1996), whose mission it was to decide the future of the dialogue and to suggest topics that might be considered if the dialogue continued.[11]

Dulles was more than likely chosen as a Catholic member of the dialogue because of his growing reputation as a fundamental theologian and ecumenist who had written much on issues of dogma and its interpretation. His skills in analyzing the relationship among scripture, tradition, and church doctrine would be of considerable usefulness to a dialogue intent on determining how best to interpret confessional statements in the new ecumenical situation. In the late 1960s and early 1970s, Dulles had repeatedly spoken of the need to reinterpret doctrine and of the need to do so in an ecumenical context. In a 1971 letter to John Hotchkin, Dulles noted that what he had previously said about dogma and infallibility might be of use in understanding the relations of Christians to the papacy.[12]

Papal Primacy and the Universal Church

The first L/RC Dialogue meeting Dulles attended discussed Carl Peter's paper on the meaning of the Catholic claim at Vatican I of the divine institution (*jus divinum*) of the papacy. Dulles agreed with Peter that *jus divinum* was a theological category and not an expression of the faith of the church. The *jus divinum* category represented a nineteenth-century Catholic ahistorical way of thinking; one had to separate the faith claim from the historical claim (namely that Jesus had himself instituted the papacy). One might be able to argue for the divine institution of the papacy without arguing that it had been divinely instituted at the foundation of Christianity or that the scriptures in fact provided solid historical evidence for the fact. Some claims, as Raymond Brown insisted, just could not be justified historically. In the midst of this discussion, the Lutheran Warren Quanbeck made the significant observation that "to accept a Petrine office as some kind of theological development which has the guidance of the Spirit in it is not impossible for Lutherans."[13]

The discussion on papal primacy moved along, and a drafting committee prepared an initial statement for discussion. In the midst of discussing the draft, Dulles prepared for the Catholic members some reactions and suggested corrections to the draft before it was published.[14] At the end of their discussion on papal primacy and the universal church, both sides were satisfied, as a prepared news release on the subject indicated, that they had reached a milestone in ecumenical relations.

> This dialogue group does not claim to have discovered completely satisfactory and final answers but it is convinced that as a result of re-examining the matter in the context of mutual concern for the faithful proclamation of the Gospel and for the unity of the church, a basis has emerged upon which, for the first time since the Reformation, fruitful discussions between the churches on this subject are possible. The group concluded that if such discussion is possible, then it is also necessary. We believe that the Holy Spirit has guided these efforts and are grateful that He is steadily drawing us closer together in Jesus Christ.[15]

The consensus statement on papal primacy that the L/RC Dialogue released on March 4, 1974,[16] was the result of some major convergences and received a significant amount of attention from the national press. The *New York Times*, among a host of newspapers, published a front-page story on the accord and excerpts from the document. The key statement, as the *Times* reported, was that papal primacy "need no longer be a 'barrier to reconciliation' of their churches." The statement envisioned a time when Lutheran and Catholic churches would be a part of a "single larger" communion: "autonomous but linked by common recognition of the Pope in Rome as a visible symbol of their underlying unity."[17] This was indeed a statement that created for a time something of a sensation in the press, and there was high interest in the topic in religious circles.

In the midst of this high interest, Dulles was invited to the John Courtney Murray Forum at Fordham University to speak to the issue. His April 18, 1974, lecture, "The Papacy: Bond or Barrier?,"[18] put the L/RC accord on the issue in a much wider context than the recent newspaper accounts, quoting the actual document, which affirmed that "papal primacy, renewed in the light of the gospel, need not be a barrier to reconciliation." He also went on to explain the document in light of numerous Orthodox and Protestant statements on the papacy in the previous five years, when the issue of papacy as an ecumenical problem came to the fore, particularly in the United States. Although Dulles explained all the provisions of agreement and continuing disagreement on the papacy, he focused much of his attention on the Petrine function in the church, indicating that in his view, the emphasis on the question of Petrine function in the New Testament and its continuing validity in the universal church was the crucial area of discussion.

The two key issues at this point in the ecumenical journey, in Dulles' view, were (1) Should there be a Petrine ministry in the universal church? and (2) Should the papacy be accepted as the concrete embodiment of that ministry? "Petrine function," in the document, was a technical term that designated "a ministry that serves to promote or preserve the oneness of the worldwide church by symbolizing unity."[19] The current emphasis on Petrine function in contemporary Orthodox, Protestant, and Catholic theology, Dulles argued, was an important advance in theology, transcending for Catholics the limitations of the older approach to the papacy, which had traditionally spoken of the papacy as directly and explicitly instituted by Christ. In the present ecumenical situation and in the present state of biblical and historical studies, Catholics needed to rethink and reformulate the doctrine of the papacy (especially noting the benefits as well as the historical limitations of the formulations of Vatican I).

The L/RC statement was a move in that direction because it emphasized the symbolic function of the papacy, but Lutherans could not at present accept the Catholic insistence on the papacy's universally valid significance (that is, that it was "permanently willed by God") for the church. Lutherans, though, could accept a Petrine ministry, renewed in the light of the gospel, and Dulles suggested, in concluding his paper, that Catholics and the papacy itself work toward that renewal by highlighting three principles: a legitimate diversity in the church and churches, a collegiality that focused on a wider and shared decision making, and a subsidiarity in the church that acknowledged Christian freedom and a legitimate authority and autonomy for the local church. There were still major ecumenical problems in the Lutheran acceptance of the papacy—universal jurisdiction and infallibility were two of the prominent ones—but the current statement on the papacy represented significant progress in Dulles' estimation.

Not everyone, of course, was happy with the new accord, limited as it was. Reginald N. Shires, pastor of the Seventh-Day Adventist Church in Reading, Pennsylvania, represented those in the American community who protested vigorously against any notion of a Petrine ministry in the universal church. Past history, the Inquisition, and other practices of an ecclesiastical monarchy had demonstrated that such an office in the church had undermined Christian freedom, and there was no reason to hope that that history would not be repeated in the future. Writing to the *New York Times* to protest against the newly released L/RC document, Shires opined that many in the United States thought that the Catholic Church under the last two popes was really a "different institution." But, he continued, "The Church has not really changed; some facelifting, perhaps some corrections, but deep down it is the same institution."[20]

Dulles could not let such opinions go by without comment. He and fellow Jesuit Walter Burghardt, both Catholic members of the L/RC Dialogue, therefore, prepared a brief response to Shires's article to "correct several misunderstandings." The dialogue had indeed struggled with the issue of Christian freedom and sought in the statement to protect the distinctive heritage of theology, polity, and worship within a larger communion. Both Lutherans and Catholics were aware, moreover, that among the historic Christian churches, Catholics did not have a monopoly on ecclesiastical repression. Shires's dismissal of change in the Catholic Church, furthermore, overlooked the "epochal shift" that had taken place, particularly with respect to the document on religious liberty. American Protestants, the two believed, would not be stampeded, as Shires implied, into "any hasty conformity that ill accords with their convictions."[21]

Teaching Authority and Infallibility

The question of papal infallibility had come up during the L/RC discussion of papal primacy, but it was not thought appropriate to bring infallibility into the discussion of primacy because that might confuse the two issues. Besides that, the issue of infallibility for the universal church had to be set within a much wider context of the issues of teaching authority in the universal church, issues that preceded, historically and logically, the issue of infallibility in the church and papal infallibility in particular. The dialogue decided to take up the issue of papal infallibility and teaching authority in 1973 and devoted nine and one-half sessions to the topic, publishing in 1980 a common statement on the topic and selected working papers. In the course of the discussion, the more general issue of doctrine and authority emerged and to some extent overshadowed the issue of papal infallibility, but some Lutherans on the dialogue, although they favored the larger discussion as a context for their more general agreements and disagreements on teaching authority within the church, wanted to keep papal infallibility in focus, because, as Karlfried Froehlich, one of the Lutheran participants, noted in one discussion, "Papal infallibility is one way (RC) of handling the problem [of the infallibility of Christian doctrine] that faces both RCs and Lutherans."[22]

In the summer of 1973, Dulles prepared an outline of issues the dialogue could consider when discussing infallibility.[23] He suggested the dialogue start by stating the problem, clarifying the terminology, providing data from the biblical and historical record, and examining current Catholic doctrine and Lutheran difficulties. For all practical purposes, the dialogue followed something of this outline; however, the issues were discussed in the much wider context of teaching authority in the local and universal churches prior to the more specific issues of the infallibility of the church and the pope.

Dulles, like some others on the dialogue, had previously spoken out on the issue of papal infallibility, reacting in part to Hans Küng's *Infallible?* (1971). The L/RC discussion of teaching authority and infallibility was set in a postconciliar Catholic theological context that had by 1973 moved well beyond the objectivist and juridical notions of infallibility. Catholic theologians in Europe and the United States had been reinterpreting the notion of infallibility within the context of an historical consciousness that had to some extent relativized the objectivist notions, making certain reformulations of what the doctrine meant in the Catholic Church more acceptable to some Lutheran theologians. Dulles contributed to this effort by presenting two papers, one clarifying terminology and the other arguing for what he and others called a "moderate infallibilism."[24]

Dulles opened the 1974 discussion on infallibility by defining it ("immunity from error" and an abiding in the truth of the gospel) in reference to inerrancy, indefectibility, irreformability (or irreversibility), reformulation, and reconceptualization. For Dulles, that which was infallibly taught was irreformable in the sense of being irreversible. Being irreversible, however, did not mean that the teaching was unable to be reformulated (that is, the mode of expression could be revised or reformulated) or possibly even reconceptualized, as long as the basic meaning was retained.[25] After defining his terms, Dulles went on to describe the various subjects of the charism of infallibility, the conditions for infallible definitions, and the sources of infallibility. This opening statement was the springboard for the new round of discussions on an issue that had received considerable attention in recent Catholic thought and was a perennial problem in Protestant-Catholic relations.

Throughout the dialogue, Dulles had identified his own position on papal infallibility as that of a "moderate infallibilist," a designation that George Lindbeck had used earlier to identify the thought of Karl Rahner and Walter Kasper. Lindbeck separated their positions from those of Hans Küng and from those he tagged "absolutistic infallibilism" and "fallibilism." The moderate infallibilists, in Lindbeck's view, were "irreversibilist." Infallibly proclaimed teachings, for these theologians, had an irreversible meaning, even though they could be reformulated in different historical and/or cultural contexts in order to preserve the meaning.[26]

Dulles acknowledged in "Moderate Infallibilism" that he accepted the doctrine of papal infallibility as necessary to preserve the church in gospel truth. "I am convinced that the occupants of the papal office do enjoy special assistance from the Holy Spirit and privileged means of access to the tradition of the whole Catholic communion of churches."[27] Although some Catholic theologians (for example, Edward Schillebeeckx) thought that the term *infallibility* could be dispensed with, Dulles considered it "still salvageable" for the sake of continuity in the tradition; but the term needed reinterpretation.[28] He conceived of papal infallibility in conditional terms. The conditions he laid down, moreover, were critical principles for determining which papal statements were indeed to be considered infallible.

The gift of infallibility in the church and in the papacy was conditioned "and therefore limited by its conditions."[29] Infallibly proclaimed papal teachings were limited by a host of specifics laid down by Vatican I, including, among other things, their agreement with scripture and tradition, the faith of the church (here he noted that the consent of the church was not the source of infallibility, but infallible decisions would evoke consent because both the faith and the consent had their origin in the Holy Spirit), the universal episcopate, and by sufficient investigation prior to proclamation. Infallibly defined teachings, moreover, had to be considered, as even the Congregation for the Doctrine of the Faith's (CDF) *Mysterium ecclesiae* (1973, 5) insisted, within the context of the mystery and transcendence of revelation and with an understanding of the historicity and limits of human formulations.[30] In the course of the discussion on his paper, Dulles admitted that anything that was infallibly proclaimed as true was so, "but it is a question of the word of God in the words of man. The expression of the truth could be so conditioned by this that some others would not be able to hear what is affirmed."[31]

The fact that some Christians could not accept the doctrine of papal infallibility as defined by Vatican I and reaffirmed by Vatican II illustrated for Dulles a fundamental fact about the reception of dogmatically formulated statements: as formulated by councils, doctrine "is a limping human effort to articulate a mystery that defies clear expression. The believer who has difficulties with the formulas may be more keenly conscious than some others are of complementary facets of the revealed mystery."[32] Infallibly proclaimed statements did not rule out the fact that the formulations themselves were historically conditioned statements that were limited in their capacity to express the fullness of the mystery of revelation. Infallibly proclaimed truths were immune from error and were irreformable doctrines that preserved the church in truth, but they were not beyond reformulations that might better capture the fullness of the mystery they intended to articulate. Dulles believed that such a prudent and moderate interpretation (or reinterpretation) of Vatican I and Vatican II on infallibility offered the most accurate understanding of the church's teaching and was "most likely to achieve both acceptability among Catholics and ecumenical usefulness."[33]

In the course of the discussions on teaching authority in the church, Lutherans wanted to know what weight Catholics assigned to infallible statements (particularly those on Mary's immaculate conception and assumption as well as on papal infallibility), and given the admittedly historically conditioned status of those statements, how much they ought to continue to be church dividing. In general, Dulles responded to questions like these by invoking the Second Vatican Council's declaration on the hierarchy of truths in the Christian tradition, repeatedly quoting the advice the Decree on Ecumenism (*Unitatis redintegratio*; UR) offered to theologians engaged in ecumenical dialogue: "When comparing doctrines, they [theologians] should remember that in Catholic teaching there exists an order or 'hierarchy' of truths, since they vary in their relationship to the foundation of the Christian faith" (UR 11).

At one point during the dialogue in 1975, Dulles asserted that the two Marian dogmas "are not central truths; they are peripheral." He was in favor, therefore, of lifting the anathemas attached to these two dogmas. Doing so would not "*eo ipso* reconcile Protestant and Orthodox Christians with Roman Catholics, but it would remove obstacles that stand in the way of that reconciliation." These two dogmas seemed to him to be "less fundamental to Catholic self-understanding than is the dogma of infallibility. In my opinion they are not necessary conditions for ecumenical reunion."[34] But, the doctrine of papal infallibility, too, was problematic "even for many Catholics, and is rather remote from the core of the gospel."[35] By 1978, Dulles was in favor of removing the anathemas attached to all three of these dogmas for the sake of removing obstacles to reunion. Removal was a gradual step in the right ecumenical direction. Such an action would "greatly help to overcome the impression that faith is a bundle of propositions divinely revealed."[36]

Dulles was willing to make some gradual adjustment in order to foster Christian unity and to emphasize what for him was the primary bond of unity among Christians: their commitment to Christ and the central Christian doctrines. In this regard, he did not see the definitions of the Marian dogmas and papal infallibility as necessarily church dividing—acceptance of these dogmas, he suggested, would not necessarily be obligatory for church unity as long as they could be accepted as not contrary to the gospel message. Even intercommunion between Lutherans and Catholics would be possible if agreements could be reached on major areas of eucharistic doctrine without requiring acceptance of the doctrine of papal infallibility—a possibility that Vatican II had already implicitly acknowledged with respect to the Orthodox, who did not accept the definition of papal infallibility.[37]

What Dulles articulated in this paper on moderate infallibilism seems to have been a position widely shared by all the Catholic members of the dialogue, as was evident in the L/RC "Common Statement" and the "Roman Catholic Reflections" on the common statement at the end of the L/RC meetings on teaching authority and infallibility.[38]

The dialogue produced in 1978 a common statement, hammered out in the course of four years of meetings, that reflected a stage of agreement on teaching authority and infallibility that could not have been imagined in the early 1970s, to say nothing of the polemical period of L/RC relations. Contemporary biblical and historical studies in both the Lutheran and Catholic theological traditions, the era of good ecumenical feeling created by the Second Vatican Council, the acknowledged limits of previous Lutheran and Catholic formulations, and the dialogical process of discovering convergences in Lutheran and Catholic positions enabled this new stage of agreement. The "Common Statement" was "not yet full agreement," but it did indicate areas in which there were considerable convergences on teaching authority (for example, the preeminent authority of Jesus, the authority of the gospel and its faithful transmission, the indefectibility of the church, the infallibility of the church's belief and teaching, and the assurance or certainty that Christian believers have always associated with their faith). There were large areas of agreement even though Lutherans and Catholics had their own ways of conceiving of these issues. Even in the area of papal infallibility, which Lutherans could not accept as a doctrine found in the Bible, Lutheran theologians were now more open to seeing papal teaching authority, which had evolved and developed over time, in a more favorable light than in the past, because they acknowledged that papal teaching authority could serve the universal unity of the church's faith. Papal infallibility was no longer to be regarded as anti-Christian.

Catholics acknowledged that papal infallibility was not the central doctrine of the faith and that Lutheran rejection of it was not "a denial of the central Christian message." The two groups of theologians could agree that the unresolved differences regarding papal infallibility "need not, of themselves, preclude a closer union than now exists between the two churches." Lutherans regretted the absence of a universal teaching magisterium in the Lutheran churches, and Catholics acknowledged that there were within the Catholic tradition no sufficient protections against abuses of the papal teaching function in the Catholic Church. On certain issues the two groups of theologians agreed to disagree, but the large areas of agreement called for more cooperation of the two churches in the future with respect to universal teaching authority. Therefore, they asked the two churches to consider the possibility of what they called "magisterial mutuality," an acknowledgment that each other's ministers were "partners in proclaiming the gospel in the unity of truth and love."[39]

Catholics called for a lifting of anathemas, a reconsideration of the Lutheran Confessions, and an exploration of the possibilities of institutional cooperation, while Lutherans called upon their churches to reject the polemical language of the past with respect to the papacy, to be willing to consult Catholics in the formulation of doctrine, and to reconsider a universal teaching function.[40] Dulles agreed with the statement and was, in fact, a contributing voice in shaping it. This was not his last effort to reconsider teaching authority within the church or within the ecumenical movement, but it did indicate the trajectory his thought would take in subsequent years.

Justification

During the discussion on church teaching and infallibility, as in many other previous discussions at the L/RC Dialogue, the issue of justification by faith came up repeatedly. For Lutherans it was not only the key issue of the Reformation period but a criteriological principle that was frequently invoked to judge most matters of church life, doctrine, and structures. Discussing justification by faith, therefore, was the next logical step to take in the dialogue. Consequently, the group decided in 1978 to address this most neuralgic issue in the dialogue, a discussion that lasted for the next five years.

It is difficult to single out any individual theologian's contributions to the discussions of specific issues like justification because the dialogue itself was a communal project; it aimed as much as possible at consensus. Theologians on both sides tried to reflect the teachings of their churches, not just their own individual theological opinions, although those opinions necessarily came into the discussion, and many times they helped to shape a way out of the theological and doctrinal impasses of the past.

Dulles' individual contribution to the discussion on justification is evident in the minutes, in two papers he presented during the course of the deliberations, in his appointment to the committee that drafted the common statement on justification, and in a paper he presented to the Lutheran School of Theology at Chicago and then shared with his dialogue partners.[41]

Dulles' paper on Vatican II and justification focused on the council's conceptions of faith, grace, and salvation in Christ through sacramental causality and the instrumentality of the church. He admitted that Vatican II, unlike Trent, "did not systematically pursue the question of justification." Nonetheless he went on to demonstrate how Vatican II's sixteen documents here and there reaffirmed and modified the positions taken at Trent. Vatican II, for example, made a significant advance beyond Trent by integrating the ministry of word and sacrament, highlighting in particular the "salvific efficacy of the word of God." After Vatican

Catholic members of the Lutheran/Catholic Dialogue,
Paoli, Pennsylvania, September 1981

II, therefore, he argued, it should no longer be possible to describe the Catholic doctrine of justification "without including some discussion of the efficacy of the written and proclaimed word." Vatican II also went beyond the narrow intellectualist view of faith found in Trent, emphasizing that faith was "in the first instance…'an obedience by which many [sic] entrusts his whole self freely to God'" (*Dei verbum*; DV 5). These and other developments at Vatican II tended to narrow the gap between Lutheran and Catholic positions, even as the council reaffirmed Trent's doctrinal definitions. Vatican II, though, went far beyond Trent by calling attention to the "cosmic and secular dimensions of justification" and the possibility of salvation outside the religious activities of preaching and sacramental ministry. By doing so, the council "helped to situate the doctrine of justification within the horizons of a Church which has burst out of its Western European confines."[42] The discussion on the paper focused on clarifying for Lutherans how Vatican II related to Reformation and Tridentine issues.[43] Dulles' paper aided in summarizing some of the issues that needed to be clarified as the dialogue moved toward some mutual understanding.

"Luther's Theology" was Dulles' reflection on justification issues from a Catholic stance, establishing where he thought Catholics and Lutherans were in fundamental agreement (for example, in their common acceptance of the essential points of Luther's theology of law and gospel), where they had acceptable theological and conceptual differences, and where their disagreements needed much further examination in order to avoid hasty agreements. Dulles advised both Catholics and Lutherans to look for the strong points in one another's systems and to allow both sides to question the weaknesses of the other side because the confessional statements of each side were constructed to meet very specific questions, some of which were perhaps no longer pertinent. There were, too, neuralgic issues from both sides that needed to be articulated clearly in order to preserve the integrity of each other's tradition. Perhaps in the present state of confessional impasses, he suggested, what was needed was "only a kind of conditional approval of one another's proposals."[44]

Dulles' paper on contemporary Catholic theology of justification focused on the new situation in Catholicism with respect to Reformation issues. The "new Catholicism" of the post–Vatican II era and significant theological and historical research prior to the council were not as influenced by the objectifying categories of scholasticism as were Trent and much of post-Tridentine Catholicism. The newer approaches possessed a much more theocentric outlook, were influenced by the mystical tradition and post-Kantian transcendental philosophy, replaced an Aristotelian anthropology with a personalist phenomenology, and considered justification in terms of uncreated (rather than created) grace and symbolic actuation. This new situation in Catholic theology opened the way for a more fruitful dialogue with Lutheranism in overcoming the impasses of the sixteenth century. Since the council, Catholics were open to the Reformation's fiduciary notions of faith and forensic notions of justification, without denying the intellectualist notions of faith and inherent justification.[45]

During the early sessions of the discussion on justification, Dulles wanted the dialogue to "take cognizance of the epochal shift since the Reformation and Counter-Reformation." From the Catholic side, however, "justification is not a crucial contemporary issue." The more pertinent question was how to relate to the absent God (as John Johnson, a Lutheran member of the dialogue, pointed out). Dulles was interested in how the gospel could be addressed to contemporary concerns. This did not mean that justification was unimportant, but it was not as crucial to Catholics as were some other issues.[46] Catholic theologians since Trent, he noted, did not have much to say about justification except in a polemical context.

It was, however, a central issue for Lutherans, and Dulles acknowledged the fact and saw the need to sort out the issues that needed to be discussed with respect to justification. Recent biblical and historical studies had moved Lutheran and Catholic theologians closer together on the issues, but lingering Catholic and Lutheran sensibilities and positions needed to be discussed on the understanding of *sola gratia, sola fide,* and *solus Christus,* among other issues that tended to divide one tradition from another: transformative notions of grace versus forensic notions of justification, simultaneity of holiness and sinfulness, the relationship of faith and love, cooperation with grace, the idea of merit, and the relationship between justification and sanctification. These and other issues came up within the dialogue, but the crucial question was to determine, in the words of George Lindbeck, whether the "doctrine of justification [was] church-dividing....Is it a legitimate proposal of dogma from the Catholic perspective? Thus, there is no request that Catholics accept Reformation talk as the best or the only form of proclaiming the gospel. But it is a request for recognition of the

Listening while George Lindbeck speaks, May 13, 1980

freedom to preach the gospel. While this is the Lutheran perspective, can it be a Catholic one, too?"[47] This was not just an appeal for mutual toleration but a plea for a genuine search for the meaning of justification in both traditions.

Some on the dialogue (for example, Lindbeck) saw justification as one of many ways of talking about salvation and did not accept justification as the organizing principle of Lutheran theology. Others (for example, Gerhard Forde) insisted on retaining justification by faith as the plumb-line principle; it was not just one of many issues. Catholics in general had difficulties in accepting justification by faith as *the* principle or criterion of doctrine and practice. Nonetheless, as Dulles indicated, Catholics in dialogue accepted justification by faith as a common principle, even though the application of that principle might differ in the Lutheran and Catholic traditions.[48]

Dulles and other Catholics on the dialogue agreed with their Lutheran partners that justification and salvation rested "solely on Christ and his obedience, not upon our love and virtues." But they had their own Catholic concerns that they wanted to preserve. Among other things, they wanted to maintain an inherent relationship between faith and love and good works, so that love and good works were not perceived, Dulles noted, simply as "a caboose detachable from justifying faith." From a Catholic perspective, love and good works were not something extrinsic or unrelated to faith and repentance; "justification, salvation will not, indeed cannot, be complete without the following of love and good works." Catholics, moreover, did not like to speak, as Lutherans did, of love being merely the fruit of faith. Catholics also wanted Lutherans to clarify other issues related to justification: the freedom of the person, the effects of original sin, internal justification, growth in sanctification, cooperation with grace, merit, and promised eschatological rewards.[49]

Lutherans also had concerns and difficulties with the Catholic transformationist approach to grace and salvation, an approach that led to issues like merit that violated the Lutheran emphasis on *sola fide*, *sola gratia*, and *solus Christus*. During the dialogue, all the issues were discussed with some passionate disagreements and some tense moments. Nonetheless, the two sides were able by 1983 to hammer out a consensus statement that indicated what significant agreements they had reached, what convergences were possible amidst continuing different theological and conceptual frameworks, and what disagreements remained. But the bottom line was that their understanding of justification by faith had led them to a mutual Christological affirmation on the doctrine of justification and salvation: "Our entire hope of justification and salvation rests on Christ Jesus and on the gospel whereby the good news of God's merciful action in Christ is made known; we do not place our ultimate trust in anything other than God's promise and saving work in Christ." After 450 years of debate over the issue, Lutherans and Catholics came to a significant level of agreement. That did not mean that full accord had been reached on justification by faith, "but it does raise the question…whether the remaining differences on this doctrine need be church-dividing."[50]

The dialogue members submitted their common statement to their respective churches for their study and their decisions, decisions that they hoped would enable the churches to confess their faith as one.[51] This American document then became part of an international discussion of the issue between representatives of the Lutheran World Federation and the Pontifical Council for the Unity of Christians. In 1994, those two bodies appointed a small group of theologians to examine the L/RC Dialogues and draw up a joint consensus statement on justification. The international group produced a common statement, which was discussed and critiqued in various national dialogues, including the American L/RC Coordinating Committee, on which Dulles served.[52] The draft of the joint statement summarized the basic agreements of various previous national and international documents and called for the lifting of the mutual sixteenth-century condemnations or anathemas on justification.

From 1994 to 1996, Dulles presented two papers to the L/RC Coordinating Committee on the applicability of the sixteenth-century condemnations and on the proposed Joint Declaration on justification.[53] From the beginning, he had some serious reservations on the advisability of declaring that all the Tridentine canons on justification were no longer applicable to the present. He reminded his dialogue partners in 1994, for example, that Catholics had a position on the question of merit and that for Catholics merit had something to do with justice and with the freedom of the will.[54] In a paper that examined whether or not the propositions on justification condemned by Trent and the Book of Concord still held, Dulles tried to distinguish between those he thought no longer applied because of the advances made in ecumenical discussions, those where there were still some disagreements but not substantial enough to be church dividing, and those that were particularly difficult and needed much further theological examination before the anathemas could be lifted.

In the last category, Dulles placed the following four issues that still seemed to separate Catholics and Lutherans: (1) whether a sinner could freely cooperate with God's grace in the process of being justified (Trent, canon 4); (2) whether an unrepentant sinner could have authentic faith (Trent, canon 28); (3) whether the justified could truly merit an increase of grace and everlasting life (Trent, canon 32); (4) whether the justified could perform works of satisfaction for their own sins and the sins of others (Trent, canon 30).[55] Whether or not these and other issues were church dividing was a major question for Dulles, and he believed that the previous Lutheran and Catholic condemnations had to be settled one at a time. Theologians had to decide, moreover, what criteria could be used in determining which disagreements were church dividing and which ones were not. As far as he was concerned, a "doctrine is church-dividing when one is not allowed to teach it" in one's church.[56] And he was not sure "whether the Catholic Church today would be willing to say that positions condemned by Trent could be freely taught in the Church today."[57]

Dulles' position on lifting the condemnations of the sixteenth century flowed over into his assessment of the 1994 draft of the declaration. Overall he liked the declaration's affirmation of the basic consensus reached on justification in the U.S. L/RC Dialogue, but he believed that the declaration's statement on mutual condemnations needed much closer examination, and, in fact, he asserted that "to say the condemnations of the sixteenth century no longer apply is to make a very sweeping statement. Is it to say that all of them do not? Some still do."[58] The four issues mentioned were discussed extensively in the coordinating committee, with Dulles leading the way in seeking for changes in the declaration or at least suggesting that revisions be included to answer objections raised particularly with reference to the declaration's statement that the sixteenth-century condemnations "no longer apply." There was no universal agreement on these objections within the coordinating committee, however, and, in fact, a considerable amount of tense give and take over the declaration.

When the committee finally put together a five-page joint response to the declaration, it singled out those Catholics on the committee who were not totally satisfied with it and wanted some changes before the declaration was published. "Three Roman Catholic members of this Committee," the response noted, "recommend that the final form of the declaration be expanded to show more clearly from the extensive work of the dialogues how Roman Catholic and Lutheran teaching on preparation for justification, the faith of unrepentant sinners, and satisfaction (Trent canons 4, 28, and 30) are not incompatible."[59] Throughout the discussion, Dulles maintained his support of the general consensus affirmation on justification, but he had opposed the declaration's assertion that the remaining differences between Catholics and Lutherans on justification, which the previous dialogues had carefully delineated, were compatible. From Dulles' perspective, the remaining differences did not appear to be compatible.

The declaration was revised somewhat and was signed by representatives of the Lutheran World Federation and the Roman Catholic Church in Augsburg, Germany, on October 31, 1999. Immediately prior to the signing ceremony, on October 26, 1999, Dulles gave a lecture on the document at Fordham University, outlining the document's evolution and some of its main features.[60] As in the past, Dulles agreed with the heart of the document, as expressed in paragraph 15: "Together we confess: By grace alone, in faith in Christ's saving work and not because of any merit on our part, we are accepted by God and receive the Holy Spirit, who renews our hearts while equipping and calling us to good works." This statement, he believed, was in clear accord with previous dialogue statements, the Augsburg Confession of 1530, and Trent's Decree on Justification. If the declaration "had stopped at this point, it would have been a breakthrough of sorts because the two churches have never in the past jointly expressed their shared convictions about justification."[61] But the declaration, Dulles argued, went on to touch upon issues that had proven divisive in the past and continued to be troublesome in the present. It was not clear in the statement, Dulles asserted, whether the doctrine of justification held a privileged position "as the criterion by which all other Christian doctrines are to be judged, or is it to be viewed as one doctrine among many?" Dulles and other Catholics on the U.S. L/RC Dialogue had raised this issue repeatedly in the dialogue and discovered that they could not come to full agreement on it. Dulles also questioned, as he had in the past, whether the Lutheran positions on the four issues listed "really escape the anathemas of the Council of Trent."[62]

After raising a series of questions on the declaration, he asserted that he found it "almost unaccountable" how the Holy See could sign the document. Nonetheless, the Vatican more than likely would sign the document, because it could do so while articulating its own caveats, acknowledging and accepting the value of varying theological formulas, and desiring to further the ecumenical movement it had initiated at the Second Vatican Council. Signing this ecumenical document, moreover, was a significant symbolic event in the midst of "a world that hovers on the brink of unbelief." Believers needed to unite for the sake of proclaiming together the gospel they accepted. In the end, Dulles accepted the declaration, even though he believed it had not overcome all difficulties. "More theological work is still needed."[63]

After the Joint Declaration[64] was signed in 1999, Dulles continued to speak and write about his fundamental support for the basic consensus and his lingering reservations or dissatisfactions about the agreement. In 2002, after he had become a cardinal, he reasserted his opinion that the declaration had tried to accomplish "too much." It had exceeded the truth by maintaining that the "remaining differences" were "acceptable." Thus, he continued to call Lutheran and Catholic theologians to the task of developing a more acceptable understanding of all the controverted points so that a fuller and truer doctrinal unity might emerge.[65]

Some theologians considered Dulles' criticisms of the Joint Declaration as inconsistent with his signing of the American L/RC 1983 joint statement on justification. Others considered it a manifestation of a reactionary turn to the right. It was neither. His criticisms, in fact, were consistent with positions he had held during the American discussion on justification when he acknowledged substantial agreement on justification but also acknowledged significant differences in the Lutheran and Catholic approaches to justification that were not entirely overcome by the agreement. His criticisms of the declaration, moreover, become all the clearer and consistent once one examines his participation in the L/RC Dialogue on the "One Mediator, the Saints and Mary," a discussion that took place prior to the publication of the declaration. That prolonged and difficult dialogue demonstrated clearly to him that the L/RC differences on justification came to the fore when both sides applied it to the issue of the cult of the saints and Mariology. The differences in his mind were not small, and in fact, help to explain his criticisms of the declaration.

One Mediator, the Saints and Mary

After the American L/RC Dialogue finished its document on justification in 1983, it began immediately to consider a discussion of Mary and the cult of the saints. The Marian dogmas and the cult of the saints had come up periodically in previous dialogues, particularly in the discussions of infallibility and justification. In the common statement on justification, for example, the Lutheran members wondered "whether official teachings on Mary and the cult of the saints, despite protestations to the contrary, do not detract from the principle that Christ alone is to be trusted for salvation because all God's saving gifts come through him alone."[66] Since the dialogue participants had already reached at least a partial agreement that the doctrine of justification was a criterion for examining church doctrine and practice, they decided to test how each side would apply that criterion to the cult of the saints and Mary. Since one of the corollaries of the doctrine of justification was the sole mediatorship of Christ, the members decided eventually to discuss the cult of the saints and the role of Mary within that context. They initiated the discussion on this issue in 1983 and continued discussions for the next seven years, concluding in 1990. The dialogue was the longest and the most contentious of all the discussions. Many of the issues relating to mediatorship and Mary and the saints proved to be intractable and beyond the theologians' ability to resolve the doctrinal issues. Nonetheless, through many painful discussions, they ultimately found the common ground they could agree upon in the midst of issues that continued to divide the two churches.

Dulles was very keenly aware throughout the many years of discussion that some of these issues on mediating salvation might be unresolvable within the current state of scholarship and convergence. He was a gradualist with respect to doctrinal unity and was satisfied to make small steps that removed obstacles to union and set the stage for later developments. This dialogue, however, proved most difficult for him to see how substantial unity could be achieved. At one point after six years of discussion, he and others in the group on both sides became exasperated with the lack of progress. He and some Catholics in the group, for example, wanted a clear statement that the cult of the saints and the two contested recent Marian doctrines, especially as understood within the context of Vatican II, did not give rise to a Lutheran charge of idolatry, a charge that had been made in some of the Reformation confessional statements. "If we cannot come up at least with some statement," Dulles complained, "I think we should resign and say that we have been unable to complete our mandate. If we have studied Vatican II for six years and not been able to conclude whether or not it recommends idolatry, again I think we have failed in our mandate and we should frankly confess that we have failed." If the current Lutheran rejection of the dogmas meant that they were "manifestly contrary to the Gospel" there would no longer be a possibility of closer communion or fellowship.[67] Ultimately this was not what the Lutherans meant by their rejection of the dogmas, but it took a considerable amount of time to erase the stereotypes of one another's positions and to reach some consensus in the midst of continuing differences.

The first few years of the dialogue on Mary and the saints lacked a central focus; instead it covered a host of issues from studies on *Mary in the New Testament*,[68] to the history and doctrine of the cult of the saints as manifested in practical piety, the invocation and veneration of the saints, the mediation of grace, the merits of the saints and the treasury of merits, the lack of biblical foundations for the Marian dogmas, and the relationship between worship and belief. The lack of a central focus frustrated the participants as they read and discussed forty-three papers on various biblical, historical, theological, and doctrinal issues that were in general tied to the issues of mediation, the cult of the saints, and Mary.

Dulles contributed to the discussion of Mary and the saints by preparing three papers and by serving on the drafting committee of the common statement that would eventually emerge from the dialogue.[69] At the beginning of the dialogue, when various topics relative to Mary and the saints were being put forth for discussion, Dulles proposed that the dialogue start with common ground before proceeding to more controversial topics. Both traditions accepted the creedal commitment to the communion of saints and he believed that would be a good place to start the conversation.[70] That suggestion, though, got buried in an unfocused multiplicity of other important converging and controversial issues. He also suggested that rather than examining Mary and the saints, as was proposed at first, the dialogue start with the saints and then Mary, focusing on areas of the common tradition, putting the examination of Mary in a much larger context than originally proposed.[71] This suggestion was eventually accepted.

As the participants prepared various papers for discussion, they asked Dulles to introduce them to contemporary Catholic theological reflection on the saints and Mariology. For his first paper, Dulles focused on Karl Rahner's understanding of the saints and mediation. Although the devotion to the saints had suffered a "notable decline" in recent years, some theologians like Rahner had upheld the traditional Catholic view of the mediation of salvation through human beings and the church. In Rahner's anthropology, Dulles argued, all human beings were bound together by reciprocal relations of interdependence. This intercommunication was part of the universal human existence and was relevant to Rahner's understanding of the mediation of salvation. Through Christ's humanity, salvation came to the human race, and therefore Christ became, as the scriptures noted, the one mediator of salvation. But the mediation did not end with Christ; other human beings and the church also mediated salvation, but that mediation was "subordinate, derivative, and instrumental." The veneration and invocation of the saints, in the Catholic tradition, was one manifestation of the principle of mediation. Catholic attention to the saints represented in an historically tangible and concrete way the ultimate victory of God's efficacious grace. The saints in the church reflect the church as the sacrament of Christ; they bore witness in their lives to the concrete triumph of Christ's salvific and continuing mission.[72]

As in most of his interventions in the L/RC Dialogue, Dulles was describing what the Catholic Church taught and how its theologians explained the teaching; he was not offering creative theological speculation or raising questions about church teachings. That was not the function of the dialogue. In the discussion that followed the paper, too, he simply reinforced Rahner's theology of the saints as one manifestation of a contemporary approach to explaining the Catholic tradition. The questions raised by the Lutheran theologians aimed at understanding what Catholics themselves understood by mediation of salvation through the saints.[73]

A second paper, which was an extension of the first, focused on Rahner's Mariology. Rahner's entire approach to Mary must be seen, Dulles argued, within the context of his view of the redeemed community, where Mary was conceived of as a type of the church and the one perfectly redeemed. Mary as the perfect Christian was a type of the church, the "historically tangible community of the redeemed, who receive the gift of Jesus Christ through the Holy Spirit."[74] She shows forth in her person what redeemed humanity is and can become. This approach to Mariology within the context of the redeemed community—a view, Dulles asserted, that was shared by other Catholic theologians and one that was consistent with Vatican II's Constitution on the Church—Rahner himself believed harmonized "fully" with the Lutheran doctrine of justification. Nonetheless, Rahner believed that there were tendencies within Protestantism that were unhealthy and unevangelical and therefore subject to correction from a Catholic perspective.[75]

Treating Mary within the context of the redeemed community, Rahner went on to discuss the various Marian dogmas (virginity, divine motherhood, immaculate conception, and assumption). When examining Mary's mediation of grace, Rahner, like most Catholic members on the dialogue, understood mediation as an analogous term. They all asserted the sole mediatorship of Christ. Mediation, understood analogously, was applied to the church, the sacraments, the saints, and Mary. When applied to the saints or Mary, mediation, Dulles repeatedly asserted in the dialogue, was a "derived mediation." Mary's mediation, as Rahner and Catholics in general held, was "not parallel to Christ's but within it." What Mary mediated was "simply the grace of God given in Christ alone."[76]

Nonetheless, Mary played a role in the objective redemption because of her perfect acceptance of Christ in faith. She is, as Rahner argued, "the highest and most radical instance of the realization of salvation, of the fruit of salvation, and of the reception of salvation." Rahner made these claims while asserting also that some claims and practices in the Catholic tradition had been excessive, and for the future he believed the task for theologians was to develop the Catholic Marian doctrines within the context of the entire doctrinal tradition. He favored simplication and clarification of those doctrines, not a multiplication of more individual doctrinal or dogmatic declarations, as some extreme Mariologists wanted.[77]

Although, for a variety of reasons, the Lutherans did not share Rahner's views, particularly on mediation, they did believe, as Robert Bertram noted, that Rahner's approach seemed to "take the sting out of traditional Mariology." Dulles thought Bertram's understanding of Rahner was correct. Rahner had perceived that "Mary is totally situated on the side of the redeemed. Even the immaculate conception could be included, in that all of us are surrounded by grace. But Rahner sees his work as strengthening the traditional dogma, not undermining it."[78] When Bertram suggested that Rahner's christocentric approach to Mary seemed to undermine the need for the Catholic preoccupation with Mary, Dulles responded with what was to him a central Catholic methodological consideration: "To emphasize Christ, one must emphasize Christ's work. Here [in Mary] Christ's work is fully operative."[79]

The discussion on the saints and Mary roamed about on a variety of related issues for another two years after Dulles' second paper. In 1987, he presented a third paper. This time on the Catholic dogma of the assumption, defined in 1950. The Marian dogmas of the immaculate conception (1854) and the assumption had been a bone of contention with Lutherans and other

Protestants for years, and they would not be acceptable to Lutherans on the dialogue for a variety of reasons but basically because Lutherans believed the dogmas had no foundation in scripture, and they considered them more like pious opinions than articles of belief. Dulles was aware of this when he wrote his paper on the assumption, an expository paper that was primarily an attempt to explain the Catholic definition and the meaning it had for Catholics. He admitted from the beginning that the two most recent Marian dogmas "represent the most problematic examples of the Catholic magisterium claiming a revealed status for doctrines having a relatively tenuous basis in Scripture and early tradition."[80]

Dulles gave an historical account of the background and a systematic analysis of the organization, method, and selection of materials for the definition of the assumption (*Munificentissimus Deus*, November 1, 1950). He identified Pope Pius XII's method in the definition as "regressive," meaning that the pope gave pride of place to the living magisterium and the existing consensus of the faith and then sought "to garner support in Scripture and tradition." The definition that "it is a divinely revealed dogma that the Immaculate Mother of God, the ever Virgin Mary, having completed the course of her earthly life, was assumed body and soul into heavenly glory" proceeded "backward from the present situation of Mary in glory rather than forward from her earthly history, thus avoiding," in Dulles' opinion, "many of the problems raised by the lack of reliable historical testimonies, and by conflicting theological speculations, about the death and entombment of Mary."[81]

Dulles dealt with the anathema attached to the definition and suggested that it said nothing about "those Catholics or non-Catholics who doubt or deny the Assumption because they are in good faith unconvinced that it has been divinely revealed." This invocation of an argument from silence was explicitly intended to make room for Lutherans who sincerely denied that there was any foundation in the Bible or early tradition for the definition. After the definition, Dulles maintained, theologians needed to explain more fully than in the past how doctrine developed in the church. He outlined how three different theologians explained the issue, favoring, to some extent, Rahner's view that the new definitions simply made explicit what was implicit in revelation from the beginning. Believers perceived the "realities of revelation with a God-given instinct." The magisterium and theologians, guided by the same Spirit, came to define the faith of Christian believers as it developed over time. For Rahner, moreover, the assumption was the fullest sign of the realization of redemption and an anticipation of the glorification that was promised to all the redeemed.[82]

In the discussion that followed Dulles' paper, Lutheran theologians asked what level of authority was assigned to such dogmatic statements and what was their foundation in the Bible. Gerhard Forde, also asked "What does Mary guarantee that is not already guaranteed in Christ?" In response to Forde, Dulles gave what was for him the central issue in Catholic approaches to Mary (and the saints): "Christ is never alone, never isolated from the redemptive effects of his work. In Mary we see the extent of Christ's redemptive power in a way that is not already seen; a dramatic instance of what is implicit in the acts of Christ himself. The redeemer implies the redeemed community."[83] Lutherans in the discussion discovered that they could understand the explanations of the dogma, but that did not mean they could accept the dogma itself because it was not grounded in revelation (as they understood it).

Dulles' paper was one of the last papers discussed in the dialogue. By 1987, most on the dialogue were weary. The discussions seemed to be leading nowhere in the direction of a common statement. Invocation of the saints and the Marian dogmas were particularly troublesome. In February 1987 George Tavard seems to have put his finger on the problem and suggested a way out of the impasse. He had been absent for the meeting at Wheeling, West Virginia, in September 1986, but after he read the minutes of that meeting, he wrote John Hotchkin to suggest a way out of the impasse. Hotchkin then sent the Tavard letter to the Catholic chair of the dialogue, Archbishop J. Francis Stafford, suggesting that he make room on the agenda of the next meeting for Tavard to present his proposal. Hotchkin did not want to send the Tavard letter to all the members "out of the blue" because he was concerned that a "certain amount of tension has begun to surround our work and it might cause unnecessary resistance if this letter came out of the blue to the Lutherans."[84]

Tavard was convinced that "our approach to the ecumenical question of 'Mary and the Saints' has been too global." The dialogue had gotten involved in a multitude of "subquestions" and needed to refocus to move toward some common statement. He suggested, therefore, that the group start with the question of holiness and then proceed to questions of "prophetic" sainthood, the ecclesial means for assessing the prophetic dimension, the saints' prayer for the church militant, veneration and invocation of the saints. From the discussion of the saints, the dialogue could then proceed to Mary, who ranked first among the prophetic saints, and then on to the Marian doctrines, the last two of which were the most controversial. Although Tavard admitted that there would be no agreement on the most recent Marian dogmas, he believed that agreement could be reached on three points: (1) that the dogmas did not detract "theoretically" from the unique mediatorship of Christ; (2) that they are not part of the heart of the gospel, but "peripheral in the hierarchy of Catholic doctrines"; and (3) that Catholic theologians have an unfinished task in demonstrating how these dogmas are consistent with revelation.[85]

The Tavard proposal did not immediately turn the dialogue toward Tavard's solution of the problem, but it did turn the discussion toward solving the issue of how each tradition applied the doctrine of justification and the sole mediatorship of Christ to the saints and Mary. At the meeting in Tampa, Florida, in February 1987, a drafting committee of two Lutherans (Eric Gritsch and John Reumann) and two Catholics (Dulles and Carl Peter) was appointed to work out an acceptable outline for a common draft. The drafting committee presented draft after draft of a common statement from 1987 to 1990 before the participants could agree on a final statement.

Lutherans from the beginning wanted the discussion of the saints and Mary to be a test case for the doctrine of justification. To Lutherans, Catholic Marian practices and doctrines appeared to violate *the* criteriological principle of justification and its corollary the sole mediatorship of Christ. Using this criterion, Lutherans had a difficult time seeing how the Catholic understanding of the mediation and invocation of the saints and Mary did not detract (or worse deny) the sole mediation of Christ. Catholics, on the other hand, while accepting justification as a (but not the only) criteriological principle, saw the gift of divine life in the saints and Mary as testifying to the reality and effectiveness of the unique mediation of Christ.

Both traditions could accept justification and the sole mediatorship of Christ, but they applied these doctrines with very different results. Lutherans continued to interpret justification in terms of simultaneity (*simul justus et peccator*) and therefore emphasized the distance between Christ and the redeemed human community; Catholics interpreted justification in terms of transformation and therefore emphasized the continuity between Christ and the redeemed human community. Mediation and invocation tended to undermine Christ's sole mediation according to the Lutherans; failure to acknowledge a derived mediation and invocation tended to undermine free agency and cooperation with the grace of the sole mediator according to the Catholics. Without free agency, cooperation with grace, and some acceptance of grace-filled merit, Catholics held, "Christ's unique mediation will be made fruitless and sterile."[86]

Lutherans, furthermore, rejected the recent Marian dogmas not only because they detracted from Christ's sole mediatorship but also because they had little or no foundation in revelation. From the Lutheran perspective, the dogma of the immaculate conception was, as one Lutheran in the dialogue maintained, "simply wrong."[87] The sixteenth-century problems with veneration and invocation, as the Lutherans noted in the common statement produced in 1990, had "not vanished" in the present.[88] For Dulles, too, all the L/RC problems in understanding justification had not vanished, and he would be reluctant, as indicated earlier, to admit that Catholics and Lutherans could remove all of the sixteenth-century condemnations until further understanding and agreement could be reached. That was a task for the future.

Despite these ongoing differences, the dialogue participants were able to list nineteen "Church-Uniting Convergences" that had emerged in the course of the long discussion of the saints and Mary.[89] The dialogue had not been fruitless, but the prolonged discussions had taken their toll upon the participants.[90] Many were convinced, too, that the next session should be much more focused and should be expedited much more efficiently than the one on the saints and Mary. The next topic, they decided, should be on the relationship of scripture and tradition, since that issue had been at the bottom of many discussions since 1965 when the participants discussed their agreements on the Nicene Creed.

Scripture and Tradition

In their common statement on scripture and tradition, the participants wrote that the "problems relating to the authority and use of Scripture and to the value of tradition surfaced several times in discussion."[91] In the most recent dialogue on the saints and Mary, the Lutherans noted that "the use of Scripture remains controversial between Lutherans and Roman Catholics." Lutherans went on to say that

> the question of Scripture and tradition lies behind much of what still separates Lutherans and Roman Catholics concerning the saints and Mary. We already signaled the importance of this question in our first round of dialogue (L/RC 1, p. 32). It was fundamental for our dialogue on Teaching Authority and Infallibility in the Church (L/RC 6). In the present round of dialogues on the saints and Mary we have again discovered the need to investigate biblical extension and magisterial tradition.[92]

All the participants were agreed that the dialogue on scripture and tradition should not be prolonged, and it was not. The dialogue began in 1990 and concluded in 1992 with a short common statement on the issues.

From the beginning of the discussion of scripture and tradition, the participants decided on very limited aims. Carl Peter, one of the Catholic members, asserted that the most that could be accomplished was to diminish caricatures of each other's positions, "which is probably all that we can expect of ecumenism at this point anyway." Others, like Dulles, wanted the dialogue to "explain as fully as we can why we have reached our respective positions."[93] The dialogue tried to address both of these objectives.

One task was to overcome limited and stereotypical notions of *sola scriptura* in the Lutheran tradition and of the two-source theory of revelation in the Catholic tradition. A second task, and probably the most persistent of the issues between Lutherans and Catholics, was to describe how each tradition understood the movement from the gospel, as the living word of God, to church doctrine and dogma. In the early part of the dialogue, Dulles wanted the group to take up the issue of the development of doctrine within the discussion of scripture and tradition because that issue had not been dealt with in depth in the past.[94] How one moved from scripture to tradition was also a key issue for Lutherans. Joseph Fitzmyer summarized the "nub of the question" as Catholics on the dialogue perceived it: "How do Scripture and Tradition function in the formation of dogma (or doctrine—whichever of those two you prefer)?"[95] On that question the participants knew they were not going to agree, but they believed it was important to describe how each church reached its different conclusions, and that is what the dialogue eventually achieved.

In the midst of discussing these issues, Dulles was asked to prepare a paper on the Catholic understanding of tradition, one of the twelve papers presented to the dialogue.[96] Later he was appointed one of the four members of the drafting committee. Dulles' paper, presented at the Erlanger, Kentucky, meeting in September 1990, argued that "at no time has a single concept of tradition prevailed in the Catholic Church."[97] His paper summarized different Catholic positions prior to Vatican II and then focused particularly on the emerging notion of tradition at Vatican II, a view that was significantly influenced by the nineteenth-century thought of Henry Cardinal Newman and Maurice Blondel and by the twentieth-century *ressourcement* theologians. Dulles' own dynamic, developmental concept of tradition was clearly in line with that of the *ressourcement* tradition and Vatican II.

Vatican II, in Dulles' interpretation, drew upon Trent in its understanding of scripture and tradition, emphasizing the objective elements in tradition, its continuity from the apostles, and its verbal transmission. But Vatican II also stressed the newer themes of subjectivity, progress, and action that were part of the *ressourcement* understanding of tradition. Dulles believed that the council, by distinguishing between tradition as the Spirit-filled process of transmission and development of the word of God, and the human traditions that were necessary (but reformable) means to make the tradition come alive and concrete in particular ages and cultures, had made significant ecumenical advances over the dominant post-Tridentine two-source theory. He concluded his paper by outlining ten positions on tradition and the traditions that he believed received nearly universal acceptance among contemporary Catholic theologians.[98]

In the discussion of Dulles' paper, some Lutherans recognized that the newer Catholic conceptions of tradition had ecumenical potential, but they also had issues with a notion of tradition that was not itself normed by scripture. Vatican II's *Dei verbum* could not imagine, the Lutheran Joseph Burgess noted, any case in which "the magisterium would be in conflict with the word of God." Kenneth Hagen, another Lutheran, thought that Vatican II's notion of the development of doctrine was something of a Catholic capitulation to the nineteenth-century zeitgeist. In response, Dulles acknowledged that the magisterium never says, "We were wrong," but it admitted that statements of the faith were not free from all deficiencies. Catholic theologians, on the other hand, acknowledged that there could be conflicts. For Dulles, moreover, the development of doctrine was not a capitulation but an ongoing reality in the history of the Christian tradition. Through preaching, worship, prayer, and meditation on the scriptures, doctrine developed but did not change. "There is a certain irreversibility to the development of doctrine. We cannot go back prior to Nicea or Vatican II. If there is an abiding presence of God in the Church, you cannot go back. New questions arise after Nicea, but they are not the same questions" as before Nicea.[99] When one Lutheran commented that Lutherans could relate to Dulles' use of Blondel and Michael Polanyi to explicate a Catholic notion of tradition as a communal and human way of knowing the tacit dimensions of the faith, Dulles responded that he found Polanyi very helpful in the area of tradition. "He has much which can be taken over. And he is in harmony with Blondel....We Catholics learned by participating in the life of the church. Lutherans learn by sharing the life of the Lutheran church."[100] For Dulles and the other Catholics, scripture never stood alone. Lutherans, too, could agree to such a statement, as long as it was qualified in a Lutheran sense.

For Dulles, the issue of tradition was important not only for the ecumenical dialogue but also for the current life of the church and the churches. In the 1960s, as Dulles interpreted the signs of the time, what was needed was an understanding of the distinction between Tradition (understood as the revealed message), tradition (as the process of transmission), and traditions (as the concrete, particular, and diverse forms of expression of the gospel).[101] Those distinctions provided a theoretical framework for reforming certain human traditions in the church that were obscuring the gospel. By the 1990s, the cultural and ecclesial situation had changed. Young Catholics in particular were growing up without any clear sense of the Catholic Tradition. The ethnic and cultural traditions of fifty years ago that had socialized Catholics into the Tradition had dissipated, and they were replaced by nothing comparable. Young people, Dulles claimed, "are so open to the world that they are almost drowning in secularity. Everything that they know came into existence yesterday and will probably vanish tomorrow. Nothing in their lives seems to be settled and secure. Not surprisingly, many of them hunger again for the richness and stability of a Catholic tradition to which they have almost lost access."[102]

A certain kind of historicism in the recent past had exaggerated the transitoriness of all things human and, in fact, had minimized the human traditions that were so important a part of socializing individuals into a community of faith. Religious traditions disposed individuals for communion with God and had a tendency to bind contemporary believers to the founding events of the apostolic age. Dulles was concerned that too little had been made of tradition and traditions in the most recent past—with devastating results for the young in particular. "Without a more effective socialization into the Church the faithful may no longer be in a position to accept or to interpret correctly the Scriptures, the normative symbols, and the statements of faith that have come down from the past."[103] The issue of tradition, therefore, was not just a theoretical issue between Lutherans and Catholics; it was an important ecclesial issue for both churches in passing on and sustaining the faith, and it was crucial if the churches were ever to have a common proclamation of and witness to the gospel. Dulles' emphasis and tone here differed considerably from his preoccupations of the mid- to late 1960s and early 1970s, when he was focused most particularly on the reforms needed within the Catholic Church.

In the 1960s, moreover, Dulles had been particularly enamored with the concept of historical consciousness and with the historical-critical method for understanding Christianity. He had not given up on the historical-critical method in the 1990s, and in fact, Lutherans and Catholics on the dialogue generally presupposed agreement on its usefulness in examining and interpreting scripture and tradition, and creedal, dogmatic, and theological statements—even though they periodically applied the method with different results. They were also well aware of the new forms of biblical and textual criticism that had surfaced in the modern period, even though the L/RC Dialogue members had not seriously considered those alternative forms of criticism within the dialogue itself.

For Dulles the historical-critical method was useful, but it had never been for him the exclusive method for interpreting scripture. Scripture for him was to be interpreted within the context of tradition—that is, an authentic interpretation of scripture presupposed a "dwelling in" the tradition (through worship, prayer, mediation, and service to others) that gave one an insight into the meaning of scripture that transcended mere historical accuracy. He emphasized repeatedly a theological interpretation of scripture, an interpretation that presupposed faith and a faithful reflection on the meaning of revelation contained in the biblical texts. Dulles' emphasis here created some tension in the dialogue with some Lutheran as well as some Catholic biblical scholars.

The participating scripture scholars did not always appreciate Dulles' approach to scripture and his periodic criticisms of an exclusive use of the historical-critical method.[104] During the discussion of scripture and tradition, Joseph Fitzmyer, for example, held that the historical-critical method was for him "*the* method. Nothing else works."[105] It was itself neutral, in the sense that anyone could use it. "What you make of it will depend on other things." The "other things," the "plus," were the elements of faith.[106]

Dulles and a few others had problems with Fitzmyer's understanding of the neutrality of the historical-critical method, or any other method. These critics asserted that all methods carried with them presuppositions that affected the use and application of the methods. Fitzmyer insisted that he was not ruling out presuppositions, just that they went beyond the text that was being examined by the historical-critical scholar. Dulles claimed in reply that the historical-critical method when applied to scripture could not get to the incarnation, the miracles, the resurrection, but only to an historical Jesus who had "very little importance for faith." Fitzmyer responded that "not everything I believe can be established by the historical-critical method. Using the method one could conclude that the tomb was found empty, but belief in the resurrection is not a result of critical interpretation."[107]

Dulles' Polanyian postcritical approach to interpretation clashed somewhat with those who claimed a methodological neutrality in approaching texts and traditions. Although Dulles and Fitzmyer were somewhat at odds on method, they were in agreement about the extension of scripture into later Catholic doctrinal developments. Both Jesuits acknowledged that scripture was the basis of doctrine in the church and that doctrine developed in the course of history but in continuity with the word of God in the Bible. Lutherans, who might have agreed with either Dulles or Fitzmyer on method, could not make the same conclusions regarding doctrinal developments.

In the midst of discussing the relationship of scripture and tradition, interpretation and an ecclesial magisterium, and the transition from the gospel to later dogmatic and confessional statements, Catholics and Lutherans discovered again multiple points of agreement and were able to pinpoint more clearly precisely where the continuing differences resided. Some stereotypes were overturned in the course of the discussion. Elizabeth Johnson, one of the Catholic members, for example, noted toward the end of the session that the typical Catholic misconception of the Lutheran *sola scriptura* idea had been significantly erased. Catholics had believed that for Lutherans only what was explicitly in scripture mattered as the source and norm of Christian doctrine and life. What Catholics discovered was that Lutherans "also hold to certain apostolic traditions, but those are also somehow found in Scripture or founded in Scripture."[108] Lutherans, on the other hand, saw convergences with Catholic emphasis on the centrality of scripture and the dynamic and developmental view of tradition. Both Lutherans and Catholics moved beyond the limits of some of their previous notions of the other's positions. Lutherans, though, continued to hold to *sola scriptura*, but not without a vital notion of tradition as the proclamation of the gospel and the continuous reception and hearing of the gospel within the church. Catholics, on the other hand, had moved beyond the two-source theory to focus on the primacy of scripture within the context of an ongoing tradition interpreted with the aid of the Holy Spirit within the church's total life and action. Catholics, too, saw authentic doctrinal development as a result of the Holy Spirit's assistance to the church's magisterium.

By the end of their discussion, Lutherans and Catholics were able to outline seven points of agreement on issues relating to scripture and tradition: (1) scripture is the preeminent word of God; (2) that word was carried by tradition prior to the written scripture; (3) scripture, under the guidance of the Holy Spirit, gave rise to oral proclamation of law and gospel; (4) the preeminence of scripture does not preclude the function of a teaching office or legitimacy of doctrinal traditions; (5) historically verifiable apostolic traditions must be attested in some way by scripture; (6) all doctrine need not be simply and literally present in scripture; and (7) teaching of doctrine is never above the word of God, but serves and must be conformed to it. They noted three major points of continuing differences: (1) scripture alone as the ultimate norm for judging traditions; (2) the infallibility of the church's magisterium; and (3) the meaning of the development of doctrine.[109] Dulles had a major hand in formulating this statement, which concluded a long series of discussions on issues that had divided the churches since the sixteenth century.

Lutheran/Catholic Coordinating Committee

As mentioned previously, members of the dialogue were tired and weary with the prolonged discussions, and some thought a break was necessary to assess what direction the dialogue might take in the future. At the end of the last meeting in 1992, therefore, the group decided to cease discussions of controverted issues, to discuss whether or not the dialogue should continue, and to take time out to assess future directions of L/RC relations.

In 1993, a group of thirty-six American and European Lutherans and Catholics met at West Palm Beach, Florida, to discuss the future of the dialogue in the United States and the possibility of lifting the sixteenth-century condemnations on justification.[110] After the participants, including Dulles, decided that the dialogue should indeed continue, they were asked to prepare a one-page paper outlining their views on future directions. Dulles suggested three options: (1) to examine, "by methods already in use," controversial issues not previously addressed; (2) to consider the ultimate aims of the dialogue and methods most appropriate for reaching those goals; (3) to investigate the "practicality of the proposals in *Facing Unity*,"[111] the 1985 document of the international L/RC commission on the models and forms of fellowship between Catholics and Lutherans. With respect to the last option, Dulles wondered whether it was realistic to speak of mutual recognition of ministries or a common ordained ministry, as *Facing Unity* did, in view of the disagreements about the ordination of women.[112]

At the end of the meeting the group decided to focus upon the church as *communio/koinonia* as a future topic for discussion. After that meeting, an L/RC Coordinating Committee was established, with new membership, including Dulles, to deal with these issues. The coordinating committee met from 1994 to 1996, and during the four meetings conducted during those years, the group concentrated on *koinonia*, proposing a constructive theology. Rather than centering on issues that divided the two traditions, the group decided, at least for the next session, to examine how each tradition conceived of the idea of communion in its theology and religious practice. The coordinating committee finished its mandate at St. Louis in April 1996, after which a new L/RC Dialogue was appointed, but Dulles was not reappointed.[113]

Dulles had been on the dialogue for twenty-five years, and according to those members of the dialogue I was able to interview, he made major contributions personally and theologically to the common statements and the general spirit of conviviality, collegiality, and openness that characterized the meetings, even those meetings where disagreements were discussed rather pointedly and sharply. The Lutheran Eric W. Gritsch, in fact, considered Dulles the "Catholic quarterback" of the L/RC Dialogue.[114]

Dulles had observed the many challenges that dialogues such as this one faced, and over the years he saw the absolute necessity of such dialogues and became hopeful about their penultimate results in creating a new atmosphere in the churches. In December 2007, he acknowledged that he personally stood "by the ecumenical statements that I have signed, including those of the Lutheran/Catholic Dialogue and of Evangelicals and Catholics Together."[115] But with respect to the lingering doctrinal differences he was less optimistic. He admitted periodically that he was a pluralist with respect to accepting theological differences and doctrinal formulations, a gradualist with respect to moving the churches little by little toward the unity that Christ desired, and a realist with respect to what could be accomplished in the present, given the long tradition of separation and suspicion that affected both churches. Some might say that Dulles turned pessimistic about the possibilities of the ecumenical movement toward the end of the 1990s, but, as a letter to one correspondent indicates, he was realistic in assessing the distance that churches needed to go to achieve significant unity. He asserted that "some reports about the advances of ecumenism minimize the length of the journey still ahead."[116] He was in the ecumenical movement for the long haul, not for instantaneous success. As a gradualist in the great movement toward ecumenical unity, he was fond of quoting Newman: "Great acts take time."[117] Experience in the L/RC Dialogue became his great teacher in this regard.

By the early 1990s, Dulles noticed in the ecumenical movement what he called an "increasing confessional self-awareness. Some deplore, but others commend, this 'reconfessionalization.'" The discussions on justification, the saints and Mary, and scripture and tradition all pointed in this direction—even though the confessionalism was less polemical and more respectful of controverted positions than in the sixteenth century. And those reconfessionalized statements provided a "platform for further advances."[118]

Dulles' participation on the L/RC Dialogue came to an end in 1996, but his work in ecumenism did not come to an end.

12

THEOLOGY FOR A POSTCRITICAL AGE, 1988–2000

IN 1988, AT THE END of the school year at Catholic University, Dulles retired from his teaching position and returned to Fordham University to become the holder of the Laurence J. McGinley chair in religion and society. His retirement was hardly a cessation of his theological work. He was seventy years old in 1988, and for the next twenty years he taught at Fordham and periodically at Dunwoodie seminary, participated in ecumenical dialogues, gave lectures and talks across the country and abroad, and served as a theological consultant on national episcopal committees and on the Vatican's International Theological Commission. Age did not slow him down. He continued to be one of the most perceptive and prolific American Catholic theologians, producing from 1988 to 2000 six more books and more than 240 articles and reviews.

Fordham and the McGinley Chair

In 1987, when Dulles was considering retirement from teaching at the Catholic University of America, he received an invitation from the president of Fordham University, Joseph O'Hare, SJ, to become the first holder of the recently endowed university chair in honor of Laurence J. McGinley, SJ, a professor of theology and president of Fordham from 1949 to 1963. In the letter of appointment, O'Hare indicated that Dulles was to hold a university professorship not identified with any department or college. The chair would give Dulles the "greatest possible freedom in working with people here at Fordham."[1] Dulles' responsibilities were limited to giving two public lectures and teaching a seminar each year. The

With Anne-Marie Kirmse, OP, his longtime research associate at Fordham, near the end of their twenty years of work together

limited responsibilities would allow him to continue his work in theology and afford him the time to address, from a theological perspective, issues in society. The chair also provided him with resources to hire a secretary and a research associate. The research associate, Anne-Marie Kirmse, OP, was particularly valuable for his work in theology, since she had herself obtained a doctorate in theology and had written a dissertation on Dulles' ecclesiology.[2] She provided him with editorial assistance on his writings but was more than a research associate. She arranged the multiple details of his very active speaking engagements across the country and his frequent trips abroad for lectures and committee meetings; for twenty years, until his death, she was his gate keeper, caretaker, and confidante.

In the course of his years at Fordham, Dulles, serving as both theologian and social critic, gave biannual McGinley lectures (all of which were published as pamphlets or in periodicals) to the general public on a host of topics. In 2007, he noted that his lectures dealt "with issues that seemed to be of current interest and in need of theological clarification." He lectured on, among other topics, the role of theology in a university, the Jesuit charism in theology, the thought of Pope John Paul II and Cardinal Newman, the role of the new catechism of the Catholic Church, Mary's role in the church, the nature and progress of ecumenism, the relationship between religion and American culture and politics, human rights and the United Nations, evolution, and the use and limits of the death penalty. He did not intend to be original but to address public and ecclesial issues from within "the great tradition of the Church." He was convinced from his studies of history that the "greatest danger for the Church and theology is to accommodate excessively to the spirit of the times." On the other hand, he tried "to make the adaptations necessary to render the wisdom of the past ages applicable to the world in which we live."³ Dulles used three criteria in selecting the topics for the lectures: they all had a theological dimension, were matters of debate among Catholic theologians, and were of general interest, "not reserved to a small clique of specialists."⁴ The lectures were classic Dulles.

Dulles had a long association with Fordham. In the early 1940s, he visited Fordham's Edwin Quain, SJ, a classics teacher there and the priest who had received him into the Catholic Church in 1940. In 1941, he attended Fordham's Summer School of Catholic Action; from 1951 to 1953, he taught philosophy; in 1970, as a member of Woodstock College, he taught a theology course at Fordham; and from 1969 to 1972, he served on Fordham's board of trustees. He had been ordained at Fordham, and since he belonged to the New York Jesuit Province he knew many of the Jesuits at Fordham and in New York City. It was familiar ground for him, but he had been living outside the province for more than fourteen years. His return to his own province enabled him to contribute again to the specific Jesuit mission in education and to reconnect with his Jesuit colleagues and Jesuit community life. While living in Caldwell Hall at the Catholic University, of course, he had associated with the Jesuits there and with those at Georgetown University, but at Fordham he returned to the Jesuit communal style of life as an everyday experience. His Jesuit colleagues at Fordham and elsewhere remarked repeatedly about how well Dulles related to Jesuit colleagues with whom he lived and worked and prayed and ate and recreated. As one Jesuit told me, "I have to say in the community he is a very humble and gracious man. He's never expected others to do his work for him, even in terms of washing his own dishes or cooking his own breakfast."⁵

Fordham publicity photograph, 1988

Numerous people who knew him well remarked upon his characteristic humility.

Dulles was returning to the city of his youth, the city he knew very well. Family and friends and acquaintances as well as Jesuit colleagues were everywhere. On December 1, 1987, prior to his coming to New York, Dulles' sister, Lillias Hinshaw, had died after a long battle with cancer. She was survived by her husband, Robert Yost Hinshaw, who lived in Manhattan, and by two sons and two daughters who lived outside of New York City. Dulles had been close to his sister, but his nieces and nephews lived at such distances from New York that he rarely had close contact with them. The Hinshaws and other members of the extended Dulles family, however, periodically spent time with Avery, particularly at the end of June and over the Fourth of July holidays, at Greyledge, the Dulles family summer home at Henderson Harbor, New York.

Well into his late eighties, Dulles recreated for a week or two at Greyledge with other members of the extended Dulles family, particularly with his nieces and nephews and cousins. These were family events that enabled the Dulleses to enjoy each other's company and to stay connected. His nieces and nephews, as I discovered in talking with some of them and with Avery's brother John, had a deep affection for their uncle, and they enjoyed their occasional summer outings with him. Having homes at Henderson Harbor gave the family a comfortable location for their occasional gatherings.

Returning to New York, Dulles was much closer, too, to his old Harvard and St. Benedict friends of the 1940s. The so-called Feeney affair had alienated him from many of those who followed Fr. Feeney at St. Benedict Center in Cambridge. In fact, he had had no contact with any of them, even his beloved godmother, Catherine Goddard Clarke, after Feeney was excommunicated and the center was interdicted. Once Feeney was reconciled to the church in 1972, and some members of the St. Benedict community were reconciled in 1974, his relationship to his former friends and acquaintances began to change.

In 1978, when Feeney died, Dulles wrote a very positive memorial, recalling Feeney's charismatic gifts and how he used them effectively at St. Benedict Center.[6] On November 26, 1980, Dulles returned to the St. Benedict Center at Still River, Massachusetts (where the community had moved after the interdiction), to celebrate the fortieth anniversary of his reception into the Catholic Church. While at Still River, Dulles visited and prayed at the graves of Fr. Feeney and his godmother, both of whom were buried on the community's grounds. It was the first time in more than thirty years that he had had any contact with the old St. Benedict group. The reunion was a joyous one, celebrated with community prayer and a Mass of thanksgiving.[7] Again, in 1990, Dulles came back to St. Benedict's with his godfather, Msgr. Christopher Huntington, who was one of the founders of the original St. Benedict Center, to concelebrate with Fr. Gabriel Gibbs of St. Benedict a Mass of thanksgiving on the fiftieth anniversary of the center's establishment. On April 18,

With Abbot Gibbs, OSB, St. Benedict's Abbey, Harvard, Massachusetts

1993, too, he returned to Still River to celebrate the installation and blessing of Abbot Gibbs, OSB, after the reconciled members of the old St. Benedict Center became a community of Benedictine monks.[8]

Throughout the 1990s, Dulles made periodic trips to Still River for short retreats and days of prayer in the quiet and peaceful surroundings of the monastery grounds. Dulles was reestablishing old ties, establishing new ones, and recollecting, one presumes, the experiences that originally brought him into the Catholic Church. These visits to Still River also reestablished his personal continuity with his own past. The emphasis on continuity would be a recurring theme in his writings during the 1990s, especially the continuity between Vatican II and the church's earlier tradition.

Neuhaus, Dulles, and the New Converts

When he arrived in New York City, Dulles reestablished contacts with Richard John Neuhaus (1936–2009), who in 1988 was a Lutheran pastor of St. John the Evangelist Church in Brooklyn, author of *The Catholic Moment* (1987),[9] organizer of the Center of Religion and Society (1984), and after 1990 a Catholic and editor of *First Things*, a journal of ecumenical opinion on religion and public life. Dulles first met Neuhaus in the early 1970s, when Dulles was a professor at Woodstock College in Manhattan. Later, in 1975, Neuhaus invited Dulles to take part in the so-called Hartford Appeal. Thereafter they met periodically, and Neuhaus frequently telephoned Dulles to consult with him on theological issues while Dulles was living in Washington, D.C.

Once Dulles moved to Fordham, Neuhaus organized what he called the "Dulles Colloquium," an informal ecumenical gathering of twenty-five to thirty professionals interested in theological issues.[10] It was called the Dulles Colloquium because of Neuhaus's affection for Dulles and his respect for his senior theological leadership in the American Catholic community. At first the colloquium met three or four times a year to discuss theological issues of mutual interest. After 1990, Neuhaus used these discussions to stimulate or generate ideas for *First Things*. Neuhaus made sure when he invited Dulles to take part in the periodic weekend symposia that he was accompanied by a fellow Jesuit from Fordham because he worried about Dulles' driving himself into Manhattan. With a gracious grin, Neuhaus reported, "He's a wild driver, and notorious, but utterly self-confident and oblivious to the danger he constitutes to himself and to the public....He doesn't pay attention to his driving, and he's totally mechanically inept."[11] Neuhaus' observation was verified by some of Dulles' Fordham colleagues.

After 1988 Dulles became increasingly associated with what some called the "neoconservative" movement of Neuhaus, Michael Novak, and George Weigel, among others. Dulles himself at times called the group neoconservatives, but he never fully identified himself with a particular ideology. His own models approach to theology prohibited him from affiliating too closely with any one system of thought or theological orientation. Theological and moral systems had their advantages and defects, and one had to avoid assimilating any one system that might in fact obscure or neglect the mystery hidden in the revealed word of God.

Nevertheless, Dulles did indeed sympathize with the so-called neoconservatives, a group with which he had some close personal friendships before and after 1988. But he was never fully comfortable with the neoconservative program. In an address to the American Catholic bishops in 1990, for example, Dulles agreed with Neuhaus and Weigel that the Catholic Church was uniquely qualified to raise public discourse in the United States to a more substantive level, and, therefore, it could be said that this was the "Catholic Moment" in history. But he cautioned that a focus on constructing a "religiously informed public philosophy" without equal attention to the fundamental tasks of evangelization, religious formation, guidance, motivation, and conversion would seem to "define the Catholic moment too narrowly." The neoconservatives were aware of such a need for religious conversion and faith, but their emphasis on a rational public philosophy seemed "to supplant the need for faith."[12]

Friendship did not bar criticism when Dulles felt it was deserved. His friend Neuhaus, for example, periodically took blanket potshots at the Jesuits in his column in *First Things*. In October 1996, he quipped that Jesuits had watered down the Catholic identity to such an extent that he proposed, in jest, a dialogue between

Catholics and Jesuits, "a proposal that has not met with the official approbation of the Society of Jesus, among whose members, we hasten to add, we count some of our best friends."[13] Dulles was obviously upset by the snide remark and shot off a letter to Neuhaus to chastise him for his flippancy at the Jesuits' expense. Dulles was not uncritical of individual Jesuits, but he did not like the wide brush that Neuhaus used to paint the Jesuits as minimizers of the Catholic tradition. "Neuhaus," Dulles wrote, "counts some Jesuits among his best friends," but if this is to continue "he would do well to lay off the irrational attacks on the Society of Jesus that appear from time to time in his column." Jesuits and others in Catholic institutions of higher education needed encouragement, "not the supercilious abuse that Father Neuhaus heaps upon them." Neuhaus was repentant, admitting that "I am chastened by the reproof of one of my best friends and apologize for any injury done the many faithful members of the society of Jesus."[14]

Dulles wrote the letter to Neuhaus, as he told the Jesuit superior general, "not simply in reply to Neuhaus but also because, at least in this country, the Society of Jesus has a general reputation for being less than faithful to the magisterium, and to Rome in particular. I receive many letters that reflect the opinion that Jesuits are arrogant, that they snipe at the pope, and distance themselves from the hierarchy." Such perceptions, Dulles believed, were in part responsible for the decline in vocations.[15] On another occasion Dulles sent the general articles that were "not untypical of what is being said and written" about the Jesuits "in many places."[16] The Jesuit general was well aware of the problem of the Jesuit image that had been created by some individual Jesuits, but he was also confident, as was Dulles, that the "vast majority of ours" were faithful to the church. Because of the image problem, the general had tried to remind all Jesuits "that when any one of us speaks, we do not speak only for ourselves as individuals, but we are perceived by others as speaking for the Society."[17]

Dulles' sympathies for the neoconservative emphasis on religion and morality in public life came to the fore in the 1990s when he was invited twice to reflect on his father's career and political philosophy. In February 1988, he participated in a Princeton University centennial conference on John Foster Dulles. In brief remarks he singled out recreation and religion as two dimensions of his father's life. "He knew how to relax, and saw the importance of doing so." His father was more reticent about religion, but after 1937 in particular, he became significantly involved in the American Protestant churches' social mission and, from the perspective of faith and morality, addressed issues of international as well as national peace and justice.[18] In 1994, Dulles gave the Flora Levy Lecture in the Humanities at the University of Southwestern Louisiana in Lafayette, Louisiana. He chose to speak on his father's religious and political heritage, outlining the principles that he believed had guided his father as a man of public affairs. He asserted in that lecture that his father's view of religion and philosophy was right on target and relevant to the contemporary world in pointing to the need for a "religiously grounded public consensus." Without such grounding, a "spiritual vacuum and moral paralysis would result." At a time of disillusionment and moral relativism, such a lesson was important to convince a nation that it could not be strong without "sound spiritual and moral principles."[19]

The Flora Levy lecture revealed much about Dulles' basic agreements with his father's views of the role of religion in public life. Religion and the churches should provide basic spiritual insights and moral principles in the formation of consciences, but the churches themselves should not be involved in applying those principles to very complicated, technical, practical problems of the political and civil order because the churches as churches did not have such competence. Dulles' reflections on his father's life and principles revealed values that he himself had learned and cherished throughout much of his life.

In the 1990s, Dulles associated not only with the neoconservatives but also with what he periodically described as the "new convert" movement since the late 1970s, a movement analogous to the convert movement in the 1930s and 1940s in the English-speaking world. Periodically he reflected on his own conversion experience in contrast to that of the new converts like Neuhaus. On November 16, 1994, for example, on the occasion of the fifty-sixth anniversary of Thomas Merton's reception into the church, Dulles gave the Merton lecture at Columbia University.[20] He noted that Merton's conversion was similar to his own, except for the fact that Dulles, unlike Merton, had developed a taste for Plato and the Platonism of the Italian Renaissance. But both he and Merton were attracted to the medievalism inherent in the neo-scholastic mentality and the sense of transcendence and purpose that seemed to govern the Catholic Church of the late 1930s and 1940s.

Dulles went on to say that Vatican II emphasized dimensions of the church's existence in the world that had been somewhat absent from the emphases of the 1940s and 1950s. The council also attempted to renew Catholic life, but in the reforming atmosphere of the immediate postconciliar years the confusion and flux within the church made it less than attractive to those outside the church. Consequently, in the decade or so after the council, few converted to the Catholic Church because it seemed not to offer much that was different from the society in which most people were living. From the late 1970s onward, however, "thoughtful inquirers" began again streaming into the church, among whom Dulles listed Harold Riesenfeld, Max Thurian, E. F. Schumacher, Malcolm Muggeridge, Alasdair MacIntyre, and Neuhaus. Dulles found himself identifying with this new group of converts for many reasons, not the least of which was his own conversion experience, but his own original attraction to the Catholic Church was not that of the new converts. These new converts were not drawn to the Middle Ages, nor did they reject their own pasts, as was the case with Merton's and Dulles' generation. Instead, they were drawn to catholicity in the qualitative sense of the fullness of Christianity they found in the Catholic tradition. They perceived their movement into the Catholic communion, moreover, to be in continuity with their previous commitments.[21] Pope John Paul II's emphasis upon a "new evangelization," dialogue, orthodoxy, and the fullness and renewal of the Catholic tradition, rather than being unattractive, as some contended, was inviting to many inside and outside the Catholic Church and was responsible, Dulles believed, for stimulating the new flood of converts into the church.[22]

Increasingly during these Fordham years, Dulles emphasized the need for orthodoxy and evangelization. He saw this emphasis as an attraction for new converts even though it might also create some defections from the church. Nonetheless, the church had to live up to a truth not its own and proclaim the "hard sayings" of the gospel. In a 1998 talk to a large audience at Loras College in Dubuque, Iowa, Dulles noted, consistent with his own personal experience and that of new converts, that

> converts do not take their faith for granted; still less do they chafe at it as something forced upon them. For them it is the treasure hidden in the field, the pearl of great price, for which they joyfully sacrifice all lesser goods. Converts tend to remain very self-motivated even within the church. They are so used to swimming against the tide that they sometimes become almost sectarian in their practice of Catholicism. They can be severely critical of other Catholics for conforming too much to the dominant culture.

Increasingly in the 1990s, Dulles favored those "countercultural Catholics" who embraced orthodoxy.[23]

In 1996, Robert Heyer, editor for Sheed & Ward, encouraged Dulles to republish his autobiography and bring it up to date by surveying his career as a Jesuit and theologian since 1946. In the updated autobiography, Dulles reflected on the course his own life had taken between 1946 and 1996, trying "to bring out the continuity within change that is so much a part of the history of the church as well as my own pilgrimage." Dulles wanted to make it clear that his conversion experience—which gave him his faith in God, Christ, and the church—had "not substantially changed," but his theology had unfolded and changed since 1940. He traced his theological developments from his early experience as a convert to his educational experience at Woodstock, where he eventually became a "convinced" philosophical Thomist, and then during the theologate his heart was drawn to the *nouvelle théologie* of Henri de Lubac, Jean Daniélou, and Yves Congar. He was thus prepared for the developments of Vatican II, but continued his allegiance to Aquinas, Ignatius of Loyola, and the great medieval and Baroque heritage.[24]

In the immediate postconciliar period, he enthusiastically backed the trajectory of conciliar thought, though he did not accept all reform proposals as "improvements." He admitted, nonetheless, that "I may have tended to exaggerate the novelty of the council's doctrine and the shortcomings of the preconciliar period." In the late 1960s, he had focused on the discontinuities, but with the "rise of the left" and secular theology, he felt called upon to insist upon "continuity with the past." His own method in theology, as expressed in his models approach, departed somewhat from the neo-scholastic method of theology, which tended to minimize or nullify the pluralism in theology itself by selecting a single image or root metaphor for explaining doctrine. He preferred to place various models of theology in conjunction with one another to underline the mystery of doctrine and to provide mutual critiques of all theological approaches, bringing out in the process the strengths as well as the weaknesses of the multiple approaches. He also admitted that he became highly critical of the excessive tendency in theology to accommodate theology "to the tastes and fashions of the day." Experience was indeed a source of theology, but experience that was informed by the gospel.[25] In 1998, in response to a reporter's question on whether or not he thought Catholic liberalism was on the decline, Dulles opined that the kind of theology that developed in the 1960s made some Catholics look favorably on other churches and religions, criticize their own tradition, and change or be prepared to change their own commitments. "What's becoming evident now is that this kind of theology engenders no posterity." Such an approach did not generate a "strong community of faith." If faith was "just a vague orientation to transcendence or a tentative opinion," few would want to become a part of that kind of community of faith.[26]

In the past, Dulles had criticized the failure of the manual and neo-scholastic theologians to dialogue with modern forms of thought; in the 1980s, he critiqued the accommodating approach. In both the immediate past and in the present period of his life, he invoked the Ignatian *agere contra* principle.[27] He applied this principle to the theological community, either implicitly or explicitly invoking the Jesuit tradition. His ultimate criterion for the validity of any theological or practical reforms or dissent in the church was always their conformity to spiritual renewal. Repeatedly he asked, as a fundamental criterion for the exercises of freedom and authority in the church, how did those exercises serve what Paul called

(Gal 5:22–23) the "fruit of the Spirit": "love, joy, peace, patient endurance, kindness, generosity, faith, mildness, and chastity." Did they build up the church or lead to the fruits of the flesh? Such questions demanded spiritual discernment.[28]

Dulles admitted in these years at Fordham that he took "a somewhat critical attitude toward the dominant secular culture." Because there was a tendency in theology to be too accommodating, Dulles believed that it was difficult to say "that Christian theology is in a very healthy condition." Dulles did not side with either the liberals or the conservatives in the Catholic Church, because the church remained for him "a communion of tradition and authority, open to dialogue and progress." Within this understanding of the church, he acknowledged that he had grown in his confidence in the "charism of truth conferred upon the hierarchical leadership."[29]

Dulles' autobiographical reflections certainly indicated tendencies and themes that were increasingly evident in his writings and talks from 1988 onward: emphasis on the continuity between Vatican II and previous church teachings; respect for ecclesiastical authority in the theological enterprise; openness to diverse theological approaches; acceptance of the need for legitimate change and the development of doctrinal formulations and theology; critique of excessive accommodation; criticisms of the dominant secular culture. These and other themes would recur throughout this period of his theological development.

Theological Issues and Method in a Postcritical Age

Prior to being named a cardinal of the Catholic Church in 2001, Dulles continued his support of John Paul II's papacy and particularly the pope's "new evangelization" motif. He also laid out the principles and methods of the Catholic theological enterprise and periodically critiqued some developments in the American Catholic theological society, in American Catholic culture, and in American society in general. As he read the signs of the times, he called for creative adaptation of theology to the new postconciliar needs, needs in the Catholic community that were very different from those in the 1960s. Although he favored a judicious accommodation of Catholic theology to the modern turn to the subject, he called more and more for a critical distance from an overidentification with a culture that was becoming, in his view, increasingly dechristianized. Periodically, too, his critics would tag him a conservative or even a reactionary. His friend and more liberal colleague, Fr. Charles Curran, for example, remarked in 1997 that Dulles had in fact wandered from the middle ground of theology. "There is no doubt that on certain issues [women's ordination and papal authority] he has been less open than he was in the past.... He's even pulled back a little on the possibility of dissent."[30] Dulles, however, continued to see himself as a moderate in the theological community. He allowed for legitimate dissent, though it should be reluctant and rare. He also continued to uphold the theological principles of the progressive wing at the Second Vatican Council, modified to some extent by giving more attention to the council's continuity with earlier Catholic teachings. He considered Pope John Paul II to be a creative interpreter of the council for the new age in which the church lived, an age of conflict, dissension, reform, and evangelization.

In the years after his retirement from Catholic University, Dulles published *The Craft of Theology* (1992), the culmination of his reflections on the nature, methods, and mission of theology.[31] During these years, too, he addressed numerous essays to issues of theological criteriology, theological dissent, the various locations of theology (in the university, the seminary, and the professional theological organizations), and described for French, German, and Italian audiences the postconciliar historical developments of American Catholic theology.

Dulles' understanding of theology owed a great deal to his appropriation of Jesuit spirituality, and periodically he drew self-consciously upon the Jesuit *Constitutions* and the *Spiritual Exercises* to speak about the role of theology in Christian life and within the church. For Dulles, theology was a form of systematic reflection within the context of prayer, a worshiping community, and an ecclesial tradition. During his theological career, Dulles applied elements of the *Exercises* to the theological enterprise. In the postconciliar period in particular, he swung back and forth between two not easily or practically reconcilable poles of spiritual development that were inherent in the *Exercises*.

From his early days as a novice, he was grounded in the practice of spiritual discernment, a regular daily self-examination of one's life and vocation in the light of the Gospels and in light of the needs of the times. Periodically Dulles applied Ignatius's "Rules for the Discernment of Spirits" to the theological enterprise and tried to determine whether suggested reforms for the Christian life and for the church would in fact lead to greater joy and fuller attachment to Christ. In his early career, he seems to have emphasized this dimension of his role as a theologian. That is, he focused upon the necessity of personal and communal discernment and, like Ignatius, worked not deductively from abstract principles but "inductively from the complex data of experience."[32] Such an approach to discernment might lead to a more penetrating discovery of the meaning of the Christian tradition and would also at times lead to a reinterpretation and reformulation of church doctrine for the times.

A second pole in the *Exercises* emphasized the "Rules for Thinking with the Church" (*sentire cum ecclesia*). Discernment could not be authentic or genuine if it did not correspond to the teachings of what Ignatius of Loyola called the "hierarchical church." The theologian's work was to be done in obedience to the church and in communion with the hierarchy. This did not mean abject conformity or passive obedience to some external rule but the active obedience of faith that flowed from an internal communion with Christ and the church and the willingness to give the presumption of truth to ecclesiastical teachings and declarations that were uncomfortable or that articulated the "hard sayings" of the gospel.

These two poles were always in some kind of dialectical tension in Dulles' approach to theology. At one time, though, as in his early career, he emphasized discernment because of the need to foster interiority and reform in the postconciliar Catholic Church; at other times, particularly in and after the 1980s, he focused on thinking with the church because he perceived a growing theological and cultural resistance to the acceptance of church teachings— a tendency he considered detrimental to Catholic theology and to the faith. Nevertheless, at no time was either pole completely absent from his approach to theology.[33]

In his courses on fundamental theology at Woodstock, at Catholic University, as well as at Fordham, Dulles had been developing his understanding of the nature and methods and mission of theology in the church. Since the mid-1970s, too, he published numerous essays on theology's role. His *Craft of Theology* (1992) defined the tasks of theology. Throughout these years, Dulles spoke of theology's responsibility to make intelligible the sound doctrine found in scripture, tradition, dogma, and the religious experience of the faith—theology perceived as a faith-derived and methodical reflection upon these sources. His attempts to define the theologian's role must be understood in the context of what was happening in the Catholic theological community during the mid-1970s and much of the 1980s and 1990s.

On several occasions, Rome condemned certain theological positions or disciplined or warned theologians about heterodox views. In 1973, the Congregation for the Doctrine of the Faith's (CDF) *Mysterium ecclesiae* sought to correct "certain errors" on the Catholic doctrine of the church—in particular, certain understandings of the formulation of dogmas and the question of infallibility (directed against Hans Küng). In 1979, Rome condemned theological positions in the works of specific theologians: in the spring Jacques Pohier was silenced for his *When I Speak of God*; in July the Catholic Theological Society of America's (CTSA) commissioned study *Human Sexuality* was condemned; in early December Edward Schillebeeckx was interrogated in Rome for his allegedly heterodox statements in recent books; in mid-December Hans Küng was declared to have "departed from the integral truth of Catholic faith and therefore can no longer be considered a Catholic theologian nor function as such in a teaching role"; and in late December some writings of the Brazilian theologian Leonardo Boff were condemned. In 1981, Cardinal Joseph Ratzinger, a German theologian, became prefect of the CDF, and the censoring of some theological movements and specific theologians continued. In 1984, for example, the CDF published its "Instruction on Certain Aspects of the 'Theology of Liberation,'" warning about misguided directions among some liberation theologies. At Catholic

University, Charles Curran's moral theology had been called into question since the mid-1960s, and in 1986 the CDF declared that he could no longer be considered a Catholic theologian and was therefore prohibited from teaching in Catholic University's theology department.

These and other Vatican actions created a tense situation in the American Catholic theological community, and some in that community interpreted the situation as a return to the pre–Vatican II Roman defensive and repressive tactics and a fundamental reversal of the dialogical and ecumenical and freedom-supporting directions of the Second Vatican Council. This new situation had created a "chill factor" in the theological community.[34] Others, while recognizing the legitimacy of some dissent in the church, saw Roman interventions as necessary corrections of theologians whose positions were seen as inconsistent with the Catholic tradition and injurious to the faith of the church.[35]

It was within this context of contention and polarization that Dulles wrote on the theologian's role, speaking out simultaneously for freedom of inquiry in theology and for the fundamental reliance on authority in the theological enterprise. In 1973, as we have seen, Dulles gave a rather negative assessment of the CDF's regressive measures in *Mysterium ecclesiae*. Nonetheless, as the years went by, he became more and more concerned that the theological community was unable or unwilling to correct the aberrations of its own members. In his own writings after 1975, he tried to balance the need for free inquiry and diversity in theology and the necessity of authority for the unity of faith. His position was not a compromise or middle ground between the extremes of liberty and authority but an attempt to bring about a synthesis that he considered integral to the theological enterprise itself.

For Dulles, theology was a creative and critical task, and creativity and criticism demanded freedom of inquiry. But creativity, odd as it may seem, also demanded authority, as almost every creative scientist, according to Polanyi, knew. To accept authority in theology was not antithetical to the critical enterprise; one did not have to give up critical thinking if one accepted the authority of the tradition out of which one worked. Critical thinking, in Dulles' view, did not operate on the presupposition of doubt, nor was it necessarily neutral with respect to the sources it examined. As a theologian, Dulles accepted the benefits of the critical age since the time of Descartes, without at the same time accepting the naive view that critical thinking had to be without presuppositions or commitments. In this respect, Dulles' approach to theology fit into a postcritical age that transcended the limits and incorporated the benefits of critical thinking.

In another respect, however, Dulles perceived that the traditional Christian notion of theology as faith seeking understanding was consistent with the postcritical thinking that prevailed in many other disciplines in the modern university. Within the Catholic Church, Dulles called for a reciprocal relationship between the ecclesiastical magisterium and eminent theologians, a relationship he perceived to be active in the church's history. "Just as the official teaching of the Church constitutes an authority for theologians, so the doctrine of eminent theologians constitutes an authority of a sort for those who strive to formulate the official positions of the Church itself."[36] Such a view of theology's dialogical role in the church would not remove all the tensions that existed, but it could lessen them and promote a deeper unity at the level of a lived faith.

Dulles made multiple attempts to define theology, but he gave one of his most concise definitions in a lecture at Boston College in 1981:

> The theologian, using the themes and symbols provided by Scripture and tradition, attempts an imaginative construing that gives meaning and direction to the Christian life. Such a construal cannot be exhaustive or adequate to the potentialities of the Christian sources, but it can be faithful, coherent, and relatively adequate to the experience of a certain number of Christians. Scripture and tradition, as theological sources, may be compared to a musical score. They challenge the creative talents of the interpreter and at the same time direct them.[37]

Dulles acknowledged that there were at least three major contemporary positions on the role of authority in theology. As indicated previously, he accepted an authoritative basis of theology—a view that was consistent with that of leading Catholic theologians like Bernard Lonergan, Karl Rahner, Edward Schillebeeckx, and other Catholic, Protestant, and Orthodox theologians. A second view, which Dulles designated "liberal," appealed to an empirical model of science and held that "theology could not defend its claim to be a science if it relied upon authority." Many in this school did not deny the role of faith and authority within the ecclesial community but insisted that theology had no right to appeal to authoritative norms; as a science it could use "only publicly verifiable criteria." A third view that Dulles tagged "critical theology," influenced significantly by ideology criticism, sought to eliminate authority completely from Christian theology.[38] Dulles' own position was eminently clear:

> I do not see how one can be a Christian without accepting authority in matters of religion, nor do I see how a Christian theologian could fulfill his task without reliance on the authorities [scripture, tradition, religious experience, the magisterium] to which he subscribes....I cannot see how a Christian theologian as a theologian can responsibly deprive himself of the resources upon which, as a believer, he relies.[39]

Nonetheless conflicts and polarization did exist in the church, and the need existed for a resolution of differences between the magisterium and theologians who had a shared responsibility for teaching sound doctrine, although their responsibilities differed according to their roles within the church. What was needed to resolve differences was an orderly discernment process, analogous to that used at the council of Jerusalem (Acts 15). That council was a biblical paradigm for corporate theological reflection. Although Dulles periodically acknowledged the legitimacy of some theological dissent from noninfallible ecclesiastical declarations, he was very leery of the good such protests could accomplish.[40]

Dulles' *Craft of Theology*, a collection of articles he had written since the early 1980s and had revised in 1992 to make a coherent and integrated argument, must be interpreted in the context of his Jesuit formation and his understanding of the times. An expanded edition came out in 1995, with two new chapters added. The text addressed theology's foundation in the church's faith and worship, the use of critical tools in the appropriation of scripture and tradition, the role of the magisterium and of dissent, the relationship of theology to philosophy and the physical sciences, theology's role in universities and the function of academic freedom, and the ecumenical nature or character of all theology. The book was the work of a master theologian in synthesizing the various approaches to theology in the modern period and in proposing a methodological approach that could transcend the confusion of the times.

By the 1990s, in Dulles' estimation, theologians themselves lacked "a common language, common goals, and common norms," and even more disturbing was the fact that civil argumentation had ceased to function. Some theologians tended, in Dulles' assessment, to glorify novelty, originality, and accommodation and took for granted "that the heterodoxy of today would become the orthodoxy of tomorrow."[41] Revisionist theologians of the period, encouraged by what they considered the council's reversal of many previous Vatican or papal declarations (for example, on the identity of the Catholic Church with the mystical body of Christ, the ends of marriage, religious liberty, ecumenism, and Christianity's relationship with world religions) were emboldened during the period to suggest even more radical reversals or reinterpretations than had been fostered by the council. The first postconciliar decade, therefore, produced radical pluralism, questioning, dissent, and confusion in the church and impotence in the ecclesial magisterium to guide the forces unleashed by the times.

The first three chapters of *Craft of Theology* dealt in a general way with theological method, and the remaining ones focused on specific areas of theology. Dulles set his own understanding of theological method within the history of theology's relationship to criticism, arguing that theology had moved from the precritical, to the critical, to the postcritical. In the precritical stage of development, prior to the rise of the new sciences in the seventeenth century, although theology used various philosophical insights to reflect critically on faith, it rarely applied criticism to the canonical sources of theology. With the rise of the new sciences and the application of observation and mathematics and critical history, theology entered into a new stage that Dulles called the "critical era." During this period, which undermined to some extent the authority of Aristotle, theology gradually applied the tools of doubt and criticism to the canonical sources. Within this period, moreover, a paracritical approach, usually associated with Protestant dialectical theology, developed; it accepted the tools of criticism but made faith itself impervious to criticism. Likewise evolved a countercritical stance, generally associated with the evidentiary tradition and Catholic neo-scholasticism, which sought to vindicate Christianity by the use of critical sources and exact syllogistic logic. In the latter half of the twentieth century, a postcritical era emerged that accepted the gains achieved by the critical enterprise but scrutinized and critiqued the presuppositions and methods of the critical enterprise. Dulles identified the postcritical movement with the works of Michael Polanyi, Hans-Georg Gadamer, Paul Ricoeur, Peter Berger, Robert Bellah, Hans Urs von Balthasar, and George Lindbeck, to name a few. Dulles placed his own developing theology within the postcritical era and relied most heavily on Michael Polanyi in his understanding of what constituted a postcritical approach. What Polanyi had done for science, Dulles wanted to do for theology.

A postcritical theology was open to the contributions of the modern turn to criticism, but Dulles noted at least five general presuppositional and methodological flaws in the critical enterprise that he periodically applied to biblical and historical scholarship. The critical approach (1) had a bias toward doubt, (2) failed to recognize that doubt itself had a fiduciary basis, (3) was incapable of applying criticism universally and consistently, and neglected the (4) social and (5) tacit dimensions of knowledge. There were indeed reasons of the heart, presuppositions, and instincts of an educated conscience that were impervious to critical analysis and beyond the human capacity to express fully. Postcritical theology, in Dulles' view, began with the presupposition of faith (conceived of in Polanyian terms as tacit knowledge); a hermeneutics of trust not suspicion or doubt; and ended with a constructive, not a destructive, purpose. Catholic theology, in particular, was an ecclesial discipline that flowed from dwelling in the church's life of faith and was a systematic methodological effort to articulate the truth

411

implied in that faith. Theology's method, therefore, could not be spelled out in terms of mathematics or syllogistic logic; it depended upon "a kind of connoisseurship derived from personal appropriation of the living faith of the Church."[42] No detached scientific approach could ever perceive the meaning of the Christian symbols; only by living within the community of those signs could one see their meaning. The problem for the theologian who dwelt within the Christian symbols was to make them intelligible, as far as possible, to those within the community of faith and to those outside it.

This theological enterprise was not an individual theologian's task but that of a community of reflectors, all of whom were accountable to the sense of the faithful, the creeds, the tradition, the liturgy, the scripture, and the magisterium. This accountability, however, was not a slavish conformity to previously articulated formulations of the faith nor to past theological syntheses, because all articulations of the faith were limited in their capacity to express adequately the mystery of God. Theology, therefore, was not a static science but one that was continually stimulated by a search to unveil the mystery and by an investigation into new problems that arose in the culture and demanded solutions that were not available in previous theological work. Postcritical theology also aimed to demonstrate to those outside the community of faith the universal meaning contained in the Christian symbols, to invite the uncommitted to enter into the universe of faith, and to foster an intellectual atmosphere for conversion.

The basic thesis of *The Craft of Theology* was contained in the subtitle, *From Symbol to System*. All genuine theology moved from divine revelation, symbolically communicated and received in faith, to articulated systems of thought that reflected in limited ways (through various root metaphors) the mystery of the revealed God. The systematic theologians themselves, initiated into and nourished by the Christian symbols, returned through prayer and worship to the sources of faith and piety to acknowledge the fact that their own systems, with their concepts and language, were inferior to the tacit knowledge they had received from the symbols themselves. Dulles' own models approach to theology was an attempt to underline this basic fact about theology by insisting that "theologians should not so confine themselves to a single school or system that they overlook elements of truth or value that are more evident from a perspective other than their own."[43] Different theological systems had different root metaphors, and it was a weakness in systematic theologians to treat their own systems as "self-enclosed."

After focusing on theological method, Dulles' *Craft of Theology* applied his understanding of symbolic communication to specific areas of theology. In *Craft* and in various essays, he addressed the uses of scripture in theology. Since the mid-1950s, Dulles had used Protestant and Catholic critical biblical scholarship in his own reassessment of revelation and faith. In fact, much of his theology was informed by his reading of biblical scholars, and biblical passages were frequently employed in his theological arguments. His participation in the Lutheran/Catholic Dialogue brought him into intimate contact with Catholic biblical scholars Raymond Brown and Joseph Fitzmyer and the Lutheran scholar John Reumann, many of whose works he had read. In the 1960s and early 1970s, Dulles had periodically invoked such biblical scholarship without much critical assessment, accepting in particular the historical-critical method as an advance over what he would call the "precritical" method of an earlier era. Nonetheless, under the influence of Polanyi, Dulles was conscious, even in his early years, of the limits of the critical methodologies. After the mid-1970s, he became increasingly more critical of historical criticism as it was applied to scripture, emphasizing the connatural relationship between faith and revelation and the need to consider the whole tradition in the interpretation of the Bible. At times this systematic preoccupation and his critical assessment of the exclusive historical emphasis created tensions between himself and some of the biblical scholars on the Lutheran/Catholic Dialogue, as we have already seen.

The historical-critical method in biblical interpretation had come under considerable censure in the 1980s. In 1983, for example, Cardinal Joseph Ratzinger had warned in a speech to catechists in France that he saw a growing and seemingly incompatible or irreconcilable conflict between dogmatic and historical-critical approaches to the Bible. Some had assigned the dogmatic approach to a prescientific or precritical era of interpretation that was no longer useful to the church.[44] Ratzinger was afraid, as he indicated in 1984, that the link between the Bible and the church was being broken by too heavy a reliance on the critical methods in place of the church's faith and tradition.[45]

In the United States, dramatically conflicting views of biblical criticisms arose in some sectors of the Catholic community. On one end of the Catholic spectrum were those who adamantly opposed biblical criticism because of its consequences for moral and religious life. George Kelly, a sociologist and Catholic social critic, leveled a series of criticisms against the *New Biblical Theorists*,[46] charging that their historical-critical approach to the Bible justified the current moral and dogmatic conflicts in the church and loosened the ties that bound Catholics to their tradition—and all this under the guise of a new scholarship. From the other end of the Catholic spectrum came those who heartily approved the new critical methods precisely because such methods destroyed what they considered outmoded traditional Catholic beliefs and practices. The Chicago Loyola University philosopher Thomas Sheehan rejected traditional Catholic readings of the New Testament on the basis of New Testament historical-critical scholarship. In his view the new scholarship had not only dismantled much of traditional Roman Catholic theology but had whittled away the "belief in the divinity of Jesus."[47]

It was within this historical context of radically opposing views of biblical scholarship that Neuhaus convoked his 1988 ecumenical conference on biblical interpretation and invited Dulles, who was still teaching at Catholic University, to attend. The symposium featured Cardinal Joseph Ratzinger,[48] whose opening address underlined the need to reassess the hermeneutical methods of biblical scholarship, maintaining that it was an "absurd abstraction" to assert the "pure objectivity" of critical scholarship. Although highly critical of some philosophical presuppositions of the critical methods, he in fact called for more concerted efforts to find a synthesis between historical and theological methods of interpreting the Bible. The exegete, he asserted, did not stand in some neutral area, above or outside of history and the church.[49] Catholic biblical scholar Raymond Brown did not respond directly to Ratzinger's criticism but focused instead on the major contributions that historical biblical scholarship had made to the church.

414

With Richard John Neuhaus and Cardinal Joseph Ratzinger, January 28, 1988

Brown did not perceive any inherent or irreconcilable conflict between faith and historical criticism.[50] Dulles—with twenty other invited theologians and biblical scholars from Protestant, Catholic, and Orthodox traditions—participated in the discussions at the conference, but the content of his participation was not recorded.

Dulles' views on biblical interpretation, however, were at the time of the conference already fairly clearly known, and they would be reinforced in subsequent years. Like Brown, he valued the contributions of historical scholarship of the Bible and saw the benefits as well as the challenges that such scholarship presented for a more adequate systematic understanding of revelation and faith and tradition. Like Ratzinger, he asserted that neutrality or pure objectivity in approaching the Bible was neither possible nor desirable. The Bible was inherently the book of the church, written out of the church's experience and interpreted within the tradition of prayer and worship. The real problem for the systematician and the biblical scholar was how to relate faith and dogma and historical scholarship. This was no easy task, but it was the task of the church since at least the age of the Enlightenment and the rise of biblical criticism.

In the years after the Ratzinger Conference, Dulles made periodic attempts to describe the relationship between critical history and scripture, an issue that he had discussed off and on since the mid-1950s. Within the Catholic Church, it had been a hot issue since the modernist-antimodernist wars of the late nineteenth and early twentieth centuries. In *Craft of Theology*, Dulles described the strengths and limits of ten different approaches to and uses of the Bible in systematic theology. The differences, which could live in coexistence with one another, were healthy and desirable in Dulles' estimation because they underlined plural perspectives that were compatible with the mystery of revelation. Among the different approaches to the Bible, he favored the historical-critical method "under the continuous guidance of tradition and magisterial teaching." An exclusive use of that method, however, would overlook the tacit meanings conveyed in the biblical stories, symbols, and metaphors. In the end, he believed that systematic theologians could do justice to the Catholic tradition by using a combination of scientific and spiritual exegesis of the scripture.[51]

In a 1992 article, republished in the 1995 expanded edition of *The Craft of Theology*, Dulles described what he considered to be four different understandings of the relationship of critical history to faith, particularly with reference to how some biblical scholars understood the reality of Christ. First was an approach that underlined the antithesis of history to orthodox faith. John Dominic Crossan's *The Historical Jesus* (1991) Dulles thought resembled this approach, a position Dulles considered unacceptable to Christian believers. A second approach separated history from dogma or faith. Such an approach made faith impervious to critical historical scholarship. In this separationist approach, history and dogma neither confirmed nor contradicted one another. Dulles asserted that John Meier's *A Marginal Jew* (1991) was not "far removed" from such a position. A third approach used history as a ground or confirmation of faith, as some Catholic neo-scholastic apologists did in the recent past and as Wolfhart Pannenberg (who had a more comprehensive view of history than the neo-scholastics) did in the present.[52]

A fourth approach, one that Dulles found the most satisfactory, asserted that Christian faith did not normally arise from or rest upon a critical examination of New Testament evidence. Faith came from God's revealing word as conveyed by the testimony of the church. But since the word of God tells us something about past events, one can say that faith itself reflects something of historical fact, a history that can transcend the tools of the historian's workshop. "Faith is an advantage because it alerts us to the particular strand of history in which God has acted decisively for our salvation." Faith cannot be insulated from history. The believer, nonetheless, can use scholarly inquiry and the critical methods of history to great advantage "to provide additional data and thereby give a better understanding" of the Christian faith. In the area of historical inquiry into the Christian faith, however, there are and will be differences of scholarly opinion about the details of historical fact even by those who share the same faith. In the end, though, the faith itself does not rest on such historical scholarship, however valuable it might be for providing additional data, for confirming faith, critically examining the church's articulation of its own faith, and contributing to the development of Christian doctrine. Like Ratzinger, Dulles concluded that faith and intelligence, dogma and history "can and must be integrated."[53] He could not accept George Kelly's uncomplicated attacks on critical biblical scholarship or Jonathan Sheehan's naive acceptance of it, but he could and did accept a faith-directed employment of tested critical methods of biblical scholarship. Those methods were historical developments for the good of the church, despite the abuse that some made of them.

Dulles returned to the issue of biblical interpretation in 1994 when he was invited to Bocum, Germany, to give a lecture in honor of the theologian Hermann Josef Pottmeyer, a fellow consultant with Dulles and others on the Vatican's International Theological Commission. On that occasion he chose to speak on the Pontifical Biblical Commission's (PBC) recently published "The Interpretation of the Bible in the Church" (November 18, 1993).[54] He was in substantial agreement with the document, pointed out some questions (particularly on the theological uses of scripture) that had been neglected, and indicated how he himself perceived the relationship between exegesis and systematic theology. The Bible, as *Dei verbum* (DV 24) indicated, was the "soul of sacred theology," and the theologian must turn to it as "a privileged source." The theologian, therefore, had to be a competent exegete or at least rely on others who were competent. The theologian's task, however, was "not just to interpret Scripture, but rather to understand the Christian faith, reflecting fully on [as the PBC acknowledged] 'all its aspects and especially that of its crucial relationship to human existence.'" Dulles, therefore, saw a difference at least in emphasis between the exegete and the theologian. "On balance, exegesis is more historical and descriptive; systematic theology is more contemporary and speculative." Exegetes served theology at times by their criticisms of weaknesses in theological systems of thought, reminding theologians of things in revelation they have neglected or forgotten. But theologians could also critique a kind of biblicism that sought "to answer modern questions in biblical categories alone."[55]

Dulles had consistently been concerned with the limits of the *sola scriptura* doctrine as interpreted by some Protestant theologians, and even though he himself emphasized the primacy of scripture for theology, he stressed the interconnectedness of revelation, scripture, tradition, and the church. "Revelation gives rise to tradition and Scripture, but Scripture and tradition, in turn, transmit revelation and make it resound in the minds and hearts of believers today."[56] It was this approach to scripture that was one of the dividing lines between Catholics and Evangelical Protestants who were becoming more and more engaged in ecumenical dialogue in the United States.

Catholic theologians used divine tradition in their theology, and Dulles devoted a chapter to it in his *Craft of Theology*. After outlining the various Catholic approaches to and understandings of divine tradition since the Council of Trent, Dulles noted that the 1990s represented a new challenge for the church and for theologians. Divine tradition produced a variety of human traditions that were intended to mediate Christian life and thought to particular peoples in different times and circumstances. At the Second Vatican Council and in the immediate postconciliar period, some theologians criticized and tried to eliminate the accumulated, outmoded, and oppressive medieval and Baroque traditions because they no longer served the purpose they were intended to serve. In the 1990s, the problem in the church was no longer oppressive outmoded traditions but a lack of effective traditions to communicate effectively the word of God. Dulles, therefore, called for a reexamination of the role that human traditions played in initiating and socializing individuals into a community of loyalty and commitment to Christian life and practice.[57] He also outlined in ten theses what he considered the consensus on the meaning of tradition among Catholic theologians in the 1990s.[58]

For Dulles, fidelity to the divine tradition required creativity and development. The theologian, living within the tradition, had to appropriate it creatively for the times in which he or she lived. That meant not a slavish conformity to the forms in which the tradition expressed itself in the past but a fidelity to the reality behind the forms and a creative insight into the reality that could be expressed in new forms that were more appropriate for the times. This did not mean that all the past forms or formulations of the tradition were subject to revision or reformulation. Although human formulations were all limited in their capacity to articulate the mystery of the revealing God, they were not all subject to change because their language did express something of the mystery and were thus to be preserved. But the theological concepts and language and formulations of the past were not immutable; they could be developed and creatively reconstructed for the sake of communicating in better ways the reality to which the older theological systems pointed.[59] Although Dulles fostered creativity in theology, he was well aware, particularly in his later years, that emphasis on theological creativity could be overdone. Some theologians overemphasized the creative aspect of theology and criticized those who stressed faithfulness to tradition: "A theologian who reaffirms the tradition and fails to challenge the received doctrine is considered timid and retrograde."[60]

From the standpoint of method, Catholic theology had to consider not only scripture and tradition but also the magisterial teachings of the church. Catholic theology was an ecclesial discipline, and within the Catholic Church magisterial teachings were an integral and inherent part of the theologians' critical reflections. "Theologians depend on the magisterium because the creeds and dogmas of the church are constitutive for their own enterprise. Theology is a reflection on the faith of the Church as set forth in the canonical Scriptures and in the official statements of the Church's belief." There were many reasons, of course, for the role of a pastoral magisterium in the church, not the least of which was "the historic experience of the Church," which in Dulles' estimation, showed "that theologians are often unable to resolve their own differences, still less to establish doctrine for the Church."[61] Theologians had a responsibility to be cognizant of the sense of the faith, but gaining a sense of the faith was not a purely individual attainment. Dulles spoke repeatedly of theology as sapiential and the need for theologians to be in tune with the wisdom of the church:

> If theologians wish to avoid an unhealthy individualism and be attuned to the mind of the Church, it is important for them to participate in the Church's prayer and worship. An intense life of prayer, nourished by the liturgy, gives intelligibility to the doctrines of the Church and in so doing assists theological speculation....A well-ordered love gives rise to the instinctive recognition of the harmony or discord between theological theories and the deposit of faith. Theology matures under the sunlight of the Holy Spirit, who gives joy and ease in assenting to the truth of Revelation.[62]

Theologians had indeed contributed to the unity of the church as they articulated the sense of the faith, but experience demonstrated the need for the living voice of a pastoral magisterium to maintain that unity. For Dulles there existed a dialectical union and tension between theologians and the magisterium. The union was constitutive of the theological enterprise; the tension was historical and could be productive of development or heterodoxy.

Theologians played an historical role in the formulation, interpretation, and reformulations of church teachings, and, therefore, it was necessary to consider not only the place of magisterial teachings in the theological enterprise but also the role of theologians and theological dissent. Addressing dissent was particularly necessary in light not only of the role that dissent played in the history of the church but also the role of theological dissent since the end of the council.

Some theologians, Dulles included, appealed to the role that legitimate dissent had played in the history of the church, particularly the role that it had played in the period immediately prior to Vatican II, when a few of the most creative theologians (Congar, de Lubac, Teilhard de Chardin, John Courtney Murray, among others) were either silenced by the Vatican or were under a cloud of suspicion because their theological positions did not correspond to the reigning Roman neo-scholastic theology. Many of those under suspicion prior to the council were vindicated by the conciliar deliberations, which a few postconciliar theologians interpreted as justification for their dissent.

The council did not in fact explicitly take up the issue of theological dissent or justify it, but it practiced loyal dissent from some previous papal declarations. This kind of loyal theological critique of papal and other Roman documents historically had brought about a certain development of doctrine. Dulles had periodically defined *dissent* in this way and at one point used standard Latin and English dictionaries to define it benignly as "to be of a different sentiment or opinion, not to agree" (Latin *dissentire*) or "to withhold assent" or "to differ in opinion."[63]

That was not the understanding of the term in Rome, as Ladislas Orsy pointed out. English-speaking theologians, in Orsy's opinion, had used that term to mean "a personal opinion different from the official one in matters where debate is permissible." Some in the Vatican, however, had a very different understanding of dissent. In the 1990 "Instruction on the Ecclesial Vocation of the Theologian," the term was used to refer to "groups that have broken their basic communion with the Church."[64] The problem of dissent, though, as Dulles and Orsy acknowledged, was not simply a matter of semantics.

In *Craft of Theology* Dulles addressed the relationship of dissent (as he interpreted it) to the magisterium—this time as a methodological issue in theology—and he continued thereafter to speak out on the legitimacy and limits of theological dissent. In the immediate postconciliar period, dissent emerged gradually and then became fairly widespread over a host of moral and doctrinal issues, with little Vatican guidance on the legitimacy and limits of such dissent in the church. In 1968, in response to *Humanae vitae* and the first major widespread public dissent from official church teaching, the American bishops in *Human Life in Our Day*[65] outlined some grounds for a legitimate dissent from official teachings, and in 1989, after some years of discussions with theologians, prepared a statement on "Doctrinal Responsibilities: Approaches to

Promoting Cooperation and Resolving Misunderstandings between Bishops and Theologians."[66] In 1990, then, the CDF issued "Instruction on the Ecclesial Vocation of the Theologian," which laid out the various levels of authoritative church teachings and outlined the corresponding levels of faithful response to them, with an understanding of dissent, as indicated earlier, that contrasted sharply with notions in the English-speaking world.

By the late 1980s, Dulles believed that a culture of dissent and what Hans Urs von Balthasar had called a "'venomous' and 'irrational' anti-Roman" feeling[67] had emerged to a considerable extent in American Catholicism and in the Catholic theological community. Although Dulles continued to acknowledge a role for differing theological opinions and positions in the church, and indeed for some theological dissent from noninfallible magisterial declarations, he worked against (in Jesuit *agere contra* fashion) what he believed to be an unhealthy and pervasive mentality of dissent. Within this context, he repeatedly advised giving the benefit of the doubt to magisterial statements, exercising thereby a hermeneutics of trust rather than of suspicion. This did not mean, however, that one treated every statement from Rome as a *de fide* statement requiring divine and Catholic faith. One had to make theological distinctions about the level of authoritative statements and the level of responses to them, as were outlined, for example, in "Ecclesial Vocation."

As he interpreted that document in the early 1990s and thereafter, there were four categories of magisterial statements and four different levels of assent: (1) dogmatic statements based on revelation, requiring divine and Catholic faith (*credenda*); (2) definitive declarations of nonrevealed truths, requiring firm assent (*tenenda*) or ecclesiastical faith; (3) nondefinitive but obligatory teaching of doctrine, requiring religious submission of intellect and will; and (4) contingent prudential applications of doctrine for particular historical situations, requiring external conformity or obedience.[68] Dissent did "not normally arise" with respect to the first two categories, even though individuals may have personal doubts about the language or appropriateness of those definitions of the faith. Legitimate dissent, however, could sometimes arise with respect to statements in the third and fourth categories, because not all of those statements were "free from all deficiencies." Even Vatican II reversed or modified some previous papal teachings and reformulated church doctrine in accord with fuller theological insights that had been developing in the church's immediate preconciliar period. Dulles interpreted "Ecclesial Vocation," though, as a justified warning against certain kinds of public opposition to magisterial statements, because some forms of objection were harmful to the church as a community of faith and trust. On occasion he made it known that he believed organizing pressure groups to˙ dissent or protest was "a poor method of arriving at the truth."[69] In his later years, he advised theologians that docility and obedience brought one closer to Christ and that dissent, though periodically justifiable, should be "rare, reluctant and respectful."[70]

Dulles and a few other theologians[71] argued that "Ecclesial Vocation," although largely negative on the role of dissent, had broken new ground in articulating the relationship between the theologians and the pastoral magisterium. The document was one of the first Vatican acknowledgments that theologians could have legitimate difficulties with magisterial statements. Its category of prudential, historically conditioned ecclesiastical applications of doctrines (as in nineteenth-century oppositions to religious liberty), for example, was a novel Vatican recognition of the time-conditioned nature of some magisterial declarations.[72] Dulles believed, however, that the CDF document had a "rather narrow" concept of dissent, limiting it almost exclusively to "public opposition to the magisterium of the Church."[73]

Dulles ended his plea for a faithful and respectful consideration of magisterial statements in theology with a five-point program of prudential advice for the magisterium to consider in exercising its legitimate authority within the church. The magisterium could generate better cooperation with theologians if it: (1) avoided issuing too many statements (magisterial statements had been rare in the church's previous history); (2) protected the legitimate freedom of theologians of different schools of thought; (3) avoided favoring any one theological school of thought and consulted widely prior to issuing statements; (4) anticipated objections to its statements and tried to avoid them; and (5) was sensitive to the variety of situations and cultures in different parts of the world in order to discover palatable formulations of magisterial statements.[74]

Dulles balanced his support for magisterial statements with advice that he believed the magisterium needed to consider to bring about better cooperation between the magisterium and the theological community. History had demonstrated that magisterial statements, particularly in the third and fourth categories, were not always well formulated or sensitive to the variety of cultural situations in which they would be interpreted, and the magisterium had not always been receptive to the variety of legitimate theological perspectives and schools of thought. Dissident theologians were not the only ones responsible for conflict in the church. Nonetheless, Dulles believed that the hierarchy could not be "infinitely permissive"; they had to set limits to what could be held and taught in the church for the sake of unity, and that was a painful duty that at times flew in the face of popular opinion.[75]

By the 1990s, theological dissent had almost become a tradition itself and had become institutionalized in the College Theology Society (CTS: approximately 895 members in 2004) and the Catholic Theological Society of America (approximately 1,511 members in 1997)[76]—both theological bodies issuing periodic statements of dissent from or doubt about certain Vatican declarations.[77] Since the mid-1970s Dulles had opposed using the CTSA to issue dissenting theological opinions, and since the publication of *Humanae vitae* in 1968 he had refused to sign theological protest statements. He was clearly disappointed with the active politicization of theology and the groupthink consensus statements that resulted from such tactics. Theologians in both the CTS and CTSA, as well as other professional societies within the church, had copied, in Dulles' view, the activist tendencies in other academic professional societies, and he became highly critical of this tendency in the theological societies. Professional groupthink had a tendency to make theologians less than critical of one another's work. Theological societies tended to become identified with the victims of the so-called Vatican authoritarians.

It is difficult to determine the accuracy of Dulles' charge that a widespread culture of dissent existed among theologians in the 1980s and 1990s. The CTS and CTSA statements questioning or protesting Vatican declarations were generally signed by a small proportion of the memberships, because those declarations were usually voted on at annual business meetings when only about 20 percent of the societies were present. In 1997, for example, the CTSA approved a statement that seriously questioned the "nature of the authority" and the theological grounds of *Ordinatio sacerdotalis* (1994), which prohibited the ordination of women. The CTSA statement was submitted to the 248 members present at the business meeting; 216 voted in favor of the statement (88 percent), 22 voted against, and 10 abstained.[78] The problem with such a statement is that it is difficult to know what it represents in terms of theological opinion in the American Catholic Church. The statement reflects the thinking of less than 20 percent of the 1,500 members, to say nothing of the large number of theologians who do not belong to this society. If in 1997 the total number of Catholic theologians in the United States was roughly 2,000 (a conservative estimate), then the representative nature of the CTSA statement becomes even more problematic.

It is true, of course, that opinion polls among American Catholics in general have demonstrated an increasing support for the ordination of women since the mid-1960s, but opinion polls do not reflect theological research or theological reflection. It may well be that a majority of theologians have seriously examined the issue within the Catholic tradition and have come to conclusions that differ from the Roman document, but at this point we have no way of knowing what was in fact the theological opinion on this particular issue. And this may also be the case for other divisive theological issues in the church. The bottom line here is that, given the present state of information, we just do not know how widespread is the theological protest and the theologians' willingness to sign protest statements. Whether or not the CTSA represented a majority of theologians in the United States was not a concern for Dulles, who considered the protests themselves to lack the ecclesial character he expected in Catholic theology.

In the mid-1960s and early 1970s, Dulles focused on the culturally and socially conditioned nature of church statements and theological systems, and he saw the need to critique and modify some past neo-scholastic formulations of the faith, and that entailed a certain amount of individual theological dissent from officially formulated positions. By the 1990s, he believed the tide had turned so much in the direction of criticism that even the fundamental doctrines of the faith were being called into question and that some theologians had excessively accommodated the biblical message and tradition to a secular mentality at odds with the Christian message. Dissent had a tendency, he wrote, "to metastasize" and in the postconciliar period it came from the right as well as the left.[79] What was needed in the 1990s was a serious critique of the mounting systematic and professional and communal criticism. Dulles' reaction was not just a specific instance of a more general pattern of the young liberal or progressive becoming the old conservative or reactionary. He had always been attached to the church's doctrinal tradition and its hierarchical authority. What he perceived in the late 1990s was a more radical departure, not just from the languages and conceptual patterns of the past, but from the truths of the doctrines themselves. The dissent, in other words, had become substantive and not merely linguistic or conceptual.

In 1999, Dulles took part in what was called the "Common Ground" project. That project, initiated by Cardinal Joseph Bernardin in 1994, was an attempt to bring together in conversation American Catholics of various opinions in order to overcome the rancor and hostility of competing ideological positions within the church.[80] The second Cardinal Bernardin Conference, to which Dulles was invited in 1999, was a continuation of discussions on issues that divided Catholics. Dulles chose to speak on the problems of the reception of *Humanae vitae* and *Ordinatio sacerdotalis*, the two Roman documents that had received the most widespread dissent in the American Catholic Church. He outlined what he considered ten arguments that had been used in rejecting both Roman documents. The positions taken on the substantive questions, he then argued, reflected a mentality that "potentially extends to an indefinite number of cases."[81]

Again, Dulles was concerned about the general mentality of resistance to Roman documents because of a "certain culture of suspicion toward Rome." He knew that the two papal declarations were countercultural, and he asserted that the church's message could not be measured by the criterion of worldly success and acceptance. He assumed "the correctness of the papal teachings on issues such as contraception, abortion, assisted suicide, homosexuality, marriage and divorce, clerical celibacy, and women's ordination," and if one accepted these teachings "it may be doubted whether there is any way of presenting the true doctrine that will win general acceptance." The tendency of secular public opinion was in the opposite direction. Dulles was here making a strong case for the distinctive and prophetic stance of the Christian message. This was a view of the relation of Christ and secular culture that he had taken in the 1940s, when he converted to Catholicism, and one that he would reiterate in the 1990s. This did not mean, however, that there was no room for legitimate dissent within the church. Dissent at times had served the development of doctrine, but not the kind of dissent fostered by defiant opposition or pressure tactics. With respect to the two papal teachings on contraception and ordination, moreover, he saw no need for the church or the bishops to demand a profession of belief. He acknowledged that people of good will and those under the power of cultural forces were not convinced by the papal teachings. Their subjective, invincible ignorance made the teachings most difficult to accept.[82]

Although Dulles never rejected the Common Ground project, as did some more conservative theologians, he was becoming increasingly disconcerted about some notions of dialogue in the church that tended to compromise doctrine. He told a reporter in 1997, prior to his involvement in Common Ground, that he could "enter into dialogue with anybody, no matter what their point of view....I can handle dialogue with an atheist, so I could certainly have dialogue with Catholics who dissent." What he could not accept was a notion of dialogue that had departed from the classical Socratic notion of dialogue as a search for the truth. He believed that some within and outside of the church conceived of dialogue as a relativist conversation that put all propositions on the same plane—where "all opinions and claims are treated as equal, neither true nor false."[83]

Locations of Theology

In the 1990s, Dulles focused not only upon the cultural influences on Catholics in general and the theological community in particular but also upon the changing location of theology in

American Catholicism. The center of theological activity in the postconciliar period had shifted from the seminaries (where most preconciliar theology took place) to the universities. By the 1990s, the greatest number of Catholic theologians resided in universities and colleges; lay theologians tended to outnumber clerical, and the most creative theology emanated from university quarters. Whether in universities or seminaries, Catholic theology shared some of the same methodological concerns; nonetheless the aims of theology in the universities and in the seminaries differed. Dulles had been educated in a seminary environment, had taught in one for more than a decade, and had taught in a major university department of theology. Periodically he reflected on what the shift in theological location meant for theology in the United States. The shift itself had advantages as well as some disadvantages, not least of which was an accommodation to prevailing trends in secular education. But the advantages were many.

Dulles' inaugural McGinley lecture at Fordham, "University Theology as a Service to the Church" (December 6, 1988), argued the thesis of the title. He pointed out in that lecture and particularly in an interview he later gave that the doctrine of the church needed to be explained in a way that was "abreast of current knowledge and in relationship to other disciplines and specializations."[84] Repeatedly during these years he spoke of the special character of university theology as a dialogical enterprise that needed freedom as well as faithfulness to meet new issues that were being raised in the various disciplines. In dialogue with other university disciplines, theologians were in a unique position to update the formulations of theology and the theological explanation of doctrine. Theologians in the universities needed to listen and learn from the other disciplines, and they needed to respond to new issues out of the context of their Catholic faith tradition. University theology was or should be a research discipline in close contact with history, literary criticism, sociology, psychology, philosophy, and the physical sciences, where new approaches and discoveries were continually raising questions to which theology had to attend.

This inaugural lecture was intended in part to meet the recurring postconciliar criticisms of theology in the Catholic universities. Dulles indicated in his opening paragraph that such criticisms had been part of the church's long history, citing as an instance John Wycliffe's (ca. 1335–1384) denunciation: "Universities, with their programs of study, their colleges, their degrees, and their professorships, are products of vain heathenism; they are as much good to the Church as the devil is." The council of Constance (1414–1417) condemned the accusation.[85]

Teaching theology at the college and university level had its own aims as an intellectual discipline. The aim of theology at this level was intelligibility, and therefore it would be "inappropriate" to demand a profession of faith from students.[86] Education, not faith formation, was the aim. University theology was not catechetical, but academic, making theology intelligible and putting it in dialogue with other disciplines to which students were exposed.

These aims of college or university theology did not mean, however, that Catholic theology was a discipline separated from the church's life and faith. Theology could be scientific, critical, and in dialogue with other disciplines without separating itself from its ecclesial base. As an ecclesial discipline, it drew its sources and principles and methods from its Catholic tradition in interaction with secular disciplines.

Ultimately the Catholic tradition benefited from this university-located theological enterprise as theologians contributed to the church's self-understanding, the communication and clarification of the faith, the development of doctrine, and dialogue with other Christian traditions, world religions, and the modern world. Theologians in Catholic universities had served these functions since the Middle Ages. By the 1990s, American Catholic university theologians had not, in Dulles' opinion, produced the kind of creative scholarship associated with the great European universities, because American scholarship was still in the early stages of development and lacked the kind of funding that would free scholars for research and creativity.[87]

Dulles was well aware of the promise that theology held out for the universities as well as for the church, but he also pointed out periodically some problems. The greatest temptation of university theology was a tendency to separate itself from the church's life of faith and to use the methodologies of the secular disciplines as the starting point of theological reflection, and if not as a starting point at least as a criterion of critical judgment parallel to the presupposition of faith. A postconciliar tendency to accommodate or put theology in dialogue with the secular disciplines produced within American Catholic theology a state of disciplinary pandemonium—with no "common language, common goals, and common norms." The pluralism and diversity that was an inherent part of the theological enterprise had by the 1990s metamorphosed into disciplinary chaos.[88] These problems arose in tandem with the successful postconciliar movement of theology into the universities.

By the late 1990s, Dulles' criticisms of Catholic university and college theology were becoming more forceful and specific, and here and there in his talks on the subject he recommended a renewal or revival of a Catholic theology that was explicitly confessional. More and more he believed the Catholic colleges and universities were copying the patterns of secular higher education. Theology was losing curricular ground within the colleges and was becoming a discipline without a distinctive Catholic identity. To Jesuit universities and colleges in particular he lamented that the Ignatian view of theology as the center and core of a Jesuit education was ignored. Following the American secular patterns of higher education, Jesuit schools had marginalized theology, conceived of it in neutral or critical terms as an academic discipline, and given students reasons for questioning faith.[89] "If religion is still taught in the colleges," he complained in one talk, "the courses are often given from an uncommitted 'scientific' point of view that makes no demands on the faith of the students."[90]

Dulles called for certain reforms in the colleges and universities. Jesuit schools in particular could oppose "certain features of the standard American pattern" of higher education and thereby salvage something of the Ignatian vision of education. Although he found the state of theology in Jesuit institutions disturbing, he believed that it was not too late to resurrect the Ignatian vision of theology as a means of "growing in the knowledge and love of God." In light of the Ignatian vision, Dulles advised a revision of the curriculum in the Jesuit schools so that students could be exposed to core courses on Catholic doctrine taught from a faith perspective. Students should also be exposed to Catholic moral theology, social teachings, business ethics, and the principles of ecumenical and interreligious dialogue. His agenda was broad, reflecting the vision of the Second Vatican Council and the needs of students who were to live and work in a very secular world. Like Ignatius, he advised teachers and researchers in theology "to follow the safer and more approved opinions" in theology. Here he was calling his Jesuit brethren back to the original charism of their society.[91] These late 1990s criticisms and recommendations were not nuanced theological arguments, as much of his previous work had been; they were prophetic pronouncements for a situation that needed a new direction.

One could envision a new direction for college and university theology, Dulles believed, if one perceived theology itself as part of the new evangelization that Pope John Paul II had called for since the early 1980s. Teaching theology at those levels had to presuppose, a presupposition not always verified by experience, that the student had "become a believer through evangelization and has learned the principal teachings of the church through catechesis." Theology's task, then, was a "systematic search for a deeper understanding."[92] There were, Dulles was well aware, many obstacles to this approach to theology at the college or university level, not the least of which was the students' own lack of adequate catechesis. In 2006, Dulles outlined seven other challenges to theological education and called upon Catholic colleges and universities to examine what they were doing in their theological programs. "Catholicism 101" was his attempt not to describe what was taking place in theology programs but "to call attention to some difficulties that must be faced in view of the dominant culture in the United States today."[93]

Dulles himself taught seminarians and graduate students during most of his career; he had never taught undergraduate theology. Nonetheless he was familiar with college and university education and was critical of some postconciliar trends in Catholic college programs that he believed had neglected the content of the faith and had moved in a direction of religious studies rather than theology. A postconciliar emphasis on a scientific approach to religion (using the social sciences, history, and various hermeneutical methods) he considered an attempt to imitate or reflect elements of the scientific and analytical approach that dominated higher education in the United States in the twentieth century and was detrimental to the specific method of theology itself, which presupposed faith as its starting point. This postconciliar focus on method and technique was one of the main reasons, he believed, for the "doctrinal decline in Catholic theology" at the college level.[94]

He pointed to six other reasons for the decline: (1) the neglect of natural theology and metaphysics, (2) the suspicion of authority, (3) a pervasive critical spirit, (4) a distaste for propositional truth in matters of religion, (5) the currency of historicism or cultural relativism, and (6) the fear of offending the conscientious convictions of some students who did not share the Catholic faith. All of these challenges, in addition to the failures in basic catechesis, presented problems for communicating the doctrinal content of the faith to students in Catholic colleges and universities. In place of what he perceived to be an undue accommodation to current trends in higher education, he proposed more emphasis in college theology on the basic doctrines of the church "from a Catholic point of view." And, on the college level, if evangelization, catechesis, and philosophy could no longer be presupposed, it would be prudent and educationally appropriate to incorporate them, "to the extent possible, in the teaching of theology itself."[95]

Dulles' "Catholicism 101" arrested the attention of those who taught theology at the college and university levels. In response to that article, the editor of *Horizons*, a journal of the College Theology Society, invited six members of the society to respond to Dulles' observations and provided Dulles the opportunity to react to them.[96] The respondents, all of whom had significant experience teaching undergraduates, were in basic agreement with Dulles' identification of the challenges; some of them added constructive supplements to what he had identified as challenges, while others offered criticisms of his perspectives. Dulles was gratified by the response he received and reiterated a theme that had appeared again and again in his writings since the late 1970s, namely, "Now that everything has been exhaustively questioned, the first priority is to rediscover and perfect the edifice of wisdom that stands firmly on the rock of faith." The discussion of his article left him "hopeful" about the future of college theology, because it appeared to him that a growing number of theologians, particularly the younger ones, recognized the challenges and were "well armed against relativism and eager to recover the best and most enduring insights of the Catholic tradition in philosophy and theology."[97] The editorial symposium on Dulles' article indicated that he had not been relegated to the pastures of theological irrelevance, where some of his most ardent critics wanted to place him.

Dulles did not think the situation of college and university theology was hopeless; leaders in Catholic higher education and in theology could salvage the situation. But things had to change, and leaders had to act. In this respect Dulles believed that Roman documents like *Ex corde ecclesiae* (Pope John Paul II's 1990 constitution on Catholic higher education) presented positive guidance for the reform of American Catholic higher education and offered a much-needed corrective for the times. Educational leaders had to recognize that they were subject to the law and discipline of the church, and theologians needed to acknowledge that the doctrine of the church was not defined by scholarly research but by the hierarchical magisterium.

Dulles was concerned with the specific mission of Catholic higher education and the need to reexamine its role in an American society that he believed was badly in need of the Catholic perspective. Again he played the role of the critic, asserting that American Catholic universities had capitulated too much to some of the dominant trends in higher education. "They have tried too hard to prove," he wrote, "that they are not committed to any truth that cannot be established by objective scientific scholarship." Like John Henry Newman, he believed that utilitarianism, fragmentation, secularism, and rationalism had pervaded the universities and that Catholic institutions of higher learning had absorbed some of these tendencies. He wanted to call Catholic universities back to their mission of integrating faith and scholarship in ways that recognized the dialectical harmony of reason and faith. Within Catholic higher education, theology and philosophy had significant roles to play in providing an integral and sapiential approach to education. Theology could remind the secular disciplines of their proper limits and "help them deal with questions that lie beyond their scope." Catholic universities needed to revitalize this mission.

Revelation and faith were not asides in the educational process but were central to it.

Dulles was not calling for a fideistic approach to education. For him the "light of revelation is no substitute for thought but is the strongest possible ally of reason and science. It can permeate the various disciplines, reenergizing them, and bringing them into an organic unity with one another." That was the enduring task of Catholic higher education, and Dulles repeatedly called for this reemphasis in Catholic higher education.[98] Toward the end of his active career as a theologian, he argued that the primary role of Catholic universities was to evangelize culture.[99]

For most of his life since his conversion, Dulles had a high regard for the role of the magisterium in defining church doctrine, protecting the unity of the church, and preserving identity amid the vicissitudes of history and culture. Like Newman, he believed that an authoritative magisterium was essential for maintaining the authority of revelation itself. This high regard for ecclesiastical authority came more and more to the fore in his later years, and he applied it to Catholic institutions of higher education—not as an external force vis-à-vis the institutions but as an internal dynamic within Catholic identity and Catholic theology. Acknowledging the role of the magisterium in college and university education, however, did not mean that bishops should treat these institutions as if they were seminaries. They were not. The role of theology in these institutions was not the same as it was in seminaries.[100]

Speaking positively on the relationship of the magisterium to the university could, Dulles acknowledged, create panic, particularly among some theologians. That anxiety among some theologians was deepened in the 1990s because of the Vatican's call for an oath of fidelity and episcopal mandates for theologians who taught in Catholic colleges. Dulles acknowledged the reluctance of many American Catholic theologians to receive from the bishops a canonical mission or *mandatum* for teaching theology, but he believed that theologians should be "willing and eager to cooperate with the magisterium as trusted associates." The *mandatum*, he believed, might be one way, but not the only one or even the most important one, for creating a closer association between theologians and the magisterium.[101]

While calling for fidelity to the magisterium and association with it in the theological enterprise, Dulles was also quick to remind bishops and theologians that freedom was absolutely essential to the work of theology and that it was one of the magisterium's responsibilities to preserve and protect that freedom. To carry out their role of research, analysis, criticism, and publication of their opinions, theologians needed academic freedom (*non ancilla nisi libera*) within the context of their faith commitments. As he had in the past, Dulles continued to affirm academic freedom for theologians and the possibility of legitimate dissent from some magisterial formulations. But he fostered a distinctively Catholic understanding of academic freedom for theologians. The secular understanding of academic freedom "requires some modifications" before being applied to Catholic or other church-related schools.[102] In the Catholic understanding, academic freedom existed in conjunction with a faith commitment and within an ecclesial context; it was not entirely autonomous.[103]

Most of Dulles' postconciliar writings on the locus of theology focused on its role in the universities, but in the late 1990s he also addressed much more specifically than in the immediate past the role of theology in the seminary and in Jesuit formation. During the 1996–1997 school year, Dulles was a scholar in residence at the New York archdiocesan seminary in Yonkers. At an academic convocation at the beginning of the school year, he outlined for the professors and students his understanding of the role of theology in the seminary. He had emphasized the critical and dialogical function of theology in the universities, and he had underlined some problems that Catholic theology encountered in accepting too uncritically the academic and scientific standards of the modern American universities. His talk at the seminary, entitled "Prospects," outlined a theological orientation that could be realized in a seminary situation, not one that was actually operative.

In the seminaries, where the primary objective was to form priests for Catholic communities, theology offered "strengths precisely at those points where university theology is most precarious." Under the guidance of the magisterium, seminary theology could develop a more holistic ecclesial approach than was possible in the modern universities and could manifest its essential ecclesial character by interrelating pure doctrine, evangelical spirituality, and liturgical piety. The spiritual formation program that was a part of theological education at the seminary, moreover, could overcome an abstract or detached approach to knowledge that sometimes characterized theology at the university level. Such a holistic approach favored an "intelligence of the heart" that enabled insight into church doctrines and traditions that was not always available in a purely scientific or abstract theology. The emphasis on liturgical piety, furthermore, brought out most clearly the symbiotic relationship between prayer and belief and underlined the doxological character of theology. The seminary's attempts to provide in its curriculum a full coverage of the doctrines of the faith, too, "compares favorably with the rather selective exposure to doctrine in many university graduate programs."[104]

Dulles was not unaware of the problems in seminary education, past and present. And by pointing out past difficulties, he was also hinting that the previous difficulties had not been entirely eradicated. Anti-intellectualism, an all-pervading American disease, had influenced American seminaries in the past, and the clergy were not immune to it. In the past, the "non-historical orthodoxy" that had shaped the neo-scholastic seminary textbooks not only contributed to the anti-intellectualism in theological education but also made it difficult for clergy, trained in such a system, to deal with change in the church and in society. Contemporary seminaries were no longer influenced by such textbooks, but Dulles worried that those seminarians who were currently educated in historical-critical approaches and the social analysis of liberation theology might, as clergy, find themselves in a situation similar to the neo-scholastic clergy once those theological trends went out of fashion. He was warning prospective clergy that theological education did not end with ordination. He also had advice for seminary professors who had failed to do the kind of research and publishing that was required in the normal American universities. Seminary professors needed more time and resources for research so that they could contribute creatively to the theological enterprise in ways that highlighted the ecclesial and pastoral character of all theology more effectively than was currently evident in university theology. Seminary professors had a role to play in the larger theological community, but, Dulles thought, that promise had yet to be realized as fully as it might be.

Dulles also addressed the issue of theological education during Jesuit formation. He had taught at Woodstock College for fourteen years, so he was familiar with the prospects, promise, and problems of theological education in the Jesuit seminary. In 1999, twenty-five years after he had last taught in a Jesuit seminary, he was asked to speak to a conference about theological education in Jesuit formation. He articulated many of the same issues he had focused on when he spoke to Jesuit university educators about the Ignatian approach to theology, but he emphasized more than before the essential need of spiritual formation as the ground for theological reflection. Theological education was not just a scientific or historical or academic exercise; it could not be fully engaged outside of a life of faith and worship. "Through prayer," he told the conference, every Jesuit should seek to attain something akin to Ignatius's "experiential knowledge" of the great mysteries of the faith "in order to have a more personal apprehension of what God has revealed." The academic study of revelation presupposed a preparation of the religious affections.[105]

Dulles then reminded conference participants of Ignatius's approach to theology, emphasizing Ignatius's rules for thinking with the church, his respect for the scholastic theologians (especially Aquinas), his advice to follow the safer theological opinions, his trust in papal guidance and respect for the papacy, his sense and art of discernment (applied to the signs of the times), and his promotion of flexibility and adaptability and accommodation to the needs of the time. "I am pleading," he told the group, "for a theology that is solidly founded on Scripture and tradition, utterly loyal to the magisterium and to the pope, nourished by reverent prayer and sacramental worship." While Jesuits should always follow the safer path, they should also courageously face the new situations of the day and creatively make the necessary adaptations (without compromising doctrine).[106]

All of these Ignatian directions, if implemented in theological education, would not only make theology faithful to its sources but creative and relevant to the needs of the day. Being faithful to the foundations and being creative were not polar opposites for Dulles.

If followed, such an approach to theological education would evoke "the gratitude and respect of all who love our holy faith and attract talented and dedicated candidates" to the Society of Jesus, and would inaugurate a "new spring time at the beginning of the new millennium."[107] The very terminology he used indicated that he saw himself leading a new crusade to renew the Jesuits and the church from within, much as the Oxford Movement had attempted to revive the church in the early nineteenth century.

Theology in the postconciliar period had its locus not only in the universities and seminaries but also in the professional theological organizations, and Dulles periodically addressed the role of theology in the professional organizations. In the period after the council, Dulles had been involved, but minimally, in the CTS, and extensively in the CTSA both before and after his 1976 presidency. By the 1990s, he had taken a more critical attitude toward what he considered advocacy theology that he saw manifested in the CTS and CTSA. Nonetheless, he did not separate himself from the CTSA in the 1990s and in fact appeared at some of the annual conventions to deliver papers focused on the criteria or principles of Catholic theology and the nature and authority of doctrine in Catholic theology.

In 1994, Robert Imbelli and Matthew Lamb, theologians at Boston College, organized for the CTSA an ad hoc group called "Criteria of Catholic Theology." The organizers convoked the group "to provide an integrative forum in face of the growing specialization of theology, with the ensuing danger of fragmentation."[108] The first meeting of the group, which drew more than 140 theologians, used Dulles' *Craft of Theology* as the background reading and heard Dulles' paper on fifteen criteria of authentic Catholic theology.

The question Dulles raised and proposed to answer was, "How can one tell whether theology is no longer Catholic even though it may claim to be so?" The question itself disturbed some in the CTSA because it implied that there were indeed some theologians who were no longer practicing Catholic theology. Dulles asserted that Catholic theology "can be identified, because faith can be identifiably Catholic and can give a special character to theological reflection." For him an authentic Catholic theology included the inclusiveness of "catholicity" (fullness or wholeness) and the specificity of "Catholicism." Catholic theologians had to respect the universal and the incarnational dimensions of Christianity. As a longtime member of the Lutheran/Catholic Dialogue, Dulles had repeatedly heard Carl Peter articulate what Peter called the "Catholic critical principle"—a principle needed to balance the Lutheran critical principle of justification by faith. Peter's principle intended to protect the Catholic substance of the Christian tradition by insisting on the here-and-now presence of the divine in visible structures (scripture, church, ministry, sacraments). Dulles understood Peter's principle to be urging a Catholic incarnationalism and sacramentalism that held that "God is normally mediated by created realities."[109]

The fifteen criteria (reason within faith, knowability of God, catholicity of Christ, missionary universalism, ecclesial context, communion with Rome, ecumenism, differentiated unity, continuity with the past, sacramentality and worship, sense of the faithful, acceptance of authority, scripture within tradition, fidelity to the magisterium, and association with the magisterium) that Dulles outlined specified what he meant by the inclusiveness and incarnate reality of the Catholic faith. He believed that by these criteria, which he had articulated here and there in his previous writings, "the work of a given theologian may be judged authentically Catholic."[110] He admitted, though, that his paper was an exploratory exercise and that his norms were still in need of clarification.

A wide-ranging discussion followed his presentation, and it was eventually decided that the group should remain in existence to continue the discussion of the criteria of Catholic theology. The group continued for a few more years (1996, 1997, 2000), but then, because of diminishing interests, it ceased to meet. The most numerous and active participation was evident at the first meeting at which Dulles held forth.

Some in this group within the CTSA believed that the CTSA was treating "authoritative church teaching simply as one more theological opinion to be challenged and even contradicted." Because of this charge, a few within the CTSA were considering forming a new theological society that would be more ecclesial in its theology. In 1994, Dulles was cool to the idea because he thought that the current mood in the society would eventually change. "Many Catholic theologians of stature," he told one correspondent in 1994, "are recognizing that there is no future in this anti-authoritarian agenda, which ends by turning theology itself into a shambles." Many competent theologians were members of the CTSA, he wrote, and it was not in principle or in practice

> value-free; it seems to me to be concerned with theological wisdom (however frequently it may fail to attain this) and, over much of its history, it has sought to promote good relations with bishops and other church authorities. In the years when I was an officer a number of bishops were members, and the Society carried out a number of projects that were requested and funded by the bishops.

Dulles preferred to work within the CTSA to foster a theology that was "authentically and identifiably Catholic."[111] Nonetheless, he could be highly critical of specific CTSA proposals.

After the 1997 CTSA convention, Dulles wrote a devastating critique of the CTSA that received a lot of attention in the Catholic theological community. Dulles' "How Catholic Is the CTSA?" dealt with the CTSA's protest against the Vatican's *Ordinatio sacerdotalis* (on the ordination of women), and with a few convention papers on the Eucharist. That CTSA meeting, in Dulles' opinion, reflected a widespread disposition to question and criticize current and traditional Catholic doctrines. The central theme of the 1997 convention was the "Eucharist for the Twenty-First Century." Speakers at the convention, Dulles noted, mounted a series of attacks on Catholic doctrine, "more radical, it would seem, than the challenges issued by Luther and Calvin." These speakers did not receive serious criticisms by fellow theologians who were the official respondents to them—reiterating a frequent critique Dulles had been making of the lack of collegial criticism within the American Catholic theological community. After outlining some of the other dissenting positions at the convention, Dulles noted that one could find in the proceedings "sound and responsible statements," but his generally negative assessment highlighted those positions that undermined significant traditional Catholic doctrines and self-consciously asserted theological positions against hierarchical authority.[112] In his exasperation, he quoted approvingly Cardinal Bernard Law, who called the CTSA "an association of advocacy for theological dissent" and a "wasteland."[113]

Dulles' criticisms created an almost immediate response in the Catholic theological community and made him a persona non grata among some of the more progressive and radical theologians. Even those who generally sided with Dulles on a host of theological issues thought that his comments were unfortunate and uncharacteristic of his approach to theologians with whom he had disagreements, and his criticisms were not as measured as they could have been.[114] The president of the CTSA, Mary Ann Donovan, characterized Dulles' assessment of the 1997 convention as "hostile," unfair, and "misleading," and she wondered what could have led such an "eminent theologian" to misrepresent the work of his fellow theologians. She ended her critique of Dulles' assault on the CTSA by quoting the "Presupposition" of Ignatius of Loyola's *Spiritual Exercises*: namely, "that every good Christian ought to be more willing to give a good interpretation to the statement of another than to condemn it as false." That is a piece of advice Dulles generally followed in many of his reviews of fellow theologians' books. But he also followed the advice of Ignatius in the sentences following the one quoted by Donovan: namely, "If he cannot give a good interpretation to this statement, he should ask the other how he understands it, and if he is in error, he should correct him with charity. If this is not sufficient, he should seek every suitable means of correcting his understanding so that he may be saved from error." More and more in the late 1990s, Dulles exercised this part of the Ignatian tradition. Corrective criticism could be helpful in the theological community, especially when it was needed to counteract a general mentality he perceived in the Society. Specific issues would have to be critiqued more carefully; a general spirit or mentality required at times a bold critical statement. Peter Steinfels, columnist for the *New York Times*, also thought that some of Dulles' interpretations had been unfair but that he was "right to flag" certain tendencies in the major convention addresses.[115]

Dulles' reference to the CTSA as a "wasteland" was not his usual approach to criticism. Usually he was more balanced. In a

441

1998 interview with a reporter, that balance came more to the fore. He told the reporter that twenty years ago, it was almost impossible for "people who had a reputation for orthodoxy" to get elected to leadership roles within the CTSA, because most of the voting theologians who attended the meetings were from the liberal or radical wings. In the recent past, too, he noted, the leadership of the CTSA had been "dominated by people who seem allergic to Rome and episcopal authority." Nonetheless the CTSA had "members whose views are orthodox," and he had the hope that the society would elect more moderate leadership and bring in speakers "more supportive of Catholic teaching." Although he was not naive about turning the association around, he based his hope on the fact that there were a "lot of sensible people" in the CTSA.[116]

Dulles did not return to the CTSA annual meeting until 1999, two years after his *Commonweal* attack on the "theological self-assertion against hierarchical authority." This time Dulles and Richard A. McCormick, SJ, a moral theologian at the University of Notre Dame, were invited by Robert Imbelli to present papers on the nature and authority of doctrine. Imbelli envisioned this session on doctrine, attended by "several hundred participants," as an attempt to create civil dialogue across differing theological positions—an attempt to put into action Cardinal Bernardin's 1996 Catholic Common Ground Initiative at the CTSA and modulate the cultural and theological divisions of the day.[117]

Dulles' paper underlined some disagreements in contemporary Catholic theology on the relationship between revelation and doctrine, differences that "constitute a major fault line." He saw the possibility of a virtual schism within the church unless theologians and others could reach some major agreement on doctrine's relationship to revelation and faith. He outlined, as he had in the past, three levels of doctrine and the corresponding three degrees of assent.[118] The talk was particularly pointed. He asserted that some prominent theologians, whose number was apparently growing (he singled out fellow Jesuit theologian Roger Haight, a past president of the CTSA), presented revelation "as an ecstatic encounter with God that has no doctrinal content." Some theologians following this understanding of revelation would be willing to deny the existence of "revealed doctrine." For Dulles, such a view violated the church's proclamation of "revealed truths" that required divine and Catholic faith. This was the first and fundamental divide within the Catholic theological community, and he posed a question to the members of the CTSA that would never have been conceived of in the 1950s or early 1960s: "Do we or do we not believe that there are revealed truths, identifiable as such on the infallible word of the Church's magisterium?"[119]

The question was radical and indicated a seriousness about theological disagreements that touched upon the faith directly. Dulles, as he had in the past, allowed room for legitimate dissent from noninfallible ecclesiastical declarations, but here again he was primarily concerned about "a general climate in which dissent from noninfallible doctrine is considered courageous, authentic, and forward looking, while submission is viewed as cowardly, hypocritical, and retrograde." He also called theologians to a collective examination of consciences, as he had in his homily at the CTSA Mass in 1975, on the issue of dissent. He singled out in particular the teachings in *Ordinatio sacerdotalis* and *Evangelium vitae* as examples of definitive, infallible statements that had received some widespread dissent. "To treat them as false or debatable within the church is therefore to dissent." Dulles was here underlining a message that he had been articulating for some time. His fundamental concern was evangelical and ecclesial. He was preoccupied with the possibility of schism. "At this critical juncture of history, union among believers must be the concern not only of popes and bishops, but of theologians as well."[120] Dulles emphasized the temptations of dissent and the actual climate of dissent within the theological community as a danger to the church's spiritual welfare, and in *agere contra* Jesuit fashion, he admonished the academic community.

Richard McCormick saw the signs of the times from a different angle. He focused on the problems in church proclamations within the context of the development of doctrine. McCormick noted that the Vatican had unnecessary fears about admitting past doctrinal and disciplinary failures, quoting Edward Cardinal Cassidy of the Pontifical Council for Promoting Christian Unity "that if you say the church has been wrong in the past, then it can be wrong today and tomorrow." Unlike Dulles, McCormick emphasized the noninfallible moral teachings of the church and the room for legitimate dissent within the church, a dissent that was perceived as one of the conditions for the development of doctrine. Although Dulles would not have agreed entirely with McCormick and "most theologians" that "the church's moral teaching is proposed noninfallibly," he would have agreed with McCormick that there was room in some of the church's previous teachings for legitimate theological dissent and that that dissent could be helpful in the correction and development of the church's teachings.[121] Dulles also agreed with McCormick that one had to give the presumption of truth to the hierarchical teaching office. McCormick, though, did not see public dissent as debilitating but as a helpful corrective within the church if done in a responsible and serious manner. Nor did he interpret the contemporary situation as one of a climate of dissent and in fact asserted that no one in the theological community dissents as a matter of policy. He believed that Pope John Paul II's and Cardinal Ratzinger's hostility to public dissent was misplaced. Here Dulles and McCormick parted company on their assessment of the conditions of contemporary ecclesial culture.

After the two papers were delivered, the discussion among the theologians turned very quickly to the roles of the hierarchical magisterium and that of the theologians—a recurring issue within the CTSA ever since *Humanae vitae* in 1968. Here there was no general consensus. Some sided with Dulles' emphasis on the need for acceptance of church teachings defined and proposed by the hierarchical magisterium; others sided with McCormick's stress on the need for respect of theological diversity and freedom in examining church teachings and the legitimate role of dissent in correcting ecclesiastical statements that lacked probative reasoning or were based on less than convincing evidence from the Catholic tradition. This was not exactly an impasse between two opposing theological positions as much as it was a matter of emphasis and a considerable difference in assessing the needs and signs of the times. Some theologians in the CTSA did not like what they characterized as Dulles' turn to the right, but they respected the man and his abilities and turned out in large numbers when he spoke at their conventions. Despite his theological differences from some in the CTSA, Dulles never alienated himself from the society, and some in the CTSA leadership continued in the early twenty-first century to invite him back to their meetings.[122] Most of the time Dulles had the personal fortitude and charity to criticize colleagues without rancor and without feeling any personal antagonism toward them.

International Theological Community

Dulles' work in the theological community was international as well as national in scope. Very early on in his career he was involved with *Concilium*, an international effort of progressive theologians. Later he wrote for *Communio*, likewise an international effort, but of more conservative theological reformers. A significant number of his books and articles, moreover, had been translated into multiple foreign languages: German, Italian, French, Polish, Spanish, Dutch, Chinese, Japanese, and Hungarian, among others. I know of no other American theologian in the twentieth and early twenty-first centuries who has received so much international attention as has Dulles. In 1992, he was appointed to the Vatican's International Theological Commission, which offered theological critiques and advice to the prefect of the CDF, Cardinal Ratzinger, who chaired the commission. Dulles served on that commission, which in one place he noted had "no magisterial authority,"[123] for the normal five-year period, during which time the commission prepared four major theological statements. Dulles was not particularly enamored with the practical workings of the commission and did not think it had much effect on the theological community.[124] Other theologians who had been on the commission shared some of Dulles' reservations about the functions and effectiveness of that international body of consultors.[125]

Periodically Dulles was invited to speak at international gatherings of theologians and other scholars in Germany, France, Italy, Poland, Mexico, and places in Africa. In some of these international gatherings, the foreign theologians were interested in what developments were taking place in American Catholic theology. On three or four occasions at international symposia, Dulles provided descriptive historical overviews of those developments in American Catholic theology since 1940, emphasizing the evolving but, especially when compared to the long history of theology in Europe, the relatively immature stage of theological development in the United States.[126] In Dulles' view, a maturing theology in the United States in the 1990s needed to pay more concerted attention to evangelization and all that that implied for a revitalized theology of faith and for a transformation of ecclesial life—issues to be taken up in the next chapter.

13
EVANGELIZATION AND FAITH, 1988–2008

DURING THE TWENTY YEARS after his return to Fordham, Dulles' work on the craft and location and stances of theology in the United States was conducted within the context of his understanding of evangelization, faith, and the church. The new global culture after the fall of the Iron Curtain, influenced (for good and for ill) by the electronic media, called for some faithful and fresh approaches to evangelization or reevangelization for the sake of reinvigorating Christian life and theology.

Evangelization

What Pope John Paul II called the "new evangelization" became a central focus in Dulles' writing, particularly during the 1990s and early twenty-first century.[1] New social, cultural, and political circumstances plus changes in the church since the Second Vatican Council required that the church reexamine the ways it handed on the faith. Dulles had, of course, been well aware that Paul VI in 1975, after a meeting of the International Synod of Bishops, had called for *Evangelization in the Modern World* (1975). John Paul II, following in Paul VI's tradition, interpreted Vatican II itself under the rubric of evangelization and in 1983 called for an evangelization "new in its ardor, its methods, and its expressions."[2] Under this huge umbrella of the "new evangelization," John Paul II located the preaching of the gospel and the call for personal repentance and conversion, catechesis, education in the faith at all levels, ecumenism and dialogue with the major religious traditions of the world, and social and cultural transformations in tune with

447

the word of God and the demands of morality and a Christian-formed conscience. The new evangelization was a comprehensive term that gave an overriding lens for interpreting the documents of the Second Vatican Council.

In Dulles' view, the papal turn to evangelization was "one of the most surprising and important developments in the Catholic Church since Vatican II." The postconciliar church had become too introverted, in Dulles' opinion. The modern papal emphasis on evangelization, therefore, had "hit upon an effective remedy for the church's present ills."[3] This new evangelical thrust pushed the church out of itself into the world, where it carried the message and gift of salvation.

The emphasis on evangelization had the added advantage of resonating and dialoguing with a huge segment of the American Protestant Evangelical tradition, the "most vigorous branch of Protestantism." Catholics and conservative Evangelicals shared many things: "a reverence for the canonical Scriptures and adherence to the central doctrines of the Trinity, the Incarnation, the atoning death and bodily resurrection of Jesus. In the realm of moral teaching, conservative Evangelicals, like Catholics, tend to be opposed to abortion and to defend traditional family values." A dialogue with these Evangelicals could, moreover, help Catholics to overcome "their excessive preoccupation with inner-church issues." Of course, major doctrinal conflicts existed between Catholics and Evangelicals in the areas of ecclesiology and sacramentality, but each tradition had something to offer to the other, and the new evangelization program could be effectively invoked to initiate a more widespread dialogue within American Christianity.[4] The new evangelization meant that the church needed to put the "highest priority" on the proclamation of the gospel of Jesus Christ, and if faithful to this evangelical mission, the church could "make its distinctive contribution in the social, political, and cultural spheres."[5]

In his public speeches,[6] Dulles outlined what he considered some obstacles to evangelization that theologians, bishops, missionaries, and Catholics in general had to face in the process of bringing about a general renewal of the evangelical spirit. At Sacred Heart University (Fairfield, Connecticut), Dulles outlined seven impediments that theologians needed to consider for the renewal of theology in accord with the new evangelization: (1) a notion of faith that made it a universal quality of the human experience and thereby minimized the need for revelation and proclamation; (2) a metaphysical agnosticism that diminished the cognitive dimension of faith; (3) a religious pragmatism that measured religion solely by its practical effects; (4) a cultural relativism that negated the universal dimension of Christian faith; (5) a radical religious pluralism that undermined the uniqueness of Christianity and a soteriological pluralism that relativized the need for Christ; (6) a false concept of freedom that minimized the value of Christian proclamation; and (7) an antiauthority complex that undermined the authoritative nature of revelation itself.[7] To a group of international scholars in Brescia, Italy, moreover, he admitted that the privatization of religion in American culture was one of the reasons that American Catholics had failed to implement Paul VI's 1975 encyclical on evangelizing culture, even though the American bishops had employed the new emphasis on evangelization in their various pastorals and episcopal statements.[8] To another group he argued that "an exaggerated form of egalitarianism" was a major obstacle to evangelization in the United States.[9]

In a talk to more than a hundred American bishops before one of their annual meetings, Dulles focused on additional obstacles and on what he considered seven major elements of Pope John Paul II's new evangelization that could be found already in Paul VI's encyclical on the subject. There were, of course, the perennial obstacles of the scandal of the cross, the hard sayings of the gospel, and Christianity itself as a sign of contradiction. In the American culture, a general openness to a vague transcendence without content, the unattractive example of non-Catholic evangelist preachers, exaggerated interpretations of the separation of church and state, and internal Catholic divisions and problems made it difficult to apply the new evangelization that the popes were advocating.[10] The difficulties, however, should not become an excuse to neglect the call for a new spirit of evangelization in the church, one that refocused the purpose of the Second Vatican Council. Like the modern popes, Dulles understood evangelization as an inclusive concept that embraced not only the proclamation of the gospel but also catechesis, witnessing, worshiping, community upbuilding, transformation of social structures, and service to others.[11]

The evangelical mission of the church, Dulles told another audience, was the "same for every generation" but "her pastoral priorities have to be continually rethought in relation to the actual condition of human society and the world."[12] At various times Dulles indicated what he thought the pastoral priorities ought to be for the church in the United States. At one point he singled out two: "to catechize Catholics in their Faith and to motivate them to evangelize others."[13]

Like some others in American Catholicism, Dulles became particularly concerned with how the faith was being passed on to the next generation. Catholics, and especially the youth, "should be helped to find in the Church and its traditions a spiritual home, a system of symbols, and a common language binding them to their fellow believers."[14] By the 1990s, it was evident to Dulles and others that Christian formation of Catholic youth was in trouble because of what some called the "lamentable decline in religious education."[15] He noted periodically that young people, the future of the church, growing up in a highly sensate culture, no longer had the Catholic cultural and ethnic customs that had in the past provided a way of socializing them into the church's tradition. Without adequate cultural forms of initiation and catechesis and continual conversion, large numbers of the young had not been able to interiorize the gospel values that came through the church. Many young Catholics were innocent of basic Christian doctrines, few of them had had anything like a conversion experience, and the church itself had few attractive structures that could provide the means for socializing young Catholics into the tradition.

The church needed to look again at its approach to catechesis. The old pre–Vatican II approach of the *Baltimore Catechism* had emphasized excessively the cognitive dimension of faith (neglecting the affective and experiential) while the immediate postconciliar approach had overemphasized the experiential or the historical (neglecting the content of revelation). The generation of Catholics raised in the post–Vatican II church were for the most part fuzzy about the substantive or objective dimensions of the faith. What was needed in the present transmission of the faith, therefore, Dulles proposed, was a consideration of the triadic structure of religious knowledge, where "the inquiring believer constitutes the subjective pole, the signs [of the Faith] constitute the objective pole, and the meaning or content of faith arises from the encounter of both."[16]

A new catechetical process that developed the whole person's commitment to Christ, moreover, had to consider the communal and liturgical and prayerful context in which faith matured. Faith deepened and was developed, furthermore, in its exercise in charity and service to others and to the common good. Catechesis was an ecclesial, liturgical, and witnessing process that aimed to bring the integral person to a knowledge and love of God in Christ. Dulles' approach to catechesis was analogous to his understanding of the reception of revelation. Religious knowledge was in fact personal knowledge, and it always came to individuals within a communal tradition of experience, reflection, and service in a way that avoided the excessive objectivism of the distant past and the dangerous subjectivism (experientialism) or historical positivism of the immediate postconciliar era.

Catholics, Dulles periodically opined, were deficient in communicating their faith to others. The church was essentially missionary, and American Catholics in the past as well as in the present had seriously neglected this side of the church's nature. Evangelical Protestants had much to teach Catholics in this regard. Sharing the faith was a matter not only of participating in the church's essential mission but also of developing and maturing one's commitment to Christ.

In a talk before a group of Catholic students at the University of Wisconsin (Madison) in 2007, Dulles outlined seven different models of evangelization: personal witness, proclamation by word of mouth and of pen (initial proclamation, catechesis, apologetics, and so on), worship, development of communities of mutual love and support, incarnation of the faith in various cultural forms, and works of charity and service to those in need. In all these ways outsiders could be attracted to the faith. The initial movement toward faith was a matter of grace, but these models of evangelization could serve as signs of the faith that manifested the grace that drew persons to the faith. To these students he emphasized that "laypersons have a special responsibility to evangelize secular society, including the workplace and the public square. The values of the Gospel can vivify and transform human relations in law, politics, business and all the professions." Dulles concluded his talk by noting that "Pope John Paul said once that faith is strengthened when it is given to others. Conversely, we may add, faith is weakened when we hoard it to ourselves."[17]

The secular and hedonistic culture was clearly a problem, but the church itself, Dulles told the American bishops in 1992, needed to do a better job of forming consciences. The need of the day was not for "more and stricter rules but to educate the consciences of the faithful so that they may be able to make reliable judgments based on personal insight and virtuous inclination." This was especially important for young Catholics, who opinion polls had shown were more likely than their Protestant peers to reject traditional moral values.[18] It was within this context, then, that he discussed the early drafts of the new *Catechism of the Catholic Church* (1994).

At the extraordinary International Synod of Bishops in 1985, Cardinal Bernard Law, among others, recommended the publication of a universal catechism for the Catholic Church, one that would be a compendium of Catholic doctrine, crystalize the developments of the Second Vatican Council, and provide guidance for the production of local- or national-language catechisms. In 1990, Dulles critiqued a draft of the proposed new catechism, pointing out in particular the weaknesses in its presentation of ecclesiology. He thought the 1990 draft deficient in many regards. He criticized, for example, its traditional four-part structure of creed, sacraments, commandments, and prayer. It failed to include or skirted, moreover, many themes of Vatican II, "such as *aggiornamento*, the reformability of the church, the importance of the word of God, the structures of collegiality, the active role of the laity, the value of the religious life, regional diversification and ecumenism."[19] Although less than satisfied with the 1990 draft, Dulles did not, as had some other theologians, reject the idea of a universal catechism.

The proposed catechism received a host of criticisms from theologians and bishops around the world. In 1992, it was revised and published in French and then in other modern languages. In the United States, and other English-language countries, the publication was delayed because of criticisms of the English translation, which, critics charged, had failed, among other things, to avoid sexist language. In 1994, even before the English text was available to him, Dulles wrote a very favorable article on the revised catechism. The article was an attempt to answer a charge made by the American bishops and some theologians that the earlier draft failed to indicate a hierarchy of truths among the various doctrines the catechism taught. According to the critics, it was difficult to decide what was essential and what was less important in the teachings of the first draft of the proposed catechism.

Dulles examined the revised text to determine if this was still the case. Prior to responding to this particular issue, he asserted his generally positive assessment of the new catechism: "I know of no comparable instrument for ascertaining the relevant data from Scripture and tradition regarding the full range of Catholic faith and morals." In fact, "the work provides a rich and harmonious synthesis of Catholic faith and moral teaching." The tone of this article was considerably more positive than his 1990 critique of the draft. Here he was trying to present the positive side of the catechism, even indicating, in contrast to his 1990 article, that the four-fold structure of the catechism brought out the "organic relationship" of the various doctrines in "connection with the central Christian mystery." Missing, too, was any criticism of the ecclesiological deficiencies in the text; rather he attempted to show how the ecclesial related to the trinitarian, christological, and pneumatological core of the catechism. After examining the catechism's structure and content, he concluded that "for the most part" there were clear distinctions between "matters of faith and other matters," and in fact the "hierarchy of truths has been duly respected." He was well aware that theologians and others might have "criticisms of detail" regarding individual passages, but there was an overall integrity in the text, and "there is no warrant for the charge that everything is taught as though it had the same degree of centrality or the same obligatory force."[20]

Having approved of the catechism did not mean that Dulles had abandoned his previous criticisms entirely. The catechetical genre had inherent limitations, and the new *Catechism* suffered from them.

Adhering closely to approved doctrine, the volume some-times fails to indicate significant theological developments that have not yet been officially received. The Scripture references are not accompanied by as much exegetical commentary as the reader might need to avoid misinter-pretation. Past doctrinal formulations are presented with little or no indication of their relative weight and the his-torical context in which they were issued. No effort is made to take account of the experiences and concerns of particular regions or groups of readers.

Dulles regretted, moreover, that the English translation of the orig-inal French used "excessive and often unnecessary...masculine lan-guage to designate human beings.[21] His criticism tempered his praise, as his praise intended to temper his earlier criticism. The *Catechism* was ultimately a human instrument in the church's life of faith. It had benefits as well as warts.

Dulles' *sic et non* approach to the *Catechism* contrasted sharply with more thoroughly negative criticisms by other theologians, some of whom predicted "with great assurance,"[22] in Dulles' characteriza-tion, that it would collapse, or that it needed to be totally rewritten, or that it presented an outmoded view of a fixed deposit of faith. The *Catechism*, in Dulles' view, was in fact needed to demonstrate that there was "an abiding deposit of faith" that some theologians were denying.[23] Dulles considered it "the boldest challenge yet offered to the cultural relativism that currently threatens to erode the contents of Catholic faith." By setting forth the church's faith, the *Catechism* "by implication takes on modern scholars who have criticized the inherited patrimony on the basis of new methodologies in exegesis, historical research, and epistemology." In particular, it challenged four very popular tendencies: positivist exegesis, historical dogmat-ics, revisionist speculation, and experienced-based catechesis. Although the *Catechism* was a "reliable compendium of Catholic doc-trine," it remained open to further investigation by exegetes, theolo-gians, and religious educators. By exercising the skills of their respective disciplines, these scholars could certainly go beyond the *Catechism*, as long as their methodologies did not reduce faith to per-sonal experience.[24] By the mid- to late 1990s, Dulles was becoming more and more forceful in asserting the need for such a universal compedium of the faith. He knew it was an imperfect instrument, but it was one that was very much needed in the cultural context of the late twentieth century. The *Catechism*, of course, was not the only means of catechesis in the Catholic Church. In 2007, Dulles outlined what he considered the strengths and weaknesses of various historical models of passing on the faith.[25]

Dulles placed not only theology but also apologetics within the new evangelization program. Giving an explanation or reason for one's faith (1 Pet 3:15) had a long history within the Christian tradition, and Dulles himself had a "lifelong interest in apologetics, which aims to show the plausibility of faith to those who do not yet believe."[26] He called for the restoration of apologetics in courses of college theology to equip students to meet the philosophical and cultural objections to religion, basic Christian doctrines, and the Catholic tradition.

Dulles believed that the beginning of the twenty-first century was a propitious time for a return to apologetics, and the need was "urgent."[27] By the 1950s, Christian apologetics had begun to collapse in both Protestant and Catholic theological circles. In Catholicism it was replaced by what some theologians called "fundamental theology," a theology of the faith meant for believers, not unbelievers. After the Second Vatican Council, apologetics, as a discipline, almost completely disappeared in American Catholicism. The reasons for the collapse were many, but one of the most significant was its attempts to prove too much, and its excesses killed it. In the early twenty-first century, Dulles saw signs of a rebirth of the discipline and for very good reasons.

Christian apologetics was an important part of the tradition that needed to be revived because it revealed the reasonableness of the act of faith. Dulles recognized that "faith [itself] is enfeebled if its rational grounds are denied." The reluctance of many Christian theologians, in both Western Europe and North America, to defend the faith, in Dulles' view, had "produced all too many fuzzy-minded and listless Christians, who care very little about what is to be believed."[28] A "prevalent agnosticism" in the modern Western world, moreover, made it imperative that Christians restore the discipline.[29]

Dulles saw signs of a return to apologetics particularly among a few Evangelical Protestants and some Catholics in the United States, and he himself republished his *History of Apologetics* (1999, 2005) and enlarged it to include historical developments since its original publication in 1971.[30] He was also well aware that this "Rebirth of Apologetics" was only in its initial stages and had not yet influenced a majority of theologians. The revival, as he saw it, resurrected some classical forms of apologetics, the philosophical approach of natural theology, and the historical, evidentiary approach. These classical forms had some value but also some severe limits.

Dulles himself did not construct his own apologetics, but he did point out what he believed were constitutive elements of a new apologetic that he found more convincing than some of the classical forms. For some years he had been advocating what he called an "apologetics of religious testimony."[31] Such an apologetic was a theological discipline that presupposed faith and tried to discern how God came to human beings who had an implicit desire and aspiration for communion with the divine. This apologetic relied on the kind of personalist epistemology that Dulles found in the thought of Pope John Paul II.[32] God came to human beings primarily through human testimony and human witnesses, and the faith that came through this testimony could find answers and reasons for belief. This personalist approach to an apologetic of religious testimony was not for Dulles a purely individual project. It also took place, as it did personally for Dulles, in a communal and sacramental context, and in fact it was the communal testimony that became most convincing.

> In becoming a Catholic, I felt from the beginning that I was joining the communion of the saints, the body to which Augustine and Aquinas, Bernard and Ignatius, belonged. I found great joy at the sense of belonging to a body of believers that stretched across the globe. The sacramental system and the authority of pastors were (and are) for me among the most attractive features of Christianity.[33]

It was the role of the apologist to establish criteria for the credibility and reliability of the witnesses in order to demonstrate the reasonableness of faith.

Dulles himself devised what he called five "rules of thumb" for evaluating religious testimony: convergence of multiple testimonies, firmness of conviction, novelty that exceeds human experience, transformative power, and illuminative insight that helps to explain the riddles of life and death.[34] Dulles did not expand on this approach; he merely outlined what he considered a valuable approach to apologetics that developed the insights of previous apologetical approaches, corresponded to his own personal experience of conversion, and met the urgent needs of contemporaries seeking reasons for belief. He outlined in 2006, in Dulles' regular fashion, seven models of apologetics (classical manual rationalism, biblical evidentialism, subjective experientialism, Augustinian yearning, objective aesthetics of Hans Urs von Balthasar, presuppositionalism, historical evidentialism), each of which provided him with insights into various ways of constructing a viable apologetic.[35] Apologetics was not absolutely necessary in the Christian tradition, but it was one way of avoiding the pitfalls of Christian superstition, fundamentalism, or fideism, on the one hand, and rationalism, skepticism, or agnosticism on the other.

Ecumenism

Ecumenism was also a dimension of the new evangelization. During the early 1990s at Fordham, Dulles worked as an ecumenist in the Lutheran/Catholic Dialogue, and after he left that dialogue in 1996, he continued in various ways to involve himself in the ecumenical movement.[36] Increasingly he came to believe that the era of convergence ecumenism, which had been so successful in the various bilateral dialogues, had come as far as it was possible to come and in fact had exhausted its potential by the late 1990s. The "convergence method" had run into the seemingly irrepressible differences that divided the churches. A new era of reconfessionalism and testimony, with a new understanding of dialogue as a mutual sharing of gifts, however, seemed to be emerging in the ecumenical movement. Reconfessionalism was not a defeat of ecumenism but an innovative approach that could move the ecumenical movement forward. When the various Christian churches identified and testified to the gifts and genuine charisms of their traditions and shared them with other churches, they could "hope to raise their voices together in a single hymn to the glory of the triune God. The result to be sought is unity in diversity....By accepting the full riches of Christ we lose nothing except our errors and defects. What we gain is the greatest gift of all: a deeper share in the truth of Christ, who said of himself, 'I am the way, and the truth, and the life.'" This entire approach could bring about mutual conversion and lead the way to the unity that Christ desired. But, Dulles was realistic enough to acknowledge that this "process of growth through mutual attestation will probably never reach its final consummation within historical time, but it can bring palpable results."[37] Dulles saw participation in the ecumenical movement as another aspect of Pope John Paul II's "new evangelization." Evangelization and ecumenism would become a major new theme in Dulles' writings in the late 1990s and early twenty-first century.

Dulles repeated many of the themes that he had previously articulated on the movement toward church unity, but in these years he emphasized the need for patience in the long-term commitment to achieving the unity Christ willed for the church. The "healing of memories," a significant part of the ecumenical and interreligious dialogues, and mutual forgiveness took time, and the dialogue partners had to await the long process of building trust to overcome the years and centuries of division and hostility.[38]

Unity could not be achieved except in truth, and Dulles believed that ecumenism involved proclamation and evangelization. It was essential to the long-term movement toward Christian unity that the dialogue partners were true to their own traditions and proclaimed the truth to one another. Compromises led to a false ecumenism that ultimately undermined unity in Christ where truth was located. Dialogues were mutual proclamations of the truth and participations in evangelization (broadly understood). The aim of bilateral dialogues and conversations was not conversion in the sense of commitment to Christ, as was the explicit intent of a narrow definition of evangelization, but conversion in the sense of a movement from misconceptions of one another's traditions to understanding and perhaps even acceptance of the truth contained in one another's traditions. In Christian bilateral conversations, the dialogue partners sought to proclaim the gospel to one another, and in this sense the dialogues participated in evangeliza-tion.[39] Being true to one's own tradition, moreover, could lead to mutual enrichment as the dialogue partners learned from one another.

Dulles was encouraged by the progress that had already been made in the bilateral conversations since the end of Vatican II, even though he had cautioned patience in the slow movement toward the fullness of church unity. He suggested, moreover, that it was perhaps time to move from bilateral to multilateral conversations (involving, for example, Reformed, Anglican, Methodist, and Orthodox traditions) on the issue of justification, which had achieved some level of mutual acceptance in the Lutheran/Catholic Dialogue. Bringing other Christian soteriological perspectives into this discussion, Dulles thought, might help to transcend the con-tinuing impasses and achieve a comprehensive resolution to an issue that had significantly divided the churches in the past.[40]

In the late 1990s and early 2000s, Dulles focused much of his ecumenical attention and became involved informally in Catholic discussions with American Protestant Evangelicals. His new involvement was part of a wider Catholic interest in dialogue with Evangelicals. Catholics had focused on evangelization since at least the 1974 meeting of the International Synod of Bishops, Pope Paul VI's subsequent encyclical *Evangelii nuntiandi* (1975), and Pope John Paul II's "new evangelization." From 1977 to 1984, moreover, the Vatican Secretariat for Promoting Christian Unity approved an international Catholic dialogue with independent Evangelicals; that international group met on a regular basis to discuss issues of Christian unity, particularly in the area of missions.[41] In 1997, too, the Pontifical Council for Promoting Christian Unity sponsored a meeting with representatives of the World Evangelical Fellowship at Tantur (Jerusalem). These pontifical directions and various Vatican-sponsored international dialogues, which Dulles com-mented on repeatedly after the mid-1980s, made him open to the emerging dialogue with American Protestant Evangelicals.

Dulles' association with Richard John Neuhaus also brought him into an informal dialogue with American Protestant Evangelical theologians. Since the mid-1980s Neuhaus had been in conversation with Evangelicals, including Charles Colson; these two in particular were drawn together by their mutual interest in the Christian influence on the public square, and by the early 1990s, after Neuhaus had become a Catholic, they shared some ethical concerns. In 1992, Neuhaus and Colson gathered together a few Catholics (Dulles included) and Evangelicals into a discussion on issues of mutual concern. For years, of course, Dulles had read and admired some of the major evangelical theological works, particularly that of Carl F. H. Henry, who had had a cordial relationship and had corresponded periodically with Dulles and Dulles' mentor, Gustave Weigel, in the 1950s.[42]

In 1994, Colson's and Neuhaus's informal and unofficial dialogue, called "Evangelicals and Catholics Together," produced on the basis of their earlier meeting in 1992 a common statement on "The Christian Mission in the Third Millennium" and in 1999 a common statement on "The Gift of Salvation." Dulles was heavily involved in writing both statements and contributed to a clarification of the agreements and continuing doctrinal divides between Catholics and Evangelicals.[43] In the midst of this new ecumenical adventure, Dulles told a London Catholic reading audience that despite their individualism, occasional anti-intellectualism, and in some cases antipathy to Roman Catholicism, the Evangelical churches were showing an "exceptional vitality." They were particularly faithful to central Christian convictions such as

> the inspiration of Scripture, the bodily resurrection of Jesus, and the identity of Jesus as the eternal Son of the eternal Father. These shared beliefs, together with a common commitment to social goals such as family stability, the protection of unborn life, parental choice in education, and the influence of Christian faith in public affairs, are increasingly being recognized as bonds between Evangelicals and Catholics.[44]

He saw hope in the dialogue with Evangelicals, even though he knew that on the doctrinal level the distance between Evangelicals and Catholics was much wider than it was currently between Catholics and Lutherans. But the dialogue with Evangelicals offered a fresh ecumenical approach. By 1999, Dulles admitted while discussing the Evangelical theologian Donald Bloesch's views of revelation that the two theologians had much in common, and while Bloesch appeared to be a Catholic Evangelical, Dulles identified himself as "a somewhat evangelical Catholic," striving "to maintain the Catholic heritage while reenergizing it with the ferment of evangelical conviction."[45]

"Evangelicals and Catholics Together" was national in scope because it drew upon Catholics and Evangelicals from various places in the United States. But it was not the only effort to engage Catholics and Evangelicals. Earlier, in California and other places, Evangelicals and Catholics were meeting to carry on high-level theological discussions.[46] These dialogues were independent of the Catholic hierarchy, and they had no standing in the official evangelical communities. It was not until 2003 that the American bishops decided to establish an official dialogue with independent Evangelicals. So Dulles' involvement in the Evangelical-Catholic dialogue can be seen as something of a precursor or preparation for this later official dialogue.

Periodically, Dulles was invited to lecture on issues of church unity to Catholic and Evangelical Protestant audiences. To a group of Evangelical Protestants at Beeson Divinity School of Samford University in Birmingham, Alabama, Dulles reiterated in 2006 his understanding of the relation of ecclesiology to ecumenism. Because Christians were baptized and had faith in Christ, they were incorporated in the body of Christ, and because of that incorporation "our ecclesiology ought to be broadly ecumenical."[47] His talk at Beeson, where his friend and colleague Timothy George was dean,[48] continued his interests in Catholic communion with Evangelicals, which he had entertained since the late 1990s. He told the Beeson audience that Catholics and Evangelicals already had "a significant measure of communion or fellowship [*koinonia* 2 Cor 13:13–14]" even though that union was imperfect. He suggested that Evangelicals and Catholics needed to combine in their ecclesiologies the ontological and the interpersonal dimensions in order to bring out the "interpersonal structure of the Church." The ontological and personal dimensions were integrated in the theology of the Trinity, and trinitarian unity was the archetype for ecclesial unity.[49] With Evangelicals Dulles was working to emphasize the essential unity that already existed as a foundation for fuller unity in the future.

Church, Contemporary Culture, and Politics

Periodically in the 1990s, Dulles spoke out on the church's social mission in the modern world. Accepting the "new evangelization" meant that the church had a mission to influence culture, become involved in issues of social justice and peace, make an impact on the political order primarily through a laity formed in gospel principles, and be aware of the massive role of the media in reflecting and shaping cultural values. In lectures and talks to various foreign as well as domestic audiences, he addressed the relationship between faith and culture.

In a talk at Louvain in 1993, Dulles defined *culture* broadly as the "general conditions of life in common, including the belief-systems, the prevalent standards of behavior, and the laws and institutions that permeate a given society." Quoting from his own *The Reshaping of Catholicism* (1988), he indicated that culture is "a system of meanings, historically transmitted, embodied in symbols, and instilled in new members of the group so that they are inclined to think, judge, and act in characteristic ways."[50] A dialectical and reciprocal relationship existed between the church and the diverse cultures of the world, and one had to be clear about the benefits and limits of that relationship.

In various lectures and in various ways, Dulles described the multifaceted nature of American culture and the historic and contemporary American Catholic strategies for dealing with it. That culture was not just one thing but many things and was in itself extremely diverse and complex. It was difficult to find a common denominator in the multiple cultures that characterized the United States. Puritanism, the Enlightenment, and Lockean philosophy had shaping influences, which were manifested in the American emphasis on freedom, independence, autonomy, personal initiative, open communication, and active participation. But the multiple ethnic and racial cultures that migrated or were transferred to American shores also helped to shape moral and religious values in the United States. Because of these values and the mixture of cul-

tures, the United States had become a model for religious tolerance, producing a vibrant religious and cultural pluralism, economic initiatives, and a wide, though not universal or even
equitable, distribution of economic goods.

Dulles also characterized contemporary American culture in a
McGinley lecture by the extreme tendencies of its own values: freedom had become a drive toward subjectivism, individualism, radical pluralism, agnosticism, secularism, and hedonism (making an
absolute out of self-satisfaction and riches). Increasingly, contemporary America was becoming a consumerist society: "Each individual is seen primarily as a consumer, and heavy consumption is
viewed as the key to social well-being....The desire for pleasure,
comfort, humor, and excitement is continually escalated." Work
became merely a means to "affluence and sensory gratification."[51]
In the United States, moreover, the courts were severely restricting
the social expressions of religion (thereby undercutting the transcendental heart of culture), questions of truth were systematically
bracketed, and a radical pluralism and polarization tended to
obscure any common goals or common societal mission. In such a
situation, he wrote in 2004, the raw new pluralism was "not an
unqualified good," and without a common purpose and a common
sense of right and wrong the "Western world, including the United
States, seems to be careening down the path toward a new age of
barbarism, this time brought on from inside rather than from outside."[52] The threats or seeds of self-destruction lay mostly within
the current Western culture, which had once been permeated by
Christianity. For Dulles, those days were gone. "The culture of
Western Europe and America in our days seemed to me like an
empty bottle still emitting the sweet scent of a perfume it had once
held. But the fragrance was diminishing since the faith from which
it arose was in recession."[53]

Dulles' mixed interpretations of the culture and of the signs of
the times influenced his historical and theological assessments of
Catholic relations to contemporary western and American society
and culture. Those relations were many and varied. Historically,
because of religious liberty, Catholics in the United States, Dulles
told a Polish audience, had built and maintained a strong institutional structure and developed, because of immigration, a vibrant

multicultural parish life that in the past had been a clear alternative to the dominant secular culture. This historical condition meant, for all practical purposes, that pre–Vatican II Catholicism was able to resist some of the secular influences, but it also meant that Catholics had little or no influence on the larger American culture (of art, architecture, music, philosophy, economics, and politics). Once American Catholics emerged from their cultural cocoons in the late 1950s and 1960s, however, and were on the verge of making an impact on American culture, they succumbed to some of the worst elements of that culture rather than transforming or elevating it.

With this historical development in the United States, a "chasm began to open up between faith and culture in American Catholicism." But the "chasm" was not like the older separation of the immigrant religious traditions from the dominant culture—a separation built upon confidence in the Catholic faith and in the various ethnic traditions that preserved that faith. By the late 1960s and early 1970s, many Catholics "lost confidence in their own religious and cultural heritage and sought to become more typically American in their attitudes." They "diluted their faith or became schizophrenic—Catholic by religion and secular by culture."[54] This historical interpretation helped Dulles to explain contemporary American Catholicism to his various audiences. But that historical shift from isolation from the dominant culture to absorption in it was only part of the story of the relationship of faith and culture.

In 1989, Dulles described four different post-1970 American Catholic strategies (traditionalist, neoconservative, liberal, and radical) for relating faith to American culture. Each of the strategies had its strengths and weaknesses; none was "simply wrong."[55] Because American culture was so complex, it required multiple responses from a faith perspective. Dulles, the pluralist, called for a dialogue between the various strategies to lessen to some extent the cultural and intra-Catholic wars that had arisen in the previous three decades, to acknowledge the multiple ramifications of the problem, and to recognize the diverse gifts of the Holy Spirit in relating faith and culture.

Dulles called for peace among the representatives of the four different Catholic strategies because as ideal types they were not incompatible. Dulles' interpretation of the contemporary situation helps somewhat to explain his own values and his own approaches to the relationship between faith and culture. It is difficult to put him in some neat box—labeled traditionalist, neoconservative, liberal, or radical—as some journalists and theologians tended to do because his approach to faith and culture in the 1990s depended on the specific issue in the culture that he was addressing.

Dulles could identify with the traditionalists when he was self-consciously countercultural, and when he emphasized, as he did periodically, respect for ecclesial authority, the need for socialization in the Catholic tradition, and the importance of an interior spiritual transformation.[56] He could side with the neoconservatives when he stressed the need for ordered liberty in society, respect for American constitutional democracy, the necessity of incarnating Catholic values in society in accord with democratic political procedures, and appreciation of the values inherent in democratic capitalism.[57] He could align himself with the liberals when he called for incorporating American liberal, republican, and democratic values into the structures of the church and for learning from and incorporating into the Catholic tradition what was good, true, and beautiful in modern cultural, intellectual, and scientific developments. He could also be radically prophetic in his calls for repentance and conversion, and his denunciations of what he perceived to be excessive Catholic appropriations and identifications with American secular and consumerist values that contradicted the gospel.

Dulles could not identify, however, with the traditionalists' attempts to restore a previous Catholic culture or their tendencies to separate themselves from the culture. Nor could he align himself fully with the neoconservatives who tended to overlook the consumerist tendencies in the culture and the necessity of evangelization, conversion, and socialization into the Catholic community of faith. Catholic liberals' preoccupation with democratic structural reform, he believed, would only increase competition for power within the church and diminish respect for and docility to traditional authority, reverence for the sacred, and esteem for sacrifice, prayer, and contemplation. Radical denunciations of American cultural values he believed tended to marginalize Catholicism and make its incarnational faith difficult, if not impossible, to implement in the culture. Because the tide had turned, though, he emphasized more and more in the 1990s the need for a distinctive Catholic voice in society that flowed from an interiorization of the gospel. His was not a law-and-order approach, but an evangelical one.

At times, as in 2001, Dulles, like some other social commentators, divided the entire country into two major camps relative to the cultural wars over a host of religious and moral issues (abortion, euthanasia, homosexual relations, divorce, and contraception, among others). On the one side were conservatives "who hold that there are transcendentally grounded and enduring moral laws, and on the other side are progressives who wish to revise all concepts of truth and falsehood, right and wrong in light of the prevailing assumptions of contemporary life." Orthodox Jews, Evangelical Protestants, and practicing Catholics, Dulles placed on the conservative side, and liberal Jews, liberal Protestants, and secular humanists he placed on the other side.[58] This simple—some might say simplistic—approach to understanding the battles occurred from time to time in Dulles' historical assessment of the religious responses to American culture wars. His theological understanding of the relationship of faith and culture, however, was more sophisticated.

The church's tasks in the culture were evangelization, proclamation, and dialogue. The church had something to give to the culture, but the way it exercised its mission of evangelization and proclamation demanded, in order to be effective, the use of various linguistic, philosophical, and aesthetic measures that it sometimes borrowed from contemporary culture. Dialoguing with the culture presupposed a willingness to learn from it and incorporate what the culture had to offer to enhance the mission of evangelization and proclamation, but the church needed to maintain something of a balance between evangelization and acculturation, realizing always the reciprocal relationship between the two. The inherent problem, as Dulles saw it, was one of discernment. How could one discover in the culture ingredients that could serve as a vehicle of faith? If the church's primary mission was evangelization and proclamation, how could it use elements of American culture that would communicate effectively the gospel message and allow that message itself to transform and elevate the culture? According to *Lumen gentium* (LG 13), the church's relationship to culture was threefold: it had to select from the culture those elements that were consistent with the gospel, purify them according to the gospel, and elevate them by associating them with the church's mission.[59]

At times the church also had to dissent from cultural values that conflicted with the gospel. But a "critical dialogue" with the culture and a Catholic "counterculturalism" had to be "measured, [and] prudent."[60] How Catholics responded to American culture demanded spiritual discernment, and such discernment required living within the church's life of evangelization, catechesis, conversion, prayer, worship, and systematic reflection upon the sources of the Tradition. How American Catholics read the culture determined to a large extent the different strategies they took to relate their faith to that culture.

The council's constitution *Gaudium et spes* set out a direction for Catholic relations with the modern world that Dulles fully accepted, with some post–Vatican II modifications. The church's mission in the world was religious, not political; its primary role, as Pope Pius XI had acknowledged, was to evangelize, not civilize. The council, though, brought a new dimension to Catholic thought by taking the secular seriously and on its own terms, by emphasizing the relative autonomy of the secular, and by a new tone of dialogue (not confrontation) with the modern world. In the immediate decade after the council, in Dulles' interpretation, what was new in that document received the most attention, and therefore theologians and others emphasized the autonomy of and dialogue with the secular, inculturation of the faith, and adaptation to modernity. After 1975, Popes Paul VI and John Paul II, wishing to restore some balance, emphasized the centrality of evangelization as proclamation and as dialogue, while not denying or neglecting the need for inculturation. Dulles followed the two popes in emphasizing the centrality of evangelization as proclamation, and he supported the need for inculturation, dialogue with the modern world, and involvement in issues of justice and peace.[61]

From time to time, Dulles lectured on the church's social mission, particularly in the areas of justice and peace. Some scholars have charged, however, that Dulles was "no friend of liberation theology or the faith and justice theme." In their view, he called for a smaller and more dedicated Catholic community, a community of committed Catholics withdrawn from a pagan society badly in need of redemption.[62] Some of Dulles' essays no doubt give this impression because of his assessment of the tendencies toward secularization, radical pluralism, and hedonism in the culture. But, in fact, he was concerned with issues of justice and peace and wanted Catholics, particularly lay Catholics, to contribute from their commitment of faith to the body politic.

What concerned him most in American society was the lack of a common consensus on basic, transcendental values. That lack of agreement on fundamental issues of truth and goodness undermined any possibilities of rational discussion about issues of social justice and peace. The radical pluralism, and even more so, the justification of a radical pluralism in society, prevented American society from reaching common judgments about what indeed was basic in any society.[63] In the past, as we have seen, Dulles had supported a legitimate pluralism in society and in Catholicism, but such pluralism presupposed in his mind fundamental agreements on basic core principles and beliefs.

As in the past, so in the early twenty-first century, Dulles called for what he in one place called a "Deist Minimum," or a civil religion that could undergird society's common purpose and mission. Rational arguments about social justice and peace needed to be grounded in a transcendental vision of the basic truths of natural and biblical religion. What he had in mind here was a common belief "in one almighty God, in providence, in a divinely given moral code, in a future life, and in divinely administered rewards and punishments."[64] That bare minimum needed to be shared by a large number of citizens in order to make genuine argument possible about moral and social and legislative issues. Otherwise, a radical pluralism would make any consensus impossible and undercut any hopes for rational discourse in society on issues of justice and peace.

Religion was not a private affair; it had a social dimension, and Catholics as well as other believers needed to join hands in addressing issues of social justice and humanitarian aid.[65] Faith-based but rationally defensible social theory could make major contributions to the body politic, and Catholics had such a body of social thought that needed to be clearly, cogently, and persuasively put forth in the public forum. This did not mean that Catholics and other believers should "impose laws that can only be recognized and enacted within the faith." In the public forum it was the responsibility of believers as citizens to make rational arguments, informed by revelation, and "bring their fellow-citizens to see what they see." In the body politic, sound arguments and rational persuasion work for the good of all. And if in some cases, Christians or Catholics or other believers could not convince the body politic of their views of what is true and just and good in society, they should at least be granted "the right of conscientious objection, so that the faithful are not compelled to go against their moral convictions," particularly in their own institutions.[66] This was Dulles' insistence that Catholics and other believers engage fellow citizens in rational dialogue; in this he was following a family tradition of public discourse. It was not a withdrawal tactic to preserve the purity of the Catholic tradition.

The relationship between religion and politics came to public discussion periodically in the United States, and especially during presidential election years. In 1992, during the presidential election, Joseph O'Hare, president of Fordham, suggested that Dulles address one of his McGinley lectures to the topic.[67] "Religion and the Transformation of Politics" argued that "although religion and politics are distinct, they are not separable." The church and individual Catholics had a role to play in the political arena. The spiritual dimension of human life had a primacy over the temporal, and

With Joseph O'Hare, SJ, who invited Dulles to Fordham

the spiritual had implications for temporal and social affairs. The church needed to be aware of the moral and religious dimensions of legislation and policy proposals, but Dulles asserted that the church's primary role in public policy issues was educational, pointing out the moral and religious dimension of legislative proposals. The American bishops were primarily pastors with an educational mission and should avoid as much as possible detailed applications of universal principles to social policies and legislative proposals.

Dulles opposed ecclesiastics who used lobbying and pressure tactics in the political arena and simultaneously warned against using ecclesiastical censures against politicians. Lobbying and pressure tactics "leave the basic situation unchanged." The church or Christian citizens might be able to create legislation against abortion, for example, but if that would happen it might be a Pyrrhic victory for the Christian and Catholic antiabortionists if the minds and hearts of the body politic had not been changed in the process. The bottom line for Dulles with respect to the transformation of politics was education in the faith and in the principles of social justice. Catholics and other religious believers needed to be personally engaged in politics, but what was most needed for a good society and good government was virtue and religion. "The church, even without directly intervening in the political process, can make a major contribution to the political order by shaping the ideas and habits of the persons who constitute society, making them morally and spiritually capable of responsible self-government."[68]

Dulles received many letters and some press reports in response to this lecture. One presumably antiabortion correspondent who was upset with what he said about abortion wrote, "The grotesque illogic of your words makes refutation seem futile. I fear for your decline....With all due charity, I suggest that you are a misfit in the Catholic Church....You are in the dark. You are wrong....You are the only covert [sic] I know of (and I know many personally) who has retained his Protestantism."[69] Periodically Dulles received letters like this, what he called "hate mail," from those who were troubled with what he had said or written. Others responding to this lecture took issue with his mild but implied criticism of the American bishops' "detailed application" of general principles to concrete social policies and legislative proposals.

Some had charged him with dualism because of his distinction between teaching principles and political activism or application to politics. Dulles responded by saying that he was simply calling for respect for the "inner workings of the political process."[70]

A reporter from the *Washington Post* called him after the Fordham lecture to interview him on the subject for an article he was writing on Dulles' talk. Dulles was even more forceful in the interview than he had been in the lecture on the absolute necessity of religion and morality for the continuation of a democratic form of government. The acceptance of common moral standards, he was reported as having said, is withering away, and "ultimately, this could bring the collapse of democracy." In fact, "It's gone pretty far." In recent years in the United States, because of the fear of religious entanglement with politics, the country had gone to the other extreme, and in effect "we're establishing secularism....Political judgments are inevitably permeated with moral and religious assumptions." The churches in the United States, he told the reporter, should be focusing primarily on "restraining the drives of hedonism, ambition and pride that everywhere threaten civil peace and order."[71] Dulles' interpretation seems more than justified in view of some of the moral sources of the economic collapse of 2008 and 2009.

During the 2004 presidential election, Dulles received many letters from people seeking his judgment on the relation of religion and politics, particularly on voting for candidates who favored abortion. Dulles tried periodically to distinguish the moral from the political question, without divorcing politics from morality. Abortion was a moral question, and Dulles opposed laws favoring abortion on demand. But he was also aware, as he told one inquirer, that it might be possible to vote for a pro-abortion candidate who in comparison to other candidates had many good qualities, and this would be particularly the case "to stave off the election of some other candidate, who was even worse. In such cases your vote would not seem to be sinful material cooperation in evil."[72] To a cousin Dulles responded that he agreed with her "that votes for candidates should be based in general qualifications, not on a single issue. I have often voted for pro-choice candidates in spite of my disagreeing with that element in their platform." In another letter to her, he tried to correct her misunderstanding of what the

American Catholic bishops held with respect to the legal dimensions of abortion. To the best of his knowledge, the bishops

> are not trying to make all abortions illegal. Many hold, as I do, that the laws of the nation should be sufficiently in line with public opinion as not to be unenforceable, as prohibition was. They also hold that the laws of the country today are too permissive. These laws authorize and support abortions that the majority of the citizens regard as immoral and unjust.[73]

On occasion Dulles addressed the religious and secular mass media, outlining his view of their role in the shaping of values in society and the church. There was something of an irony here, as he admitted, because he rarely watched television or listened to the radio, and he was technologically challenged when making his way around the Internet. He preferred, for example, to correspond by snail mail rather than electronic mail.[74] The mass media played a major role in reflecting and creating a new electronic and technological American culture that was "highly sensate, fluid, and consumer-oriented" and in intensifying the culture wars and the polarizations that existed in the church and society,[75] but they were also potentially powerful instruments "at the service of truth, justice and moral decency."[76]

Between 1994 and 1999, Dulles gave lectures that focused on the church's communication of the faith and the media's reporting and/or interpretation of religious issues. The church, Dulles argued, had not been terribly successful with the news media; that was the case, he believed, because of the very different perceptions of what was crucially important and because the methods and aims of the church and the media differed considerably. The church's message, for example, was primarily a spiritual message about the mystery of God's presence, and that mystery was to be approached with faithful and reverent worship. The news media, on the other hand, was almost by nature "investigative" and even "iconoclast."[77]

Naturally, therefore, tensions of substance and style existed between the news media and the church, and the church itself was not entirely free from blame about this situation. Roman doctrinal pronouncements, on the one hand, were sometimes insensitive to contemporary Western culture because they "are often expressed in precise, juridical terms and issued in an authoritative tone that is disconcerting to people accustomed to discussion and argument." On the other hand, the news media's reporting of these pronouncements sometimes makes it difficult for them to get a fair hearing. The news media had a tendency to offset the Roman statements by recording, as was its right and custom, the dissenting opinions that it "had managed to gather up." The news media "go by preference to people who will disagree [whether liberal or conservative] because this will generate a more interesting story."[78]

There were barriers to communications on both sides of the divide between the church and the news media, and efforts needed to be made to bridge the gap, even though, Dulles was aware, there were some permanent and inbuilt tensions because of the different functions of the church and the news media, and because the church's message was not always going to be popular or acceptable. But, he believed, the gap between the news media and the church could be bridged somewhat with a little effort on both sides. The church could be more sensitive to the way in which its message might be received in the different cultures of the world, and many of the news institutions could hire more reporters and journalists (like Peter Steinfels of the *New York Times* and Ken Woodward of *Newsweek*) who were qualified and knowledgeable in the field of religion. But, he advised church leaders, Christ himself, with all of his communication skills, "met with misunderstanding and hostility"— the church could expect no less.[79]

Dulles advised the Catholic Press Association to give fuller coverage to church teachings, providing their readers with the grounds for these teachings to counter the inadequate and sometimes biased or unfaithful reporting that periodically took place in the secular press. He suggested, moreover, that the Catholic press should frankly, forthrightly, and honestly acknowledge the failures and sins of the church's clerical and lay members. The church's faithful "are pained and embarrassed when bishops, priests and religious are found guilty of fiscal, sexual or other misconduct," and the press, without minimizing the gravity of their crimes, could help the faithful to give a Christian response to such scandals.

Dulles thought, moreover, that the Catholic press in the United States could have a medicinal role in the American Catholic Church if it took measures "to heal the scandalous polarization between the backward-looking integrism and an irresponsible progressivism." The press could also play a significant role in "countering the corrosive secularism of the day" and in evangelizing or reevangelizing the culture. They could take up such a role, for example, by advising their readers "about what to accept and what to reject in the dominant culture, including literature, films and television programs."[80] The media had an important role to play in shaping the culture, for good or for ill.

To a group of technically competent communications students at Xavier University, Dulles advised that though technical skill was important and could be used for the church's evangelization of the culture, and that young people could contribute to this effort, technical competence was not as important or as necessary for the evangelical process as adherence to the word of God, an interior union with Christ, and a holy life. The church could never use the young people's skills in communication for evangelization if communication were purely technical. The kind of Christian communication that got to the heart of the matter was a saintly life. Dulles told these young people that it was his impression that the productions of the technically proficient new culture industries of the mass media tended to produce

> a rather passive consumer, who is content to be a spectator rather than an actor, a follower rather than a leader….We thus forfeit our independence of judgment. Accustomed to surfing, we lose our ability to focus on anything in particular….Having more choices at our finger tips than we can seriously appraise, we lose our capacity for profound and permanent commitments and our taste for sustained analysis….All too often, we allow our humanity to be debased by representations of brutal violence and sexual licentiousness.[81]

Dulles had no intention of undercutting the importance of the media, but he believed that the church's efforts were best placed in works that aimed at genuine evangelical conversion of the heart and socialization into the community of the faith, a recurring theme in his late-1990s writings and talks.

Faith

In the midst of examining the new evangelization, Dulles completed two major books explicitly on a theology of faith: *The Assurance of Things Hoped For* (1994) and *The New World of Faith* (2000). The first was a thorough systematic study intended for students of theology and professionals; the second was more evangelical, intended for a larger and more popular audience of lay readers. Research and reflection on the theology of faith had become a central focus for Dulles in the 1990s. He had addressed the issue in connection with apologetics in the early 1960s and in connection with revelation in the mid-1960s and early 1970s, and he had focused particularly on various models of revelation in the 1980s.

Prior to the publication of *Assurance*, Dulles prepared a seminal article on "Faith and Revelation" in a textbook intended for students of theology. That essay became the basis upon which the book was constructed. Revelation, he argued, constituted and evoked Christian faith, and thus revelation and faith were of "constitutive importance" for both Christian life and theology. "Without a prior revelation on God's part faith would be impossible, for it would have no basis and no object. And without faith, the whole edifice of Christian existence would collapse."[82] The article then described revelation as Dulles had done many times in the past but most effectively in *Models of Revelation*; outlined the characteristics of faith as a supernatural gift and an affirmative, free, intellectual, volitional, and highly personal response to revelation; and then delineated the transmission of revelation through personal witnesses, scripture, tradition (understood broadly as prayer, worship, catechesis, and other acts of the church's activity in history), the sense of the faithful, and teachings of the hierarchical magisterium. This article, intended to introduce students to the issues, focused primarily on theological reflection at the Second Vatican Council and thereafter. It was not intended to be a full-scale theology of faith, but an introduction to contemporary issues.

Dulles decided to do a comprehensive systematic analysis of the understandings of faith contained in the Bible and tradition because no such examination existed in the English-speaking world. As a teacher he discovered, as others had, that he could find no substantial English-language text on the subject that he could recommend to his students. The book was clearly intended to serve as a comprehensive survey and retrieval of the biblical and traditional notions of faith and a systematic analysis of faith intended for believers in the modern world. His method was thus historical retrieval followed by systematic reflection. He was convinced of this method because "the most creative advances in theology are made by thinkers who have appropriated the wisdom of the past." An individual theologian's personal insights could be "no more than a footnote to the work of others."[83] Theology was always a matter of profound reliance on the sources of the tradition coupled with a systematic reflection that used contemporary disciplines in service to the sources for the sake of deepening contemporary reflection and contemporary Christian life.

The contemporary need for a solid theology of faith was particularly urgent in light of the challenges presented by an all-pervasive secularism in its obvious and subtle forms. In Dulles' view, "secularism, which centers human trust and aspirations on things that can be touched and seen, is an acute temptation in the present age. The achievements of human science and technology seem to promise many of the satisfactions that religion has been thought to offer." Christian faith was also imperiled by "the erosion of traditional sociological supports, the rapidity of cultural change, the aggressive propagation of alternative belief-systems, and the bewildering variety of contemporary options."[84] Unbelief or agnosticism or the inability to make final commitments, Dulles noted, was growing in contemporary society, particularly in the Western world, and those who accepted the fullness of the Christian faith were increasingly becoming a minority tradition. The systematic theologian had to address and confront these and other contemporary challenges, some of which were rather perennial, if he or she were to present a meaningful concept of Christian faith that could be perceived as an alternative to the multiplicity of contemporary choices.

Dulles sought to understand the nature and meaning and

claims of faith on the basis of scripture and the tradition of theological reflection from the early fathers of the church to contemporary postconciliar theologians. It was not "an irrational act," but
it was also "not a matter of human minds climbing up toward the
divine." Faith was a "welcoming" of "the gracious manifestation that
God has given of himself. Faith itself is, in the words of Scripture,
'the assurance of things hoped for, the conviction of things not
seen' (Heb 11:1)."[85] The book was an extended explication of this
definition.

In *Assurance*, Dulles presented the biblical and traditional
notions of faith, compared and contrasted various models of faith,
and offered his own constructive theology of faith in dialogue with
the tradition and other contemporary theologies of faith. The first
section of the book surveyed the understanding of faith from the
biblical foundations to the most recent developments in theology.
The second was a short chapter in which he described what he perceived to be seven models (the propositional, transcendental, fiducial, affective-experiential, obediential, praxis, and personalist) of
faith in this tradition.[86] Each model had its own strengths and
weaknesses, but in general all the models were in agreement that
faith was a gift of God, that it rested on revelation, and that it was
necessary for salvation. Although each model stressed a different
aspect of faith, the models themselves were complementary, not
contradictory.[87] In consistent Dulles fashion, then, he proceeded to
the third section of his theology of faith, providing a systematic
analysis that put the different models into dialogue with one
another, assessing again the strengths and weaknesses of each and
developing in the process a theology of faith that he believed gave
students of Christian life and theology a good introduction to the
reality of faith. He concluded his study by listing thirty-six characteristics of faith under five headings (the nature, attributes, and life
of faith, the universal call to faith, and Christian faith).

In the midst of presenting the act of faith as assent, trust, and
obedience, Dulles distinguished his own theology of faith from that
of other contemporary theologians. He wanted to emphasize the
harmony of the objective and the subjective dimensions of faith,
and in his attempt to do so, he distinguished his own theology of
faith from, among others, that of Karl Rahner and the transcen-

dental theologies that followed him. For much of Dulles' earlier career he had relied on Rahner's theology and shared much of his post-Kantian transcendental turn to the subject, but gradually, as he developed his own voice in theology, he began to see some weaknesses in Rahner's approach, and here and there in his articles Dulles noted where he was parting company with this giant of twentieth-century Catholic theology.

In *Assurance*, Dulles quotes, approvingly, it seems, von Balthasar's criticism of Rahner's transcendental theology "for being too anthropocentric, too much focused on the subjective component of faith." In Dulles' opinion, von Balthasar was unsympathetic to theories, like Rahner's anonymous Christianity, that seemed to minimize the importance of explicit belief in Christ.[88] Dulles himself interpreted Rahner's transcendental notion of faith as "a radicalization of the trend inaugurated by Blondel and Rousselot" by emphasizing the interior light of faith "as being by itself a kind of subjective or transcendental revelation, and thus as permitting an act of faith even where unaccompanied by the explicit transmission of any specific revealed truths." Although Rahner's transcendental notion of faith acknowledged that the human spirit had an intrinsic dynamism to realize itself explicitly, Rahner seemed to be saying that the explicit acceptance of Christ or the Christian proclamation was of secondary importance with respect to salvation. "If one accepts that proclamation, one does so because it is seen as the best articulation of what one already believed in an implicit or nonthematic way." Dulles found Rahner's transcendental notion of faith hard to square with the New Testament and traditional notions of faith as an explicit acceptance of the gospel. He noted, too, other general criticisms and remarked that although Rahner's views and theories were shared by large segments in postconciliar Catholicism and had a great "appeal to critical minds,"[89] "his synthesis, brilliant and comprehensive as it is, has not as yet won anything like a consensus, even among Catholics."[90] Ultimately Dulles found Rahner's transcendental notion of faith and his theory of the supernatural existential "vulnerable" because it tended "to subordinate without eliminating the historical and conceptual aspects of faith."[91]

By 1994, Dulles no longer spoke, as he had in 1983, of the "dialectical balance" in Rahner's notions of transcendental and categorical revelation.[92] He still accepted Rahner's notion of the human spirit's inner dynamism toward the transcendent, but Dulles put much more emphasis on the necessity of categorical revelation than he thought Rahner was willing to do. In his personal correspondence, Dulles remarked to a fellow theologian in 1997 that "my emphasis falls less on the religious question of how we get to God [as with Rahner and Tracy] than on the relational question of how God gets to us."[93]

Dulles' synthetic skills came to the fore again in this book and received the plaudits of numerous peers in theology. Reviewers asserted that Dulles was, in Lawrence S. Cunningham's opinion, "one of the truly distinguished Catholic theologians of our time," or in John Macquarrie's view, "probably the leading Catholic theologian in the United States at the present time." The book provided the reader with the sweep of the tradition and was ecumenically sensitive and fair in describing differing theological positions. Some reviewers wished Dulles had included modern Orthodox theologians in his survey or that he had dealt with the contemporary phenomenon of Pentecostalism and the charismatic renewal, and others faulted him for failing to criticize more sharply than he had certain positions that he described. But almost all the reviewers noted that this was a book very much needed in the English-speaking world and would be a standard introductory text for years to come.[94]

The book was, in my estimation, the major theological achievement of this period of Dulles' career as a theologian and as a teacher concerned with communicating the fullness of the tradition. Understanding the meaning of Christian faith and conversion had been an abiding concern of his life since his days as a Harvard undergraduate. The book revealed not only the abilities of a synthetic mind but the depths of his personal insights and his enduring concern to keep differing theological systems in a kind of dialectical tension that allowed the mystery of Christian faith to break forth in those tensions and in the limited perspectives of the various systems.

The *New World of Faith* was a different kind of book.[95] It was more evangelical in tone and style and language than *The Assurance*. It focused on contemporary issues in Christian life and on the current situation of believers in the modern world. Dulles could address the systematic issues of his peers in the field of theology, but he could also, and frequently did, address a larger reading audience, hoping to provide some general guidance for believers in a time of confusion and radical change. His clarity and lack of theological jargon in his many essays in *America, Commonweal,* and other widely distributed journals of opinion were intended to make theological reflection available to the general public. In his later years he became even more concerned with the state of belief in society and in the church, and his essays and this book reveal his evangelical as well as theological concern. He emphasized more and more that theology was a part of evangelization.

The *New World* demonstrated this evangelical emphasis. Dulles acknowledged that

> for some years I have had a growing conviction that believers, in a country like our own, are unsettled by the great plethora of ideas and options presented to them and by the allurements of instant satisfaction, which incline them to neglect the claims of eternal life. Yet they somehow sense within them that truth must be coherent, permanent, and universal. They long for communion with the transcendent and the divine.[96]

Dulles' book depicted the new situation and the challenges to faith and presented in readable prose the deep human desire for communion and the permanence of truth and freedom that came from commitment to Christ, the medium of communion with the divine.

The new world of faith, demanding a radical conversion, met three major impediments in American and Western societies: a historical consciousness, pluralism, and free market economy that relativized the very notion of faith and undermined the radical change needed in order to reach for the true, the good, and the beautiful. The book focused on the creedal structure of faith and the realities of evangelization and ecumenism. Dulles called for a new emphasis on handing the faith on to the new generation, believing that the youth of today were shaped so much by peer pressure and a secular culture (advertising and consumerism of the mass media) that was preponderantly antithetical to Christian revelation. To accept the new world of faith in such an atmosphere demanded the creation of an alternative environment that was guided by masters of Christian doctrine and life. Since one could no longer presuppose that the young received the faith from a culture that had previously been somewhat influenced by Christianity, it was necessary to employ a "strenuous type of catechesis."[97]

In the secular environment, a new catechesis and a new evangelization were necessary for the current generation in order to challenge young people and other potential members of the church to believe and to change. A radical conversion was necessary not to separate new Christians from their culture but to get them to see the difference between the demands of the gospel and the allurements of their consumerist culture and then to get them to transform that culture in light of the gospel. In faith one could discover the objectivity, universality, and permanence of what was true, good, and beautiful. Faith helped to discover answers to the yearning of the human soul. *The New World of Faith*, influenced by Vatican II and by more than sixty years of study, called for a response to secular culture that was not that different from Dulles' writings at St. Benedict Center in Boston shortly after he returned from World War II. He was always quite conscious of the radical demands of the gospel, even though his prescriptions for the times shifted periodically. By 2000, he had clearly returned to his 1946 call for a radical distinction between the Christian life of faith and the life of consumerist self-satisfaction. One could see what was new in the new world of faith only with the eyes of faith.

14
INTERPRETING VATICAN II AND THE CHURCH, 1988-2008

DULLES PRODUCED NO NEW systematic study of the church in the 1990s, but he addressed ad hoc ecclesiological issues. The most important of these included the interpretation of Vatican II, the papacy of Pope John Paul II, the nature and functions of the priestly office, and the ordination of women. He continued to employ his models approach to ecclesiology, but he was increasingly aware of the limits of trying to combine "a typological with a systematic approach."[1]

Models in Theology

In the *Craft of Theology* Dulles had dealt with various objections to his use of a models approach to theology.[2] Objections, however, continued to be raised here and there and in private correspondence. Some theologians, notably Joseph Komonchak, critiqued Dulles' models method for its failure to distinguish sufficiently between models and images, his resistance to developing a super-model or a systematic stance that integrates "all that needs to be integrated" in the various models, and his failure to acknowledge that in fact by using universal criteria to examine various models he was implying a methodology that transcended the models approach. Komonchak was also apprehensive about the popular misuse of Dulles' models approach. Some had taken Dulles' criticisms of the institutional model, for example, as a criticism of the institutional church; some had mistaken the five models of the church as five churches; and others had taken the approach to reinforce a general relativism, saying, "Well, that's your model; it's not mine."³ Dulles, of course, was not responsible for the abuses of his method, but the method itself had weaknesses that tended in these directions.

In response to Komonchak, Dulles was most adamant in rejecting the charge of relativism. "To attribute to me the thesis that one cannot go beyond the pluralism of models is totally to misunderstand the book [*Models of the Church*], since the book is one long plea for partisans of different models to recognize the limitations of the models on which they are operating and to open their minds to the values in other models." Dulles' own epistemology, he wrote, was influenced by Henri de Lubac, John Henry Newman, and Michael Polanyi, who contended repeatedly that "the mind is greater than the models that it employs as tools. In its affirmations, the intellect transcends its own images and concepts." Or, as Dulles wrote in another letter, "We can know more than we can say, and say more than we can define," and that is why we can say "that the mind can transcend any one of its models without being able to concoct a supermodel that includes all the insights embodied in all the models." The exchange between the two theologians indicated systematic differences, but in the end Dulles believed that on most major issues "we are probably very close to full agreement."⁴

The popular American tendency to use the models approach to theology received a devastating criticism from the cardinal archbishop of Vienna, Christoph Schönborn. The *Houston Catholic Worker* published Schönborn's critique as "A Time of Desert for Theology." Many English handbooks of theology, he wrote, "use the method of models like a catalog of car models....Choose your model according to your tastes!...The models are presented as a matter of choice, without an organic analysis of the faith. Yet the study of theology is not a question of models, it is a question of truth."⁵

Dulles was very disturbed by this critique because, as he told Schönborn, in the United States Schönborn's criticisms "will be interpreted as a rejection of a method with which I am identified. But I vigorously deny that I am guilty of the deviations you point out. I have constantly attacked relativism and the choice of a model according to one's taste." Dulles went on to suggest that Schönborn explain that he was "targeting an abuse of the method by irresponsible theologians, not a proper use of the method. Your remarks will otherwise be interpreted as a judgment on the method itself, as I have proposed it." Dulles had worked with Schönborn on the International Theological Commission and on the *Catechism*, and he felt free to be frank with the archbishop in defense of his own theological method. The archbishop responded that he did not "attack single theologians and certainly not your person....Be sure that I have not the slightest doubts about the firm orthodoxy of your large theological opus."[6]

Interpreting Vatican II

As we have already seen, Dulles saw himself as one of the interpreters of Vatican II for English-language countries. By the 1990s, he acknowledged that in the early days after the council, he, like other progressive theologians of the period, stressed the discontinuities with the immediate preconciliar period, the need for internal reforms, accommodation to American culture and modern scholarship, a freedom of expression that naturally gave rise to internal pluralism of perspective and opinion, and at the same time, he minimized or overlooked the continuities. In the 1980s and 1990s, after the rise of some radical reform proposals, the loss of an internal sense of unity and tradition, and a splintering of the church into opposing ideological camps, Dulles emphasized Vatican II's continuity with its preconciliar past, the need to focus on the contents of the faith, and the necessity, benefits, and charism of the hierarchical order as a divinely given means for preserving the integrity of revelation itself. In 1987, he wrote that the "theological liberalism of the past two decades is no longer triumphant. Efforts are being made to reread Vatican II in the context of the entire tradition."[7] He opposed in particular the rather "common" but "false" impression that (1) the Vatican Council brought to an end a basic certitude about the doctrines of the church, and that (2) it had "reversed so many strongly held positions that it was difficult to give unquestioning allegiance to what remained."[8]

At times, too, Dulles took issue with the misreading of the council as a transformation of the church "in a democratic direction, introducing constitutional checks and balances."[9] These all-too-popular notions, of course, had a grain of truth to them, but they were one-sided misreadings. The council's decree on religious liberty, for example, did indeed reverse some previous papal positions; the decree itself was promoted by those who argued that religious liberty was consistent with the larger Catholic tradition and part of what John Courtney Murray had called the "growing edge" of the tradition. Blanket statements about Vatican II reversals, however, did not do justice to the continuities that were evident in almost all the conciliar documents.[10]

In the period since the council, there arose a host of conflicting interpretations of its meaning by those who rejected it as well as by those who accepted it. Repeatedly after the 1985 extraordinary International Synod of Bishops, Dulles emphasized what he and some others, notably Cardinal Joseph Ratzinger, called a "hermeneutics of continuity," with admonitions to those who rejected the council and to those who accepted only what was new in the council and minimized or neglected the continuities with the church's previous doctrines. Dulles believed that those who stressed the novelty or the so-called spirit of the council, as he had himself done in the late 1960s, had distorted what the council in fact had accomplished. The council documents were, he insisted, compromise statements that incorporated the older scholastic and manual theology alongside of (or juxtaposed to) statements of the progressive theologians.

The central focus of the council was, as many admitted, the church's self-understanding, and Dulles frequently outlined what he considered the essential elements of that self-understanding. At one point in 1999, in an attempt to counter what he considered compromising interpretations of the council, Dulles delineated the basic teachings of the council, drawing attention to ten conciliar principles that were "unquestionably endorsed by the Council." He contended that

> whoever does not accept all ten of these principles [that is, *aggiornamento*, reformability of the church, renewed attention to Scripture, collegiality, religious freedom, active role of the laity, regional and local variety, ecumenism, dialogue with other religions, and the social

mission of the church]...cannot honestly claim to have accepted the results of the Council.[11]

The council had provided some norms and guidance for the post-conciliar church.

In October 2002, forty years after the opening of the council, Dulles lectured on what he called the "Myth and the Reality of the Council" at Loyola University in New Orleans and at Georgetown University. That lecture, published in *America*,[12] drew a considerable amount of response from the magazine's readers. He outlined two major competing interpretations of the council in its immediate aftermath. One group of interpreters, called "reformers," saw the preconciliar period as tyrannical and obscurantist, and the council as a movement of liberation from such a past. A second group, called "traditionalists," saw the preconciliar period as an idealized lost paradise from which the council had departed. The council documents, however, reflected neither view of the past and in fact were compromise statements including continuity with the past as well as some novelty or innovation. Some of the early reformers (many associated with the journal *Concilium*), however, suggested that the documents of the council contained revolutionary implications that were not apparent on the surface of the documents, believed that the ambiguities in the documents should be resolved in favor of discontinuity, or emphasized what they called the "spirit of the Council."

By the mid-1970s a new school of interpretation emerged—the leading members of which were de Lubac, Hans Urs von Balthasar, Ratzinger (all associated with the new international journal *Communio*), and Pope John Paul II. They preferred a hermeneutics of continuity—that is, that Vatican II was in continuity with other councils (particularly Trent and Vatican I) on substantive doctrinal issues. After 1975, in particular, Dulles thought that Ratzinger, who was a force for the progressives during the council, became increasingly critical of those progressives who wanted to go beyond the council and those conservatives who wanted to retreat behind it—an interpretation very similar to the one Dulles fostered. That school's interpretation of the council was articulated clearly in the 1985 International Synod of Bishops, where the bishops agreed upon six principles for a sound interpretation of the council. Like some others, Dulles agreed that the council "needs to be understood in conformity with the constant teaching of the church. The true spirit of the council is to be found in, and not apart from, the letter."[13]

Dulles' critics asserted in the late 1980s that he had joined the school of retrenchment, but he insisted that he did not want to restore some kind of idealized preconciliar past. He asserted that he found the teaching of Vatican II "very solid, carefully nuanced, and sufficiently flexible to meet the needs of our own time and place."[14] While emphasizing continuity, he did not deny the council's call for reform and change, an emphasis in his earlier years.

In the same issue of *America* where Dulles had presented his interpretation of Vatican II, John O'Malley, SJ, a professor of church history at Weston Jesuit School of Theology in Cambridge, Massachusetts, offered an alternative view of the council, focusing on what he called Vatican II's "significant break with the past." O'Malley argued that the radical nature of the council had not been fully accepted or understood, and "for all its continuity with previous councils," Vatican II "was unique in many ways but nowhere more than in its call for an across-the-board change in church procedures or, better, in church *style*."[15]

These two very different assessments of the council evoked from readers some angry and some substantive responses, most of whom took issue with Dulles' approach. A few saw Dulles' article as a Vatican-like retrenchment or a "defense of conservative Catholicism's interpretation" or a "distressing and depressing" caricature of the misinterpretations of the council. Others, though, focused on what they considered Dulles' excessively restrictive interpretation of *Lumen gentium*'s *subsistit in* (LG 8). Dulles had argued that when Vatican II said that the church of Christ subsisted in (*subsistit in*) the Catholic Church, it did not mean that the church of Christ was "wider and more inclusive" than the Roman Catholic communion as some seemed to have interpreted it. He agreed with Cardinal Ratzinger's view that because the church of Christ subsisted in the Roman Catholic Church, it could not subsist anywhere else.[16] Fellow Jesuit theologian Francis Sullivan suggested a slightly different interpretation, asserting that *subsistit* needed to be understood within the context of the entire council and in light of subsequent declarations from the Vatican's Congregation for the Doctrine of the Faith (CDF). He argued that *subsistit* was accurately translated as "to continue to exist" and thus, following *Dominus Iesus*, he explained that Vatican II declared that the church of Christ "continues to exist fully only in the Catholic Church." By this translation, he maintained that Vatican II wanted to recognize "that the universal church of Christ is wider and more inclusive than the Roman Catholic Church."[17]

Dulles continued to argue in other places that *subsistit in* meant "to remain present in its substantial completeness." In classical metaphysics, it meant "full and substantial existence." By using *subsistit in* to describe the relationship between the church of Christ and the Catholic Church, the council was in fact in continuity with *Mystici corporis* and *Humani generis*, which held that the "Mystical Body of Jesus Christ and the Roman Catholic Church are one and the same thing."[18] Vatican II continued this tradition while simultaneously developing it in light of a sacramental ecclesiology that acknowledged the presence of ecclesial elements outside the Catholic Church that were impelled toward Catholic unity. Dulles found confirmation for this interpretation in a study by Alexandra von Teuffenbach. This study modified Dulles' earlier hermeneutic of discontinuity where he contrasted Vatican II's *subsistit* with *Mystici corporis*'s identification of the church of Christ with the Catholic Church. As we have seen, he emphasized in his earlier career that *subsistit* meant that the church of Christ was not exclusively identified with the Catholic Church.[19] Teuffenbach's study helped him modify his position. She had done an extensive examination of the various drafts of *Lumen gentium* (8) and concluded, in Dulles' paraphrase, that

> in the penultimate draft the Constitution had said simply that the Church of Christ was present in (*adest in*) the Catholic Church. The members of the Doctrinal Commission considered this affirmation too weak; some wanted to go back to an earlier "*est*," which had been dropped because it seemed to exclude the presence of ecclesial elements elsewhere. Sebastian Tromp, as

Secretary, proposed substituting "subsistit in," and this suggestion gained general approval. It is unthinkable that Tromp, who had adamantly defended the doctrine of *Mystici corporis*, would have proposed a term that in his judgment contradicted that encyclical.[20]

Dulles concluded, therefore, that the "Church as sacrament exists fully in the Catholic Church and no where else. But the sacrament is imperfectly realized in other Christian communions, in different degrees and modalities."[21]

The exchanges between theologians on *subsistit in* did not solve the problem of interpreting Vatican II. A popular journal of opinion like *America* was not the place for substantive argumentation, but, in fact, the debate over continuity and discontinuity, letter and spirit, continued in *America*[22] throughout the first decade of the twenty-first century. Neither O'Malley nor Dulles denied the presence of continuity and discontinuity or the importance of paying attention to the letter and spirit (or style) of the council. But in terms of emphases, they agreed to disagree.

Ecclesiological Issues

The Papacy

The papacy became one of the significant ecclesiological issues in the postconciliar period. We have already seen the ecumenical dimensions of that issue in the Lutheran/Catholic Dialogue. The papacy and especially the papacy of John Paul II received wide attention in the world press and became something of a source of internal Catholic contention in the 1980s and 1990s. As a world traveler and super-evangelist, John Paul II had attracted large audiences wherever he went, proclaiming the gospel and a message of hope and moral regeneration, one that at times countered popular opinions. His periodic youth days, celebrated in different countries, drew significant numbers of young people to listen to his message. His papacy, though, was variously interpreted within the Catholic community. Some progressive theologians and journalists interpreted it as a return to preconciliar authoritarianism and a reversal of the advances made by the Second Vatican Council. His papacy was perceived as a turn to the right, a theological and ecclesial movement analogous to the political leanings of Margaret Thatcher in England and Ronald Reagan in the United States.[23] On the other hand, for neoconservatives like George Weigel, the pope was "the most compelling public figure in the world, the man with arguably the most coherent and comprehensive vision of the human possibility in the world ahead."[24] For still others, particularly George A. Kelly, a sociologist priest and founder of the Fellowship of Catholic Scholars, John Paul II's papacy was the right medicine needed to heal the diseased American Catholic body, broken apart by postconciliar liberal and progressive theologians and bishops who had undermined the church's tradition.[25]

Dulles, in the camp of the postconciliar progressive theologians, had on occasion criticized decisions emanating from the papacies of Paul VI and John Paul II, but he was by no means a persistent and inveterate critic of the postconciliar papacy. Nor did he side with those who believed that a rigorous exercise of ecclesial authority and the enactment of more stringent rules and regulations was the right medicine to heal the wounds that afflicted the contemporary church. By the 1990s, though, he was becoming more and more concerned that continual and vigorous criticisms of Roman and papal decisions were contributing to the breakdown of ecclesial and doctrinal unity.

Dulles reminded Jesuits, especially young Jesuits, that Ignatius of Loyola's "Rules for Thinking with the Church" called for obedience to the church, devotion to the papacy, and trust in papal guidance.[26] He was well aware that the emphasis on obedience to the papacy was countercultural in American society; however, he was not speaking of obedience as abject intellectual slavery but a commitment that flowed from faith and that acknowledged a presumption in favor of divinely guided authority within the church.

Thinking with the church was a Jesuit charism in Dulles' mind, and he demonstrated this in his admiration of the Jesuit theologian Robert Bellarmine (1542–1621), a doctor of the church and "patron of my own studies," whose given name Dulles took as his confirmation name. Bellarmine lived in a time of confusion and crisis, and in the midst of his times, he was a "model of moderation and rationality, open to new developments but deeply attached to the Catholic heritage." Dulles focused on Bellarmine's virtue of loyalty. According to Dulles, Bellarmine "did what was asked of him; he spoke frankly when consulted, but he never urged his own opinions to the detriment of the church itself. He was loyal to his religious order, loyal to the Holy See, loyal to the church, and loyal especially to God, in whom he placed all his trust and confidence."[27] What Dulles admired in Bellarmine he emulated in his own life, and this was especially evident in the 1990s, as Dulles became the leading American theological exponent and interpreter of John Paul II's papacy and his theological and ecclesial vision.

In the course of the 1990s, Dulles became a supporter of John Paul II's papacy at a time when some in the American Catholic theological community considered his papacy a disaster. Unlike some theologians, Dulles did not interpret John Paul II's papacy as part of a restorationist movement, because the pope saw Vatican II as a providential preparation for the church as it moved toward the third millennium.[28] Dulles conceived of John Paul II as an authentic interpreter of Vatican II, in line with his predecessors Paul VI and John XXIII, but Dulles also perceived John Paul II's papacy as a necessary corrective or remedy for the spiritual and intellectual disorder that distressed the postconciliar church.

Dulles devoted much energy and attention to explicating the thought of Pope John Paul II in the late twentieth and early twenty-first centuries. He treated the pope as a philosopher and a theologian and considered him and Cardinal Joseph Ratzinger, as he once noted, the "intellectual equals of any other religious thinkers of our day."[29] According to Dulles, John Paul II was "in the view of many competent observers, the preeminent religious and moral leader of the world in our day." The pope provided "more than any other theologian…a brilliant and comprehensive restatement of Catholic doctrine in which the teaching of the council is expounded in relation to the contemporary world situation."[30] He was not only the preeminent articulator of the "new evangelization" but also the "leading evangelizer in our day" and the "model of evangelization." He presented his message, even when it went against contemporary trends, "so winsomely" that it made a deep impression. "His intellectual brilliance, his mastery of languages, and his skill in handling the mass media all contributed to his success" in his visits to the United States and other places around the world.[31]

From 1990 to 2000, Dulles wrote more than twenty articles and published a book on the pope's thought. In 1996, as a visiting scholar at St. Joseph's Seminary in Yonkers, New York, Dulles gave a series of lectures on the pope's theology, and those who heard the lectures suggested that he develop them into a book for wider distribution. *The Splendor of Faith: The Theological Vision of Pope John Paul II* (1999, revised in 2003), which incorporated some of Dulles' previous lectures and articles, systematically laid out the unity, coherence, and structure of the pope's theological vision, from his understanding of the triune God to his views of history and eschatology. The new evangelization provided a hermeneutical key for Dulles' interpretation of the pope's thought. The book reflected Dulles' clarity and synthetic skills in putting the pope's theology, articulated in numerous ad hoc philosophical, theological, pastoral, and papal publications, into an integrated framework that one usually finds in systematic summas or textbooks. It was a constructive exposition of the pope's theology as well as a theological synthesis and interpretation. The pope had neither the theological erudition of theologians like Henri de Lubac or Yves Congar, nor the speculative acumen of a Karl Rahner, but like the patristic episcopal theologians (for example, Gregory of Nyssa, Ambrose, Augustine) and other doctors of the church, he fashioned a theology that communicated the life and experience of the Christian tradition in a modern idiom to large audiences who were not technical theologians. Formed in the crucible of Nazi occupation and communist regimes, John Paul II knew that Christian theology served the real aspirations of human persons in need of faith, hope, love, mercy, and justice.

Dulles, like many other commentators, emphasized the pope's "metaphysical personalism" and Christian or christocentric humanism as other keys for unlocking the pope's thought.[32] Combining the metaphysical realism of Aristotle and Aquinas, Max Scheler's phenomenology of human experience, the philosophy of Maurice Blondel, and the emphasis on the dignity and destiny of the human person in the scriptures, the pope had constructed an integral view of the subjectivity, freedom, and solidarity of the human person that transcended both subjectivism and objectivism. The pope used reason and revelation together to construct a personalism that undergirded his understanding of the Trinity, Christology and Mariology, the church, the experiences of sin and human suffering and redemption, religion and culture, Catholic social thought, the political order, ecumenism and interreligious dialogue, and eschatology and history.

After examining the key areas of this thought (which are impossible to summarize in the space allotted to a biography), Dulles concluded that the pope's contribution lay primarily in the area of pastoral leadership. He addressed numerous current devotional and practical issues in the church and in the world, expounding clearly and systematically the fundamental doctrines of the church following the agenda of Vatican II, interpreted in the light of "the perennial Catholic tradition" and his "personalist phenomenology." In doing all this, moreover, the pope avoided "technical disquisitions on the fine points of speculative theology" and refrained from settling open questions that were "legitimately disputed in the [various theological] schools."[33]

In 1995 the pope published *Ut unum sint*, an encyclical on ecumenism. In it he acknowledged that the papacy was an ecumenical problem impeding fuller unity among Christians and invited those inside and outside of the Catholic Church to find ways of exercising papal primacy so that the papacy could better serve the unity of the church. In response, a host of suggestions and reform proposals came forth in the American Catholic community as well as elsewhere in the world. One of the major responses came from the retired archbishop of San Francisco and past president of the National Conference of Catholic Bishops, John R. Quinn. In June 1996, he delivered a lecture at Campion Hall, Oxford, on the relationship between the pope and the bishops, offering some acute assessments of the current situation in the church and some bold proposals for the reform of the papacy.[34]

On three different occasions, Dulles reviewed various Catholic proposals for the reform of the exercise of the papal office and argued that the new global situation demanded more, not less, emphasis on papal primacy.[35] Quinn's proposals and those of others boiled down to a recommendation for a more collegial exercise of the primacy by implementing in practice the principles of subsidiarity and inculturation. By allowing a certain legitimate autonomy to episcopal conferences, a deliberative vote to the International Synod of Bishops, and local or regional elections of bishops, and by a more thorough reform of the curia and restructuring of the College of Cardinals, Quinn and others thought that collegiality could be more clearly manifested in the church. Although Dulles believed that some of the critiques of current Vatican practices were not entirely unwarranted and some of the proposals merited careful consideration, he was hesitant in the end to give his full support to any of the proposals because he did not see how they could safeguard the truth of revelation and the unity of the church.[36] Dulles' hesitancy to give full support to the critiques of centralization and the advocacy of more regional and local diversity stemmed from his own assessment of what he called "The Papacy for a Global Church."

The centrifugal pull of many of the proposals, he believed, was at odds with the new global world order created by the mass media and instant communications across the world. What the new situation demanded was more emphasis upon the papacy's capacity to maintain and promote the church's universal unity in doctrine, worship, and governance while supporting the need for regional and local adaptations for the incarnation of the gospel. He did not fear, as he believed some did, that the papacy had become too active and powerful. On the contrary, he asserted that "in our electronic age, when information travels with the speed of light, global authority is more important than ever....Rome cannot wait silently while doctrinal issues are debated on the local level, as it might have done when communications were slow and transportation was difficult." He was not calling for a return to the pre–Vatican II situation but for a new way for the church to enter the globalized universe. The legitimate Vatican II emphases on inculturation, collegiality, and local diversity enabled the church to meet the needs of the new global circumstances, but he wanted to maintain a balance between the centrifugal and centripetal forces in the church and believed that the new post–Vatican II situation placed greater burdens upon the Roman center to simultaneously protect legitimate differences and make sure the differences contributed to unity.[37]

Ladislas Orsy, a Jesuit canon lawyer, reviewed what he called Dulles' "partial" assessment of the current situation. The church was strong at its center, as Dulles indicated, but weak at its "provinces," Orsy argued. All was not well in the "provinces," and part of the reason for such a state of affairs was the "unduly restrictive nature of several legal provisions" that emanated from the Roman center, a situation that Dulles had neglected to describe.[38] Orsy's disagreement with Dulles was not about faith or the doctrine of the papal office but about its relationship to the particular churches and its exercise of authority. In this respect the two men read the signs of the times in very different ways and thus came to different conclusions about the remedies needed for the ills of the times.

Dulles saw the ills in terms of the doctrinal confusion and excessive accommodations in the postconciliar period that demanded a firm and decisive exercise of the papal office for the sake of protecting the truth of revelation. Orsy emphasized the restrictive nature of postconciliar papal and Roman declarations (for example, canonical regulations that restricted the freedom of bishops in episcopal conferences, the purely consultative nature of the Roman synod of bishops, the 1989 extended profession of faith required for ordination or for an ecclesiastical office and the oath of fidelity) that tended to weaken the local churches and put too high a premium on conformity and uniformity. Such papal and Roman decisions, he thought, had a negative impact on the ecumenical movement. By neglecting to deal with these troublesome exercises of the papal office, he maintained that Dulles' argument for a strong papacy in the new global context, which Orsy did not deny, had simply turned out to be a piece of advocacy that implied that no reforms of the papal office were currently needed. Orsy saw such a view as an unrealistic assessment of the current situation in the church.[39]

Dulles did not back down from his own reading of the times. In response to Orsy's critique, he reaffirmed his earlier position, noting that he was critiquing some Catholic reform proposals "that did not take sufficient account of the new situation of the church in a global age dominated by electronic communications." This situation put "new demands on the papal office as well as on regional and diocesan churches within the Catholic community." The postconciliar emphases on inculturation and regional diversity required "a stronger office of unity to prevent mutual alienation among Catholics of different regions." Dulles did not oppose changes in the church, he insisted, but he wanted to "make sure that the change is for the better." Orsy, too, did not back down. He thought the new situation of globalization should not be the occasion for the papacy to copy the ways of the multinational corporations in governing the church.[40] The exchange between the two Jesuits reflected the divergent assessments of the times within the larger American Catholic communion.

In the 1990s, Dulles carried a torch for a papacy that was very much under fire in American Catholic theological circles. He was trying, *agere contra*, to bring about a balanced perspective by emphasizing the positive contributions of John Paul II's papacy. It had attracted many converts from the intellectual class, and it had received a sympathetic response from many outside the Catholic Church even while it had become a barrier to Christian unity among many others. Many outside the Catholic Church, of course, had rejected Vatican I's and Vatican II's doctrine of the papacy, and thus the exercise of the papacy was not the crucial issue for them. Dulles was trying to be realistic about the papacy's concrete ecumenical possibilities.

The Universal and the Local Church

Dulles' theological support for the papacy came out repeatedly in debates over the relationship between the universal and the local church and in his post–Lutheran-Catholic ecumenical reflections on the role of the papacy in the universal church.[41] In April 2001, *America* published an article by the German theologian and bishop Walter Kasper that focused on his debate with Joseph Ratzinger on the relationship between the local and the universal church.[42] The debate reflected theological concerns in Germany and other places about the excessive centralization initiatives in the Vatican.[43] As bishop of Rottenburg-Stuttgart, Kasper, sensitive to the practical pastoral needs and practices of the local churches (for example, Communion for divorced and remarried Catholics and eucharistic sharing with those outside of the Catholic Church), saw

Roman prohibitions against such pastoral practices as excessively juridical and tending toward a postconciliar centralization that he considered unhealthy for the church. For Kasper the universal church existed, as he believed the Second Vatican Council held, "in and from" the local churches.⁴⁴ Ratzinger accepted the conciliar phrase but took issue with Kasper's position by emphasizing, as he had done in the CDF's "Letter to the Bishops of the Catholic Church on Some Aspects of the Church Understood as Communion" (1992), that "in its essential mystery, the universal church is a reality ontologically and temporally prior to every individual church."⁴⁵ In this Ratzinger was countering certain theologians who had been emphasizing the primacy of the local church over the universal church. That emphasis was not Kasper's, but Kasper did not agree with Ratzinger's position on the ontological priority of the universal church. The debate over the relationship between the local and the universal church was not confined to Germany. Some theologians and bishops in the United States periodically spoke out about what they considered the excessive tendencies to centralization emanating from Rome during the papacy of John Paul II.

Dulles weighed in on the issue periodically in the early twenty-first century. Like Ratzinger, Kasper, other theologians, and the Second Vatican Council, Dulles emphasized the theological importance of the local church. Even though the council made an advance by resurrecting the significance of the local church as the locus and instantiation of the universal church, the local was not identified with the universal. Dulles sided with Ratzinger in emphasizing the priority of the universal over the local church by arguing for a bishop's prior identification with the College of Bishops (who shared responsibility for the universal church) over his identification with a particular or diocesan church. A bishop was first a member of the College of Bishops before he became head of a local church.⁴⁶ "The ontological priority of the church universal appears to me to be almost self-evident, since the very concept of a particular church presupposes a universal church to which it belongs, whereas the concept of the universal church does not imply that it is made up of distinct particular churches."⁴⁷ Dulles made it clear in another article that even though he shared

Ratzinger's view of the primacy of the universal church, he did not argue for that primacy on the basis of "the patristic idea that the universal church precedes creation" as Ratzinger did.[48]

Dulles objected to Kasper's particular emphasis on the local church and his pastoral grievances about Vatican restrictions regulating eucharistic hospitality because in Dulles' view, the Vatican needed to protect the nature of the Eucharist as a sacrament of unity and of communion.[49] While Dulles admitted the need for adaptation and accommodation and freedom in the local church, he was hesitant to give any priority to the local church because of his view of the excessive contemporary tendency to localism, freedom, and diversity at the expense of universal unity and communion. For him, the local church existed always within the context and communion of the universal church. His *agere contra* mentality once again came to the fore as he sided with Ratzinger against certain prevailing tendencies he saw in the American Catholic community.

Dulles reiterated his position on the relationship between the local and the universal church in a talk he gave in Paderborn, Germany. He argued that the decentralizing reformers, who identified themselves as progressive, were in fact, "restorationists" who were proposing reforms appropriate for the primitive period of the church's history. The real progressives, those most in tune with the currents of a more global culture, were those who realized the times had changed and required more than ever before an emphasis on the universal church and the primacy of the papal office to meet the needs of an emerging global culture that demanded strong vigilance for the unity of the faith and of communion.[50]

Dulles was conversant with the debates on subsidiarity and inculturation and acknowledged that they had not been satisfactorily resolved within the church. Although he acknowledged the necessity and value of inculturation, for example, he preferred the contemporary papal emphasis on evangelization over inculturation. That preference arose from his own assessment that inculturation could and at times did lead to excesses that undermined the significance of the universal church. Those dangers were evident in the United States, where the national spirit of independence made some susceptible to an "anti-Roman complex," which resented Roman control and regarded it "as undue interference, forgetting that the Pope has ordinary responsibility for the life of the Church in every nation." An excessive degree of inculturation was evident, too, in some Protestant and Anglican churches in the United States that had become so "thoroughly Americanized that they retained very little capacity to challenge the culture."[51] In the early twenty-first century, Dulles believed the pendulum had swung too far in the direction of accommodation, and what was needed was a more thorough evangelization of the local churches. He believed that the Catholic Church, precisely because of the Petrine office and its hierarchical government, had the capacity to "stand as a sign of contradiction. No other church has comparable universality." That countercultural potential, in fact, was one of the things that originally attracted him to Catholicism, and it continued to attract contemporary converts.[52] Thus, Dulles' emphasis upon the primacy of the universal church was grounded theologically, culturally, and experientially.

The universal church was particularly manifested in the local eucharistic community, but some theologians, the Russian Orthodox Nicholas Afanassieff in particular, had, in Dulles' view, so emphasized the idea that the church was fully realized in the eucharistic worshiping community that there was no theological justification or need for ecclesiastical superstructures. Afanassieff and other theologians exaggerated the fullness or catholicity of the local church and neglected the fact that the eucharistic celebration had an inner catholicity that identified the local community with the body of Christ, which indeed transcended the local community. The eucharistic prayers themselves, moreover, pointed to the fact that the Eucharist was celebrated in union with the whole body of bishops and the pope. The universal was present in the local, but the totality of the church, Dulles argued, was not identified with the local church.[53]

Dulles continued to argue for the importance of papal primacy during a talk at the University of Salford (Salford, England) in 2002. He examined various ecumenical statements on papal primacy, maintaining that the Petrine office is "a gift held in trust for all churches and all Christians." Popes Paul VI and John Paul II had from 1967 to 1995 clearly acknowledged that the papacy was one of the "gravest obstacles" to the church's unity. Since the end of Vatican II, great strides were made in acknowledging the need for unity in the church and the role the Petrine function had played, or might play in the future, in articulating and maintaining that unity.[54]

In 2002 no consensus existed among the churches on papal primacy. While acknowledging the ecumenical problem the papacy presented and the proposals for the reform of the papacy, Dulles affirmed that the Catholic acceptance of "papal primacy must depend on a decision of faith." The papacy for him remained a gift of the Holy Spirit to the church and the churches: "We cannot rigorously prove the truth of the pope's utterances. Nor can we control what the pope will teach or do in the future." In the end Catholics accepted the papacy in faith and that act of acceptance demanded a "renunciation of private judgment, trust in duly appointed superiors and a will to solidarity with the larger community." In ecumenical dialogues Catholics needed to give witness confidently to the "symbolic and effective value of papal primacy" for the sake of Christian unity.[55] Dulles was well aware of the historical, theological, and practical problems presented by the papacy, but he was also aware that the papacy had served the cause of Christian unity in the past, and without it in the future he could not see how the cause of Christian unity could progress.

Although Dulles emphasized papal primacy in his later years, he did not neglect the role of the episcopacy, national episcopal conferences and collegiality. Since the late 1960s, Dulles had a long-standing relationship with the United States Catholic Conference of Bishops and with numerous individual American bishops. He served as theological advisory for many of their statements and gave individual bishops advice when they sought him out. He had a deep respect for the episcopal office and for the persons and capacities of bishops he knew personally. Contact with the American bishops and with others in Rome and elsewhere surely contributed to his high, apostolic view of the episcopate. Like Newman, Dulles recognized that the apostolic authority of the bishops rested not in individuals but in the College of Bishops, and like Vatican II, he acknowledged the individual bishop's priestly, prophetic, and regal functions (unlike Newman, who assigned these functions to different persons) within the church. Like Newman, however, he never doubted the divine institution of the episcopacy and the bishops' responsibility for defining obligatory doctrine and prescribing right conduct.[56] He supported the postconciliar establishment and role of national episcopal conferences, but he was critical of those who sought to interpret episcopal collegiality in a democratic way or who sought to magnify the authority of local episcopal conferences or the International Synod of Bishops.[57] He saw the postconciliar conferences and the synods as valuable pastoral and consultative bodies but not deliberative ones for defining doctrine.

Vatican II, unlike Vatican I, had spelled out the principle of collegiality, and Dulles followed Vatican II in this respect while acknowledging continuity with Vatican I's emphasis on primacy. The problem was trying to establish the relationship between the primacy of the pope within the College of Bishops, because both the pope and the College of Bishops shared the same identical full and supreme power. In the course of history, that relationship has been interpreted, Dulles asserted following Congar, in three different ways: the monarchical, the collegial, and the theory of "two inadequately distinct subjects." Dulles seems to have preferred the third theory of that relationship. The third theory held that the pope could act either extracollegially (as the monarchical position emphasized) or collegially (as the collegial position maintained). The third view acknowledged the benefits of the other two positions while not being so exclusive as to minimize the authority of the College of Bishops or to deny the independence of the pope. In any of these positions, though, Dulles admitted, the College of Bishops "is inseparable from the Pope because it includes him as a member and indeed its chief member." Some theologians and bishops complained that the idea of collegiality had been severely limited in practice in the post–Vatican II era by the popes' exercise of primatial ministry independent of consultation with the College of Bishops. Dulles did not see it that way. The postconciliar popes exercised their office "consistent with Vatican II's teaching on collegiality," which understood the "dialectical relationship" between the pope and the College of Bishops.[58]

The Priesthood

Another ecclesiological issue that Dulles tackled in the late twentieth and early twenty-first centuries was that of the priesthood, and particularly the ordination of women. He taught periodically at the Gregorian seminary in Rome and at the New York diocesan seminary, and he delivered keynote addresses and several lectures to various groups of priests on the theology, identity, and mission of the priesthood.[59] The decline in the number of clergy, the pedophilia scandals, and the advocacy for the ordination of women created the need for a rejuvenated theology of the priesthood, and Dulles prepared essays on the subject, emphasizing, as in other cases, his theological continuity with the church's long tradition on the priesthood and demonstrating, in continuity with Trent and Vatican II, a theology of the priesthood that was at once traditional, pertinent to the needs of the church in the twenty-first century, and countercultural.

Dulles' *Models of the Church* (1974) had examined "Ecclesiology and Ministry."[60] By the 1990s, his terminological shift from "ministry" to "priesthood" indicated something of a transformed emphasis in his approach. Although he did not deny the multiple functions of ministry within the church, he, like Pope John Paul II, reemphasized the sacerdotal office and the public functions (preaching, eucharistic celebration, and pastoral leadership) that flowed from that ordained office within the church.

Some of Dulles' major lectures on the priesthood, collected in *The Priestly Office* (1997), reflected his negative and positive assessments of many postconciliar theological reinterpretations of the priesthood, but they also emphasized those elements in the traditional view of the priesthood that were reiterated at the Second Vatican Council and tended to be minimized or rejected by some in the postconciliar church. In a sense he was again calling for an understanding of the continuity of the Second Vatican Council with previous church teachings as well as an understanding of newer theological reformulations.

Dulles believed that some in the church had misread or read out of context what the Second Vatican Council had proclaimed about the priesthood. The council had indeed emphasized the multiple functions of the priest (as preacher, teacher, pastoral governor, and fellow witness with the laity) instead of focusing almost exclusively on the priest's cultic role, which had been the emphasis in the most recent pre–Vatican II Catholic tradition. But after the council some priests and some theologians, believing that the priesthood had become too exclusively cultic and isolated from secular life, sought to update the priesthood by accommodating it to the modern world, which in effect meant to secularize or demythologize the cultic priesthood, bringing about a decline of the cultic dimension that was so much a part of the church's continuous tradition.[61] Some postconciliar progressive theologians, moreover, trying to advance beyond Vatican II, sought to escape from what they called the "medieval fabrication" of a priestly character that distinguished ordained priests from the baptized laity, and in the process some of them emphasized almost exclusively a functional view of the priesthood that distinguished priests from laity only in the functions they served within the church. Some, too, went so far as to hold that, in emergency situations the congregation or local community could ordain a priest to serve them.[62]

Dulles was well aware that there were many and complex causes for the so-called crisis of the priesthood in Western Europe and North America, but one cause was the "uncertainty about the role and identity of the priest arising from the introduction of new theological paradigms."[63] Hans Küng's *Why Priests?* (1972), which called for the abolition of the term *priest* when applied to ministers, Edward Schillebeeckx's *Ministry: Leadership in the Community of Jesus Christ* (1981), which also rejected the ontological understanding of the priestly character,[64] and other more radical theological attempts either to reject the concept of a ministerial priesthood or to redefine it in ways that scarcely distinguished it from concepts of ministry in Protestant Congregationalism had led in part to a confusion in priestly identity.

Dulles found these views inconsistent with the Catholic tradition on the priesthood, and he sought to restore some balance. In 1990, he constructed five models of the ministerial priesthood that corresponded to his five models of the church: the clerical or authoritative leader model (corresponding to the institutional model of the church); pastoral or community builder (communal); sacramental or cultic figure (sacramental); herald or evangelical preacher (herald);and servant or promoter of peace and justice in society (servant). The Second Vatican Council wanted to go beyond the previous neo-scholastic emphasis on the cultic priesthood. Part of the reason for the crisis in priestly identity in the postconciliar period was that "many functions that did not seem to require ordination were now attributed to the priest as such." In order to get beyond the limits of functionalism, Dulles proposed a "representational" model that emphasized an "ontology of the priesthood." Through ordination the priest became a sign of Christ's presence in the church. Christ gave his priest authority to represent him and to speak and act in his name. The sacramental identification with Christ through ordination made it possible for the priest to act upon and live out the grace conferred in the sacrament. The sacramental approach provided a basis for the five ministerial functions Dulles had identified.[65]

Vatican II was in fundamental continuity with Trent on this sacramental view of the priesthood even though it developed the tradition beyond Trent's concerns. Vatican II put the cultic in conjunction with the prophetic and regal dimensions of the priesthood, but it did not diminish the priestly or cultic dimension. Dulles argued that the council was clear about the centrality of the eucharistic celebration in the church's life, and "at its heart," therefore, the priest's role was cultic, and it was not just one of many functions; in fact, the priest's other functions took on their full significance only where the priority of the Eucharist and the cultic was acknowledged.[66]

Dulles' many lectures stressed the important point that the office of the priesthood, that by which the priest was sacramentally configured to Christ in a special way, preceded and gave direction to the priest's public functions of preaching, sacramental celebrations, and pastoral governance and leadership. Dulles emphasized that

> the Thomistic concept of configuration to Christ through sacramental ordination illuminates the representative role of the priest. Through the sacrament of ordination the priest is enabled to share in a specific way in the many-faceted work of mediation by which Christ accomplished our redemption. By reason of his public persona, the priest is par excellence the man of God and of the church.[67]

This view was consistent, he argued throughout, with the biblical witness, the church's tradition, and the documents of Vatican II.

And in his mind it countered the all-too-widespread or exclusive emphasis on a merely functional ministry. The sacramental dimension of the priest's configuration to Christ, though, Dulles argued in conjunction with his own personalism, needed to be complemented by a life of holiness. "Unless a high level of holiness is achieved, it will not be possible to preach and teach effectively, to preside fruitfully over the worship of the community, or to direct the people of God toward its appointed goal."[68]

Dulles wanted to reemphasize, in continuity with Trent and Vatican II, the nature of the priestly character that was conferred by ordination. By ordination the priest acted *in persona Christi*, participating ontologically in the priesthood of Christ. The priestly character was no mere medieval fabrication but a Catholic doctrine that reinforced the essential difference between the ordained ministry and the laity with respect to the celebration of the Eucharist. In continuity with *Lumen gentium* (10), Dulles reasserted the church's teaching that the common priesthood of the faithful and the hierarchical priesthood differed from one another "in essence and not only in degree."[69]

Dulles also exercised an *agere contra* stance against those who he thought were trying to clericalize the laity, as some had tried to secularize the priesthood. Over and over he emphasized the universal call to holiness, as had Vatican II, while emphasizing, as had the council (LG 31, 33), that the laity's role was indeed that of exercising their priestly, prophetic, and regal baptismal offices in their families and in their attempts to transform the secular world in accord with gospel principles. Nonetheless, he believed the laity could and should play a significant role within the church, and that when they did that, they could properly be called "ministers" of the gospel. Some in the church objected to the term *lay ministers*, believing that the term *ministry* should be applied only to ordained priests or members of the hierarchy. Emphasizing lay ministry, some thought, obscured the laity's proper secular mission. Dulles did not buy that argument and in fact argued that the term *lay ministry* was consistent with the New Testament (*diakonia* in Greek, *ministerium* in Latin), the tradition, and the writings of Pope John Paul II. *Ministry* had very wide connotations and referred to a variety of services within the Christian community and to the world.

Dulles, moreover, did not want to draw too sharp a distinction between ministry in the church and mission to the world. The laity were ordained by their baptism and their call to holiness and discipleship to become involved in both dimensions of ministry. He lamented, though, that Vatican II's hope for the laity's mission to transform the world of politics and culture was "largely unfulfilled."[70]

Time and again Dulles stressed the countercultural nature of the Catholic priesthood. He told a group of priests in Fort Wayne, Indiana, in 1998 that "there is an opposition between the traditional Catholic concept of priesthood and the prevalent mentality of our day, as we experience it in western Europe and North America." By that he meant that the traditional Catholic concept of the priesthood clashed in ten major ways with the prevalent spirit of the times: (1) the idea of mediation of priests clashed with egalitarianism; (2) sacrifice with the decline in the sense of sin as an offense to God; (3) divine vocation with equal opportunity; (4) sacred hierarchical powers with a democratic culture; (5) limitation to men with equal opportunity for women; (6) priestly character configured to Christ with the empirical and pragmatic mentality; (7) permanent indelible character with social mobility and the exchange of roles and missions; (8) ecclesial office and fidelity to the church with perceptions of conformism; (9) evangelical counsels with a self-indulgent and consumerist society; and (10) pursuit of holiness with an American utilitarianism. Dulles argued that the "survival and vigor of the Catholic priesthood requires strong confidence in the Church's distinctive heritage and a healthy suspicion of the axioms of secular modernity." In fact, the whole church "must be motivated to oppose the reigning ethos in order to evangelize our culture. This countercultural posture is especially incumbent on priests as sacramentally ordained leaders."[71]

Ordination of Women

The ordination of women to the priesthood in the Catholic Church had been discussed here and there in American Catholicism since at least 1965, became more broadly advocated in the 1970s, and became a hot topic in the 1990s. The Vatican prohibitions against the ordination of women to the priesthood (*Inter insigniores* in 1976 and *Ordinatio sacerdotalis* in 1994), like Pope Paul VI's 1968 encyclical *Humanae vitae* against artificial birth control, raised a storm of protests in certain segments of the American Catholic community. Dulles had been relatively removed from the 1968 internal public protests on birth control.

Gradually Dulles became significantly involved in the ecclesiological controversy over the ordination of women. In 1976, the Detroit Call to Action conference recommended the ordination of women in the Catholic Church. Dulles, a participant, responded to a reporter's question on the issue with characteristic academic reserve. It needed to be investigated, he observed, to determine whether or not the ordination of men only was a culturally and historically conditioned part of the church's tradition that could be changed.[72] Even after the publication of *Inter insigniores* (October 15, 1976), Dulles told a correspondent in a private letter that the reasons against ordination were mostly "sociological and psychological" not theological.[73] In another letter in 1983, he told a correspondent that he was waiting for the right moment to address the issue. "At present the atmosphere is so charged that a defense of either [women's ordination or a married clergy] could appear to be provocative, and just make the situation worse." He was in favor of letting the matter of ordination evolve gradually. Besides that, he reported, "my own mind is not all that clear on the subject."[74] Dulles considered *Insigniores* a declaration, not a decree, as he told another correspondent in 1986. Decrees decide something previously undecided, while declarations simply reiterate what was previously taught. He believed, though, that Rome would not be satisfied if a theologian asserted, after such a declaration, that the ordination of women continued to be an open question, but he did not reveal at the time where he stood on the issue.[75] To a correspondent in 1993, Dulles summarized the converging arguments (from scripture, tradition, and "representational symbolism") that the CDF and the magisterium had used to limit ordination to men, but then indicated that "no dogmatic declaration regarding the impossibility of ordaining women has been made."[76]

After the 1994 publication of *Ordinatio sacerdotalis*, and in opposition to the public outcry against it, Dulles argued in seven explicit essays that the limitation of ordination to men only was not in fact simply a historically conditioned part of the tradition. The church had grounds in Christ's will, in the scripture, and in tradition and theology to declare that it had no authority to change.[77] These essays differed considerably from his earlier uncommitted or uncertain stance, but they were consistent with his views of magisterial authority. He became after 1994 a forceful, articulate supporter of the Vatican position and perceived *Ordinatio* as "definitive" church teaching.

Dulles' responses to *Ordinatio* and the reactions that followed were part of his emphasis on the church's continuity with its tradition. Almost as soon as the apostolic letter was published, Dulles supported it and declared that the teaching was irreversible Catholic teaching to be definitively held, and, therefore, theologians, "I would judge, are no longer free to advocate opposed positions." He acknowledged, too, that the papal teaching confirmed that the ordination of men only was based upon scripture and tradition. The theological arguments in the letter, in Dulles' opinion, did not preclude all possible objections, but he insisted that few, if any, doctrines of the faith could be ultimately confirmed without reliance on arguments from authority. He admitted, too, that *Ordinatio* was particularly a "hard saying," like some of the gospel sayings, because the cultural support for women's ordination was part of legitimate societal calls for equal opportunity, and because of the apparent growing support within the American Catholic population.[78] To one correspondent in 1994, he outlined ten reasons for supporting the church's teaching on ordination and ended the letter by saying, "I hope it is clear that I am aware that serious arguments can be made in favor of women's ordination," but it was necessary to "walk with the Church."[79]

American bishops, wondering how they might communicate this "hard saying" to women in their dioceses who felt marginalized in their church, questioned the pastoral value of the letter, and in October 1995 the National Conference of Catholic Bishops (NCCB) raised a question (a *dubium*) with the CDF regarding the definitive authority of the apostolic letter. In November 1995, the CDF responded to the *dubium* by reaffirming that the church had no authority to ordain women to the priesthood and that the declaration was to be definitively held. Thereafter the president of the NCCB, Bishop Anthony Pilla of Cleveland, announced the Roman decision and called upon all Catholics to accept the teaching as belonging to the deposit of faith that was "to be held always, everywhere, and by all."[80]

After the CDF's decision, Dulles wrote in the London *Tablet* against some theologians who thought that the grounds of the apostolic letter were unsound. He argued that the teaching was to be definitively held and that a case could be made for the infallibility of the statement, even though the pope had not explicitly invoked his prerogative of infallibility. The pope asserted only that it was infallibly present in the church's teaching, which he merely acknowledged and proclaimed. He did not make an *ex cathedra* statement.[81] Although Dulles accepted the teaching, he acknowledged that it was possible that the pope and the CDF might "have erred in their estimation of the state of the doctrine" in the church. Difficulties continued to be raised, but Dulles asserted that presumption must be on the side of a tradition that was not entirely conditioned by culture.[82]

The interpretation of *Ordinatio* continued to raise objections from theologians and others, and, therefore, Dulles decided to meet the objections straight on in a lecture he gave at Fordham on April 10, 1996. Answering objections in an American culture that had stressed equal opportunity for women in all phases of life was no easy task. The church had taught the equal dignity and rights of men and women in nature and society but had not perceived ordination itself as a right within the church or society. Making such a distinction was not only difficult to make intelligible in the United States; it was difficult to make imaginable. *Ordinatio*, Dulles opined, was the "most controversial statement" from John Paul II's pontificate.[83]

In the Fordham address, Dulles outlined and answered what he considered the ten most serious theological objections to the exclusion of women from ordination to the priesthood: (1) Jesus ordained no one, and there was no indication that he prohibited women; (2) evidence on the practice of ordination in the apostolic church had been contested, and the Pontifical Biblical Commission in 1975 found no difficulty against ordaining women; (3) the argument from tradition did not meet the issue because the question itself was new and more time was needed before the magisterium could properly decide the issue; (4) the teachings of the past prohibiting ordination of women were socially and culturally conditioned; (5) the state of biological science (for example, Aristotle's view of women as genetically inferior) in the earlier centuries was outmoded; (6) priestly representation did not require, as the iconic argument insisted, natural resemblance; (7) exclusion of women from ordination was unjust toward women; (8) the prohibition was unecumenical and contributed to the ongoing disunity of Christianity; (9) the question remained open in spite of magisterial statement; and (10) John Paul II did not consult the world's bishops prior to this teaching.

Some of these objections were more serious than others, but Dulles considered the objections and dissenting opinions seriously and in fact called for toleration of those who could not give firm assent to the teaching in the present. Theologians of "acknowledged professional competence" had raised some serious objections that could not be "written off as merely flippant." Such theological objections, moreover, could "contribute to real doctrinal progress and provide a stimulus to the magisterium to propose the teaching of the church in greater depth and with a clearer presentation of the arguments," a view of the theologian's role that the CDF itself acknowledged in the "Ecclesial Vocation of the Theologian" (1990). For Dulles this did not mean that the truth of the teaching was flawed, but that the arguments and evidence for it could be less than convincing.[84] Because the biblical and historical evidence was complex and at some points obscure, Dulles advised that bishops and others not be quick to judge as renegades or heterodox those who had legitimate difficulties with the teaching.

Significant numbers of the faithful as well as theologians had objected to the teaching. Dulles believed that the contemporary climate of opinion, which affected large segments in society and the church, was "predominantly hostile to the biblical and Catholic heritage" on sexual ethics and gender. He called for tolerance of the faithful's culturally conditioned objections to the teaching as he had called for tolerance of serious theological objections. He was not calling for dissent, but for tolerance of dissent in very difficult cultural circumstances. He thought that it was still an open question whether or not *Ordinatio* was to be accepted on the motive of faith or with what he and others called "firm assent." In the end, though, Dulles advised those in "pastoral leadership" to recognize the "complexity of the theological issues and the inevitability of dissenting views" and to be "patient with Catholics who feel unable to accept the approved position."[85] While accepting the teaching himself, he counseled prudent pastoral acceptance of those faithful who did not understand the teaching and were not able to give firm assent to it.

Although he acknowledged the theological and cultural objections to *Ordinatio*, he supported it himself, believing, as he said in 1996, that the classical theological method "strongly supports the Holy See in the present instance." In fact, he argued, particularly in his Fordham address, that "the standard theological *loci* of Scripture, tradition, theological reason and magisterial authority are manifestly opposed to women's ordination."[86] At Fordham, he argued, like Newman and in conjunction with Vatican II, that these separate *loci* were "not to be taken in isolation but in convergence, since none of them is an independent authority."[87] He saw in the convergence of probabilities strong evidence for the teaching and responded to each of the objections raised against the prohibition by an analysis of the contrary evidences, too extensive to indicate here, that he found in the church's long tradition. For him the ordination of men only was "not based on time-conditioned sociological factors and on ideas about the inferiority of women that no longer obtain." In fact, he noted in 1998:

> A deeper inquiry into the dynamics of Christian doctrine will show...that the traditional teaching is based on fidelity to the sources of revelation and that it could not be changed without impairing the authentic Christian understanding of God, of Christ, and of the church. The reservation of apostolic office to men, moreover, leaves ample scope for women to develop and deploy their talents in the church, the family, and the world.[88]

Much was at stake in this issue, but it was not, as he said repeatedly, an essential doctrine of the Christian faith.

511

Theologians of the Catholic Theological Society of America (CTSA) took up the issue in 1996, forming a study committee to examine the CDF's clarifications on the authority of the prohibition against ordaining women.[89] After a yearlong study, the committee submitted a document, eventually entitled "Tradition and the Ordination of Women,"[90] to the entire CTSA for examination and emendation, after which the committee created the final draft in 1997. The vast majority of members present at the June 1997 annual meeting voted to approve the document before it was sent to the NCCB. The CTSA resolution agreed with the conclusion of the study statement that "there are serious doubts regarding the nature of the authority of this teaching [namely, the teaching that the church's lack of authority to ordain women to the priesthood is a truth that has been infallibly taught and requires the definitive assent of the faithful] and its grounds in Tradition."[91]

Dulles was not present at the 1997 meeting of the CTSA, but, of course, he did not agree with his fellow theologians, and he said so quite publicly, claiming that it was correctly perceived as a dissent from "the pope's call for definitive adherence to his teaching." He was upset at the CTSA's apparent "urge for theological self-assertion against hierarchical authority," an urge that widened "the gap" and constituted "a kind of alternative magisterium for dissatisfied Catholics."[92] Although he could accept the fact that theologians of "acknowledged professional competence" had raised serious objections to the arguments and evidences supplied for the teaching on ordination, he could not stomach the herd mentality that opposed the church's teaching in this instance. He thought the CTSA theologians were overstepping the boundaries of their own competence in this case.

Between 1988 and 2000, while he held the endowed McGinley chair at Fordham University, Dulles published about 250 articles and seven books. He was invited to give numerous public lectures and talks, both in the United States and abroad, many of which were published. He continued his ecumenical work on the Lutheran/Catholic Dialogue until 1996, and thereafter entered more fully into Catholic dialogues with conservative Protestant Evangelicals. He served as an advisor on the NCCB's Committee on Doctrine and on the International Theological Commission. He was widely recognized as one of the foremost theologians in the United States, and even though he had had some very critical assessments of the state of Catholic theology in the United States, he was still respected in the theological community, even by those who did not share his perspective and disagreed with his assessment of the current situation of the American church and his view of remedies for troublesome divisions in the church. More and more he had become an Evangelical Catholic who called for a spiritual regeneration in the American church. Rome was well aware of the conflicts in the American church and the need for spiritual renewal. Sometime in 2000, Pope John Paul II decided that Dulles should be made a cardinal as a reward, some thought, for his work as the prominent American Catholic theologian and an orthodox supporter of the church's teaching and evangelical mission.

15
THE CARDINAL, 2001–2008

AT THE BEGINNING OF 2001, Dulles was created a cardinal of the Catholic Church and served in the College of Cardinals as a priest theologian for the next seven years. During those years he continued to give talks and lectures, publishing more than 150 articles and three books on issues in the church and society that required theological analysis and reflection. He continued his emphasis on orthodoxy and became increasingly more evangelical in his public talks and lectures, especially those given to college students.

Becoming a Cardinal

At the end of 2000, Dulles was eighty-two years of age. He continued, though, to put in long hours at his desk as well as on the lecture circuit, giving of himself tirelessly to the cause of Catholic theology for the good of the church. He was a Catholic theologian with a well-deserved national and international reputation. Even at his advanced age, he was regularly invited to give keynote addresses, delivering about twenty formal lectures a year, and participated in numerous international theological meetings. Many of his books and articles continued to be translated into multiple foreign languages. In the previous decade, as already observed, he became one of the foremost interpreters and supporters of the teachings of Pope John Paul II. Nonetheless, it was a great "surprise," as the *New York Times* acknowledged, when it was announced in January 2001 that Dulles had been named a cardinal of the Catholic Church and was to receive the red hat in February of that year.[1]

Dulles was named a cardinal together with two other Americans, Edward Michael Egan, the archbishop of New York, and Theodore

E. McCarrick, archbishop of Washington, D.C., both of whom because of their positions in the church were expected to receive the red hat. Unlike the two bishops, Dulles, at eighty-two, would be ineligible to vote for the next pope, and because he was a priest and not a bishop, he requested an indult from the pope to remain a priest and continue his work as a theologian within the College of Cardinals—a request that was granted. Dulles had prior associations with the two American bishops, and he had known Archbishop McCarrick for nearly fifty years. Dulles had directed McCarrick in a Fordham devotional group in the early 1950s when McCarrick was an undergraduate there. As a seminarian in 1956, moreover, McCarrick had served at Dulles' first Mass. These and other stories about Dulles and the other new cardinals came to the fore in the newspapers. The press was particularly interested in the nomination of Dulles because he was the first nonepiscopal theologian and the first Jesuit in the United States ever to be named to the cardinalate, a nomination that some thought particularly revealing because of the ideological tensions that had been going on for some time between the Vatican and a few American Catholic theologians and Jesuits.

The rumors had been going around for some time that Dulles was to be made a cardinal. In the early 1990s some were saying that he would be made a cardinal, and in 2000 there were some clear indications that something was brewing in Rome. The New York Jesuit Provincial in the fall of 2000 requested from Dulles' office his complete bibliography, and at that time Dulles' research associate, Anne-Marie Kirmse, OP, suspected that the provincial's request originated at the Vatican. Some Jesuit superiors at Fordham believed in 2000 that Dulles' elevation was imminent and began preparing for that eventuality. Dulles, too, was well aware of the rumors, but he put no stock in them.[2]

The Fordham Jesuits were particularly proud that one of their own had been named to the College of Cardinals and called a press conference to celebrate the event. At the press conference Dulles, with characteristic humor and humility, is reported to have said, "At my relatively advanced age, I will have the task of trying to learn how to look and act cardinalatial. I am very much accustomed to my informal and rather plebian manners." Joseph A. O'Hare, SJ, president of Fordham, beaming with pride, tried to summarize the meaning of Dulles' career as a theologian rewarded with the red hat: "Faith seeking understanding defines the mission of the theologian, even as it has consistently defined the life of Avery Dulles, whose intellectual integrity, fairness of judgment and lucidity of style set a high standard for all theologians." In response to a reporter's question about how it felt to be named to the exclusive Catholic club, Dulles replied, "It's very gratifying to think that my theology is considered somewhat important, not only in the United States but for the world's church." Dulles also wanted to reflect the honor of his nomination on those with whom he had been associated for more than three-quarters of his life. "In a wider perspective, I would see it [the nomination] as a gesture of encouragement for American theologians and for my order, the Society of Jesus." The *New York Times* reporter at the news conference saw in Dulles' acknowledgment some truth. Although Dulles himself had been a papal supporter, the reporter noted, he had tried to keep the door opened between the Vatican and theological dissenters in the United States.[3]

Prior to his trip to Rome for the reception of the red hat, Dulles generously granted reporters interviews and tried to define his role as a theologian in the church, although the reporters did not have the time or space to do justice to his own nuanced understanding of the theologian's role. To one reporter he said that the "church looks to the theologian for prudent advice." It was the theologian's job "to show why the church is teaching what she is." Some reporters contrasted this definition with that of other American Catholic theologians who emphasized the more exploratory role of theology, but Dulles had never denied this side of the theologian's task. In the circumstances of the 1990s, though, Dulles believed that some in the American Catholic Church thought that "everything was up for grabs, and that every doctrine could be challenged." In such a situation, the theologian had to act in the church's interest. "The mentality I was rejecting [when I was] at Harvard [in the 1940s] was very much the mentality of the 1990s—relativism, skepticism, agnosticism." Christianity was a corrective for these tendencies, in Dulles' view, and he believed it was necessary in the present circumstances to "pay attention to what is permanent and universal." He knew, too, that this approach was a hard sell in the United States. "It goes against the American mentality."[4]

Before going to Rome for the installation, Dulles chose, as was customary for those named to the College of Cardinals, a coat of arms, which was designed by Fr. Thomas Slon, SJ. Dulles selected as his motto, *Scio cui credidi* ("I know the one in whom I have put my trust," a verse from 2 Timothy 1:12). The shield in the coat of arms is divided in half, the upper half depicting his ecclesiastical family, the Jesuits, at the center of which is the symbol of Jesus crucified and in the upper right-hand corner is an eight-pointed star symbolizing the Blessed Virgin Mary in her title as "Star of the Sea." The lower half of the shield depicts the Dulles family, symbolized by a blue field with three gold fleur-de-lis, a hint that the Dulles name "may derive from 'De-lis,' a title and emblem given by the King of France to the family for its services to the Crown."[5] By this designation of the roots of the family name, the cardinal sided with those in the family who traced the family name back to France.

Cardinal Dulles' coat of arms and motto: *scio cui credidi* ("I know the one in whom I have put my trust," 2 Timothy 1:12)

The trip to Rome for Dulles' installation was a memorable event for him, his immediate family and relatives, his Jesuit colleagues, and his other 150 invited guests, including his longtime research associate and secretary, Dr. Anne-Marie Kirmse, OP, and Abbot Gabriel Gibbs, OSB, the superior of St. Benedict Abbey in Still River, Massachusetts. His sister-in-law, Eleanor Ritter Dulles, his nephews and nieces, his longtime friend from the Cambridge St. Benedict Center, Mrs. Louise Mercier Des Marais, her daughter and son-in-law, Monica Des Marais and John Murphy, Richard John Neuhaus, George Weigel, and some of his former students were among those who came to Rome to celebrate with him. Fr. Gerald Blaszczak, SJ, the former rector of the Fordham Jesuit com-

With Louise Mercier Des Marais, Rome, 2001

munity, helped Dulles to prepare for the events in Rome and acted as his assistant and press secretary throughout the trip. Joseph O'Hare, the president of Fordham, hosted many of the events while in Rome. A generous donor had provided funds for the Jesuits who accompanied Dulles to Rome.

The trip to Rome included for the guests not only the attendance at the Consistory at St. Peter's Basilica on February 21, 2001, but also a private tour of Ignatian Rome, a Mass of Thanksgiving followed by a reception at the Gregorian University in Cardinal Dulles' honor, a first Mass in Dulles' titular church, Gesù e Maria, followed by a banquet at the Gregorian University, and before departing, a tour of the Vatican Observatory, the Papal Gardens, and Castel Gandolfo.

Dulles belonged to the largest class in history (forty-four) to be made cardinals. He was the last and oldest of the nominees to receive the red hat during the impressive installation ceremony at St. Peter's. When his name was announced, as one press report recorded, "rousing cheers" went up from many of those attending the ceremony.[6] Dulles walked to the papal throne with a cane because, by the time of his elevation, he had been suffering from post-polio syndrome, which considerably weakened the muscles in his left leg. After embracing the pope, he knocked his biretta off his own head, a clumsiness he would joke about later. In a press conference after the ceremony, he was asked what it felt like to be installed before the large crowd at St. Peter's. He replayed the clumsy incident, and "with a wry smile, he said it was humbling."[7]

At the banquet at the Gregorian in his honor, three of Dulles' guests, representing different phases of his life, spoke and toasted or roasted him. Richard John Neuhaus spoke on behalf of his theological and professional colleagues; John Murphy, a New York City lawyer and longtime close friend, represented his steadfast loyalty to his lay acquaintances; and Joan Buresch-Talley, a cousin, represented Dulles' extended family. Murphy had prepared a speech comparing Dulles to John Henry Newman and Robert Bellarmine, but Neuhaus and others had made the comparison before he got up to speak, so he tore up the talk and simply spoke extemporaneously of Dulles as a man and a friend.[8] Joan Buresch-Talley delighted the guests with tales of Dulles' character and of his family life. She told one story about Avery's driving. At one point when he was driving in New York City he stopped quickly at a light, and another car ran into his car, wrecking it. Joan reported humorously that he was so "advanced in his spiritual life that he had become invisible to the common man."[9] As a young child, she also is reported to have said, she overheard her father, Allen Dulles, her

With Pope John Paul II on the day Dulles was created a cardinal, February 21, 2001

aunt Eleanor, and her uncle, John Foster, discussing Avery's decision to become a Catholic, complaining that the best and the brightest of the family's next generation seemed determined to throw his promising life away. "And, of course, they were right," she said. "He did throw that life away. He threw it away for God."[10] The affair was a joyous occasion for family, friends, colleagues, and members of the Fordham community. John Foster Dulles II, the cardinal's nephew, reported that "being in Rome for his elevation was one of the great highlights of my life!"[11]

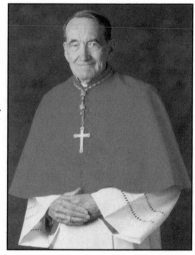

Official portrait as cardinal, 2001

The press enjoyed Dulles' candor, humor, and self-deprecating demeanor during the press conferences before and after the Consistory. He did not know what he was expected to wear, how he was expected to act in liturgical ceremonies, and how he was to be perceived. As far as he was concerned, though, he was still a simple Jesuit priest and, in response to one of many letters of congratulations he received on being elevated to the College of Cardinals, he asked the well wisher to "pray for me that I may continue to serve the church in this new capacity."[12] The honorific title had not changed his priestly and theological mission. When he returned to his Fordham Jesuit community after the installation, he wanted his colleagues to treat him as they had previous to this new honor and to address him, as they had before, as "Avery." And when some of his Jesuit colleagues toyed with him with "Good morning, your Eminence," he replied with a characteristic grin, "Thank you, your lowliness."[13]

In the American Catholic theological community Dulles' elevation was perceived by some not as a reward for "his undeniable achievements and contributions as a Catholic theologian" but as a prize for what one theologian called his lurch to the right.[14] Others, like Joseph Komonchak, Dulles' colleague at Catholic University in the 1980s, put Dulles in the camp of previous eminent theologians (Yves-Marie Congar, Jean Daniélou, Henri de Lubac, Alois Grillmeier, Pietro Pavan, and Hans Urs von Balthasar) who had also been given the red hat precisely for their theological works. In Komonchak's view, Dulles' work "has been marked largely by a commitment to conversation, which, of course, involves listening as much as it does speaking. And he has been a good listener, first, in the sense that he has attended to the voices of the past in large works on the history of theology, to separated Christians in several ecumenical dialogues, and to fellow Catholics in analyses of postconciliar church life and theology." He had critiqued the conservative neo-scholastics when he thought their theological paradigm needed revision, and in most recent years he had come to criticize the liberal paradigm because he believed that it most needed to be challenged. In Komonchak's view, Dulles' "respect for the tradition and for the church's doctrinal integrity is nothing new in him." Komonchak was unwilling to reduce Dulles' theological work to one or another of the shibboleths of the age: either conservative or liberal.[15] Without access to the Vatican's decision-making process, this historian cannot determine the motivation for elevating Dulles, but Komonchak's view seems closer to the known facts than other more suspicious hermeneutics.

Death Penalty Controversy

In his first years as a cardinal, Dulles became involved in three events that received considerable public attention. The first was the public controversy over the death penalty, with particular reference in some quarters to the death sentence of Timothy McVeigh, the convicted mass murderer who had bombed the Oklahoma City Federal Building. The second and most disturbing internal Catholic event was the pedophilia crisis that came to the fore after the *Boston Globe* published a series of articles in January 2002 detailing the pedophilia abuses and cover-ups in the archdiocese of Boston. The third event was the death of Pope John Paul II in April 2005.

Between 2000 and 2004, Dulles gave public lectures, which were subsequently published, on the death penalty in Catholic doctrine. He chose to address the issue because it had become a topic of concern in American life and in Catholic theology. In the United States, capital punishment had been of some concern for years. It had been outlawed in the United States between 1972 and 1977, but was resumed in 1977, making the United States one of only a few world powers to continue the practice. After 1977, however, the death penalty was prohibited for federal prisoners. That restriction was lifted after a four-decade hiatus in 2001, when Timothy McVeigh became the first federal prisoner to be executed in more than forty years. Catholic leaders periodically discussed the justice and necessity of capital punishment. The American Catholic bishops in 1980 had argued vigorously against it, and in *Evangelium vitae* (EV; 1995) Pope John Paul II had indicated that cases in which it would be absolutely necessary "are very rare, if not practically non-existent" (EV 56), and in a talk at St. Louis in 1999 he called the death penalty "cruel and unnecessary."[16] Some Catholic theologians and a few others believed that the classical Catholic doctrine in support of the state's right to take life needed to be reversed in light of the Catholic right to life insistence, the improved conditions of the modern penal system, and the sociological statistics that revealed many cases of innocent people or an inordinate number of minority persons being put to death. In these circumstances, Dulles thought it advisable to speak out on the issue as a Catholic theologian who had been called to Fordham's McGinley chair precisely to address the intersection of religion and society.

In the fall of 2000, Dulles' McGinley lecture was entitled "The Death Penalty: A Right to Life Issue?" As a theologian, he examined the classical biblical texts and the teachings of the tradition to argue that Catholic doctrine upheld in principle the state's right to take the life of criminals as punishments for their serious crimes. The death penalty served four traditional purposes of punishment (rehabilitation—as in death-bed conversions, defense against future criminal action, deterrence, and retribution). The death penalty was "not in itself a violation of the right to life." Here he was arguing against those who called for the reversal of the classical Catholic doctrine on the death penalty and who supported the absolute abolition of the death penalty. His argument, however, did not end here, because he acknowledged that it was one thing to uphold a principle of Catholic moral doctrine and another thing to apply it to contemporary circumstances. Was the death penalty the appropriate and necessary means of punishment in the present?[17]

After examining some of the more and less powerful arguments against capital punishment (for example, convictions of the innocent, whetting the appetite for revenge and vindictiveness, cheapening the value of life, and incompatibility with Jesus' teaching on forgiveness), he upheld the classical Catholic doctrine in principle and asserted that capital punishment had some "limited value, but its necessity is open to doubt." He found himself, therefore, in agreement with Pope John Paul II, who had become "increasingly vocal in opposing the practice of capital punishment," even though he did not deny in principle the state's right. The pope and the American bishops, in coming to their conclusions on the current practice of capital punishment, had exercised their "prudential" judgments in applying classical Catholic doctrine to current circumstances, determining that the current practice "on balance" did "more harm than good." Dulles was in entire agreement with that magisterial prudential judgment.[18]

The discussion on the death penalty between Dulles' supporters and opponents continued in lectures, journals, and newspapers from 2000 to 2004. Dulles' McGinley address was subsequently used by some American Catholic bishops to oppose the execution of Timothy McVeigh. In April 2001, for example, Indianapolis Archbishop Daniel M. Buechlein, whose diocese included Terre Haute, where the execution of Timothy McVeigh was to take place, used Dulles' McGinley address extensively to argue that the Catholic Church opposed the death penalty even in cases like McVeigh's because it could cause society more harm than good by feeding a demand for revenge and increasing the cycle of violence (which he thought was "alarming"). The church did not deny government the right in principle, but the church's understanding of the circumstances in which capital punishment could be used had changed in recent years.[19]

Dulles' view of the death penalty was challenged by a few. Some of his opponents thought that he had seriously misinterpreted what was "fundamentally new" in the 1997 edition of the *Catechism of the Catholic Church*. The *Catechism* and Pope John Paul II's *Evangelium vitae* laid a clear foundation for a change, not just a development, of the church's teaching—meaning that retribution was never a sufficient condition for inflicting the death penalty and that death as a punishment was never legitimate. The arguments against the death penalty were moral and not merely prudential, as Dulles argued. Other opponents argued that the *Catechism* and the pope were departing from a long-standing Catholic tradition on the death penalty when arguing against its use in contemporary circumstances.[20]

Supreme Court Justice Antonin Scalia in particular took issue with Dulles' interpretation. Both Scalia and Dulles delivered papers on the subject at a Pew Foundation–sponsored symposium on Religion and the Death Penalty at the University of Chicago Divinity School in January 2002.[21] In addresses in Chicago and at Georgetown University in February 2002, Justice Scalia challenged the current Catholic teaching that opposed the death penalty, saying in effect that it was contrary to the long Catholic tradition that had supported it. He observed, furthermore, that if he agreed with what Pope John Paul II had taught in *Evangelium vitae* on capital punishment he would, as a believing Catholic, have to resign as a justice. But he would not resign, because what the pope taught was not consistent with the long-held Catholic doctrine on the subject. He also disagreed with Dulles that *Evangelium vitae* was consistent with the longer Catholic tradition. According to Scalia, the pope's position did not intend to "sweep away" two thousand years of tradition, but in fact it did so. Scalia interpreted the encyclical to mean that "retribution is not a valid purpose of capital punishment."[22]

In February the *National Catholic Register* editorialized against "Scalia's Dissenting Opinion," arguing that Scalia should stick to being a jurist instead of trying to interpret Catholic doctrine in the public fashion he did. The *Register* opined that Scalia provided "an example of a powerful man persuading a crowd of people that the Church is wrong."[23] Scalia responded to the editorial, and the *Register* invited others, including Dulles, to offer their assessments of the pope's teaching and Scalia's position.[24]

Dulles agreed with Scalia's view that the death penalty was consistent with the "constant Catholic tradition" but disagreed with Scalia's interpretation of *Evangelium vitae*. The pope had not condemned in principle the state's right to capital punishment; his view in that encyclical, as Dulles had argued before, was, in the technical language of theology, a "prudential judgment" on the current practice. He was applying Catholic moral doctrine to concrete cases. Dulles then went on to offer seven reasons (prudential judgments) why the United States should not execute criminals (inequitable application, unequal legal representation for poor and uneducated, likelihood of innocent persons being condemned, difficulty of judging subjective guilt, tendency to inflame revenge, failure of modern states to embody a transcendent order of justice for exercising retribution, and urgency of manifesting respect for the value and dignity of human life). On these reasons persons of good will and intelligence could disagree. "If the Pope [as Dulles believed] allows for capital punishment in some cases, to be determined by prudent considerations, his position is not contrary to the American Constitution and the Bill of Rights and raises no problem" for Catholic judges. They would not have to resign their positions in order to be in conformity with Catholic teaching.[25]

The discussion with Scalia continued when Fr. Richard John Neuhaus, editor of *First Things*, invited scholars, Dulles included, to comment on Scalia's position.[26] Dulles reiterated his view that he and Scalia agreed on the irreversible church doctrine on the death penalty but disagreed on their interpretation of *Evangelium vitae*—Dulles maintaining that it was consistent with the traditional doctrine and Scalia arguing that it unintentionally contradicted that doctrine. While reconciling the pope's view with that of the classical tradition, Dulles invoked a "hermeneutics of continuity" that he had been consistently using for some years in interpreting other church doctrines. "My desire is to be faithful both to the past and to the present teaching of the Magisterium." The pope's view that the death penalty should be used rarely, moreover, was a prudential judgment that was not binding Catholic doctrine, and to dissent from such "prudential judgments" was not in itself "to dissent from Church teaching."[27] Scalia continued to disagree with Dulles' interpretation of continuity, insisting that the pope's restrictions on the death penalty were not merely prudential judgments and that he had repudiated retribution as justification for the death penalty.

Scalia had consistently held that retribution was in fact one of the primary purposes for the death penalty in the tradition. Dulles had attempted to show that retribution was indeed a part of the pope's position, indicated by his quotation from the *Catechism of the Catholic Church* (CCC), which in fact had mentioned the expiatory value of punishment in order to redress the disorder caused by the criminal offense (CCC, 1997, 2266). According to Scalia, Dulles' interpretation "fits neither the text nor the reasoning of the document." If the pope had seriously considered retribution as one of the goals of capital punishment, he could not have held, as he did, that capital punishment was no longer necessary in the improved situation of the modern penal system. Scalia acknowledged that the pope supported the death penalty when absolutely necessary for the defense of society, but Scalia's primary point was "whether the retributive element *justifies* the punishment in the *absence* of a 'defense of society' rationale."[28] Scalia had the last word in this symposium. In the end the two disagreed fundamentally on the interpretation of the pope's views.[29]

After the exchange with Scalia, Dulles continued to articulate his own interpretation and in 2004 put that interpretation into what he called the three different schools of thought in contemporary theological literature. The first school, called "abolitionist," maintained that the Catholic Church had indeed reversed its earlier teaching and now absolutely opposed the death penalty. A second school, called "developmentalist," held that the pope and the *Catechism* had not repudiated but refined the earlier teaching, asserting that capital punishment was valid only when the physical protection of society required it (and therefore it would be extremely rare, given the condition of the modern penal system). The third school, to which Dulles belonged and which he believed was the best available interpretation the church's doctrine in the light of the present magisterial teaching, scripture, and tradition, left the traditional doctrine unchanged (meaning, in particular, that retribution was still considered one of the reasons for the death penalty), but the application of that doctrine in the present circumstances seemed to him to be practically rare for the reasons he had previously given. He saw drastic consequences for other church doctrines (for example, abortion, euthanasia) if one admitted that the traditional doctrine on the death penalty were reversed or reversible. What his position meant in practice, however, was not the abolition of the death penalty. "It should remain in law, and its implementation should be a real possibility." It should be imposed, however, only when serious guilt is certain and where the restoration of the social order and moral health of society required it. In this case the prudential judgment belonged to "competent secular agents, including judges and juries, who are guided by sound principles."[30]

Clerical Sexual Abuse

The second major issue during Dulles' first year as a cardinal was the scandal of clerical sexual abuse. And, as a cardinal, he would become directly involved in the church's attempt to address the issue. Unlike the other American cardinals, however, he was not directly or even indirectly implicated in the scandal because he, unlike them, was not responsible for the ecclesiastical supervision of any diocese. Sexual abuse by Catholic clergy in the United States, and especially abuse of minors, had been public knowledge since at least 1985 but came to explosive national attention in January 2002 when the *Boston Globe* revealed the story of pedophilia in the Archdiocese of Boston and of the diocese's secrecy and refusal to reveal the crimes to competent secular authorities.[31]

Previous to 2002, Dulles said very little publicly about the sexual abuse scandal within the priesthood. Interviewed in 2002, after the *Boston Globe* revelations, he is reported to have said that "the sexual abuse scandal was a creation of a news media feeding frenzy," a view that was initially shared by some other Catholics in the early months of 2002.[32] The abuse, however, was very real, not a creation of the news media, and implicated not only the predatory priests who violated their vows of celibacy but their bishops who failed to report their crimes and continued to assign them to pastoral responsibilities. The pope, who was informed on the American crisis, saw the seriousness of the issue for the victims and for the credibility of the church and its own moral authority. In an attempt to restore credibility and renew confidence in the church's moral authority, the pope called all the American cardinals, including Dulles, to Rome to discuss ways of responding to the victims, disciplining the abusers, and establishing guidelines for the prevention of future abuse. In April 2002, Dulles, together with the other American cardinals, flew to Rome for an emergency meeting with the pope on the scandal.

After the meeting in Rome, the pope, the American cardinals, and leading bishops in the United States Conference of Catholic Bishops (USCCB) reaffirmed Catholic teaching on sexual abuse, stating that "the sexual abuse of minors is rightly considered a crime by society and is an appalling sin in the eyes of God, above all when it is perpetrated by priests and religious whose vocation is to help persons to lead holy lives before God and men." They also confirmed the need to stand in solidarity with the victims of abuse and their families and to provide appropriate assistance in recovering faith and receiving pastoral care for the physical, psychological, and spiritual damage that they had incurred from priests. The Americans, moreover, promised to send the Vatican a set of new national standards and policies to deal with the crisis after the June meeting of the USCCB in Dallas.[33]

Before the June meeting, Dulles wrote an op-ed piece for the *New York Times*, commenting on a draft policy statement the American bishops were preparing for discussion at Dallas. He wrote that the April meeting in Rome acknowledged the church's past failures but concentrated upon the future, agreeing to adopt a national policy to be reviewed by the Vatican. He then described for his readers the proposed American episcopal policy on sexual abuse and suggested that the bishops add to their statement "ways of supporting young priests in the observance of their commitments." The draft reflected two schools of thought on dismissing priests, but both sides agreed that any priest who committed a single act of abuse of a minor and all those who in the past had committed more than one such offense should be defrocked.[34]

One group within the episcopacy, as the proposed draft indicated, favored a zero tolerance of sexual abuse, "one strike and you're out" of the priesthood. A second school cautioned against such hasty and simplistic solutions. This school asked, "Is it fair, for example, to remove priests from the ministry if the accusations against them are unproved and if they protest their innocence (as did Cardinal Joseph Bernardin when he was falsely accused a decade ago)?" The second school insisted on a difference between serious offenses and lesser offenses. This school wanted to make some provisions for repentant and reformed priests who committed crimes long ago and had not repeated them, and it wanted the church to take responsibility for the clerical abusers rather than dismissing them and putting them back in society. They could be put in a monastery for life instead of being returned to society without ecclesiastical supervision.

It was clear from Dulles' article that he favored the second school because it was more in conformity with equity and justice. Dulles added that the draft did not "explicitly raise the question of homosexuality, but it is a matter of obvious concern." The bishops who noted the large portion of sexual abuses against adolescent boys, Dulles supposed, would want to screen out all "homosexually inclined seminarians." Dulles believed, too, that the issue of clerical celibacy would be discussed at the Dallas meeting. But in his view celibacy itself was not the problem. "The problem comes from the ordination of men who are not convinced of the value of celibacy or are unable to observe it. In our sex-saturated society it is difficult to transmit the church's tradition on this point....A married priesthood, while it might diminish certain problems, would bring in a host of others, like adultery, divorce or contraception." Dulles was afraid that the bishops would be stampeded into an excessively rigorous policy. "They should take care not to lock the church into positions that will later prove to be unwise."[35]

Two readers of the *Times* responded to Dulles' statement on a married priesthood, commenting sarcastically that it seemed that a celibate clergy could not imagine being married "without wanting to control the timing and number of their children." Perhaps, a married clergy might also want "safe places for their children." A married clergy, another wrote, might make priests "more empathic and to do a better job."[36]

At the June meeting, the bishops decided by an overwhelming majority (239 for, 13 against, and 32 abstentions) on the more rigorous, zero-tolerance policy. But before the voting, they listened to bishops' speeches on the draft statement. Dulles, too, spoke up, saying, "If I did have a vote, which I don't,...I think I'd have to vote against it because of some flaws that have shown up, particularly this morning." The definition of sexual abuse was not restrictive enough; taking priests out of ministry for minor infractions of sexual abuses seemed to him "awfully harsh."[37] As the *New York Times* reported, when Dulles took the microphone, the bishops "fell silent." Because he was not a bishop, he had no vote, but he "wields tremendous influence." He cautioned the bishops, thinking the policy statement was too strong and would create "a very adversarial relationship between the bishop and the priest....The priest can no longer go to his bishop in confidence with a problem that he has. He has to be very careful what he says to the bishop because the bishop can throw him out of the ministry for his entire life."[38] Both before and after the Dallas meeting, Dulles warned the bishops against such a consequence, but the vast majority of bishops, needing to restore some order and confidence in the church, thought that price was worth paying if the new policy did what it was intended to do.[39]

Dulles was not happy with the lack of nuance in the bishops' zero-tolerance policy because he did not believe it adequately protected the rights of priests, and he said so on two occasions after Dallas. He told a clerical colleague that at the Dallas meeting he was the only priest who had a voice and the only priest who tried to defend the rights of accused priests to a fair hearing.[40] On May 27, 2004, Dulles delivered a keynote address to the Thomas More Society[41] in Fort Lauderdale, Florida, and called for a revision of the Dallas policies in order to protect more adequately the rights of accused priests. The bishops, in Dulles' opinion, had "hastily adopted, after less than two days of debate," under intense pressure from media and survivors' networks, an "extreme response" to the crisis, adopting in the process policies and principles that they had condemned in their 2000 declaration on the secular juridical system.[42] Dulles then outlined fifteen principles (presumption of innocence, confidentiality, access to trial, prospect of reinstatement, conformity to universal legislation, and others) that he believed would give more equitable treatment to accused priests and that should be incorporated into any revision of the Dallas decisions, which Rome had approved for a two-year period.[43]

Not many bishops or theologians agreed with Dulles' position,[44] and there were only a few others within the Catholic community who spoke out for clerical rights in the circumstances of the horrendous revelations of crimes against children and adolescents. Dulles, of course, was not speaking for tolerance of the crimes or the criminals who committed them but for priests who might have repented and been living a virtuous life after a single crime in the distant past and for those unjustly accused. He wanted policies and procedures that would protect their rights.

Germain Grisez, a moral theologian at Mount St. Mary's University in Emmitsburg, Maryland, agreed with Dulles on the need to protect the innocent (or those priests accused falsely), but he disagreed with Dulles' comparison of the principles of justice in the secular juridical system with those that needed to be applied to priests in the church and with Dulles' opposition to the zero-tolerance policy that bore on future sexual abuses of minors. Grisez's principal argument seemed to be that sexual abuse of a minor by a cleric is graver than similar wrongdoing by a layperson because of the sacred order the priest represents in his person, making it an offense against the church as well as against the child. The act damages the child and the church's sacred mission. The severest penalty, exclusion from the ministry, therefore, ought to be the law. Grisez presumed in his argument that immoral acts against minors made clerics permanently disabled and unqualified for the ministry because such cases seemed to be incurable. The church should not, as in the past, take a chance against recidivisim.[45]

In response to Grisez, Dulles tried to clarify his own position. Like Grisez, Dulles noted where the two were in agreement but then went on to insist that his main objection to zero tolerance was integrally connected to his view that the definition of sexual abuse in the bishops' policy statement was too comprehensive. "Zero tolerance is most questionable if the definition of sexual abuse is broad or ambiguous." Dulles agreed that no sexual abuse of a minor should be tolerated and that there were acts of sexual abuses of minors for which the exclusion from the ministry was the appropriate penalty, but such acts needed to be defined more clearly than in the current episcopal policy because not every act (for example, indecent solicitation of a child, obscenity, child pornography) ought to be punished in the same way. He saw degrees of sexual abuse with minors and wanted the church's policy to acknowledge the degrees of difference, as the secular courts acknowledged the differences between misdemeanors and felonies. Dulles, too, continued to insist that there were cases in which forgiveness and rehabilitation were possible for some priests, as was evident in cases where a single act in the past was followed by years of exemplary service in the ministry. Recidivism was not universal and was particularly improbable if the priest were aged and infirm. In such cases, he opined, removal from the ministry would seem to be unjust and contrary to the gospel. As in the past, Dulles argued for the possibility of rehabilitation and restoration of ministry in some one-time, less than grave sexual abuse cases, and called for a revision of the bishops' policies to reflect such distinctions.[46] Most bishops and theologians like Grisez considered such an approach too risky, given the human fallibility in making such distinctions in concrete cases, especially in the abuse of minors.

Dulles' position on zero tolerance did not seem to change in subsequent years, but the sexual abuse scandal did influence what he had to say about the limits of ecclesiastical authority. At one point when outlining those limits, he mentioned that bishops were "bound to respect civil governments," an explicit acknowledgment that had not appeared in his theology prior to the revelations of the sexual abuse scandals. The exercise of ecclesiastical authority could be abused by omission as well as commission. "Perhaps," he noted, "the antiauthoritarian climate of the nation in the 1960s and 1970s was partly responsible for the failure of some bishops to act decisively" in the sexual abuse scandals.[47]

Death of John Paul II and Election of Benedict XVI

In the midst of the discussion of sexual abuse by priests, Pope John Paul II's health was rapidly declining because of Parkinson's disease and other complications. On April 2, 2005, he died, and Dulles along with all the other cardinals was called to Rome for the funeral, the days of mourning, the cardinals' consistory meetings on the state of the church, and the conclave for the election of a new pope (although because he was eighty-six at the time, Dulles was ineligible to vote for the new pope). Dulles was teaching at Fordham when he received the announcement of the pope's death, and he had to give some lectures in Philadelphia before going to Rome. He arrived in Rome in time to take part in the funeral ceremonies before an estimated 1.4 million mourners in Rome.

Fr. Gerald Blaszczak, SJ, accompanied Dulles to Rome a second time and served as his assistant for the ceremonies and as a kind of press secretary who tried to arrange meetings with the many reporters who were, in Dulles' words, "desperate" for any news about the election of a new pope, but "of course there was no news during those two weeks."[48] He granted interviews to the *New York Times*, *Time*, *Atlantic Monthly*, EWTN, and other news media who were seeking his view of the church's future and his assessment of Pope John Paul II's papacy. But no cardinal commented on the *papabili*.

Dulles was impressed with the great outpouring of grief during and after the funeral and told a reporter, "It has occurred to me that this great wave of enthusiasm, especially among young people, and love for the pope and sense of loss at his death, certainly shows their great faithfulness to him, but also their indebtedness." But he went on to comment that it remained to be seen whether or not that enthusiasm would be sustained. "It depends on discipleship taking hold....Faith is communicated from teachers to followers, and they in turn communicate it to their followers."[49]

Dulles had a great love for Pope John Paul II, as Fr. Blaszczak has said and as is evident in Dulles' theology. During the days of mourning, Avery was staying at the Jesuit curia across from the Vatican. He wanted to pray before the pope's body, but Blaszczak could not get a car to take him there because there were so many people camped out in front of St. Peter's and in the streets around the Vatican that a car could not get through. Dulles, who had difficulties walking because of the post-polio effects on his left leg, insisted on walking with his cane over the cobble stones to venerate and pray over the pope's body. According to Blaszczak, "he knelt devoutly for a good stretch of time honoring the remains of John Paul II."[50]

After the funeral on April 8, Dulles participated in cardinals' meetings every morning for the next nine days, discussing the state of the church throughout the world and celebrating Mass each day for the pope. Dulles attended all the long liturgical ceremonies, but he was always the theologian and continued working on articles and proofs during those days of mourning. He sent Blaszczak all over Rome hunting down books and articles he needed to finish writing articles he was working on during the time he was not occupied with his official duties as cardinal. In Blaszczak's view, "He was the servant of the Church, but it was never more apparent to me that Avery was first of all a theologian, and he knew what he was about."[51]

During the days of the consistory meetings, the international press speculated on the *papabili*, those cardinals considered to be front runners in the election. Dulles and other cardinals were interviewed repeatedly on the *papabili* but refused to offer their opinions. Dulles, however, did tell the American press that the church in the future needed to "continue" to forge "closer ties with other religions and other Christian denominations." He suggested, in fact, that ecumenism and efforts to evangelize the West should be two priorities for the next pontiff. One reporter, among many, asserted that one major candidate for the papacy was Cardinal Joseph Ratzinger, "an older interim figure, someone who would help the Church pause for breath in the aftermath of one of history's longest and most eventful papacies." He was "deeply respected for his learning and decisiveness." He would provide continuity with the aims of the previous papacy.[52]

The conclave chose Ratzinger as the next pope on April 19 after only four ballots. Ratzinger was labeled by the *New York Times* as a conservative and a theological hardliner.[53] Dulles, of course, had known Ratzinger personally for some time, and he considered the election a good choice, but not always for the reasons the secular press periodically indicated. Dulles had first met Ratzinger at the World Council of Church's Faith and Order Commission, August 2–12, 1971, in Belgium, when Ratzinger was still a relatively young but already internationally known theologian. He met Ratzinger again in the early 1980s after he had become the cardinal prefect of the CDF and more significantly at a three-day New York conference on the interpretation of scripture in the church, organized by Richard John Neuhaus in 1988. Both Ratzinger and Dulles addressed the American bishops in Dallas in 1991 on freedom and formation of conscience and dissent. From 1992 to 1997,

With Pope Benedict XVI at the time of his election, April 2005

Dulles served on the International Theological Commission that was chaired by Ratzinger. And, of course, he had been reading many of Ratzinger's theological treatises since the 1960s. So Dulles was no stranger to the new pope.

When asked what direction Dulles thought the new pope would take, he responded by saying:

> Well he has a rather long paper trail....I think he is interested in the re-Christianization of Europe, and a re-emphasis on the sacred, and receptivity to the revelation of Christ in the tradition and Scriptures and so forth. He is interested in the theology of creation, Christology, in the centrality of the Eucharist, and he believes that being a Christian requires a reverence towards the divine and the sacred. I think he will emphasize worship more than in the past; he has definitely a theological perspective on things; he will bring theology to bear on issues more than philosophizing as John Paul II did.[54]

Dulles would not label Ratzinger, except to say that he was definitely Augustinian in his theology. He was a faithful supporter of Vatican II, as was Pope John Paul II, though the emphases of the two men were different. John Paul II was a social ethicist, anxious to shape the world order, favoring *Gaudium et spes*; Ratzinger, the theologian, favored the other three constitutions on the liturgy, revelation, and the church.[55] Unlike the secular press, Dulles interpreted the new pope in terms of his theology, not in terms of his supposed relationship to the liberal-conservative cultural wars in the United States, as the secular press, with some exceptions, tended to do.

Newman

After the election of the new pope, Dulles returned to the United States to resume his teaching and his theological work, which had not ceased since his elevation to the cardinalate. Shortly after his elevation, in the midst of the sexual abuse scandal, Dulles published *Newman*, a book on Cardinal John Henry Newman, the nineteenth-century convert to Catholicism and a major theologian in the period between the Council of Trent and the Second Vatican Council.[56] Ever since his days as an undergraduate at Harvard, Dulles had been reading and commenting on Newman's works, publishing, during his career as a theologian, especially since 1990, several explicit articles on Newman and repeatedly citing him in his own works on fundamental theology throughout his career.

There were parallels between the lives of the two theologians. Both were raised in upper-middle-class families with considerable means, and both had access to the best educations available in their times. Both were converts to Catholicism,[57] although as Dulles pointed out on occasion, his own conversion to Catholicism was unlike that of Newman's. Newman's conversion had a greater continuity with his former life. Dulles' conversion was from agnosticism to real belief, and therefore he found more discontinuity between his former life and his life in Catholicism than did Newman. Newman's issues were those of the development of Christian doctrine; Dulles' were those of a fundamental commitment to Christ and the church.

Dulles and Newman opposed what they called liberalism. For both men, *liberalism* was a code word for the "anti-dogmatic principle and its developments" or religious indifferentism in matters of doctrine, an excessive attempt to accommodate the Christian tradition to contemporary forms of life and thought without concern for the continuity of Christian doctrine, and/or a reduction of religion to private sentiment.[58] Both supported church doctrine in their times when that doctrine was in various ways challenged or called into question. Both were recognized widely as theologians of the church with well-deserved reputations for insight, creativity, and clarity. Both, finally, were made cardinals in recognition of their theological and churchly achievements. The parallelism was not exact because they lived in different times, faced different specific issues, and did not share all of the same theological education.

Dulles had adopted the modern philosophical turn to the subject, a turn to personalism he attributed to Newman and Michael Polanyi, among others. Newman's religious epistemology was a major advance in the Catholic theological tradition, a precursor to what Dulles called, using terminology he had appropriated from Polanyi, "post-critical personalism."[59] This emphasis on the subject, with a modern sense of historicity, made Dulles, following Newman, open to the conditioned nature of human consciousness and to the relative value of all theological linguistic constructions. Influenced by Newman, moreover, Dulles gave significant attention to the subject's reception of revelation and church doctrine. Newman's views also made Dulles open to a person's and a Christian community's gradual and developmental appropriation of revelation and church doctrine. This Newmanian posture in the twentieth and early twenty-first centuries meant that Dulles accepted theological pluralism and the possibilities of legitimate dissent in the church, and he counseled churchmen to exercise patience and tolerance within the church of Christ for those who were unable in the present to accept the fullness of Catholic doctrine and discipline—and this without forfeiting the church's hard and difficult doctrines. When he counseled tolerance, he was accused of relativism. When he advocated the fullness of Catholic doctrine, he was accused of intransigence and a return to pre–Vatican II closed-mindedness. Dulles discovered that he could identify with Newman in many, but not all, respects.

In 2000, Brian Davies, OP, a philosophy professor at Fordham and general editor of the "Outstanding Christian Thinkers" series, knowing of Dulles' previous work on Newman, asked him to write a book on Newman.[60] Previous books in the series had been published on Augustine, Aquinas, Søren Kierkegaard, Karl Barth, Paul Tillich, and Karl Rahner, among others. Newman would be in good company in this series. But with so many books on Newman already filling library shelves, Dulles considered what new approach could be taken. He decided that since there were already many good biographies and studies of specific issues in Newman's thought, he would write a book that surveyed "in a comprehensive and systematic way" Newman's teaching "about the classical theological questions" and critically analyze them in light of the documents of the Second Vatican Council.[61] The book was intended for theologians and for a more general reading audience. After a brief description of Newman's life, Dulles summarized Newman's views on eight topics (redemption, justification, and sanctification; faith and reason; apologetics; revelation, doctrine, and development; the church; the roles of theologians and the laity; ecumenism; and the function of the university) and then evaluated those positions using the teachings of the Second Vatican Council as the criteria of judgment. Newman was, very much like Dulles himself, a fundamental theologian rather than a traditional systematic theologian. They were both interested in exploring the nature of faith in the individual and the communal experience with revelation.

The small book of about 170 pages was an exemplary illustration of Dulles' well-known synthetic skills, incisive depiction, and luminous clarity. Dulles was not an expert Newmanian scholar, but he had the ability to demonstrate how and why Newman was a classical theologian whose works, amid their time-conditioned limitations, had insights that transcended the times in which he wrote and anticipated developments that were reflected in the theology of the Second Vatican Council. Dulles remarked, for example, that Newman would have welcomed Vatican II's positions "on universal revelation, on the centrality of Christ, on the place of Mary in salvation history, on biblical inerrancy, on the indispensability of tradition, on the authority of bishops, on the consensus of the faithful, and on freedom of conscience."[62] The council, though, went well beyond where Newman had gone in the areas of liturgy, sacramental ecclesiology, episcopal collegiality, the threefold office of the bishops, and ecumenism. Newman, though, had emphasized some issues that the council had not. Among these issues, Dulles listed the need for more emphasis on the relationship between faith and reason, the role of theologians in the church, and the homogeneous development of doctrine—areas Dulles believed the council had not addressed adequately and needed to be reasserted in the twenty-first century.

What Dulles admired in Newman he emulated, with some accommodations to his own times. Many of Dulles' judgments on what was valuable in Newman's life and thought could well be applied analogously to Dulles himself. Within the Catholic Church, for example, Dulles wrote, Newman tried "in vain" at certain times in his life to mediate "between the conservative hierarchy and the liberal faction of the laity, personified by Lord Acton."[63] Dulles, too, attempted a mediating role in the American church between liberals and conservatives.

Although Newman critiqued autonomous reason (whether in Enlightenment or neo-scholastic forms), believing that in concrete matters reason depended on presumptions that were "by no means self-evident" or explicit, he did not as a result accept the all-too-prevalent twenty-first-century shift from objectivism to subjectivism. Although his religious epistemology invited criticisms of subjectivism and relativism with regard to the truth, he upheld the fact that religious faith had firm rational grounds and evidences that were convincing in the light of the presuppositions of faith. Especially in his later years, Dulles was also concerned with what he saw as the popular shift in religious consciousness from objectivism to subjectivism, and his own religious epistemology tried, with some of the same problems in Newman's approach, to provide a way out of subjectivism as well as objectivism. Faith was not just an inner impulse of individual experience.[64]

Newman perceived the historically conditioned nature of the development of doctrine, but he upheld the irreversibility of the church's dogmas "not necessarily in their wording, but in their meaning." Dulles' theology, like Newman's, rejected both "a fluid historicism and a rigid dogmatism."[65] Newman, conscious of the concrete historical circumstances in which revelation was received in the church, acknowledged not only the need for unity and harmony but also the inevitability of tension. Unlike some continental Catholic theologians of his day, he did not place the priestly, prophetic, and regal ecclesial functions exclusively in the hierarchy but held that those functions stood in tension in the church between the laity (priestly), the theologians (prophetic), and the hierarchy (regal). That fact led him to emphasize mutual understanding and, at times, tolerance and compromise within the church when differences arose. "The hierarchical leaders," for example, "may have to refrain from condemning relatively innocuous doctrinal deviations so that the theological community may enjoy a proper freedom and autonomy, relying on its own self-corrective mechanisms."[66]

Dulles' models approach to theology and his well-known theory of a dual magisterium served the same purposes he attributed to Newman's views of the threefold offices within the entire church. In Dulles' view, Vatican II, like the nineteenth-century continental theologians, dealt adequately with harmony in the church; it was less successful in dealing with the concrete tensions and dissensions than Newman had been. "If Newman's realism were put into practice, the church might be spared some of the bitter controversies that have recently arisen over questions such as the ordination of women and the supervision of the liturgical translations."[67]

Newman was an archenemy of liberalism and a supporter of dogmatic religion, the authority of the apostolic office, and the infallibility of the magisterium, as well as a "champion of liberty," "the inviolability of conscience, the dignity of the laity, and the freedom of theological investigation."[68] Newman, therefore, should not be pigeonholed; one had to take in the full range of his thinking. The same could be said of Dulles. For Dulles, as for Newman, it was not so much a balancing of freedom and authority in the church as it was a recognition of a certain constitutional order within the church. That constitutionalism, moreover, was grounded ultimately not in canon law or juridical structures but in the mystery of revelation, where it is sometimes difficult to reconcile apparent contradictions. It could be said of Dulles, moreover, as Dulles said of Newman, that "in his letters and diaries, and to a great extent in his works written for publication, we see the mind of the theologian at work, torn by his attraction for each of several incompatible positions."[69] Some of Newman's strengths and weaknesses were also those of Dulles.

Doctrine, Development, Reversals, and Reform

In his mid-eighties, Dulles continued to be a productive, publishing scholar in fundamental theology, ecclesiology, and ecumenism and periodically served as social critic and prophet of the word. What he wrote on fundamental theology (on revelation, faith, scripture, tradition, the nature of doctrine, and apologetics) reiterated much of what he had previously taught on these issues, but he gave much more attention to the hermeneutics of continuity. He took on more than in the immediate past those who stressed the reversal of previous church teachings or who emphasized the discontinuity between the present and past teachings of the church.

The nature and development of doctrine was a key issue for Dulles in the early twenty-first century. He discussed the nature of doctrine in dialogue with George Lindbeck, many of whose positions he shared, and the development of doctrine with Judge John Noonan and others. By the early 2000s, Dulles had known and had worked with George Lindbeck for more than twenty-five years. They were part of the Hartford Appeal (1975), and they both served together for years on the Lutheran/Catholic Dialogue (L/RC). For years, too, both men had shared a view that society was becoming increasingly secular and that the churches needed to take on some sectarian features in order to transmit the Christian heritage to new members. The Hartford Appeal had demonstrated something of their shared views in this regard. In 2003, Dulles reviewed one of Lindbeck's books,[70] and that review initiated an irenic and gentlemanly exchange between the two senior theologians on their respective understandings of the nature and meaning of doctrine. Although the book under review was an anthology of Lindbeck's writings, Dulles focused most of his review on Lindbeck's well-known theory of doctrine, first systematically presented in *The Nature of Doctrine: Religion and Theology in a Postliberal Age* (1984).[71]

Dulles and Lindbeck both accepted something of a models approach to revelation and were both keenly aware of the inadequacies of some previous and contemporary approaches to Christian doctrine. Lindbeck had argued that two models of doctrine dominated in contemporary Christianity: the cognitive or propositional (conservative) and the experiential-expressive (liberal). He proposed instead what he called the cultural-linguistic (seeking to transcend the other two). Doctrine, in his view, was not a mere medium for transmitting some antecedent conceptual truth nor the expression of an experience that was independent of doctrine itself. The cultural-linguistic approach to doctrine was inseparable from doctrinal content and shaped the experience for those who submitted to its power.

Dulles was "enthusiastic" about aspects of what he called Lindbeck's "project." Lindbeck's cultural-linguistic approach had the great advantage of pointing out how religious knowledge was not just a matter of information. Dulles, however, did not like the way Lindbeck used models in his theology. He said at one point in the L/RC dialogue that Lindbeck made one choose between the cognitive, subjective, and regulative approaches to dogma. "I think that all three are valid.…I think that all three are dimensions of dogma."[72] Dulles, the pluralist, preferred to keep all the models (of the church or of revelation or of theology) in dialectical tension so that they might mutually correct and enrich each other. At another point in the dialogue, Dulles charged that Lindbeck's three models tended "to end in relativism. [That charge was periodically made against Dulles' own use of models.] A precritical, primitive narrative theology is not an option. Neither is a naive critical position."[73]

Following Polanyi, Dulles preferred a postcritical approach to doctrine. In his review of Lindbeck's book, he reiterated his charge that Lindbeck's cultural-linguistic and narrative or regulative understanding of doctrine tended to become relativistic. Dulles was afraid that Lindbeck's approach to doctrine undermined the ability of language to symbolize the truth and the reality in which the symbol participated. "While rightly rejecting univocal literalism, Lindbeck seriously undermines, if he does not dismiss, the propositional truth of dogma." In the final analysis, Dulles believed that although Lindbeck wished to overcome the limitations of the liberal or critical program, his own project conceded "too much to postmodernist relativism." Dulles ended his review by expressing the hope that Lindbeck "could amend his cultural-linguistic theory to give greater attention to the capacity of religious language to disclose the reality of God."[74]

In response to Dulles' critique, Lindbeck clarified his position by admitting that his language and conceptual framework in some places led to the kinds of misunderstandings that Dulles identified and to misinterpretations of his intentions with respect to understanding doctrine's regulative role in Christianity. Doctrinal statements, as cultural-linguistic statements, important as they are for protecting the truth of the faith, are not the primary dimension of Christian faith. Nonetheless, they correspond to the reality they symbolize in the context of Christian worship and prayer. Lindbeck demurred, therefore, from Dulles' characterization of his position as postmodernist relativism. Dulles was satisfied with Lindbeck's explanation of his own theory because he gave "greater attention to the capacity of religious language to disclose the reality of God" than Dulles had previously seen in Lindbeck's work.[75] The two theologians had analogous views not only of the current situation of theology in American culture but also of religious epistemology.

Dulles also had recurring debates and discussions with Catholic scholars on changes in church doctrine. Was contemporary church doctrine in some cases (on issues like slavery, usury, religious liberty, divorce, capital punishment, just war, salvation in world religions) a reversal of previous teachings, or was it a development? On all of these issues, Dulles outlined three contemporary Catholic positions (total reversal; development and refinement of teachings; tradition unchanged but changing prudential judgments in applying tradition to the modern context). Depending on the issues, Dulles came down on the side of development or changing prudential judgments in his general "hermeneutic of continuity."

Dulles' view came to the fore particularly in his "Development or Reversal?"—a review of John T. Noonan Jr.'s *A Church That Can and Cannot Change: The Development of Catholic Moral Teaching* (2005).[76] Noonan's book dealt with changes in church teaching on usury, religious freedom, divorce, and especially on slavery. Dulles admitted that in these areas of social ethics, church teachings were more susceptible to change than in areas of revealed doctrine, but he thought that Noonan had overstepped the boundaries of evidence by claiming that the magisterium's doctrinal change in these cases was "an about-face, repudiating the erroneous past teaching of the magisterium itself." In these specific cases of social ethics, Dulles admitted changes in the magisterium's teaching, but he saw those changes as developments of previous teachings, not reversals. What remained unchanged were universal principles of morality; what changed were the applications to changing concrete social circumstances. While examining the changes, Noonan overlooked "important qualifications" because he failed to note adequately the historical and social context of previous teachings. Repeatedly Dulles acknowledged a certain level of novelty in contemporary church teachings, as he acknowledged in Vatican II's doctrine of religious liberty, but not reversals of previous teachings that had to be interpreted within their historical and social contexts in order to appreciate what was time bound in them and what transcended the particular applications.[77] He acknowledged development, but in continuity with elements of previous teachings.

Dulles made analogous assessments of what some theologians had to say about Vatican II's understanding of world religions. Some, like Paul Knitter, had argued that Vatican II reversed the church's previous teaching on non-Christian religions as mediators of revelation or grace; other theologians denied that the council had made any changes in its teaching about the world's religions. Dulles argued that the council was cautious in what it had to say about world religions (for example, making "no mention of non-Christian religions as mediators of revelation or grace"), but it was open to new developments that were consistent with Catholic tradition. The council admitted, for example, the presence of "rays of divine truth" and "seeds of the Word" in the world's religions, but it never minimized the salvific role of the church itself. It called for dialogue with the religions of the world without eschewing the church's missionary mandate.[78]

The traditional Catholic just war theory ran into similar problems of reversal or development. Dulles acknowledged, in continuity with the tradition, the validity of the just war principles, but he also recognized the difficulties of applying those principles in modern social circumstances (for example, the existence of nuclear weapons, total warfare, and terrorism).[79] Dulles did not accept a reversal of the just war theory because of the universally valid moral principles involved in the teaching, but he was very cautious about justifying modern warfare.

Dulles could be, and has been, accused of turning to the right on a host of issues in the Catholic Church because of his emphasis on continuity and organic development. But he defended himself by saying that his method had been in his early career as in his later one a historical-critical method that tried to examine church teachings in their contexts in order to discern what was permanently valid in the light of revelation and universal moral principles and what was socially and culturally conditioned. He criticized the static traditionalists as well as the modern accommodationist reformers. In his later years he was more critical of the reformers because he believed their tendency was toward relativism, which he countered wherever he met it.

The issue of reform in the church was analogous to that of reversal or development in doctrine, and Dulles at times spoke out on it. He acknowledged that "reform" had a bad taste in Catholicism after the Protestant Reformation and the Council of Trent. The Second Vatican Council to some extent sweetened the taste for reform and in fact exemplified it, but it was very much aware of the extent and limits of reform within the church. Dulles frequently quoted the Decree on Ecumenism (*Unitatis redintegratio*; UR 6) to indicate the cautious way the council approached reform in the church:

> Christ summons the Church, as she goes her pilgrim way, to that continual reformation of which she is always in need insofar as she is an institution of men here on earth. Therefore, if the influence of events or of the times has led to deficiencies in conduct, in Church discipline, or even in the formulation of doctrine (which must be carefully distinguished from the deposit itself of faith), these should be appropriately rectified at the proper moment.[80]

In the postconciliar period, however, reformatory caution was sometimes thrown to the wind on both the left and the right. Both extremes in Dulles' view had faulty notions of reform. On the left, groups like We Are Church and Call to Action emphasized an egalitarian democracy in the church that went contrary to the hierarchical nature of the church. On the moderate right were those who sought to reform the reformers or on the far right those who sought to undo the reforms of Vatican II and restore a Tridentine cultural Catholicism. Dulles asserted that the church in the United States needed intellectual, spiritual, and moral reforms because of a growing religious illiteracy, rampant dissent, failures in evangelization, flouting of liturgical laws, declining religious practices, excessive extraneous encumbrances upon pastoral offices, confusion in regard to lay and clerical roles, and the immoral and scandalous behavior of numerous Catholics whose standards of morality fell well behind that of observant Protestants and unbelievers.

But reforms and reform movements needed to be evaluated in light of Vatican II, and the very concept of reform required unpacking. For Dulles, "to reform is to give new and better form to a preexisting reality, while preserving the essentials."[81] He emphasized that all reforms needed to retain an organic continuity with the tradition without identifying tradition itself with the many contingent and historically conditioned ethnic, disciplinary, spiritual, or intellectual traditions or styles of leadership that have emerged in the course of the church's history. Genuine reforms, whether restorative or progressive, aimed to make the gospel more clearly manifest in the life of the church.

Ecclesiological Issues

Widely known for his work on ecclesiology, Dulles did not develop his understanding of the church significantly during his years as a cardinal. He did, though, take up and weigh in on various ecclesiological issues as they emerged in the theological debates in journals of opinion or in response to Vatican initiatives. He discussed, for example, the relationship between the church and the Eucharist, the pastoral teaching office (magisterium) in the church, the place of Mary in ecclesiology, and other ecclesial issues.

Church and the Eucharist

Dulles focused much of his writing during the early years of the twenty-first century on the relationship between the church and the Eucharist, giving considerable attention to it because it had become a focus of Pope John Paul II's papacy in his last years. In fact, the pope declared the year between October 2004 and October 2005 to be the "Year of the Eucharist," which culminated with a meeting of the Synod of Bishops focusing on "The Eucharist: Source and Summit of the Life and Mission of the Church." Like the pope, Dulles wrote repeatedly on the intimate relationship between the church and the Eucharist, revived an understanding of the Mass as sacrifice, and focused attention again on the Real Presence and communion.

Like the pope, Dulles repeatedly quoted Henri de Lubac's view that "the Church produces the Eucharist but the Eucharist also produces the Church." It is in the celebration of the Eucharist where the church most fully realizes and symbolizes its identity because of its intimate communion with the body of Christ. Christ founded both the church and the Eucharist, and therefore there was a reciprocal causal relationship between church and Eucharist. "Unless there were a Church, there would be no one to celebrate the Eucharist, but unless there were a Eucharist, the Church would lack the supreme source of her vitality."[82] In the eucharistic celebration, the universal church as the body of Christ was present in the local community, but it transcended the local and the temporal. Past, present, and future came together in the eucharistic celebration, in terms of the *anamnesis* of the death and resurrection, the communication of grace, and the pledge of future glory.

Prior to and during the "Year of the Eucharist," Dulles seized an opportunity to reaffirm some traditional Catholic teachings on the Mass as sacrifice, as communion, and as Real Presence. In lectures between 2003 and 2005, he attempted to restore these notions in a society, as he noted, that had become increasingly deaf to certain notions of sin and retribution, sacrifice, and Real Presence. The postconciliar emphasis on the Eucharist as meal, valuable as that was, had tended to neglect the sacrificial dimension. A new focus on traditional doctrines of the Eucharist in the church, moreover, was crucial for a church "in dire need of renewal....She is sinful in her members and in constant need of being purified. Many of the faithful are ignorant of her teachings; some few defiantly reject them. Even the clergy are not exempt from grave and scandalous sins, as we have learned all too well in these recent years."[83]

For some time Dulles had spoken of the necessity of retrieving the biblical notion of the sacrificial death of Jesus.[84] As a cardinal he focused, too, on the Mass as Christ's sacrifice and the church's sacrifice. The Bible, the tradition, and the eucharistic prayers themselves could not be understood without an understanding of sacrifice. But some misunderstandings of sacrifice (for example, scapegoat theories), some Protestant objections to the Mass as sacrifice, and some contemporary assertions that the biblical notions of sacrifice reflected primitive thinking had to be overcome in any restoration of the genuine notion of sacrifice in Catholicism. The death of Jesus as a sacrifice purified notions of sacrifice. "The Christian theology of Sacrifice, while it does not authorize killing the innocent, maintains that unearned suffering, when accepted with patient love, can be redemptive." Jesus' sacrifice was completed not with his death but with his resurrection and ascension. His once-and-for-all sacrifice was made present sacramentally and repeatedly in the Eucharist. The church, too, was said to offer the sacrifice, as was evident in the eucharistic prayer where the priest addressed the people, saying, "Brothers, pray that my sacrifice and yours may be acceptable to God the Father almightly." The sacrifice was completed in those who partook of the Eucharist in the sacrifice of praise and faith. Dulles' attempt to restore the notion of sacrifice was a combination, as he maintained, of "biblical realism with ecclesial personalism. It insists on the intrinsic connections among the sacrifice of Christ on the cross, the sacrificial meal of the Last Supper, the liturgical sacrifice of the church, and the personal sacrifice of those who participate."[85]

Dulles also focused his attention on recovering the Catholic notion of the Real Presence of Christ in the Eucharist, a doctrine, according to some opinion polls, that was not shared by large numbers of American Catholics in the postconciliar period. Dulles devoted one of his McGinley lectures to this topic, and the lecture was reprinted in a few other venues, indicating how important and timely some thought the lecture to be.[86] Vatican II, Dulles argued, had rightly restored a sense of the multiple presences of Christ: in the congregation when it prays, in the word of God when proclaimed, in the priest when he presides, and in the sacraments when they are administered. In the postconciliar period these presences were rightly emphasized but, in Dulles' view, to the neglect of the primary and substantial presence of Christ in the Eucharist. There was a tendency among some postconciliar theologians and catechists to minimize the church's earlier emphasis on Christ's true, real, and substantial presence in the Eucharist, as taught, for example, by the Council of Trent, and indeed by the Second Vatican Council itself. Dulles wanted to reemphasize the true, real, substantial, and sacramental presence of Christ, but in a way that avoided the naive realism or maximizing inclinations of some in the past and the minimizing or reductionist tendencies of some Catholics in the postconciliar period. Both dispositions were out of tune with the orthodox positions of Trent and Vatican II.

The Magisterium

Dulles produced no major sustained examination of ecclesiology in his last years except for his *Magisterium: Teacher and Guardian of the Faith* (2007),[87] which reflected much of what he had been saying on the topic for the previous twenty years. That text was intended for a general audience and as an introductory manual for understanding the role of the magisterium in the Catholic Church. The text focused on the pastoral or hierarchical magisterium. Describing the teaching office in the church—that of the pope and the College of Bishops and that of theologians—had been one of Dulles' longtime theological preoccupations, as was evident in 1970 and 1976 in particular when he began speaking of a dual magisterium in the church.[88] In those years he distinguished clearly between the role of the pastoral or hierarchical magisterium and that of the theologians who taught by reason of their academic proficiency, but it was clear that he wanted to highlight and resurrect the theologians' teaching role because of a modern (nineteenth- and early twentieth-century) narrow conception of the magisterium that had excluded theologians. His intent in those years was to expand the notion of magisterium to include theologians, even though he distinguished clearly two different roles within the magisterium.

As Dulles read the signs of the times in the 1980s and thereafter, there was a new need to refocus on the nature and function of the pastoral magisterium without denying what he had previously written about the teaching role of theologians. Post–Vatican II developments and cultural forces made it necessary in his view to be clear about the hierarchical magisterium's nature and functions. Postconciliar Catholics, for example, lacked clarity on "the respective authority of various teachers in the Church," and many were confused about the "biblical sources and the historical development of the Magisterium as a normative organ of doctrinal authority." Catholics and others in the United States, moreover, living in a liberal democratic society, had serious "misgivings" about the "very idea of an authoritative Magisterium." Popular and theological dissent to magisterial statements, furthermore, and a lack of knowledge of the degrees of authority within magisterial statements made it opportune to clarify the Catholic understanding of magisterium.[89]

Even though the "standard book in English" on the subject had been published by Francis A. Sullivan in 1983, Dulles believed that the times called for a new "concise, up-to-date manual on the subject."[90] In 2006, he was invited to prepare such a theological textbook on the magisterium to introduce students and a general Catholic readership to the biblical grounds, history, doctrine, and theology of the magisterium. It was to be primarily a book in doctrinal, not apologetical, theology. He wrote *Magisterium* (2007) for Catholic believers who wished to know more about the "authoritative transmission" of the Christian faith in their church. The book was a concise introduction but also the most extensive and sustained statement on the topic that Dulles had made up to this point in his career as a theologian.[91]

The need for an official or hierarchical magisterium was obvious to Dulles. Undoubtedly there was no need for a magisterium in the eschaton, but here on earth, because of the limitations of the human condition, there was a need for a charismatic office that preserved revelation whole and integral and passed it on with faithfulness and with the assurance and promise of the Holy Spirit. The very act of faith itself, an act that required submission to the word of God, made intelligible the need for an office that authentically preserved and transmitted the content of the word of God. For years Dulles had argued, in conjunction with Newman, that it was logical "that if God deems it important to give a revelation, he will make provision to assure its conservation." That authoritative role of conserving and transmitting revelation and its meaning belonged to the hierarchical and spirit-led magisterium of the pope and bishops in the Catholic Church. The passing on of revelation belongs to the prophetic office, as distinguished from the priestly and governing offices within the hierarchy. In their prophetic role, hierarchical authorities "speak not in their own name but on behalf of God, whose word they transmit with whatever explanations may be necessary."[92] Although the teaching function in the church is shared by others—parents, religious educators, and professional theologians—it is authoritative only in the hierarchical magisterium, which possesses the charism of the teaching office.

Dulles' *Magisterium*, as a compendium for Catholics on the subject, outlined not only the nature and functions of the teaching office in the church but also the biblical grounds for it in the New Testament, the historical evolution and development of the office, the distinctive contributions of the hierarchical and nonhierarchical (including theologians) to the church's teaching mission and their relationships to one another, the various organs within the pastoral magisterium, the infallibility of the pastoral office and the degrees of authority within various magisterial statements, the response owed to the magisterium, and the reception of magisterial teachings. Within the text Dulles made his usual careful distinctions, distinguishing in particular the faith of the church from doctrinal formulations that were historically conditioned and in need of theological interpretation. The theologian, moreover, as this text demonstrated in practice, had a crucial role to play not only in using the magisterium as "an essential resource for theology itself" but also in explaining and interpreting magisterial pronouncements. Theologians, therefore, were not mere servants of the hierarchy because they had a certain freedom indigenous to the theological task—they had what Dulles called "a certain margin for interpretation."[93]

Magisterial and papal pronouncements in particular required interpretation because those statements could range from *de fide* statements to prudential pastoral judgments. Statements coming from the Vatican, for example, carried different levels of authority and evoked different levels of response, and it was the task of theologians to point out these things. Their interpretive role (making the appropriate distinctions), moreover, could not be brushed aside without burdening the consciences of the faithful. Like other teachers in the church, furthermore, they had a responsibility to be witnesses to the faith they investigated and explained, and their authority within the church derived from their academic competence, an acquired competence, and not from a sacramental office. Unlike the hierarchical magisterium, though, they had no authority to bind the consciences of the faithful. Their authority, as Thomas Aquinas held, stemmed from their faithful use of the sources of the faith and from the force of their human argumentation.

As a theologian of the church, Dulles had a high regard for the role of the hierarchical magisterium, and as a Jesuit he was always ready to give a presumption in favor of magisterial teaching. He also had a great knowledge and sense of the church's history, and he knew of times when magisterial statements were mere prudential pastoral judgments that required respectful attention but were not binding for all time because they were so time conditioned. Other statements in the history of the church were binding upon the faithful, even though they were rejected by various factions in the church. In certain periods of history, the church's doctrines and moral positions were so contrary to the social and ethical values of the times that they were not fully received. During such times "this evil [of rejection]," he counseled, "must be patiently endured."[94]

The church had to be patient in proclaiming the meaning of the gospel in every age, whether or not the age was prepared to accept its pronouncements. Church teachers appealed to the intellect and to faith, and the response to their teaching was the free response of faith. It was this notion of teaching and faith that made Dulles counsel various elements in the American Catholic Church to be patient with the lack of full reception of certain church teachings. On the other hand, for him, patience was not an excuse for a failure to proclaim the truth and hold to it. He could be and was firm in holding to unpopular magisterial teachings (for example, against the ordination of women or contraception).

Mary and the Church

After receiving the red hat, Dulles focused some of his ecclesiological attention on the relationship between Mary and the
church. Mary had played an insignificant role in Dulles' *Models of
the Church* and in some of his other early reflections on ecclesiology, but she came to more prominence in his thinking during and
especially after the Lutheran/Catholic Dialogue (1983–1990) that
produced *The One Mediator: The Saints and Mary*. The Vatican
Council had placed Mary in an ecclesiological and eschatological
context, and Dulles had followed suit in his treatment of Mary in
his own earlier ecclesiology. He admitted, too, that his own
involvement in ecumenism in the mid-1970s led him to propose
eliminating the anathemas attached to Marian dogmas. That proposal was thought to be ecumenically fruitful, but in hindsight,
Dulles acknowledged in 2002, it could be seen as a participation in
the immediate postconciliar decline in Marian devotion and theological attention to Mary.[95]

By 2002, although Dulles saw the justification and fruitfulness
of treating Mary in the context of ecclesiology as the exemplary
Christian disciple and the model of the church's receptivity to
Christ, he believed that the theological shift away from the previous, almost exclusive emphasis on Mary's special and unique pre-
rogatives had unintentionally precipitated the decline in Marian
piety—an overreaction to the maximalist tradition of Mariology
that had characterized much of Catholicism in the nineteenth and
early twentieth centuries.

In the late 1970s, after a decade of decline, a new attention to
Mary emerged. Some theologians developed a renewed maximalist
approach, while others, criticizing the new maximalist tendencies
to "divinize" Mary, tended to minimize Mary's role in the history
of redemption. In his later years, Dulles himself seemed to favor
von Balthasar's and John Paul II's analyses of the Marian or feminine side of the church. Von Balthasar and John Paul II had each
noted the Petrine or masculine (that is, hierarchical and sacramental) and Marian or feminine (that is, active, internal receptivity)
dimensions of the church. The biblical bridal imagery of the
church underlined the interpersonal character of the church and
the fact that "the Church as a whole has a predominantly feminine

character. She is receptive to the word of God, which comes to her from outside, and in responding to the word, she gives herself in love to him who first loved her, and enters into mystical union with him."[96] At Mass, the congregation acts like Mary, saying "Yes" to the sacrifice of Jesus.[97] This emphasis on the feminine, interpersonal, covenantal dimension of the entire church also underlined the free consent that characterized Mary's own reception of Christ, making her the exemplary model of the church and of Christian discipleship.

Dulles saw a new need in the early part of the twenty-first century to reemphasize Mary's manifestation of the "mystery of victorious grace" and her singular position in God's saving plan. But he called for more balance in Catholic theology, emphasizing not only Mary as a model of the church but also her unique privileges and position in the plan of salvation. "There can be no cleavage," he wrote, "between the Mary of history and the Mary of dogma. By a neglect of history one can open the path to a divinized Mary in whom mythical projection overcomes theology. By a neglect of dogma one can deprive Mary of her distinctive role in salvation history and reduce her to the common level of our humanity."[98] Dulles noted, too, a resurgence of interest in Mary in ecumenical circles.

Interreligious Dialogues

As a cardinal, Dulles continued his interest and involvement in the ecumenical movement. Prior to becoming a cardinal he had never been explicitly involved in any of the interreligious dialogues (with Jews, Muslims, and other world religions) that were taking place in the United States. Periodically, however, he was called upon to address the issue, and after the September 11, 2001, attacks on the World Trade Center and the Pentagon in particular he emphasized the need, as did others, for interreligious dialogue because of the linking of terrorism and religion. On occasion he asserted that interreligious dialogue was no longer a luxury but an essential task not only because it was a response to Vatican II's *Nostra aetate* (NA; the Declaration on Non-Christian religions) but also because it was important "to prevent disastrous collisions between opposed religious groups" and to foster world peace and harmony among different peoples and cultures.[99] Interreligious conversation could decrease the hostilities of the past and heal raw memories.

The dialogue with Jews was uppermost for Christians because, as Pope John Paul II said frequently, they were the Christians' elder brothers and sisters. For Dulles it was obvious that Judaism "holds a special position among the non-Christian religions, since the faith of Israel is the foundation on which Christianity rests (cf. NA 4). The Hebrew Bible is a permanently valid and inspired record of God's revelation to his elect People before the coming of Christ (*Dei verbum*; DV 14)."[100] On two or three occasions Dulles addressed issues that arose between Catholicism and the Jewish community. In 1998, the Vatican's Commission for Religious Relations with the Jews published "We Remember: A Reflection on the Shoah." In 1987, Pope John Paul II had invited the commission to prepare this document on the Holocaust, which was intended to be a Catholic meditation and reflection on the catastrophe against the Jewish people that would lead to an examination of consciences for responsibility for past evils, a purification of Catholic hearts through repentance, and a healing of wounds caused by the past atrocities. It was hoped that the document would produce a new spirit in Catholic-Jewish relations, but in fact it received much criticism for being entirely too ambivalent about the Shoah and for its failures to acknowledge fully the Catholic Church's complicity in the Holocaust.[101]

Dulles was invited to comment on the controversial document shortly after it was published. In the midst of controversy over the document, Dulles, the theologian, made four comments on the significance of the document: (1) as had Vatican II, the document spoke of the church containing sinful members but avoided speaking of the church itself as sinful—a distinction some frowned upon; (2) it distinguished between anti-Judaism (which had a long and regrettable tradition in Catholic religious thought) and anti-Semitism (which was cultural, nationalistic, and racist in origin); (3) it acknowledged Catholic protection of Jews during the catastrophe but failed to mention Catholics who had collaborated in the persecution of Jews, and in this failure it fell short of the French and German episcopal statements on the Shoah; (4) it called forth, though, the need for repentance, a repentance addressed to God for the sake of restoring right order in society; and because the repentance was addressed to God it called for a firm purpose of amendment so that such tragedies would not happen in the future. But, in Dulles' view, acknowledging collective guilt for the Holocaust on the part of the present generation was problematic, because in the past Christians themselves had invoked such a concept of collective guilt to blame Jews for the death of Christ. That belief had fostered Catholic anti-Judaism.[102]

Dulles also became involved in a theological discussion of the relationship between the Old Covenant with Israel and the New Covenant. The National Council of Synagogues and the Catholic Bishops' Committee for Ecumenical and Interreligious Affairs had appointed a group of scholars to examine the relationship between the two covenants. In 2002 they published "Reflections on Covenant and Mission," which asserted in the preface that "campaigns that target Jews for conversion to Christianity are no longer theologically acceptable in the Catholic Church."[103] That particular statement, Dulles asserted, although not an official document of the USCCB, was theologically "ambiguous, if not erroneous." The crux of the problem for Dulles was the implication that the Jewish people were already in a saving covenant and need not consider Christ, who, for Christians, was the only way to salvation. For Dulles that bald statement could not be justified by the biblical record and undermined the universal evangelical mission of the church. "Reflections" itself, however, was much more nuanced than the statement in the preface had indicated, but Dulles thought that the document as a whole needed revision. That the divine promises to Judaism were permanently valid and that Jews could be saved, though somehow through Christ, Dulles had no doubt. In his analysis of "Reflections" and in some of his other writings on the two covenants, Dulles relied extensively upon the letter to the Hebrews, which asserted that "Jesus has obtained a more excellent ministry [than the Jewish high priest] now, just as he is mediator of a better covenant, founded on a better promise" (Heb 8:6).[104] Because of his emphasis on the superiority of the new covenant and the sole mediatorship of Christ, Dulles has at times been accused of a "soft supersessionism."

Because of the article he wrote on "Reflections," Dulles was invited to address a group of Jews and Catholics on the relationship between the Old and New Covenants at Catholic University in 2005. The group included members of the American Jewish Committee under the leadership of Rabbi David Rosen, director of the Department of Interreligious Affairs, and some of the Jewish and Catholic authors of "Reflections." Dulles' talk, "The Covenant with Israel," was an attempt to steer between supersessionism (that is, the view that God's relationship with Christians supersedes or replaces the prior relationship with the Jews) and the assertion that the Old Covenant in and of itself is salvific without relationship to Christ. Dulles held that it was an open question whether or not the Old Covenant remained in force today. But in saying that, he made distinctions about what in the Old Covenant with Israel was permanent and irrevocable (for example, the election of and promises to Israel, God's gifts, and the Ten Commandments) and what was conditional and provisional (for example, ceremonial and ritual laws, circumcision). Nonetheless, he opposed those who, rejecting a crude supersessionism, gave independent validity to the Old Covenant as a permanently salvific instrument and thereby argued that there were two separate but equal paths to salvation. Such a view, Dulles maintained, countered the church's teaching on the one mediatorship of Christ for the salvation of all. The New Covenant, in other words, was not a separate covenant with God independent of the Old Covenant but the fulfillment and culmination of the promises given in the Old Covenant.[105]

Dulles' talk was followed up by a very heated discussion from members of the audience. In Dulles' interpretation, the reactions were "uniformly negative. And angry." One rabbi in the audience caught Dulles "off guard by saying that there really was no covenant with the Jews anyway. He said that it would be undemocratic for God to make a special covenant with any particular people; he must treat everybody alike. So, if there was any covenant, it was with the whole of humanity. So, obviously, I [Dulles] had not received that as a position with which I was in dialogue."[106] The discussion did not help to bring clarity. Some in the audience, without paying attention to the theological distinctions that he had made, thought that Dulles held the view that the covenant with the Jews was no longer in force. He had asserted only that certain elements of the covenant were no longer in force but were fulfilled in the New Testament. This he believed to be consistent with Catholic teaching. That particular meeting of Jews and Catholics ended on a sour note and failed to advance ecumenical understanding. Misconceptions and suspicions continued to arise from some quarters in Jewish-Catholic relations.

Interreligious dialogue included other world religions besides Judaism, even though for Catholics like Dulles, Judaism retained its primacy in interreligious relations. Dulles, however, lectured and wrote periodically on the Catholic Church's relationship to other world religions, although he did so more generically than he did with respect to Judaism. Immediately after the attacks on the World Trade Center and the Pentagon, he devoted a McGinley lecture to what he called *Christ Among the Religions* (2001). In the "present crisis" it was important, he thought, to address the issues of religious tensions and hostilities that had so much contributed to worldwide instability and wars. The lecture called for tolerance among all religions of the world, outlined four models for understanding how religions related to one another, and suggested six strategies for achieving a more adequate tolerance that could contribute to world peace and harmony.

Before proceeding to outline his models of interreligious relations, however, Dulles speculated on some of the reasons that might have motivated Osama bin Laden's and other Islamic terrorists' hatred of the global effects of Western culture:

> They resent the power of the United States and its allies, which they perceive as arrogant and brutal. Even more fundamentally, they are repelled by what they perceive as the culture of the West. Their quarrel is not primarily with Christianity as a religion but much more with what they regard as the loss of religion in the West: its excessive individualism, its licentious practice of freedom, its materialism, its pleasure-loving consumerism. They see this hedonistic culture as a threat since it exercises a strong seductive power over many young people in the

traditionally Islamic societies of Asia, Africa, and other continents.[107]

This characterization seems remarkably close to Dulles' own assessment of the deficiencies of contemporary life in the West (the United States and Western Europe in particular).

Dulles outlined four models (coercion, convergence, pluralism, and tolerance) for understanding the relations of different religions to one another. The talk pleaded for worldwide tolerance and offered the United States as a model of a tolerant society in which different world religions coexisted historically in relative harmony. The first model, coercion, which predominated in much of the past before the rise of modernity, used the state to enforce a single religion on its citizens. Those who called for convergence (for example John Hick and Paul Knitter) among the world's religions did so either because they believed that all religions were mere human constructs or they asserted that all religions agreed in essentials. Convergence allowed all religions to live in peaceful coexistence without any consideration for the issues that divided them. The third model, pluralism, considered the differences in religion a blessing, not just a fact of world history; since all religions were partially true, they should all be given opportunity to flourish. Pluralism of this type appealed primarily to philosophical and religious relativists. Tolerance, the fourth model and the one that Dulles supported, acknowledged and accepted the peaceful coexistence of various religions in society for the sake of peace and justice, but it did not mean that different and contradictory religious truth claims were approved—tolerance was not the same as approval or religious indifference to the truth. The U.S. experiment in tolerance, Dulles argued, had worked well enough "to offer a possible model for the global international community."[108] Tolerance allowed Christians to maintain their claims about the absolute uniqueness of Christianity and Catholics to assert the truth of the Catholic tradition while appreciating and tolerating, for the sake of justice and peace in society, the presence of other world religions.

In a society where tolerance was operative, Dulles suggested six strategies for bringing about better relations between the world's religions. These strategies flowed from his understanding of Vatican II's documents (UR, NA) and his own experience in the ecumenical movement. He suggested (1) study of one another's religious traditions to gain knowledge of the other and to eliminate prejudices of the past; (2) cooperation among the world's religions in responding to the needs of the poor and dispossessed around the globe; (3) common witness to the religious truths that united the various religious traditions; (4) common prayer and worship when appropriate; (5) the healing of historical memories through mutual repentance and forgiveness; and (6) theological dialogues between the religions that avoided both proselytization on the one hand and a false irenicism on the other.[109]

In 2003, Dulles was invited to prepare an article on interreligious dialogues for a festschrift dedicated to Jacques Dupuis, a friend, theological colleague, fellow classmate, and longtime professor at the Gregorian University, and a theological expert on relations between the Catholic Church and the world's religions. Dupuis's *Toward a Christian Theology of Religious Pluralism* (1997) was censured in 2001 by the CDF for certain "ambiguities."[110] Because of his friendship and his belief in the freedom necessary for the theologian, freedom even to be wrong in speculation, Dulles contributed to the festschrift in honor of Dupuis.

Using the documents of Vatican II (especially the four major constitutions and *Nostra aetate*) as his guides, Dulles underlined a Catholic understanding of the relationship of Christianity to other religions in the new millennium. On the issue of world religions, Dulles held, the documents of Vatican II were cautious and yet open to new developments. One could not argue, however, as some had done in the postconciliar era, that Vatican II had reversed or mitigated Catholic teaching on the uniqueness and privileged status of Christianity; nor could one maintain that other world religions, containing grace and revelation, were alternate ways of salvation or hold that the church was unnecessary for salvation or that the Christian missionary mandate was inconsistent with ecumenism and interreligious dialogue. Those relativizing positions, upheld by persons like Paul Knitter and John Hick, whom Dulles characterized as radical religious pluralists, undermined "traditional teaching on the absolute primacy of Christ."[111] The four basic constitutions of Vatican II were clear on the sole mediatorship of Christ for all human beings and on the church as the instrument of redemption for all.

Nonetheless, Vatican II made some important new clarifications on the relationship of other world religions to Christ and the church. What was particularly new in the council was the acknowledgment that non-Christian religions contained elements of truth and goodness, and that the enlightening "rays of divine truth" and "seeds of the word" were providential gifts in other world religions that "could find their fulfillment in Christian faith." The religions of the world may indeed embody signs and symbols of God's gracious presence, and "these tokens may be called rays of divine truth, seeds of the word, and preparations for the gospel." Vatican II, in Dulles' interpretation, made it clear that God's universal, salvific will extended to all but in such a way that in order to be saved, all persons must in some way be oriented to Christ and the church. The possibility of salvation for those within the world's religions, however, did not require "that non-Christian religions mediate the grace of God, nor does it exclude the possibility that religions may play a salvific role in the process."[112]

None of these conciliar acknowledgments, however, eliminated the need for explicit Christian proclamation and for the missionary mandate. The traditional missionary mandate, moreover, did not preclude the possibility of dialogue with the world's religions for the sake of building up trust, eliminating prejudices, learning from one another, and mutually contributing to the world's welfare. Dialogue, unlike proclamation and missionary work, was not a direct call for conversion, but it could involve mutual proclamation and help prepare the ground for future conversion.[113]

In his approach to other world religions, as on most other issues, Dulles exercised his "hermeneutics of continuity" and simultaneously acknowledged what John Courtney Murray had called the "growing edge of the tradition." Although Dulles hoped that his essay on world religions would be "convergent, or perhaps fully concordant" with Dupuis's positions,[114] nowhere in the essay did Dulles mention or cite Dupuis's positions. Dulles' own position was closely aligned with the CDF's position as articulated in *Dominus Iesus* (2000) and other recent Vatican documents.

Avery Cardinal Dulles

An Evangelical Catholic Theologian

Dulles had become something of an itinerant Evangelical Catholic theologian especially in his later years. In his correspondence, his lecturing and sermons, and in his many trips to theological conventions in the United States and abroad, he carried the message of the new evangelization to various audiences. He kept up a lively and extensive correspondence with publishers, theological colleagues, relatives, former students, and friends. Like John Henry Newman, he took great care in composing responses to the inquiries of his correspondents. He had letters from all sides of the theological spectrum. Whether his correspondents approved or criticized his positions, they received courteous and at times frank and lengthy responses to their missives. Most of the time, though, he did not respond to what he called "hate mail." He received multiple invitations for visiting professorships, to review books, and to examine manuscripts intended for publication; bishops, too, frequently asked him to critique papers and documents they were writing either as individual bishops or as chairs of USCCB committees. Throughout his career as an active theologian, moreover, he received about two or three invitations a month for speaking engagements. Most of these invitations he had to turn down because of his very busy teaching, public lecturing, and publishing schedule.

Dulles also engaged in what could be called a "pastoral ministry of correspondence," spending hours each week of his life responding to the many people who wrote to him seeking advice, for example, about joining the Catholic Church, children who had left the church, matters of conscience, colleges and universities where one could find sound Catholic doctrine, proposed dissertations and publications, marriages on the brink of failure or already in divorce, vocations to the priesthood, and a host of other issues requiring spiritual and/or theological direction. Dulles took all of this correspondence seriously and wrote sometimes lengthy responses offering pastoral advice. To one lay correspondent who had requested information on a series of theological issues, Dulles wrote a four-page reply, detailing his response to the questions and indicating bibliography where more information on the topics could be located. The correspondent was "delighted and horrified" with the response: delighted because of the time and care Dulles took to respond; horrified that she had taken so much of his time. "Had I known that you would not simply pass on a short list of sources to an assistant to forward to me but would, rather, take a great block of precious time to compose a long and carefully considered letter in response to my requests, I would never have had the temerity to present my questions to you."[115]

Some correspondents simply wanted to tell him that they had read one of his works and wanted further clarifications, which he provided. Periodically he received a manuscript from an author who either wanted him to endorse it or to comment on it prior to publication. He could be at times quite frank in his response. To a Mexican Benedictine who had written in Spanish a short historical account of Dulles' relationship with Fr. Leonard Feeney, Dulles responded, after pointing out mistakes in the text, "I find it remarkable that you have managed to combine so many errors and misleading statements in one sentence. I hope that your theological scholarship is more careful."[116] Other correspondents wrote to acknowledge their indebtedness to him for something he had written. In 2002, for example, a fellow convert told him that he had been converted to Catholicism many years ago and that he was influenced to make this decision after he had read Dulles' *Testimonial to Grace.*[117]

Various young men sought his advice about discerning their vocations to the priesthood or about how young Jesuits ought to function in the Jesuit community.[118] To one college student seeking advice about a vocation, he described his own discernment process as a young man and then gave him the following advice:

> You will not find an ideal community anywhere. I think that some Jesuits (and some non-Jesuits) made false moves in the wake of Vatican II, and the Society, like most branches of the clergy, is paying a price. But I am impressed with the quality of the younger Jesuits, those in the under-forty group, who seem to be much more committed to faithful service in the Church. If you join the clergy or a religious order, it will not be for the sake of a career. You will be serving in the way that others

think you can be of best service. I have never asked for any assignment in the Society of Jesus, and if I did ask I should be prepared for a refusal, since by my vows I am bound to obey. That is part of the gift of self to God which one makes as a religious. It helps to rid one of the temptations of selfishness and pride, to do God's work rather than live according to one's own choice. In that one can find great peace.[119]

The letter was typical of the kind of response he gave to young people seeking his wisdom about a vocation.

To a Catholic laywoman troubled with "today's morality" and confusion in the church, he wrote:

In many places I find a strong devotion to moral principle and a resurgence of vitality in the Church which are very encouraging. In other places there seems to be a spirit of boredom and discouragement. But if one knows any history, one will hesitate to deplore our own times as the worst. There have been times of gross immorality and infidelity from which the Church has, in part recovered. So I continue to rely on the grace and providence of God. Even if we suppose that we are entering into the "last times" as described, for instance, in 2 Timothy 3:1–5, this would not affect our obligation to adhere to Christ and his principles....One gift which we converts may have more than others is that of not taking Christ and the Church too much for granted. If there is anything I can do to assist you to grow in the faith and love of God, please let me know. In any case, I shall keep you in my prayers.[120]

Shortly after he was named a cardinal in 2001, Dulles received numerous letters from former students he had taught at Fordham in the 1950s, from old Navy buddies, from old friends from St. Benedict Center, and a host of others—all congratulating him on his elevation to the cardinalate. Dulles responded to most of these letters with a personal touch to each.[121] One former Fordham student he had taught in the 1950s wrote to thank him for the "irrepressible joy" in reading Dulles' *New World of Faith*, and recalled the "joy and thrill" of casual conversations he and other students had had with him in Fordham's Ramskeller.[122]

The thousands of letters in his personal archives indicate that he spent a significant portion of his week responding to correspondents and preaching the gospel in this way—a practice that he had entertained throughout his career. Most of his letters, moreover, were not perfunctory responses but thoughtful and specific messages to those seeking his particular advice. He was a high-profile figure in church and society, and numerous people of all ages, theological orientations, and religious affiliations sought out his counsel.

Dulles' pastoral ministry of correspondence was a side of his private life unknown to most of his Jesuit confreres, although well known to his dedicated research associate and secretarial assistant, Dr. Anne-Marie Kirmse, OP, and Mrs. Maureen Noone. On one of my trips to Fordham to interview Dulles and examine his personal papers, I invited him out to dinner after a long day of interviews and research in his papers. We returned from dinner at about 9:00 p.m. I was exhausted from the day. Dulles, though, said he still had a couple of hours of correspondence to finish. So he returned to his office to complete the day's work. He was in his late eighties at the time.

Being elevated to the cardinalate did not change Dulles' work habits or his ministry of correspondence; in fact, the correspondence multiplied after he received the red hat. A Jesuit colleague asked him how he thought the red hat might change his life. He told him that his new title was purely honorary and he hoped he would be left alone to teach and lecture and write.[123] He in fact continued to work as a theologian, focusing his attention, as he had done for more than forty years, on explicating and interpreting the documents of the Second Vatican Council.[124]

For the first few years after his elevation to the cardinalate, Dulles continued, as he had in the past, his many trips to Germany, Poland, France, and Italy, among other countries, lecturing on theology and spreading his evangelical message. Many of his books and articles, too, were translated into various foreign languages.

His public lectures at Fordham, which were published for a wider distribution, his evangelical and autobiographical talks to students at various colleges and universities, and his addresses to numerous other groups, including the Harvard alumni at the Harvard Catholic Club (New York City), kept him on the go from 2001 until 2007, when his health began to fail him.

16
THE LAST YEARS

FOR SOME YEARS AFTER he moved to Fordham, Dulles, in his seventies, had begun to feel the effects of post-polio syndrome.[1] He paid little attention, however, to an increasing weakness in his legs. Fr. Gerald Blaszczak, SJ, the rector of the Fordham Jesuit community at the time, became concerned and noticed that Dulles' "legs were weakening, and he was falling with greater frequency. And it was very, very hard to get him to the point of getting any physical therapy."[2] Dulles was never solicitous about his health prior to 2007, and he did not want to get the medical attention his rector thought he needed. Nonetheless, the difficulties became so serious that in November 2001 he was forced to get a brace on his left leg that would allow him to walk without falling. His health continued to be a problem from time to time, and periodically he was placed in the hospital for various conditions: prostate surgery in 1994 and two heart operations after 2004. On each occasion he bounced back and returned to his teaching, writing, and lecturing. In 2007, however, after a wound became infected because of a serious fall, he was moved from Spellman Hall, where Jesuits actively employed at Fordham were living, to Loyola Hall, another Jesuit residence (for elderly and retired Jesuits), making it easier for him to walk with a cane or walker to his office in Faber Hall, which was attached to Loyola.

From January to the end of the summer 2007, Dulles kept up his hectic pace of research, writing, lecturing, and publishing. By the end of the summer, he had published one book, *Magisterium: Teacher and Guardian of the Faith*, and sixteen articles and reviews, and delivered eight public lectures. On April 14, for example, he traveled to Madison, Wisconsin, to give a lecture on evangelization to University of Wisconsin students at the St. Paul Catholic

Receiving an honorary doctorate at Marquette University, 2007

Center, which was celebrating its hundredth anniversary.[3] On the following day, the Second Sunday of Easter, he gave a homily at the center, preaching on the so-called doubting Thomas Gospel (John 20:19–31). He identified himself with the students in the pews, as he frequently did in talks to college students: "The years of study in college are often decisive for giving direction to one's life as a whole. In my own case I can say that my transition from a vague agnosticism to the Catholic faith corresponded to the four years of my undergraduate education at a secular university."[4]

Dulles went on to say that "in every generation the faith has to be rediscovered." He used the apostle Thomas as an example of what it meant to discover or rediscover the faith. Thomas had personal doubts, "not unlike the ones that we experience from time to time." Doubt was a part of the Christian life, and he assured students that believing was not easy for Thomas or for any generation of Christians: "The doctrines of our faith are so strange as to be practically incredible. Who could imagine that God would be present on this earth as a man, that one man would be the Savior of the world, that he would rise gloriously from the dead, and that he would give his body and blood to be eaten and drunk by his followers?" To believe in such things is miraculous. "The doubts of St. Thomas, far from embarrassing us, give us assurance that he and the other apostles did not believe lightly." Thomas had personal doubts, but his faith was sustained by his contact with his fellow apostles. Faith is not, therefore, a simple individual discovery but an act of the believing church that sustains personal belief in Christ as Savior: "Unlike Judas, who lost faith and separated himself from the other apostles, Thomas remained in contact with the group," and in spite of his personal incredulity he kept up his association with the Eleven. His experience "reminds us that the church is not a collection of isolated individuals but a community in which the members support one another....Every individual is capable of losing the faith, but the faith of the Church is indefectible. In our moments of doubt, therefore, we must turn to the Church to support us."

Thomas was a model for students to make a "total surrender of faith." He challenged students to make this act of faith within the community of faith.

> In the name of St. Thomas, therefore, I beg you not to become half-hearted Christians, uncertain of what you stand for....Do whatever it takes to settle in your minds whether Christianity is true, if once you have answered this question, let Jesus be your Lord and your God, and cast your whole life in the balance. If you give yourselves totally to God, you will find a joy and peace that are not of this world. Even if you die, you will live.[5]

The homily, not unlike other talks he gave to college students in his later years as a cardinal, was vintage Dulles, who personally knew the struggles of college-aged students.

Immediately after Dulles returned from Madison, he gave his spring McGinley lecture, "Evolution, Atheism, and Religious Belief" (April 17, 2007),[6] and continued working on other articles and lectures. From July 19 to 23, he attended with Fr. James Massa, his former student and the director of the Bishops' Committee in Ecumenical and Interreligious Affairs (BCEIA), his last ecumenical meeting at Oberlin, Ohio. In 1957, his own mentor, Gustave Weigel, had attended at Oberlin the Faith and Order meeting of the National Council of Churches of Christ in U.S.A. The meeting that Dulles attended in 2007 was a fiftieth anniversary celebration of that first meeting. He spoke on the visions of Christian unity and reiterated his view that the bilaterals had done as much as they could at the present and that the ecumenical movement, which was becoming increasingly reconfessionalized, was in a new stage of its development, which called for a mutual enrichment through shared testimony. This meeting was in fact Dulles' swan song as an ecumenist.[7]

By the end of July, when I visited him, he was still working vigorously on articles to be published. He was able to walk, but with more difficulty than the previous summer, and he could speak with clarity, although he was beginning to slur some of his speech. By August 25, 2007, when he presided at the marriage of Christine Marie Julep and Dylan John Murphy, the son of his good friends Monica and John Murphy, he was unable to preach. John recalled that Dulles "did a very good job of doing the ceremony, but you could tell it was an effort. So, I was glad that one of the other Jesuits agreed to give the homily."[8]

By the fall of 2007, Dulles' health was declining sharply. He was diagnosed with pseudobulbar palsy, a part of the post-polio syndrome, which affected the muscles in his neck and throat. His speech had become almost unintelligible at times, and he was having difficulties swallowing. He continued, however, to do his research and writing. On October 11 he traveled to Assumption College in Worcester, Massachusetts, the last trip he was able to make, where he was slated to deliver a lecture during the inauguration of Assumption's new president, Francesco Caesareo, who had known Dulles and who had been a graduate student in Fordham's Department of History. Dulles gave a brief oral introduction to the lecture on the nature of a Catholic college and the special role of theology within a college. Because he had some difficulties with his speech, he had asked a Fordham colleague, Fr. Louis Pascoe, SJ, Caesareo's professor in medieval church history, to read the lecture for him as he sat on the stage.[9]

On October 20 and 21, Dulles was supposed to deliver a lecture on catechesis to groups in Lansing and Ann Arbor, Michigan, but his health made it impossible for him to be in attendance. Instead, he sent his lecture, which was read to the diocesan conferences by others.[10] Shortly thereafter, on November 7, his McGinley lecture at Fordham, "Who Can Be Saved?," was read by Thomas E. Smith, SJ, superior of Fordham's Loyola Hall, because Dulles was unable to speak clearly.[11] Dulles, however, responded to questions after the lecture.

By the end of 2007 and the beginning of 2008, Dulles' health was declining rapidly, and, after he fell again, requiring hospitalization and some stitches in his arm, his Jesuit superiors decided in February to move him to Murray-Weigel Hall, the Jesuit residence for the infirm. He could no longer speak or swallow, had a feeding tube, and was losing weight, but he continued to go to his office to work on his publications. In the midst of these health problems, he retired from the McGinley chair. He prepared, though, his last McGinley lecture for the spring semester of 2008, a lecture summarizing his life as a theologian that was read by Fordham's ex-president Joseph O'Hare, SJ, while Dulles sat on the stage.[12] He acknowledged in the talk that a "benign providence has governed my days," and he accepted his current suffering and diminishment of capacities as part of a "full human existence" and the "normal ingredients in life, especially in old age." He ended his lecture with an interpretation of his own weakened condition in light of his understanding of the Gospels:

Final McGinley lecture, 2008

As I become increasingly paralyzed and unable to speak, I can identify with the many paralytics and mute persons in the Gospels, grateful for the loving and skillful care I receive and for the hope of everlasting life in Christ. If the Lord now calls me to a period of weakness, I know well that his power can be made perfect in infirmity. "Blessed be the name of the Lord!"[13]

After O'Hare read the talk, Fr. Robert Imbelli, a Boston College theologian, gave a response, summarizing Dulles' personal journey of faith seeking understanding and his major contributions to theology.[14] The president of Fordham University, Fr. Joseph McShane, SJ, then asked Cardinal Dulles for a blessing upon the large audience in attendance. In silence, and with considerable difficulty, Dulles raised his arm to bless those present—a moving moment that demonstrated the power of grace in weakness. This event was Dulles' last public appearance.

Dulles had repeatedly spoken about suffering in the past, particularly in his correspondence with those who were in bad health. To one Jesuit, for example, he wrote in 1993:

The illnesses of many friends these days makes me think increasingly of the fragility of all our lives and the importance of looking beyond. It becomes increasingly important to understand that diminishment as well as growth can be part of the spiritual life. The public life of Christ apart from his passion and death would not have been the world's salvation.[15]

After the McGinley lecture, Dulles was supposed to give an address at Mundelein Seminary outside of Chicago for a conference on "The Theological Contribution of Avery Cardinal Dulles, SJ." Because of his health, he could not attend, so the organizers of the conference invited Dulles' research associate, Sr. Anne-Marie Kirmse, to present a paper. She asked Dulles if he had a paper she could deliver, but he told her to prepare one of her own. She delivered a paper on his contributions to theology.[16]

When Pope Benedict XVI visited New York in 2008, he

requested a meeting with Dulles. On April 19, the two theologians met at St. Joseph's Seminary (Dunwoodie, New York), where the pope was to speak to a large crowd of young people. Dulles was taken to the seminary and had a brief visit with the pope, a theologian he had first met in 1971. Sr. Anne-Marie Kirmse was present at the meeting and recorded that the "pope literally bounded into the room with a big smile on his face. He went directly to where Cardinal Dulles was sitting, saying, 'Eminenza, Eminenza, I recall the work you did for the International Theological Committee in the 1990s.'" Unable to speak, Dulles

With Pope Benedict XVI at St. Joseph's Seminary, Dunwoodie, Yonkers, New York, April 2008

smiled back and kissed the papal ring. Fr. Thomas R. Marciniak of the Fordham Jesuit Community served as Dulles' assistant at the meeting and read to the pope a greeting Dulles had prepared, detailing the various times that the two theologians had met in the past. Marciniak then handed the pope a gift from Dulles, his recently published *Church and Society* with a handwritten inscription. Before the pope left, he blessed Dulles, assured him of his prayers, and encouraged him in his sufferings.[17]

Dulles returned to Fordham's Murray-Weigel Hall, where his deteriorating body trapped a still active mind that remained very alert. He continued his daily routine of attending Mass and prayer, but he was totally incapacitated physically and could communicate only by nodding his head in response to questions or typing with extreme difficulty his answers or questions on a Lightwriter (a text-to-speech communication device) programmed for him. His research associate, Sr. Anne-Marie, and his part-time secretary, Maureen Noone, continued to care for him, and Sr. Anne-Marie continued to help him get his previously written manuscripts ready for publication. For someone who had an enormous capacity for intellectual work and who spent hours each day in writing (either in personal correspondence or in preparing articles and books for publication), this current incapacity to do such work and his total dependence on others must have been most excruciating. He had to rely on Sr. Anne-Marie totally to prepare for publication manuscripts he had intended to publish before his physical condition worsened.

As Dulles struggled with his own physical incapacities, he was aware that his brother John and John's wife, Eleanor, were very seriously ill. They both died within four days of each other in late June 2008, and immediately Sr. Anne-Marie informed Dulles of their deaths. As he mourned their deaths, he must have realized that his own death was imminent. Almost every muscle and bodily function was shutting down, and he was totally dependent upon his health care providers. His prospects for recovery, moreover, were not good because pseudobulbar palsy would eventually shut down his respiratory system. He knew these were the expected effects of his condition.

Even as his paralysis increased, his mind remained sharp, and he kept his sense of humor. In late September his godson Andrew Curry visited him. By then Dulles could barely nod his head. Andrew commented to him that "it must be difficult for you to be trapped in that body of yours." Dulles signaled, no, and then blinked at the machine in front of him, indicating that he wanted Andrew to type out a message on the Lightwriter keyboard. Andrew pointed to keyboard letters, and when he pointed to the right ones Dulles nodded his head. Through this torturous process Andrew typed out, "Very difficult for a liberation theologian."[18]

On December 12, 2008, the feast of Our Lady of Guadalupe, after a little more than nine months in the Jesuit infirmary, Dulles died. He had succumbed to a period of weakness and suffering and purification, as he wrote months prior to his death; he interpreted those last days as another dispensation of divine providence. "If the Kingdom is the pearl of great price, the treasure buried in the field," he once wrote, "one should be prepared to give up everything else to acquire it."[19] He gave up his life in the hope of acquiring it. What he wrote in 1946, after returning from World War II, illustrates the unbending aim of his life: "May we, on departing this life, be able to echo on our lips and in our hearts the glorious boast of the Apostle of the Gentiles, "Cursum consummavi, fidem servavi" [I have finished the race, I have kept the faith, 2 Tim 4:7].[20]

Pope Benedict XVI sent Edward Cardinal Egan of New York a telegram of condolences immediately after Dulles' death, noting the church's "immense gratitude for the deep learning, serene judgment, and unfailing love of the Lord and his Church which marked his entire priestly ministry and his long years of teaching and theological research."[21] Newspapers across the United States and in various other countries announced his death and rehearsed the major accomplishments of America's only cardinal theologian who was not a bishop. "A scion of diplomats and Presbyterians," the *New York Times* reported, Dulles made his mark as a theological diplomat within the Catholic Church during times of rapid change and conflict.[22] Many other obituaries noted his prominence as an American theologian with worldwide influence, calling attention particularly to the moderating tone of his theology, his respect for diverse opinions, his "creative fidelity," and the changes that took place in his theology during the period after the Second Vatican Council.[23]

Cardinal Theodore McCarrick, Dulles' former student and longtime friend, paid him a tribute that many of Dulles' admirers could affirm: "He was a holy man, totally without guile or pretense. The great theologian saints of the Jesuits would be very proud of him. American Catholics and all who seek the truth in holiness will thank God for Avery's many years of gentle and extraordinary service to the Church."[24] McCarrick noted also that Dulles was a "faith filled and a faithful theologian." When asked to assess Dulles' contribution to the universal church, McCarrick suggested that "after the Council, because of men like Dulles, I think theology, Catholic theology in America became a very important part of the life of the Church."[25] Prior to the council, few in the universal church would have paid any attention to American theological contributions. Dulles' life as a theologian reflected the emergence of theology as a significant part of the American Catholic tradition, having all the earmarks of a developing discipline.

Three funeral Masses of Christian burial were celebrated for Dulles, as was customary for a cardinal of the Catholic Church. Two were celebrated at the Fordham University Church, where

Dulles was ordained and where he periodically celebrated Mass: one of them primarily for the New York Province Jesuits, the other for the Fordham University community. The third Mass was at St. Patrick's Cathedral in Manhattan where Cardinal Egan officiated, joined by five other cardinals and a large number of archbishops, bishops, abbots, and priests, as well as more than 750 other mourners, including Archbishop Demetrios, Primate of the Greek Orthodox Church in America, representatives from American Protestant denominations, and members of Dulles' family.[26]

The homilies at these Masses focused upon Dulles' creative fidelity, as John J. Cecero, SJ, and the other homilists noted. "As Jesuits," Cecero pointed out, "we are called to live at the heart of the church and at the same time at the frontier." Dulles' life was a fulfillment of that vocation. At the Mass for the university community, Joseph O'Hare, SJ, former president of Fordham, called Dulles not only a prince of the church but a citizen of the academy: "Through his extraordinary gifts of insight and expression, he has left us a guide to his own personal pilgrimage that can enlighten the search of others, whether they be men and women of faith, seeking understanding, or citizens of the academy, where understanding is often searching for faith." Dulles was always the teacher, O'Hare pointed out, even in his last days when he suffered in identification with the one in whom he believed (*Scio cui credidi*). His "fidelity to the truth of the Catholic tradition, what he believed, was rooted in his deep and confident trust in the one in whom he believed, the ultimate source of that tradition, Our Lord and Savior Jesus Christ, who now has welcomed him to everlasting life." In the course of the homily, O'Hare recalled a humorous event that he cherished. He told the university audience that when he read Dulles' last McGinley lecture, he asked Dulles if he could make any changes in the text. Dulles "replied in writing, 'Only if they are improvements.'" O'Hare read the text exactly as it was written, but when he had finished reading the text, Dulles, no longer able to speak, wrote him a note: "Thanks for the improvements."[27]

Cardinal Egan, who had grown fond of Dulles and identified with him in his later years because both of them suffered from the effects of polio they had contracted in their earlier years, delivered the homily at St. Patrick's Cathedral. He recalled that as a young seminarian in Italy, he visited one day a church in Umbria that had an ancient crucifix. When viewed from one side, the face of Christ appeared "contorted in pain"; from the other, it had "a clear unmistakable, and—indeed—challenging smile." Egan used this image to summarize Dulles' life: one of suffering and triumph. He experienced pain as a result of the reaction of his family to his conversion, his polio during World War II, and his immobility and almost total physical incapacities in the months prior to his death. But his life also manifested the elements of triumph. His conversion story was an emblem of the triumph of grace. When he contracted polio in the Navy, he was told he would never write again because of the paralysis in his right arm. "He proved them monumentally wrong," becoming the author of twenty-five books and more than eight hundred articles. His many services to the church and to theology, universal as well as local, were exemplary: "You have the example of a triumphant life-story, never matched, to my knowledge, by any other American Catholic theologian." The suffering and incapacities of Dulles' last days also demonstrated something of a testimonial to grace. Cardinal Egan, who was lame because of his earlier polio, recalled that when he wheeled Dulles' "bed on wheels" up the aisle of the Fordham chapel for the celebration of his ninetieth birthday, Egan, thinking the ride might be too bumpy because of his own limp, turned to Dulles and said, "Forgive me if the procession was not as smooth as it should have been. I am afraid it's a case of the 'lame pushing the lame.'" Dulles broke into a wide smile that reminded Egan of the illuminating face on that ancient crucifix.[28]

The Jesuits' New York Provincial, David S. Ciancimino, SJ, also spoke at the St. Patrick's Mass of Christian burial. He noted what Dulles meant to the Jesuits. He was to them, "Avery, our brother—our older, wiser brother. He loved the Society and took common life very seriously....He taught our scholastics—both in the classroom and in life. He prepared us for ministry. He modeled Jesuit and priestly life and service for us."[29]

After these remarks, Cardinal Egan intoned the *Salve Regina*, the most celebrated Marian hymn that Dulles would have recited in the Breviary every year from Holy Trinity Sunday to Advent. The entire congregation joined in singing the hymn, filling the cathedral with joyous sound. The final procession then moved out onto Fifth Avenue, during which a thunderous applause broke out from the congregation.

In the early twenty-first century, it is difficult to assess the historical significance and contributions of Dulles' life, but there is little doubt that he was a model to many in his life, in his last sufferings, and in his death. We are too close, however, to his life to get a bird's-eye view of his long-lasting theological contributions. That assessment is for another generation to make. Nonetheless, some things are clear about his life as a whole. That life was shaped by the Dulles family heritage, his conversion experience at Harvard, his formation in and identification with Ignatian spirituality, his Jesuit education, and by the Second Vatican Council, which became the defining event of his life as a theologian. He became a primary theological interpreter of that council for American Catholics and for many others, not only in the English-speaking world but also in many other parts of the world where his books and articles have been translated.

There are those who say that Dulles was not a particularly creative theologian, like Karl Rahner or Hans Urs von Balthasar. Dulles was, however, a theologian for his times, and he creatively appropriated and analyzed and reinterpreted the Catholic theological traditions in the light of developments at the Second Vatican Council and communicated his own theological perspective with clarity and effectiveness to large segments of the postconciliar Catholic and Protestant communities in the United States. What he communicated to his theological colleagues and to the reading public about the council's message changed in emphasis as he responded to the changing times in which he lived. Throughout the changing emphases, however, was a major constant: his commitment to thinking with the church as that thinking was articulated by the hierarchy and its greatest theologians (some of whom were not always in step with every pronouncement of the hierarchy).

Development in continuity characterized his approach to the theological enterprise in the postconciliar period. In this endeavor, as Joseph Komonchak once wrote, Dulles could be placed within the company of many of the greatest Catholic theologians of the twentieth century, many of whom were also nominated or created cardinals: Yves Congar, Jean Daniélou, Alois Grillmeier, Pietro

Pavan, Hans Urs von Balthasar, and Henri de Lubac.[30] What Dulles once wrote about de Lubac could very well be used to summarize the meaning of Dulles' own life as a theologian:

> He was emphatically a man of the Church, deeply involved in the pastoral problems of the day. He was also a man of tradition, seeking to retrieve earlier insights that could be of help for our own time. A master of the apt quotation, he often cited the words of others to express his own thoughts. He did so partly out of modesty, no doubt, but also because he believed that good theology stands within the great tradition.[31]

NOTES

Preface

1. "The Faith of a Theologian," in *Believing Scholars*, ed. James L. Heft (New York: Fordham University Press, 2005), 157–58.

2. Dulles to Charles R. Morris, June 10, 1997, in Dulles Papers, Fordham University (hereafter DPFU).

3. Dulles to Christopher M. Bellitto, March 10, 2003; copy of letter in my possession.

4. Dulles to James A. Kalbaugh, April 3, 2002, in DPFU.

5. John Bolt, "Calvinism, Catholicism and the American Experiment: What Is the Question?" *Journal of Markets and Morality* 5 (Spring 2002): 183.

Chapter 1. Dulles Family Heritage

1. Avery Dulles dropped his Christian name Charles in the late 1930s.

2. My information on the Dulles family comes primarily from an unpublished family document, "Dulles and Related Family Records," based on public records and compiled in 1946 by Heatly Courtonne Dulles. That document is in DPFU. Further data on Joseph Dulles is available from Robert P. Stockton, "Dulles' House Built in 1780s," Charleston, SC, *News and Courier* (May 28, 1979): B1, and Samuel Gaillard Stoney, *The Dulles Family in South Carolina* (Columbia: University of South Carolina, 1955). I also received helpful information on the Dulles family from Mrs. Judith Dulles, wife of John Foster Dulles II, who gave me private family records that are located in the Harry Ransom Humanities Research Center, the University of Texas at Austin (hereafter HRHC,TX): "The Record of My Ancestry: The Avery-Pomeroy Family Book of Origins" and "The Record of My Ancestry: The Dulles-Foster Family Book of Origins." Other evidence of family history came from Philip A. Crowl's interview with Avery Dulles for the John Foster Dulles Oral History Project, Princeton University: "A Transcript of a Recorded Interview with Father Avery Dulles," Woodstock College, Maryland, July 30, 1966 (hereafter this document is cited as "Crowl interview"), the transcript and other Dulles family papers are available at the Mudd Library at Princeton University; Avery Dulles, *John Foster Dulles: His Religious and Political Heritage*, Flora Levy Lecture in the Humanities, 1994 (Lafayette: University of

Southwestern Louisiana, 1994), and from interviews I conducted with Avery Cardinal Dulles, SJ (June 8–10, 2004, August 2–5, 2005, and July 24, 2007, at Fordham University) and his brother John Watson Foster Dulles (November 19, 2004, and June 9, 2006, at University of Texas, Austin).

3. On Union Theological Seminary, see Robert T. Handy, *A History of Union Theological Seminary in New York* (New York: Columbia University Press, 1987), ix, 45, 47.

4. *Life in India: Or, Madras, the Neilgherries, and Calcutta* (Philadelphia: American Sunday School Union, 1855). John Welsh was actively engaged in various Presbyterian projects, as is indicated in other books and pamphlets he wrote, among which were *The Soldier's Friend* (Philadelphia: C. S. Luther, 1861); *Life by the Ganges, Or, Faith and Victory* (Philadelphia: Presbyterian Publication Committee, 1867); *Historical Report of the Yale Class of 1844: From 1844 to 1874, With a Notice of Its Third Decennial Re-union, June 24, 1874* (Philadelphia: n.p., 1874); *The Ride through Palestine* (Philadelphia: Presbyterian Board of Publication, 1881); *Westminster Sabbath-School Hymnal: A Collection of Hymns and Tunes for Use in Sabbath-Schools and Social Meetings* (Philadelphia: Presbyterian Board of Publications and Sabbath-School Work, 1883); *The Forty-Year Gathering of the Yale Class of 1844. Briefly Reported for the Class by Its Secretary, John W. Dulles* (Philadelphia: n.p., 1884); and, posthumously, *The Office of Ruling Elder in the Presbyterian Church in the United States of America* (Coatesville, PA: Council of Ruling Elders' Associations, 1929).

5. For background on Allen Macy Dulles, see *Biographical Catalogue of Princeton Theological Seminary 1815–1954*, compiled by Orion Cornelius Hopper (Princeton, NJ: Trustees of the Theological Seminary of the Presbyterian Church, 1955), 83, and *General Biographical Catalogue of Auburn Theological Seminary, 1919–1940* (New York: Auburn Theological Seminary, 1960), 7.

6. For a good study of Foster, see Michael J. Devine, *John W. Foster: Politics and Diplomacy in the Imperial Era, 1873–1917* (Athens: Ohio University Press, 1981). See also Devine's biographical sketch in *American National Biography* and Foster's obituary in the *New York Times*, November 16, 1917.

7. On Lansing, see Thomas H. Hartig, *Robert Lansing: An Interpretive Biography* (New York: Arno Press, 1982), and a biographical sketch by Lawrence E. Gelfand in *American National Biography*.

8. On the lectures, see John Quincy Adams, *A History of Auburn Theological Seminary 1818–1918* (Auburn, NY: Auburn Seminary Press, 1918), 160. See also Allen Macy Dulles' *The True Church: A Study (Historical and Scriptural)* (New York: F. H. Revell, 1907).

9. Adams, *Auburn Theological Seminary*, 164.

10. For Allen Macy's inaugural, see "The Inauguration of Allen Macy Dulles," *Auburn Seminary Record* 1 (November 10, 1905). For "The New Apologetic," see 303–21; quotations at 304 and 290.

11. For Allen Macy Dulles' theological background, I am indebted to Mark G. Toulouse, *The Transformation of John Foster Dulles: From Prophet of Realism to Priest of Nationalism* (Mercer, AL: Mercer University Press, 1985), 3–5.

12. See Avery Dulles, "The True Church: In Dialogue with Liberal Protestantism," in *A Church to Believe In* (New York: Crossroad, 1982), 53–66; see in particular 54, 57, 58, 62.

13. Auburn had prominent Presbyterian scholars on its faculty, including Robert Hastings Nichols, a nationally recognized historian of the church's life and theology and a leader of the liberal Presbyterian wing against the Fundamentalists. On Auburn before its union with Union Theological Seminary in 1939, see R. T. Handy, *Union Theological Seminary*, 198–99.

14. Allen Macy Dulles et al., *What Shall I Believe?: Addresses* (Philadelphia: Presbyterian Board of Publication, 1908); Allen Macy Dulles, *Test of Truth* (n.p., 1912); *Eucken's Philosophy: A Lecture* (n.p., 1913); *What is Necessary in the Christian Religion, A Sermon…Preached at Rome, NY, October 21, 1919* (Auburn, NY: n.p., 1919), and *Lectures on the History and Nature of Apologetics* (1930). Both the Dulles and the Foster sides of the family had developed a tradition of writing and publishing that would be passed on to the next two generations. Avery would also write *A History of Apologetics* (Washington, DC: Corpus, 1971).

15. On the liberal-fundamentalist battles of the period, see the fine study by Bradley J. Longfield, *The Presbyterian Controversy: Fundamentalists, Modernists, and Moderates* (New York: Oxford University Press, 1991). On the "Auburn Affirmation" in particular, see 77–79, 100–102, 159–60; quotation at 78.

16. Joan Dulles Talley to me, March 31, 2009. Letter in my possession.

17. Information on Dulles is available in numerous sources, only a few of which can be mentioned here. Richard H. Immerman's brief biographical sketch is available in *American National Biography*. Dulles' obituary is in the *New York Times*, May 25, 1959. Also valuable are John Robinson Beal, *John Foster Dulles: A Biography* (New York: Harper & Brothers, 1957), Ronald W. Pruessen, *John Foster Dulles: The Road to Power* (New York: Free Press, 1982), and Frederick W. Marks III, *Power and Peace: The Diplomacy of John Foster Dulles* (Westport, CT: Praeger, 1993). Especially useful on the religious dimension of Dulles' life, in addition to Avery Dulles' *John Foster Dulles*, are Toulouse's, *Transformation of John Foster Dulles*, and Richard H. Immerman's *John Foster Dulles: Piety, Pragmatism, and Power in U.S. Foreign Policy* (Wilmington, DE: Scholarly Resources, 1999). Also interesting, but unreliable in many particulars and unconvincing as an interpretation, is Leonard Mosley's *Dulles: A Biography of Eleanor, Allen, and John Foster Dulles and Their Family Network* (New York: Dial, 1978).

18. Quoted in Mosley, *Dulles*, 31.

19. John W. F. Dulles—a graduate of Princeton University (BA, 1935), Harvard Business School (MBA, 1937), and the University of Arizona (BSMedE, 1943)—became a mining engineer, and later a historian, author, and professor at the University of Texas, Austin, and the University of Arizona. For eighteen years (1943–1961), he was an engineer and executive with Mexican and Brazilian mining companies, making his residence in Monterrey, Mexico. While in Mexico and Brazil he studied Mexican and Brazilian history, and when he returned to the United States he obtained teaching positions at the University of Texas, where between 1961 and 2008 he published twelve books on Mexican and Brazilian his-

tory, including *Yesterday in Mexico: A Chronicle of the Revolution, 1919–1936* (Austin: University of Texas Press, 1961), *Sobral Pinto: The Conscience of Brazil: Leading the Attack against Vargas (1930–1945)* (Austin: University of Texas Press, 2002), and *Resisting Brazil's Military Regime: An Account of the Battles of Sobral Pinto* (Austin: University of Texas Press, 2007). Most of his twelve books have been translated into Portuguese and one into Spanish. Lillias Dulles received her BA from Bennington College in Bennington, Vermont. After graduation she married Robert Hinshaw, who was at the time of their marriage working for the Republican Party. He was drafted into the Army during World War II and after the war became a businessman in New York City. Lillias became a mother and housewife, and after her children were raised, she enrolled at Union Theological Seminary in New York and obtained a master's degree in theology so that she could teach religion to children in her Presbyterian parish in New York City. As her brother John tells it, she frequently discussed theological issues with her brother Avery before and after she had obtained her theological degree.

20. On their participation in the war, see Mosley, "The Trio Abroad," *Dulles*, 44–62.

21. Interview with Mosley, see *Dulles*, 82.

22. Avery Dulles gave various interviews in which he was questioned about his relationship to his father. See, e.g., the Crowl interview, upon which I based much of my characterization of Dulles' home life. My own interviews with Dulles on June 8–10, 2004, August 2–5, 2005, and July 24, 2007, also provided insights into his relationship with his parents and siblings. Dulles' interpretation of his home life was confirmed by his brother John, whom I interviewed on November 19, 2004, and June 9, 2006. The Dulles family papers, especially the multiple letters between John Foster Dulles and his son John W. F. Dulles, at the HRHC,TX, also support the Dulles brothers' characterizations of their home life. Mosley's *Dulles* (e.g., pp. 54, 72, 80, 81, 83, 202, 203)—which frequently characterized strained and distant relationships between the Dulles parents and the children, and the tense inner dynamics of the Dulles home life—is essentially distorted, lacking a foundation in unpublished interviews and the available archival sources.

Chapter 2. Home and Education, 1920–1940

1. Avery Dulles, *John Foster Dulles*, 8–9.

2. *A Testimonial to Grace and Reflections on a Theological Journey: 50th Anniversary Edition* (1946; Kansas City: Sheed & Ward, 1996), 38.

3. On these and other cases, see Toulouse, *Transformation of John Foster Dulles*, 17–26, and Avery Dulles, *John Foster Dulles*, 9.

4. Avery Dulles, *John Foster Dulles*, 9.

5. A. M. Dulles to Master Charles Avery Dulles, August 29, 1930, in DPFU.

6. "The Contribution of Christianity to Culture: An American Perspective," *Chrzescijanstwo Jutra*, Proceedings of the Second Congress of Fundamental Theology (Lublin, Poland: Towarzystwo Naukowe, 2001), 158.

7. My interviews with Avery Dulles, June 8–10, 2004.

8. For some background on the school, see Geoffrey Perret, *Jack: A Life Like No Other* (New York: Random House, 2001), 27–41.

9. Charles Avery Dulles, "Perugino," *Supplement to the Choate Literary Magazine* 7 (November 1932): 5.

10. Quoted in Lorraine Fraser, "Charles Avery Dulles '36: On the Sea of Faith," *Alumni Magazine* [of Choate Rosemary Hall] (1993). See Dulles to Lorraine Fraser, February 24, 1993, in DPFU.

11. *Choate Literary Magazine* 21 (May 1935): 60–62.

12. Letter of F. S. Fitzpatrick, circulation manager of the *Atlantic Monthly*, to C. Avery Dulles, May 8, 1935, in DPFU. Mention of the prize is in the *Atlantic Monthly* 155 (June 1935): 22. In 1990, one of his high school poems, "Song among Machines," was republished in *Choate Rosemary Hall Literary Magazine: A Celebration of Writing 1910–1990* (October 5, 1990): 21.

13. "The Modern Artist and Tradition," *Choate Literary Magazine* 22 (November 1935): 49–54; "Paul Cézanne: A Traditionalist Artist," idem 22 (February 1936): 10–14; and "Individualism and World Drama: A Study of Four Plays," idem 22 (May 1936): 47–54.

14. "Paul Cézanne," 10.

15. "Harvard as an Invitation to Catholicism," in *The Catholics of Harvard Square*, ed. Jeffrey Wills (Petersham, MA: Saint Bede's, 1993), 119.

16. "Faith of a Theologian," 151.

17. "The Modern Artist and Tradition," 50, 51.

18. *Testimonial to Grace*, 59.

19. Crowl interview, transcript, 19.

20. On these trips, see the *Menemsha* log, August 12–31, 1933, as "Recorded by the Ship's Historian Charles Avery Dulles." The log is available from the John Foster Dulles Room in HRHC,TX. Detailed maps of journeys the Dulleses took in 1933, 1935, 1938, 1939, and 1940 also hang in the John Foster Dulles Room. I used the log and the maps to identify the excursions. Logs for the trips after 1933 have apparently been lost.

21. Crowl interview, transcript, 10.

22. Ibid., 11.

23. James Laughlin to Avery Dulles, March 4, 1936, in DPFU.

24. For background on the Lowell administration of Harvard, see Samuel Eliot Morrison, *Three Centuries of Harvard, 1636–1936* (1936; Cambridge, MA: Harvard University Press, 1946), 439–81; see the appendix for the statistics.

25. For a sample of Catholic Harvard alumni who have testified about religion at Harvard, see *Catholics of Harvard Square*. See also John C. Cort, "A Bizarre Conversion," in *The New Catholics: Contemporary Converts Tell Their Stories*, ed. Dan O'Neill (New York: Crossroad, 1987), 1–19. Cort's story of his conversion to Catholicism in 1935 as a consequence, among other things, of his studies at

Harvard was analogous to Dulles' experiences at Harvard. In fact, they were influenced on their journeys of faith by some of the same professors. Dulles read Cort's account in 1987 and wrote Cort, marveling at the similarities of their Harvard encounters with history, literature, and art that contributed to their conversion stories. See Dulles to John C. Cort, December 17, 1987, in DPFU.

26. Quoted in *Catholics of Harvard Square*, 91.

27. "Harvard as an Invitation to Catholicism," 119.

28. Avery records the incident in *Testimonial to Grace*, 8. In interviews with him on June 8–10, 2004, and August 3, 2005, transcript, 5, in DPFU, where Dulles informed me of the crime.

29. *Testimonial to Grace*, 5, 8, 10. Dulles was more a religious skeptic or agnostic than an atheist during his teenage years, as is evident in some of his writings at Choate.

30. "Harvard as an Invitation to Catholicism," 119.

31. A 1927 Catholic Harvard graduate, William Doherty, corroborated the fact that Merriman's introductory course was a positive assessment of the Catholic Church's role in history. He recalled that the course made "the sprinkling of Catholics among us feel that we had something [in the Catholic Church]." Quoted in *Catholics of Harvard Square*, 90.

32. On Avery's father's change, see Toulouse, *Transformation of John Foster Dulles*, especially 47–59. See also Crowl interview transcript, 23–24, where Avery asserts that the trip to Paris and to Oxford was a significant turning point in his father's thinking and convinced him that "Christianity was of tremendous importance for the solution of world problems of peace and international justice." See also his later reflections on his father's positive experience at Oxford: Dulles to John M. Metzger, February 7, 2006, in DPFU.

33. Years later, Dulles told a correspondent that the Oxford Conference "was very important for my father. He found that the representatives of the various countries were able to communicate and work together because they shared a Christian vision and commitment, which had not been the case at the Paris meeting on 'Peaceful Change.'" See Dulles to John M. Metzger, February 7, 2006, in DPFU.

34. My interview with Avery Dulles, June 8–10, 2004.

35. Avery Dulles to Mrs. J. F. Dulles, July, 19, 1937, in DPFU.

36. *Testimonial to Grace*, 41. During World War II, Dulles wrote to a friend that he fell in love with Plato. "My first introduction to Plato, my freshman year in college, brought about revolutionary changes in my whole attitude to life for he it was who taught me that virtue is to be prized above all other things. Formerly I had been a materialist. I had thought that the best life was a life full of experiences, intense and varied, and had subscribed to the doctrine of [Walter] Pater [1839–1894] that man's highest aim is 'to *burn* always with a hard gemlike flame.'" On this, see Avery Dulles to Beda [Louise Mercier], November 30, 1943, in DPFU. The letter to Mercier inaccurately refers to his freshman year, but it accurately records the impact of his first readings of Plato.

37. *Testimonial to Grace*, 15, 21.

Notes

38. On Merton's 1937 discovery of Gilson's *The Spirit of Medieval Philosophy* and his uncovery of a Catholic notion of God as *aseitas* (that is, that God exists *a se*, from himself), see Merton's *The Seven Storey Mountain* (New York: Harcourt, Brace, & Company, 1948), 169–71.

39. On Dulles' assessment of Doolin, see *Testimonial to Grace*, 22–28, and "Harvard as an Invitation to Catholicism," 120.

40. "A Constitution for the Amalgamated Molders of the Upper Crust," an unpublished paper in DPFU.

41. Most of the AMUC Bulletins from 1936 to 1945 and unpublished papers are preserved in DPFU.

42. Paper presented for the Fifth Official Meeting of the AMUC, September 19, 1937; see also "Notes from C[rumb]. Dulles," Bulletin Number Three, AMUC, September 1937, 5; both papers in DPFU.

43. On John Foster Dulles' early internationalism, see Toulouse, *Transformation of John Foster Dulles*, 42.

44. See, e.g., Bulletin Number Six, AMUC, September 8, 1938, ed. C[rumb]. Dulles, 4, and "Contribution of Avery Dulles," Bulletin Number Seven, AMUC, September 8, 1938, ed. C. [David] Simboli, n.p., in DPFU.

45. "Contribution of Avery Dulles: Some Personal Reflections on the Present Crisis," Bulletin Number Nine, AMUC, September 12, 1939, ed. C. [Henry] Angel, 3–5, in DPFU.

46. "Contribution of Avery Dulles: Liberalism in Retrospect," Bulletin Number Ten, AMUC, December 1939, ed. C. Dulles, n.p., in DPFU.

47. That definition could be found, Dulles noted, in Leo XIII's encyclical *Libertas praestantissimum* (June 20, 1888). For the encyclical, see Claudia Carlen, *The Papal Encyclicals: 1878–1903* (Raleigh, NC: Pierian Press, 1990), 173.

48. Dulles did not identify the source of the quotation, but it comes from Karl Adam's *The Spirit of Catholicism* (1924; Eng. trans. 1929; reprint, Garden City, NY: Image Books, 1960), 9.

49. Printed in Bulletin Number Twelve, AMUC, November 6, 1940, ed. C. Angel, 1–4, in DPFU.

50. Ibid.

51. Bulletin Number Thirteen, AMUC. No date provided, but after March 16, 1941, ed. C. [James or Richard] Young, n.p., in DPFU.

52. Avery Dulles to Mrs. J. F. Dulles, February 9, 1939, in DPFU.

53. *Three Centuries of Harvard*, 376.

54. See, in particular, "Does the Ecclesiastical Establishment of Edward VI...?" November 1938, 34, in DPFU.

55. Kristeller to Dulles, December 11, 1939, in DPFU.

56. *Princeps Concordiae: Pico della Mirandola and the Scholastic Tradition* (Cambridge, MA: Harvard University Press, 1941), xi–xii.

57. *Three Centuries of Harvard*, 449.

58. See *Orestes A. Brownson: A Pilgrim's Progress* (Boston: Little, Brown, 1939).

59. During the summer Dulles again sent Kristeller a copy of his revised thesis, seeking Kristeller's reactions and suggestions. Kristeller responded to Dulles on September 28, 1940 with a detailed list of minor corrections and indicated, as he had in his earlier letter, that he could not subscribe entirely to Dulles' main thesis. He thought Dulles overemphasized the scholastic influence. But, the older scholar continued, that professional judgment "must not discourage you. You state your case and make a valuable contribution by emphasizing an aspect largely neglected." Letter in DPFU.

60. M. B. McNamee reviewed the book in *Modern Schoolman* 18.1 (November 1941): 17–18, judging that Dulles had successfully defended his thesis that Pico was a scholastic and that the idealist interpretations were wrongheaded. In 1943, Anton C. Pegis also reviewed the book, agreeing that Dulles had achieved his objectives "admirably." Pegis believed, however, that Dulles needed "greater precision" in his interpretation of medieval doctrine, being "guilty of several misinterpretations and confusions." See *Thought* 18 (September 1943): 553. During World War II, Dulles read Pegis's review and had to agree that he needed a more thorough knowledge of medieval philosophy and theology. See Dulles to Beda [Louise Mercier], November 30, 1943, in DPFU.

61. "Faith of a Theologian," 153.

62. Aidan Nichols, "Avery Dulles: Theologian in the Church," *Chicago Studies* 47 (Summer 2008): 135–38. Nichols's paper was given at a conference on "The Theological Contribution of Avery Cardinal Dulles, SJ," the Albert Cardinal Meyer Lecture Series at St. Mary of the Lake College, Mundelein, Illinois, April 10, 2008.

63. Some of the other colleges at the conference were Yale (France), Wellesley (Italy), Bowdoin (Mexico), Boston University (Argentina), Columbia (Chile and Venezuela), Radcliffe (USSR), Vassar (Romania), Wheaton (Brazil), Clark (Netherlands), Tufts (India and Ireland).

64. For background on the conference, see the published brochure, "Harvard Foreign Relations Club Conference on Peace Through a New International Order," April 12–14, 1940—Littauer Center, Harvard University. For the unpublished letter of invitation to the colleges, see "Harvard Foreign Relations Club Conference on Peace through a New International Order," from George McTurnan Kahin and Eric Warner Johnson, president and secretary of the club. Both documents are in the DPFU.

65. Other speakers were Francis Deák, former Hungarian representative at the League of Nations, Rafael de la Colina, Mexican Consul General at New York, and Waldo Heinrichs, professor of Middlebury College and an advocate of Clarence K. Streit's *Union Now: A Proposal for a Federal Union of the Democracies of the North Atlantic* (New York: Harper & Brothers, 1939).

66. "German Economic Cooperation," in DPFU.

67. The Yale delegation walked out because, it protested, it could not accept any proceedings that "did not rest on the assumption of a French victory in the war." See George M. Kahin's report in "Conference on Foreign Affairs Stresses Collaboration in Spheres of Economics," a newspaper clipping in the

DPFU, that I could not identify. It was published after the April 12–13, 1940, conference but it was not in the *Harvard Crimson*. A summary of the conference stated, "At the opening of the [second] session, France declared that she found the Conference 'paradoxical' and could proceed only upon the assumption of a French victory. She thereupon withdrew, the delegation refusing to continue informally as individuals, and was censured by 12 nations on the motion of the United States [Cornell]. See "Harvard Foreign Relations Club Conference on Peace through a New International Order, April 12–13, 1940, Littauer Center, Harvard University, *Summary of Proceedings*," 3, in DPFU. This was a report at the conference's conclusion that the club sent to all the participating college delegates.

68. "Harvard Foreign Relations Club Conference...*Summary of Proceedings*," in DPFU.

69. "Faith of a Theologian," 154.

70. "Rome Is the Center and Touchstone of Unity," Thomas Aquinas College Newsletter (Summer 2005): 3–4.

Chapter 3. Becoming a Catholic, 1937–1941

1. *A Testimonial to Grace*, 30.

2. Ibid., 36.

3. Ibid., 38.

4. Ibid., 60.

5. Ibid., 62.

6. Ibid., 62–65.

7. The original manuscript of "A Testimonial to Grace" (1944), 56b, located in Avery Dulles Woodstock Papers, Georgetown University Library, Special Collections Division, Washington, DC (hereafter ADGUSC), Box 11.

8. "The Contribution of Christianity to Culture: An American Perspective," 160.

9. "Harvard as an Invitation to Catholicism," 121.

10. For background on the bookstore, see Louise M[ercier]. Des Marais, "An Early History of the St. Thomas More Lending Library and Bookshop," 4, an unpublished and undated paper in DPFU. See also Margaret M. Kelly, "St. Thomas More—Bookseller," *Catholic Transcript* (March 24, 1938), 2; Martha Bowers Doherty, "Do People Read Religious Books," *Publishers Weekly* (March 25, 1939): 2.

11. Numerous entries in the diary illustrate the relationship and her preoccupation with Avery. Unpublished diary of Louise Mercier Des Marais (1936–1948). The typescript manuscript is in the Archives of the Archdiocese of Boston. Used with permission of Louise Mercier Des Marais. I would like to thank James O'Toole for drawing my attention to this source. On July 6, 1946, she records, "At last I know. Avery is to be a Jesuit. God bless him." Shortly thereafter, she ceases to write in her diary.

12. As a Jesuit, many years after these events, Dulles presided over the marriage of Louise and Philip's daughter Monica Des Marais to John Murphy. The Murphys continued the Des Marais tradition and frequently invited Dulles to their home to celebrate Thanksgiving and other family events, including the marriage of their own son, over which Dulles also presided.

13. Shortly after the store was organized, Mary Stanton and Evangeline Mercier entered the Carmelite Monastery in Roxbury, Massachusetts, taking the names of Sr. Mary Elizabeth of the Trinity and Sr. Evangeline of Jesus.

14. The Belgium artist, Ade de Bethune, was a frequent visitor to and patron of the store. She also designed the bookplate for each of the lending library books.

15. *Testimonial to Grace*, 64, 66.

16. "The Contribution of Christianity to Culture: An American Perspective," 160. See also "Faith of a Theologian," 154.

17. For one example, see "Faith of a Theologian," 151–63.

18. Crowl interview, transcript, 20–21. Six extant reports are available in the DPFU: "Circumstances of Wilson's Nomination" (June 22, 1939); "Wilson's Campaign in the Election of 1912" (July 6, 1939); "The Presidential Campaign of 1916, Wilson V. Hughes" (n.d.); "The Presidential Campaign of 1920, Harding V. Cox" (n.d.); "Neutrality Legislation (1933–1939)" (after June 1939); and "Preparedness and Foreign Policy in the Presidential Campaign of 1916, Wilson V. Hughes" (May 17, 1940).

19. "Circumstances of Wilson's Nomination" (June 22, 1939), 16.

20. "Presidential Campaign of 1920, Harding V. Cox" (n.d.), 8.

21. "Neutrality Legislation (1933–1939)" (after June 1939), 8.

22. Ibid., 18.

23. Dewey to Dulles, July 29, 1940, in DPFU, and in Dewey Papers, University of Rochester (New York) Library.

24. "The American Independence League," unpublished paper [September 1940], n.p., in DPFU.

25. *Testimonial to Grace*, 69–77.

26. Ibid., 71, 72.

27. Ibid., 65.

28. Ibid., 80, 81.

29. Ibid., 82.

30. Avery Dulles, "Catholics in Secular Colleges," *Catholic Mind* 49 (September 1951): 561–62.

31. *Testimonial to Grace*, 88, 89.

32. Ibid., 60.

33. Dulles, "Models of Apologetics" [2006], in *Evangelization for the Third Millennium* (New York: Paulist, 2009), 120.

34. *Testimonial to Grace*, 89.

35. My interview with Dulles, June 8–10, 2004.

36. Unpublished diary of Louise Mercier Des Marais (1936–1948); see November 1, 1940, and November 26, 1940, 4.

37. Dulles to Mrs. John Foster Dulles, 3 November 1940, in DPFU.

38. My interviews at the University of Texas, Austin, with John Watson Foster Dulles, November 19, 2004, and June 9, 2006, transcript, 21, in my possession: "It seems to me I recall my father taking my brother to lunch in New York at some club and giving him arguments that might dissuade him from becoming a Catholic. I think my father mentioned to me one of his arguments," which John Watson could not remember.

39. Dulles' interview with William Bole in *Our Sunday Visitor* (May 25, 1997): 11.

40. Crowl interview, transcript, 27–28.

41. My interview with Dulles, June 8–10, 2004.

42. Dulles to Mother & Daddy, November 25, 1940, in DPFU. Quotations in the next three paragraphs are from this letter.

43. On Huntington's conversion story, see his "The Voice of Authority," in *The Way to Emmaus: The Intimate Personal Stories of Converts to the Catholic Faith*, ed. John A. O'Brien (New York: McGraw-Hill, 1953), 133–59.

44. Mrs. Allen M. Dulles to Avery Dulles, December 14, 1940, in DPFU.

45. John W. Foster, *Diplomatic Memoirs*, 2 vols. (New York: Houghton Mifflin, 1909), 1: 314–28, recorded this event in great detail. He also indicated that his two young daughters were particularly impressed with Archbishop Rampolla. According to Foster's wife, the two girls raved "about the Pope's Nuncio, who had just been here making a visit....They declared him the most interesting, intelligent, fascinating man they had ever met, and I am afraid if he comes often they may be wanting to change their religion" (268).

46. Edith Foster Dulles, "The Story of My Life" (privately printed, 1934), in DPFU.

47. This and the next paragraph rely on Mrs. Allen M. Dulles to Avery Dulles, December 14, 1940, in DPFU.

48. Mrs. Allen M. Dulles to Avery Dulles, January 13, 1941, in DPFU.

49. Mrs. Allen M. Dulles to Avery Dulles, April 3, 1941, in DPFU.

50. See Mrs. Allen M. Dulles to Avery Dulles, April 3, 1941, and Mrs. Allen M. Dulles to Avery Dulles, March 10, 1941, both in DPFU.

51. Eleanor Lansing Dulles, *The French Franc, 1914–1928: The Facts and Their Interpretation* (New York: Macmillan, 1929).

52. Mrs. Allen M. Dulles to Avery Dulles, April 3, 1941, in DPFU.

53. Mrs. Allen M. Dulles to Avery Dulles, April 28, 1941, in DPFU.

54. John W. Davis to Janet [Mrs. John Foster Dulles], April 6, 1941. For another favorable and equally enthusiastic assessment of the book, see Mrs. [Margaret] Charles W. MacMullen to Mrs. John Foster Dulles, April 28, 1941, both in DPFU.

55. Avery Dulles, "Saint Robert Bellarmine: A Moderate in a Disputatious Age," *Crisis* 12 (December 1994): 39.

56. On the controversy, see, e.g., Catherine Goddard Clarke, *The Loyolas and the Cabots: The Story of the Boston Heresy Case* (Boston: Ravengate Press, 1950); idem, *The Gate of Heaven* (Cambridge, MA: St. Benedict Center, 1952); George B.

Pepper, *The Boston Heresy Case in View of the Secularization of Religion: A Case Study in the Sociology of Religion* (Lewiston, NY: E. Mellen Press, 1988); Mark S. Massa, "Boundary Maintenance: Leonard Feeney, the Boston Heresy Case, and the Postwar Culture," in *Catholic and American Culture: Fulton Sheen, Dorothy Day, and the Notre Dame Football Team* (New York: Crossroad, 1999), 21–37; and Patrick Carey, "Avery Dulles, St. Benedict's Center, and No Salvation Outside the Church, 1940–1953," *Catholic Historical Review* 93 (July 2007): 553–75.

57. In the Boston archdiocese in the 1940s, as in many Catholic dioceses across the country, bishops were reluctant to recognize Catholic centers on secular campuses because they did not want to give the impression that they approved of higher education at secular institutions. Much of this hesitancy is detailed in John Whitney Evans, *The Newman Movement: Roman Catholics in American Higher Education, 1883–1971* (Notre Dame, IN: University of Notre Dame Press, 1980).

58. Information on St. Benedict Center is available in James M. O'Toole's interview with Avery Dulles, June 22, 1982. A printed account of the interview is located in the archives of the Archdiocese of Boston, and in the DPFU.

59. Avery Dulles to Mrs. [Louis] Mercier, no date, but the context indicates spring of 1941, after the publication of Leonard Feeney's *Survival Till Seventeen* (1941), which Professor Mercier had sent to Avery as a gift. Letter in DPFU.

60. Dewey to Commandant, Third Naval District, August 21, 1941, in DPFU.

61. Daddy to John W. F. Dulles, July 22, 1941, in HRHC,TX, and John Foster Dulles Papers (hereafter JFDP).

62. My interview with John W. F. Dulles, at Austin, Texas, November 19, 2004. See also my interview with John W. F. Dulles, June 9, 2006, transcript, 11, in my possession.

63. Daddy to John W. F. Dulles, September 23, 1941, in HRHC,TX, and JFDP.

64. Daddy to John W. F. Dulles, May 27, 1942, in HRHC,TX, and JFDP.

65. Daddy to John W. F. Dulles, April 26, 1943, in HRHC,TX, and JFDP.

66. "Revelation and Discovery," in *Theology and Discovery*, ed. William J. Kelly (Milwaukee: Marquette University Press, 1980), 12.

67. Tom Brokaw, *The Greatest Generation* (New York: Random House, 1998).

Chapter 4. The Navy Years, 1941–1946

1. Unpublished diary of Louise Mercier Des Marais (1936–1948), see December 7, 1941 and December 19, 1941, 12, 13.

2. On January 4, 1942 Dulles informed Thomas Dewey, who had written a letter of recommendation for him to the Naval Reserve, that he had gone into the Navy. See also Dewey to Dulles, January 7, 1942. Letters in DPFU, and in Dewey Papers, University of Rochester Library.

3. Unpublished paper, in DPFU, 1.

4. Ibid., 2.

5. Ibid., 4.

6. Dulles to Christopher Huntington, June 28, 1942, in personal archives of Mark J. Williams.

7. Dulles to Christopher Huntington, June 28, 1942, in Mark J. Williams's archives.

8. Margaret Knapp to Dulles, July 2, 1942, in DPFU.

9. Dulles to Christopher Huntington, May 31, 1942, in Mark J. Williams's archives.

10. For one account of a subchaser's mission during the war, see J. Henry Doscher Jr., *Subchaser in the South Pacific: A Saga of the USS SC 761 During World War II* (Austin: Eakin Press, 1994).

11. For the Catholic statement, see Hugh J. Nolan, ed., *Pastoral Letters of the United States Catholic Bishops: Volume 2 1941–1961* (Washington, DC: NCCB/USCC, 1984), 42. On the controversy and John Foster Dulles' intervention, see "Protestants Ask Freedom for Faith," *New York Times* (December 12, 1942): 12. See also the letters of Avery Dulles to Christopher Huntington and to Daddy, Feast of the Epiphany [January 6] 1943, in Mark J. Williams's archives.

12. "Notes on Religious Tolerance," and Dulles to Christopher Huntington, January 11, 1943, in Mark J. Williams's archives.

13. On the earlier trip, see unpublished diary of Louise Mercier Des Marais, October 9, 1942, 25.

14. On Dulles' fond appreciation of Feeney's talents and personal charm as well as his assessment of Feeney's unfortunate later developments, see Avery Dulles, "Leonard Feeney: In Memoriam," *America* 138 (February 2, 1978): 135–37.

15. He read, e.g., François Mauriac's *Thérèse Desqueyroux* (1927), Charles Péguy's *Les Prières* (1934), Jean De LaVarende's *Le Centaure de Dieu* (1952), Roger Vercel's *Jean Villemour* (1939), Henri Ghéon's *La Jambe Noire* (1941), and Alphonsine Vavasseur-Acher Simonet's *La nuit nuptiale* (1940).

16. Unpublished diary of Louise Mercier Des Marais, July 4, 1944, 49.

17. Dulles to Catherine Clarke, July 31, 1944, in Archives of St. Benedict Abbey, Still River, Massachusetts (hereafter ASBA). The archives contain twenty-three letters of Dulles to Clarke and thirty-five letters of Clarke to Dulles. These letters are used by permission of Abbot Gabriel Gibbs, OSB.

18. His letters, like most letters Navy personnel sent home, were censored by the Navy; some passages that were apparently too descriptive in a few of his letters home were blotted out by the Navy censors.

19. During World War II, V-Mail was used to reduce the weight and space of sending correspondence to the United States. V-mail correspondence worked by photographing large amounts of mail reduced to thumbnail size onto reels of microfilm, which weighed much less than the original would have. Only very short messages could be sent in this fashion.

20. These letters are in the DPFU.

21. *A Message to the Church*, from the National Study Conference on the Churches and a Just and Durable Peace (Cleveland, OH: Commission on a Just and Durable Peace, January 16–19, 1945).

22. Lieutenant Avery Dulles to John Foster Dulles, February 25, 1945, in DPFU. See also "Church and State," *Time* (February 19, 1945): 85.

23. Avery to Mrs. John Foster Dulles, November 10, 1944, in DPFU.

24. Avery Dulles to Mrs. Robert Hinshaw, November 7, 1944, in DPFU.

25. My interview with Dulles, August 3, 2005, transcript, 10, in DPFU.

26. On his uncle, see Avery's letters to his mother and to Beda [Louise Mercier], both dated September 25–26, 1945, in DPFU. On Allen Dulles' role in the surrender of the Germans from northern Italy, see Mosley, *Dulles*, 174–88.

27. Avery Dulles to St. Benny's, November 12, 1943. Printed copy of letter in DPFU. See also Dulles to Catherine Clarke, November 14, 1943, in ASBA.

28. Ibid.

29. Dulles to Catherine Clarke, feast of the Apparition of Our Lady at Lourdes [February 11] 1944, in ASBA.

30. "Prayer for Lent 1944," in ASBA.

31. See, e.g., Margaret Knapp to Avery Dulles, July 2, 1942, and Peggy Dorgan to Avery Dulles, August 11, 1946, in DPFU.

32. Avery Dulles to Sr. Evangeline of Jesus, October 29, 1942, in DPFU.

33. Sr. Evangeline of Jesus to Louise Mercier, November 1, 1942, in DPFU.

34. A scapular is a small devotional artifact cloth draped over the shoulders and usually worn under the wearer's top layer of clothes. Catholics consider these artifacts sacramentals because they reminded them of some spiritual reality.

35. Sr. Evangeline of Jesus to Avery Dulles, 2nd day in the Octave of the feast of St. Teresa of Jesus [16 October] 1942, in DPFU.

36. Leonard Feeney to Avery Dulles, October 28, 1943, in DPFU.

37. Dulles to Ruth M. Snow, July 22, 1986, in DPFU.

38. He read, e.g., Dom Columba Marmion's various spiritual treatises, Anna Katharina Emmerich's *The Dolorous Passion of Our Lord Jesus Christ*, Paul Claudel's *Présence et Prophétie* (1942), and Maisie Ward's *The Splendor of the Rosary* (1945).

39. Among other studies, he read Luigi Sturzo's *Spiritual Problems in Our Times* (1945), Raïssa Maritain's *Adventures in Grace* (1945), and Paul Claudel's *Les Figures et paraboles* (1926).

40. He read Plato's *Protagoras* as well as Walter Pater's anthology of *Marius the Epicurean* (1945), which he enjoyed reading even though he had difficulties with Pater's philosophy and that of Marius. See Avery Dulles to Beda [Louise Mercier], November 30, 1943, in DPFU.

41. While in Italy he purchased the complete works of Dante and began to read them. He also read, among a host of other literary works, Bruce Marshall's *The World, the Flesh, and Father Smith* (1945), Jean Staffords' *Boston Adventure* (1944), Willa Cather's *Death Comes for the Archbishop* (1927), Evelyn Waugh's *Brideshead Revisited* (1944), and Helen C. White's *Watch in the Night* (1933).

42. He noted that he had read a life of St. Paul but did not indicate which one. He also read Evelyn Waugh's *Edmund Campion* (1946) and sent his mother a copy of the book. He was enthralled with John Moody's *John Henry Newman* (1945). Newman became one of Dulles' favorite writers, and he published *Newman* (New York: Continuum, 2002) when he was in his eighties.

43. Avery Dulles to Mother, July 18, 1944, in DPFU.

44. John F. O'Hara to Avery Dulles, February 17, 1943, in DPFU.

45. Dulles to Catherine Clarke, Nativity of John the Baptist [June 24], 1945, in ASBA.

46. Avery Dulles, "Letter to a Prospective Inductee," *America* 85 (May 5, 1951): 119–21.

47. Avery Dulles to John Foster Dulles, February 9, 1943, in DPFU. See also Avery Dulles to Catherine Clarke, February 21, 1943, in ASBA, where Dulles indicated that he did not think the paper was appropriate for publication, but he would not object to its being published. It was, he said, "too boring and abstruse" for a popular magazine and "not suited" for a scholarly one because he was not a trained philosopher or theologian.

48. 16 (1946): 489–504.

49. Ibid., 504.

50. Dulles to Catherine Clarke, feast of St. John the Baptist [June 24] 1944, in ASBA.

51. Dulles to Beda Venerabilis [Louise Mercier], June 24, 1944, in DPFU.

52. Dulles to Beda [Louise Mercier], April 4, 1945, in DPFU.

53. Dulles to Catherine Clarke, September 10, 1945, in ASBA.

54. See Dulles to Catherine Clarke, January 17, 1944, in ASBA, where Dulles gives a long description of his second trip to Rome and his audience with the pope, at which were many hundreds of the Allied Forces.

55. My interview with Dulles, August 3, 2005, transcript, 24, in DPFU.

56. Dr. David Deavel, one of Dulles' students, related this story to me, December 19, 2008, e-mail in my possession.

57. On the meetings and their failures, see Toulouse, *Transformation of John Foster Dulles*, 158–69.

58. Mosley, *Dulles*, 202–3. See also Avery to Mother, September 25–26, 1945, in DPFU.

59. On Avery's desire to see his parents in London and to spend some time "together quietly for a while" with his mother, see Avery to Mother, September 19, 1945, and September 25–26, 1945, in DPFU. The September 25–26 letter indicates that Avery had just received a dispatch telling him "to report to London for temporary duty in carrying out my basic orders whatever they may be. So please try to stay in London another week." Mosley, *Dulles*, 202–3, records interviews he held with Avery on the London trip. Mosley has wrongly dated the London conference as taking place in 1947 and has made a few assertions that cannot be substantiated. Mosley says, e.g., that during the London trip Avery failed to tell his parents that he was considering becoming a Catholic priest—another example, in Mosley's view, of the strained relationship between parents and child.

Avery had indeed considered becoming a Jesuit during the war years, but he had made no firm plans at the time of his London visit, and, as was his practice, he did not reveal to others what he had not yet had a reasonable expectation of achieving. He did not reveal to his parents, e.g., that he was going to become a Catholic until after he had made a firm decision and had made arrangements for his reception into the church.

60. Avery Dulles to Mother, October 17, 1945, in DPFU.

61. Ibid.

62. In the next few paragraphs, I am relying on Dulles' characterization of the center in 1946. See his interview with James O'Toole, 15–17, 20–21, in DPFU.

63. A doctor of the church is usually a theologian, canonized as a saint, whose eminent teachings and sanctity the pope sanctioned as beneficial for the entire church. By 1946, twenty-nine saintly scholars had been publicly acknowledged as doctors of the church.

64. "Chapter I. St. Athanasius" (April 1946); "St. Ephraem," *From the Housetops* 1 (December 1946): 50–60; "Chapter III. Saint Hilary" (May 1946); "Chapter IV. Saint Cyril of Jerusalem" (May 1946). The three unpublished texts are in DPFU.

65. "Chapter I. St. Athanasius" (April 1946), 13, in DPFU.

66. "Chapter III. Saint Hilary," 7.

67. Ibid., 8.

68. "St. Bernard—*Love of God*" (April 1946) and "St. Bernard—*Canticle of Canticles*" (May 1946), in DPFU. Previous to the discussion of *Love of God*, the group had read and discussed Aristotle's *De Anima*.

69. "St. Bernard—*Love of God*," 6–7.

70. For background on the journal, see O'Toole interview with Dulles, 11–12.

71. "A Prelude to Faith," *From the Housetops* 1 (September 1946): 3–12.

72. "On Keeping the Faith," *From the Housetops* 1 (September 1946): 60–66. When he entered the Jesuits, Dulles left behind three other manuscripts that were eventually published in the journal: "St. Ephraem," "Beauty," and "Outline of Art" in *From the Housetops* 1 (December 1946): 50–60, (March 1947): 27–36, and (June 1947): 16–21. *From the Housetops* started out with a few subscribers, but by January 1947 the center was distributing fifteen hundred copies. On the increase, see Feeney to Dulles, January 2, 1947, in DPFU.

73. "On Keeping the Faith," 60.

74. Ibid., 63.

75. Ibid., 66.

Chapter 5. Becoming a Jesuit, 1946–1958

1. James O'Toole interview with Dulles, 17, in DPFU.

2. Dulles to Huntington, Vigil of the Assumption [August 14] 1946, in Mark J. Williams's archives.

3. Dulles to Mother, June 15, 1946, in DPFU.

4. Dulles to Mother, June 22, 1946, in DPFU.

5. *Boston Evening Globe* (August 14, 1946): 1, 15.

6. "Avery Dulles, Jesuit Novice, Pens Book on Conversion," *Boston Pilot* (August 24, 1946): 2.

7. The report on the family gathering I received in a conversation with Eleanor Ritter Dulles on November 19, 2004, in Austin, Texas.

8. Saint Ignatius of Loyola, *The Constitutions of the Society of Jesus*, trans. George E. Ganss (St. Louis: Institute of Jesuit Sources, 1970), 77, *Cons* [3].

9. F. A. McQuade, SJ, Provincial, to Dulles, July 2, 1946, in DPFU.

10. For these statistics, see my *Catholics in America: A History* (Westport, CT: Praeger, 2004), 93.

11. On the Jesuit statistics, see Edmund Granville Ryan, "An Academic History of Woodstock College in Maryland (1869–1944): The First Jesuit Seminary in North America" (PhD dissertation, Catholic University of America, 1964), 149.

12. Of the thirty-eight members of the novice class of 1946, twenty-two were eventually ordained as priests. Seven of those ordained were still living in 2004.

13. For the profile of these Jesuit novices, I am indebted to Fr. Frederick O'Brien, SJ, archivist of the New York Jesuit Province, who had access to the New York Jesuit Province Annual Catalogue of 1946. See O'Brien's letter to me, December 16, 2004. Letter in my possession.

14. Avery Dulles, "Letter to a Prospective Inductee," *America* 85 (May 5, 1951): 119.

15. See the *Spiritual Exercises*, especially the "Presupposition" [22], Annotation #13, the "Rules for the Discernment of Spirits" [13, 313–36], and the "Rules for Thinking with the Church" [352–70].

16. *Cons* [66 to 69].

17. Dulles to Catherine Clarke, April 22, 1948, in DPFU.

18. Thirty-five extant letters from Clarke to Dulles (1942 to 1947) are available in ASBA.

19. Dulles to Catherine Clarke, May 2, 1948, in DPFU. After one of his mother's earlier visits, Dulles told Clarke, June 27, 1947, in ASBA, that the visit went well enough, "of course nothing of a fundamental nature was touched upon. The rest was pleasant enough." He could not share his deep personal faith with members of his family, and that was painful for him.

20. On the early history of Woodstock, see Patrick J. Dooley, *Woodstock and Its Makers* (Woodstock, MD: College Press, 1927), and Edmund Granville Ryan, "An Academic History of Woodstock"; and for a briefer account and the quotation, see Michael J. Fahey, "A Last Look: Woodstock Closing after 109 [sic] Years," *National Jesuit News* 4 (April 1975): 5. See also idem, "Woodstock: 'Vale atque Ave,'" *America* 132 (May 31, 1975): 414–17.

21. On Weigel, see Patrick W. Collins, *Gustave Weigel: A Pioneer of Reform* (Collegeville, MN: Liturgical Press, 1992).

22. Suarezianism takes its name from the thought of the Jesuit philosopher and theologian, Francis Suárez (1548–1617), whose systematic treatment of metaphysics departed somewhat from the thought of Thomas Aquinas by denying the real distinction between essence and existence, by reworking the theory of relations, and placing great emphasis on the unity of finite being. The Suarezian ahistorical and abstract approach to reality also departed from the emerging philosophical transcendentalism, historical consciousness, personalism, and existentialism of the nineteenth and twentieth centuries.

23. My interview with Dulles, August 3, 2005, transcript, 21–22, in DPFU.

24. *Testimonial to Grace*, 102.

25. Avery R. Dulles, "Three Years of Philosophy: The Key to Reality," *Jesuit* (Maryland Province; March 1950): 5–6.

26. Ibid., 7.

27. See, e.g., Dulles' *Craft of Theology: From Symbol to System* (1992; New York: Crossroad, 1995), 128.

28. *The Intimate Personal Stories of Fourteen Converts to the Catholic Faith* (Garden City, NY: Doubleday, 1950), 63–81.

29. John A. O'Brien to Dulles, August 2, 1949, in DPFU.

30. "Coming Home," in *Where I Found Christ*, 63–81, and *Catholic Digest* (October 1950): 45–54.

31. See O'Brien's untitled comments on the first draft, in DPFU.

32. "Coming Home," *Catholic Digest* (October 1950): 52.

33. Daddy to Avery Dulles, SJ, August 15, 1949, in DPFU.

34. Daddy to Avery Dulles, SJ, September 19, 1949, in DPFU.

35. Daddy to Brother Avery Dulles, March 3, 1949, in DPFU.

36. Daddy to Brother Avery Dulles, April 20, 1949, in DPFU.

37. On John Foster Dulles' opposition to McCarthy's methods, see Eleanor Lansing Dulles, *John Foster Dulles: The Last Year* (New York: Harcourt, Brace & World, 1963), 87–92. Avery's own views were expressed in my interview with him, August 3, 2005, transcript, 22, in DPFU: "I would say that McCarthy's tactics certainly violated Christian principles. My father definitely did not like him. And he reacted to him in his own way, using an indirect approach. He did not make any public statements against McCarthy because he did not want to alienate any of McCarthy's supporters in the Senate....My father worked in a private way to oppose McCarthy."

38. Many of the New York papers carried the photos with captions that clearly indicated that Avery was a Jesuit. See, e.g., "Tough-Campaigning Mrs. Dulles Proves One of the Girls," *New York World-Telegram* (November 3, 1949): 3, with the caption "Avery is studying to be a Jesuit Priest at Woodstock College in Maryland." See also the same picture in the *New York Herald Tribune* (November 4, 1949): 2, and the *New York Sun* (November 4, 1949): 2, where the *Sun* noted that Avery was "a convert to Roman Catholicism and [is] now studying at the Jesuit Seminary."

39. Quoted in Mosley, *Dulles*, 220.

40. Daddy to A. R. Dulles, November 28, 1949, in DPFU.

41. *Cons* [417].
42. Quoted in Raymond A. Schroth, *Fordham: A History and Memoir* (Chicago: Loyola Press, 2002), 218.
43. For the statistics on Fordham, see Schroth, *Fordham*, 162, 189, 195.
44. On Dulles' philosophical anti-communism, see his review of *The Anatomy of Communism* (1951), by Andrew MacKay Scott, and *The Philosophy of Communism* (1952), by Giogio La Pira et al., *Best Sellers* (January 15, 1952): 218–19. The authors of these texts, especially the Italians, in Dulles' view, saw communism as "anti-God because it is anti-human, and anti-human because it is anti-rational." But in their criticisms of communism they avoided an "exaggerated individualism and unrestricted capitalism."
45. "Catholics in Secular Colleges," *Catholic Mind* 49 (September 1951): 560. See also Dulles' review of *God and Man at Yale* (1951), by William F. Buckley Jr., *Best Sellers* 11 (November 1, 1951): 141.
46. Schroth, *Fordham*, 203.
47. Fifty-five percent of Catholics voted for Adlai Stevenson in 1952, but that was 11 percent fewer than those who had voted for Harry Truman in 1948. By 1956, according to the Gallup poll, 49 percent of Catholics (53 percent, according to a University of Michigan poll) voted for Eisenhower. Catholics, traditionally in the Democratic column, were moving in a Republican direction during the Eisenhower era. On these statistics, see Albert J. Menendez, *Religion at the Polls* (Philadelphia: Westminster, 1977), 62, 214.
48. (May 19, 1952): 146, 148, 151–52, 154, 157–58, 160.
49. Schroth, *Fordham*, 213.
50. *Introductory Metaphysics: A Course Combining Matter Treated in Ontology, Cosmology, and Natural Theology* (New York: Sheed & Ward, 1955), preface.
51. Ibid., 3.
52. Ibid., 10, 13, 153, for the authors' moderate realism.
53. In book reviews of philosophical texts while he was a faculty member at Fordham, Dulles criticized those in the modern scholastic tradition who overemphasized the passivity of the human intellect in Aquinas's theory of knowledge and praised those who upheld the intellect's implicit awareness of its own capacity for truth in every judgment. See, e.g., Dulles' reviews of *The March toward Matter* (1952), by John MacPartland, *Best Sellers* 12 (May 15, 1952): 50, and *Reality and Judgment according to St. Thomas* (1952), by Peter Hoenen, *Best Sellers* 12 (July 1, 1952): 81.
54. My interview with Theodore Cardinal McCarrick, January 5, 2009, transcript, 1, in my possession.
55. See my "A Model Theologian," *Fordham* (Winter 2008): 27.
56. Anthony L. Adolino to Dulles, March 14, 1972, in DPFU.
57. Abbott R. Morgan to Dulles, October 29, 2001, in DPFU.
58. When Dulles reviewed Sheed's *Society and Sanity*, he asserted that "it would be difficult to name a living man who has contributed more to the growth of the Catholic mind in the English-speaking world than F. J. Sheed." While evaluating the book, however, he noted that Sheed's arguments were hardly adequate,

because Sheed had failed to emphasize the Christian's constructive participation in the formation of the social order at the domestic and international levels. He had not sufficiently appealed to the reader's "social conscience." See *Best Sellers* 13 (March 15, 1953): 271–72.

59. On Murray, see Donald E. Pelotte, *John Courtney Murray: Theologian in Conflict* (New York: Paulist, 1975).

60. On Burghardt, see David G. Hunter, ed., *Preaching in the Patristic Age: Studies in Honor of Walter J. Burghardt, SJ* (New York: Paulist, 1989). See in particular the article by Gerald P. Fogarty, "Walter J. Burghardt, SJ: An Appreciation," 3–18.

61. My interview with Dulles, June 8–10, 2004.

62. "Gustave Weigel, SJ: Voices of Tribute," *Baltimore Catholic Review* (January 10, 1964): 4.

63. Ibid.

64. On the definition of the term *fundamental theology* and the great debate on the existence of apologetics after Vatican II, see Avery Dulles, *A History of Apologetics* (1971; San Francisco: Ignatius Press, 2005), 326–28. In 1965, for the first time, as far as I know, Jesuits called a meeting at Rockhurst, Kansas, chaired by Dulles, to discuss the curriculum of theology and devised a plan, the so-called Rockhurst Plan, that radically reconceived the discipline and renamed the theological specialities (e.g., biblical, historical, systematic, theologico-pastoral), leaving almost no room for apologetics except under the discipline of fundamental theology, which was a subsection of systematics. See "Inter-Faculty Program Inquiry Report," *Woodstock Letters* 95 (Summer 1966): 335–56, and chapter 6 of this book for a description of the Rockhurst Plan. For information on the conceptual changes in the curriculum, which were followed by most seminaries and Catholic colleges and universities after 1966, see Joseph Lienhard, "Historical Theology in the Curriculum," in *Theological Education in the Catholic Tradition*, eds. Patrick W. Carey and Earl C. Muller (New York: Crossroad, 1997), 266–67.

65. Christian Pesch (1853–1925), Hermann Dieckmann (1880–1928), Joseph Pohle (1852–1922), and Reginald Garrigou-Lagrange (1877–1964) had all written large manuals of fundamental and dogmatic theology that were widely used in Catholic seminaries in the pre–Vatican II era.

66. "Faith of a Theologian," 155.

67. (1924; Eng. trans., London and New York: Sheed & Ward, and Macmillan, 1929, and many subsequent English editions).

68. "Faith of a Theologian," 155.

69. On Dulles' own assessment of his theological education in the 1950s, see *Craft of Theology*, 44. My interview with Dulles, June 8–10, 2004, indicated how much he had "devoured" Rahner.

70. "Church Unity and Roman Primacy in the Doctrine of St. Cyprian," *Theologian* 9 (1954): 33, 36, 37. Dulles followed the opinion of Dom John Chapman in arguing, against certain nineteenth-century Protestant scholars, that both the earlier version (called by some "the primacy" version) of the text and the later were from Cyprian's pen and that the primacy version, which acknowledged

the necessity of unity with Rome, was not a later Roman interpolation of the text but a reflection of Cyprian's attempts to bring about unity in a church divided over the issue of reconciling the lapsed to the church after the Decian persecutions. In Dulles' view, the later (shorter) version of the text, reedited by Cyprian himself with several important changes, reflected his conflict with Pope Stephen in the rebaptism controversy. In this opinion, Dulles agreed with patristic scholars Maurice Bévenot and Johannes Quasten.

71. Ibid., 39, 40, 43.

72. Ibid., 43 n. 49.

73. "Church Unity," *Worship* 29 (October 1955): 509–17.

74. On Tavard and his approach to ecumenism, see Marc R. Alexander, *Church and Ministry in the Works of G. H. Tavard* (Leuven: Leuven University Press: Uitgeveruij Peeters, 1994) and Kenneth Hagen, ed., *The Quadrilog: Tradition and the Future of Ecumenism: Essays in Honor of George H. Tavard* (Collegeville, MN: Liturgical Press, 1994).

75. "The Protestant Concept of the Church," *American Ecclesiastical Review* 132 (May 1955): 333.

76. Ibid., 334–35.

77. 239 (January 1957): 38–54. The article was actually written before he was ordained.

78. Ibid., 42, 54.

79. Ibid., 53.

80. "The Theological Significance of Paul Tillich," *Gregorianum* 37 (1956): 34–54. See also the republication in Thomas A. O'Meara and Celestin D. Weisser, eds., *Paul Tillich in Catholic Thought* (Dubuque, IA: Priory Press, 1964), 3–24. Tillich's response to Weigel's analysis was published at the end of the article, demonstrating Tillich's appreciation of Weigel's view and correcting some of his misconceptions.

81. 17 (September 1956): 345–67. This article was written in 1955 before Dulles was ordained; *TS* waited a year before publishing it because of its policy against publishing works of unordained scholastics. Reprinted in TO'Meara and Weisser, *Paul Tillich*, 109–32.

82. "Paul Tillich and the Bible," 367.

83. Ibid., 345.

84. On the revival in the 1950s, see Gerald P. Fogarty, *American Catholic Biblical Scholarship: A History from the Early Republic to Vatican II* (San Francisco: Harper & Row, 1989), 250–80.

85. "Some Recent Trends in Pentateuchal Criticism," *Theologian* 10 (1954): 18–28.

86. Ibid., 28.

87. Ibid., 22.

88. On the ordination, see "Dulles Here to See Ordination of Son," *New York Times* (June 16, 1956): 1; and "Dulles and Wife See Son Ordained a Jesuit Priest," *New York Times* (June 17, 1956): 1.

89. My interview with Theodore Cardinal McCarrick, January 5, 2009, transcript, 2, in my possession.

90. Christopher Huntington, "Sermon Delivered at the First Solemn Mass of the Reverend Avery Robert Dulles, SJ, Dahlgren Memorial Chapel, Georgetown University, Washington, DC, Sunday, June the Twenty-Fourth, 1956," in Mark J. Williams's archives.

91. "The Legion of Decency," *America* 95 (June 2, 1956): 240–42.

92. "The Contemporary Flight from Ideas," *Loyola Law Review* 8 (1955–1956): 41, 43, 44, 47, 49, 57.

93. *Cons* [516].

94. Daddy to the Reverend Avery Dulles, February 26, 1957, in DPFU. John Foster Dulles had become good friends with Konrad Adenauer (1876–1967), chancellor of West Germany from 1949 to 1963.

95. See Dulles' account of the trip in "Protestants and Catholics in Germany," *America* 100 (January 24, 1959): 493–95; see also Dulles' "Protestant-Catholic Relations in Germany," *Epistle* 27 (Winter 1961): 2–11.

Chapter 6. From the Gregorian to Woodstock, 1958–1965

1. See, e.g., "Cardinals Name a Leader Pending Election of Pope; Rites for Pius Begin Today," *New York Times* (October 10, 1958): 1.

2. "Truman and Hoover Join Many Other U.S. Leaders in Homage to Late Pontiff," *New York Times* (October 10, 1958): 12.

3. For a perfunctory description of the papal election, one that had no indication of changes that were to come, see Arnaldo Cortesis, "Cardinal Roncalli Elected Pope," *New York Times* (October 29, 1958): 1.

4. A church in Rome named after St. Sylvester, bishop of Rome from 314 to 335, and, according to legend, the first bishop of Rome to be given the Lateran Basilica as his cathedral.

5. "Dulles' Son in Debut as Jesuit Preacher," *New York Times* (November 10, 1958): 4.

6. Dulles to Mother, November 21, 1958, in DPFU. Sermon enclosed.

7. Ibid.

8. Dulles, *The Craft of Theology: From Symbol to System* (New York: Crossroad, 1992, exp. ed., 1995), 152. I am using the 1995 edition of this text.

9. My interview with Dulles, August 3, 2005, transcript, 29, in DPFU.

10. "Protestant Churches and the Prophetic Office," STD dissertation, Pontifical Gregorian University, Rome, 1960, in DPFU.

11. Dulles' illness was a matter of press comments in December 1958. Avery received two letters from his mother informing him of his father's bad condition. On January 19, 1959, his mother wrote, "Daddy has been suffering from different ailments and says he feels like Job." After a brief hospital stay at Walter Reed, John Foster and Janet went to Florida for some recuperation, but on April

7, 1959, Janet reported to Avery that his father's health had not improved, and, in fact, he was very weak. Both letters in DPFU.

12. "Remarks of Avery Dulles, SJ," in *John Foster Dulles: The Leader and the Legend* (Princeton, NJ: Woodrow Wilson School of Public and International Affairs, 1988), 7.

13. "John Foster Dulles Dies; Special Funeral Decreed; Geneva Talks to Suspend," *New York Times* (May 25, 1959): 1. See also "Thousands Visit at Dulles' Bier; Burial Is Today," ibid. (May 27, 1959): 1; "Dulles Is Buried; World's Leaders Attend Services," ibid. (May 28, 1959): 1; "Dulles Dies in His Sleep," *Washington Post* (May 25, 1959): 1, A6, A7, A8, A10; "President Leads World Notables in Paying Tribute at Dulles' Bier," ibid. (May 27, 1959): 1, A8; "Thousands Pay Tribute at Dulles Rites," ibid. (May 28, 1959): 1, A16.

14. "Pope, Queen Elizabeth Extend Their Sympathy," *Washington Post* (May 26, 1959): A8.

15. "His Passing Mourned as Tragic Loss," *Washington Post* (May 25, 1959): A6.

16. For historical background on the conference, see C. J. Dumont, "La Conférence Catholique Internationale pour les questions oecuméniques," *Vers l'unité chrétienne* 14 (1961): 18–20; Yves M.-J. Congar, *Dialogue between Christians* (Westminster, MD: Newman Press, 1966), 40–41; Jan Grootaers, "Jan Cardinal Willebrands," *One in Christ* 6 (1970): 23–44.

17. *De Spiritu Sancto anima corporis mystici*, 2 vols. (Rome: Gregorian University, 1948–1952).

18. *Testimonial to Grace*, 105.

19. "Protestant Churches and the Prophetic Office," 16.

20. Ibid., 1–4.

21. My interview with Dulles, August 3, 2005, transcript, 33, in DPFU.

22. "Protestant Churches and the Prophetic Office," 29.

23. Murray to Dulles, May 5, 1960, in DPFU.

24. See "The Protestant Preacher and the Prophetic Mission," *TS* 21 (December 1960): 544-80. See also *Protestant Churches and the Prophetic Office* (Woodstock, MD: Woodstock College Press, 1961).

25. *Protestant Churches and the Prophetic Office*, 15, 38.

26. Ibid., 16, invoking Aquinas's *Summa theologiae*, II–II, q. 177, a. 2, c.

27. Ibid., 41–43.

28. *Testimonial to Grace*, 106. Dulles was cautious by temperament, and in the dissertation intentionally so because he was writing, on the one hand, for Witte, who was open to arguments about the *vestigia*, and, on the other hand, for Charles Boyer, who was more conservative theologically. Before the defense, Dulles received somewhat contradictory recommendations for changes from both men. When he took the suggested changes to each of them, they each vetoed the changes suggested by the other. So, Dulles made none of the changes. See my interview with Dulles, August 4, 2005, transcript, 30, in DPFU.

29. Pius XII's approach, though, had not been universally accepted in the United States, as was evident in Fr. Leonard Feeney's, SJ, and St. Benedict

Center's rigorous interpretation of the dictum "No salvation outside the church," excluding all but faithful Catholics from salvation and denying the possibility of belonging to the church through implicit or explicit desire or intention.

30. *Catholic Ecumenism: The Reunion of Christendom in Contemporary Papal Pronouncements* (Washington, DC: Catholic University of America, 1953).

31. "Vestigia Ecclesiae: Their Meaning and Value," in *One Fold: Essays and Documents to Commemorate the Golden Jubilee of the Chair of Unity Octave (1908–1958)*, eds. Edward F. Hanahoe and Titus F. Cranny (Garrison, NY: Chair of Unity Apostolate, 1959), 272–383; see especially 297–308.

32. *That They May Be One: A Study of Papal Doctrine* (Westminster, MD: Newman, 1958), 38–44, 112.

33. *A la rencontre du Protestantisme* (Paris: Le Centurion, 1954), 80; see also the English translation, *The Catholic Approach to Protestantism* (New York: Harper & Brothers, 1955), 94, 96, and 132, where Tavard asserted that Catholics needed to study the *vestigia ecclesiae* to understand the various ways in which Protestants were related to the church in a filial fashion.

34. *Testimonial to Grace*, 108.

35. Schutz's *Unity: Man's Tomorrow* (1962) in *TS* 24 (June 1963): 345–46.

36. See Dulles' review of Thurian's *Visible Unity and Tradition* (1962) in *America* 108 (January 19, 1963): 109.

37. "Protestant-Catholic Relations in Germany," *Epistle* 27 (Winter 1961): 10–11.

38. Dulles to the Honorable Richard Nixon, November 22, 1988, in DPFU.

39. "Protestant Unit Wary on Kennedy," *New York Times* (September 8, 1960): 1; see also "Protestant Groups' Statements," *New York Times* (September 8, 1960): 28.

40. *A Roman Catholic in the White House* (New York: Doubleday, 1960), 133.

41. See, e.g., Weigel's angry response in "Bishop Pike and a Catholic President," *Ave Maria* (May 28, 1960): 20–21.

42. "Remarks on Church and State," in *Church and State in American History*, ed. John Wilson (Boston: D. C. Heath, 1965), 188–90, at 188, and "Refutation of Bigotry" in *"Let the Word Go Forth": The Speeches, Statements, and Writings of John F. Kennedy*, ed. Theodore C. Sorensen (New York: Delacorte, 1988), 130–36. See also *New York Times* (September 13, 1960): 22.

43. On this, see Donald E. Pelotte, *John Courtney Murray: Theologian in Conflict* (New York: Paulist, 1976), 76–77.

44. "On Raising the Religious Issue," *America* 103 (September 24, 1960): 702.

45. Collins, *Gustave Weigel*, 161.

46. "Excerpts from Address by Theologian," *New York Times* (September 28, 1960): 28; see also the fully published speech in "Church-State Relations: A Theological Consideration," *Catholic Theology in Dialogue* (New York: Harper, 1961), 101–17. See also "Jesuit Rules Out Church Control over a President," *New York Times* (September 28, 1960): 1.

Notes

47. "Church-State Relations," 115.

48. Collins, *Gustave Weigel*, 163.

49. Rynne was a pseudonym for Francis Xavier Murphy (1914–2002), a Redemptorist priest and Patristics scholar at the Alphonsian Academy in Rome from 1959 to 1971.

50. My interview with Dulles, August 3, 2005, transcript, 42, in DPFU. See also "Reflections on Revelation," in *Vatican II: Forty Personal Stories*, eds. William Madges and Michael J. Daley (Mystic, CT: Twenty-Third Publications, 2003), 117–18.

51. Letters from Vatican City," *New Yorker* 38 (October 20, 1962): 95–23; (December 29, 1962): 34–59, and multiple other letters nearly every month until the last one in the *New Yorker* 44 (November 2, 1968): 131–47. The letters were later expanded and republished in a series of books on the council happenings. See Xavier Rynne, *Letters from Vatican City: Vatican Council II (First Session): Background and Debates* (New York: Farrar, Straus & Company, 1963); *The Second Session: The Debates and Decrees of Vatican Council II, September 29 to December 4, 1963* (New York: Farrar, Straus & Company, 1964); *The Third Session: The Debates and Decrees of Vatican Council II, September 14 to November 21, 1964* (New York: Farrar, Straus & Company, 1965); *The Fourth Session: The Debates and Decrees of Vatican Council II, September 14 to December 8, 1965* (New York: Farrar, Straus & Company, 1966). Later these texts were published in a single volume, Xavier Rynne, *Vatican Council II* (Maryknoll, NY: Orbis, 1999).

52. For a description and enthusiastic reactions to Küng's tour, see "Fr. Küng in America," [London] *Tablet* 217 (April 27, 1963): 468; Leonard Swidler, "The Catholic Historian and Freedom," *American Benedictine Review* 17 (June 1966): 152–53; John B. Sheerin, "Interview with Hans Küng," *Catholic World* 197 (June 1963): 159–63; and editorial in *Commonweal* 78 (June 21, 1963): 343.

53. Trans. from *Konzil under Wiedervereinigung* (Freiburg im Breisgau, 1961) by Cecily Hastings (New York: Sheed & Ward, 1962).

54. Ibid., 184–85.

55. The French translation in *TS* 22 (December 1961): 704–6, and the English translation in *America* 106 (March 31, 1962): 861–62, and the *Catholic Book Reporter* (April–May 1962): 11.

56. See Dulles' review of Küng's *That the World May Believe* in *Woodstock Letters* 92 (1963): 305–6.

57. *Catholic Mind* 63 (April 1965): 32–35, quotation on 35. The article was originally given as a talk at the National Shrine of the Immaculate Conception in Washington, DC, January 21, 1965, on the fourth day of the Chair of Unity Octave. The original sermon, "Luther's Unfinished Reformation," is in ADGUSC, Box 6.

58. See, e.g., "Finding God's Will," *Woodstock Letters* 94 (1965): 139–52, and "The Ignatian Experience as Reflected in the Spiritual Theology of Karl Rahner," *Philippine Studies* 13 (1965): 471–94. Both essays were reprinted in *Jesuit Spirit in a Time of Change*, eds. Raymond A. Schroth et al. (Westminster, MD: Newman Press, 1968), 9–41. I am using *Jesuit Spirit* in what follows.

59. "Finding God's Will," in *Jesuit Spirit*, 25, 26, 33.

60. My interview with Patrick Burns, SJ, May 29, 2008, transcript, 2, in my possession. Burns was a scholastic at Woodstock from 1960 to 1964. He also finished his doctoral dissertation at Woodstock, under Dulles, during the 1967–1968 school year.

61. On these rough statistics, see Joseph M. Becker, *The Re-Formed Jesuits: A History of Changes in Jesuit Formation during the Decade 1965–1976*, Vol. 2, *Changes in Religious Lifesytle, Dress and Demographics* (San Francisco: Ignatius Press, 1997), 44–45. See also my interview with Patrick Burns, SJ, May 29, 2008, transcript, 2–3, in my possession.

62. My interview with Dulles, August 3, 2005, transcript, 43, in DPFU. The use of Latin in the liturgy would be a contentious point during the first session of Vatican II, with clerical scholars like Godfrey Diekmann of St. John's University in Minnesota and Frederick McMannus of the Catholic University of America, both American *periti* on the Preparatory Liturgical Commission, pleading for the use of the vernacular in public worship.

63. "*De Revelatione Christiana (Tractatus dogmatico–apologeticus)*" [1961–62]. The Latin lecture notes of more than eighty-five single-spaced typed pages, with substantial bibliographies and more than sixty pages of English translations are located in DPFU. To some extent the excursus on "Non-Catholic Notions of Christian Revelation" begins a history of the theology of revelation on which he would work for the next decade, until he published his *Revelation Theology: A History* (New York: Herder & Herder, 1969).

64. See, e.g., "The Catholic Notion of Christian Revelation" in Dulles' 1961–1962 class notes for *De Revelatione Christiana*, in DPFU. The article was Latourelle's "Notion de révélation et magistère de l'Eglise," *Sciences ecclésiastiques* 9 (1957): 20–21.

65. TS 25 (March 1964): 43–58, quotation at 44.

66. Ibid., 49, 52–58.

67. Latourelle to Dulles, April 14, 1964, in DPFU.

68. See Dulles' 1961–1962 class notes for *De Revelatione Christiana*, in DPFU. "The Historical Component in Christian Revelation" was a translation of G. Söhngen's "Das Mysterium des lebendigen Christus und der lebendige Glaube…" in *Die Einheit in der Theologie* (München, 1952), 344–48.

69. Ibid., 2.

70. "Non-Catholic Notions of Christian Revelation," in 1961–1962 class notes for *De Revelatione Christiana*, 40, in DPFU.

71. *The Open Church: Vatican II, Act II* (New York: Macmillan, 1964), 52–70.

72. Ibid., 56, 57.

73. Ibid., 55.

74. Periodically Dulles referred to the "Pesch-Dieckmann tradition" of manual theology. See "Revelation and the Apostolate," in *Apostolic Renewal in the Seminary in the Light of Vatican Council II*, eds. James Keller and Richard Armstrong (New York: Christopher Books, 1965), 113. On the limits of manual

theology, see also Dulles' review of W. Bulst's *Revelation* in *TS* 26 (June 1965): 307–8.

75. *Apologetics and the Biblical Christ* (1963; Westminster, MD: Newman Press, 1967). I am using the 1967, eighth printing of the text.

76. Ibid., ix.

77. See, e.g., "The Gospels and Apologetic Method," *Proceedings*, CTSA 19 (1964): 151.

78. Dulles' review in *TS* 24 (December 1963): 675.

79. "Method in Biblical Theology," in *The Bible in Modern Scholarship*, ed. J. Philip Hyatt (Nashville, TN: Abingdon, 1965), 210–11, 212, 213.

80. Ibid., xi.

81. Ibid., viii–ix.

82. Ibid., 73.

83. "Gospels and Apologetic Method," 153.

84. See, e.g., reviews in *Downside Review* 82 (March 1964): 281–92; *TS* 25 (June 1964): 260–63; *Heythrop Journal* 6 (January 1965): 85–7; *Tablet* (London) 218 (August 29, 1964): 974–75; *Studies* (Dublin) 54 (Summer–Fall 1965): 259–61; *Catholic Biblical Quarterly* 26 (April 1964): 263–64; *American Ecclesiastical Review* 150 (June 1964): 453–56.

85. "Jesus as the Christ: Some Recent Protestant Positions," *Thought* 39 (Autumn 1964): 362.

86. Ibid., 367, 379.

87. "The Council and the Sources of Revelation," *America* 107 (December 1962): 1176–77.

88. Dulles' review of Blondel's *Letter on Apologetics and History and Dogma* in *TS* 26 (September 1965): 499.

89. Review in *America* 108 (May 25, 1963): 783.

90. Review in *America* 109 (November 2, 1963): 529–30.

91. Gabriel Moran to Avery Dulles, September 12, 1964, in DPFU.

92. Ibid.

93. Dulles to Br. Gabriel Moran, FSC, September 17, 1964, in DPFU.

94. Ibid.

95. "Revelation and the Apostolate," 121.

96. "Comments," *America* 104 (January 14, 1961): 461–62.

97. "Catholic Ecumenism," *Catholic Reporter* (May 4, 1962): 11.

98. "Ecumenism: A Catholic Concern," *Proceedings of the National Catholic Educational Association* (August 1962): 144.

99. "Pope Paul's Ecumenical Perspective," *Catholic World* 200 (October 1964): 15–21.

100. See, e.g., Dulles' review of Gregory Baum's *Progress and Perspectives* in *TS* 24 (March 1963): 159, and Dulles' "A Different Reading," *Commonweal* 81 (January 22, 1965): 530–31, reacting to Robert McAfee Brown's apprehensions about the council.

101. Samuel H. Miller and G. Ernest Wright, eds., *Ecumenical Dialogue at Harvard: The Roman Catholic–Protestant Colloquium* (Cambridge, MA: Harvard University Press, 1964), vii.

102. Dulles' review of *Ecumenical Dialogue at Harvard* in *TS* 25 (December 1964): 672.

103. James Keller and Richard Armstrong, "Introduction," in *Apostolic Renewal in the Seminary* (1965), 8, 16.

104. See, e.g., Brown's "Apprehensions about the Council," *Commonweal* 81 (December 25, 1964): 442–45.

105. Brown to Dulles, December 28, 1965, in DPFU.

106. On the historical significance of the congregation, see John W. Padberg, *Together as a Companionship: A History of the Thirty-First, Thirty-Second, and Thirty-Third General Congregations of the Society of Jesus* (St. Louis: Institute of Jesuit Sources, 1994), and *Documents of the Thirty-First General Congregation* (Woodstock, MD: Woodstock College, 1967).

107. See "Excerpt from the Minutes of Committee on Theologates, JEA Commission on Houses of Study, Fordham University, New York, April 18–20, 1965," in ADGUSC, Box 8.

108. Dulles, "Report on Woodstock Curriculum Discussions Sept.–Oct. 1965," October 17, 1965, in ADGUSC, Box 8.

109. For the report, see *Woodstock Letters* 95 (Summer 1966): 335–56. Jesuit theologates, of course, had periodically through the centuries experienced some minor transformations here and there. The original, unedited document, "Report: Inter-Faculty Program Inquiry, Rockhurst College, 7–13 November 1965," is available in ADGUSC, Box 8.

110. My interview with Dulles, August 3, 2005, transcript, 44, in DPFU. For a detailed account of the meeting, see "Minutes of Inter-Faculty Program Inquiry, Rockhurst College, November 7–13, 1965," fifty pages in manuscript, in ADGUSC, Box 8.

111. *The Re-Formed Jesuits*, Vol. 1, *A History of Changes in Jesuit Education during the Decade 1965–1975* (San Francisco: Ignatius Press, 1992), 140, see also 55–59.

112. "Toward a New Theology: The Implications of Rockhurst," *Woodstock Letters* 95 (Summer 1966): 357.

113. "Inter-Faculty Program Inquiry Report," *Woodstock Letters* 95 (Summer 1966): 338. The Rockhurst Report did not actually recommend a move, but most Jesuits took its "Resolution 8" as such. The resolution stated, "Adequate implementation of the proposed program, especially in its graduate phase, demands close contact with a full university complex to insure a proper range of offerings." See "Inter-Faculty Program Inquiry," 6, in ADGUSC, Box 8.

114. Ibid., 349.

115. "Toward a New Theology: The Implications of Rockhurst," *Woodstock Letters* 95 (Summer 1966): 362, 365.

116. Later in his career, Dulles, like some other theologians in the late twentieth and early twenty-first centuries, criticized the fragmentation that had taken

place in theology and the shift from dogmatic to systematic theology and defined historical theology not as an autonomous discipline, but as a part of "faith seeking understanding by reference to faith's own past.…Historical theology, like all theology, must submit to the norm of living tradition, but it has a certain normative value of its own, since past expressions of the church's faith are authoritative for the present." See Dulles' "Wisdom as the Source of Unity for Theology," in *Wisdom and Holiness, Science and Scholarship (Essays in Honor of Matthew L. Lamb)*, eds. Michael Dauphinais and Matthew Levering (Naples, FL: Sapientia Press of Ave Maria University, 2007), 59–71, quotation at 69.

117. "Inter-Faculty Program Inquiry Report," 358–60.

118. "Minutes of Inter-Faculty Program Inquiry, XI Session, November 12, 1965," 45.

119. My interview with Dulles, August 3, 2005, transcript, 45, in DPFU. In a handwritten note in his papers, entitled "Why? My reasons" (n.d. but 1965 or 1966), Dulles indicated his understanding of historical theology that was considerably more nuanced than that of Justin Kelly's. He wrote that historical theology was "not just a history of theology, but a theological treatment of development of understanding of revelation." Document in ADGUSC, Box 8.

120. On de Pauw and his movement, see William D. Dinges, "'We Are What You Were': Roman Catholic Traditionalism in America," in *Being Right: Conservative Catholics in America*, eds. Mary Jo Weaver and R. Scott Appleby (Bloomington: Indiana University Press, 1995), 241–69, especially 241–44.

Chapter 7. From Vatican II to the Closing of Woodstock, 1966–1974

1. The original proposal was entitled "Toward an American Institute of Spirituality," February 1964; see 5 for quotation. The document is in ADGUSC, Box 8.

2. Dulles to the Very Reverend Fathers Provincial of Buffalo, Maryland and New York, November 3, 1964, in ADGUSC, Box 8.

3. Dulles to Andrew Brady, December 16, 1964, in ADGUSC, Box 8.

4. "Theology Curriculum Proposals" (n.d., but January 1966); see also Dulles' Memorandum to Prefect of Studies, January 24, 1966, on the implementation of Rockhurst on the undergraduate courses in theology. Both documents in ADGUSC, Box 8.

5. "Recommendations of the Student Committee to the Woodstock Faculty on the Implementation of the Rockhurst Report at Woodstock" (February 1966). See also "Minutes of the Faculty-Student Meeting of March 2, 1966" (March 4, 1966). Documents in ADGUSC, Box 8.

6. "Comments on Curriculum Section of Evaluation Report," October 29, 1967, in ADGUSC, Box 1.

7. Dulles memo to Dean, "Why Comprehensives?" April 12, 1969, in ADGUSC, Box 2.

8. My interview with Joseph Lienhard, SJ, a student at Woodstock in the late 1960s and early 1970s, August 5, 2005, transcript, 1, in my possession.

9. Ibid.

10. Andrew Greeley was the first, as far as I know, to tag seminarians of the 1960s the "new breed." See his "A New Breed," *America* 110 (May 23, 1964): 706–9. See also Raymond A. Schroth, SJ, "The Trouble with the Younger Men," *Woodstock Letters* 94 (Winter 1965): 45–54, who asserted (45) that "changing opinions, tastes, and concepts of the religious life itself [among the younger generation of Jesuits] can be more disturbing than usual."

11. Greeley, "New Breed," 708–9.

12. For statistics on the general decline of Jesuit scholastics in the entire American Assistancy, see Joseph M. Becker, *The Re-Formed Jesuits*, Vol. 2 (1997), 44–45, and Vol. 1 (1992), 193.

13. The information in this paragraph comes primarily from my interview with Philip Rossi, SJ, a student at Woodstock at the time, October 5, 2005, transcript, 5, in my possession.

14. My interview with Dulles, August 3–4, 2005, transcript, 44, in DPFU.

15. My interview with Lienhard, August 5, 2005, transcript, 2, in my possession.

16. My interview with Rossi, October 5, 2005, transcript, 5, in my possession.

17. On the FBI investigations, see my interview with Patrick Burns, SJ, May 29, 2008, transcript, 4, in my possession.

18. My interview with Dulles, August 3–4, 2005, transcript, 44, in DPFU.

19. Dulles to Matthew Lamb, May 10, 1994, in DPFU.

20. Dorothy McCardle, "Wife of John Foster Dulles Dies at 78," *Washington Post* (May 15, 1969): B6; see also "Mrs. John Foster Dulles, 77, Dies; Widow of the Secretary of State," *New York Times* (May 15, 1969): 47.

21. Carlos P. Rombo to Dulles, May 16, 1969, in DPFU.

22. My interview with Dulles, August 3–4, 2005, transcript, 57, in DPFU.

23. "Report to Woodstock College," by Taylor Lieberfeld and Heldman Inc. The report was delivered to Woodstock in December 1967. Document in ADGUSC, Box 1.

24. My interview with Patrick Burns, SJ, May 29, 2008, transcript, 10, in my possession.

25. My interview with Dulles, August 3–4, 2005, transcript, 58, in DPFU. See also Mooney's "Relocation of Woodstock: Fundamental Issues," August 17, 1967 (document not paginated). Among the many arguments he offered for relocating in New York, he suggested that New York was the entertainment center of the nation and offered Jesuits an opportunity to become involved in such attractions. On his personal copy of this report, Dulles wrote after reading this argument, "God help theology." The document with Mooney's letter to Dulles, August 17, 1967, is in ADGUSC, Box 1.

26. "Introductory Letter from the Provincial Superiors [James L. Connor and Robert A. Mitchell] of the Maryland and New York Provinces" (n.d., but 1970), in ADGUSC, Box 1.

27. My interview with Lienhard, August 5, 2005, typescript, 5, in my possession.

28. Dulles memo to Brian H. Smith, SJ, March 4, 1971, in ADGUSC, Box 1.

29. George Dugan, "Woodstock Future Jesuits to Study Theology at Union Seminary," *New York Times* (September 28, 1969): 64.

30. Will Lissner, "Protestants Greet Jesuits Here," *New York Times* (October 23, 1969): 49.

31. My interview with Joseph Lienhard, SJ, August 5, 2005; typescript, 5, in my possession.

32. Garry Wills, "The New Jesuits vs. the Heavenly City," *New York Magazine* 4 (August 2, 1971): 20–27.

33. Ibid., 22.

34. Ibid., 24.

35. Ibid., 24.

36. Ibid., 27.

37. Edward B. Fiske, "Jesuit Seminarians Adjust to City Life," *New York Times* (December 28, 1971): 31, 36.

38. Dulles to Rev. George Driscoll, SJ, January 8, 1972, in DPFU.

39. Dan Lyons, "Protestant Catholicism," *Twin Circle* (August 11, 1972): 7.

40. Dulles to Reginald Fuller, August 7, 1972, in ADGUSC, Box 1.

41. Fuller to Dulles, August 12, 1972, in ADGUSC, Box 1.

42. On these statistics, see Becker, *Re-Formed Jesuits*, Vol. 2 (1997), 43; see also 19–21.

43. Pedro Arrupe to James L. Connor, March 3, 1973. For information on the chain of events leading to the decision to close Woodstock, see letter from James L. Connor and Eamon Taylor [Maryland and New York provincials] to Pedro Arrupe, February 21, 1973; "Excerpt from Minutes of the Meeting of the Board of Trustees, Woodstock College, January 19, 1973"; and Burghardt memo to Fr. General, Proposed Agenda re Woodstock, March 7, 1973. Documents in ADGUSC, Box 1. On the details of the decision, see also Becker, *Re-Formed Jesuits*, Vol. 1, 129–38.

44. Robert Mitchell, SJ, to Patrick Carey, February 22, 2006. Letter in my possession.

45. Becker, *Re-Formed Jesuits*, Vol. 1, 134 n. 29.

46. Eleanor Blau, "Woodstock Jesuit College Here, Experimental Seminary, to Shut," *New York Times* (January 9, 1973): 1, 36; "A Death in the Family," *Time* (January 22, 1973): 47–48; Raymond A. Schroth, "The End of Woodstock," *Commonweal* (January 26, 1973): 364–65.

47. My interview with Dulles, August 3–4, 2005, transcript, 59, in DPFU.

48. Burghardt prepared an eleven-page memo on the meeting with the general for the Woodstock faculty and superiors, outlining the discussions that took place. See Walter J. Burghardt to Woodstock Faculty and Superiors, on

"Dulles-Burghardt at Curia re Woodstock, March 7–10, 1973." Dulles prepared a hand-drawn sketch of the discussion table, indicating where each person at the meeting sat and summarizing the positions of the general and each of the curia members. See also Dulles to Fr. General, Pedro Arrupe, March 11, 1973, in which Dulles indicates his acceptance of the general's decision and indicated that "the discussions did throw some helpful light on the decision process that took place last summer and fall, and particularly on the role which you had played in that process. I think that the earlier reports had given some false impressions on these matters." These three documents are in ADGUSC, Box 1.

Chapter 8. Models Theology for Turbulent Times, 1966–1974

1. "The New Atheism," *Sign* (June 1968): 9.
2. *Revelation and the Quest for Unity* (Washington: Corpus Books, 1968), 275. The text is from an earlier unpublished lecture, "The Death-of-God Theologies: Symptom and Challenge," which Dulles had delivered at Purdue University, November 2, 1966.
3. Ibid., 270.
4. "The Contemporary Magisterium," *Theology Digest* 17 (Winter 1969): 303.
5. "The Open Church," *Chicago Studies* 8 (Spring 1969): 19. This interpretation of the closed church of the preconciliar era is representative of Dulles' essays during the period. For another example, see "Faith Come of Age," *America* 117 (August 5, 1967): 137.
6. "Les catholiques américains à l'ère 'post-protestante,'" *Christus* (Paris) 9 (Octobre 1962): 542–44. See also "I cattolici americani nell'era 'post-protestante,'" *Aggiornamenti sociali* (Milano) 14 (Marzo 1963): 207–16.
7. "Les catholiques américains," 541.
8. In 1996, Dulles admitted that in this period "I may have tended to exaggerate the novelty of the Council's doctrines and the shortcomings of the preconciliar period." See his 1996 edition of *Testimonial to Grace*, 110. For a later, but more positive, assessment of pre–Vatican II American theology, see Dulles' "Theological Orientations, American Catholic Theology, 1940-1962," *Cristianesimo nella storia* 13 (Giugno 1992): 361–82.
9. Avery Dulles, "The Meaning of Revelation," in *The Dynamic in Christian Thought*, ed. Joseph Papin (Villanova, PA: Villanova University Press, 1971), 55.
10. For Dulles' 1989 characterization of his progressive interpretation of the Council, see "A Half Century of Ecclesiology," *TS* 50 (September 1989): 430–31.
11. "The Modern Dilemma of Faith," in *Toward a Theology of Christian Faith: Readings in Theology*, compiled by Michael Mooney et al. (New York: P. J. Kennedy & Sons, 1968), 16–17.

12. For one example of Dulles' view, see *Revelation and the Quest for Unity*, 83–84.

13. The books envisioned here are *Revelation and the Quest for Unity* (1968); *Revelation Theology: A History* (New York: Herder & Herder, 1969); *A History of Apologetics* (New York: Corpus; Philadelphia: Westminster; and London: Hutchinson, 1971); and *The Survival of Dogma* (Garden City, NY: Doubleday, 1971).

14. *Revelation and the Quest for Unity*, 16.

15. Ibid., 11.

16. For one of many examples of this view of the task, see "Symbol, Myth and Biblical Revelation," *TS* 27 (March 1966): 23. For the reference to the pope's opening message, see *The Documents of Vatican II*, ed. Walter M. Abbott (New York: American Press, 1966), 715.

17. "The Theology of Revelation: Recent Catholic Books in English," *Woodstock Letters* 96 (1967): 133.

18. Review of J. H. Gill's *The Possibility of Religious Knowledge* in *TS* 33 (March 1972): 148.

19. "Symbol, Myth and Biblical Revelation," 6.

20. Review of Gabriel Moran's *Theology of Revelation* in *Commonweal* 84 (September 16, 1966): 591–92.

21. "Theology of Revelation," 131; see also "Theological Table Talk: Revelation in Recent Catholic Theology," *Theology Today* 24 (October 1967): 364.

22. More than twenty years after *Survival*, Dulles indicated to a correspondent that his main concern in that book "was to get Catholic readers to accept the possibility of development of doctrine and to take personal responsibility for their faith....Since authoritarianism and blind conservatism are always a danger, the book may still have some relevance....I am still opposed to authoritarianism, but I dislike the current tendency to label any exercise of authority as authoritarian. Christian doctrine is normally accepted on authority—that of Christ, the Scriptures, or the teaching Church." See Dulles to Jim Roth, June 8, 1999. In a letter to Gil Costello, October 13, 2002, Dulles wrote that his *Survival* reflected the times in which it was written, "when many of us were uncertain about how far the changes introduced by Vatican II were going to go. In arguing for the changeability of dogmas, I had in mind the formulated statements, not the truths that these statements intended to convey." Since the publication of that book "I have become more cautious in my statements," emphasizing the continuity of church teachings. There might be statements, he continued, in *Survival*, "that I would want to retract today." In 2004, Dulles told another correspondent that he still believed in the "reformability of dogma," but he "would be inclined to add some words of caution about reformulation and reconceptualization. Often the old formulas and concepts were better than those proposed as replacements." See Dulles to Patrick G. D. Riley, February 23, 2004. Letters in DPFU.

23. On Michael Polanyi, see Richard Gelwick, *The Way of Discovery: An Introduction to the Thought of Michael Polanyi* (New York: Oxford University Press, 1977); Scott Drusilla, *Everyman Revived: The Common Sense of Michael Polanyi*

(Grand Rapids: Eerdmans, 1995); Andy F. Sanders, *Michael Polanyi's Post-Critical Epistemology: A Reconsideration of Some Aspects of "Tacit Knowing"* (Amsterdam: Rodopi, 1988); Mark T. Mitchell, *Michael Polanyi: The Art of Knowing* (Wilmington, DE: Intercollegiate Studies Institute, 2006); Andrew T. Grosso, *Personal Being: Polanyi, Ontology, and Christian Theology* (New York: Peter Lang, 2007). In the 1971 fall semester at Woodstock College, Dulles gave a seminar on "Discernment and Discovery in Theology" and spent a month reading with the students Polanyi's *Personal Knowledge*, and found it "very rewarding." See Dulles to Fr. Manno, December 17, 1971, in DPFU. For one of Dulles' later assessments of Polanyi's influence, see "Faith, Church, and God: Insights from Michael Polanyi," *TS* 45 (September 1984): 537-50.

24. My interview with Dulles, August 3–4, 2005, transcript, 52, in DPFU.

25. "Faith and Doubt," *America* 116 (March 11, 1967): 350; "Faith and Dogmatic Pluralism," *America* 116 (May 13, 1967): 728; "Faith Come of Age," *America* 117 (August 5, 1967): 137; "Faith and New Opinions," *America* 117 (October 28, 1967): 479; "Faith and Meaning," *America* 118 (January 13, 1968): 41; "Faith and Its Contents," *America* 118 (April 13, 1968): 484. This series of articles was then combined in "The Modern Dilemma of Faith," 11–32.

26. "Modern Dilemma of Faith," 16–17.

27. "Faith and Dogmatic Pluralism," 728.

28. "Faith and New Opinions," 479.

29. "Faith Come of Age," 137.

30. "Faith and Meaning," 41.

31. "Faith and Its Contents," 484.

32. *The Documents of Vatican II* (Abbott), 715. See also one example of Dulles' frequent use of this passage, "The Contemporary Magisterium," *Theology Digest* 17 (Winter 1969): 306.

33. In August 1973, Dulles granted Fr. Jozef Krasinski, a Polish seminary professor, an interview on his theology that was later published in Polish. In it Dulles summarized the intent of his *Survival of Dogma*. In that book, "I devoted my attention principally to the question of the continuity and discontinuity in the ways in which the Church understands and expresses its faith. That is one of the questions that most interests me. By identifying too closely faith and the formulations of faith, Christians can prevent the Church from adjusting to the times and from availing itself of the good things that modern thought has to offer." See Dulles to Joseph Krasinski, August 29, 1973, letter in DPFU.

34. For this description, see "Dogma as an Ecumenical Problem," *TS* 29 (September 1968): 400, and *Survival of Dogma*, 13.

35. *Survival of Dogma*, 112–13.

36. Ibid., 11.

37. "Symbol, Myth, and the Biblical Revelation," 2–3.

38. *Survival of Dogma*, 185–203.

39. Ibid., 192.

40. See Dulles' conclusion to "Contemporary Understanding of the Irreformability of Dogma," *Proceedings*, CTSA 25 (June 1970): 134–36.

41. *Survival of Dogma*, 203.
42. Ibid., 192–93.
43. "Contemporary Understanding of the Irreformability of Dogma," 129–30.
44. "How Sound is Avery Dulles?" *Twin Circle* (August 4, 1972): 7, 10. See also Dulles' response in "Fr. Avery Dulles Replies," *Twin Circle* (August 25, 1972): 4, 5. In an earlier interview with *Twin Circle*, Dulles asserted that people were afraid of change because they lacked a sense of history. "True fidelity to the past includes a readiness to move forward, inspired by the example of our predecessors." In the interview, he recommended an asceticism of flexibility in the current state of the church. See "Father Dulles Gives His Theories on Church," *Twin Circle* (July 14, 1972): 9. For another, later, charge against Dulles' relativism, see Robert F. Christian, "A Rebuttal to Avery Dulles," *Homelitic and Pastoral Review* (March 1979): 62–67.
45. "How Sound Is Avery Dulles?" 10.
46. Another Catholic in a conservative journal charged that Dulles held that "it is alright [sic] to deny the dogma of the Virgin Birth." See Henry Ives Cobb Jr., "Avery Dulles and the Virgin Birth," *Triumph* 3 (January 1968): 6. In a brief article, "Faith and New Opinions," *America* (October 28, 1967): 479, Dulles had asserted that a few years ago hardly any Catholic would have felt free to deny "that Jesus was conceived without the co-operation of a human father." The *Triumph* correspondent believed that this implied that Dulles had denied the virgin birth. Dulles protested to the editor of *Triumph* that he had never denied the virginal conception of Jesus Christ. He had mentioned only in passing that "some Catholic writers feel free to deny the physical interpretation of Mary's virginity, which is the interpretation on which older Catholics have been brought up." But, Dulles retorted, he had not pronounced on the validity of such interpretations. Here it was not dogma, but the interpretations of dogma that was the issue, he insinuated. See Dulles to Editor of *Triumph*, January 26, 1968, in DPFU. See also "Fr. Dulles Objects," *Triumph* (March 1968): 3–4. The editor of *Triumph* was not impressed with Dulles' explanation.

John J. Mulloy, "The Dulles Changes: Developments or Corruption?" *Wanderer* (November 16, 1972): 5, and (December 21, 1972): 8, also charged that Dulles' views on changes in or reformulations of doctrine lacked fundamental criteria for laypeople to determine which theologians' reformulations were authentic developments and which ones were corruptions of doctrine. Dulles, Mulloy continued, was largely favorable to change and to adaptation, but he failed to point out which contemporary "signs of the times" were valuable and which were detrimental to the church. Dulles and other theologians of his type were "elitists" who were imposing changes upon ordinary laypeople who would just "have to get used to them," as Dulles wrote in one of his articles [the one cited above in *America*]. What specific responsibility, moreover, did theologians have to the Magisterium? In response to these and other charges Dulles responded that "history is not all progress, that change is not automatically for the better, and that criteria are necessary to evaluate proposed changes" as he had argued in his works, particularly in

Survival of Dogma, 161. See Dulles to editor of *The Wanderer* (December 21, 1972): 8, and responses to Dulles' defense by John J. Mulloy. In that same issue of *The Wanderer*, William A. Marshner's "Culture, Concept and Dogma in Avery Dulles" took issue with *Survival's* notion of concept as culturally conditioned; Marshner maintained that concepts were not, as Dulles and Rahner understood them, phantasms, but "expressed species," and as such they expressed the intelligibility of things. Concepts were not, as Dulles asserted, simply conditioned by experience and history; they tended to transcend history and culture; otherwise there would be no possibility of communication across cultural or historical boundaries.

In another letter to the editor of *Triumph* 5 (March 1970): 38, R. L. Davis charged that Dulles was a latter-day Sabellian and that his position as teacher of seminarians at Woodstock was particularly dangerous because of his potential to create "a lot of little Sabellians, who, in turn, would form other little Sabellians." The charge was made because of what Dulles had written in his "Dogma as an Ecumenical Problem," *TS* 29 (September 1968): 405 (later republished in *Survival of Dogma*): "To safeguard Trinitarian orthodoxy, one might raise the question whether it would not be preferable to call God a single person with three modes of being." The suggested language was not well formulated and was open to the charge, but Dulles was not saying that this was his position; he was simply arguing that the contemporary understanding of "person" did not correspond to ancient Christian usage of that language. In the context in which this statement occurred, he was arguing for the "principle of variability in language." That Dulles was orthodox on the doctrine of the Trinity is evident in many of his works, but see in particular *The Catholicity of the Church* (Oxford: Clarendon Press, 1985), 31–32.

47. See, e.g., Michael Fahey's review in *America* 125 (September 25, 1971): 214–15; Marthaler's in *American Ecclesiastical Review* 166 (June 1972): 425; and James Langford's in *Catholic World* 214 (December 1971): 136.

48. *History of Apologetics* (Washington, DC: Corpus Instrumentorum, 1971); republished (Eugene, OR: Wipf & Stock, 1999); and revised and enlarged (San Francisco: Ignatius Press, 2005), xxiii. Generally, I am using the 2005 edition.

49. Dulles' course on revelation gave significant attention to apologetics. For Dulles' analysis of the post–Vatican II Catholic debates on the meaning of fundamental theology and the role of apologetics within it, see *History of Apologetics* (San Francisco: Ignatius Press, 2005), 326–29.

50. See, e.g., *Apologetics and the Biblical Christ* (1963).

51. For one lament over the loss of apologetics, see Arnold Lunn, "A Dirty Word [Apologetics]," *Triumph* 5 (March 1970): 22–23.

52. Prior to the council, undergraduate theology, especially as presented through neo-scholastic philosophical courses in natural theology, had been apologetic, aiming to give students reasons for belief.

53. My interview with Dulles, August 3–4, 2005, transcript, 24, in DPFU.

54. In Dulles' 1973 interview with Fr. Jozef Krasinski, one of the questions focused on the contemporary role of apologetics in Catholicism. "Some theologians," Krasinski asserted, "think that the era of apologetical approach to theo-

logical questions has passed away. Even the word 'apologetics' is unpleasant to their ears and belongs to the epoch of Trent, they say. As an expert in this area do you see a real profound difference between methods of traditional Apologetics and the new Fundamental Theology?" Dulles responded, "Personally I think that the apologetical quest is a good and necessary one, but that many of the past forms of apologetics are no longer suitable. Perhaps some other word is necessary. The new fundamental theology differs from the traditional apologetics in several important respects: It speaks not only to non-believers but to believers. It seeks to explore from a position within faith the reasonableness of believing. It does not seek to erect compelling arguments based on undeniable evidences but rather to assist in the interpretation or discernment of the signs of the working of God in history. It does not assume that the content of faith is antecedently clear, but it seeks to establish what Christians should believe partly on the basis of what it is reasonable to believe. Thus apologetics becomes a dimension of dogmatic theology itself." See Jozef Krasinski to Dulles, November 12, 1973, and Dulles to Joseph Krasinski, August 29, 1973, letters in DPFU.

55. See, n. 48 above.

56. *History of Apologetics* (2005), 268.

57. *Models of the Church* (Garden City, NY: Doubleday, 1974). A British edition came out in 1976; it was reprinted in 1977 and 1978 in the United States and England; reprinted and expanded editions in 1987 and 2002; and foreign translations were published in Spanish (1975), Portugese (1978), Indonesian (1990), Hungarian (2003), and Italian (2005).

58. My interview with Dulles, August 3–4, 2005, transcript, 48, in DPFU.

59. Dulles, "The Church," in *Documents of Vatican II*, 9–13, quotations at 10–11, 13. This English translation of the documents, published by different presses, had little competition in the publishing world until 1975 when Austin Flannery, as general editor, produced *Vatican Council II: The Conciliar and Postconciliar Documents* (Boston: St. Paul Books & Media, 1975).

60. Dulles, "The Church," 11–13.

61. *The Dimensions of the Church: A Postconciliar Reflection* (New York: Newman Press, 1967), 1, viii, l03.

62. Ibid., 20, 114.

63. Rosemary Ruether's review in *Cross Currents* 18 (Winter 1968): 110–13.

64. Carl S. Meyer's review in *Christianity Today* 12 (May 10, 1968): 31–32.

65. "The Changing Nature of Mission," *American Ecclesiastical Review* 157 (December 1967): 367, alluding to GS 1.

66. For examples of some of the themes in this paragraph, see "The Changing Nature of Mission," 366–72; "Christian Missions in Transition," in *The Word in the Third World*, ed. James P. Cotter (Washington, DC: Corpus Books, 1968), 261–69, and "Current Trends in Mission Theology," *Studies in the International Apostolate of Jesuits* 1 (January 1972): 21–37.

67. For one example of this, see Dulles' "Comments on Paper by C. C. West," *Word in the Third World*, 74–81.

68. Quoting GS 42 in "The Church and Civil Society," *Studies in the International Apostolate of Jesuits* 3 (November 1974): 99.

69. Dulles, "The Church as Eschatological Community," in *The Eschaton: A Community of Love*, ed. Joseph Papin (Villanova, PA: Villanova University Press, 1974), 88–89.

70. Ibid., 97–99.

71. Justin Kelly to Dulles, June 24, 1994, in DPFU.

72. Dulles to Justin Kelly, August 1, 1994, in DPFU.

73. My interview with Dulles, August 3–4, 2005, transcript, 53, in DPFU.

74. Ibid.

75. "Karl Rahner on Human Life," *America* 119 (September 28, 1968): 250–52.

76. "Contemporary Magisterium," 304–5.

77. For a brief introduction to the movement, see my *Catholics in America: A History* (Westport, CT: Praeger, 2004), 137.

78. For an example of such thinking, see "The Succession of Prophets in the Church," in *Apostolic Succession: Rethinking a Barrier to Unity. Concilium* 34, ed. Hans Küng (Paramus, NJ: Paulist, 1968), 52–62.

79. For these emphases, see "Charisms for the Whole Church," *New Covenant* 3 (April 1974): 31, and "Now That the Honeymoon Is Over," *Origins* 3 (April 11, 1974): 649–56, especially 653.

80. Review of Küng's *The Church* in *America* 118 (April 20, 1968): 545-46, quote on 545.

81. Letters to the Editor, *America* 118 (May 25, 1968): 686.

82. Dulles to Küng, March 20, 1969, in DPFU.

83. John J. Kirvan, ed., *The Infallibility Debate* (New York: Paulist, 1971). See also Michael A. Fahey, "Europe's Theologians Join the Debate," and George A. Lindbeck, "A Protestant Perspective," both in *America* 124 (April 24, 1971): 429–31, 431–33.

84. Dulles to O'Donovan, March 10, 1971, in DPFU.

85. "Hans Küng's *Infallible? An Inquiry*: The Theological Issues," *America* 124 (April 24, 1971): 427–28.

86. "The Theology of Hans Küng: A Comment," *Union Seminary Quarterly Review* 27 (Spring 1972): 137–42.

87. "Infallibility Revisited," *America* 129 (August 4, 1973): 56.

88. "Reforming the Church, Reviving Religion" [Review of R. P. McBrien, *The Remaking of the Church*], *America* 129 (November 10, 1973): 358–59.

89. Dulles may have had in mind here some of his own Woodstock Jesuit colleagues who had left the priesthood or even the British priest Charles Davis, who left the church.

90. McBrien to Dulles, November 13, 1973, in DPFU.

91. Dulles to McBrien, November 16, 1973, in DPFU. McBrien responded to Dulles by assuring him that his criticisms had not offended. See McBrien to Dulles, November 20, 1973, in DPFU.

Notes

92. Francis F. Brown, Director of Public Relations for the National Federation of Priests' Councils, to Dulles, January 29, 1974, in DPFU; and McBrien to Dulles, February 12, 1974, in DPFU.

93. Albert J. Nevins, ed., "Odds and Ends," *Our Sunday Visitor* (December 23, 1973): 4.

94. Dulles to Editor of *Our Sunday Visitor*, February 14, 1974, and Dulles to McBrien, February 14, 1974, in DPFU.

95. See, e.g., Dulles to Msgr. Wilfrid H. Paradis, April 27, 1975; Paradis to Dulles, June 1, 1976; Dulles to Paradis, June 17, 1976, and Paradis to Dulles, June 21, 1976, in ADGUSC, Box 5.

96. My interview with Dulles, August 3–4, 2005, transcript, 54, in DPFU.

97. On these suggestions, see, e.g., Dulles to Msgr. J. Paul O'Conner, April 22, 1970, in ADGUSC, Box 3; Dulles' "National Pastoral Council Booklet," October 23, 1970, in ADGUSC, Box 9; Dulles to William Toomey, February 4, 1974, in ADGUSC, Box 4; "NCCB Documentation: Catholic-Muslim Dialogue" (n.d. but 1974), in ADGUSC, Box 4; Dulles to Bishop James S. Rausch, March 25, 1976, in ADGUSC, Box 5. Dulles preserved (in ADGUSC, Boxes 3, 4, 5, and 9) multiple papers and minutes of meetings of the Advisory Council that detailed its activities and suggestions to the bishops.

98. "Minutes of Meeting of Steering Committee of USCC Advisory Council," May 2, 1970, 10, in ADGUSC, Box 3.

99. "The Idea of a National Pastoral Council," in *A National Pastoral Council: Pro and Con*, Proceedings of an Interdisciplinary Consultation August 28–30, 1970, in Chicago, IL (Washington, DC: United States Catholic Conference, 1971), 3–20.

100. Document written on October 23, 1970, in ADGUSC, Box 9.

101. The recommendation is made in a report of September 14, 1971, to the USCC's Administrative Board and is found in ADGUSC, Box 9.

102. On the Dutch church, see John Coleman, *The Evolution of Dutch Catholicism, 1958–1974* (Berkeley: University of California Press, 1978), and Jan Bots, *Documentation on Dutch Catholicism on the Eve of the Papal Visit, 11–15 May 1985* (Gaithersburg, MD: Human Life International, 1985).

103. My interview with Dulles, August 3–4, 2005, transcript, 54, in DPFU.

104. "The Church, the Churches, and the Catholic Church," *TS* 33 (June 1972): 199–234. The text was also published in *The Dublin Papers on Ecumenism: Fourth Congress of Jesuit Ecumenists*, Cardinal Bea Studies II, ed. Pedro S. de Achutegui, SJ (Manila: Loyola School of Theology, Anteneo de Manila University, 1972), 118–58, and in *Dimensions in Religious Education*, ed. John R. McCall (Havertown, PA: CIM Books, 1973), 3–35.

105. "The Church and Salvation," *Missiology: An International Review* 1 (April 2, 1973): 71-80.

106. My interview with a student in Dulles' 1971 ecclesiology class, Joseph Lienhard, SJ, August 5, 2005, transcript, 2, in my possession.

107. My interview with Philip Rossi, SJ, October 5, 2005, transcript, 3, in my possession.

108. My interview with Dulles, August 3–4, 2005, transcript, 47, in DPFU.

109. Dulles to John M. McDermott, July 21, 1987, in DPFU.

110. Dulles to J. M. McDermott, August 10, 1987, in DPFU.

111. For Dulles' own explication of his method, see "Umrisse meiner theologischen Methode," in *Entwürfe der Theologie*, ed. Johannes B. Bauer (Graz, Austria: Verlag Styria, 1985), 51–70.

112. *Models of the Church*, exp. ed. (1974; New York: Doubleday, 2002), 5.

113. For an introduction to Dulles' intentions, see ibid., 1–25.

114. Dulles to Claude N. Pavur, October 10. 1984, in DPFU.

115. *Models of the Church*, 191–93.

116. In a letter to a Polish correspondent, Joseph Krasinski, August 29. 1973, Dulles outlined in brief his intent in *Models*: "I am concerned with keeping alive the variety of ecclesiological options that exists in the Church today. Too many believers, including some theologians, speak as though the Church itself were identical with their own concept of the Church, and thus they become imperialistic and intolerant, and they fail to profit from the good things that others have to say, from other points of view. In short, I am favoring openness and dialogue, and am trying to be faithful to the essential thrust of Vatican II, as I interpret it." Letter in DPFU.

117. For a sample of these diverse opinions, see the reviews by K. Baker in *Homiletic and Pastoral Review* 75 (October 1974): 74–76; H. B. Green in *Expository Times* 88 (April 1977): 220; J. P. Mackey in *Furrow* 28 (February 1977): 118–19; Robert Murray in *Heythrop Journal* 19 (January 1978): 79–81; J. Pelikan in *Commonweal* 102 (April 25. 1975): 90; Carl J. Peter in *Review for Religious* 33 (September 1974): 1209; J. R. Sheets in *America* 130 (March 23. 1974): 224; Jerome P. Theisen in *Worship* 48 (October 1974): 500–501.

118. S. McKenna in *Best Sellers* 34 (May 1, 1974): 67.

119. Richard P. McBrien in *NCR* 10 (March 29, 1974): 7.

120. "Christian Missions in Transition," 269.

121. On the establishment, see "Baltimore Initiatives," *America* 106 (January 20, 1962): 493–94. On Baltimore's leadership in the area of ecumenism and its early ecumenical activities, see Thomas W. Spalding, *The Premier See: A History of the Archdiocese of Baltimore, 1789–1989* (Baltimore: Johns Hopkins University Press, 1989), 420–24.

122. For the secretariat's objectives and directives, see Cardinal König's "Dialogue with Non-Believers" (August 28, 1968), *L'Osservatore Romano* [Eng. ed.] (October 10, 1968): 6. On the creation of the secretariat, see Peter Hebblethwaite, *Paul VI: The First Modern Pope* (New York: Paulist, 1993), 423–24, and his *The Council Fathers and Atheism* (New York: Paulist, 1966).

123. My interview with Dulles, July 24, 2007, transcript, 1, in DPFU.

124. For a summary of the meeting and the common text produced at the meeting, see "Intercommunion: Evaluation and Recommendations," *Journal of Ecumenical Studies* 7 (Summer 1970): 699–701. On Dulles' intervention, see "Intercommunion and the Decree on Ecumenism," *Diakonia* 5:2 (1970): 101–14.

125. "Intercommunion and the Decree on Ecumenism," 106.

126. "Ministry and Intercommunion," *TS* 34 (December 1973): 693–78.

127. For the publication of their lectures at John Carroll, see Wolfhart Pannenberg, Carl E. Braaten, and Avery Robert Dulles, *Spirit, Faith and Church* (Philadelphia: Westminster, 1970). In May 2006, Dulles himself reported to me the John Carroll concelebration. In my interview with him on July 23, 2007, transcript, 3–4, in DPFU, he confirmed the concelebration, saying: "I don't know how unusual it was, all kinds of crazy things were going on in that period....There was that period of confusion in the first years after Vatican II." For a report on the conference that emphasized the historical relativity of doctrine and church structures, see Joseph Kopko, "Interterm Tuohy Chair Conference Considers Contemporary Theology," *The* [John] *Carroll* [University] *News* (January 31, 1969). I am indebted to Joseph Kelly of John Carroll for bringing the article to my attention.

128. "Ministry and Intercommunion," 648, 660, 675.

129. Ibid., 675.

130. Ibid., 667.

131. "The Church, the Churches, and the Catholic Church," 199–234.

132. Dulles to Jan Cardinal Willebrands, March 16, 1971, in DPFU.

133. "Faith and Order at Louvain," *TS* 33 (March 1972): 35-67.

134. Ibid., 63.

135. See Dulles' report, "Toward a Christian Consensus: The Lima Meeting," *America* 146 (February 20, 1982): 126–29.

136. The other members of the committee were Myles M. Bourke, Agnes Cunningham, Maurice C. Duchaine, Richard P. McBrien, and Austin B. Vaughan.

137. The eight bilaterals were with the American Baptists, Disciples of Christ, Episcopalians, Southern Baptists, Orthodox, Lutherans, Methodists, and Presbyterians.

138. "The Bilateral Consultations Between the Roman Catholic Church in the United States and Other Christian Communions: A Theological Review and Critique by the Study Committee Commissioned by the Board of Directors of the Catholic Theological Society of America, Report of July 1972," *Proceedings*, CTSA 27 (1973), 177–232, letter quoted, 178.

139. "Secretary's Report," *Proceedings*, CTSA 27 (1973), 173.

140. "Bilateral Consultations," 228, 229, 231.

141. Ibid., 229.

142. He spoke, e.g., to a Baptist-Catholic Regional Conference at Marriotsville, Maryland, on February 4–6, 1974, and to a National Workshop of Christian Unity at Charleston, South Carolina, on March 11–13, 1974. See "The Church Always in Need of Reform," in *The Church Inside and Out* (Washington, DC: United States Catholic Conference, 1974), 37–50, for the Marriotsville talk; and "Now That the Honeymoon Is Over," for the Charleston talk.

143. "Reflections on Doctrinal Agreement," in *Episcopalians and Roman Catholics: Can They Ever Get Together?*, eds. Herbert J. Ryan and J. Robert Wright (Denville, NJ: Dimension Books, 1972), 51–66, quote on 64.

144. "A Proposal to Lift Two Anathemas," *Origins* 4 (December 26, 1974): 417–21. Later, in *A Church to Believe In: Discipleship and the Dynamics of Freedom*

(New York: Crossroad, 1982), 148, Dulles added the anathemas attached to the doctrine of papal infallibility.

145. "Infallibility Revisited," 58.

146. Ibid., 55.

147. "The State of the Question—Infallibility Revisited," *America* 129 (September 22, 1973): 192–93, quote at 192.

148. "The Changing Nature of Mission," *American Ecclesiastical Review* 157 (December 1967): 366–72, see especially 369–70.

149. For an example of Dulles' "secular" approach to ecumenism, see *American Christians and Ecumenism* (Hudson, NY: Graymoor Unity Apostolate, 1966).

150. Bill Macomber to Dulles, November 17, 1969, in DPFU. Dulles received other letters from fellow Jesuits and other clergy complaining about his criticisms of past orthodoxy, the historicizing and democratizing of the church and doctrine, the polarization in the church, and a host of other complaints that they found in Dulles' essays and books and in those of other theologians. See, e.g., Albert Smith, SJ, to Dulles, September 26, 1971, in DPFU.

151. Bill Macomber to Dulles, November 17, 1969, in DPFU.

152. Dulles to J. Madison King, November 4, 1970, in DPFU.

153. Dulles to Bede Reynolds, OSB, May 20, 1976, in ADGUSC, Box 6.

154. "Theology of Revelation," 133.

155. Dulles to Pedro Arrupe, March 11, 1973, in ADGUSC, Box 1.

156. See, e.g., Dulles' memo to Donald R. Campion, SJ, October 15, 1973; his memo to Bert Collopy, SJ, October 26, 1973, both memos in ADGUSC, Box 2. See also his "The Apostolate of Theological Reflection," *The Way* (Supplement 20, 1973): 114-23, in which he indicates the possibility of using the Ignatian spiritual discernment process to reflect on various problems in the modern world from an explicitly theological stance.

157. Dulles to Rev. Robert F. Trisco, October 24, 1972, in DPFU. Dulles was responding to an invitation from Bishop William W. Baum, Chair of the Search Committee in Religious Studies, October 13, 1972, in DPFU.

158. Dulles to Mike [Boulette], October 20, 1974, in DPFU.

159. My interview with Dulles, August 3–4, 2005, transcript, 60, in DPFU.

160. "Woodstock's Pentecost," *America* 132 (May 31, 1975): 417.

Chapter 9. A Chastened Progressivism, 1974–1988

1. "Woodstock: 'Vale atque Ave,'" 414.

2. *The Reshaping of Catholicism: Current Challenges in the Theology of Church* (San Francisco: Harper & Row, 1988), 153.

3. Ibid., 17. The citation is from a reprint of an article Dulles wrote in 1982.

4. Dulles' memos to Ed Glynn, April 12, 1974, and April 29, 1975, in ADGUSC, Box 12, which contains multiple documents relative to Dulles' participation at various events sponsored by the Woodstock Theological Center.

5. Dulles to Ed Glynn, May 7, 1975, containing memo (July 16, 1974) to Woodstock Theological Center Staff, outlining his suggestion for a study of freedom, in ADGUSC, Box 12.

6. Dulles' unpublished introductory comments ("Your eminences ..."), November, 16 1975, are located in ADGUSC, Box 12. The symposium eventually produced *Religious Freedom, 1965 and 1975: A Symposium on a Historic Document*, ed. Walter J. Burghardt (New York: Paulist, 1976). See also "Theology of Freedom—Suggestions for Project," February 9, 1976; "The Church as a Free Society: Theses Inspired by Michael Polanyi," June 24, 1976; memo to Members of Woodstock Theological Center Freedom Project," December 1, 1976; all these unpublished documents in ADGUSC, Box 12.

7. "Freedom" (n.d., but 1975 or 1976), in ADGUSC, Box 12.

8. "The Situation of the Church: 1965 and 1975," in ADGUSC, Box 12, p. 7.

9. Ibid., 16, 24–25.

10. "The Meaning of Faith Considered in Relationship to Justice," in *The Faith That Does Justice: Examining the Christian Sources for Social Change*, ed. John C. Haughey (New York: Paulist, 1977), 10–46.

11. See *Personal Values in Public Policy: Essays and Conversations in Government Decision-Making*, ed. John C. Haughey (New York: Paulist, 1979), and *Claims in Conflict: Retrieving and Renewing the Catholic Human Rights Tradition*, ed. David Hollenbach (New York: Paulist, 1979).

12. "Earthen Vessels: Institution and Charism in the Church," in *Above Every Name: The Lordship Of Christ and Social Systems*, ed. Thomas E. Clarke (Ramsey, NJ: Paulist, 1980), 155–87. See also "The Lordship of Christ and Social Systems: Marginalia by Avery Dulles" (n.d. but 1966 or 1967); "Theses" on the institutional and charismatic (n.d. but 1978); "Christ as Lord of the Church: Reflections on the Charismatic and the Institutional," April 15, 1978; "Theses on the Lordship of Christ—Distilled by A. Dulles" (n.d. but 1978). These unpublished discussion papers in ADGUSC, Box 12.

13. Dulles to Gerald J. Campbell, January 31, 1983, in DPFU.

14. See, e.g., "Aquinas and Consumerism," *America* 131 (November 2, 1974): 258; "The Revolutionary Spirit of Thomas Aquinas" *Origins* 4 (February 13, 1975): 543–44; and "The Spiritual Community of Man: The Church According to St. Thomas," in *Calgary Aquinas Studies*, ed. Anthony Parel (Toronto: Pontifical Institute of Medieval Studies, 1978), 125–53.

15. "The Church and Civil Society," *Studies in the International Apostolate of Jesuits* 3 (November 1974): 100.

16. Berger and Neuhaus to Langdon Gilkey, March 21, 1974, quoted in Gilkey's "Anathemas and Orthodoxy: A Reply to Avery Dulles," *Christian Century* 94:36 (November 9, 1977): 1028.

17. Memo to Peter L. Berger and Richard John Neuhaus, March 15, 1974, in DPFU.

18. Dulles and Peter, "Antitheses For the Theological Affirmation Conference," n.d. [but between June and December 1974], in DPFU.

19. The manifesto was published in the *Humanist* 33 (September–October 1973): 4–9, quoted in Carl J. Peter, "A Creative Alienation," in *Against the World for the World: The Hartford Appeal and the Future of American Religion*, eds. Peter L. Berger and Richard John Neuhaus (New York: Seabury, 1976), 97.

20. "Unmasking Secret Infidelities: Hartford and the Future of Ecumenism," in *Against the World for the World*, 53. Dulles was quoting here the executive secretary of the WCC Department on Studies in Evangelism, Walter J. Hollenweger, ed., *The Church for Others* (Geneva: WCC, 1968), 20.

21. Those attending were Elizabeth Ann Bettenhausen, William Sloane Coffin Jr., Neal Fisher, George W. Forell, James N. Gettemy, George A. Lindbeck, Ileana Marculescu, Ralph McInerny, Richard J. Mouw, Carl J. Peter, Alexander Schmemann, Gerard Sloyan, Lewis B. Smedes, George H. Tavard, and Robert Wilken, in addition to Berger, Neuhaus, and Dulles. Six others who could not attend signed the final statement: Stanley Hauerwas, Thomas Hopko, E. Kilmer Myers, Randolph W. Nugent Jr., Bruce Vawter, and John D. Weaver.

22. My interview with Neuhaus, May 13, 2005, transcript, 4, in my possession.

23. Published as "The Church Today/A Challenge to Popular Notions," in *Origins* 4 (February 6, 1975): 522–23, and as "An Appeal for Theological Affirmation," in *Worldview* 18 (April 1975): 39–41, and in other places. It is most easily accessed in *Against the World for the World*, 1–7.

24. "Finding God and the Hartford Appeal," *America* 132 (May 3, 1975): 335.

25. "18 Christian Leaders Attack 'Debilitating' Secular Influences," *New York Times* (January 28, 1975): 30. See also Briggs' "Protestant Churches Returning to Basic Beliefs," *New York Times* (March 9, 1975): 1, 33.

26. *Time* 105 (February 10, 1975): 47.

27. "No Christological Center," *Worldview* 18 (May 1975): 22.

28. "Silence on Issues of High Priority," *Worldview* 18 (May 1975): 23–24.

29. "On Not Asking the Right Questions," *Worldview* 18 (May 1975): 25–26.

30. "On the Human Locus of the Divine," *Worldview* 18 (May 1975): 26–27.

31. Besides the *Worldview* articles cited above, see, e.g., comments by Ernest Campbell, Joseph Fletcher, Letty M. Russell, Richard Shaull, and Peter Berger in *Theology Today* 32 (July 1975): 183–91. Other journals, too numerous to cite, gave space to those who agreed and disagreed with Hartford.

32. "The Relevance of Attacking Relevance," *Christian Century* 63:136 (February 19, 1975): 183. See also the responses to this column in "On Attacking the Relevant Reverends," *Christian Century* 63 (April 2, 1975): 336–37.

33. *Proceedings*, CTSA 30 (1975): 239–50.

34. Ibid., 248.

35. Homily for Convention Eucharist, *Proceedings*, CTSA 30 (1975): 267-69.

36. "Unmasking Secret Infidelities: Hartford and the Future of Ecumenism," in *Against the World for the World*, 57–58.

37. "Method in Fundamental Theology: Reflections on David Tracy's *Blessed Rage for Order*," *TS* 37 (June 1976): 303-16.

38. David Tracy, *Blessed Rage for Order: The New Pluralism in Theology* (New York: Seabury, 1975), 3, 4, 10, 34.

39. Tracy, "Theological Classics in Contemporary Theology," *Theology Digest* 25 (Winter 1977): 348.

40. *Blessed Rage*, 27, 45.

41. "Method in Fundamental Theology," 310, 311. Dulles consistently argued this position. On this, see Dulles to Francis Schüssler Fiorenza, December 10, 1997; see also Dulles to Laurence Hemming, October 4, 1999, in DPFU.

42. "Authority and Criticism in Systematic Theology," *Theology Digest* 26 (Winter 1978): 392.

43. *The Resilient Church: The Necessity and Limits of Adaptation* (Garden City, NY: Doubleday, 1977), 1, 5.

44. Ibid., 64, 65, 66.

45. Immediately after Hartford, Dulles had critiqued Gilkey as well as Tracy. See his review of Gilkey's *Catholicism Confronts Modernity* in "Modernizing or Dismantling the Church," *Review of Books and Religion* 4 (Mid-June 1975): 1, 16.

46. *Resilient Church*, 68.

47. Ibid., 78–79, 80.

48. Ibid., 91.

49. "Secular Theology and the Rejection of the Supernatural: Reflections on Recent Trends," *TS* 38 (March 1977): 39–56.

50. For Tracy's response, see *NCR* (November 4, 1977): 10, and for Gilkey's see "Anathemas and Orthodoxy: A Reply to Avery Dulles," *Christian Century* 94:36 (November 9, 1977): 1026–29.

51. Dulles' responses in *NCR* (November 4, 1977): 11, and in "'Latent Heresy' and Orthodoxy," *Christian Century* 94:37 (November 16, 1977): 1053-54.

52. Adam Bernstein, "Langdon Gilkey Dies; Theologian, Author, Educator," *Washington Post* (November 22, 2004): B06.

53. "'Latent Heresy' and Orthodoxy," 1053.

54. I call this a "new emphasis" because it would be inaccurate to say that he had failed to critique excessive accommodationists in the 1960s. He had supported as well as criticized among others Hans Küng in the 1960s, and he continued that approach to Küng after 1975. See "Küng—An Assessment of His Work since 1965," *NCR* (October 21, 1977): 13.

55. The five theologians were William Carroll, Agnes Cunningham, Anthony Kosnik (the general editor of the report), Ronald Modras, and James Schulte.

56. Anthony Kosnik et al., *Human Sexuality: New Directions in American Catholic Thought* (New York: Paulist Press, 1977), xi.

57. "Summary Report of the CTSA Committee on the Study of Human Sexuality," *Proceedings*, CTSA 30 (1975), 221–37.

58. See, e.g., Steve Hefter, "A New Catholic View of Sex," *Detroit Free Press* (September 5, 1975): 1C, 5C, who observed that the report "would surprise and even shock many who are familiar with the Catholic Church's traditional attitudes toward human sexuality." Hefter quoted Kosnick as saying that the report would offer Catholics "an alternative" to the Church's views on premarital sex, homosexuality, masturbation, and contraception. In Kosnick's view, the report presented a legitimate dissent from Catholic teachings in the area of sexual morality. See also Frank Teskey, "A New Catholic View of Sex," *Wanderer* (October 2, 1975): 1, 5; Brian McNaught, "Church Study Debunks Roman Catholic Stand," *Advocate* (July 16 1975): 40, 41. See also Kosnik to Dulles, October 11, 1975, in CTSA Papers, Archives, the Catholic University of America (hereafter ACUA), Box 2, folder 65 (88–2–65), where he protested that he had always "presented our report as being written in continuity with tradition and developing it and not as condemning or departing from it." He had also written a letter to the *Detroit Free Press* expressing this view after its report on September 5, 1975.

59. "New Catholic Attitude on Sex Urged," *Detroit News* (August 17, 1975).

60. My interview with Dulles, June 8–10, 2004. On Dulles' reservations, see Dulles to Michael Novak, July 5, 1977, in DPFU. The board members at the time were Richard McBrien, Agnes Cunningham, Francis Fiorenza, Suzanne Noffke, David Tracy, as well as Dulles.

61. Dulles to Kosnik, January 11, 1976, in CTSA Papers, ACUA, Box 2, folder 66 (88–2–66). Dulles was referring to the CDF's *Persona Humana*, that is, the Declaration on Certain Questions Concerning Sexual Ethics (December 29, 1975).

62. Mark Winarski, "Theologians Reassess Sexual Morality," *NCR* (May 27, 1977): 1, 15, 20, quotation at 20.

63. Minutes, CTSA Board Meeting, June 10, 1976, in CTSA Papers, ACUA, Box 2, folder 68 (88–2–68).

64. Dulles to Kosnik, August 31, 1976, in CTSA Papers, ACUA, Box 3, folder 1 (88–3–1).

65. May to Colleagues, May 25, 1977, in CTSA Papers, ACUA, Box 3, folder 3 (88–3–3); see also a report of May's objections to the study in "Society Study Under Fire," *NCR* (May 27, 1977): 1, 15. Other theologians' letters in the CTSA Papers outline the deficiencies, problems, and poor theology in the report. See ACUA, Box 2, folders 66 and 67 (88–2–66 and 67).

66. *Proceedings*, CTSA 32 (1977), 254.

67. See Giles Milhaven to Kosnik, January 20, 1976, in CTSA Papers, ACUA, Box 2, folder 67 (88–2–67). See this same box and folder 66 as well as 67 for other positive evaluations of the study.

68. Kosnik, *Human Sexuality*.

69. See, e.g., John Farrelly, "An Introduction to a Discussion of 'Human Sexuality,'" *Proceedings*, CTSA 32 (1977), 221–33.

70. Winarski, "Theologians Reassess Sexual Morality," 20.

71. On this, see May's and John F. Harvey's critical review of *Human Sexuality* in *NCR* (June 17, 1977): 7, 8. See also their *On Understanding Human*

Sexuality (Chicago: Franciscan Herald Press, 1977); and "Rebuttal of Catholic Theological Society Report," *National Catholic Register* (May 22, 1977): 3.

72. For some immediate episcopal reactions to *Human Sexuality*, see Mark Winarski, "Theological Society 'Grateful' for Report," *NCR* (July 1, 1977): 1, 6.

73. NCCB/Committee on Doctrine, "Statement Concerning *Human Sexuality*" (November 15, 1977), in *Pastoral Letters*, 4: 228.

74. CDF to John R. Quinn, July 13, 1982, CTSA Papers, ACUA, Box 3, folder 5 (88–3–5).

75. On those who left the society, see James Hitchcock, "The Fellowship of Catholic Scholars: Bowing Out of the New Class," in *Being Right: Conservative Catholics in America*, eds. Mary Jo Weaver and R. Scott Appleby (Bloomington: Indiana University Press, 1995), 186–210; see also Kosnik to Luke Salm, December 20, 1982, in CTSA Papers, ACUA, Box 3, folder 5 (88–3–5), indicating that his removal from the seminary was a "small price to pay for the good done by the book."

76. Novak to Dulles, June 13, 1977. For Dulles' agreement, see Dulles to Novak, July 5, 1977. Letters in DPFU.

77. "'Humanae Vitae' and the Crisis of Dissent," *Origins* 22 (April 22, 1993): 774–77; "*Humanae Vitae* and *Ordinatio Sacerdotalis*: Problems of Reception," in *Church Authority in American Culture* (New York: Crossroad, 1999), 25–26.

78. *Testimonial to Grace*, 123–24. See also, my interview with Dulles, July 24, 2007, transcript, 8–9, in DPFU, where Dulles repeats what he said in *A Testimonial to Grace*: The CTSA Board of Directors were unhappy with the report, but "the board was faced by a dilemma, and we couldn't exactly reject the report, since they [the authors] had done what they were asked to do, to present their own conclusions."

79. In 2002, Dulles told a correspondent, "If the Board had rejected the study, its actions would have been contested on the floor at the general meeting and presumably overruled." He did not think that *Human Sexuality* had "any great influence." He reiterated what he had said in 1976 and 1977, namely that "the contents of the book...were not untypical of what many Catholic teachers of ethics and moral theology were saying at the time. The report was a sign, not a cause of what people were thinking." Dulles to George Weigel, May 14, 2002, in DPFU.

80. "Intercommunion between Lutherans and Roman Catholics?" *Journal of Ecumenical Studies* 13 (Spring 1976): 250.

81. See Lindbeck's "A Lutheran View of Intercommunion with Roman Catholics," *Journal of Ecumenical Studies* 13 (Spring 1976): 242–48, and Lindbeck's response to Dulles in ibid., 255–57, and Dulles' response to Lindbeck in ibid., 248–49.

82. For background, history, and sociological analysis of Call to Action, see Joseph A. Varacalli, *Toward the Establishment of Liberal Catholicism in America* (Washington, DC: University Press of America, 1983), the title of which indicates the thesis.

83. *Liberty and Justice for All*, First Preparatory Hearing "Humankind" (Washington, DC: National Conference of Catholic Bishops/Committee for the Bicentennial, 1975), 1.

84. Ibid., 2. No title for this talk is given.

85. Ibid., 2–7.

86. For Dulles' responses to other questions raised about his talk, see ibid., 7–10.

87. There were seven other writing committees on issues of ethnicity and race, neighborhoods, families, personhood, work, nationkind, and humankind.

88. The resolutions and issues are listed in Varacalli, *Toward the Establishment of Liberal Catholicism*, 263–94.

89. Kenneth Briggs, "Catholics Weigh Proposals to Alter Policies of Church," *New York Times* (October 22, 1976): 12.

90. See, e.g., Kenneth Briggs, "Aid for Divorced Catholics Urged," *New York Times* (October 23, 1976): 32; idem, "Conference of Catholics Supports Resolution on Ordaining Women," *New York Times* (October 24, 1976): 26; idem, "Catholic Meeting's Proposal Stirs Backers of Women's Ordination," *New York Times* (October 25, 1976): 25; idem, "Catholic 'Call to Action': A Diversified Group of Delegates Took Full Advantage of a Chance to Recommend Changes," *New York Times* (October 27, 1976): 18; idem, "Catholic Bishops Stirred to Debate by the Proposals of 'Call to Action,'" *New York Times* (November 11, 1976): 18. See also "A 'Call' by Catholics," *Time* (November 8 1976): 100.

91. See, e.g., the NCCB's "The Bicentennial Consultation: A Response to the Call to Action" (May 5, 1977) and "To Do the Work of Justice" (May 4, 1978), both in *Pastoral Letters*, 4: 215–26, 243–54.

92. Kenneth Briggs, "Catholic Meeting's Proposal Stirs Backers of Women's Ordination," 25. Dulles' statement came after the publication of *Inter Insigniores* (October 15, 1976), the Vatican declaration against the ordination of women, a document Dulles probably had not read at the time of his comments. Dulles' later, more systematic reflections on the ordination of women are treated in chap. 14 of this book.

93. Later in his career he reported that "the people who came [to Detroit] were social action types, and many were not concerned with doctrine." My interview with Dulles, August 4, 2005, transcript, 55, in DPFU.

94. "The Gospel, the Church, and Politics," *Origins* 16 (February 19, 1987): 645.

95. *Testimonial to Grace* (1996), 116.

Chapter 10. The Moderate Middle in Theology, 1974–1988

1. "An Unfolding Process," in *What Faith Has Meant to Me*, ed. Claude A. Frazier (Philadelphia: Westminster, 1975), 60, 61.

2. Ibid., 63.

3. "The Meaning of Faith Considered in Relationship to Justice" in *The Faith That Does Justice*, ed. John C. Haughey (New York: Paulist, 1977), 10–46.

4. "Faith, Justice, and the University," *Catholic Mind* 76 (October 1978): 25–32, quotation at 31.

5. Preface to the 1992 edition of *Models of Revelation* (New York: Orbis, 2003), vii. My interviews with Dulles, June 8–10, 2004, and August 4, 2005, transcript, 49, in DPFU.

6. *TS* 41 (March 1980): 51-73.

7. Ibid., 55–56.

8. Dulles to John M. McDermott, July 21, 1987, and July 9, 1987, in DPFU. Dulles was becoming more and more independent of Rahner's transcendental Thomism, at least in respect to how Dulles saw the role of revelation (faith comes from hearing, Romans 10:14) in transforming human consciousness. In 1998, he told a reporter, "We need an epistemology that shows how we can hear the word of God and grasp its real meaning. Much of the recent neo-Kantian epistemology, even as filtered through great intellects such as Karl Rahner and Bernard Lonergan, is weak in this respect. It is not enough to say that God is absolute mystery or that we speak of him only in metaphors." See Gabriel Meyer's interview with Dulles in "Into the Millenium [sic] and Beyond," *National Catholic Register* (August 9–15, 1998): 1, 10.

9. "The Symbolic Structure of Revelation," 73. John Lamont, "The Nature of Revelation," *New Blackfriars* (August 1991): 335–45, especially 337, 339, argued that for Dulles "much of revelation is not propositional." Lamont could not accept that view as consistent with Christianity and proposed instead that revelation was essentially propositional, and that propositions were still the "main thing about revelation."

10. "Revelation and Discovery," in *Theology and Discovery*, ed. William J. Kelly (Milwaukee: Marquette University Press, 1980), 2.

11. *Models of Revelation*, 98.

12. Ibid., 35.

13. "Pannenberg on Revelation and Faith," in *The Theology of Wolfhart Pannenberg*, eds. Carl E. Braaten and Philip Clayton (Minneapolis: Augsburg, 1988), 169.

14. *Models of Revelation*, 271–72.

15. Ibid., 131.

16. Dermont Lane, "A Review Essay: Dulles on Revelation," *Living Light* 21 (October 1984): 74–76, quotation at 74.

17. See, e.g., William Loewe's review in *New Catholic World* 226 (July–August 1983): 185; William E. Thompson's review in *TS* 45 (June 1984): 357–59; Thomas Hughson, "Dulles and Aquinas on Revelation," *Thomist* 52 (July 1988): 445–71; and Carl F. H. Henry, "The Priority of Divine Revelation: A Review Article," *Journal of the Evangelical Theological Society* 27 (March 1984): 77–92.

18. "Faith, Church, and God: Insights from Michael Polanyi," *TS* 45 (September 1984): 537.

19. Ibid., 539.

20. Ibid., 540, where Dulles quoted Polanyi's *Personal Knowledge*.

21. "Faith, Church, and God: Insights from Michael Polanyi," 540.

22. (Washington, DC: National Catholic Educational Association, 1985).

23. Ibid., 8, 9, 11.

24. Ibid., 14.

25. "*Sensus Fidelium*," *America* 115 (November 1, 1986): 240-42, 263, quotation at 263.

26. "Authority in the Church," in *Civilizing Authority: Society, State, and Church*, ed. Patrick McKinley Brennan (Lanham: Lexington Books, 2007), 47. See also Dulles' response to a question on the meaning of *sensus fidelium* during a 1998 discussion at the Common Ground Project in *Church Authority in American Culture* (The Second Cardinal Bernardin Conference) (New York: Crossroad, 1999), 119. During that same discussion, Joseph Komonchak maintained, 120–21, that the sense of the faith was a spiritual insight. "As people make progress in faith, hope, and love they develop a sensitivity, an instinct, that enables them to judge what is to be done as a Christian or to think 'Christianly' about new problems as they arise." As such the *sensus fidelium* is "very difficult to quantify. It becomes very difficult to turn into a criterion."

27. "Scripture: Recent Protestant and Catholic Views," *Theology Today* 37 (April 1980): 26. For similar remarks, see "The Authority of Scripture: A Catholic Perspective," in *Scripture in the Jewish and Christian Traditions: Authority, Interpretation, Relevance*, ed. F. E. Greenspahn (Nashville: Abingdon, 1982), 13–40.

28. "The Bible in the Church: Some Debated Questions," in *Scripture and the Charismatic Renewal*, ed. George Martin (Ann Arbor: Servant Books, 1979), 26.

29. "Foundation Documents of the Faith: X. Modern Credal Affirmations," *Expository Times* 91 (July 1980): 291-96, especially 295–96.

30. "How Can Christian Faith Be Justified Today?" *Communio* 2 (Winter 1975): 343-56.

31. "The Church: Sacrament and Ground of Faith," in *Problems and Perspectives of Fundamental Theology*, eds. René Latourelle and Gerald O'Collins (New York: Paulist, 1982), 259–73.

32. "Fundamental Theology and the Dynamics of Conversion," *Thomist* 45 (April 1981): 175-93.

33. *Resilient Church*, 1.

34. Ibid., 5.

35. Dulles cited some of the following studies in his articles on discipleship in the 1980s: Karl L. Schelke, *Discipleship and Priesthood* (New York: Herder & Herder, 1965); Eduard Schweizer, *Lordship and Discipleship* (Naperville: Allenson, 1960); Raymond E. Brown, *Priest and Bishop: Biblical Reflections* (New York: Paulist, 1970).

36. Fernando F. Segovia, ed., *Discipleship in the New Testament* (Philadelphia: Fortress, 1985).

37. (Washington, DC: U.S. Catholic Conference, 1979).

38. Carl Bernstein and Marco Politi, *His Holiness: John Paul II and the Hidden History of Our Time* (New York: Doubleday, 1996), 214.

39. *Redemptor Hominis*, 21.

40. See, e.g., "Revelation and Discovery," in *Theology and Discovery*, 24–28; "Imaging the Church for the 1980s," *Thought* 56 (June 1981): 121–38; "Ministry and Discipleship," in *Extending Our Benedictine Tradition*, ed. Philip Timko (Lisle, IL: St. Procopius Abbey, 1981), 33–43; *A Church to Believe In: Discipleship and the Dynamics of Freedom* (New York: Crossroad, 1982); and "Community of Disciples as a Model of Church," *Philosophy and Theology* 1 (Winter 1986): 99-120.

41. "Imaging the Church for the 1980s," 129.

42. "Ministry and Discipleship," 39.

43. "Community of Disciples as a Model of Church," 113.

44. *A Church to Believe In*, x.

45. "Ministry and Discipleship," 34.

46. *Models of the Church* (New York: Doubleday, 1987), 6. See also chap. 13, "The Church: Community of Disciples," a slight revision of his "Community of Disciples as a Model of Church," 99–120.

47. Since the middle 1970s, Dulles admitted, he had been concerned by the development of a generation of Catholics "who are not securely rooted in the Catholic tradition, which I presupposed in my readership in earlier works." Hence his more recent works may have sounded more conservative than his earlier works, but "my perception of my reading public and its needs has changed somewhat." See Dulles to John M. McDermott, August 10, 1987, in DPFU.

48. Review of Francis A. Sullivan's *Magisterium* in *America* 150 (May 26, 1984): 403.

49. *The Papacy in Transition* (New York: Doubleday, 1980).

50. The papacy as an ecumenical problem is discussed in chap. 11 of this book.

51. For a good selected bibliography of studies on the papacy prior to 1980, see Patrick Granfield's *Papacy in Transition*, 204–16.

52. "Authority: The Divided Legacy–Charting a Course: From the Council to the Synod," *Commonweal* 112 (July 12, 1985): 401.

53. Cardinal Alfredo Ottaviani (1890–1979) was secretary of the Vatican's Holy Office and Pro-Prefect of the CDF from 1959 to 1968. He was also the leading conservative voice at Vatican II.

54. "Authority: The Divided Legacy," 403.

55. See, e.g., his "Toward a Renewed Papacy," chap. 6 of his *Resilient Church*, 111–31. See also "Papal Authority in Roman Catholicism," in *A Pope for All Christians? An Inquiry into the Role of Peter in the Modern Church*, ed. Peter J. McCord (New York: Paulist, 1976), 48–70.

56. *Resilient Church*, 119.

57. Ibid., 127.

58. "The Teaching Authority of Bishops' Conferences," *America* 148 (June 11, 1983): 453–55.

59. Ibid., 455. Dulles consistently supported the American bishops' consultation process prior to the publication of pastoral letters. See also "Bishops' Conference Documents: What Doctrinal Authority?" *Origins* 14 (January 24, 1985): 533; "What Is the Role of a Bishops' Conference?" *Origins* 17 (April 28, 1988): 796.

60. "Bishops' Conference Documents: What Doctrinal Authority?" 532.

61. "What Is the Role of a Bishops' Conference?" 793.

62. "The Extraordinary Synod: IV," *America* 153 (September 28 1985): 158. By the principles of Vatican II, Dulles meant a reassertion of *aggiornamento* (or openness to the modern world), reformability of the church, renewed attention to scripture, collegiality, religious freedom, lay participation, regional and local diversity, ecumenism, dialogue with other religions, and the social mission of the church. See "Vatican II Reform: The Basic Principles," *Church* 1 (Summer 1985): 3–10, and *Vatican II and the Extraordinary Synod* (Collegeville, MN: Liturgical Press, 1986), 7, where Dulles argued that failure to accept these principles "signifies a lack of agreement with Vatican II."

63. *Vatican II and the Extraordinary Synod*, 5, 6.

64. Ibid., 31–33.

65. See, e.g., "Successio apostolorum—Successio prophetarum—Successio doctorum," in *Who Has the Say in the Church? Concilium* 148, eds. Jürgen Moltmann and Hans Küng (New York: Seabury, 1981), 62.

66. The above paragraphs rely on Dulles' "Earthen Vessels: Institution and Charism in the Church," in *Above Every Name: The Lordship Of Christ and Social Systems*, ed. Thomas E. Clarke (Ramsey, NJ: Paulist, 1980), 155–87.

67. "The Magisterium and Authority in the Church," in *Theology in Revolution*, ed. George Devine (Staten Island, NY: Alba House, 1970), 29–45.

68. "The Magisterium and Authority in the Church," 31.

69. Ibid., 33, 37.

70. Ibid., 41.

71. "The Theologian and the Magisterium," *Proceedings*, CTSA 31 (1976): 235–46, quotations at 245, 239, 237.

72. Ibid., 235.

73. Ibid., 243.

74. Ibid., 245.

75. Dulles to Higgins, June 21, 1976, in the Higgins Papers, ACUA.

76. Higgins to Dulles, August 17, 1976, in Higgins Papers, ACUA.

77. "Saint Robert Bellarmine: A Moderate in a Disputatious Age," *Crisis* 12 (December 1994): 39–44.

78. "Loyalty and Dissent after Vatican II," *America* 122 (June 27, 1970): 673.

79. "The Magisterium in History: A Theological Reflection," *Chicago Studies* 17 (Summer 1978): 264–81.

80. "Authority and Criticism in Systematic Theology," 387–99. See also "Tradition and Theology: A Roman Catholic Response to Clark Pinnock," *TSF* [Theological Students Fellowship] *Bulletin* 6 (January–February 1983): 6–8.

Notes

81. "Hermeneutical Theology," *Communio* 6 (Spring 1979): 16–37.

82. "Ecumenism and Theological Method," in *Consensus in Theology? A Dialogue with Hans Küng, Edward Schillebeeckx, and Others*, ed. Leonard Swidler (Philadelphia: Westminster, 1980), 40–48.

83. "Saint Ignatius and the Jesuit Theological Tradition," *Studies in the Spirituality of Jesuits* 14 (March 1982): 1–21.

84. There were a host of published statements by bishops and theologians on the relationship between theologians and the hierarchy. The American bishops' pastoral "Human Life in Our Day" (1968), published in the aftermath of *Humanae vitae*, indicated briefly some conditions for legitimate theological dissent, and in 1969 the bishops passed a "Resolution on Due Process" that intended to protect rights and duties within the church. See *Pastoral Letters*, 3:173–74, and 486.

85. Edited by Leo J. O'Donovan (Washington, DC: CLSA, 1982).

86. "Doctrinal Responsibilities: Procedures for Promoting Cooperation and Resolving Disputes between Bishops and Theologians" in *Proceedings*, CTSA 39 (1984): 209–34.

87. *Doctrinal Responsibilities: Approaches to Promoting Cooperation and Resolving Misunderstandings between Bishops and Theologians*. See *Pastoral Letters*, 7:43–72, for the statement.

88. *Proceedings*, CTSA 36 (1981): 155.

89. Ibid., 159.

90. For Curran's assessment of the controversy in the context of his autobiography, see Charles E. Curran, *Loyal Dissent: Memoir of a Catholic Theologian* (Washington, DC: Georgetown University Press, 2006), quotation at 132.

91. Dulles to Ratzinger, September 26, 1984, in DPFU. See also Dulles to William E. May, December 22, 1986, in DPFU.

92. Review of William E. May, ed., *Vatican Authority and American Catholic Dissent: The Curran Case and Its Consequences* (1988), *Crisis* 6 (June 1988): 47–48.

93. *Church to Believe In*, 40 and 48, for two of the many appeals to Polanyi in this regard.

94. "The Theologian and the Magisterium," 240. See also *Resilient Church*, 108–12.

95. "Authority and Conscience: Two Needed Voices in the Church," *Church* 2 (Fall 1986): 8–15, quotation at 15.

96. "The Meaning of Freedom in the Church," *Gettysburg Lutheran Theological Seminary Bulletin* 57 (1977): 21–22.

97. *Church to Believe In*, 117, quoting *GS*, 62.

98. "'Glorified Unorthodoxy' or Orthodoxy as Status Quo: Neither Is Good for the Church," *NCR* 20 (July 20, 1984).

99. Dulles to Lydia Englebert, January 10, 1988, in DPFU.

Chapter 11. The Ecumenist, 1971–1996

1. For one example of his enthusiasm and optimism, see his "Contribution to a Round Table: Where Are We in Ecumenism?" *America* 126 (January 22, 1972): 55–56. In response to an interview in 1973, Dulles gave his assessment of the state of ecumenical affairs in the following terms: "On the theological level the ecumenical movement is continuing to progress very well. Since Vatican II we have a growing body of consensus statements resulting chiefly from bilateral conversations. We are beginning to get a large ecumenical consensus about many controversial subjects, notably eucharist, ministry, and intercommunion. We are beginning to get into the questions of Church structure, including the papacy. The main crisis in the ecumenical movement is that as soon as one tries to get any concrete action to follow up the theoretical agreement, there are groups in each Church that feel such action would threaten their power. Often in good faith, they resist any recommendations that would change the actual relationships of the churches to one another. The best hope of overcoming this difficulty is to have a more widely disseminated theological educational program. Without this, people will simply be shocked by the results of the dialogues." Dulles to Joseph Krasinski, August 29, 1973, in DPFU.

2. In 1971 the NCCB's Office of Ecumenical Affairs asked Dulles to become a member of that dialogue, but he requested that he not receive an official appointment to the dialogue until after he finished the CTSA's study of the various bilaterals. Although he attended the 1971 meetings of the group, he was not officially appointed to the dialogue until 1972 and served on it until 1996.

3. Dulles to John W. Klein, November 22, 1980, in DPFU.

4. For background on the origins, see my interview with Fr. George Tavard, a charter member of the dialogue, May 15, 2006, transcript, 16, in my possession. See also Tavard's "Reflections on the Lutheran/Catholic Dialogue," *Ecumenical Trends* 34 (September 2005): 113–16.

5. Statements on the Nicene Creed (1965), Baptism (1966), Eucharist as Sacrifice (1967), and Eucharist and Ministry (1970).

6. During Dulles' time Raymond E. Brown, Walter Burghardt, Godfrey Diekmann, Joseph Fitzmeyer, Elizabeth A. Johnson, James F. McCue, Kilian McDonnell, Carl J. Peter, Walter Principe, Jerome D. Quinn, Jill Raitt, and George Tavard, among other Catholics, served on the dialogue. Lutheran theologians Joseph A. Burgess, Gerhard O. Forde, Karlfried Froehlich, Eric W. Gritsch, Kenneth Hagen, George A. Lindbeck, Arthur Carl Piepkorn, Warren A. Quanbeck, and John Reumann, among others, were also members.

7. See, e.g., Paul C. Empie, T. Austin Murphy, and Joseph A. Burgess, eds., *Teaching Authority and Infallibility in the Church: Lutherans and Catholics in Dialogue VI* (Minneapolis: Augsburg, 1980), 38.

8. All members of the dialogue have copies of the minutes. They are also located in the archives of the American Catholic Bishops' Committee for Ecumenical and Interreligious Affairs (BCEIA) in Washington, DC, and in the archives of the Evangelical Lutheran Church of America, with offices in Chicago,

Illinois. I have read the minutes and documents from the bishops' Ecumenical office, and much of what I say about the dialogue comes from interpretations of these statements. Those minutes were not catalogued in 2006 when I had access to them. They were located in manila folders for the years in which they were published. I refer to all unpublished minutes as well as other documents from the dialogue according to the year of the folder. Documents cited in the text, therefore, list the title and the location in the bishops' Ecumenical office (e.g., BCEIA Ecumenical, folder 1971, for the folder containing the documents of that year).

9. Copy of Hotchkin to Baum, March 6, 1974, in BCEIA Ecumenical, folder 1974.

10. Copy of Villot to Baum, March 5, 1976. See in particular attached evaluations, "Note on 'Ministry and the Universal Church—Differing Attitudes towards Papal Primacy,'" and "Results of the Examination of the Document 'Ministry and the Universal Church—Differing Attitudes towards Papal Primacy.'" Documents in BCEIA Ecumenical, folder 1976.

11. For background on the discussions, see my interview with John Reumann, a Lutheran participant on the dialogue, September 25, 2005, transcript, 2, in my possession. For his more general comments on the dialogues, see Reumann's "The Development of the Ecumenical Vision of Vatican II: A Lutheran's Reflections on the First 40 Years of Lutheran-Catholic Dialogue USA," *Ecumenical Trends* 34 (September 2005): 117–23.

12. Dulles to John Hotchkin, April 29, 1971, in BCEIA Ecumenical, folder 1971.

13. For this discussion, see L/RC Dialogue, Minutes of the Greenwick, Connecticut, Meeting, September 24–27, 1971, 1–3, in BCEIA Ecumenical, folder 1971. Dulles was in favor of reinterpreting the *jus divinum* category, with its ahistorical implications, in order to preserve the sense of the faith that the category was attempting to retain: namely that the development of the papacy was not just a human invention, but a divinely guided development. For this discussion, see also L/RC Dialogue, Minutes of the New Orleans Meeting, February 10, 1972, 7–8, in BCEIA Ecumenical, folder 1972.

14. See "Roman Catholic Reflections Prompted by the Consensus Statement on Ministry and the Church Universal" (July 13, 1973), in BCEIA Ecumenical, folder 1973. See also Dulles' original draft: "Roman Catholic Reaction to Consensus Statement on Papal Ministry" (June 1973), in DPFU.

15. L/RC Dialogue, Minutes of the Allentown, Pennsylvania, Meeting, September 21–24, 1973, 4, in BCEIA Ecumenical, folder 1973.

16. Paul C. Empie and T. Austin Murphy, eds., *Papal Primacy and the Universal Church: Lutherans and Catholics in Dialogue V* (Minneapolis: Augsburg, 1974). Prior to this statement, the L/RC Dialogue had commissioned a study of the Petrine ministry in the New Testament, which served as a biblical foundation for their common statement. See Raymond E. Brown, Karl P. Donfried, and John Reumann, eds., *Peter in the New Testament* (Minneapolis and New York: Augsburg Publishing and Paulist Press, 1973).

17. Edward B. Fiske, "Lutheran-Catholic Accord Voted; Accord Reached on the Papacy," *New York Times* (March 4, 1974): 1, 61; "Excerpts from Text on Primacy of Pontiff," *New York Times* (March 4, 1974): 25. See also "Papal Primacy," *New York Times* (March 6, 1974): 36.

18. Later published under that title in *Origins* 3 (May 2, 1974): 705–12, reprinted, with revisions, in *Catholic Mind* 72 (July 1974): 45–59.

19. "The Papacy: Bond or Barrier," *Origins* 3 (May 2, 1974): 706.

20. "On Christian Unity under the Pope," *New York Times* (April 24, 1974): 41.

21. "To the Editor," *New York Times* (May 22, 1974): 42.

22. L/RC Dialogue, Minutes of the Gettysburg Meeting, September 16–19, 1976, 15, in BCEIA Ecumenical, folder 1976.

23. "The Problem of Infallibility: Agenda for a Lutheran-Catholic Study" (September 1973), in BCEIA Ecumenical, folder 1973.

24. See "Infallibility: The Terminology" and "Moderate Infallibilism," in *Teaching Authority and Infallibility in the Church*, 69–80, 81–100.

25. "Infallibility: The Terminology," 75.

26. George A. Lindbeck, *Infallibility* (Milwaukee: Marquette University Press, 1972), 58–59.

27. "Moderate Infallibilism," 99.

28. Ibid., 97.

29. L/RC Dialogue, Minutes of the Princeton Meeting, September 19–22, 1974, 37, in BCEIA Ecumenical, folder 1974.

30. "Moderate Infallibilism," 89–93.

31. L/RC Dialogue, Minutes of the Scottsdale, Arizona, Meeting, February 19–22, 1976, 55, in BCEIA Ecumenical, folder 1976.

32. "Moderate Infallibilism," 93.

33. L/RC Dialogue, Minutes of the Scottsdale, Arizona, Meeting, February 19–22, 1976, 42, in BCEIA Ecumenical, folder 1976. In 2005, to a correspondent who inquired about his understanding of "moderate infallibilism," Dulles wrote that it should be remembered that his statement "was done toward the beginning of the Lutheran-Roman Catholic Dialogue on the subject, and was presented in 1974, more than thirty years ago, when a lot of questions seemed to be open in Catholic theology." At the time, Dulles wanted to keep as many questions as possible open "to help get the Lutherans interested in even discussing the question of infallibility. I did not agree with all the opinions I mentioned." It was more difficult in 2005, after the Vatican publications of a new Profession of Faith (1989) and *Ad tuendam fidem* (1998), "to defend the position that infallibility extends only to revealed truths [as Dulles had contended in 1974]." See Dulles to Jim Roth, September 23, 2005, in DPFU.

34. L/RC Dialogue, Minutes of the Washington, DC, Meeting, September 18–21, 1975, 17, 18, in BCEIA Ecumenical, folder 1975.

35. "Moderate Infallibilism," 99.

36. L/RC Dialogue, Minutes of the Washington, DC, Meeting, September 18–21, 1975, 24, in BCEIA Ecumenical, folder 1975.

37. "Moderate Infallibilism," 99–100.
38. For the two statements, see *Teaching Authority*, 11–38, 38–59.
39. For the "Common Statement," see *Teaching Authority*, 11–38; quotations at 32, 35.
40. Ibid., 36.
41. Two of these papers are unpublished: "Vatican II and the Problem of Justification" [1979] is available in DPFU, "Luther's Theology: A Modern Catholic Reflection" (October 1980) is available in BCEIA Ecumenical, folder 1980, as well as in DPFU. "Justification in Contemporary Catholic Theology" is published in *Justification by Faith: Lutherans and Catholics in Dialogue VII*, eds. H. George Anderson, T. Austin Murphy, and Joseph A. Burgess (Minneapolis: Augsburg, 1985), 256–77.
42. "Vatican II and the Problem of Justification," 1, 5, 11, 20.
43. L/RC Dialogue, Minutes of the Princeton, New Jersey, Meeting, September 13–16, 1979, 2–8, in BCEIA Ecumenical, folder 1979.
44. "Luther's Theology: A Modern Catholic Reflection," unpublished paper given at the Lutheran School of Theology at Chicago, October 20, 1980, 20, in BCEIA Ecumenical, folder 1981.
45. "Justification in Contemporary Catholic Theology," in *Justification by Faith*, 277.
46. L/RC Dialogue, Minutes of the Princeton Meeting, September 13–16, 1979, 35, in BCEIA Ecumenical, folder 1979.
47. L/RC Dialogue, Minutes of the Cincinnati Meeting, September 19–22, 1981, 18, in BCEIA Ecumenical, folder 1981.
48. For the discussion of this issue, see L/RC Dialogue, Minutes of the Gulf Park, Mississippi, Meeting, February 18–21, 1982, 10, 11, 14, 30, in BCEIA Ecumenical, folder 1982.
49. "Memorandum" from Avery Dulles to Roman Catholic Members of the Lutheran-Catholic Dialogue, July 29, 1980, 2, in BCEIA Ecumenical, folder 1980.
50. "Common Statement," in *Justification by Faith*, 16.
51. Ibid., 74.
52. In 1993, after the conclusion of its discussion on scripture and tradition, the L/RC dialogue created a Coordinating Committee to reconsider its achievements and set goals and an agenda for future meetings. The coordinating committee met between 1994 and 1996, and in the course of these meetings, it discussed a draft of the joint international statement on justification.
53. The two unpublished papers were "Condemnations of the Reformation Era regarding Justification: Some Remaining Problems" for the New Orleans meeting (March 25, 1995), and "Comments on Joint Declaration on the Doctrine of Justification Between the LWF and the RCC" for the Chicago meeting (November 3, 1995). Both papers are in BCEIA Ecumenical, folder 1995. Later Dulles published "On Lifting the Condemnations," *Dialog* 35 (Summer 1996): 219–20.

54. L/RC Dialogue, Minutes of the Chicago Meeting, October 21–23, 1994, Session III, 3, in BCEIA Ecumenical, folder 1994.

55. "Condemnations of the Reformation Era regarding Justification," 17.

56. L/RC Dialogue, Minutes of the Chicago Meeting, October 21–23, 1994, Session III, 3. In BCEIA Ecumenical, folder 1994.

57. "Condemnations of the Reformation Era Regarding Justification," 18.

58. For these judgments see the following: L/RC Dialogue, Minutes of the New Orleans Meeting, March 24–27, 1995, 16; L/RC Dialogue, Minutes of the Chicago Meeting, November 3–5, 1995, Session 4, (no pagination, but 1); and "Comments on Joint Declaration on the Doctrine of Justification between the LWF and the RCC," 1.

59. "Response by the Lutheran-Roman Catholic Coordinating Committee in the USA to the Proposed 'Joint Declaration on the Doctrine of Justification Between the Lutheran World Federation and the Roman Catholic Church,'" 4, in BCEIA Ecumenical, folder 1995. The three Roman Catholics, as the minutes of 1995 indicate, were Dulles, Patrick Granfield, and Archbishop J. Francis Stafford.

60. *Justification Today: A New Ecumenical Breakthrough* (New York: Fordham University Press, 1999).

61. Ibid., 8, 9.

62. Ibid., 10.

63. Ibid., 13, 15, 16.

64. For the "Joint Declaration on the Doctrine of Justification" (1997), the "Official Catholic Response to Joint Declaration" (June 25, 1998), "The Official Common Statement" and the "Annex" (June 1999), see *Origins* 28 (July 16, 1998): 120–26, 130–32; 29 (June 24, 1999): 85–92.

65. "Justification: The *Joint Declaration*," *Josephinum Journal of Theology* 9 (Winter/Spring 2002): 115; for other post-declaration writings, see "Justification: The Growing Consensus," in *Story Lines: Chapters on Thought, Word, and Deed*, ed. Skye Fackre Gibson (Grand Rapids, MI, and Cambridge, UK: Eerdmans, 2002), 16–21; "A Roman Catholic View of Justification in Light of the Dialogues," in *By Faith Alone: Essays on Justification in Honor of Gerhard D. Forde*, eds. Joseph A. Burgess and Marc Kolden (Grand Rapids, MI: Eerdmans, 2004), 220–31.

66. "Common Statement," in *Justification by Faith*, 57.

67. L/RC Dialogue, Minutes of the New Orleans Meeting, September 20–24, 1989, 51–52, in BCEIA Ecumenical, folder 1989.

68. The dialogue commissioned *Mary in the New Testament*, eds. Raymond E. Brown, Karl P. Donfried, Joseph A. Fitzmyer, and John Reumann (Philadelphia: Fortress; New York: Paulist, 1978), after the authors of *Peter in the New Testament* suggested in 1975, when the dialogue was in the midst of discussing papal infallibility and teaching authority, that such a study might be useful for future ecumenical work. The volume became particularly valuable in providing biblical background for the discussion of Mary and the saints.

69. Two papers were unpublished: "Karl Rahner on the Mediation of the Saints" [February 1985] and "Karl Rahner's Mariology" [September 1985]. Both papers are available in DPFU. The third paper, prepared for the February 1987

meeting, was published as "The Dogma of the Assumption," in *The One Mediator, the Saints and Mary: Lutherans and Catholics in Dialogue VIII*, eds. H. George Anderson, J. Francis Stafford, and Joseph A. Burgess (Minneapolis: Augsburg, 1992), 279–94.

70. L/RC Dialogue, Minutes of the Seguin, Texas, Meeting, February 23–26, 1984, 30, in BCEIA Ecumenical, folder 1984.

71. L/RC Dialogue, Minutes of the Cincinnati Meeting, September 20–23, 1984, 29, in BCEIA Ecumenical, folder 1984.

72. "Karl Rahner on the Mediation of the Saints," 2, 3, 4, 15.

73. L/RC Dialogue, Minutes of the Bon Secours Spiritual Center, Marriottsville, Maryland, Meeting, February 21–24, 1985, 26–30, in BCEIA Ecumenical, folder 1985.

74. "Karl Rahner's Mariology," 8.

75. Ibid., 1. Without being polemical, Rahner put questions to Protestants who were scandalized by the excesses of Catholic Mariology and devotional practices. All the questions reflected Rahner's view that Protestants did not take seriously enough the fact that salvation had already been realized to a considerable extent in the redeemed community. An excessive Protestant preoccupation with the theology of the cross, he thought, obscured the theology of glory. See, ibid., 22–23. This kind of Catholic hermeneutic of suspicion was a recurring theme in this particular dialogue.

76. Ibid., 20.

77. Ibid., 23, 26.

78. L/RC Dialogue, Minutes of the Techny, Illinois, Meeting, September 19–22, 1985, 28, in BCEIA Ecumenical, folder 1984. Bertram listed six ways in which Rahner "domesticated" Mariology: (1) by appealing to a hierarchy of truths; (2) though sinlessly conceived she still needs redemption; (3) her assumption is related to the future of all faithful Christians; (4) Rahner is periodically critical of Mariological excesses; (5) he emphasizes features with which Protestants could easily identify; and (6) his emphasis on simplication not multiplication of Marian privileges.

79. Ibid., 29.

80. "The Dogma of the Assumption," in *One Mediator, the Saints and Mary*, 279.

81. Ibid., 285–86, 289.

82. Ibid., 290, 291.

83. L/RC Dialogue, Minutes of the Tampa, Florida, Meeting, February 19–22, 1987, 10, in BCEIA Ecumenical, folder 1987.

84. Hotchkin to Stafford, February 6, 1987, in BCEIA Ecumenical, folder 1987.

85. Tavard to Hotchkin, February 2, 1987, in BCEIA Ecumenical, folder 1987.

86. "Common Statement," in *One Mediator, the Saints and Mary*, 45, no. 63.

87. L/RC Dialogue, Minutes of the Dayton Meeting, September 23–25, 1988, 18, in BCEIA Ecumenical, folder 1988.

88. "Common Statement," 35.

89. Ibid., 60–61.

90. See, e.g., L/RC Dialogue, Minutes of the New Orleans Meeting, September 20–24, 1989, 44, 47, 64, in BCEIA Ecumenical, folder 1989.

91. Harold C. Skillrud, J. Francis Stafford, and Daniel F. Martensen, eds., *Scripture and Tradition: Lutherans and Catholics in Dialogue IX* (Minneapolis: Augsburg, 1995), 19.

92. "Lutheran Reflections," in *One Mediator, the Saints and Mary*, 129–32, quotations at 129, 131–32.

93. L/RC Dialogue, Minutes of the Lantana, Florida, Meeting, March 6–10, 1991, Session 14, 2, in BCEIA Ecumenical, folder 1991.

94. L/RC Dialogue, Minutes of the Lantana, Florida, Meeting, February 14–18, 1990, Session 15, 1, in BCEIA Ecumenical, folder 1990.

95. L/RC Dialogue, Minutes of the Lantana, Florida, Meeting, March 6–10, 1991, Session 14, 1–2, in BCEIA Ecumenical, folder 1991.

96. Unlike previous sessions, none of the position papers were published with the common statement in *Scripture and Tradition*.

97. "The Catholic Concept of Tradition: With Special Reference to Vatican II," in BCEIA Ecumenical, folder 1990.

98. Ibid., 11, 26–28.

99. L/RC Dialogue, Minutes of the Erlanger, Kentucky, Meeting, September 20–23, 1990, September 20, 2:30 p.m. Session, 2, in BCEIA Ecumenical, folder 1990.

100. Ibid., 3.

101. Dulles frequently distinguished between Tradition, tradition, and the traditions. Following in part the Faith and Order meeting of the WCC in Montreal in 1963, he defined *Tradition* (with a capital *T*) as "God's action in handing over Jesus Christ for our salvation and the work of the Holy Spirit maintaining Christ's presence in the life of the Church." By *tradition*, he meant the process by which the life and message of Christ was handed over from generation to generation. By *traditions* he meant the "various expressions of the gospel in different churches and different cultures." For one example of these definitions, see Dulles' "The Role of Tradition in Catholic Christianity," *Emmanuel* 96 (January/February 1990): 4–13, 21, 28–29, especially 10.

102. "Catholic Concept of Tradition," 24.

103. Ibid., 25–26, quote on 26.

104. The Lutheran John Reumann charged that "Dulles [in the late 1980s], like a few other systematicians, became increasingly critical of New Testament scripture scholars as "mere philologists"—a criticism that was "not generously accepted by the Scripture scholars." My interview with Reumann, September 25, 2005, transcript, 3, in my possession. The Catholic Joseph Fitzmyer shared analogous criticisms. He reported that Dulles was unhappy with the way the biblical scholars applied the historical critical method to the Bible on the issue of Mary and the saints. Dulles "sees the value of a certain amount of historical critical method, but he always wants to bring in what he calls spiritual interpretation. And

to me spiritual is a weasel word. Because you never know how people are using the term." My interview with Fitzmyer, November 30, 2006, transcript, 19–20, in my possession. See also Fitzmyer's published reflections on Dulles' approach to scripture in Fitzmyer's *The Interpretation of Scripture: In Defense of the Historical-Critical Method* (New York: Paulist, 2008), 96–99, 116, 133–35. After reading Fitzmyer's book, Dulles wrote to him, April 3, 2008, in DPFU, commending him and mentioning that the differences they had with one another were "minor."

105. L/RC Dialogue, Minutes of the Lantana, Florida, Meeting, February 14–18, 1990, 33, in BCEIA Ecumenical, folder 1990.

106. L/RC Dialogue, Minutes of the Erlanger, Kentucky, Meeting, September 20–23, 1990, September 21, 2:00 p.m. Session, 2–3, in BCEIA Ecumenical, folder 1990.

107. Ibid., September 21, 3:45 p.m. Session, 1–2.

108. L/RC Dialogue, Minutes of the Chicago Meeting, September 17–19, 1992, September 19, Session 15, 4, in BCEIA Ecumenical, folder 1992.

109. *Scripture and Tradition*, 49–50.

110. Among the European participants were Edward Cardinal Cassidy, president of the Vatican's Pontifical Council for Promoting Christian Unity; Heinz-Albert Raem of the Pontifical Council; Dr. Eugene Brand, assistant general secretary for ecumenical affairs at the Lutheran World Federation; and Drs. Harding Meyer and Michael Root from the Institute for Ecumenical Research, Strasbourg, France.

111. Roman Catholic/Lutheran Joint Commission, *Facing Unity: Models, Forms and Phases of Catholic-Lutheran Church Fellowship* (Geneva: Lutheran World Federation, 1985).

112. "Statement on Advancement of Lutheran-Roman Catholic Relations," February 18–21, 1993, in BCEIA Ecumenical, folder 1993.

113. It is not entirely clear why he was not reappointed, but some on the dialogue suggested that new members were periodically appointed to replace older members, and in Dulles' case two younger Catholic ecclesiologists, Margaret O'Gara and Susan Wood, were appointed to replace Dulles. In 1996 Dulles was seventy-eight years old, and still in good health, mentally and physically. Nevertheless, it was thought best to appoint younger members to carry on the dialogue into the distant future. For confirmation that "new blood" was needed on the dialogue, see my interviews with Joseph Fitzmyer, November 30, 2006, transcript, 14–15; John Reumann, September 25, 2005, transcript, 7–8; and Jeffrey Gros, June 10, 2006, transcript, 6, all in my possession. My interview with George Tavard, May 15, 2006, transcript, 8–9, indicated that Dulles was not reappointed because of his opposition to the Joint Declaration, an interpretation Gros has contested. I could find no official records confirming or denying these interpretations.

114. Gritsch to Dulles, July 17, 2006, and Dulles to Gritsch, July 24, 2006, in DPFU.

115. "Saving Ecumenism from Itself," *First Things* 178 (December 2007): 24.

116. Dulles to Michael Rubino, January 5, 1996, in DPFU.

117. *The Catholicity of the Church* (Oxford: Clarendon Press, 1985), 105, quoting Newman's *Apologia pro vita sua* (Garden City, NY: Doubleday Image, 1956), 264.

118. "Statement on Advancement of Lutheran-Roman Catholic Relations," February 18–21, 1993, in BCEIA Ecumenical, folder 1993.

Chapter 12. Theology for a Postcritical Age, 1988–2000

1. "Interview with Rev. Avery Dulles, SJ," in *As I Remember Fordham: Selections from the Sesquicentennial Oral History Project*, ed. Jerry Buckley (New York: Fordham University, Office of the Sesquicentennial, 1991), 61, quoting letter from O'Hare to Dulles, April 9, 1987.

2. Anne-Marie Rose Kirmse, "The Church and the Churches—A Study of Ecclesiology and Ecumenical Developments in the Writings of Avery Dulles, SJ" (PhD diss., Fordham University, 1989). In 1989, when she defended her dissertation at Fordham, Dulles was at a meeting in Rome. He wrote to her, quipping, "Good luck defending the indefensible." See Dulles' interview with William Bole in *Our Sunday Visitor* (May 25, 1997): 11.

3. Avery Cardinal Dulles, *Church and Society: The Laurence J. McGinley Lectures, 1988–2007* (New York: Fordham University Press, 2008), xxi, xxii, xxiii.

4. "A Life in Theology," *America* 198 (April 21, 2008): 10.

5. My interview with Joseph Lienhard, SJ, August 5, 2005, transcript, 8, in my possession.

6. "Leonard Feeney: In Memoriam," *America* 138 (February 25, 1978): 135–37.

7. My interview with St. Benedict's Abbot Gabriel Gibbs, OSB, April 7, 2006, transcript, 2–3, in my possession. See also the unpublished diary, 68, of Louise Mercier Des Marais, in the archives of the Archdiocese of Boston.

8. For the story of the establishment of the monastery and the blessing of the new abbot, see Gabriel Gibbs, *Harvard to Harvard: The Story of Saint Benedict Center's Becoming Saint Benedict Abbey* (Still River, MA: Ravengate Press, 2006), especially 189–223.

9. *The Catholic Moment: The Paradox of the Church in the Postmodern World* (San Francisco: Harper & Row, 1987).

10. Members of the group included, e.g., George Lindbeck, Robert Wilken, and David Novak.

11. My interview with Richard John Neuhaus, May 13, 2005, transcript, 5, in my possession.

12. "Is This the Catholic Moment for the Future?" in *The Twenty-Fifth Anniversary of Vatican II: A Look Back and a Look Ahead*, ed. Russell E. Smith (Braintree, MA: Pope John Center, 1990), 307–8.

13. "While We're At It," *First Things* 66 (October 1996): 84–85.

14. Letter to the Editor, "Lay Off the Jesuits," *First Things* 69 (January 1997): 11. See also Joseph O'Hare to Dulles [n.d. but September 1996], commending Dulles for his admonitions to Neuhaus and complaining about Neuhaus's assaults on the Jesuits. See also Dulles' entire, unexcerpted, letter to Neuhaus, September 27, 1996, where Dulles complained, "Broadsides against whole orders in the Church, however whimsically intended can do great harm. They are unjust of the vast majority...who labor faithfully, and often against great odds, in missions, universities, high schools, retreat houses, and parishes all over the world." See also Dulles' assertion that his complaint against Neuhaus was not just against "a single column" but against a "series of sallies" that made Jesuits the "butt of his humor," in Dulles to John R. Dunlap, January 5, 1997. Letters in DPFU.

15. Dulles to Peter-Hans Kolvenbach, January 6, 1997. See also Dulles to Thomas H. Smolich, President of Jesuit Conference, December 8, 2006, on the Jesuit image problem in the United States. Dulles enclosed in the letter George Neumayr's "The Pope and Jesuit Education: Ravages in the Vineyard of the Lord," *Catholic World Report* (December 2006): 1, 28, 32, 44, showing that some American Jesuits were "sowing confusion in the Church." Letters in DPFU.

16. Dulles to Peter-Hans Kolvenbach, February 21, 1997, in DPFU. The articles were an editorial on Vincent O'Keefe, SJ, in *First Things* 70 (February 1997): 70, and "The Drinan Affair, Again," *First Things* 71 (March 1997): 58–59.

17. Peter-Hans Kolvenbach to Dulles, February 6, 1997, in DPFU.

18. "Remarks of Avery Dulles, SJ," in *John Foster Dulles: The Leader and the Legend*, ed. Richard H. Immerman (Princeton University: Woodrow Wilson School of Public and International Affairs, 1989), 6–7.

19. *John Foster Dulles: His Philosophical and Religious Heritage* (Lafayette: University of Southwestern Louisiana, 1994), 21, 23.

20. "The Lure of Catholicism," *New Oxford Review* 52 (March 1995): 6–14.

21. Ibid. Michael Novak, "The New Allure of Rome," *Crisis* 12 (January 1994): 4–6, made comments analogous to Dulles' about the new convert movement, attributing the allure to the papacy of John Paul II and Rome's guardianship of truth.

22. Six years after his Columbia speech, Dulles wrote that between 1965 and 1975 Catholicism in the English-speaking world "seemed to be losing its nerve and seeking to minimize its most distinctive features." In such a situation, conversions slowed to a trickle. Under the energetic leadership of Pope John Paul II and his interpretations of Vatican II, however, "Catholic doctrine has regained its balance and clarity. The Church is once more in a position to evangelize the modern world. And the flow of conversions has resumed." See "Foreword" to Oliver Barres's *One Shepherd, One Flock* (San Diego: Catholic Answers, 2000), 13. An examination of the *Official Catholic Directory* indicates that the peak year in the United States for conversions to Catholicism was 1960 (146,212); steadily thereafter the numbers declined until about 1989 (82,409), the last year when the *Directory* used the category of "converts." The decline was gradual in the 1960s and fell considerably in the 1970s and 1980s. From 1994 to 2000, however, a significant increase occurred in adult baptisms and receptions into full communion,

the categories used to indicate growth of those who were perhaps called converts in the past. In those years, 1,137,965 adults entered the church, averaging about 162,500 per year. Dulles' historical assessment was not exactly correct, but he did sense that a change had been taking place by the end of the century. I thank Mark B. Chapman, my faithful graduate research assistant, for collecting and analyzing these statistics for me.

23. See, e.g., "Orthodoxy and Social Change," *America* 178 (June 20, 1998): 14.

24. *Testimonial to Grace*, quotations at ix, 97.

25. Ibid., 109, 110, 125.

26. Dulles' interview with Gabriel Meyer in "Into the Millenium [sic] and Beyond," *National Catholic Register* (August 9–15, 1998): 1.

27. For one of Dulles' explicit invocations of the Ignatian *agere contra* principle applied to the temptations of the culture, see "Theological Education in Jesuit Formation," *Review for Religious* 59 (May–June 2000): 239. For an explanation of the principle, see chap. 6 of this book.

28. "An Ecclesial Model for Theological Reflection: The Council of Jerusalem," in *Tracing the Spirit: Communities, Social Action, and Theological Reflection*, ed. James E. Hug (Ramsey, NJ/New York: Paulist, 1983), 237.

29. *Testimonial to Grace*, 127, 131, 137.

30. Curran quoted by William Bole in *Our Sunday Visitor* (May 25, 1997): 11.

31. *The Craft of Theology: From Symbol to System* (New York: Crossroad, 1992, 1995). The text was expanded in 1995 and translated into Spanish in 2003. Here, I am using the 1995 edition.

32. "Appreciation and Challenge: Remarks at the Opening Celebration of Woodstock's 20th Anniversary" (Washington, DC, February 18, 1994), *Woodstock Report* 39 (October 1994): 8.

33. I am relying here on articles Dulles wrote on Jesuit spirituality and its relevance to theology. See, in particular, "Jesuits and Theology: Yesterday and Today," *TS* 52 (December 1991): 524–38; "The Ignatian 'Sentire cum Ecclesia' Today," *CIS: Review of Ignatian Spirituality* 25 (1994): 19–35; "Saint Robert Bellarmine: A Moderate in a Disputatious Age," *Crisis* 12 (December 1994): 39–44; "Appreciation and Challenge: Remarks at the Opening Celebration of Woodstock's 20th Anniversary"; "The Ignatian Charism and Contemporary Theology," *America* 176 (April 26, 1997): 14–22; republished in "What Distinguishes the Jesuits? The Ignatian Charism at the Dawn of the 21st Century," *America* 196 (January 15–22, 2007): 20–25; "Authentic Prayer," in *The Power of Prayer*, ed. Dale Salwak (Novato, CA: New World Library, 1998), 138–43; "Theological Education in Jesuit Formation," *Review for Religious* 59 (May–June 2000): 230–40; Preface to *The Spiritual Exercises of St. Ignatius* (New York: Random House Vintage Books, 2000), xiii–xxiii.

34. For a representative example of this interpretation, see Leonard Swidler and Hans Küng in *Consensus in Theology? A Dialogue with Hans Küng and Edward Schillebeeckx*, ed. Leonard Swidler (Philadelphia: Westminster, 1980), vi,

159, and Richard A. McCormick, "The Chill Factor: Recent Roman Interventions," *America* 150 (June 30, 1984): 475–81.

35. See, e.g., especially for the Curran case, the articles by Archbishop Roger M. Mahony, James Hitchcock, Michael Novak, and William E. May in *Vatican Authority and American Catholic Dissent: The Curran Case and Its Consequences*, ed. William W. May (New York: Crossroad, 1987), 16–26, 56–62, 74–103.

36. "Authority and Criticism in Systematic Theology," *Theology Digest* 26 (Winter 1978): 399.

37. "Saint Ignatius and The Jesuit Theological Tradition," *Studies in the Spirituality of Jesuits* 14 (March 1982): 1.

38. "Authority and Criticism in Systematic Theology," 392.

39. Ibid., 393–94, 395.

40. Dulles to Br. Tolbert McCarroll, March 27, 1984, on the uselessness of protesting Roman decisions because such protests only confirm anti-Roman sentiments. Dulles to Thomas E. Clarke, January 1, 1984, on his opposition to symbolic-action protests in the political order on very complex and technical issues of war and disarmament. Letters in DPFU.

41. *Craft of Theology*, ix, x.

42. *Craft of Theology*, 8.

43. "From Symbol to System: A Proposal for Theological Method," *Pro Ecclesia* 1 (Fall 1992): 43. This article is a summary of *Craft of Theology*.

44. "Transmission de la Foi et Sources de la Foi," *La Documentation Catholique* 80 (March 6, 1983): 260–67. English translation in "Sources and the Transmission of the Faith," *Communio* 10:1 (1983): 17–34, especially 22–23.

45. *The Ratzinger Report* (San Francisco: Ignatius Press, 1984), 75, 164.

46. *New Biblical Theorists: Raymond E. Brown and Beyond* (Ann Arbor: Servant Publications, 1983).

47. See "Revolution in the Church," *New York Review of Books* 31 (June 14, 1984): 35–39. See, too, responses to this article by Louis Dupré and Steven Englund and Ralph McInerny, among others, ibid., 31 (November 22, 1984): 56–57. See also Sheehan's *The First Coming: How the Kingdom of God Became Christianity* (New York: Random House, 1986).

48. Richard John Neuhaus, ed., *Biblical Interpretation in Crisis: The Ratzinger Conference on Bible and Church* (Grand Rapids, MI: Eerdmans, 1989). Other addresses were given by Raymond E. Brown, William H. Lazareth, and George Lindbeck.

49. See Ratzinger's "Biblical Interpretation in Crisis: On the Question of the Foundations and Approaches of Exegesis Today," in *Biblical Interpretation in Crisis*, 1–23. For Dulles' reflections on the synthesis, quoting Ratzinger, see "Vatican II on the Interpretation of Scripture," *Letter and Spirit* 2 (2006): 17–16.

50. Raymond E. Brown, "The Contribution of Historical Biblical Criticism to Ecumenical Church Discussion," in *Biblical Interpretation in Crisis*, 24–50.

51. *Craft of Theology*, 85.

52. "Historians and the Reality of Christ," *First Things* 28 (December 1992): 20–25, quotation at 24. See also *Craft of Theology*, "Historical Method and the Reality of Christ," 211–24.

53. "Historians and the Reality of Christ," 24, 25.

54. *Origins* 23 (January 6, 1994): 497, 499–524. Dulles' talk, "The Interpretation of the Bible in the Church: A Theological Appraisal," in *Kirche sein: Nachkonziliare Theologie im Dienst der Kirchenreform* (Festschrift for Hermann Josef Pottmeyer), eds. Wilhelm Geerlings and Max Seckler (Freiburg im Breisgau/Basel/Wein: Herder, 1994), 29–37.

55. "The Interpretation of the Bible in the Church," 34–35.

56. "Revelation as the Basis for Scripture and Tradition," *Evangelical Review of Theology* 21 (April 1997): 120.

57. *Craft of Theology*, 101–2.

58. Ibid., 103–4.

59. "Tradition and Creativity in Theology," *First Things* 27 (November 1992): 20–27.

60. "Wisdom as the Source of Unity for Theology," in *Wisdom and Holiness, Science and Scholarship (Essays in Honor of Matthew L. Lamb)*, eds. Michael Dauphinais and Matthew Levering (Naples, FL: Sapientia Press of Ave Maria University, 2007), 60.

61. "The Freedom of Theology," *First Things* 183 (May 2008): 19–23, quotations at 21.

62. "Wisdom as the Source of Unity for Theology," 60.

63. *Craft of Theology*, 115.

64. "Magisterium and Theologians: A Vatican Document," *America* 163 (July 21, 1990): 32.

65. (Washington, DC: United States Catholic Conference, 1968), 18.

66. See *Pastoral Letters*, 6: 43–71.

67. "The Ignatian Charism and Contemporary Theology," *America* 176 (April 26, 1997): 21.

68. Dulles would continue to maintain this fourfold distinction of the levels of authoritative statements of the faith, although the fourth category would recede into the background in later years. In 1998, after Pope John Paul II published *Ad tuendam fidem* (June 30, 1998), Dulles gave an interview to a reporter and reaffirmed the first three levels of authoritative statements and asserted that the pope in this case was doing nothing new but simply "tidying up" canon law because canon law had only made provisions for categories one and three. *Ad tuendam fidem* helped to clarify the second category. What made the papal declaration controversial, Dulles told the reporter, was the fact that the CDF put the prohibition against women's ordination in the second category, which required firm assent to those propositions that were necessarily or logically connected with revelation, even though not themselves revealed. On this, see Dulles' interview with Gabriel Meyer in "The Finer Points of the Faith," *National Catholic Register* (August 2–8, 1998): 1, 13.

Notes

69. See, e.g., "The Magisterium, Theology, and Dissent," *Origins* 20 (March 28, 1991): 692–96, quotation at 694.

70. "Authority in the Church," in *Civilizing Authority: Society, State, and Church*, ed. Patrick McKinley Brennan (Lanham: Lexington Books, 2007), 42; see also Dulles to Emil J. Bodart, April 16, 1998, in DPFU.

71. See, e.g., Dulles' "The Place of the Theologian: 1. The Question of Dissent," *Tablet* (London) 244 (August 18, 1990): 1033–34; Joseph A. Komonchak, "The Magisterium and Theologians," *Chicago Studies* 29 (November 1990): 307–29. For a balanced focus on the limits of the document, see Ladislas Orsy, "The Limits of Magisterium," *Tablet* 244 (August 25, 1990): 1066–69.

72. In a letter to Thomas Guarino, August 26, 2002, in DPFU, Dulles indicated that he believed Ratzinger was placing some nineteenth-century condemnations, like that against Antonio Rosmini-Serbati, in the category of "prudential admonitions."

73. *Craft of Theology*, 105–18, quotations at 113, 115.

74. Ibid., 118.

75. Ibid. For further comments on dissent, see Dulles, "The Place of the Theologian: 1. The Question of Dissent," 1033-34; "The Magisterium, Theology, and Dissent," 692-96.

76. Membership statistics taken from Sandra Yocum Mize, *Joining the Revolution in Theology: The College Theology Society, 1954–2004* (New York: Rowman & Littlefield, 2007), 257, and Matthew Lamb, "Catholic Theological Society of America: Theologians Unbound," *Crisis* 15 (December 1997): 36–37. The fiftieth anniversary edition of *Proceedings*, CTSA 50 (1995): 301–5, also provided some membership profiles and statistics. *Proceedings* indicated that the CTSA had grown from 670 members in 1963 to 1,098 in 1982 to 1,347 in 1992 (the last year of available statistics at the time).

77. For a moderate, self-critical assessment of such tactics, see Dan Finn's June 2007 presidential address to the CTSA "The Catholic Theological Society of America and the Bishops," *Origins* 37 (June 21, 2007): 88–95.

78. *Proceedings*, CTSA 52 (1997), 194.

79. "Motives and Types of Dissent," *New Oxford Review* 56 (January–February 1989): 8–9, quotation at 9.

80. Bernardin invited Dulles to participate in the project. See Bernardin to Dulles, April 17, 1996, but Dulles, "although sympathetic with the goals" of the project, had to decline "at the present time" to participate because of multiple other commitments. See Dulles to Bernardin, April 30, 1996. Letters in DPFU.

81. "*Humanae Vitae* and *Ordinatio Sacerdotalis*: Problems of Reception," in *Church Authority in American Culture* (New York: Crossroad, 1999), 14–28, quotation at 21.

82. Ibid., 25–26, and 80. In a talk to the American bishops, "'Humanae Vitae' and the Crisis of Dissent," *Origins* 22 (April 22, 1993): 774–77, Dulles outlined seven deleterious consequences of the encyclical and the public dissent from it and suggested five prudential steps that could be taken that might alleviate the disastrous consequences of the entire situation, including advice to the dissenters

that public dissent weakens the community of faith and witness, and to the magisterium that it might learn a lesson from the massive disagreement that the encyclical occasioned.

83. See Dulles interview with William Bole in *Our Sunday Visitor* (May 25, 1997): 11.

84. "Interview with Rev. Avery Dulles, SJ," in *As I Remember Fordham*, 62. See also *University Theology as a Service to the Church* (New York: Fordham University Press, New York, 1989), and *Church and Society*, 1–15.

85. *University Theology*, 3. See Dulles' citation of Constance from Henry Denzinger and Adolf Schönmetzer, *Enchiridion Symbolorum*, 23rd ed. (New York: Herder, 1965), no. 1179: "Universitates, studia, collegia, graduationes, et magisteria in iisdem sunt vana gentilitate introduca; tantum prosunt Ecclesiae, sicut diabolus."

86. *University Theology*, 16.

87. Ibid., 17.

88. Dulles makes these criticisms in the 1980s and 1990s. For one example, see "Theological Education in the Catholic Tradition," in *Theological Education in the Catholic Tradition: Contemporary Challenges*, eds. Patrick W. Carey and Earl C. Mueller (New York: Crossroad, 1997), 18.

89. "Theology in the Jesuit University," in *Jesuit Education 21: Conference Proceedings on the Future of Jesuit Higher Education*, ed. Martin R. Tripole (Philadelphia: Saint Joseph's University Press, 2000), 167–69.

90. "The Magisterium, the University, and the Catholic," *Prism* (Institute of Catholic Studies and John Carroll University): no. 5 (Summer 2000): 10.

91. "Theology in the Jesuit University," 166–71, quotations at 166, 169. For other essays on theology's role in the university, see "The Place of Theology in a Catholic University" (1991 Justin D. McClunn Inaugural Lecture, Marymount University, Arlington, VA), reprinted in *Catholic Theology in the University: Source of Wholeness*, ed. Virginia M. Shaddy (Milwaukee: Marquette University Press, 1999), 59–71.

92. "Catholicism 101: Challenges to a Theological Education," *Boston College Magazine* (Winter 2006): 48–50. The article was originally presented as a talk at Boston College on October 12, 2005.

93. "Catholicism 101: Challenges to a Theological Education" (with author's response to six reviewers), *Horizons* 33 (Fall 2006): 303–8, 324–29, quotation at 325.

94. Dulles, "Catholicism 101," *Boston College Magazine*, 50, and "Catholicism 101," *Horizons*, 329.

95. Ibid.

96. The respondents were William L. Portier, Lawrence S. Cunningham, Anne M. Clifford, John C. Cavadini, Mary Ann Hinsdale, and Christopher Ruddy. For their responses, see *Horizons* 33 (Fall 2006): 308–24.

97. Ibid., 328–29.

98. See, e.g., "Newman's *Idea of a University* and Its Relevance to Catholic Higher Education," *Conversations* 22 (Fall 2002): 16–18, quotations at 16, 18, and

"Faith and Reason: From Vatican I to John Paul II," in *The Two Wings of Catholic Thought: Essays on Fides et Ratio,* eds. David Ruel Foster and Joseph W. Koterski, SJ (Washington, DC: Catholic University of America Press, 2003), 193–208, quotation at 208.

99. "The Evangelization of Culture and the Catholic University," *Journal of Law, Philosophy and Culture* 1 (Spring 2007): 1–11; see also Dulles to Leo J. O'Donovan, September 18, 1995, in DPFU.

100. "The Magisterium, the University, and the Catholic," 8–11.

101. "Criteria of Catholic Theology," *Communio: International Catholic Review* 22 (Summer 1995): 314–15. This essay was a talk Dulles gave to Catholic theologians at the 1995 CTSA convention. Association with the magisterium was one of fifteen criteria of Catholic theology that he delineated. In 1981, as we have already seen, Dulles argued that a "canonical mission" was not necessary for the theological enterprise. See "The Two Magisteria: An Interim Reflection," *Proceedings,* CTSA 36 (1981): 159.

102. As early as 1951, Dulles weighed in on the secular notion of academic freedom when he reviewed William F. Buckley Jr.'s *God and Man at Yale* in *Best Sellers* 11 (November 1, 1951): 141–42. Dulles agreed that Buckley "rightly condemns that false notion of academic liberty which would grant an 'equal hearing' to views which are demonstrably false and immoral." Buckley, however, rested his case on an "unsound principle" when he asserted that the alumni should be the "ultimate arbiters of teaching policy," which would make them, in Dulles' opinion, judges in areas where they lacked competence.

103. See, e.g., Dulles' talk at the 1989 Duquesne University Symposium on Academic Freedom, "The Teaching Mission of the Church and Academic Freedom," *America* 162 (April 21, 1990): 397–402. Full text also available in *Academic Freedom in a Pluralistic Society: The Catholic University,* ed. Nicholas P. Cafardi (Pittsburgh: Duquesne University Press, 1990), 10–19; and in *Issues in Academic Freedom,* ed. George S. Worgul (Pittsburgh: Duquesne University Press, 1992), 42–56.

104. "Prospects for Seminary Theology," [Dunwoodie] *Seminary Journal* 2 (Winter 1996): 12–19, quotations at 14, 15, 16.

105. "Theological Education in Jesuit Formation," *Review for Religious* 59 (May–June 2000): 230–40, quotation at 231.

106. Ibid., 239–40.

107. Ibid.

108. *Proceedings,* CTSA 50 (1995): 277.

109. "Criteria of Catholic Theology," *Communio: International Catholic Review* 22 (Summer 1995): 303, 304. Later Dulles expanded this talk, but delineated ten instead of fifteen critical principles. See "Principles of Catholic Theology," *Pro Ecclesia* 1 (Winter 1999): 73–84, an article that was translated into Polish. On Peter's principle, see Carl J. Peter, "Justification and the Catholic Principle," *Lutheran Theological Seminary Bulletin* [Gettysburg, PA] 61 (1981): 16–32, and "Justification by Faith and the Need of Another Critical Principle," in

Justification by Faith. Lutherans and Catholics in Dialogue 7, ed. H. George Anderson et al. (Minneapolis: Augsburg, 1985), 304–16.

110. "Criteria of Catholic Theology," 315.

111. Dulles to Matthew Lamb, May 10, 1994, in DPFU.

112. "How Catholic Is the CTSA?" 13–14.

113. Bernard Law, "The CTSA: A Theological Wasteland," *Boston Pilot* 168 (June 20, 1997): 2.

114. See my interview with Br. Jeffrey Gros, FSC, June 10, 2006, transcript, 15–17, in my possession.

115. Mary Ann Donovan and Peter Steinfels, "How Catholic Is the CTSA?" *Commonweal* 125 (March 27, 1998): 14–16, 16–17.

116. Dulles' interview with Gabriel Meyer in "The Finer Points of the Faith," *National Catholic Register* (August 2–8, 1998): 13.

117. *Proceedings*, CTSA 54 (1999): 81.

118. Dulles was following here Pope John Paul II's Apostolic letter, *Ad tuendam fidem* (May 28, 1998). See *Origins* 28 (July 16, 1998): 113–16, and *Ad tuendam fidem* (Boston: Pauline Books & Media, 1998).

119. "Catholic Doctrine: Between Revelation and Theology," *Proceedings*, CTSA 54 (1999): 83–91, quotations at 83 and 85. Earlier Dulles had presented Dermot Lane as well as Haight as representatives of those theologians who had distinguished too sharply between faith and particular beliefs contained in doctrinal propositions. See *The Assurance of Things Hoped For: A Theology of Christian Faith* (New York/Oxford: Oxford University Press, 1994), 194–95.

120. "Catholic Doctrine," 89, 91.

121. "Moral Doctrine: Stability and Development," *Proceedings*, CTSA 54 (1999): 92–100, quotation at 93.

122. See, e.g., Jon Nilson, president of the CTSA, to Dulles, January 7, 2003. Dulles could not accept the invitation to attend, however, because of prior commitments to talks he had to give in Italy, Poland, and England that year. See Dulles to Nilson, March 21, 2003. Both letters in DPFU.

123. "The Church and Universal Catechism," *America* 162 (March 3, 1990): 203.

124. My interview with Dulles, August 3–4, 2005, transcript, 67, in my possession: "I think the effect [of the commission on American Catholic theology] is minimal. I think there must be a better way of using the theologians....I was put on the committee that worked on the theology of redemption, but I am not an expert on the theology of redemption. Other scholars not on the International Theological Commission had devoted their lives to it and knew the area more thoroughly than our committee. We were supposed to come up with an authoritative statement on the theology of redemption; but we had only one meeting to discuss the topic, and the next meeting we had to submit the paper. So on the committee, we had people from at least eight different nationalities, Irish, American, German, Dutch, French, Swiss, Croatian, Hungarian. We didn't have a common language; not all spoke English. It was difficult to communicate. And it was, therefore, hard to get a coherent document."

125. See, e.g., Walter H. Principe, "The International Theological Commission," in *Modern Catholicism: Vatican II and After*, ed. Adrian Hastings (New York: Oxford University Press, 1991), 194–99.

126. See, e.g., "Theological Orientations, American Catholic Theology, 1940–1962," *Cristianesimo nella storia* 13 (Giugno 1992): 361–82; "La théologie catholique nord-américaine depuis 1965," *Transversalités* (*Revue de L'Institut catholique de Paris*) 68 (Octobre–Décembre 1998): 9–28; "Les États-Unis," in *Le devenir de la théologie catholique mondiale depuis Vatican II*, ed. Joseph Doré (Paris: Beauchesne, 2000), 319–39; "Le statut de la théologie dans les universités catholiques aux États-Unis," in *La Responsabilité des théologiens Mélanges offers à Joseph Doré*, eds. François Bousquet, Henri-Jérôme Gagey, Geneviève Médevielle (Paris: Desclée, 2002), 295–302.

Chapter 13. Evangelization and Faith, 1988–2008

1. For the posthumous collection of his favorite articles on evangelization, see Dulles' *Evangelization for the Third Millennium* (New York: Paulist, 2009).

2. Pope John Paul II's speech at Port-au-Prince, Haiti. See "The Task of the Latin American Bishop," *Origins* 12 (March 24, 1983): 659–62, quotation at 661.

3. *John Paul II and the New Evangelization* (New York: Fordham University Press, 1992), 13, 15. See also *Church and Society*, 87–102. Dulles had spoken on the theme of evangelization in the late 1970s, too, but it came to a more central focus in his thought in the 1990s. For his earlier writings, note, e.g., "Mass Evangelization through Social Media," *Origins* 8 (March 29, 1979): 649–52.

4. For Dulles' more extensive treatment of the Evangelical-Catholic relationship, see "The Unity for Which We Hope," in *Evangelicals and Catholics Together: Toward a Common Mission*, eds. Charles Colson and Richard John Neuhaus (Dallas, TX: Word, 1995), 115–46.

5. *John Paul II and the New Evangelization*, 17.

6. "The New Evangelization and Theological Renewal," *Sacred Heart University Review* 15 (Fall 1994/Spring 1995): 14–26; "The Reception of *Evangelii nuntiandi* in the West," in *L'Esortazione Apostolica di Paolo VI Evangelii Nuntiandi. Storia, Contenuti, Ricezione* (Brescia: Istituto Paolo VI, 1998), 244–50; "Seven Essentials of Evangelization," *Origins* 25 (November 23, 1995): 397–400; "The New Evangelization: Challenge for Religious Missionary Institutes," in *Word Remembered, Word Proclaimed: Selected Papers from Symposia Celebrating the SVD Centennial in North America*, eds. Stephen Bevans and Roger Schroeder (Nettetal: Steyler, 1997), 17–31.

7. "The New Evangelization and Theological Renewal," 18–25.

8. "The Reception of *Evangelii Nuntiandi* in the West," 303.

9. "Current Theological Obstacles to Evangelization," in *The New Evangelization: Overcoming the Obstacles*, eds. Steven Boguslawski and Ralph Martin (Mahwah, NJ: Paulist, 2008), 13–25, quotation at 13.

10. "Seven Essentials of Evangelization," 400.

11. Ibid., 397–99.

12. "The Mission of the Church in *Gaudium et Spes*," in *The Church and Human Freedom: Forty Years after Gaudium et Spes*, ed. Darlene Fozard Weaver (Villanova, PA: Villanova University Press, 2006), 36.

13. "Contemporary Mission Priorities," *Catholic Extension* 100 (November 2005): 20.

14. "The Four Faces of American Catholicism," *Louvain Studies* 18 (Summer 1993): 107.

15. Dulles to Sandra Y. Rueb, January 13, 1994, in DPFU.

16. "The Catechetical Process in the Light of the *General Directory for Catechesis*," in *Hear, O Islands: Theology and Catechesis in the New Millennium*, ed. John Redford (Dublin: Veritas, 2002), 27.

17. The University of Wisconsin Catholic students called their group the Evangelical Catholic Institute, which aimed to find and form "leaders who will then evangelize, establish and equip their fellow parishioners for the new evangelization." For Dulles' talk on April 14, 2007, see "Models of Evangelization," *Origins* 37 (May 17, 2007): 8–12, quotations at 10, 11.

18. "The Bishop, Conscience, and Moral Teaching," in *Catholic Conscience Foundation and Formation*, ed. Russell E. Smith (New Haven, CT: Knights of Columbus, 1992), 146, 161.

19. "The Church and Universal Catechism," *America* 162 (March 3, 1990): 219.

20. "The Hierarchy of Truths in the Catechism," *Thomist* 58 (July 1994): 369–88, quotations at 370, 387, 377, 388.

21. "Books on the New Catechism," *America* 171 (October 22, 1994): 21.

22. *The Challenge of the Catechism* (New York: Fordham University Press, 1994), 8. See also *Church and Society*, 157–74.

23. "The New Catechism: A Feast of Faith," *Theology Today* 53 (July 1996): 148–51, quotation at 148.

24. *Challenge of the Catechism*, 3, 8, 15, 21.

25. "Historical Models of Catechesis," *Origins* 37 (November 8, 2007): 347–52.

26. "The Faith of a Theologian," in *Believing Scholars*, 162.

27. "The Rebirth of Apologetics," *First Things* 143 (May 2004): 23.

28. Ibid., 20.

29. "Mere Apologetics," *First Things* 154 (June/July 2005): 15–20, quotation at 15.

30. *A History of Apologetics* (1971; Eugene, OR: Wipf & Stock, 1999; San Francisco: Ignatius Press, 2005).

31. "Rebirth of Apologetics," 23.

32. Ibid., 21; see also "The Enrichment and Transmission of Faith in the Theology of John Paul II," in *Creed and Culture: Jesuit Studies of Pope John Paul II*, eds. Joseph W. Koterski and John J. Conley (Philadelphia: Saint Joseph's University Press, 2004), 8–9; "The Legacy of John Paul II—The Theologian,"

Notes

America 192 (April 18, 2005): 20–21; and *The Splendor of Faith: The Theological Vision of Pope John Paul II* (New York: Crossroad, 1999; new and rev. ed., 2003), vii, 6–7, 27–29, 173–74, 194, 248–62, and passim.

33. "Mere Apologetics," 20.

34. "Rebirth of Apologetics," 22–23.

35. "Models of Apologetics," 115–27.

·36. See, e.g., Dulles, "Receiving and Handing on the Faith: Dialogue between the Catholic Church and the Disciples of Christ: Comment," *Information Service* of the Pontifical Council for Promoting Christian Unity 111 (2002): 252–55; "Florovsky and the New Orthodox Ecumenism," in *Twenty-Five Year Commemoration to the Life of Georges Florovsky*, ed. G. O. Mazur (New York: Semenenko Foundation, 2005), 34–56.

37. "Saving Ecumenism from Itself," 23–27, quotations at 27.

38. "When to Forgive," *America* 187 (October 7, 2002): 6–10.

39. "Ecumenism and Evangelization," *Origins* 33 (November 13, 2003): 399–401.

40. "Justification and the Unity of the Church," in *The Gospel of Justification in Christ*, ed. Wayne C. Summer (Grand Rapids, MI: Eerdmans, 2006), 125–40.

41. Basil Meeking and John Stott, eds., *The Evangelical Roman Catholic Dialogue on Mission 1977–1984: A Report* (Grand Rapids, MI: Eerdmans, 1986).

42. A collection of letters from Weigel to Henry are available in the Carl F. H. Henry Papers in the archives of the Rolfing Memorial Library, Trinity International University, Deerfield, Illinois. I am grateful to Professor Douglas Sweeney of Trinity International for drawing my attention to this correspondence.

43. Both statements were initially published in *First Things* 43 (May 1994): 15–22, and 79 (January 1998): 20–23. On the dialogue, see also Colson and Neuhaus, *Evangelicals and Catholics Together*. Dulles published "The Unity for Which We Hope," 115–46, as a contribution to that early dialogue.

44. "Season of Grace," *Tablet* (London) 248 (October 22, 1994): 1341. For Dulles' view of the traditional marks of the church and the need for Catholics and Evangelicals to grow into greater unity on these issues, see, e.g., "The Church as 'One, Holy, Catholic and Apostolic,'" *One in Christ* 35:1 (1999): 12–26, and "Church, Ministry and Sacraments in Catholic-Evangelical Dialogue," in *Catholics and Evangelicals: Do They Share a Common Future?* ed. Thomas P. Rausch (New York/Mahwah, NJ: Paulist, 2000), 101–21.

45. "Donald Bloesch on Revelation," in *Evangelical Theology in Transition: Theologians in Dialogue with Donald Bloesch*, ed. Elmer M. Colyer (Downers Grove, IL: InterVarsity, 1999), 75–76.

46. See, in particular, Thomas Rausch's "Introduction," in *Catholics and Evangelicals*, 5–10.

47. "Trinity and Christian Unity," in *God the Holy Trinity: Reflections on Christian Faith and Practice*, ed. Timothy George (Grand Rapids, MI: Baker Academic, 2006), 61–82, quotation at 71.

48. George, the executive editor of *Christianity Today*, had written the foreword to the 2005 expanded edition of Dulles' *A History of Apologetics*.

49. "Trinity and Christian Unity," 72, 73, 82.

50. "Four Faces of American Catholicism," 100, quoting from *The Reshaping of Catholicism: Current Challenges in the Theology of Church* (San Francisco: Harper & Row, 1988), 40.

51. *Catholicism and American Culture: The Uneasy Dialogue* (New York: Fordham University Press, 1990), 4–6. That lecture was widely distributed and translated into Italian, German, Polish, and Chinese. See also *Church and Society*, 27–42.

52. "Faith and Civility," *Josephinum Journal of Theology* 11 (Summer/Fall 2004): 217, 218.

53. "The Contribution of Christianity to Culture: An American Perspective," *Chrzescijanstwo Jutra*, Proceedings of the Second Congress of Fundamental Theology (Lublin, Poland: Towarzystwo Naukowe, 2001), 160.

54. Ibid., 162.

55. *Catholicism and American Culture*, 11. In 2001, he suggested that there were three major American Catholic approaches to culture since 1970: neoconservativism, traditionalism, and popular ethnic religious engagements with their neighborhoods. See "Contribution of Christianity to Culture,"168. In addition to these two essays, I am relying on the following articles in the paragraphs that follow: "The Four Faces of American Catholicism," *Louvain Studies* 18 (Summer 1993): 99–109; "Narrowing the Gap: Gospel and Culture," *Origins* 23 (March 17, 1994): 677–80; "The Radicalism of the Gospel: The Evangelical Counsels in the Teaching of Pope John Paul II," *Religious Life* 29 (July/August 2004): 3–10.

56. See, e.g., "Orthodoxy and Social Change," *America* 178 (June 20–27, 1998): 8–17.

57. See, e.g., "And Yet…: A Counterproposal," *Discovery: Jesuit International Ministries* 2 (December 1992): 22–25.

58. "Contribution of Christianity to Culture," 163–64.

59. Ibid., 156.

60. "Narrowing the Gap," 679; *Catholicism and American Culture*, 16.

61. "The Mission of the Church in *Gaudium et Spes*," 26–37, see especially 29–31, 34. Cf. also "The Universal and the Particular Church," in Proceedings of the Sixty-Fifth Annual Convention of the Canon Law Society of America (Washington, DC: Canon Law Society of America, 2004), 37–39.

62. See, e.g., David J. O'Brien, *From the Heart of the American Church: Catholic Higher Education and American Culture* (Maryknoll, NY: Orbis, 1994), 190, 194–95.

63. "Faith and Civility," *Josephinum Journal of Theology* 11 (Summer/Fall 2004): 216–25.

64. "The Deist Minimum," *First Things* 149 (January 2005): 30. See also "Religious Freedom and Pluralism," *Journal of Markets and Morality* 5 (Spring 2002): 176, 180; "The Indirect Mission of the Church to Politics," *Villanova Law Review* 52:2 (2007): 241–52, especially 247–48.

65. "Christianity and Humanitarian Action," in *Traditions, Values, and Humanitarian Action*, ed. Kevin M. Cahill, MD (New York: Fordham University Press, 2003), 5–20, especially 19–20.

66. "Indirect Mission of the Church to Politics," 247.

67. Dulles to James Massa, January 22, 1993, in DPFU.

68. "Religion and the Transformation of Politics," McGinley lecture in *Church and Society*, 116–29, quotations at 116, 123, 127.

69. Laura Winterroth to Dulles, December 19, 1992, in DPFU. Some correspondents charged that Dulles was heretical on the issue of contraception, that his ecclesiology was the ground for widespread dissent in the church, and that his views on revelation (replacing concepts with symbols) played havoc in catechesis. See, e.g., Anthony Sistrom to Dulles, February 6, 1997; Dulles to Sistrom, February 5, 1997, and Sistrom to Richard Neuhaus, January 24, 1997, in DPFU. For some of these charges, see also John Lamont, "The Nature of Revelation," *New Blackfriars* (August 1991): 335–45.

70. See, e.g., Dulles to Sr. Anne-Marie Kirmse, November 13, 1992; Michael Phayer to Dulles, December 12, 1992; Dulles to Phayer, December 22, 1992; Dulles to Jane L. Curry, January 14, 1993. Letters in DPFU.

71. George W. Cornell, "Theologian Fears for the Future of Democracy; Self-Government Is Losing Its Reliance on a Moral Standard, Catholic Scholar Says," *Washington Post* (October 24, 1992): B7.

72. Dulles to Lourne J. Durward, June 1, 2004, in DPFU.

73. Dulles to Sybilla A. Cook, July 13, 2004, and May 28, 2004, in DPFU.

74. See, e.g., Dulles' "Catholics in the World of Mass Media," *Fellowship of Catholic Scholars Quarterly* 22 (Summer 1999): 15.

75. "The Four Faces of American Catholicism," 101. See also "The Church and the Media—Towards Mutual Understanding," *Media Report* [Newsletter of the Family and Media Association, Dublin, Ireland] 8 (Autumn, 1997): 1, 3, 8.

76. "Religion and the News Media: A Theologian Reflects," *America* 171 (October 1, 1994): 6.

77. "The Church, A Complex Reality: A Theologian Reflects on News Reporting," in *Religion and the Media* (Washington, DC: FADICA, 1994), 45.

78. Ibid.

79. "Religion and the News Media," 7, 9.

80. "The Catholic Press and the New Evangelization," *Origins* 27 (June 12, 1997): 62–63.

81. "Catholics in the World of Mass Media," 17, 21.

82. "Faith and Revelation," in *Systematic Theology: Roman Catholic Perspectives*, eds. Francis Schüssler Fiorenza and John Galvin (Minneapolis: Fortress, 1991), 91–128, quotation at 92.

83. *The Assurance of Things Hoped For: A Theology of Christian Faith* (New York/Oxford: Oxford University Press, 1994), 4.

84. Ibid., 279.

85. Ibid., 5.

86. In an earlier article Dulles argued for six models of faith (intellectual assent, transcendental orientation of the human spirit to God, trust, personal act of ultimate concern, obedience, and solidarity with the poor and commitment to the cause of justice). See "Models of Faith," in *Fides quaerens intellectum. Beiträge zur Fundamentaltheologie*, eds. Michael Kessler, Wolfhart Pannenberg, and Hermann Josef Pottmeyer (Tübingen: Francke, 1992), 412.

87. *Assurance of Things Hoped For*, 181.

88. Ibid., 150, 151.

89. Ibid., 165.

90. Ibid., 152, 153.

91. Ibid., 267; see also 166, 172–74.

92. *Models of Revelation* (1983; Maryknoll, NY: Orbis, 1992, 2003), 101.

93. Dulles was here commenting on how he understood fundamental theology. He maintained that "fundamental theology might be understood as a reflection from within faith on the dynamics of conversion. Such conversion, as I see it, depends upon God reaching us through real symbols of his presence and especially on the testimony of committed believers (who themselves become pre-eminent symbols)." See Dulles to Francis Schüssler Fiorenza, December 10, 1997; see also Dulles to Laurence Hemming, October 4, 1999, both letters, uncatalogued, in DPFU.

94. See reviews of the book by Cunningham in *Commonweal* 122 (May 1995): 38, John Macquarrie in *Journal of Theological Studies* 46 (October 1995): 802–4, Oliver Davies in *Theology* 98 (September/October 1995): 374–75, Richard McBrien in *Worship* 69 (September 1995): 462–63, Donald K. McKim in *Pro Ecclesia* 5 (Summer 1996): 365–67, Patrick O'Connell in *New Oxford Review* 62 (1995): 26–27, Thomas G. Weinandy in *New Blackfriars* 76 (November 1995): 515–16.

95. *The New World of Faith* (Huntington, IN: Our Sunday Visitor, 2000).

96. Ibid., 11.

97. Ibid., 163.

Chapter 14. Interpreting Vatican II and the Church, 1988–2008

1. Dulles' review of Gabriel Fackre's *The Doctrine of Revelation: A Narrative Interpretation* in *TS* 59 (September 1998): 527–29.

2. *Craft of Theology*, 50–52.

3. Joseph Komonchak to Dulles, April 21, 1999, in DPFU.

4. Dulles to Komonchak, May 11, 1999, and October 19, 1999, in DPFU.

5. *Houston Catholic Worker* (December 1999): 3.

6. Kardinal Dr. Christoph Schönborn to Dulles, February 5, 2000, in DPFU.

7. *The Reshaping of Catholicism: Current Challenges in the Theology of Church* (San Francisco: Harper & Row, 1988), 205.

8. "Reversals at Vatican II?" *America* 180 (May 29, 1999): 22. Dulles was responding here to Thomas Reese's "Of Many Things," *America* 180 (May 15, 1999): 1.

9. "Authority in the Church," in *Civilizing Authority: Society, State, and Church*, ed. Patrick McKinley Brennan (Lanham, MD: Lexington Books, 2007), 42–43.

10. To one correspondent who thought that Dulles' emphasis on continuity with respect to religious liberty "leaves little room for development," Dulles responded, "I have always thought that development presupposed continuity, because it is an unfolding of implications or potentialities in what is already given; it is not sheer innovation nor is it a repudiation of previous doctrine....But I would hold fast to my position that development requires continuity and does not exclude it. Continuity does not mean identity; it implies going beyond what was already there." Dulles was dealing with official teaching, not with theological opinions. Vatican II did not fully endorse the opinions of John Courtney Murray, and the opinions of Cardinal Ottavini were not Catholic doctrine. See Dulles to Joseph Komonchak, May 21, 2007, in DPFU. Dulles was responding to Komonchak's "An Unfinished Agenda," *Commonweal* 134 (May 18, 2007): 18–20, a review of *An Unfinished Agenda: Catholicism and Religious Freedom*, where Komonchak charged that Dulles' emphasis on continuity was a "curious abstraction."

11. "The Basic Teaching of Vatican II," in *Sacred Adventure: Beginning Theological Study*, ed. William C. Graham (New York: University Press of America, 1999), 125–37. The ten principles, which he had articulated at other times and in slightly different terminology, were points of departure for the life of the church and for continuous theological reflection. They were not hard and fast conclusions. They left room for many open questions. Earlier, Dulles had emphasized Vatican II's continuity with neo-Thomism. See, in particular, "Is Neo-Thomism Obsolete?—Vatican II and Scholasticism," *New Oxford Review* 57 (May 1990): 5–11.

12. "Vatican II: The Myth and the Reality," *America* 188 (February 24, 2003): 7–11.

13. "From Ratzinger to Benedict," *First Things* 160 (February 2006): 24–29, at 25 and 28. This is a reprint of Dulles' McGinley lecture of October 25, 2005. See *Benedict XVI: Interpreter of Vatican II* (New York: Fordham University, 2005), and *Church and Society*, 468–84. On the younger Ratzinger's participation at the council, see W. Jared Wicks, *Prof. Ratzinger at Vatican II: A Chapter in the Life of Pope Benedict XVI*, The Yamauchi Lectures in Religion, Spring 2007 (New Orleans: Loyola University, 2007). Wicks argued, 16, that Ratzinger applied a hermeneutics of reform to the council, combining a "demanding synthesis of fidelity" with "a dynamic movement of change."

14. "Vatican II: The Myth and the Reality," 9, 11.

15. "The Style of Vatican II," *America* 188 (February 24, 2003): 12–15, quotations at 12.

16. "Vatican II: The Myth and the Reality," 10. For further clarification of what Dulles meant by *subsistit*, see "Vatican II: Substantive Teaching: A Reply to John W. O'Malley and Others," *America* 188 (March 31, 2003): 16–17; "Clarifying the Council," *America* 197 (October 1, 2007): 43; and "Saving Ecumenism from Itself," 23–27.

17. For reactions to Dulles' view, see "Further Reflections on Vatican II," *America* 188 (March 17, 2003): 14–15, 29–30, quotations at 15, 29.

18. "The Sacramental Ecclesiology of *Lumen Gentium*," *Gregorianum* 86:3 (2005): 557. See also "Clarifying the Council," *America* 197 (October 1, 2007): 43.

19. For his earlier interpretations, see "Ecclesiological Issues" in chap. 8 of this book. See also his *Dimensions of the Church*, 10; *Models of the Church*, 44–45, 136–37; "The Church as Eschatological Community," in *The Eschaton: A Community of Love*, ed. Joseph Papin (Villanova, PA: Villanova University Press, 1974), 88–89; and "Infallibility Revisited," *America* 129 (August 4, 1973): 55. For Dulles' claim that he had since 1967 consistently taught that the church of Christ subsists only in the Catholic Church and nowhere else, see his letter to Emil Bodart, August 16, 1995. In a later letter to Bodart, Dulles said that he was insisting "even more than I did in 1972 that subsistence requires permanence in integral form. I believe that outside the Roman Catholic Church the Church of Christ is not integrally present, and hence that it does not subsist in other churches. This is not a departure from my 1972 position, or, for that matter my 1967 position." See Dulles to Bodart, August 31, 1995. Letters in DPFU.

20. "Sacramental Ecclesiology of *Lumen Gentium*," 557. Dulles was referring here to Teuffenbach's Gregorian University dissertation, *Die Bedeutung des 'subsistit in' (LG 8): Zum Selbstverständnis der katholischen Kirches* (Rome: Gregorian University, 2002), 380–88, which was later published as a book under the same title (München: Herbert Utz, 2002). See also Dulles to Fr. Patrick Bonner, November 28, 2007, in DPFU, where he expands on Teuffenbach's interpretation and the change that that study had made in his own interpretation of the phrase.

21. "Sacramental Ecclesiology of *Lumen Gentium*," 557.

22. See, e.g., John O'Malley, "Vatican II: Official Norms: On Interpreting the Council with a Response to Cardinal Avery Dulles," *America* 188 (March 31, 2003): 11–14, and Avery Dulles, "Vatican II: Substantive Teaching: A Reply to John W. O'Malley and Others," *America* 188 (March 31, 2003): 14–17.

23. For examples of this interpretation, see Charles E. Curran, *Loyal Dissent: Memoir of a Catholic Theologian* (Washington, DC: Georgetown University Press, 2006), 237, and Thomas F. O'Meara, *A Theologian's Journey* (New York: Paulist, 2002), 309. See also Alessandra Stanley, "John Paul Moves to Stifle Dissent on Heated Issues; Slap at Church Liberals," *New York Times* (July 1, 1998): A1; and Arthur Jones, "John Paul Acts to Muzzle Dissent," *NCR* 34 (July 17, 1998): 14.

24. George Weigel, *Witness to Hope: The Biography of Pope John Paul II* (New York: HarperCollins/Cliff Books, 1999), 10.

25. George A. Kelly, *Inside My Father's House* (New York: Doubleday, 1989), 275–78. Kelly, one of Dulles' persistent critics, charged that Dulles' progressive theological relativism and historicism and his emphasis upon a second magisterium undermined the church's credibility, contributing to the malaise and confusion in postconciliar American Catholicism; see, 274–76, 279–80. For Kelly's attack on the American bishops, see his *The Crisis of Authority: John Paul II and the American Bishops* (Chicago: Regnery Gateway, 1982).

Notes

26. "Theological Education in Jesuit Formation," *Review for Religious* 59 (May–June 2000): 232–33.

27. "Saint Robert Bellarmine: A Moderate in a Disputatious Age," *Crisis* 12 (December 1994): 39–44, quotes on 39, 44.

28. "John Paul II Theologian," *Communio: International Catholic Review* 24 (Winter 1997): 719.

29. *Challenge of the Catechism*, 3.

30. *The Splendor of Faith: The Theological Vision of Pope John Paul II* (1999; New York: Crossroad, 2003), x, 19.

31. "Seven Essentials of Evangelization," 400. See also *John Paul II and the New Evangelization* (New York: Fordham University, 1992), 15; *Splendor of Faith*, 69–76; "John Paul II and the New Evangelization—What Does It Mean?" in *John Paul II and the New Evangelization*, eds. Ralph Martin and Peter Williamson (San Francisco: Ignatius Press, 1995), 25–39; "John Paul II and the New Millennium," *America* 173 (December 9, 1995): 9–15; "John Paul II and the New Evangelization," *Studia Missionalia* 48 (1999): 165–80; "*Fides et Ratio* and the New Evangelization," *Theologie und Glaube* 90 (Fall 2000): 412–16.

32. *The Splendor of Faith*, vii, 5–6. On the metaphysical realism, see also "The Metaphysical Realism of Pope John Paul II," *International Philosophical Quarterly* 48 (March 2008): 99–106, where Dulles argued against the charge that the pope was a pure phenomenologist who resorted to authoritarianism to settle disputed issues in the church.

33. *Splendor of Faith*, 244–45.

34. John R. Quinn, "The Exercise of the Primacy and the Costly Call to Unity," in *The Exercise of the Primacy: Continuing the Dialogue*, eds. Phyllis Zagano and Terrence W. Tilley (New York: Crossroad, 1998), 1–28. The book also contains a selection of other responses to the pope's invitation as well as assessments of Quinn's proposals. Quinn expanded his initial lecture and published it in *The Reform of the Papacy: The Costly Call to Christian Unity* (New York: Crossroad, 1999).

35. See Dulles' reviews of P. Zagano and T. W. Tilley, *The Exercise of the Papacy: Continuing the Dialogue*; M. Buckley, *Papal Primacy and the Episcopate: Toward a Relational Understanding*; H. J. Pottmeyer, *Towards a Papacy in Communion: Perspectives from Vatican Councils I and II* in *Thomist* 63 (April 1999): 307–13; "What Price Reform?" Review of *The Reform of the Papacy: The Costly Call to Christian Unity* by John R. Quinn, *First Things* 104 (June/July 2000): 60–64; "The Papacy for a Global Church," *America* 183 (July 15–22, 2000): 6–11; and "In Dialogue: Avery Dulles and Ladislas Orsy Continue Their Conversation about the Papacy," *America* 183 (November 25, 2000): 12–13.

36. See, e.g., "What Price Reform?" 64.

37. "Papacy for a Global Church," 9. See also *Church and Society*, 318–31.

38. Ladislas Orsy, "The Papacy for an Ecumenical Age: A Response to Avery Dulles," *America* 183 (October 21, 2000): 9–15.

39. Ibid.

40. Dulles and Orsy, "In Dialogue," 12–15.

41. Untitled article in "The Future of the Papacy: A Symposium," *First Things* 111 (March 2001): 31–32; "Die Universalkirche und die Lokalkirche im Zeitalter der Globalisierung," *Theologie und Glaube* 91:4 (2001): 543–46; "The Petrine Office in the Service of Unity," *Origins* 31 (April 4, 2002): 704–8; "Florovsky and the New Orthodox Ecumenism," in *Twenty-Five Year Commemoration to the Life of Georges Florovsky*, ed. G. O. Mazur (New York: Semenenko Foundation, 2005), 34–56; "Primacy and Collegiality," in *John Paul II on the Body: Human, Eucharistic, Ecclesial*, eds. John M. McDermott and John Galvin (Philadelphia: St. Joseph's University Press, 2007), 179–94. Since 1988, many of the McGinley lectures at Fordham focused on papal documents and particularly on the thought of John Paul II and Benedict XVI. See *Church and Society*, 87–102, 142–57, 191–204, 414–29, 443–54, 468–84.

42. Walter Kasper, "On the Church: A Friendly Reply to Cardinal Ratzinger," *America* 184 (April 23–30, 2001): 8–14.

43. For a theological assessment of the debate, see Kilian McDonnell, "The Ratzinger/Kasper Debate: The Universal Church and Local Churches," *TS* 63 (June 2002): 227–50. The early Ratzinger, the Ratzinger of the council years, placed great importance on the theology of the local church. For a variety of reasons, he focused more and more in his later years on the theology, importance, and primacy of the universal church. On this, see Avery Dulles, "From Ratzinger to Benedict," 28.

44. Kasper, "On the Church," 11.

45. Letter in *Origins* 22 (June 25, 1992): 108–12, quotation at 109.

46. "The Universal and the Particular Church," in *Proceedings of the Sixty-Fifth Annual Convention of the Canon Law Society of America* (Washington, DC: Canon Law Society of America, 2004), 31–41.

47. "Ratzinger and Kasper on the Universal Church," *Inside the Vatican* 9 (June 2001): 12–14, quotation at 13.

48. "Universal and Particular Church," 31.

49. "Ratzinger and Kasper on the Universal Church," 12–14.

50. "Die Universalkirche und die Lokalkirche im Zeitalter der Globalisierung," 543–46.

51. "The Universal and the Particular Church," 39.

52. Ibid., 41.

53. *A Eucharistic Church: The Vision of John Paul II* (New York: Fordham University Press, 2004), 12–14. See also *Church and Society*, 443–54.

54. "Petrine Office in the Service of Unity," 708.

55. Ibid.; see also "Authority in the Church," 44–46.

56. "Newman and the Hierarchy," *Newman Studies Journal* 2 (Spring 2005): 8–19, especially 18.

57. See, e.g., "Die Universalkirche und die Lokalkirche im Zeitalter der Globalisierung," 545; "Petrine Office in the Service of Unity," 707; "Universal and Particular Church," 34–36; "Primacy and Collegiality," 188–89, 189–92.

58. "Primacy and Collegiality," 182–83, 192–93.

59. "Models for Ministerial Priesthood," *Origins* 20 (October 11, 1990): 284–89; "The Priest and the Great Jubilee," *The Priest* 54 (June 1998): 31–39; *The Priest and the Eucharist* (Weston, MA: Blessed John XXIII National Seminary, 2000); *The Priestly Office: A Theological Reflection* (New York: Paulist, 1997); "The Priest and the Eucharist," *Emmanuel* 108 (May 2002): 222–41; "Philosophy and Priestly Formation," *Theology Digest* 50 (Winter 2003): 343–52; "The Radicalism of the Gospel: The Evangelical Counsels in the Teaching of Pope John Paul II," *Religious Life* 29 (July/August 2004): 3–10; "John Paul II and the Priesthood," in *Creed and Culture: Jesuit Studies of Pope John Paul II*, eds. Joseph W. Koterski and John J. Conley (Philadelphia: Saint Joseph's University Press, 2004), 195–210; "The Church as the Body of Christ," in *John Paul II on the Body: Human, Eucharistic, Ecclesial*, 160–62.

60. *Models of the Church*, chap. 10.

61. "Priest and the Eucharist," 230; "The Radicalism of the Gospel," 5–6; "John Paul II and the Priesthood," 207–8.

62. "John Paul II and the Priesthood," 196, 197.

63. *Priestly Office*, 1.

64. Ibid., 3.

65. "Models for Ministerial Priesthood," 287, 288. In a letter to Edward F. Malone, May 28 1996, in DPFU, Dulles wrote that he did not intend to deal significantly with the problem of the "functional versus ontological" approaches to the priesthood. He did not like the purely functional approach, "but I am not quite comfortable to speak of ordination as effecting an ontological change, since it seems to suggest that a man is made into a superman and removed from solidarity with the rest of the human race." The ontological change, he argued, is in the supernatural or sacramental order rather than in the order of nature.

66. "Priest and the Eucharist," 230, 232.

67. Ibid., 58.

68. Ibid., 59.

69. "John Paul II and the Priesthood," 195–96.

70. "The Mission of the Laity," in *Church and Society*, 485–96, quotation at 494.

71. "The Priest and the Great Jubilee," 38, 32, 33.

72. Kenneth Briggs, "Catholic Meeting's Proposal Stirs Backers of Women's Ordination," *New York Times* (October 25, 1976): 25.

73. Dulles to Sr. Paula Richard, January 15, 1979, in DPFU.

74. Dulles to Peter J. McCord, May 22, 1983, in DPFU.

75. Dulles to Michael Buckeley, July 7, 1983, in DPFU.

76. Dulles to Karl P. Donfried, April 7, 1993, in DPFU.

77. See, e.g., "Women's Ordination: A Response," *Commonweal* 121 (July 15, 1994): 10–11; "Tradition Says No," *The Tablet* 249 (December 9, 1995): 1572–73; "Gender and Priesthood: Examining the Teaching," *Origins* 25 (May 2, 1996): 778–84; "Pastoral Response to the Teaching on Women's Ordination," *Origins* 26 (August 29, 1996): 177–80; "How Catholic Is the CTSA?" *Commonweal* 125 (March 27, 1998): 13–14; "Women Priests—The Case Against," *Studies* 87 (Spring 1998):

43–50; *"Humanae Vitae* and *Ordinatio Sacerdotalis*: Problems of Reception," in *Church Authority in American Culture* (New York: Crossroad, 1999), 14–28.

78. "Women's Ordination," *Commonweal* 121 (July 15, 1994): 10–11. Opinion polls indicated that in 1974 only 29 percent of Catholics favored the ordination of women; by 1985 47 percent favored it. See George Gallup Jr. and Jim Castelli, *The American Catholic People: Their Beliefs, Practices, and Values* (Garden City, NY: Doubleday, 1987), 56. A Gallup poll in 1992 revealed that 67 percent of Catholics favored ordination of women.

79. Dulles to Justin J. Kelly, August 1, 1994, in DPFU. Dulles carried on an extensive correspondence with Kelly, who could not accept the teaching of *Ordinatio* as an authentic part of the tradition. See, e.g., Kelly to Dulles, June 24, 1994, and August 12, 1994, in DPFU. Kelly concluded his August 12 letter by noting, "I hope you know that our lack of agreement here doesn't in any way diminish my affection for you and respect for your enormous contribution to the Church." To Walter Burghardt, September 4, 1996, in DPFU, Dulles wrote that he acknowledged the need for further examination of the constancy of the magisterial teaching, but that the "argument from convergence" of historical evidences seems to support the church's teaching. At any rate, the interventions of Popes Paul VI and John Paul II were "sufficiently weighty to remove prudent doubts." He was convinced by Newman "that history can rarely if ever prove the truth of dogma, and by the Ignatian rules for thinking with the Church." See also Dulles to James R. Roth, January 15, 1997, in DPFU.

80. On the CDF's response to the *dubium*, see "Inadmissibility of Women to Ministerial Priesthood," *Origins* 25 (November 30, 1995): 401, 403–5, and on American bishops' replies, see "Statements on Doctrinal Congregation's Action," *Origins* (November 30, 1995): 406–9.

81. In 2001, Dulles was asked why the pope did not make an *ex cathedra* statement. "I can only speculate," he replied to a correspondent. "I suspect that he may have felt that the doctrine is not so clearly contained in the apostolic deposit of revelation that all the faithful should be bound to accept in [sic] on a motive of divine and catholic faith. He perhaps sees it as a doctrine closely connected with revelation, to be accepted on the authority of the Church." Dulles to Jim Roth, August 27, 2001, in DPFU.

82. "Tradition Says No," 1572–73.

83. "Gender and Priesthood: Examining the Teaching," *Origins* 25 (May 2, 1996): 778–84, quotation at 779. See also *Church and Society*, 205–20.

84. Ibid.

85. Ibid., 782–83. See also Dulles' June 22, 1996 talk to the nation's Catholic bishops, "Pastoral Response to the Teaching on Women's Ordination," *Origins* 26 (August 29, 1996): 177–180.

86. "Pastoral Response to the Teaching on Women's Ordination," 178.

87. "Gender and Priesthood," 778.

88. "Women Priests—The Case Against," 43.

89. In 1996, moreover, Dulles was part of a panel of five theologians who addressed *Ordinatio*, and, as he reported to one correspondent, he was the only one

on the panel who "defended the infallibility of the Pope's decision." See Dulles to William F. Macomber, August 23, 2005, in DPFU.

90. *Origins* 27 (June 19, 1997): 74, 76–79. A first draft of the statement was presented in 1996. See *Proceedings*, CTSA 51 (1996): 332–42.

91. *Proceedings*, CTSA 52 (1997): 194.

92. "How Catholic Is the CTSA?" 13–14.

Chapter 15. The Cardinal, 2001–2008

1. "37 New Cardinals Selected by Pope," *New York Times* (January 22, 2001): A1.

2. My interview with Anne-Marie Kirmse, June 24, 2008; see also my interview with Fr. Gerald Blaszczak, SJ, July 25, 2007, transcript, 4–5, in my possession.

3. Robert D. McFadden, "A Theologian at Fordham Gets Red Hat," *New York Times* (January 22, 2001): A1.

4. Gustav Niebuhr, "Reward for Faithful Service," *New York Times* (February 17, 2001): B9.

5. See "The Coat of Arms of His Eminence, Avery Cardinal Dulles of the Society of Jesus," March 29 2001, in DPFU.

6. "Pope Installs 44 Cardinals," *Milwaukee Journal* (February 22, 2001): 1.

7. Alessandra Stanley, "American Cardinals Handle Reporters and Flying Birettas," *New York Times* (February 22, 2001): A4.

8. See my interview with John and Monica Murphy, June 25, 2008, transcript, 8, in my possession.

9. Letter of Joan Talley to author, December 8, 2008, in my possession.

10. Story recounted in "Cardinal Avery Dulles: Roman Catholic Theologian," *London Times* (December 13, 2008), at http://www.timesonline.co. uk/tol/comment/obituaries/article5332887. Joan Talley does not remember this story, as she told me in a letter of January 24, 2009. Letter in my possession.

11. John Foster Dulles II to Patrick Carey, July 19, 2008, letter in my possession.

12. Avery Cardinal Dulles to Sr. M. Christine Athans, BVM, May 13, 2001. Copy of letter in my possession.

13. Interview with Joseph Lienhard, SJ, August 5, 2005, transcript, 8, in my possession.

14. Richard P. McBrien, "Red Hat after Lurch to Right," *NCR* (February 16, 2001): 17. Others shared McBrien's suspicion that Dulles was rewarded for his defense of "disputed papal teachings." See, e.g., "All Dressed Up," *Commonweal* 128 (March 23, 2001): 5–6.

15. "All Dressed in Scarlet: Avery Dulles Goes to College," *Commonweal* 128 (February 23, 2001): 9.

16. See *Origins* 28 (February 11, 1999): 60l. Homily in the Trans World Dome, St. Louis, January 27, 1999.

17. *The Death Penalty: A Right to Life Issue?* (New York: Fordham University Press, 2000), 11. See also *Church and Society*, 332–47.

18. Ibid., 14, 17, 18.

19. For Buechlein's address, see *Origins* 30 (April 26, 2001): 727–28.

20. Twelve opponents as well as supporters of Dulles' views published their reactions in "Avery Cardinal Dulles and His Critics: An Exchange on Capital Punishment," *First Things* 115 (September 2001): 7–14.

21. Dulles' talk at the Chicago symposium was "Catholic Teaching on the Death Penalty: Has it Changed?" *Criterion* 41 (Autumn 2002): 10–15; see also "Catholic Teaching on the Death Penalty: Has It Changed?" in *Religion and the Death Penalty: A Call for Reckoning*, eds. Erik C. Owens, John D. Carlson, and Eric P. Elshtain (Grand Rapids, MI: Eerdmans, 2004), 23–30. Dulles' talk reiterated the argument of his McGinley lecture. An adapted version of Scalia's talk at the Chicago symposium was published as "God's Justice and Ours," *First Things* 123 (May 2002): 17–21.

22. Scalia, "God's Justice and Ours," especially 20–21, where he disagreed with Dulles' interpretation of *Evangelium vitae*.

23. *National Catholic Register* (February 17–23, 2002): 8. See also "Scalia Defends Death Penalty," ibid. (February 17–23, 2002): 2.

24. The editorial symposium was entitled "Pope John Paul's Teaching on Capital Punishment," *National Catholic Register* (March 24–30, 2002): 7.

25. "Seven Reasons America Shouldn't Execute," *National Catholic Register* (March 24–30, 2002): 7.

26. "Antonin Scalia and His Critics: An Exchange on the Church, the Courts, and the Death Penalty," *First Things* 126 (October 2002): 8–18. The scholars were Robert H. Bork, Archbishop Charles J. Chaput, Douglas W. Kmiec, David Smolin, Steven Long, Judie Brown, Robert Fastiggi, and Michael Neumann. Scalia, then, responded to the various scholars.

27. Ibid., 8.

28. Ibid., 17.

29. In a letter to Gil Costello, October 13, 2002, in DPFU, Dulles indicated that his differences with Scalia "are rather narrow."

30. "Catholic Teaching on the Death Penalty," 26–27, 30.

31. For some background on the crisis, see my *Catholics in America: A History* (Westport, CT: Praeger, 2004), 145–56.

32. Laurie Goodstein, "A Mission to Restore Credibility," *New York Times* (April 21, 2002): 1, 30.

33. For details of the meeting, see "Final Communique of Vatican–U.S. Church Leaders Summit," *Origins* 31 (May 2, 2002): 771–72; see also John Paul II, "Address to Summit of Vatican, U.S. Church Leaders," *Origins* 31 (May 2, 2002): 757, 759; "Final Communiqué" (April 24, 2002) at http://vatican.va/roman_curia/cardinals/documents/rc_cardinals-20020424-fin. The American church leaders also wrote a "Letter to U.S. Priests," in *Origins* 31 (May 2, 2002): 772, on the subject of clerical abuse and indicated their support for the many priests who were scandalized by the abuse cases. Cardinal McCarrick was involved

in preparing the statement. He did not remember if Dulles participated much in the Roman discussions but he did not play a major role in the formation of the statement. My interview with McCarrick, January 5, 2009, transcript, 10, in my possession.

34. "The Bishops and the Vatican," *New York Times* (June 10, 2002): A25.

35. Ibid.

36. Comments of Nan Marie Astone, *New York Times* (June 11, 2002): A28, and Edd Doerr, ibid. (June 13, 2002): A38.

37. See Dulles to Peter Stravinskas, June 20, 2002, a memo that contains his unpublished talk before the bishops. Dulles received numerous letters on clerical sexual abuse and the bishops' zero-tolerance policy, and he responded to all of them. See, e.g., Dulles to Jim Roth, July 31, 2002, a letter that reveals Dulles' strongest reactions to the bishops' zero-tolerance policy. The "bishops seem to have been influenced more by the media pressure than by the gospel and canon law....I also see no reason except vindictiveness for removing elderly priests who may have committed some offence in their early years but who have served without any allegations against them for several decades." See also Dulles to John F. Harrington, August 9, 2002. Memo and letters in DPFU.

38. Laurie Goodstein and Sam Dillon, "Bishops Set Policy to Remove Priests in Sex Abuse Cases," *New York Times* (June 15, 2002): A1.

39. Cardinal McCarrick and a few other bishops sided somewhat with Dulles' warnings. McCarrick "spoke in favor of his position" and told the bishops "we really have to consider" Dulles' good points, but his objections were not favored by the majority. See my interview with McCarrick, January 5, 2009, transcript, 11, in my possession.

40. My interview with Msgr. Thomas Shelley, May 22, 2008.

41. The Thomas More Society, Pro-Life Center, founded in 1997, is a not-for-profit, public interest law firm based in Chicago and dedicated to fighting for the rights and dignity of all human life.

42. He was referring here to the American bishops' *Responsibility, Rehabilitation, and Restoration: A Catholic Perspective on Crime and Criminal Justice* (Washington, DC: United States Conference of Catholic Bishops, 2000).

43. "Rights of Accused Priests: Toward a Revision of the Dallas Charter and the 'Essential Norms,'" *America* 190 (June 21–28, 2004): 19–23.

44. Archbishop Harry J. Flynn of St. Paul and Minneapolis, chairman of the Bishops' Committee on Sexual Abuse, e.g., argued for no revisions of the zero-tolerance policy for a variety of reasons but primarily because of the church's inability to identify those who would not again commit abuses of minors. See "What Has the Charter Accomplished," *America* 191 (October 18, 2004): 8–11.

45. Germain Grisez, "Sin, Grace, and Zero Tolerance: An Exchange," *First Things* 151 (March 2005): 27–33.

46. Avery Dulles, "Sin, Grace, and Zero Tolerance: An Exchange," *First Things* 151 (March 2005): 33–36.

47. "Authority in the Church," in *Civilizing Authority: Society, State, and Church*, ed. Patrick McKinley Brennan (Lanham, MD: Lexington Books, 2007),

45, 53. In a letter to Richard J. Clarkson, October 30, 2003, in DPFU, Dulles indicated that he was unwilling to judge the bishops for their failure to report the sexual abuse cases, but in his judgment "more harm and dishonor to the Church is wrought by concealment than by disclosure of the truth." On the other hand the bishops' behavior, he believed, may have been partly determined by the "evangelical motives" of Matthew 18:15–17, which indicated that "if an offence can be handled privately there is no need to go public with it." Dulles was not sure his judgment "would have been any better than" that of the bishops under their circumstances. He was not excusing the episcopal failures but giving a benign interpretation of what might have motivated them.

48. My interview with Dulles, August 3, 2005, transcript, 64, in DPFU.

49. Laurie Goodstein, "Where Chariots Raced, a Modern Spectacle Brings Together, if Briefly, a Diverse Church," *New York Times* (April 9, 2005): A10.

50. My interview with Gerald Blaszczak, July 25, 2007, transcript, 8–9, in my possession.

51. Ibid., 14.

52. Laurie Goodstein, "Cardinals Hint at the Profile of a New Pope," *New York Times* (April 10, 2005): 1.

53. Ian Fisher, Elisabetta Povoledo, and Jason Horowitz, "German Cardinal Is Chosen as Pope," *New York Times* (April 20, 2005): A1.

54. My interview with Dulles, August 3, 2005, transcript, 68, in DPFU.

55. "From Ratzinger to Benedict," *First Things* 160 (February 2006): 29.

56. *Newman* (London/New York: Continuum, 2002).

57. For Dulles' analysis of Newman's conversion, see "Newman: The Anatomy of a Conversion," in *Newman and Conversion*, ed. Ian Ker (Edinburgh: T. & T. Clark, 1997), 21–36.

58. For these and other Newmanian definitions of liberalism, see Dulles, *Newman*, 14, 72–73.

59. Ibid., 44–45.

60. Davies to Dulles, February 22, 2000, in DPFU.

61. Dulles to Davies, March 2, 2000, in DPFU, and *Newman*, ix.

62. *Newman*, 163.

63. Ibid., 10.

64. Ibid., 44–45.

65. Ibid., 79.

66. Ibid., 112.

67. Ibid.

68. Ibid., 112–13, 151.

69. Ibid., 164.

70. Review of George Lindbeck's *The Church in a Postliberal Age*, ed. James J. Buckley, in *First Things* 136 (October 2003): 57–61.

71. For Dulles' earlier assessments of that work, see "Zur Überwindbarkeit von Lehrdifferenzen—Überlegungen aus Anlass zweier neuerer Lösungsvorschlage," *Theologische Quartalschrift* 166 (1986): 278–89; and *The Reshaping of Catholicism: Current Challenges in the Theology of Church* (San Francisco: Harper & Row, 1988),

140–41. An extended review symposium of Lindbeck's book by other theologians is also published in the *Thomist* 49 (1985): 392–472.

72. L/RC Dialogue, Minutes of the Tampa, Florida, Meeting, February 19–22, 1987, 15. In BCEIA Ecumenical, folder 1987.

73. L/RC Dialogue, Minutes of the Erlanger, Kentucky, Meeting, September 20–23, 1990, n.p. but the September 21, 10:45 a.m. meeting. In BCEIA Ecumenical, folder 1990.

74. Review of Lindbeck, *Church in a Postliberal Age*, 61.

75. George Lindbeck, "George Lindbeck Replies to Avery Cardinal Dulles," and Avery Dulles, "Avery Cardinal Dulles Replies," *First Things* 139 (January 2004): 13–15.

76. *First Things* 156 (October 2005): 53–61.

77. See, e.g., Dulles, "*Dignitatis humanae* and the Development of Catholic Doctrine," in *Catholicism and Religious Freedom*, eds. Kenneth L. Grasso and Robert P. Hunt (Lanham, MD: Rowman & Littlefield, 2006), 43–46.

78. See, e.g., "World Religions and the New Millennium," in *In Many and Diverse Ways: In Honor of Jacques Dupuis*, eds. Daniel Kendall and Gerald O'Collins (Maryknoll, NY: Orbis, 2003), 3–13, quotations at 5, 10.

79. "Catholic Just War Doctrine," *Living Pulpit* 14 (October–December 2005): 4.

80. "True and False Reform," *First Things* 135 (August/September 2003): 14–19, quotation at 15.

81. Ibid., 16.

82. "Church as the Body of Christ," in *John Paul II on the Body*, eds. McDermott and Galvin, 158, quoting Henri de Lubac, *The Splendor of the Church*, trans. Michael Mason (1956; rpt. ed. San Francisco: Ignatius, 1986), 134. See also Dulles, "Reflections on *Ecclesia de Eucharistia*," *L'Asservatore Romano* (Eng. ed.) (July 30, 2003): 3; "The Eucharist Builds the Church," in *At the Altar of the World* (Washington, DC: Pope John Paul II Cultural Center, 2003), 55–56; *A Eucharistic Church: The Vision of John Paul II* (New York: Fordham University Press, 2004), 4.

83. *Eucharistic Church*, 16.

84. See, e.g., "The Death of Jesus as Sacrifice," *Josephinum Journal of Theology* 3 (Summer/Fall 1996): 4–17.

85. "The Eucharist as Sacrifice," in *Rediscovering the Eucharist: Ecumenical Conversations*, ed. Ruch A. Kereszty (New York/Mahwah: Paulist, 2003), 175–87, quotations at 177, 182, 185.

86. "How Real Is the Real Presence?" in *Church and Society*, 455–67. See also reprints in "Christ's Presence in the Eucharist," *Origins* 34 (March 17, 2005): 627–31; and under different titles in *Adoremus Bulletin* 11 (April 2005) 5–6, 9; *Our Sunday Visitor* (May 29, 2005): 9–12; 30 *Giorni* 23 (2005): 74–79, 82–86; *30 Days* 23 (2005): 56–66.

87. (Naples, FL: Sapientia Press, 2007).

88. On this, see chap. 10 of this book.

89. John C. Cort, a Catholic socialist and a Harvard-educated convert to Catholicism, regretted that some Catholic laity and clergy "seem to be losing their

faith in the magisterium....I keep telling them, I've been where you are heading and, believe me, you wouldn't like it." See Cort's "A Bizarre Conversion," in *The New Catholics: Contemporary Converts Tell Their Stories*, ed. Dan O'Neill (New York: Crossroad, 1987), 19. Dulles shared Cort's feeling "about the undue loss of confidence on the part of some of our coreligionists today." See Dulles to John C. Cort, December 17, 1987, in DPFU.

90. *Magisterium*, vii, 2n. 3, 3, 6. Sullivan's book was *Magisterium: Teaching Authority in the Catholic Church* (New York: Paulist, 1983).

91. *Magisterium*, however, was based upon and followed the outline of an earlier article Dulles had written on the subject: "Lehramt und Unfehlbarkeit," in *Handbuch der Fundamentaltheologie*, eds. Walter Kern, Hermann J. Pottmeyer, and Max Seckler, 4 vols. (Frieburg: Herder, 1988), 4: 153–78; rep. 2nd, imp. and upd. ed. (Tubingen und Basel: Francke, 2000), 109–30.

92. *Magisterium*, 2, 4, 5.

93. Ibid., 41.

94. Ibid., 107.

95. "Mary since Vatican II: Decline and Recovery," *Marian Studies* 52 (2002): 13.

96. "Church as the Body of Christ," 162.

97. "Eucharist as Sacrifice," 184.

98. "Mary since Vatican II," 21.

99. *Christ Among the Religions* (New York: Fordham University Press, 2001), 19. See also *Church and Society*, 360–72; "World Religions and the New Millennium," 3–13.

100. *Christ among the Religions*, 13. Dulles found it strange that the CDF's 2000 declaration *Dominus Iesus* (on Christianity's relationship to other world religions and Catholicism's relations with other Christian churches) was "conspicuously silent on Judaism. I doubt that Judaism is being classified as just one of the world's religions, like Buddhism and Hinduism." See "*Dominus Iesus*: A Catholic Response," *Pro Ecclesia* 10 (Winter 2001): 5–7, quotation at 6.

101. For some of the criticisms and evaluations, see editorial "The Vatican's Holocaust Report," *New York Times* (March 18, 1998): A20; Gustav Niebuhr, "A Vatican Peace Offering Reopens War Wounds," *New York Times* (March 29, 1998): 4; Peter Steinfels, "A Year after a Much-Criticized Vatican Document on the Holocaust, Jewish and Christian Scholars Find Even its Weaknesses a Tool of Reconciliation," *New York Times* (April 3, 1999): A12.

102. Commentary on *We Remember* in *The Holocaust, Never to Be Forgotten* (New York/Mahwah: Paulist, 2001), 47–72.

103. *The Hebrew Catholic* 77 (Fall 2002): 39–47.

104. "Covenant and Mission," *America* 187 (October 21, 2002): 8–11, "ambiguous" quotation at 9. Later, in a letter to Gerald Anderson, January 16, 2004, Dulles suggested that "experts in exegesis would call to task people who think that the passage [Rom 9–11] warrants something like a two-covenant theory." On the same subject, see Dulles to Daniel J. Kutys, February 16, 2007, and Dulles to John Van Coppenolle, November 8, 2006. Letters in DPFU.

105. "The Covenant with Israel," *First Things* 157 (November 2005): 16–21.
106. My interview with Avery Cardinal Dulles, July 24, 2007, transcript, 31–32, in DPFU. See also Dulles' "Current Theological Obstacles to Evangelization," in *The New Evangelization: Overcoming the Obstacles*, eds. Steven Boguslawski and Ralph Martin (Mahwah, NJ: Paulist, 2008), 13.
107. *Christ among the Religions*, 3.
108. Ibid., 11.
109. Ibid., 15–16.
110. On the censures, see John L. Allen Jr., "Theologian Dupuis Says He's Free at Last," *NCR* (March 9 2001): 11, and Christa Pongratz-Lippitt, "Writer Witnessed Conversation between Cardinal [Franz König] and Censured Theologian Jacques Dupuis," *NCR* (March 21, 2008): 17–18.
111. "World Religions and the New Millennium," 5. Dulles had in mind books like Paul F. Knitter's *No Other Name?* (Maryknoll, NY: Orbis, 1985) and John Hick and Paul F. Knitter, eds., *The Myth of Christian Uniqueness: Towards a Pluralistic Theology of Religions* (Maryknoll, NY: Orbis, 1987).
112. "World Religions and the New Millennium," 10, 11.
113. Ibid., 12.
114. Ibid., 3.
115. Constance Archambault to Dulles, May 15, 1997, and Dulles to Archambault, May 14, 1997, in DPFU.
116. Dulles to Ansgar Santogrossi, June 29, 2007, in DPFU.
117. Robert C. Mathes, November 5, 2002, and Dulles to Mathes, November 26, 2002. Letters in DPFU.
118. Among the many letters he wrote on vocations to the priesthood or on Jesuit life, see, e.g., Dulles to Robert Grosse, June 30, 1998; to Gregory Jordan, August 13, 1998; to Christopher Hadly, June 9, 1999; to Scott Moringiello, February 5, 2002. Letters in DPFU.
119. Dulles to Jason Smith, March 25, 2002, in DPFU.
120. Dulles to Mrs. Ruth M. Snow, July 22, 1986. See also Dulles to James Akin, June 3, 2003, on the relationship between sin, punishment, retribution, and due satisfaction. Letters in DPFU.
121. See, e.g., Abbott R. Morgan to Dulles, October 29, 2001; Henry O. Belanger to Dulles, July 11, 2001; Dulles to Markus Graulich, April 14, 2002. Letters in DPFU.
122. Edward I. Condren to Dulles, May 6, 2003, in DPFU.
123. James Martin, "Reason, Faith and Theology," *America* 184 (March 5, 2001): 14.
124. "Faith of a Theologian," 156.

Chapter 16. The Last Years

1. The effects of the polio he had had in the mid-1940s returned in the 1990s, making his left leg weakened and incapable of walking without an iron brace and a cane.

2. My interview with Fr. Gerald Blaszczak, SJ, July 25, 2007, transcript, 11, in my possession.

3. The lecture was later published as "Models of Evangelization," *Origins* 37 (May 17, 2007): 8–12.

4. Unpublished homily, "Second Sunday of Easter, St. Paul Catholic Center, University of Wisconsin, Madison, April 15, 2007." I am grateful to Dr. Constance Nielsen, who was present at the Mass, for giving me the original text, which had handwritten corrections and additions on it. The manuscript is also available in DPFU.

5. Ibid.

6. In *Church and Society*, 509–21.

7. "Saving Ecumenism from Itself."

8. My interview with Monica and John Murphy, June 25, 2008, transcript, 20, in my possession. More than twenty years previously, Dulles had also presided at Monica Des Marais and John Murphy's wedding.

9. Information on the assumption event comes from a letter by Louis Pascoe, SJ, to me, November 30 2008, and from Bronislaus B. Kush, "Popular NY Cardinal Joins Assumption Gala," *Worcester Telegram and Gazette* (October 13, 2007), and Tanya Connor, "Cardinal Dulles," *The Catholic Free Press* (October 19, 2007). For Dulles' lecture, "Catholic Colleges and Universities Today," see http//www.assumption.edu/inauguration/dulles-address.html, accessed December 1, 2008.

10. The lecture was published as "Historical Models of Catechesis," *Origins* 37 (November 8, 2007): 347–52.

11. Lecture published in *Church and Society*, 522–34.

12. Lecture published as "Farewell Address as McGinley Professor," *Origins* 37 (April 17, 2008): 697–701, and reprinted as "A Life in Theology," *America* 198 (April 21, 2008): 9–12.

13. "Life in Theology," 12.

14. Robert Peter Imbelli, "Avery Dulles, *Vir Ecclesiasticus*," in *Church and Society*, ix–xx.

15. Dulles to Kenneth Bogart, January 21, 1993; see also Dulles to Christopher Huntington, March 30, 1998, in DPFU.

16. For the conference papers, except that of Sr. Anne-Marie Kirmse, see "The Theological Contribution of Avery Cardinal Dulles, SJ," in *Chicago Studies* 47:2 (Summer 2008): 129–254. Kirmse's paper, "Avery Cardinal Dulles, SJ: From Convert to Cardinal," was published in *Here Comes Everybody*, ed. William C. Graham (Lanham, MD: University Press of America, 2008), 158–69.

17. Anne-Marie Kirmse, OP, "My Visit with the Pope" (n.d. but April 19, 2008), unpublished manuscript in my possession and in DPFU.

18. My conversation with Andrew Curry, December 17, 2008. Dulles' comment was intended to be humorous and not a summary of his views of liberation theology. Although he was critical of some aspects of liberation theology, he saw the positive dimensions of this new movement in theology. For one example of his standard evaluation, see *Assurance of Things Hoped For*, 155–61, 177–79.

19. *Testimonial to Grace*, 143.

20. "On Keeping the Faith," *From the Housetops* 1 (September 1946): 66.

21. Telegraph and obituary in "Unfailing Love for the Lord Marks Cardinal Dulles' Life," *L'Osservatore Romano* (Eng. ed.) (December 17, 2008): 20.

22. Robert D. McFadden, "Cardinal Avery Dulles, 90, Elder Statesman of Catholic Theology in America," *New York Times* (December 13, 2008): B10.

23. See, e.g., John L. Allen Jr., "Avery Dulles, 'Giant' of Theology Dies at 90," *NCR* (December 26, 2008): 8; "Cardinal Avery Dulles: Roman Catholic Theologian," *London Times* (December 13, 2008), at http://www.timesonline.co.uk/tol/comment/obituaries/article5332887.ece; Michelle Boorstein, "Avery Dulles, 90; Prominent Catholic Cardinal, Theologian," *Washington Post* (December 14, 2008): C8; Gary Stern, "Cardinal Dulles, Noted Theologian, Dies at 90," *Journal News* [Westchester, NY] (December 13, 2008), on line at http://m.lohud.com/news.jsp?key=181412; Robert Imbelli, "Il teologo creativo nella fedeltà," *L'Osservatore Romano* (14 dicembre 2008): 7; "A Man Who Lived to Seek Christ, 'The pearl of Great Price,'" *L'Osservatore Romano* (Eng. ed.) (December 24/31, 2008): 8; and "Model of the Church: Cardinal Avery Dulles, SJ," *Commonweal* (January 16, 2009): 6–9; Raymond J. De Souza, "Memories of Cardinal Dulles," and "A Great American Mind," *National Catholic Register* (January 4–10, 2009): 1, 10; "Avery, Richard, Paul and the Rest of Us," *National Catholic Register* (January 25–31, 2009): 8.

24. Cardinal McCarrick's communication to the Catholic News Service, December 12, 2008. Susan Gibbs of the communication office of the Archdiocese of Washington sent me this communication, January 7, 2009, which was published in various Catholic and secular newspapers.

25. My interview with McCarrick, January 5, 2009, transcript, 12, in my possession.

26. For an account of the Mass at St. Patrick's, see Glenn Collins, "For a Modest Cardinal, A Farewell Full of Majesty," *New York Times* (December 19, 2008): A35; see also "St. Patrick's Cathedral Farewell for Cardinal Avery Dulles," CathNewsUSA (December 19, 2008), at http://www.cathnewsusa.com/article.aspx?acid=10861.

27. John J. Cecero, SJ, "Homily for Avery Cardinal Dulles, SJ," December 16, 2008, and Joseph A. O'Hare, SJ, "Avery Cardinal Dulles," December 17, 2008. Copies of homilies in my possession.

28. Cardinal Edward Egan, Sermon, untitled, December 18, 2008; unpublished text in my possession.

29. "Remarks at the Funeral of Avery Cardinal Dulles, SJ," December 18, 2008; unpublished text in my possession.

30. "All Dressed in Scarlet," 9.

31. Foreword to *De Lubac: A Guide for the Perplexed* by David Grumett (London: T. & T. Clark/New York: Continuum, 2007), ix.

CHRONOLOGICAL OUTLINE

1918	August 24	Born to John Foster Dulles and Janet Pomeroy Avery Dulles Auburn, New York
1936		Graduated Choate
1940		Received AB, Harvard College, Phi Beta Kappa Award
	Fall	Entered Harvard Law School (1940–1941)
	November 26	Received into Catholic Church
1941	Fall	Established St. Benedict Center, Cambridge, MA
		Published *Princeps Concordiae* (on Mirandola)
1941	December	Called into U.S. Naval Reserve
	March	Served as Navy lieutenant during World War II in Atlantic, Caribbean, and Mediterranean, until Spring 1946
1945	February	Awarded Croix de Guerre, with silver star, for contributions to French Navy during World War II
	October	Hospitalized with polio, U.S. Army hospital in Caserta, Italy
		Transferred to Naval Hospital, Bethesda, Maryland
1946	February	Released from Bethesda Naval Hospital; rejoined St. Benedict Center
	July	Discharged from active duty in Naval Reserve
		Published articles in *From the Housetops*
		Published *A Testimonial to Grace*
		Left St. Benedict Center

Jesuit Formation Years

1946	August	Entered Jesuits (Novitiate of New York Province, St. Andrew-on-Hudson)
1948–1951		Attended Woodstock College, for philosophy; 1951, PhL. Woodstock College, Maryland
1951–1953		Served Jesuit Regency, teaching philosophy, Fordham University
1953–1957		Attended Woodstock College, for theology

673

1955	Published with James Demske and Robert O'Connell *Introductory Metaphysics*
1956 June 16	Ordained priest
1957–1958	Served Tertianship in Münster, Germany

Gregorian University Years

1958–1960	Attended Gregorian University (Rome) for doctoral studies in theology
1959 May 25	Death of John Foster Dulles
	Attended Paderborn, Germany, Catholic Conference for Ecumenical Questions
1960	Received STD, Gregorian University, Rome; visited Taizé; returned to Woodstock to teach

Woodstock College Years, Maryland

1960–1974	Served as professor of systematic theology, Woodstock College, Maryland (1960–1970), Woodstock College, New York City (1970–1974)
1962 January	Appointed to the Baltimore Archdiocesan Commission on Christian Unity
1962–1965	Vatican Council II
1963–1992	Served on Advisory Editorial Board for Ecumenism, *Concilium*
1966–1973	Consultor to Papal Secretariat for Dialogue with Non-Believers
1968	Pope Paul VI's *Humanae vitae* published; Dulles does not sign protests
1969 May 14	Death of Janet Pomeroy Avery Dulles
1969–1975	Served as member of the USCC's Advisory Council

Woodstock College, New York City

1969 Summer	Woodstock moved to Morningside Heights, New York City
1970 November	Received CTSA's Cardinal Spellman Award for Distinguished Achievement in Theology
1971	Elected member of the American Theological Society
1972–1996	Served as member of U.S. Lutheran/Catholic Dialogue (1972–1992) and Lutheran-Catholic Coordinating Committee (1992–1996)

1973		American Jesuit Provincials decide to reduce the number of theologates and to close Woodstock College in New York City

Catholic University of America Years

1974		Woodstock theological library moved to Georgetown University, Washington, D.C., where Dulles helped set up Woodstock Theological Center
		Published *Models of the Church*
1974–1983		Served as research associate, Woodstock Theological Center
1974–1988		Served as professor of systematic theology at the Catholic University of America, Washington, D.C.
1975		Signed Hartford "Appeal for Theological Affirmation"
1975–1976		Served as president, CTSA; CTSA report on *Human Sexuality* "received"
1976		Dulles/Tracy controversy
	October	Served as observer at Bicentennial "Call to Action," Detroit
1977		Named Fellow, Woodrow Wilson International Center for Scholars, Washington, D.C.
		Published *The Resilient Church*
1978–1979		Served as president, American Theological Society, member since 1971
1981–1982		Served as visiting professor, Thomas J. Gasson Chair, Boston College
1982		Attended and participated in Faith and Order Conference, Lima, Peru
1983		Served as Martin D'Arcy lecturer, Campion Hall, Oxford, England
		Catholicity of the Church published D'Arcy lectures
1984–1987		Charles Curran controversy at the Catholic University of America; Dulles refused to sign corporate protests or to join public protests; Curran removed from his teaching position in Department of Theology
1985	Fall	Served as visiting professor, John A. O'Brien Chair, University of Notre Dame
1987	December 1	Death of Lillias Dulles Hinshaw, his sister
1988	January	Attended Ratzinger Conference on Biblical Interpretation, New York City

Fordham University Years

1987	September	Appointed Laurence J. McGinley, SJ, Chair on Religion and Society, Fordham University, New York City
		Dulles Colloquium organized by Richard John Neuhaus
1989		Fall of Iron Curtain
1990		Pope John Paul II's *Ex corde ecclesiae* and the CDF's *Ecclesial Vocation of Theologians* published
	Fall	Appointed visiting professor, Gregorian University, Rome
1991	January	Persian Gulf War
	September	Attended International Symposium on Theology in Latin America, Mexico City
1991–2007		Served as Consultor, Committee on Doctrine of the NCCB, USCCB
1992		Contributed to "Evangelicals and Catholics Together" Published *The Craft of Theology* (rev. 1994); won Catholic Book Award for Theology (1993)
	Fall	Appointed visiting professor, North American College, Louvain, Belgium
1992–1997		Served as member of the Vatican International Theological Commission
1993	Fall	Appointed visiting professor, Gregorian University, Rome
1994		Published *Assurance of Things Hoped For* Pope John Paul II's *Ordinatio sacerdotalis* published Hospitalized for prostate surgery
1995		Pope John Paul II visited United States and addressed United Nations
	September	Attended Istituo Paolo VI Conference, Brescia, Italy Pope John Paul II's *Ut unum sint* published
1996	Spring	Appointed visiting professor, Yale University, New Haven, Connecticut
		Republished *A Testimonial to Grace* in expanded edition
		Common Ground Project launched
		Presented Campion Hall Lecture on Reform of Papacy, Oxford, England
	Fall	Appointed Scholar in Residence, St. Joseph's Seminary, Dunwoodie, Yonkers, New York
1997		Published *Priestly Office*
1998		Pope John Paul II's *Fides et ratio* published
	March	Attended Second Common Ground Meeting
1999		Published *Splendor of Faith*
2000		Published *New World of Faith*

	October	Presented lecture at Oxford University, Oxford, England
		Presented lecture on *Fides et ratio*, Paderborn, Germany
2001	February 21	Created Cardinal in Rome
		Prepared lecture for Second Congress of Systematic Theology, Lublin, Poland; lecture sent but could not attend because of terrorist attacks of September 2001
2002		Presented lecture on the state of Catholic theology in the United States, Paris, France
		Published *Newman*
2003		Dulles/O'Malley controversy on meaning of Vatican II
2004		Participated in debate with George Lindbeck
		Hospitalized for heart surgery
2005	April	Presented lecture at University of Wisconsin, Madison
		Death of Pope John Paul II, call to Rome, Conclave, and election of Benedict XVI
2007	April	Presented lecture and homily at the University of Wisconsin, Madison
	Fall	Diagnosed with pseudobulbar palsy, a part of the post-polio syndrome
2008	February	Placed in Murray-Weigel Infirmary, Fordham University
	June 19	Death of Eleanor Ritter Dulles, his sister-in-law
	June 23	Death of John Watson Foster Dulles, his brother
	December 12	Died at Murray-Weigel Infirmary, Fordham University

ESSAY ON THE SOURCES

Unpublished Works

I HAVE RELIED ON different kinds of sources in preparing this biography: primarily on Dulles' unpublished and published works, on archival deposits relating to Dulles' life and career as a theologian, on newspaper accounts of significant events affecting his life and that of the church and Society of Jesus, and on some recent histories of American Catholic life and thought. In this essay I am not providing a full bibliography of Cardinal Dulles' published works because, prior to his death, he decided to publish it himself and asked that I honor his decision and not publish it in the biography. After his death, Sr. Anne-Marie Kirmse inherited the task of publishing it. His bibliography itself, moreover, is more than seventy-five pages in manuscript form and would tax the resources for this biography. At the end of this essay on his unpublished sources, I am including only some of his most significant published materials, arranged topically and chronologically.

Dulles' multiple unpublished sources (personal correspondence, high school and college papers, family histories, doctoral dissertation, public lectures, class syllabi and notes, sermons, drafts of books and articles, newspaper clippings about his and his family's history, handwritten notes he took at various conferences, minutes of meetings, papers and drafts of professional statements and documents he participated in writing, various other documents and statements produced by others, awards and honorary degrees, and so on) are contained in fifteen 4-foot file cabinets located at Fordham University. Dulles kept copies of almost all the letters he sent and the correspondence he received from others, even during the World War II years. When I examined these uncatalogued papers I did so in his university offices. Those papers will eventually be catalogued and placed in Fordham's University Archives. An archivist in the future will undoubtedly collect correspondence that he did not preserve but was preserved by others.

The John Foster Dulles Papers, containing family correspondence as well as collections of state documents, are located at the Seeley G. Mudd Manuscript Library at Princeton University, Princeton, New Jersey. The John Watson Foster Dulles Papers—containing his father's papers as well as Avery Dulles' own extensive correspondence with his father and others in the family, maps and logs of sailing trips, family memorabilia and histories—are located in the Harry Ransom Humanities Research Center at the University of Texas in Austin. The papers in the Harry Ransom Center have been especially helpful in preparing this biography. Prior to his death, John Watson Foster Dulles also sent me copies of his personal correspondence with his brother Avery. Those papers from his personal archives will eventually be deposited in the Harry Ransom Humanities Research Center.

Papers relating to Dulles' experiences at St. Benedict Center in Cambridge, Massachusetts, and his correspondence with his godmother Catherine Goddard Clarke during World War II and shortly thereafter are located at St. Benedict's Abbey, Still River, Massachusetts. The daily diary of Louise Mercier Des Marais relating to the St. Benedict Center and to Dulles (1938–1948) is located at the archives of the Archdiocese of Boston. Dulles' correspondence with his godfather, Christopher Huntington, during and after World War II is in the possession of Mark Williams of Mendham, New Jersey.

Twelve boxes of Dulles' papers relating to his experiences at Woodstock College, particularly from the late 1960s to its closing in the mid-1970s, are housed in the archives of Georgetown University, Washington, D.C. A 1944 draft of his *A Testimonial to Grace* is also located in this collection. These papers or copies of them will eventually be placed in the Avery Cardinal Dulles Papers at Fordham University. The Georgetown papers, too, were uncatalogued at the time I had access to them.

Six boxes of catalogued papers relating to Dulles' role as vice president, president, and board member in the Catholic Theological Society of America during the mid- to late 1970s are located in the archives of the Catholic University of America. Multiple file cabinets containing papers relating to Dulles' participation in the Lutheran/Catholic Dialogue (1970–1996) are in the office of the Bishops' Committee on Ecumenical and Interreligious Affairs, located in the USCCB office building, Washington, D.C.

Although I had generous access to the archives mentioned, I did not have access to other archives that may contain papers and information that might have been helpful for the biography. I mention this to alert later biographers that they might want to consult those archival deposits once they are freed from the fifty-year time restrictions. Because of these normal archival restrictions, I did not have access to personnel files in the New York and Maryland Jesuit archives nor to papers relating to Woodstock College in the Jesuit archives in Rome; time-bound restrictions, moreover, were placed on papers relating to activities and personnel in the Theology Department at the Catholic University of America; documents relating to Dulles' participation in the International Theological Commission and to his involvement in committees of the United States Conference of Catholic Bishops (for example, the Committee on Doctrine) were also unavailable. Future biographers will have access to these sources and will be able to provide interpretations that uncover elements of the mystery of the man that I do not or cannot see.

Published Writings

A selected bibliography of Dulles' published works is presented, arranged chronologically under the following topics: autobiographical materials, and works on the aims and methods of theology, revelation, faith, church, ecumenism, and the relations of church and culture.

Autobiographical Writings

Periodically Dulles wrote about his life and particularly his conversion experience as was evident in these major works: *A Testimonial to Grace* (New York: Sheed & Ward, 1946), 50th anniv. ed. with afterword; *Reflections on a Theological Journey* (Kansas City, MO: Sheed & Ward, 1996); "Coming Home," in *Where I Found*

Christ, edited by John A. O'Brien (Garden City, NY: Doubleday, 1950), 63–81; "Harvard as an Invitation to Catholicism," in *The Catholics of Harvard Square*, edited by Jeffrey Wills (Petersham, MA: St. Bede's Publications, 1993), 119–24; "Vatican II and My Self," in *Vatican II: Forty Personal Stories*, edited by William Madges and Michael J. Daley (Mystic, CT: Twenty-Third Publications, 2003), 117–19; "The Faith of a Theologian," in *Believing Scholars*, edited by James L. Heft (Bronx, NY: Fordham University Press, 2005), 151–63; "Farewell Address as McGinley Professor," *Origins* 37 (April 17, 2008): 697–701.

Theology

Most of what Dulles wrote was a reflection on the art, aims, and methods of theology, but he gave explicit attention to this topic in the following sources: "Method in Biblical Theology (Response to Krister Stendahl)," in *The Bible in Modern Scholarship*, edited by J. Philip Hyatt (Nashville, TN: Abingdon, 1965), 210–16; "The Ignatian Experience as Reflected in the Spiritual Theology of Karl Rahner," *Philippine Studies* 13 (1965): 471–94; "Method in Fundamental Theology: Reflections on David Tracy's *Blessed Rage for Order*," *Theological Studies* 37 (June 1976): 303–16; "Authority and Criticism in Systematic Theology," *Theology Digest* 26 (Winter 1978): 387–99; "Hermeneutical Theology," *Communio: International Catholic Review* 6 (Spring 1979): 16–37; "Fundamental Theology and the Dynamics of Conversion," *Thomist* 45 (April 1981): 175–93; "Saint Ignatius and the Jesuit Theological Tradition," *Studies in the Spirituality of Jesuits* 14 (March 1982): 1–21; "Faith, Church, and God: Insights from Michael Polanyi," *Theological Studies* 45 (September 1984): 537–50; "Umrisse meiner theologischen Methode," in *Entwürfe der Theologie*, edited by Johannes B. Bauer (Graz, Austria: Styria, 1985), 51–70; *University Theology as a Service to the Church* (New York: Fordham University Press, 1989); "The Place of the Theologian: 1. The Question of Dissent," *Tablet* (London) 244 (August 18, 1990): 1033–34; "Science and Theology," in *John Paul II on Science and Religion: Reflections on the New View from Rome*, edited by Robert John Russell, William H. Stoeger, and George V. Coyne (Notre Dame, IN, and Vatican City State: University of Notre Dame

Press/Libreria Editrice Vaticana, 1990), 9–18; "The Magisterium, Theology, and Dissent," *Origins* 20 (March 28, 1991): 692–96; "Theology for a Post-Critical Age," in *Theology Toward the Third Millennium: Theological Issues for the Twenty-First Century*, edited by David G. Schultenover (Lewiston, NY: Edwin Mellen Press, 1991), 5–21; "Magisterium and Theological Method," *Seminarium* 31 (1991): 289–99; *The Craft of Theology: From Symbol to System* (New York: Crossroad, 1992); "Tradition and Creativity in Theology," *First Things* 27 (November 1992): 20–27; "From Symbol to System: A Proposal for Theological Method," *Pro Ecclesia* 1 (Fall 1992): 42–52, with "Rejoinder to George Lindbeck," 61–62; "Theology and Worship: The Reciprocity of Prayer and Belief," *Ex Auditu* 8 (1992): 85–94; "The Ignatian 'Sentire cum Ecclesia' Today," *CIS: Review of Ignatian Spirituality* 25 (1994): 19–35; "The Interpretation of the Bible in the Church: A Theological Appraisal," in *Kirche sein: Nachkonziliare Theologie im Dienst der Kirchenreform* (Festschrift for Hermann Josef Pottmeyer), edited by Wilhelm Geerlings and Max Seckler (Freiburg im Breisgau/Basel/Wein: Herder, 1994), 29–37; "Criteria of Catholic Theology," *Communio: International Catholic Review* 22 (Summer 1995): 303–15; "Evangelizing Theology," *First Things* 61 (March 1996): 27–32; "Prospects for Seminary Theology," *Seminary Journal* 2 (Winter 1996): 12–19; "The Ignatian Charism and Contemporary Theology," *America* 176 (April 26, 1997): 14–22; "Principles of Catholic Theology," *Pro Ecclesia* 1 (Winter 1999): 73–84; *The Splendor of Faith: The Theological Vision of Pope John Paul II* (New York: Crossroad, 1999, new and rev. ed., 2003); *Newman* (London/New York: Continuum, 2002); "Wisdom as the Source of Unity for Theology," in *Wisdom and Holiness, Science and Scholarship* (Essays in Honor of Matthew L. Lamb), edited by Michael Dauphinais and Matthew Levering (Naples, FL: Sapientia Press, 2007), 59–71; *Magisterium: Teacher and Guardian of the Faith* (Naples, FL: Sapientia Press, 2007); "The Freedom of Theology," *First Things* 183 (May 2008): 19–23.

Revelation

Dulles wrote repeatedly on the doctrine of revelation and its relation to the Bible, tradition, the church, and dogma. Some of his more important works on this subject are included in the following: "Some Recent Trends in Pentateuchal Criticism," *Theologian* 10 (1954): 18–28; "The Council and the Sources of Revelation," *America* 107 (December 1, 1962): 1176–77; *Apologetics and the Biblical Christ* (Westminster, MD: Newman Press, 1963); "The Theology of Revelation," *Theological Studies* 25 (March 1964): 43–58; "The Gospels and Apologetic Method," in *Proceedings of the Catholic Theological Society of America* 19 (1964): 151–60; "Symbol, Myth, and the Biblical Revelation," *Theological Studies* 27 (March 1966): 1–26; "The Constitution on Divine Revelation in Ecumenical Perspective," *American Ecclesiastical Review* 154 (1966): 25–27; "Theological Table Talk: Revelation in Recent Catholic Theology," *Theology Today* 24 (October 1967): 350–65; *Revelation and the Quest for Unity* (Washington, DC: Corpus Books, 1968); *Revelation Theology: A History* (New York: Herder & Herder, 1969); *A History of Apologetics* (New York: Corpus; Philadelphia: Westminster; and London: Hutchinson, 1971); *The Survival of Dogma* (Garden City, NY: Doubleday, 1971, rpt. Garden City, NY: Doubleday Image Books, 1973); "The Bible in the Church: Some Debated Questions," in *Scripture and the Charismatic Renewal*, edited by George Martin (Ann Arbor: Servant Books, 1979), 5–27, 119–21; "The Symbolic Structure of Revelation," *Theological Studies* 41 (March 1980): 51–73; "Revelation and Discovery," in *Theology and Discovery*, edited by William J. Kelly, SJ (Milwaukee: Marquette University Press, 1980), 1–29; *Models of Revelation* (Garden City, NY: Doubleday, 1983); "From Images to Truth: Newman on Revelation and Faith," *Theological Studies* 51 (June 1990): 252–67; "Revelation as the Basis for Scripture and Tradition," *Evangelical Review of Theology* 21 (April 1997): 104–20; "Catholic Doctrine: Between Revelation and Theology," *Proceedings of the Catholic Theology Society of America* 54 (1999): 83–91; "Vatican II and Myself" [reflections on revelation], in *Vatican II: Forty Personal Stories*, 117–19; "Models of Evangelization," *Origins* 37 (May 17, 2007): 8–12; *Evangelization for the Third Millennium* (New York: Paulist, 2009).

Faith

The relationship between revelation and faith had been a recurring concern in Dulles' writings since his conversion to Catholicism in 1940. Some of his more important reflections on the structure and meaning of faith are included here: "The Modern Dilemma of Faith," in *Toward a Theology of Christian Faith*, edited by M. Mooney and others (New York: P. J. Kenedy, 1968), 11–32; "Faith, Reason, and the Logic of Discovery," *Thought* 45 (Winter 1970): 485–502; "The Meaning of Faith Considered in Relationship to Justice," in *The Faith That Does Justice*, edited by John C. Haughey (New York: Paulist, 1977), 10–46; "Foundation Documents of the Faith: X. Modern Credal Affirmations," *Expository Times* 91 (July 1980): 291–96; *The Communication of Faith and Its Content* (Washington, DC: National Catholic Educational Association, 1985); "The Systematic Theology of Faith: A Catholic Perspective," in *Handbook of Faith*, edited by James Michael Lee (Birmingham, AL: Religious Education Press, 1990), 142–63; "Faith and Experience: Strangers? Rivals? Partners?" *The Priest* 46 (1990): 19–22; "Faith, Justice, and the Jesuit Mission," in *Assembly 1989: Jesuit Ministry in Higher Education. Faith/Justice Mission in Higher Education 1. Theological and Educational Dimensions* (Washington, DC: Jesuit Conference, 1990), 19–25; "Faith and Revelation," in *Systematic Theology: Roman Catholic Perspectives*, edited by Francis Schüssler Fiorenza and John Galvin (Minneapolis: Fortress, 1991), 89–128; "Handing on the Faith through Witness and Symbol," *The Living Light* 27 (1991): 295–302; "Models of Faith," in *Fides quaerens intellectum: Beiträge zur Fundamentaltheologie*, edited by Michael Kessler, Wolfhart Pannenberg, and Hermann Josef Pottmeyer (Tübingen: Francke, 1992), 405–13; *The Assurance of Things Hoped For: A Theology of Christian Faith* (New York/Oxford: Oxford University Press, 1994); "The Ecclesial Dimension of Faith," *Communio* 22 (Fall 1995): 418–32; "Seven Essentials of Evangelization," *Origins* 25 (November 23, 1995): 397–400; "The Cognitive Basis of Faith," *Philosophy and Theology* 10 (1998): 19–31; *The New World of Faith* (Huntington, IN: Our Sunday Visitor, 2000); "Reason, Philosophy, and the Grounding of Faith: A Reflection on *Fides et Ratio*," *International Philosophical Quarterly* 40 (December 2000): 479–90; "Receiving and Handing on the Faith: Dialogue between the Catholic Church and the Disciples of Christ: Comment," *Information Service* of the Pontifical Council for Promoting Christian Unity 111 (2002): 252–55; "Faith and Civility," *Josephinum Journal of Theology* 11 (Summer/Fall 2004):

216–25; "Historical Models of Catechesis," *Origins* 37 (November 8, 2007): 347–52.

The Church

Dulles was most widely recognized nationally and internationally as an ecclesiologist, and his writings on the church are voluminous. Some of his more important studies are included in the following: "Church Unity and Roman Primacy in the Doctrine of St. Cyprian," *Theologian* 9 (1954): 33–48; introduction and commentary to *Lumen Gentium*, in *Documents of Vatican II*, edited by William M. Abbott, SJ (New York: America Press, 1966), 9–13; *The Dimensions of the Church* (Westminster, MD: Newman Press, 1967); "The Magisterium and Authority in the Church," in *Theology in Revolution*, edited by George Devine (Staten Island, NY: Alba House, 1970), 29–45; "The Church, the Churches, and the Catholic Church," *Theological Studies* 33 (June 1972): 199–234; "The Church and Salvation," *Missiology: An International Review* (1973): 71–80; *Models of the Church* (Garden City, NY: Doubleday, 1974; exp. ed., Garden City, NY: Doubleday Image Books, 1987; exp. ed. with new appendix, New York: Doubleday Image Books, 2002); "The Papacy: Bond or Barrier?" *Origins* 3 (May 2, 1974): 705–12; "The Theologian and the Magisterium," *Proceedings of the Catholic Theological Society of America* 31 (1976): 235–46; *The Resilient Church: The Necessity and Limits of Adaptation* (Garden City: Doubleday, 1977; Dublin: Gill & Macmillan, 1978); "Earthen Vessels: Institution and Charism in the Church," in *Above Every Name: The Lordship Of Christ and Social Systems*, edited by Thomas E. Clarke (Ramsey, NJ: Paulist, 1980), 155–87; "The Two Magisteria: An Interim Reflection," *Proceedings of the Catholic Theological Society of America* 36 (1981): 155–69; *A Church to Believe In: Discipleship and the Dynamics of Freedom* (New York: Crossroad, 1982); "Vatican II Reform: The Basic Principles," *Church* 1 (Summer 1985): 3–10; *The Catholicity of the Church* (Oxford, UK: Clarendon Press, 1985); "Catholic Ecclesiology since Vatican II," in *Synod 1985: An Evaluation. Concilium* 188, edited by Giuseppe Alberigo and James Provost (Edinburgh: T. & T. Clark, 1986), 3–13; *Vatican II and the Extraordinary Synod* (Collegeville, MN:

Liturgical Press, 1986); "The Reception of Vatican II at the Extraordinary Synod of 1985," in *The Reception of Vatican II*, edited by Giuseppe Alberigo, J. P. Jossua, and Joseph A. Komonchak (Washington, DC: Catholic University of America Press, 1987), 349–63; *The Reshaping of Catholicism: Current Challenges in the Theology of Church* (San Francisco: Harper & Row, 1988); "A Half Century of Ecclesiology," *Theological Studies* 50 (September 1989): 419–42; "Models for Ministerial Priesthood," *Origins* 20 (October 11, 1990): 284–89; *The Priestly Office* (New York/Mahwah, NJ: Paulist, 1997); "*Humanae Vitae* and *Ordinatio Sacerdotalis*: Problems of Reception," in *Church Authority in American Culture* (New York: Crossroad, 1999), 14–28; "The Sacramental Ecclesiology of *Lumen Gentium*," *Gregorianum* 86 (2005): 550–62; "*Dignitatis humanae* and the Development of Catholic Doctrine," in *Catholicism and Religious Freedom*, edited by Kenneth L. Grasso and Robert P. Hunt (Lanham, MD: Rowman & Littlefield, 2006), 43–67.

Ecumenical Writings

Dulles was one of the more important American Catholic ecumenists. He participated in the creation of a number of joint ecumenical statements and wrote extensively on the subject, as the following major statements indicate: "Paul Tillich and the Bible," *Theological Studies* 17 (September 1956): 345–67; "The Orthodox Churches and the Ecumenical Movement," *Downside Review* 239 (January 1957): 38–54; "Protestants and Catholics in Germany," *America* 100 (January 24, 1959): 493–95; "The Protestant Preacher and the Prophetic Mission,"*Theological Studies* 21 (December 1960): 544–80; "Protestant-Catholic Relations in Germany," *Epistle* 27 (Winter 1961): 2–11; "Pope Paul's Ecumenical Perspective," *Catholic World* 200 (October 1964): 15–21; "Luther's Unfinished Reformation," *Catholic Mind* 63 (1965): 32–35; *American Christians and Ecumenism* (Hudson, NY: Graymoor Unity Apostolate, 1966); "Faith and Order at Louvain," *Theological Studies* 33 (March 1972): 35–67; *Church Membership as a Catholic and Ecumenical Problem* (Milwaukee: Marquette University Press, 1974); "Unmasking Secret Infidelities: Hartford and the Future of Ecumenism," in *Against the World for the World*, edited by Peter L. Berger and Richard John

Neuhaus (New York: Seabury, 1976), 44–62; "Ten Principles of Ecumenism: Part I," *New Covenant* 5 (1976): 29–33; "Ten Principles of Ecumenism: Part II," *New Covenant* 6 (1976): 26–29; "Ius divinum as an Ecumenical Problem," *Theological Studies* 38 (December 1977): 681–708; "Ecumenism: Problems and Opportunities for the Future," in *Toward Vatican III: The Work That Needs to Be Done*, edited by David Tracy, Hans Küng, and Johann B. Metz (New York: Seabury, 1978), 91–101; "What Belongs in a Future Ecumenical Creed? A Catholic Answer," in *An Ecumenical Confession of Faith? Concilium* 118, edited by Hans Küng and Jürgen Moltmann (New York: Seabury, 1979), 77–81; "Moderate Infallibilism," in *Teaching Authority and Infallibility in the Church*, edited by Paul C. Empie, T. Austin Murphy, and Joseph A. Burgess (Minneapolis: Augsburg, 1980), 81–100; "Ecumenism and Theological Method," in *Consensus in Theology? A Dialogue with Hans Küng, Edward Schillebeeckx, and Others*, edited by Leonard Swidler (Philadelphia: Westminster, 1980), 40–48; "Toward a Christian Consensus: The Lima Meeting," *America* 146 (February 20, 1982): 126–29; "Justification in Contemporary Catholic Theology," in *Justification by Faith*, edited by H. George Anderson, T. Austin Murphy, and Joseph A. Burgess (Minneapolis: Augsburg, 1985), 256–77; "Paths to Doctrinal Agreement: Ten Theses," *Theological Studies* 47 (March 1986): 32–47; "Ecumenism without Illusions: A Catholic Perspective," *First Things* 4 (June–July 1990): 20–25; "The Decree on Ecumenism: Twenty-Five Years After," *New Catholic World* 233 (September/October 1990): 196–201; "The Unity for Which We Hope," in *Evangelicals and Catholics Together: Toward a Common Mission*, edited by Charles Colson and Richard John Neuhaus (Dallas, TX: Word, 1995), 115–46; *The Travails of Dialogue* (New York: Fordham University Press, 1997); "Two Languages of Salvation," *First Things* 98 (December 1999): 25–30; *Christ among the Religions* (New York: Fordham University Press, 2001); "Justification: the Joint Declaration," *Josephinum Journal of Theology* 9 (Winter/Spring 2002): 108–19; "World Religions and the New Millennium," in *In Many and Diverse Ways: In Honor of Jacques Dupuis*, edited by Daniel Kendall and Gerald O'Collins (Maryknoll, NY: Orbis, 2003), 3–13; "Ecumenism and Evangelization," *Origins* 33 November (13, 2003): 399–401; "Saving Ecumenism from Itself," *First Things* 178 (December 2007): 23–27.

The Church and Culture

On several occasions Dulles wrote on the relationship between the church and culture, and in particular on the relationship of Catholicism to American society and social values. Some of his more important statements are included here: "Les catholiques Américains à l'ère 'post-protestante,'" *Christus* [Paris] 9 (1962): 533–45; "The Church as Multimedia," *New Catholic World* 215 (1972): 22–24, 43–46; "Mass Evangelization through Social Media," *Origins* 8 (March 29, 1979): 649–52; "The Gospel, the Church, and Politics," *Origins* 16 (February 19, 1987): 637–46; "Catholicism and American Culture: The Uneasy Dialogue," *America* 162 (January 27, 1990): 54–59; "Religion and the Transformation of Politics," *America* 167 (October 24, 1992): 296–301; "The Four Faces of American Catholicism," *Louvain Studies* 18 (Summer 1993): 99–109; "Narrowing the Gap: Gospel and Culture," *Origins* 23 (17 March 1994): 677–80; "John Paul II as a Theologian of Culture," *Logos* 1 (Summer 1997): 19–33; "Ethics of Culture: Faith and Culture in the Thought of John Paul II," in *Prophecy and Diplomacy: The Moral Doctrine of John Paul II*, edited by John J. Conley and Joseph W. Koterski (New York: Fordham University Press, 1999), 175–89; "The Contribution of Christianity to Culture: An American Perspective," in *Chrzescijanstwo Jutra* (Lublin, Poland: Towarzystwo Naukowe, 2001), 150–77; "The Deist Minimum," *First Things* 149 (January 2005): 25–30; "Catholicism and the American Experience," in *Religion and the American Experience*, edited by Frank T. Birtel (Hyde Park, NY: New City Press, 2005), 3–16; "The Mission of the Church in *Gaudium et Spes*," in *The Church and Human Freedom: Forty Years after Gaudium et Spes*, edited by Darlene Fozard Weaver (Villanova, PA: Villanova University Press, 2006), 26–37; "The Indirect Mission of the Church to Politics," *Villanova Law Review* 52:2 (2007): 241–52; "The Evangelization of Culture and the Catholic University," *Journal of Law, Philosophy and Culture* 1 (Spring 2007): 1–11; *Church and Society: The McGinley Lectures 1998–2007* (Bronx, NY: Fordham University Press, 2008).

INDEX